Political Change
in France Under
Richelieu and Mazarin

Political Change
in France under
Richelieu and Mazarin
1624–1661

BY

RICHARD BONNEY

1978

OXFORD UNIVERSITY PRESS

Oxford University Press, Walton Street, Oxford OX2 6DP

OXFORD LONDON GLASGOW
NEW YORK TORONTO MELBOURNE WELLINGTON
IBADAN NAIROBI DAR ES SALAAM LUSAKA CAPE TOWN
KUALA LUMPUR SINGAPORE JAKARTA HONG KONG TOKYO
DELHI BOMBAY CALCUTTA MADRAS KARACHI

British Library Cataloguing in Publication Data
Bonney, Richard
    Political change in France under Richelieu and
    Mazarin, 1624–1661.
    1. France—Politics and government—17th century
    I. Title
    354'.44   JN2341   77–30298
    ISBN 0–19–822537–7

Printed in Great Britain by
Butler & Tanner Ltd
Frome and London

Preface

THE TERMS 'absolutism' and *ancien régime* are widely used by historians to describe the political and social structure of France which endured until 1789. Precisely because the issues involved are complex, these terms are given a variety of meanings—some more accurate than others—which hinder rather than facilitate comparison with other political systems prevailing in Europe at the time. One of the aims of this book is to arrive at a more precise definition of these terms from a detailed examination of the political changes introduced by Richelieu after 1624 and continued by Mazarin. There is little agreement among historians over the date at which 'absolutism' could be said to have become established in France. It has recently been argued that the changes during the reign of Henri IV (chiefly the years of peace between 1598 and 1610) 'were more radical than any in the two . . . centuries before the Revolution'.[1] Yet intractable problems of government remained on the death of Henri IV in 1610, so much so that another historian has viewed the 1620s as 'the crucial phase' in the development of 'absolutism' in France.[2]

In this study emphasis is placed on the working of central government and the intendants, the new provincial administrators established during Richelieu's ministry. From this basis, it is hoped to provide a new perspective on the period of Richelieu and Mazarin and on Louis XIV's personal rule after 1661. Throughout, the word 'political' is not used in any restrictive, institutional sense: indeed many of the changes introduced had economic as well as social consequences. If it is axiomatic that the social process cannot properly be understood without reference to politics, it is equally the case that politics rapidly becomes devoid of significance as a subject of enquiry if it is not related to the experience of social groups which did not participate directly in the process of government.

[1] J. H. M. Salmon, *Society in crisis: France in the sixteenth century* (1975), p. 326.
[2] A. D. Lublinskaya, *French absolutism: the crucial phase, 1620–1629* (Cambridge, 1968).

This is especially true at the time of Richelieu and Mazarin, when the government had to defeat popular rebellion while staving off criticism from privileged social groups such as the nobles and office-holders.

This book is the outcome of an extended period of research in France between 1969 and 1971 and intermittent visits since that time. The costs of research abroad—especially at Paris—are so immense that they could not have been supported without the generosity of a number of award-giving bodies. I thank the Leverhulme Trust, the Centre National de la Recherche Scientifique, the Harmsworth Trust at Merton College, Oxford, the Research Board of the University of Reading, and the Twenty-Seven Foundation for their assistance. I would like to thank particularly Mrs. Menna Prestwich of St. Hilda's College, Oxford, who supervised work on my D.Phil. thesis between 1968 and 1973, and has been kind enough to comment on other pieces of my work since then. I owe a great debt to French historians—most notably Professors Roland Mousnier, Emmanuel Leroy-Ladurie, and Yves-Marie Bercé—for their advice and encouragement at various stages. My thanks to Robin Briggs of all Souls College, Oxford, for his helpful comments at the difficult last stage of preparing the book for publication, and to Julian Richards for preparing the maps. This book is dedicated to my parents and to my wife. Without the support of my parents I might never have gone to university or embarked on research. Without my wife, who read this manuscript painstakingly and was an acute and knowledgeable critic, my research might never have reached fruition.

R.J.B.

July 1976

Contents

Tables

List of Figures

List of Maps

Abbreviations

A.A.E. France	Archives des Affaires Étrangères, Mémoires et Documents, France
A.D.	Archives Départementales
A.G.	Archives de la Guerre (Château de Vincennes, Service Historique de l'Armée, Ancien Dépôt de la Guerre)
Annales E.S.C.	*Annales, Économies, Sociétés, Civilisations*
a.p.	archives privées (Archives Nationales, Fonds privés)
B.L.	British Library
B.M.	Bibliothèque Municipale
B.N. MS.fr.	Bibliothèque Nationale, Manuscrits français
B.N. n.a.f.	Bibliothèque Nationale, nouvelles acquisitions françaises
B.N. p.o.	Bibliothèque Nationale, pièces originales
Dr.	Dossier
Min.	Minute

N.B.: All manuscript references are to the Archives Nationales unless otherwise stated. All printed works in English are published at London unless otherwise stated. All printed works in French are published at Paris unless otherwise stated.

PART ONE

CENTRAL GOVERNMENT AND THE INTENDANTS

CHAPTER 1

Central Government

IN THE years between 1624 and 1661, there was a broad measure of continuity in the organization of central government and in the process of decision-making. From 1624 until 1661, the central government was dominated by a chief minister: Richelieu from 13 August 1624 until his death on 4 December 1642, and Mazarin from 18 May 1643 until his death on 9 March 1661. The *ministériat*[1] thus encompassed a period of personal rule by Louis XIII (15 December 1621–14 May 1643), a period of Regency (18 May 1643–7 September 1651), and a period when Louis XIV was declared to have come of age but did not govern (7 September 1651–9 March 1661). It ended only when Louis XIV expressed the wish, on the death of Mazarin, to rule without a chief minister.

Unlike their immediate predecessors as chief minister— Concini and Luynes—both Richelieu and Mazarin laid the foundations for their future power by first attaining the position of cardinal. This position was of great significance, for as Richelieu took the trouble to demonstrate, cardinals had precedence in the king's council over other dignitaries of the crown such as the Chancellor and the Constable, the head of the army.[2] Appointment to a position of such importance was naturally the outcome of long intrigue. A particular candidate needed powerful political support before the king would apply pressure on the papacy to agree to the promotion. Richelieu was appointed cardinal on 5 September 1622, to fill the vacancy left by the death of Cardinal de Retz. The crucial factor in

---

[1] A term used by contemporaries: E. Thuau, *Raison d'état et pensée politique à l'époque de Richelieu* (1966), pp. 239–40. P. R. Doolin, *The Fronde* (Cambridge, Mass., 1935), pp. 73–4, 152–6. Cf. J. Bérenger, 'Pour une enquête européenne. Le problème du ministériat au xviie. siècle', *Annales E.S.C.*, xxix (1974), 166–92.

[2] *Lettres, instructions diplomatiques et papiers d'état du Cardinal de Richelieu*, ed. D. L. M. Avenel (8 vols., 1853–77), ii. 6–12. *Les papiers de Richelieu. Section politique intérieure. Correspondance et papiers d'état. I. 1624–1626*, ed. P. Grillon (1975), pp. 84–8. Memorandum of Richelieu, May 1624. Cf. B.N. n.a.f. 7228, fo. 63/2. Remonstrances of Constable Lesdiguières, rejected by Louis XIII on 9 May 1624.

Richelieu's promotion was the support of Marie de Médicis, and the need of Louis XIII to conciliate his mother. Richelieu had negotiated reconciliations between the king and Marie de Médicis on 30 April 1619 and 10 August 1620, and in each of these agreements his appointment as cardinal had been envisaged.[1] Mazarin was appointed cardinal on 16 December 1641, as a result of the political pressure applied by Richelieu on Pope Urban VIII, who needed to avoid a schism with the French church.[2]

The cardinalate was important in itself and as a way of gaining the presidency of the king's council. Neither Richelieu nor Mazarin saw any incompatability in their responsibilities as both minister and cardinal. If indeed there was any such incompatability, it was officially removed by papal dispensation granted respectively on 9 December 1624 and 6 February 1644.[3] Nevertheless, the right of entry of cardinals into the king's council was criticized. So too was the right of precedence of cardinals which made it likely that they would gain the presidency of the council. In 1651, the *Parlement* of Paris made a concerted effort to exclude cardinals and foreigners from the king's council, while in the same year the *Frondeurs* negotiated at Rome to deprive Mazarin of the cardinalate.[4] Once they attained the position of chief minister, both Richelieu and Mazarin were extremely difficult to oust because of the support their position as cardinals brought them. The French clergy interpreted any attack on the position of cardinals in the king's council as an attack on the clergy itself. Provided that the chief minister continued to enjoy the support of the king or Regent, therefore, he was extremely difficult to remove from power.

The difficulty was in gaining the support of the king. Richelieu's appointment in 1624 had virtually been forced upon a reluctant king. His outstanding ability was well known

[1] J. A. Clarke, *Huguenot warrior: the life and times of Henri de Rohan, 1579–1638* (The Hague, 1966), pp. 67, 69.

[2] P. Blet, 'Richelieu et les débuts de Mazarin', *Revue d'Histoire Moderne et Contemporaine*, vi (1959), 241–68.

[3] M. Laurain-Portemer, 'Le statut de Mazarin dans l'église. Aperçus sur le haut clergé de la contre-réforme', *Bibliothèque de l'École des Chartes*, cxxviii (1970), 21–2.

[4] ibid., pp. 46–52. P. Blet, *Le clergé de France et la monarchie. Étude sur les assemblées générales du clergé de 1615 à 1666* (2 vols., Rome, 1959), ii. 66–73.

and was a major obstacle to his attaining power.[1] Louis XIII
had spoken bitter words against Richelieu before exiling him
to his diocese of Luçon in 1617.[2] Richelieu had to combat an
incumbent chief minister in La Vieuville, albeit only a *de facto*
chief minister, who owed his position chiefly to the power
vacuum after the dismissal of the Brûlarts on 4 February 1624.
In order to secure the dismissal of the Brûlarts, La Vieuville
had had to fall back upon support from the Queen Mother. The
price of this support was to allow Richelieu entry into the
king's council as the nominee of the Queen Mother (29 April
1624).[3] La Vieuville's foreign policy had taken an increasingly
anti-Habsburg turn which offended Marie de Médicis and the
dévot party, who wanted a policy of co-existence abroad and a
crusade against the Protestants at home. Richelieu was thus
nominated with the intention that he should oppose this
tendency in foreign policy. La Vieuville hoped that Richelieu's
importance would be no greater than that enjoyed by another
cardinal, De la Rochefoucauld. La Vieuville's apparent lack of
ability, the charge of peculation against him, the opposition of
Marie de Médicis to his policies, and above all the suspicion
of Louis XIII that his chief minister was acting with too much
independence—all these factors led to his arrest on 12 August
1624 and the appointment of Richelieu as his successor.[4]

In contrast, Mazarin had no chief minister to combat in
1643, because a triumvirate—comprising himself, Chavigny,
and Sublet des Noyers—had controlled policy after the death of
Richelieu. If Richelieu had needed merely to influence the
king against La Vieuville to secure his rise to power, Mazarin
had the much more complicated task of reassuring a king
whose health was rapidly failing, while retaining the support of

[1] 'Cet homme est redouté de chacun comme en sachant trop et comme trop
habile . . .' B. Zeller, *Richelieu et les ministres de Louis XIII de 1621 à 1624* (1880),
p. 281.
[2] *Lettres . . . de Richelieu*, ed. Avenel, i. 537. Richelieu was exiled on 15 June 1617
to Luçon and on 7 Apr. 1618 to Avignon. E. Griselle, *Louis XIII et Richelieu.
Lettres et pièces diplomatiques* (1911, reprinted Geneva, 1974), pp. 164, 185.
[3] Zeller, op. cit., p. 241.
[4] *Lettres . . . de Richelieu*, ed. Avenel, ii. 4: 'il a pleu au roy me donner la charge de
son premier ministre à la prière de la reine'. Richelieu to Père Joseph, *c.* 13 Aug.
1624, but misdated by Avenel as end of April or beginning of May 1624. A. D.
Lublinskaya, *French absolutism, the crucial phase, 1620–1629* (Cambridge, 1968),
pp. 267–8.

the future Regent. An indication of Mazarin's success is that, of his two rivals, Sublet des Noyers was dismissed by Louis XIII because he sided too early with the future Regent, whereas Chavigny was demoted by Anne of Austria because he appeared to remain loyal to the king's wish that a regency council be set up after his death.[1] Mazarin had to face competition from dangerous rivals of proven ability: but his major debt was to Richelieu, which carried with it no commitment into the future.[2]

The chief minister had also to retain royal support. This was less of a problem for Mazarin than for Richelieu. Richelieu had predicted that Anne of Austria would like Mazarin because he had something of the air of Buckingham, her erstwhile platonic lover. Anne of Austria had promised her husband that she would 'never abandon' Mazarin. His continuance as chief minister appeared the best guarantee not only of her Regency, but of her son's future accession to absolute power.[3] The problem for Mazarin, therefore, arose less from his rivals— Châteauneuf, Chavigny, and De Retz—whom Anne of Austria disliked, than from other influences on her, such as the *dévots*, who were hostile to Mazarin.[4] In contrast, Richelieu was never the favourite of Louis XIII. This role was filled first by François de Baradas, then by Claude de Saint-Simon and finally by Cinq-Mars, whose influence over the king Richelieu encouraged until he used his position to conspire against the chief minister in 1642. This was a fundamental source of weakness in Richelieu's position. Despite Louis XIII's protestations of support after the Chalais conspiracy in 1626, after the Day of Dupes (10 November 1630), and after the Cinq-Mars conspiracy, Richelieu could never rely on the king's total commitment to his position as chief minister. Incapable of filling the role of favourite, Richelieu might have used his unquestioned religious authority to control the conscience of the

---

[1] G. Dethan, 'Mazarin avant le ministère', *Revue Historique*, ccxxvii (1962), 33–66.

[2] Mazarin entered the council on 5 Dec. 1642, possibly at the request of Richelieu on his death-bed. Cf. Griselle, op. cit., pp. 57–8.

[3] Laurain-Portemer, 'Le statut de Mazarin', pp. 75–6.

[4] R. Allier, *La cabale des dévots, 1627–1666* (1902, reprinted Geneva, 1970), pp. 339–40, 346, 358–61. For Anne of Austria's dislike of Châteauneuf: A.A.E. France 888, fo. 37.

king. Yet Richelieu did not choose to combine his political role
with that of confessor, with the result that the confessor could
present a political danger to his position.[1]

The role of Richelieu and Mazarin in domestic policy-

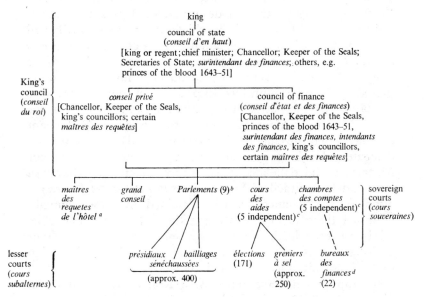

FIG. 1. The King's council and the judicial and financial courts, 1624–1661.

[a] The *Parlement* of Paris (e.g. on 17 Aug. 1648) denied the *maîtres des requêtes de
l'hôtel* the status of a sovereign court. A number of *maîtres des requêtes* were
allowed to sit in the *Parlement*. In 1669, the *Parlement* tried to limit this number to
four.

[b] Ten after the establishment of the *Parlement* at Metz in 1633.

[c] Three of these courts were amalgamated as a *cour des comptes* (Aix, Montpellier,
and Pau). Two *cours des aides* (Dijon, Vienne) were linked with *Parlements*
(Dijon and Grenoble, respectively in 1630 and 1658).

[d] The *bureaux des finances* claimed to be sovereign courts, but Chancellor Séguier
denied them this status in 1653. They claimed also to be superior to the *élections*,
but this claim was not recognized except in the years 1640–2.

making has to be elucidated issue by issue. Certain generaliz-
ations may be made, however. The chief minister was responsible for the detailed instructions issued to ambassadors,
military commanders, and governors. He carried on an

[1] D. P. O'Connell, *Richelieu* (1968), p. 366.

enormous correspondence with bishops, nobles, office-holders, and intendants. The burden was extremely heavy. On 26 June 1626, because of ill health, Richelieu was discharged from the tasks of receiving visits from private individuals and hearing private grievances and requests so that he could concentrate on '[affaires] des estrangères et des générales et plus importantes qui seront dans l'Estat . . .'[1] The chief minister undoubtedly had a preponderant voice in the small council of state (*conseil d'en haut*).

He was responsible for conveying ministerial advice to the king or Regent: it was unusual for the chief minister to be by-passed by the other ministers. In practice, of course, there were limitations on the power of the chief minister. After 1630, the subordination of domestic policy to foreign policy meant inevitably that the chief minister concentrated on the latter and delegated decisions on the former. Neither Richelieu nor Mazarin attended the meetings of the lesser councils[2]—the *conseil privé* and the council of finance (*conseil d'état et des finances*)—although the Chancellor, who presided in these councils, informed them of decisions taken there. (Fig. 1.) The chief minister left the details of financial administration to the finance ministers (*surintendants des finances*). Richelieu declared in 1640 that 'il n'avoit aucune cognoissance des finances [mais] il s'en rapportoit à ceux ausquels le Roy en avoit donné la direction . . .'[3] Mazarin had a similar attitude. Foucquet remarked that Mazarin 'ne donna jamais d'ordre précis' in financial questions.[4] Nevertheless, in a crisis the chief minister might demand a review of financial policy: Richelieu did so in 1637; so too did Mazarin in 1655.

The long period of political predominance of a chief minister had a profound effect upon the structure of government. Not

[1] *Les papiers de Richelieu*, ed. Grillon, i. 368.
[2] When Mazarin signed decrees in the council of finance in the first week of Nov. 1643, it was regarded as exceptional: A.A.E. France 847, fo. 90ᵛ, 7 Nov. 1643. E 184c, fos. 1–120, 4 Nov. 1643. Richelieu, when writing to Bouthillier on 28 Aug. 1639, referred to 'vostre conseil des finances'. *Lettres . . . de Richelieu*, ed. Avenel, vi. 501. O. A. Ranum, *Richelieu and the councillors of Louis XIII. A study of the secretaries of state and the superintendents of finance in the ministry of Richelieu, 1635–1642* (Oxford, 1963), p. 124, n. 1.
[3] B.N. MS.fr. 16218, fo. 418. Cf. Ranum, op. cit., p. 136.
[4] P. Clément, *La police sous Louis XIV* (1866), p. 29. B.L. Add. MS. 39673, fo. 74.

the least of the consequences was a reduction in the status of the Chancellor. In the sixteenth century the Chancellor himself had not infrequently been the chief minister—Duprat and De l'Hôpital were good examples.[1] During the reign of Henri IV, Bellièvre had attempted to gain the position of chief minister as well as Chancellor, but by 1605 had lost the political struggle with Sully.[2] During the years 1624–61, the Chancellorship lost much of its independence and the political disgrace of Chancellors became a feature of French life. Brûlart de Sillery was disgraced on 1 January 1624, thus preparing the way for the ascendancy of La Vieuville.[3] D'Aligre was disgraced in 1626.[4] Séguier was disgraced twice during the Fronde.[5] It was impolitic to depose, let alone prosecute, a Chancellor (although there were precedents, notably from the reign of Francis I).[6] Thus the seals were transferred to a Keeper of the Seals (*Garde des Sceaux*), of whom six were appointed between 1624 and 1661. Three Keepers of the Seals also ended up in disgrace for opposing the chief minister (Marillac in 1630;[7] Châteauneuf in 1633[8] and again in 1651).[9] Mathieu Molé was the only Keeper of the Seals in this period to co-exist with a Chancellor for any significant period of time—he had proved his loyalty during

[1] A. Buisson, *Le chancelier Antoine Duprat* (1935); A. Buisson, *Michel de l'Hôpital* (1950).

[2] R. Mousnier, 'Sully et le conseil d'état et des finances', *Revue Historique*, cxcii (1941), 68–86. R. Mousnier, *La vénalité des offices sous Henri IV et Louis XIII* (2nd ed., 1971), pp. 600–3.

[3] Zeller, *Richelieu et les ministres de Louis XIII*, p. 239. B.L. Harleian 4472b, fo. 288, Aligre's letters as Keeper of the Seals and *serment* of 6 Jan. 1624.

[4] Aligre was exiled to his estates at La Rivière in the Perche for apparent sympathy with Gaston d'Orléans. He continued to call himself Chancellor of France and Navarre until his death on 11 Dec. 1635. B.N. p.o. 36, nos. 132, 133, 139. Cf. B.L. Harleian 4472b, fo. 285, Marillac's letters as Keeper of the Seals and *serment* of 1 June 1626.

[5] '. . . m'esloign[é] de la cour deux fois'. A.A.E. France 882, fo. 72, Séguier to Anne of Austria, 18 Mar. 1652. Séguier was disgraced on the first occasion between 2 Mar. 1650 and 13 Apr. 1651, and on the second occasion between 8 Sept. 1651 and 30 Sept. 1652.

[6] Chancellor Poyet was arrested in 1542 and removed from office two years later. H. Michaud, *La grande chancellerie et les écritures royales au seizième siècle, 1515–1589* (1967), p. 25. B.L. Harleian 4472b, fo. 234ᵛ.

[7] B.L. Harleian 4472b, fo. 283, Châteauneuf's letters as Keeper of the Seals and *serment* of 14 Nov. 1630.

[8] 01 7, fo. 18ᵛ, Séguier's letters as Keeper of the Seals and *serment* of 25 Feb. 1633.

[9] B.L. Harleian 4472b, fo. 278, Molé's letters as Keeper of the Seals, Apr. 1651. He held the Seals from 3 April to 13 April.

the Fronde and could not be removed for the sake of administrative convenience.[1]

There could be no doubt that Richelieu and Mazarin were the masters among their respective ministers. This did not, however, preclude the Chancellor from retaining important areas of governmental responsibility. This was especially true under Richelieu, when the exceptionally frequent and important political trials set in motion by him gave the Chancellor or Keeper of the Seals a vital role both in selecting suitable candidates to sit on the judicial commissions and in exploring the legal precedents for the prosecution case.[2] It was this activity—with its implied subordination to Richelieu's whim— which made Séguier extremely unpopular by 1643.[3] The Chancellor also received the oath of loyalty from the councillors of state.[4] Historically, he had a special relationship with the *maîtres des requêtes*.[5] He was also, except in the years 1643–51, *ex officio* president of the lesser councils (the *conseil privé* and the *conseil d'état et des finances*).[6] The Chancellor usually appointed the *rapporteurs* of decrees in the lesser councils, and proposed suitable candidates for promotion as intendants or senior councillors of state. When the political influence of Séguier declined in the 1650s, these rights of proposal and nomination were increasingly threatened by other ministers.

[1] Molé was Keeper of the Seals from 8 Sept. 1651 until his death on 3 Jan. 1656, despite the return of Séguier to favour on 30 Sept. 1652. Séguier protested at this situation: A.A.E. France 885, fo. 291, Oct. 1652. B.L. Harleian 4472b, fos. 212, 228, n.d. and 2 May 1653.

[2] W. F. Church, *Richelieu and reason of state* (Princeton, N.J., 1972), pp. 331, n. 117, 332, n. 119. J. Richou, *Histoire des commissions extraordinaires sous l'ancien régime* (1905), p. 47, calls Richelieu's ministry 'l'époque par excellence des commissions extraordinaires'.

[3] Omer Talon considered that Séguier was 'dans la haine publique' at this date. Talon, *Mémoires*, ed. J. F. Michaud and J. J. F. Poujoulat, 3rd ser., vi (1839), p. 91.

[4] Michaud, *La grande Chancellerie*, p. 51. Bellièvre as Chancellor received the *foys et hommages* of fief-holders and oaths of councillors of state, as did Brûlart de Sillery. But Molé as Keeper of the Seals was allowed to retain this power on 2 May 1653, despite the protests of Séguier: B.L. Harleian 4472b, fos. 206, 228, 242. For an example of the oath of a councillor of state, dating from 1593: *Lettres et mémoires adressés au Chancelier Séguier, 1633–1649*, ed. R. Mousnier (2 vols., 1964), ii. 1038–9.

[5] Michaud, *La grande chancellerie*, p. 50.

[6] Between 1643 and 1651 Gaston d'Orléans and Condé (father and son), as princes of the blood summoned to the council by the Regent, had the right of presidency. Séguier accepted their rights, which were exercised infrequently. Séguier opposed the claim of Vendôme, a bastard of Henri IV, who was only a duke. A.A.E. France 853, fos. 170, 171. Cf. Michaud, *La grande chancellerie*, p. 38.

The Chancellor had the right of signature to all decrees and orders emanating from the council. As late as 1658, when he was about to set out to Lyon, Séguier had to leave behind specific instructions to the secretaries of the council, empowering them to sign decrees in his absence.[1] This right of signature gave the Chancellor a power of veto—a power which was used rarely, and then only with discretion. In a celebrated incident, Bellièvre used it in the question of the *droit annuel* in 1602.[2] As late as 1656, Séguier refused to sign an edict ordering the sale of royal forests in the Île-de-France, because this constituted an alienation of the royal domain which was contrary to the ordinances.[3] The Chancellor also had certain legislative powers, though the extent of these depended on the zeal of the incumbent and the legislative activities of the other ministers. Before 1661, the reform of the council—in the sense of reorganization of its structure—had depended essentially on the attitude of the Chancellor. André Lefèvre d'Ormesson, a reliable witness since he was longest-serving councillor (*doyen*) by 1661, noted the difference between the Chancellors in their involvement in reform of the council. According to D'Ormesson, Chancellor Sillery (10 December 1607–1 January 1624) initiated few reforms and a major ruling on 12 October 1622 was drawn up against his advice. The important ruling of Compiègne (1 June 1624) was issued while Étienne d'Aligre was Keeper of the Seals. Yet according to D'Ormesson, the ruling was issued at the instigation of Marillac and against the wishes of D'Aligre, who frequently remarked that he had not wanted the measure to pass. In contrast, nine rulings were issued during Marillac's period as Keeper of the Seals (1 June 1626–10 November 1630).[4] The record of Séguier's Chancellorship in this respect was not particularly impressive, the chief achievements being the rulings of 16 June 1644[5] and 1 May 1657.[6] The reform of 15 September 1661 was the work of

[1] E 317b, fo. 262, 26 Oct. 1658.
[2] Mousnier 'Sully et le conseil', p. 73; Mousnier, *La vénalité*, pp. 234–6.
[3] A.A.E. France 900, fo. 157ᵛ, 12 July 1656.
[4] Marillac was known as a 'grand faiseur de règlemens': B.M. Rouen MS. Léber 5767 (3252 t.i), fo. 230ᵛ. The rulings are in R. Mousnier, 'Les règlements du Conseil du Roi sous Louis XIII', *Annuaire-Bulletin de la Société de l'Histoire de France* (1948), pp. 93–211.
[5] E 1688, fo. 111 and A.A.E. France 849, fo. 282.
[6] B.N. 500 Colbert 194, fo. 291.

Colbert.[1] So too was the reform of the *conseil privé*, which was implemented on 3 January 1673, after the death of Séguier.[2] It was Colbert, too, who was the driving force behind the civil and criminal law codes of 1667 and 1670.[3]

Up to 1661, the presidency of the council of finance (*conseil d'état et des finances*) gave the Chancellor at least a negative role with regard to financial legislation. Séguier agreed to, or opposed, legislation proposed by the finance ministers. When Séguier went to Normandy to suppress the revolt of the *Va-Nu-Pieds* in 1640, the council of finance and the finance ministers had to follow him to Rouen.[4] The Chancellor kept his own copy of the cash payments (*comptants*) made by the crown, which was quite distinct from the copy kept by the finance ministers.[5] The establishment of a new council—the *conseil royal des finances*—on 15 September 1661, to which the Chancellor was summoned at the discretion of the king, removed these important powers. However, the decline of the Chancellorship had been foreshadowed under Richelieu and Mazarin by its subordination to the requirements of a system of government based upon a chief minister.

There was a significant development of the secretaryships of state between 1624 and 1661, although the situation was not clear-cut because older forms of secretarial organization survived. A great deal of the work of the secretaries of state was traditionally concerned with issuing letters patent and decrees of the council and carrying out the king's commands as *secrétaire en mois*.[6] In addition, the king might delegate the signing of these papers to his secretaries of state and others during his unavoidable absence from Paris.[7] After 1643, the secretaries of state acted with considerable independence in

---

[1] 'C'est M. Colbert qui l'a dressé.' B.N. Clairambault 651, fo. 355.

[2] M. Antoine, *Le conseil du roi sous Louis XV* (Paris–Geneva, 1970), p. 64.

[3] R. Pillorget, 'Henri Pussort, oncle de Colbert, 1615–1697', *Le conseil du roi de Louis XII à la Révolution*, ed. R. Mousnier (1970), pp. 262–3.

[4] E 154a, fo. 15, council of finance at Rouen with Bullion and Bouthillier present.

[5] B.L. Harleian 4472b, fos. 413–17, 'Inventaire des Estatz de comptant qui sont ès mains de Monseigneur le Chancelier'.

[6] Ranum, *Richelieu and the councillors of Louis XIII*, pp. 53, 60–1, 102, n. 2. Michaud, *La grande chancellerie*, pp. 149–50. Antoine, *Le conseil du roi*, p. 278.

[7] Richelieu and Servien, the secretary of state for war, were empowered to sign all letters patent and ordinances during the absence of Louis XIII at the frontier of Champagne: A.G. A1 26, fo. 83, Aug. 1635. Condé, Séguier, and Loménie de

issuing the orders of Anne of Austria and Mazarin on behalf of a king who had not come of age. In 1661, as one of the first acts of his personal rule, Louis XIV reversed this tendency. The king prohibited his secretaries of state from issuing *arrêts en commandement* without receiving specific orders from himself.[1] The secretaries of state were office-holders. They bought and sold their positions, each office being valued at approximately 300,000 *livres*.[2] They could transmit their offices to their heirs.[3] The positions of minister of the crown and *surintendant des finances* could not be bought and sold, however. They were held by virtue of letters patent,[4] appointments and dismissals being made by the king, subject to the advice of the chief minister. When a minister was given departmental responsibility for war or foreign affairs, he usually bought the office of secretary of state. This was often a lengthy process, however: Le Tellier received his letters patent as war minister on 13 April 1643, but was unable to buy a secretaryship of state until 22 October 1645, after the death of Sublet des Noyers.[5] The

---

Brienne, a secretary of state, were empowered to sign despatches and *lettres de commandement* during the king's absence at Lyon: 01 7, fo. 36, 26 Jan. 1642.

[1] Decree of 3 Aug. 1661: *Mémoriaux du conseil de 1661*, ed. J. M. de Boislisle (3 vols., 1905–7), iii. 8.

[2] Payment of this sum to the heirs of Potier d'Ocquerre: Ranum, op. cit., p. 36, n. 3. Acquisition of Sublet's office for this sum by Le Tellier: *Lettres . . . au Chancelier Séguier*, ed. Mousnier, ii. 1214. Cf. Mousnier, *La vénalité*, pp. 341, 343. Michaud, *La grande chancellerie*, p. 138, n. 7. Servien bought his office for 500,000 *livres* on the death of Beauclerc, but recognized that this was 'à titre onereux': A.A.E. France 890, fo. 184, 1652.

[3] *Survivance* of Louis-Henri Loménie de Brienne: A.A.E. France 878, fo. 294, 24 Aug. 1651. *Survivance* of Louis III Phélypeaux de la Vrillière: A.A.E. France 877, fo. 385, 10 Dec. 1651. Confirmed: 01 7, fo. 36ᵛ, 15 Apr. 1654. *Survivance* of François Le Tellier, marquis de Louvois: *Lettres . . . au Chancelier Séguier*, ed. Mousnier, ii. 1214 (ref. to 13 Dec. 1655). Additional permission was needed for the heir to carry out the duties of secretary of state: 01 7, fo. 35, 28 May 1658 (permission to Louis-Henri Loménie de Brienne).

[4] Either a *brevet* or a commission. The *surintendance* was described as a commission when abolished on 15 Sept. 1661: E 1713, fo. 173. Cf. B.N. MS. fr. 18152, fo. 81. Jean Bochart and Marillac were appointed as joint *surintendants* 'par commission du 2 sept. 1624'.

[5] L. André, *Michel Le Tellier et l'organisation de l'armée monarchique* (Montpellier, 1906), pp. 98–101. A.A.E. France 846, fo. 127, 13 Apr. 1643, commission to Le Tellier. A.A.E. France 852, fo. 170, 22 Oct. 1645, provisions of secretary of state for Le Tellier. Even then, Le Tellier's claims were contested by Servien, who argued that he and not Sublet had the right to the office. Servien contended that his resignation had been 'exigé par menaces à la poursuitte dud. Sr. Denoyers deux ans après sa retraite de la cour'. A.A.E. France 847, fo. 136, 25 Dec. 1643.

appointment as minister was the avenue to real power. Whereas ministers usually bought the office of secretary of state, it was unusual for secretaries of state to be promoted minister.[1] In general, the ministers with the greatest political power were those who were secretaries of state and whose departments were least subject to scrutiny by the chief minister. The influence of Richelieu and Mazarin was greatest over foreign affairs. It was rather less over the war minister, particularly after Le Tellier assumed control in 1643 and demonstrated his loyalty to Mazarin during the Fronde. Where the finance ministers were concerned, the influence of Richelieu and Mazarin was minimal.

In part, this varying degree of independence enjoyed by the different government departments reflected their stage of development before 1624. There had been finance ministers of a sort during the wars of religion—first, Artus de Cossé, Pomponne de Bellièvre, and François d'O; later, under Henri IV, Sully.[2] The development was interrupted on two occasions, however, when responsibility for finance was vested in a commission of the council (25 November 1594; 5 February 1611).[3] Thus a continuous line of *surintendants des finances* is traceable only from the ministry of Jeannin,[4] with the first letters of appointment being those of Schomberg on 6 September 1619.[5] By 1630 Le Bret could describe the post as 'maintenant une des plus importantes du Royaume'.[6] Few of the finance ministers were dismissed, and most of the (relatively frequent) changes resulted from death in office. Despite his

[1] Loménie de Brienne and Phélypeaux de la Vrillière were secretaries of state between 1629 and 1643, but not ministers. Ranum, op. cit., pp. 68–71. De Bailleul remained a minister of state after he resigned as *surintendant*: A.G. A1 101, no. 344, 18 July 1647. Abel Servien held no secretaryship of state under Mazarin, nor did he have departmental responsibilities before January 1653. Yet he was one of the most important ministers between 1649 and 1653. Cf. E 234c, fo. 158, 9 Jan. 1649: 'Le Sr. de Servien ministre d'estat . . .'

[2] H. de Jouvencel, *Le contrôleur-général des finances sous l'ancien régime* (1901), p. 15. B. Barbiche and D. J. Buisseret, 'Sully et la surintendance des finances', *Bibliothèque de l'École des Chartes* cxxiii (1965), 538–43.

[3] Mousnier, *La vénalité*, p. 101; Mousnier, 'Les règlements du conseil', pp. 128–31. B.N. MS. fr. 16218, fos. 121, 225, 25 Nov. 1594, 5 Feb. 1611.

[4] Jeannin referred to himself as 'naguères surintendant'. B.N. p.o. 1578 (Dr. 36,199), no. 12, 1 Dec. 1621.

[5] Barbiche and Buisseret, art. cit., p. 542, n. 7. B.N. MS. fr. 18152, fo. 77. Before this date, Barbiche and Buisseret conclude, the *surintendance* was 'plus une situation de fait qu'une charge bien déterminée'.

[6] Cardin Le Bret, *De la souveraineté du roy* (1632), p. 172.

threats to Bullion, Richelieu never dismissed a finance minister. Mazarin did so only once, when he rid himself of D'Hémery as the storm clouds of the Fronde gathered in 1648. Other dismissals coincided with changes in royal policy. Louis XIII imprisoned La Vieuville in 1624. Bouthillier lost his place in 1643 because he wanted a regency council as set out in the last will and testament of Louis XIII. Louis XIV imprisoned Foucquet in 1661. There can be little doubt that most of the finance ministers enjoyed a prestige greater than that of other ministers. Something of the special position of the finance minister is suggested by his mediation in 1631–3 in the departmental conflict between the secretaries of state for foreign affairs and war.[1] Furthermore, while the other ministers might attempt to block a particular candidate from the vacant position of minister of finance,[2] they were never able to force the resignation of an incumbent minister. By contrast, the experienced Bullion had little difficulty in 1636 in forcing the resignation of Servien, the war minister, after a dispute over the war estimates.[3]

An independent war ministry emerged later than the finance ministry, as the ruling of 29 April 1619 bears witness.[4] Not until the appointment of Beauclerc (4 February 1624) was there, properly speaking, a secretary of state for war at all, while the true emergence of the war ministry as a separate department of government coincided with the entry of France into the Thirty Years' War. If the ministry of war developed relatively late, that of foreign affairs emerged earlier. The immense prestige of Villeroy—secretary of state under Charles IX, Henri III, Henri IV, and Louis XIII—ensured this.[5] After Villeroy's

[1] A.G. A1 16, fo. 701, Servien to D'Effiat, 22 Nov. 1631, requesting his mediation in Servien's dispute with Bouthillier, 'sachant le pouvoir que vous avez auprès de M. Bouthillier'.
[2] A.A.E. France 891, fo. 56 and 892, fo. 148. Memorandum of Servien to Mazarin, 25 Jan. 1653, accusing Le Tellier of trying to block his candidacy for the *surintendance*.
[3] Ranum, op. cit., p. 161. A.G. A1 41, fo. 117, 27 Feb. 1636. Servien commented: 'le Roy . . . fust réduit à choisir [celui] qu'il voudroit conserver . . . ce grand homme de bien M. Bullion n'eust pas manqué d'artifices ny de moyens avec les finances du Roy dont il dispose pour attaquer mon honneur.'
[4] H. Michaud, 'Aux origines du secrétariat d'état à la guerre. Les "règlements" de 1617–1619', *Revue d'Histoire Moderne et Contemporaine* xix (1972), 389–413. Cf. Michaud, *La grande chancellerie*, pp. 146–7. Ranum, op. cit., pp. 53–5.
[5] J. Nouaillac, *Villeroy. Secrétaire d'état et ministre de Charles IX, Henri III et Henri IV, 1543–1610* (1909).

death, however, foreign affairs became linked with domestic politics. The Brûlarts dominated politics after the death of Luynes (15 December 1621) by controlling the Chancellorship and the secretaryship of state for foreign affairs. After the dismissal of the Brûlarts in February 1624, responsibility for the conduct of foreign policy was divided between three secretaries of state, thus leaving first La Vieuville, and later Richelieu, in real control. In his brief experience of government in 1616–17, Richelieu had been in charge of foreign affairs.[1] The attempt of La Vieuville to exclude him from foreign affairs in 1624[2] ensured that this area of government would be subject to his close scrutiny once he gained predominance in the council. After 11 March 1626, Richelieu filled the secretaryship of state for foreign affairs with loyal supporters. The chief minister's control of foreign policy was ensured by the fact that the council of state (*conseil d'en haut*)—with the king or regent and chief minister present—was the forum for all major decisions in foreign policy: this was much less true of military questions, and scarcely true at all of financial questions.[3] It is therefore difficult to conceive of a forceful and independent foreign ministry as long as there was a chief minister. The executive authority enjoyed by Pomponne, Colbert de Croissy, and Torcy was the direct result of Louis XIV's decision in 1661 to rule without a chief minister.[4]

Almost all the ministerial appointments at the time of Richelieu and Mazarin were made from the Parisian *noblesse de robe*,[5] and

[1] V. L. Tapié, *La politique étrangère de la France et le début de la guerre de Trente Ans, 1616–1621* (1934), p. 13.

[2] Richelieu was prohibited from negotiating 'dans sa maison n'y traiter avec personne des affaires de Sa Majesté'. Zeller, *Richelieu et les ministres de Louis XIII*, p. 281. Lublinskaya, *French absolutism*, pp. 262–4.

[3] Ranum, op. cit., p. 93. Cf. B.M. Rouen Léber 5767, fo. 223. Council of state, Feb. 1643. 'Le conseil du Roy estoit composé pour les affaires d'estat, affaires de la guerre, affaires estrangères du Cardinal Mazarin, du Chancelier, du surintendant Bouthillier, de Messieurs de Chavigny et des Noyers, secrétaires d'estat.'

[4] C. G. Picavet, *La diplomatie française au temps de Louis XIV, 1661–1715. Institutions, mœurs et coutumes* (1930), pp. 11–69. J. C. Rule, 'Colbert de Torcy, an emergent bureaucracy, and the formulation of French foreign policy, 1698–1715', *Louis XIV and Europe*, ed. R. M. Hatton (1976), pp. 261–88.

[5] J. F. Bluche, 'L'origine sociale des secrétaires d'état de Louis XIV, 1661–1715', *XVIIe Siècle*, xlii–xliii (1959), 10 [translated in *Louis XIV and absolutism*, ed. R. M. Hatton (1976), p. 86], stresses the continuity between the ministers before and after 1661 in terms of social origins.

the exceptions came from the higher, not lower, levels of political society. In the case of the war ministers, a particular type of expertise was valued, it seems: three of the four war ministers of Richelieu and Mazarin had previously been intendants of the army.[1] No previous diplomatic experience was essential for foreign affairs, however, while a particularly varied picture emerges with regard to the finance ministers. All finance ministers were required to command the support and co-operation of the financiers, but there was great diversity of previous experience. Some—Schomberg, D'Effiat, and La Meilleraye—were career soldiers, not, properly speaking, administrators at all.[2] Since a great deal of government expenditure went on military affairs, such appointments made sense provided the men chosen could win the support of the financiers. For others—notably De Bailleul in 1643 and Servien ten years later—the post was an honourable retirement, conferred as a reward for years of loyal service.[3] Of only three finance ministers—Bochart de Champigny in 1624, Bullion in 1632, and D'Hémery in 1647—could it be said that their appointments were the result of proven experience in financial administration.[4]

On occasions, more than one minister was appointed to the same department. This was true of foreign affairs between 1624 and 1626 and of military affairs before 1626. It was true of finance in the years 1624–6, 1632–40, 1643–7, and 1653–9. The appointment of joint finance ministers sometimes led to

[1] Servien served as intendant in Guyenne in 1628 and in the army of Italy in 1630. Sublet was an *intendant des finances* serving on the frontier of Picardy in 1632–6: C. Schmidt, 'Le rôle et les attributions d'un "intendant des finances" aux armées. Sublet des Noyers de 1632 à 1636', *Revue d'Histoire Moderne et Contemporaine*, 1st ser., ii (1900–1), 156–75. Le Tellier was an intendant of the army in Lombardy in 1640–3: N. L. Caron, *Michel Le Tellier. Son administration comme intendant d'armée en Piémont, 1640–1643* (Paris–Nantes, 1880).

[2] Cf. D'Ormesson's judgement of La Meilleraye: 'tout le monde demeurant d'accord qu'il estoit bien meilleur capitaine que financier'. *Journal d'Olivier Lefèvre d'Ormesson et extraits des mémoires d'André Lefèvre d'Ormesson*, ed. P. A. Chéruel (2 vols., 1860–1), i. 738.

[3] Servien stated categorically of the *surintendance* that there was 'point de charge où il faut moins de travail et l'exercice de celle-cy consiste plus à avoir de la prévoyance et de la fermeté et de la probité qu'à estre laborieux'. A.A.E. France 891, fos. 54–5 and 892, fo. 148, 25 Jan. 1653.

[4] Bochart had served previously as *contrôleur-général des finances*. Bullion had been a member of the finance commission of 5 Feb. 1611. D'Hémery had been an *intendant des finances* since 1631.

conflict, and—in 1645[1] and 1654[2]—created artificial divisions of responsibility which weakened the central direction of the finance ministry. On 22 December 1654, Servien complained to Mazarin of the 'obstacles et . . . longueurs qui arrivent ordinairement dans les employs de cette nature quand ils sont partagez'. He asserted that Foucquet was not prepared to take second place and that 'on ne doit plus chercher ailleurs la cause de la froideur des traitants, ny l'humeur qu'ils ont prise de fermer leurs bourses . . .'[3]

It was clearly preferable in war, finance, and foreign affairs to appoint ministers who had a 'connaissance du mestier'.[4] Without specialist knowledge, a minister might lose control over the subordinate officials in his department. This was perhaps less likely in war and foreign affairs, but in finance it was an issue of the gravest importance. Under Richelieu there had never been more than four *intendants des finances*, chiefly because Richelieu distrusted these officials. The financial crisis of the Fronde led Mazarin to throw such caution to the winds. By June 1649, the number of *intendants des finances* had been increased to eight; by July 1654 there were twelve. The government desperately needed the funds provided by the sale of these offices, and assumed that further loans from these officials would be forthcoming at a later date. Mazarin thus sacrificed the long-term interests of the state to a short-term gain. The new *intendants des finances* obtained their offices because they were rich: there was little investigation of the qualities of the new appointees. Doubtless, in theory, the double function of financier and *intendant des finances* was incompatible: an act renouncing former financial associates had to be signed and handed over to the Chancellor.[5] But was

---

[1] J. Dent, *Crisis in finance. Crown financiers and society in seventeenth-century France* (1973), pp. 94–6. B.N. MS.fr. 4222, fo. 197, 7 Oct. 1645. Despite the appointment of De Bailleul and Mesmes d'Avaux as joint *surintendants* on 5 June 1643, real financial control had passed to D'Hémery, the *contrôleur-général des finances* after 8 Nov. 1643.

[2] ibid., p. 68. E 272b, fo. 565; B.N. MS.fr. 4222, fo. 195; A.G. A1 144, fo. 299, 24 Dec. 1654.

[3] A.A.E. France 893/2, fo. 385 and 893/3, fo. 457.

[4] cf. the objection to René Longueil de Maisons's appointment as *surintendant* in May 1650, that he had 'nulle connaissance du mestier': A.A.E. France 871, fo. 69.

[5] B.N. MS.fr. 18510, fo. 297, 22 July 1654. Act of renunciation by Claude Boylesve, an *intendant des finances*, who specifically disavowed continued association

this 'self-denying ordinance' effective? Whether or not the *intendants des finances* practised fraud on a widespread scale, it is evident that they divided responsibility within the finance ministry to an unacceptable extent.[1] Each official was given his own geographical area, within which he was responsible for negotiating loan contracts with the financiers, making reports to the council, and drawing up the necessary documents. These officials could also be sent into the provinces to supervise the levy of taxation and the accounting procedure. Certain *intendants des finances* took, on their own initiative, decisions of great importance.[2] Thus although the finance ministers were often the most important members of the government after the chief minister, they were by no means firmly in command of their department. Divided financial leadership at the time of Richelieu and Mazarin worsened the fiscal problems of the French crown.

The growth in power of the secretaries of state was to a certain extent balanced by an unprecedented growth in government by council. The increase in the amount of business coming before the two lesser councils—the *conseil privé* and the council of finance (*conseil d'état et des finances*)—illustrates this development. At the peak of its activity, it was not at all unusual for the council of finance to issue 200[3] or even 295[4] decrees on a single day. On 30 September 1656, the *conseil privé* issued 347 decrees.[5] The increase in council business was related to the general political situation and public confidence in the government. There was thus a noticeable decline in activity during the Fronde, as is clear from the number of decrees issued by the

with his financial consortium (Guillaume Languet, Marchant, Desbordes, and François Jacquier).

[1] E 1710, fo. 56, 12 Oct. 1660. It was declared to be 'presque impossible d'empescher les abus quand le maniement en est dispersé entre plusieurs . . .' Cf. J. Dent, 'An aspect of the crisis of the seventeenth century: the collapse of the financial administration of the French monarchy 1653–1661', *Economic History Review*, 2nd ser., xx (1967), 241–56.

[2] For example, Claude Cornuel's decision to burn the minutes of treasury payments which greatly hampered subsequent financial investigations: Ranum, *Richelieu and the councillors of Louis XIII*, p. 153.

[3] E 289c, 31 May 1656.

[4] E 288b, 29 Apr. 1656.

[5] V6 332 and 333.

council of finance. 484 decrees were issued in June 1647, but the figure fell well below three hundred until after the Fronde. In June 1653, the figure reached 440 decrees. By June 1654, it had risen to 579; in June 1655, it reached 657 decrees. There were other, structural causes for an increase in council activity under Richelieu and Mazarin. One of these was the extension of the sale of offices, particularly in the first third of the seventeenth century. This brought with it problems of disputed ownership, which were referred to the king's council.[1] It also increased the numbers from individual families holding office in any one local court, thus making the transfer of lawsuits (*évocations*) to the king's council, or to other impartial courts, a more frequent occurrence.[2] The sale of offices also led to an increase in the number of courts[3] and this created new possibilities for disputes over jurisdiction between different courts in which the king's council acted as mediator. The increase in taxation at the time of Richelieu and Mazarin was a further reason for increased council activity.[4] The council of finance came to deal with cases of 'tax rebellion' and with the problem of arrears of taxation. Later, it transferred responsibility in fiscal questions from the finance courts to the provincial intendants.

As president of the two lesser councils, Séguier wrote proudly to Mazarin in 1656: 'il n'i a point de compagnie dans le Royaume qui sert mieux le Roy . . . ou qui traiste les affaires avec plus de règles'.[5] The situation was not quite as idyllic as Séguier suggested. In practice, the different responsibilities of the *conseil privé* and the council of finance were not clearly defined. In 1632 Le Bret defined the role of the *conseil privé* as one of adjudicating disputes between the sovereign courts, of protecting the rights and authority of the crown, of transferring lawsuits from one court to another by the process of *évocation*, and of allocating cases to particular courts by the process known

---

[1] Mousnier, *La vénalité*, pp. 167–8.

[2] ibid., pp. 189–92.

[3] In particular, new *élections* and *cours des aides* were established during Richelieu's ministry.

[4] '. . . la misère des troubles, la qualité des affaires, les finances, les nouvelles élections, les grandes fermes et le mesnage des finances ont obligé et obligent tous les jours de retenir au conseil plusieurs causes qu'il seroit mal aisé de juger ailleurs . . .' B.L. Egerton 1680, fo. 45ᵛ. Anon. memorandum on the council, variously attributed to Michel de Marillac or André Lefèvre d'Ormesson.

[5] B.L. Harleian 4489, fo. 43ᵛ, 23 Aug. 1656.

as *règlement de juges*. However, already by this date some of these functions were being assumed by the council of finance. Moreover, Le Bret attributed to the *conseil privé* powers in financial administration and revenue raising which belonged to the council of finance.[1] The membership of the *conseil privé* was basically the same as that of the council of finance (except that the *surintendants* and *intendants des finances* did not attend the *conseil privé*), the meetings merely taking place on different days.[2] Exactly why some cases appeared before one council rather than another was not always clear, however. There were instances of plaintiffs who had lost their case before one of the lesser councils seeking to reverse the decision before the other. On one such occasion, 30 August 1646, the council of state (*conseil d'en haut*) issued a clarification to the effect that it alone could annul a decree of one of the lesser councils.[3]

In other respects, too, Séguier's claim was not entirely accurate. The size of the lesser councils was a serious problem. During the Regencies of Marie de Médicis and Anne of Austria, an increase in appointments to the council by the Regent was an obvious way of gaining political support. 'Sous la minorité de Louis XIII', it was said, 'le nombre des conseillers commenca à s'accroistre et a depuis continué jusques au nombre effrené.'[4] There were 31 members of the council on 1 June 1624,[5] 35 on 3 January 1628,[6] 44 in 1630,[7] 38 in 1633[8] and 1637.[9] Membership rose rapidly after 1640, and especially after the declaration of the Regency of Anne of Austria. There were 63 councillors on 14 December 1640,[10] and 67 in February

---

[1] Le Bret, *De la souveraineté du roy*, p. 157. On the basis of the rulings of the council, Mousnier argues that after 1630 the *conseil privé* increased its importance at the expense of the council of finance: R. Mousnier, *La plume, la faucille et le marteau. Institutions et société en France du moyen âge à la Révolution* (1970), p. 161. A comparison of the decrees issued by these two councils suggests that the reverse was true.

[2] Antoine, *Le conseil du roi*, p. 63.

[3] E 214c, fo. 454, on the subject of a disputed election at Mende. The previous decree was issued on 22 Aug. 1646: E 214c, fo. 12.

[4] B.L. Egerton 1680, fo. 21. There were attempts to limit the number of *brevets* on 22 June 1611, 31 Jan. 1612, 30 Jan. 1613, 3 Mar. 1614, and 1 Feb. 1622. B.N. MS.fr. 16218, fos. 182–5, 198.

[5] Mousnier, 'Les règlements du conseil', pp. 180–1.

[6] ibid., pp. 176–7.

[7] B.N. MS.fr. 18152, fo. 132.

[8] B.N. MS.fr. 18152, fo. 130.

[9] B.N. MS.fr. 18152, fo. 133.

[10] B.M. Rouen MS. Léber 5767 (3252 t.i), fo. 136.

1643.[1] The Regency was established on 18 May 1643. There were 74 councillors on 27 June 1643,[2] 107 on 18 April 1644,[3] and 122 on 30 April 1644.[4] Between 30 April 1644 and 5 May 1657, 75 new members were appointed while only 50 places became vacant through the death of the incumbents:[5] in theory, therefore, the number of council members rose to 147. Guy Patin remarked with justice that Anne of Austria did not have 'cette vertu de Plutarque de refuser hardiment'.[6] In 1644, Séguier lamented 'la grande confusion et désordre' resulting from the fact that 'chaque jour produisait un conseiller d'état'.[7]

However, not all the members of the council were eligible to attend council meetings at the same time. Grades of councillor were established in the 1620s.[8] A political career in the council entailed an extremely long period of waiting for promotion. The first promotion was to the position of *quadrimestre*, which conferred the right of entry to the lesser councils for three months in a year. Later, the position of *conseiller semestre* would be attained—the right to attend the lesser councils for six months in the year. Finally, the councillor became a *conseiller ordinaire*, which conferred automatic right of entry into the lesser councils. Seniority depended on the date of the letters of appointment (*brevet*) as councillor, and the date of the oath of loyalty (*serment*) given to the Chancellor or Keeper of the Seals. Eventually, after thirty or forty years in the council and a few well-timed deaths or disgraces of other candidates, the position of longest-serving councillor (*doyen*) was reached,[9] conferring the right of precedence over all other councillors within the lesser councils, with the exception of officers of the crown such as the Chancellor.

[1] Ormesson, *Journal*, ed. Chéruel, ii. 635–7. B.M. Rouen MS. Léber 5767, fo. 223.

[2] Ormesson, *Journal*, i. 78; B.M. Rouen MS. Léber 5767, fo. 226.

[3] B.M. Rouen MS. Léber 5767, fo. 231.

[4] B.M. Rouen MS. Léber 5767, fo. 232.   [5] B.N. MS.fr. 18155, fo. 29.

[6] Guy Patin, *Lettres pendant la Fronde*, ed. A. Thérive (1921), p. 187.

[7] Mousnier, *La plume*, p. 166. B.L. Egerton 1680, fo. 24ᵛ: 'moins de conseillers sont plus forts qu'un plus grand nombre, ce qui semble paradoxe. Mais le petit nombre a plus de dignité, de poids et plus d'authorité, sont plus respectés. Le grand nombre avilit le corps et est plus mesprisé et est plus aisément rendu ennuyeux au prince...'

[8] Mousnier, *La plume*, p. 165. B.L. Egerton 1680, fo. 23. Notably by the rulings of 12 Oct. 1622 and 26 Aug. 1626.

[9] J. J. de Mesmes de Roissy called himself 'doyen des conseillers d'estat'. Minutier Central Li 491, marriage of Cazet de Vautorte, 30 Jan. 1634. Cf. Antoine, *Le conseil du roi*, p. 194.

Attempts were made throughout the ministries of Richelieu and Mazarin to reduce the size of the councils, and to abolish the position of *conseiller quadrimestre*. The basic problem was one of implementation. André Lefèvre d'Ormesson confirmed this impression: 'enfin, j'ai tousjours veu', he wrote in 1644, 'que les règlemens du Conseil excitent tousjours beaucoup de bruict et peu de fruict'. D'Ormesson inclined to Jeannin's view that 'confusion valoit mieux que mescontentement', pointing out that any attempt to reduce council membership pleased only the longest-serving councillors, while it put the Chancellor in an impossible position.[1] A detailed investigation of *brevets* was carried out on 12 April 1644.[2] Châteauneuf hoped for a reduction of council membership in April 1650.[3] Le Tellier proposed the same measure in September 1652.[4] It was not until May 1657, however, that the membership of the council was limited to 32 and the subordinate grade of *conseiller quadrimestre* was abolished.[5]

Between 1624 and 1661, under the direction of the chief minister and his subordinates, the central government developed a sense of its own identity and purpose. There was a growing distinction between membership of the council and membership of the sovereign courts. The position of king's councillor was not an office, but an appointment by letters patent regarded increasingly as incompatible with office in the sovereign courts. Although there were exceptions to this rule, its implications were clear above all in the crisis years of the Fronde. When René Longueil de Maisons was considered for the post of *surintendant* in 1650, it was objected that as a *président* in the *Parlement* of Paris he would be 'un espion dans le conseil d'en haut . . . qui scauroit le fonds du secret pour s'en servir un jour contre le Roy à l'avantage du Parlement'.[6] The crucial distinction between membership of the sovereign courts and membership of the council was one of executive power. However junior the member of the council, he participated to a certain

[1] 'S'il y a confusion au conseil, c'est [sa] faute; si l'ordre apporte du mescontentement, c'est [sa] faute. B.M. Rouen MS Léber 5767, fo. 230ᵛ.
[2] B.M. Rouen MS. Léber 5767, fos. 229-30.   [3] Guy Patin, loc. cit.
[4] A.A.E. France 884, fo. 222, 4 Sept. 1652.   [5] B.N. 500 Colbert 194, fo. 291.
[6] A.A.E. France 871, fo. 68. The oath of loyalty taken by a king's councillor included a clause pledging secrecy, however, and Maisons was appointed.

extent in the decision-making process. The members of the sovereign courts did not. All decisions in the sovereign courts were subject to correction by the king's council, although the *Parlement* of Paris claimed the special privilege of having its decrees annulled by the council of state only, and not by the lesser councils (the *conseil privé* and council of finance).[1] In contrast, the sovereign courts were not entitled to annul decrees of the council, although they assumed this power on occasion before 1661. No member of the council, or *maître des requêtes* who had presented business to the council, could be summoned before the sovereign courts. When the *Parlement* of Paris tried to innovate in this area by summoning before it two *maîtres des requêtes* in 1656, its attempts were rejected.[2] In contrast, any member of a sovereign court could be summoned before the council and upbraided.

The corollary of strong executive government was the exclusion of the sovereign courts from participation in affairs of state. The crown maintained a consistent attitude in this respect in a number of *causes célèbres* in the first half of the seventeenth century. On 28 March 1615, the *Parlement* of Paris criticized the king's foreign policy and his choice of ministers. It asserted that its decrees in judicial questions should no longer be suspended by the council. It demanded also the reform of the royal finances. The council of state issued a decree condemning the court's action and declaring that since the *Parlement*'s role was purely judicial, it was not authorized to intervene in political affairs unless explicitly invited to do so by the sovereign.[3] On 26 April 1631, the *Parlement* of Paris refused to register a royal declaration against Gaston d'Orléans, who had gone into exile in Lorraine. The council of state annulled its decree and informed the *Parlement* that it had no right to intervene in affairs of state.[4] On 21 February 1641, Louis XIII and Richelieu

---

[1] X1b 8854 and X1a 8388, 17 Aug. 1645. The *Parlement* of Paris was not wholly successful, however. Cf. Mousnier, *La plume*, p. 177.

[2] A. N. Hamscher, *The Parlement of Paris after the Fronde, 1653–1673* (Pittsburgh, Pa., 1976), pp. 102–3. X1a 8390, fos. 418, 434ᵛ, 442ᵛ, 18 Aug., 1 Sept., 4 Sept. 1656. A.A.E. France 900, fo. 324, 23 Aug. 1656. B.L. Harleian 4489, fos. 39ᵛ, 42, 22 and 23 Aug. 1656.

[3] E. Glasson, *Le Parlement de Paris. Son rôle politique depuis Charles VII jusqu'à la Révolution* (2 vols., 1901), i. 123–7. *Négociations, lettres et pièces relatives à la conférence de Loudun*, ed. L. F. H. Bouchitté (1862), pp. 202–3.

[4] Glasson, op. cit., i. 137–9. E 1685, fo. 128, 12 May 1631.

went further. At a *lit de justice*—a special session of the *Parlement*
presided over by the king—Louis XIII prohibited the *Parlement*
from intervening in affairs of state, and also limited its powers of
issuing remonstrances.[1]

It is sometimes stated that the Regency of Anne of Austria
saw a reversal of this policy. It is certainly true that on 18 May
1643 the *Parlement* of Paris was invited by Anne of Austria to
annul the last will and testament of Louis XIII. While this was
an intervention in affairs of state, it was an exceptional incident.
The Regent did not formally remove the limitations imposed by
Louis XIII on 21 February 1641. Nor did she offer to consult
the *Parlement* of Paris on issues of policy. The office-holders
were quite mistaken in believing that they had been invited to
participate in government. The action of the Parisian sovereign
courts in demanding a meeting at the *Chambre Saint-Louis* in
1648—where the government would be criticized—was condemned by the council of state as 'injurieuse à l'autorité
royalle qui ne [la] peut souffrir sans sa diminution . . .'[2] The
collapse of government followed this revolt of the office-
holders, but in the years after the Fronde, similar arguments
were used. On 22 October 1652, the *Parlement* of Paris was
prohibited from interfering in affairs of state, in financial
questions, and in the work of the ministers of the crown.
Previous interventions in such matters were annulled retrospectively.[3] The council of state, acting at the request of
Chancellor Séguier, confirmed its supremacy over the *Parlement*
of Paris on 19 October 1656.[4] Louis XIV remained 'mal
satisfaict de la conduite de toutes les compagnies souveraines
du royaume', however.[5] As one of the first acts of his personal
rule, on 8 July 1661, he confirmed 'la suprême autorité du
Conseil' over the sovereign courts.[6]

The years between 1624 and 1661 saw a broadening of the
concept of 'affairs of state'. Inevitably this meant some loss of

[1] Glasson, op. cit., i. 167–71, who misdates this event. X1a 8387, 21 Feb. 1641.
[2] E 1693, fo. 132, 15 June 1648.
[3] Doolin, *The Fronde*, p. 80. A. L. Moote, *The revolt of the judges. The Parlement of Paris and the Fronde, 1643–1652* (Princeton, N.J., 1971), p. 352. U 30, fo. 356.
[4] E 1704, fo. 52.
[5] X1a 8392, fo. 399, 5 Aug. 1661—the verdict of the *Parlement* of Paris.
[6] *Mémoriaux du Conseil de 1661*, ed. Boislisle, i. 374–6. Hamscher, *The Parlement of Paris after the Fronde*, pp. 130–1. E 1714, no. 95.

status for the sovereign courts, whose activities were increasingly restricted to the realm of private law (*jus privatum*). Whereas the courts tried to extend the scope of their jurisdiction, the king's council tried to restrict them to the *juridiction contentieuse*, that is to say cases between contending parties where the interests of the crown were not affected. The growth of government by council implied a growth in public law (*jus publicum*).[1] Cardin Le Bret defined the theory underlying this tendency in his treatise entitled *De la souveraineté du roy*, which was published in 1632 and became virtually the textbook of government at the time of Richelieu and Mazarin. France enjoyed a customary constitution, interpreted theoretically by the king and in practice by the king's council. According to Le Bret, the king could modify the constitution, altering the powers of the sovereign courts and other jurisdictions in the land, if necessary removing powers from some courts and transferring them to others. Could the king change laws and ordinances and grant commissions on his own authority, without discussing these measures with the sovereign courts? Le Bret's answer was an unqualified yes. The king was the only sovereign power in his kingdom: despite the title *cours souveraines*, sovereignty, in Le Bret's view, was 'no more divisible than the point in geometry'. The sovereign courts could issue provisional rulings 'selon les occasions qui se présentent'— but these were subject to correction by the king and the king's council. The courts 'ne peuvent rien définir par une loy générale'. Legislation was the prerogative of the king, although in Le Bret's view it was seemly (*bienséant*) for a king to have his laws and edicts approved by the *parlements*.[2]

Le Bret argued that in an edict issued by Charles VIII (1483–98), the king had reserved for himself powers over 'des affaires publiques et qui touchent l'état'—a decision taken, in Le Bret's view, under the influence of Roman Law.[3] In such affairs of state, the king had complete freedom of action, and could issue

---

[1] For the origins and use of this term: G. Chevrier, 'Remarques sur l'introduction et les vicissitudes de la distinction du "jus privatum" et du "jus publicum" dans les oeuvres des anciens juristes français', *Archives de Philosophie du Droit*, new ser., i (1952), 5–77.

[2] Le Bret, *De la souveraineté du roy*, pp. 69–73.

[3] ibid., p. 149. Cf. Doolin, *The Fronde*, p. 100, who notes the difficulty in tracing this edict.

commissions of a temporary nature as he saw fit. The royal commissioners were the direct representatives of the king and thus could assume superiority over other office-holders. The

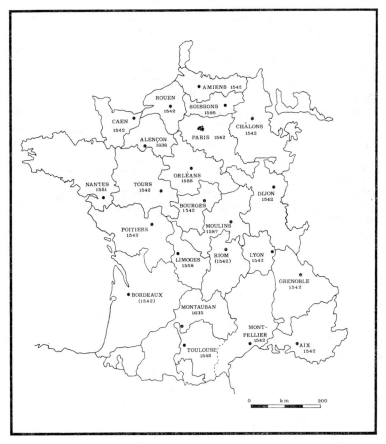

MAP I. The *généralités* of France at the time of Richelieu and Mazarin.

The date indicates the year in which the *généralité* was established. *Bureaux des finances* were established at Agen and Issoire in 1542 and subsequently transferred to Bordeaux and Riom respectively.

king did not enjoy such freedom of action in 'affaires privées et qui ne vont qu'à l'intérêt des particuliers . . .' Article 98 of the ordinance of Blois (1579) had prohibited the granting of commissions in such matters and thus preserved the rights of the sovereign courts. The implications of Le Bret's theory were clear. Any matters at issue between private persons and the crown could be viewed as questions of public law, and thus the preserve of the king's council or royal commissioners such as the intendants. Accordingly, the sovereign courts might be limited to 'affaires privées', the realm of private law. Indeed, Louis XIII told the *Parlement* of Paris in 1632: 'vous n'êtes établis que pour juger entre maître Pierre et maître Jean . . .'[1] It is scarcely an exaggeration, therefore, to view this growth of public law at the time of Richelieu and Mazarin as the first real development of administrative law in France. De Tocqueville was later to see this establishment of a body of administrative law as a characteristic feature of the *ancien régime*.[2]

[1] Glasson, op. cit., i. 144. A.A.E. France 802, fo. 31ᵛ, 30 Jan. 1632.
[2] A. de Tocqueville, *L'ancien régime et la Révolution* (1856), bk. ii, chapter 4. Cf. also the important discussion of A. V. Dicey, *Introduction to the study of the law of the constitution* (10th ed., 1961), chapter 12: 'rule of law compared with *droit administratif*'.

CHAPTER II

The Intendants before the Fronde

CONTEMPORARIES WERE confused on the origins of the intendants and the related, but separate, question of the date at which the intendants became an integral part of the administrative system. At the Assembly of Notables of 1626–7, the *présidents* of the *Parlements* protested at 'un nouvel usage d'intendants de la justice'.[1] Their statement implied either that the intendants had been introduced relatively recently, or alternatively that there had been intendants for a long time but by 1626–7 they were acting in a new way. In 1648, when the *Chambre Saint-Louis* was pressing for the abolition of the intendants, Chancellor Séguier defended Anne of Austria, the Regent, from the charge of having established them. The introduction of the intendants could not be imputed to the Regent, Séguier argued, because they had been 'establis par le feu Roy en 1635'. But again, he was reported as saying in 1648 'il y a quinze ans [i.e. since 1633] que selon les occasions ils y ont été ordonnés et depuis onze ans entiers [i.e. since 1637] il y en a dans toutes les provinces'.[2] Séguier ought to have been well informed on this subject, since he was appointed Keeper of the Seals in 1633 and Chancellor two years later. At the same time, however, there is an evident contradiction in Séguier's dates, while the issue of when the intendants became permanent administrators is left obscure. By 1648 the ministers regarded the recall of the intendants as a 'mutation . . . grande et soudaine' because they had taken over a large part of the work formerly undertaken by over 3,000 financial officials. When this had happened was not clarified in their statement.[3]

The views of the *présidents* of the *Parlements* in 1626–7 and of Chancellor Séguier in 1648 cannot be taken as objective

[1] J. Petit, *L'assemblée des notables de 1626–1627* (1936), pp. 266–7. B.L. Egerton 1666, fo. 224.

[2] Mousnier, *La plume*, pp. 181–2. Talon, *Mémoires*, ed. Michaud and Poujoulat, p. 246, gives a résumé of Séguier's speech.

[3] Mousnier, *La plume*, p. 182.

statements. Both statements were produced at moments of exceptionally probing political debate and they were distorted for this reason. In 1626–7, the *Parlements* wanted to assert their own position in the constitution and to reverse any tendencies towards a strengthening of the central government.[1] In 1648, Séguier defended the Regent from the charge of introducing the intendants because most contemporaries believed that during a royal minority no new laws could be introduced.[2] Moreover, the collapse of government was predicted if the intendants were recalled. Thus neither statement can be interpreted as representing the historical reality. The origins of the intendants, and the date at which they became permanent administrators are separate, but related, problems, which may be elucidated only by studying the number of intendants serving in the provinces at any one time, the continuity of service in the provinces, the size of their administrative areas and the evolution of their powers. Lists of intendants are therefore essential[3] as is a study of their commissions: but the evolution of the powers and function of the intendants must be related to the problems faced by the central government and its attempts to remedy these problems.

There were intendants before Richelieu became chief minister in 1624, but there were relatively few of them. Indeed, Richelieu appointed relatively few before 1630. In the seventy years between 1560 and 1630, there were about 120 appointments as intendant. In contrast, in the eighteen years between 1630 and 1648 there were between 120 and 150 appointments as intendant.[4] After 1560, there were intendants in the sense of officials

---

[1] Mousnier, *La vénalité*, pp. 647–9. Lublinskaya, *French absolutism*, p. 324.

[2] Doolin, *The Fronde*, pp. 75–6, 149.

[3] These lists, established from manuscript sources, are presented in diagrammatic form in Fig. 2. They are presented in tabular form in R. J. Bonney, 'The intendants of Richelieu and Mazarin, 1624–1661' (Oxford Univ. D.Phil., 1973), pp. 252–8, 269–85, 309–15, 317–28. To the lists add—Antoine Aguesseau (Grenoble, 1627): B.N. p.o. 14, no. 4, 20 Sept. 1627. Jacques Ollier, sieur de Verneuil (Limoges, 1611): V6 1191, no. 44, 18 Mar. 1612. Paul Hay du Châtelet (Dijon, 1631): A.A.E. France 1490, fo. 250, 8 May 1631.

[4] It is not meaningful to give a precise figure. Much depends, particularly in the years 1560–1630, on definition, about which there may be debate. Moreover, a number of joint intendants were appointed. The higher figure for the years 1630–48 counts the members of a joint commission as two intendants. The lower figure counts them as one intendant.

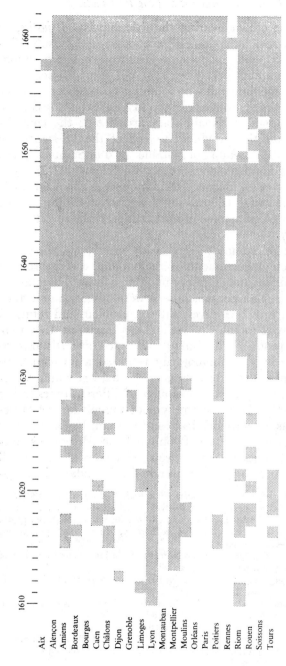

FIG. 2. The presence of intendants in the *généralités*, 1610–1661.

Source: Bonney, loc. cit. N.B.: each symbol indicates at least one reference to an intendant in the sources, but does not necessarily imply direct continuity of intendants. The *généralités* of Montauban and Alençon were established respectively in 1635 and 1636. Toulouse is counted with Montpellier; La Rochelle with Poitiers. The commissioners of the *cour des aides* during the Fronde are omitted.

sent out by the crown bearing the title *intendant de justice*, or *intendant de finance*, later—during the reign of Louis XIII—*intendant de justice, police, et finances*.[1] There were also occasions when royal commissioners were sent out into different provinces at the same time and with a similar purpose, for example the commissioners sent out after 1570 to ensure that the edict of pacification of Saint-Germain was carried out; the commissioners sent into the provinces to collect the grievances to be debated in the Assembly of Notables held at Saint-Germain in 1583; the commissioners sent out by Henri III in 1588 'afin d'éclairer et de déconcerter les desseins des Ligueurs'; the various financial commissioners sent out in the 1590s; finally, the commissioners sent out to suppress the revolt of the nobles in 1617.[2]

Not all these commissioners were intendants, however. Moreover, these appointments were sporadic, a response to a particular problem and certainly not a new form of permanent administration. The commissioners were investigators: they were sent to a province, investigated a problem and returned to Paris to report to the Chancellor. On occasions, they took executive decisions. Some intendants acted as assistants to the governors or even temporarily replaced a law-court. In general, however, these developments lacked unity and coherence, there being many commissioners of different types rather than a gradual evolution of one type of commissioner.[3] Moreover, there was no chronological continuity in the experiments —with the exception of the Lyonnais,[4] the Auvergne,[5] Burgundy,[6] and Languedoc[7] there were no commissioners at all between 1602 and 1615. There were a few intendants in 1615–

[1] G. Hanotaux, *Origines de l'institution des intendants des provinces* (1884). E. Esmonin, 'Observations, critiques sur le livre de M. Hanotaux . . .' (1910), reprinted in Esmonin, *Études sur la France des xviie et xviiie siècles* (1964), pp. 13–17.

[2] Information on these commissioners in Bonney, 'Intendants', pp. 31–40, 45–9, 247–51, 259–62.

[3] D. J. Buisseret, 'A stage in the development of the intendants: the reign of Henry IV', *Historical Journal*, ix (1966), 27–38.

[4] Méric de Vic (1597–1601), Eustache de Refuge (1601–7), and Guillaume de Montholon (1607–17) served as intendants.

[5] Jacques Mérault served as intendant in 1603–4 and from 12 Sept. 1607 until 1611. Perhaps Jean de Génicourt served as intendant in 1611–12.

[6] Gilles Le Mazuyer served as intendant in 1612.

[7] François du Faure served as intendant after 1613: D. J. Buisseret, 'Les précurseurs des intendants du Languedoc', *Annales du Midi*, lxxx (1968), 85–6.

16, but by no means one intendant for each province. When the government put to the Assembly of Notables of 1617 its proposal to send a *maître des requêtes* to each province, this provoked a storm of protest. The government was accused of attempting 'un nouvel establissement de justice exécutoire en toutes les provinces du royaume'.[1] By implication, there was no common system of administration by intendants at this date.

Between 1617 and 1627 intendants were present in only twelve provinces for even part of the time.[2] Only in the Lyonnais[3] and Languedoc[4] can it be said that there was a direct continuity of intendants: perhaps the commercial and financial importance of Lyon—which had made it the object of Sully's reforming energies[5]—and the size of the Protestant minority within Languedoc made the continued presence of intendants necessary. There was relatively little financial investigation in the years between 1617 and 1624. On 27 April 1623, an investigation into the *taille* was ordered for Normandy.[6] By July, commissioners charged with this task (*commissaires pour le régalement des tailles*) had been sent also into Poitou, Aunis (i.e. La Rochelle), and Guyenne.[7] In the Lyonnais, however, the task was not carried out by the intendant, but by the *trésoriers de France*.[8] It had been expected that this investigation would be extended throughout the *pays d'élections*; but on 29 July 1623 a decree of the council of finance halted further development along these lines.[9] Part of the explanation for the change in policy may be found in the ministerial struggle between La Vieuville and the Brûlarts; part may also be

---

[1] C. J. Mayer, *Des États-Généraux et autres assemblées nationales* (18 vols., The Hague, 1788–9), xviii. 108–10. B.L. Egerton 1666, fo. 93ᵛ–95ʳ. B.L. Add. MS. 30555, fos. 247ᵛ–250ᵛ.

[2] Some of these provinces were linked, however. For example, Thévin served in the Auvergne and the Bourbonnais in 1617–18.

[3] Jacques Ollier, sieur de Verneuil, served as intendant from 1617 to 1624 and was succeeded by Maximilien Granger.

[4] François du Faure continued to serve in Languedoc until his death in 1628. He was joined by François Bitault de Chizé between 10 July 1618 and 1622, Charles Machault d'Arnouville in 1622, and Jacques Favier in 1623.

[5] J. Permezel, *La politique financière de Sully dans la généralité de Lyon* (Lyon, 1935).

[6] *Cahiers des États de Normandie sous les règnes de Louis XIII et Louis XIV*, ed. C. de Robillard de Beaurepaire (3 vols., Rouen, 1876–8), ii. 36–7.

[7] Bonney, 'Intendants', p. 263.

[8] E 79c, fo. 257, 25 Sept. 1624.

[9] Z1a 206, p. 597 and E 75b, fo. 317.

found in the strength of the opposition among the office-
holders to this investigation.

What effect did Richelieu's entry into the king's council
(29 April 1624) and his replacement of La Vieuville as chief
minister of Louis XIII (13 August 1624) have upon the
intendants? Clearly it is an exaggeration to contend that at the
moment of Richelieu's rise to power the intendants 'were
almost everywhere ... and in charge of almost everything'.[1]
There were at most intendants in seven provinces in 1623–4, and
if anything there were probably fewer intendants in the years
1624–30 than in the years 1617–24. At the same time, it is
probably an overstatement to say that Richelieu reduced the
number of intendants as a deliberate act of policy.[2] Richelieu's
attitude was far too equivocal for such an assertion: for while
Richelieu thought it 'très utile d'envoyer souvent dans les
provinces des conseillers d'état ou des maîtres des requêtes
bien choisis', he apparently thought that the task of 'intendant
de justice dans les villes capitales ... peut plus servir à leur
vanité qu'à l'utilité du public ...'[3] This statement could be
taken to mean nothing more than that Richelieu envisaged the
commissioners playing an active role throughout the provinces
rather than remaining in the major urban centres. Alternatively, it could be interpreted as a fundamental distinction between temporary investigations—of which Richelieu approved—
and permanent administrators, which he opposed.

A similarly equivocal standpoint is to be found in the *Code
Michaud* of January 1629[4] and the ruling of the council of 18
January 1630,[5] both of which are usually taken to be the
work of Michel de Marillac, the Keeper of the Seals, whose
influence on the direction of government policy was substantial.
Marillac was certainly not opposed to the use of intendants.

[1] Lublinskaya, *French absolutism*, p. 319.
[2] Mousnier, *La vénalité*, pp. 648–9, based on Hanotaux's inaccurate lists.
[3] A. J. du Plessis, Cardinal de Richelieu [?], *Testament politique*, ed. L. André
(1947), pp. 246–7. The problem of authenticity of this work is unresolved, but it
appears to be a collection of Richelieu's writings compiled by his secretaries and
dating from the years 1639–40.
[4] Articles 58, 81, 404. *Recueil général des anciennes lois françaises depuis l'an 420
jusqu'à la Révolution de 1789*, ed. A. J. L. Jourdan, Decrusy, and F. A. Isambert
(28 vols., 1821–33), xvi. 241–2, 250–1, 322.
[5] Article 30. Mousnier, 'Les règlements du conseil', p. 101.

He had served as a *maître des requêtes* after 25 January 1595 and as a royal commissioner in Normandy and Guyenne. As Keeper of the Seals, he was responsible for the appointment of twenty-four intendants. However, there is little doubt that Marillac viewed the intendants as investigators, sent to a province to deal with a particular problem and then report back to the council. Both the *Code Michaud* and the ruling of the council of 18 January 1630 contain references to the traditional circuit-tours of the *maîtres des requêtes* in the provinces. In addition, the *Code Michaud* contained a clause concerning 'charges d'intendants de la justice ou finance que nous députons en nos armées ou provinces'. This clause has been interpreted as the nearest the government came to setting up the intendants by a formal edict of creation,[1] but this is an obvious exaggeration. It would in any case have been paradoxical for the government to have set up a system of intendants by an edict, for this was how offices were established. All intendants needed were their commissions. The context of the clause makes it clear that the main concern of the government was with the clientage ties of the nobility rather than a new system of intendants: 'que nul ne puisse être employé ès charges . . . qui soit domestique, conseiller, ou employé aux affaires ou proche parent des généraux des distes armées ou gouverneurs desdites provinces . . .' Finally, the *Code Michaud* appeared to envisage no more than intendants of justice in the provinces and intendants of finance in the army—both types of official had existed during the reign of Henri IV.[2] There was no mention of conferring powers of *police*, that is to say general administrative powers, to the intendants. Marillac did not envisage the intendants becoming permanent administrators in a province, nor was such a development the logical outcome of his policies.

Marillac opposed an aggressive French foreign policy and particularly the military intervention in the Valtelline in 1624–6. He argued that the war was neither just nor useful, while it would lead to the bankruptcy of the crown. In 1626, Marillac was 63 years old, and his experience of the Catholic League had taught him the need to 'éviter l'extrême indignation

---

[1] Mousnier, *La vénalité*, pp. 650–1, probably overestimates its significance.
[2] Hanotaux, *Origines*, pp. 227–31.

de tout le clergé, les parlements, les villes, et le peuple'. This
could be achieved only by a policy of low taxation. In Marillac's
view, heavier taxes would alienate the population as a whole,
who would claim that the ministers had abnegated their chief
responsibility, which was the maintenance of peace. Factions
within the state would exploit this discontent, Marillac argued,
and 'il y a beaucoup de choses à prévoir et à craindre . . .'[1]
In contrast, a policy of co-existence abroad would permit
reform at home: 'il est principalement de la gloire du bon
gouvernement de penser au soulagement des sujets et aux
bons règlements de l'état, qui ne se peuvent faire que par la
paix'.[2]

Marillac thus wanted the modification of existing institutions,
not the introduction of new forms of government. Moreover,
his objective of low taxation would have permitted the existing
institutions to function properly. War, above all the fiscal
demands of war, was to prove the decisive factor in the establishment of the intendants. Only Marillac's religious policy
might have led to a system of permanent intendants. Marillac
wanted to 'ruisner l'hérésie et la faction huguenote en France'.
This might have led to permanent intendants in the Huguenot-
dominated regions of the Midi. It was on 16 November 1628,
during Marillac's Keepership of the Seals, that the first of a
line of intendants was appointed to serve at La Rochelle. The
war against the Protestants in Languedoc led to a succession of
intendants in that province in the 1620s.

Where did Richelieu stand on the issue of war versus domestic
reform in his early years as chief minister? He certainly wanted
reform. The 'mémoire au roi' and 'règlement pour toutes les
affaires du royaume' of 1625 demonstrate Richelieu's concern
for reform.[3] He wanted the abolition of the sale of offices and
hoped that the budgetary deficit could be eliminated by new
revenues following the resumption of crown lands. He ruled out

[1] A. J. du Plessis, Cardinal de Richelieu, *Mémoires*, ed. G. Lacour-Gayet and
R. Lavollé (10 vols., 1907–31), v. 320–5. Speech of Marillac to the council, 1626.
The existence of rival parties for and against the war is indicated by Richelieu in a
letter to Marie de Médicis dated 16 Aug. 1625. *Les papiers de Richelieu*, ed. Grillon,
i. 205.

[2] G. Pagès, 'Autour de "Grand Orage". Richelieu et Marillac. Deux politiques',
Revue Historique, clxxix (1937), 66.

[3] *Lettres . . . de Richelieu*, ed. Avenel, ii. 159–62, 168–83. *Les papiers de Richelieu*, ed.
Grillon, i. 248–69.

the possibility of heavier taxes: 'les peuples ne sçauroient plus porter', he declared.[1] He recognized the validity of Marillac's objection to war: 'en matière de guerres', he advised Louis XIII, 'on sçait comment et quand elles commencent, mais nul ne peut prévoir le temps et la qualité de leur fin.'[2]

Unlike Marillac, however, Richelieu believed that there were great issues at stake in the Valtelline and in Italy. He wanted a defensive League against the Habsburgs,[3] and recognized 'la difficulté . . . de faire la paix avec l'Espagne en sorte qu'elle soit sure, honorable et que tous nos alliés y puissent avoir l'avantage que raisonablement ilz peuvent désirer . . .'[4] This desire for a permanent settlement, resolving all the issues at stake, accounts for Richelieu's repudiation of the text of the treaty of Regensburg (22 October 1630).[5] The *dévot* party had seen this treaty, which had been signed on 13 October, as the great triumph of their policy of co-existence with the Habsburgs. Marillac bitterly denounced Richelieu's repudiation of the treaty and it was this event which precipitated the trial of strength between the two men. Richelieu was twenty-two years younger than Marillac, without first-hand knowledge of the Catholic League, and his politics were more aggressive. While he wanted reform, Richelieu believed that the demands of French foreign policy had to take precedence over all domestic considerations. If bad peace conditions were to be accepted simply because of domestic political pressures, 'la réputation du roi est blessée, ce qui peut avoir beaucoup de mauvaises suites pour l'état'.[6]

On the Day of Dupes (10 November 1630), it appeared at first that Louis XIII had capitulated to the Queen Mother, and replaced Richelieu by Marillac as his chief minister. Later the same day, however, after weighing up the consequences of such an action on the conduct of his foreign policy, Louis XIII declared his intention of retaining Richelieu.[7] Marillac was arrested and four days later Châteauneuf was appointed Keeper

[1] Lublinskaya, *French absolutism*, p. 299.
[2] *Lettres . . . de Richelieu*, ed. Avenel, ii. 83.
[3] ibid., ii. 81. [4] ibid., ii. 84.
[5] D. P. O'Connell, 'A *cause célèbre* in the history of treaty making. The refusal to ratify the peace treaty of Regensburg in 1630', *British Yearbook of International Law*, xlii (1967), 71–90.
[6] Pagès, 'Richelieu et Marillac', p. 92.
[7] L. Batiffol, *La journée des Dupes* (1925). G. Mongrédien, *10 Novembre 1630. La journée des Dupes* (1961).

of the Seals. The Queen Mother was held virtually in captivity at Compiègne. The most important consequence of the Day of Dupes was that it left Richelieu in political control. D'Effiat, the *surintendant des finances*, was a loyal supporter; Châteauneuf, while less certain in his allegiance, was demonstrably a Richelieu appointee; so too was Bouthillier. Richelieu was thus able to pursue his anti-Habsburg foreign policy with greater vigour. On 13 January 1631, he signed the treaty of Barwälde, a subsidy alliance with the Lutheran Gustavus Adolphus of Sweden, who was about to strike at the heartlands of Germany. In terms of practical politics, the *dévot* policy was dead.

The Day of Dupes had important domestic consequences. The most significant of these was that Gaston d'Orléans, the younger brother of Louis XIII, broke with Richelieu (30 January 1631). Gaston had rebelled in 1629 and on that occasion had gone into self-imposed exile in the duchy of Lorraine—duke Charles IV of Lorraine was an ally of the Habsburgs. The quarrel had been patched up in January 1630. In 1631, however, Gaston was much more dangerous. He interpreted the Day of Dupes as an act of treason committed by Richelieu against the Queen Mother.[1] Gaston tried to raise his province, the Orléanais: when this failed, he fled to Lorraine. On 31 May 1631, he issued a manifesto at Nancy which denounced Richelieu's absolute control over Louis XIII, the government, and the kingdom of France. He criticized the war of the Mantuan succession, 'qui a coûté plus de 50 millions, laquelle il a entreprise pour sa vanité, son ambition et son intérêt, au détriment de la France'. Gaston denounced also the domestic consequences of the war. In his view, Richelieu 'a voulu exprès appauvrir l'état par tributs, impôts et dépenses excessives . . .' This policy, he concluded, had reduced the peasants to misery.[2] In July 1631, Marie de Médicis escaped from Compiègne and fled to the Spanish Netherlands. As a result of these events, domestic security became an issue of paramount importance to the government. Richelieu laid a memorandum before the council of state at the end of March 1632 which argued that Spain, the Empire, and Lorraine were in league against France and hoped

---

[1] For Gaston's motives: G. Dethan, *Gaston d'Orléans. Conspirateur et prince charmant* (1959), pp. 83–101.   [2] Mongrédien, op. cit., pp. 215–18.

to instigate a rising within the kingdom. Letters intercepted from Brussels and Nancy indicated, in Richelieu's view, that there were many potential rebels about whom the government had no information.[1]

A central tenet in Richelieu's philosophy was the belief that in a crisis, prompt and effective action must be taken. The ordinary course of justice might require proof and evidence of guilt, but a question of state could not wait for this, since delay in a case of conspiracy or sedition might be disastrous.[2] Richelieu believed that one man was more effective than a group of men in weighing up the issues and taking remedial action.[3] It would not be a great step in logic for Richelieu to conclude that one intendant might be more effective in dealing with a crisis than a group of lawyers gathered together in a sovereign court. Necessity, Richelieu said, 'oblige souvent à être impitoyable'. The intendants of 1631–3 were a clear example of his maxim being translated into action.[4]

The security measures began at once. The events of the Day of Dupes precipitated an attack by Richelieu on the provincial governors. Gaston's departure from France had been facilitated by the duc de Bellegarde, the governor of Burgundy. Richelieu dismissed Bellegarde, replaced him by Condé, and sent Hay du Châtelet as intendant to the province.[5] After the extremely serious revolt of the *Cascaveoux* at Aix in the autumn of 1630, Provence was not left without an intendant until the Fronde. In Languedoc, Poitou, Guyenne, and Normandy intendants were present between 1630 and 1633. In June 1632 Gaston d'Orléans invaded France with 2,500 cavalry, crossing Burgundy and the Auvergne and entering Languedoc, where he met up with Montmorency who had timed his rebellion to coincide with the invasion. This was exactly the sort of uprising that Marillac had feared. Richelieu, Châteauneuf, and Bullion (D'Effiat died on 27 July 1632) responded to the

---

[1] *Lettres . . . de Richelieu*, ed. Avenel, iv. 270. O'Connell, *Richelieu*, p. 242.

[2] Richelieu, *Testament politique*, ed. André, p. 343. G. Hanotaux, 'Maximes d'état et fragments politiques du Cardinal de Richelieu', *Mélanges Historiques. Choix de documents* (3 vols., 1880), iii. 770, 784 (maxims nos. 80, 124). Richelieu, *Mémoires*, ed. Lacour-Gayet and Lavollé, vi. 37.

[3] Richelieu, *Testament politique*, ed. André, pp. 249, 305–6.

[4] A. J. du Plessis, Cardinal de Richelieu, *Mémoires . . .*, ed. J. F. Michaud and J. J. F. Poujoulat, 2nd ser., viii (1838), 454.

[5] A.A.E. France 1490, fo. 250, 8 May 1631.

challenge with vigour. On 22 July 1632, Machault was given a commission as intendant of Languedoc, and he was also given the presidency of a roving tribunal (*chambre de justice ambulatoire*) in the Velay, the Vivarais, and the Gévaudan. Mangot de Villarceaux, Le Maître de Bellejambe, and Dyel de Miroménil were all empowered to arrest and prosecute the supporters of Montmorency. D'Argenson in the Limousin and the Auvergne and Laffemas in Champagne had similar powers to prosecute Gaston's supporters. The commitment of Richelieu and Châteauneuf to the suppression of rebellion is further demonstrated by the extent of the powers conferred in these commissions in 1632–3, which were greater than had previously been granted, or indeed were to be granted subsequently. The sending out of intendants was an exceptional response to crisis conditions: where there was no threat of rebellion—in Brittany, Berry, the Bourbonnais, the Orléanais, the Île-de-France, and the Soissonnais—no intendants were employed. This presumably was what Chancellor Séguier meant in 1648 when he told Omer Talon that the intendants had been employed since 1633 'selon les occasions'.

Between 1630 and 1633, the usefulness of the intendants in suppressing rebellion had been demonstrated, and it can hardly be without significance that the three major new appointments to the government after November 1630 (Servien as war minister on 11 December 1630; Bullion as joint, but senior *surintendant des finances* on 4 August 1632; Séguier as Keeper of the Seals on 25 February 1633, after the arrest of Châteauneuf) had all served previously as intendants.[1] Séguier appreciated the political usefulness of intendants, instructing them to 's'instruire dans leurs provinces . . . qu'ils puissent en rendre bon compte dans les occasions'.[2] For his part, Bullion was intent on achieving D'Effiat's aim of 'un bon règlement des tailles'[3]—which was given force of law in January 1634—and

---

[1] Bullion had served as intendant of justice and finance in the army of the ducs de Guise and Lesdiguières in 1620. Cf. E 104, fo. 279, 11 Sept. 1630. He had also served as intendant of justice, police, and finance in the army of Lesdiguières after 13 August 1624. B.N. MS.fr. 26477, fo. 53.

[2] Ormesson, *Journal*, ed. Chéruel, i. 402. *Lettres . . . au Chancelier Séguier*, ed. Mousnier, ii. 1135.

[3] A. M. de Boislisle [untitled communication], *Revue des Sociétés Savantes*, 7th ser., iii (1881), 176–80. B.N. MS. Dupuy 94, fo. 167, 18 May 1630.

envisaged sending out commissioners who would 'corriger les abus qui s'y trouveront, procéder contre les contravenans par condemnation d'amende et interdiction de leurs charges ou autrement extraordinairement ainsi qu'ils verront bon être . . .'[1] The appointments of Séguier and Bullion in 1632–3 were thus of crucial importance for the development of the use of intendants, resulting directly on 25 May 1634 in the issuing of commissions for the reform (*régalement*) of the *taille* in seventeen *généralités*.[2] Bullion wanted the implementation of the edict of January 1634 on the *taille*, and this was the purpose of issuing these commissions. Séguier, who had carried out a similar commission when intendant in Guyenne in 1623, appreciated the difficulties and obstacles that would have to be faced by the commissioners. Unlike the previous investigations in 1598–9 and 1623–4, the commissioners in 1634–5 all received standardized powers as intendants of justice.[3] They were thus empowered to deal with both judicial and financial questions, or rather to deal with financial questions by judicial procedure.

It might appear that this investigation, which was carried out in the greater part of France—seventeen of the twenty-two *généralités*—marks the arrival of the intendants as permanent administrators. Important as the investigation was, such a view would exaggerate the extent of institutional innovation in 1634–5. The investigation was of a temporary nature only—all work had ceased by March 1636 and the commissioners sent to Alençon, Amiens, Bourges, Caen, Châlons, Limoges, Lyon, Moulins, Orléans, Paris, Poitiers, and Rouen had returned to Paris by this date. By definition also, the investigation could not have been extended into the *pays d'états*, where the system of *taille réelle* (except in Burgundy) precluded swift adjustment of the tax-rates, which was one of the tasks of the commissioners. Finally, the intendants were investigators, not administrators. Unlike their counterparts in Languedoc, for example, they had no powers of *police*, that is to say administrative powers.[4]

---

[1] AD + 226.

[2] Bordeaux, La Rochelle, Riom, Tours, Alençon (although not yet a *généralité*), Amiens, Bourges, Caen, Châlons, Limoges, Lyon, Moulins, Orléans, Paris, Poitiers, Rouen, Soissons. Bonney, 'Intendants', pp. 264–6.

[3] A.G. A1 21, no. 121, 25 May 1634.

[4] Those intendants who were already serving in the provinces when they received their commissions for the *régalement des tailles*—Verthamon at Bordeaux,

The investigation in 1634–5 had been based on the assumption that the *taille* could be reduced by 25 per cent even though the crown saw the 'nécessité . . . d'armer puissamment pour prévenir les mauvais desseins de ceux qui voudroient affoiblir notre autorité . . .'[1] Events overtook both the investigation and the thinking behind it. The situation in Germany had deteriorated rapidly after the death of Gustavus Adolphus at Lützen (16 November 1632). Richelieu had continued the subsidy alliance with Sweden, but it was clear even before news of the disaster at Nördlingen (6 September 1634) reached Paris that greater French military assistance would be necessary. Such assistance was delayed because of Oxenstierna's refusal to ratify the treaty of Paris, which had been signed on 1 November 1634. The treaty of Compiègne in April 1635 envisaged immediate French entry into the war; and on 16 May 1635 war against Spain was declared officially. A rapid increase in government expenditure was made inevitable by the size of the armies and subsidies to allies that were envisaged. In 1630 total expenditure had stood at 41 million *livres*. By 1633 it had risen to 65 million. In 1636, the Spanish army invaded France from the Low Countries and from Franche-Comté. The army of invasion reached Corbie, a town situated on the Somme about eighty miles from Paris. In this year, the cost of the war effort reached 108 million, and every available source of revenue was used.[2]

A direct consequence of the national emergency was that in the summer of 1636 several intendants obtained forced loans from the municipalities. There was a significant increase in the number of intendants operating on the northern frontier in 1635–7: Laffemas in Picardy in 1635 and the Île-de-France in 1636; Bellejambe in Picardy after 12 March 1636; Claude Vignier at Troyes after 16 August 1636; Sève in the counties of Ponthieu and the Boulonnais after 4 February 1637—quite apart from the intendants in the separate armies. The year 1636,

---

Villemontée at La Rochelle (N.B. that for the purposes of this task, La Rochelle and Poitiers had separate commissioners), Argenson at Riom, and Étampes de Valençay at Tours—were possibly exceptions to this rule.

[1] The assumption was that a reduction in taxation would facilitate the tax-returns and thus leave the crown better off.

[2] R. J. Bonney, 'The secret expenses of Richelieu and Mazarin 1624–1661', *English Historical Review*, xci (1976), 829, n. 1.

therefore, was one of quite exceptional effort: more money was spent by the government in that year than ever before in French history; more intendants were sent out than in any previous year apart from 1634. It was of this crisis following the entry of France into the Thirty Years' War that Chancellor Séguier was probably thinking when in 1648 he claimed that the intendants had been 'establis par le feu Roy en 1635 . . .'

The effort was still not enough. Already in June 1636, the cost of the troops in Germany, Italy, the Netherlands, and the Valtelline had exhausted the revenues of the crown.[1] By December, the armies in Italy and the Valtelline could be paid only by anticipating future receipts from the tax-farms.[2] What was needed was an immediate inflow of cash—and only the towns could provide this, since the countryside, especially in northern and eastern France, was impoverished. A declaration of 18 December 1636 ordered a forced loan on the towns— Bullion, the finance minister, calculated that this would bring in 20 million *livres*[3]—while half the *taille* due to be paid by the countryside was remitted. The rate for each town was to be decided by the council of finance, and the tax-rolls sent to the mayors and *échevins* who were to carry out the levy. After considerable pressure, Paris and Rouen paid up, and Bullion hoped that they would 'donner . . . le bransle à tout le reste'.[4] His expectations, however, proved too high, for the town oligarchies refused to carry out the levy. This stalemate continued until March 1637 when there was a disaster on the war front. Jenatsch led a rising of the Grisons which brought about a collapse of the French position in the Valtelline, and threatened also the other theatres of war. Richelieu reserved his anger for Bullion, whom he told categorically: 'ce mal est arrivé faute d'argent'.[5] Bullion, fearful that he might be dismissed from office, decided upon coercion of the towns through the employment of commissioners. This decision was taken in the

[1] E 131b, fo. 76, 28 June 1636.

[2] E 134c, fo. 201, 20 Dec. 1636.

[3] A.A.E. France 826, fo. 227, 25 Mar. 1637. Y. M. Bercé, *Histoire des croquants. Étude des soulèvements populaires au xviie siècle dans le sud-ouest de la France* (2 vols., Paris–Geneva, 1974), i. 90, 404–5. Bercé demonstrates that despite Bullion's optimism, the taxes levied on the parishes in fact increased.

[4] A.A.E. France 826, fo. 244, 29 Mar. 1637.

[5] *Lettres . . . de Richelieu*, ed. Avenel, v. 763.

council of finance on 28 March 1637,[1] and two days later a commission was drawn up for François de Villemontée in Poitou which formed the model for the other fifteen commissions that were issued.[2] Villemontée was conferred 'plain et entier pouvoir d'intendance de justice, police et finances'. The preamble of his commission announced that similar commissioners would be sent 'en chacune de nosd[ites] provinces'. It was of these commissioners for the levy of the forced loan, therefore, that Chancellor Séguier was thinking in 1648 when he told Omer Talon that 'depuis onze ans entiers' there had been intendants 'dans toutes les provinces'. But the intendants did not remain in the provinces after the levy of the forced loan in the fiscal year 1636–7: most had returned to Paris by May 1638. At Bourges, Châlons, Limoges, Montauban, Moulins, Orléans, Paris, Rouen, and Tours, the intendant left the province before his successor was appointed. There was no attempt to levy the forced loan in the *pays d'états*. Indeed, there was bound to be dissimilarity in the responsibilities of the intendants in the *pays d'élections* and the *pays d'états*, because of the existence of two different fiscal *régimes*. There had been more stability in the role of the intendants in the *pays d'états*, since an intendant had been present continuously in Languedoc since the 1620s, in Provence since 1630, and in Burgundy since 1635.

Events between 1638 and 1641 went some way towards diminishing the differences in the functions of the intendants in the *pays d'états* and the *pays d'élections*. In July 1638, there was a fresh crisis at the Treasury. Bullion warned Richelieu that the troops could not be paid, 'les receptes ne venant pas comme elles devroyent'.[3] Special funds would have to be found to pay for the troops during the winter quarter, and this meant a further levy of 9·6 million *livres*. A ruling of 24 July 1638 envisaged sending out intendants 'en chacune des

---

[1] AD + 247 and E 136a, fo. 147.

[2] At Amiens, Bordeaux, Lyon, Poitiers, Riom, Soissons, and Tours—where intendants were already present. At Caen, Rouen, Bourges, Châlons, Limoges, Montauban, Moulins, Orléans, and Paris—where intendants had not been present: Bonney, 'Intendants', pp. 295–6. A.G. A1 41, no. 257, 30 Mar. 1637, commission of Villemontée. A version of this commission, dated 31 Mar. 1637, was published by A. Barbier, 'Les intendants de province et les commissaires royaux en Poitou', *Mémoires de la Société des Antiquaires de l'Ouest*, xxvi (1902), 611 f.

[3] A.A.E. France 830, fo. 266, 21 July 1638.

provinces' with the task of levying these *subsistances* for the troops.[1] In fact, this task was carried out in nineteen provinces, including two *pays d'états*—Burgundy and Languedoc.[2] It was also carried out elsewhere—in Alsace and Franche-Comté, which at this time were not part of France. The levy of the *subsistances* was extremely important in that it necessitated an increase in the number of intendants—fourteen intendants were sent out in addition to those who were already in the provinces. Even more important was the fact that this tax was levied each year thereafter until the Fronde, thus requiring the continuous presence of intendants in provinces where there had been no such continuity before. Finally, the tax was levied —albeit with very great difficulty—in two areas of *taille réelle*, the provinces of Languedoc and the Dauphiné.

For a short period of time, it seemed that fiscal experimentation by the government might lead to administrative uniformity in France, and the disappearance of the distinction between the *pays d'états* and the *pays d'élections*. This tendency was apparently confirmed when, in February 1641, commissions were issued to a number of intendants to levy a 5 per cent sales tax (*sol pour livre*), which was to apply to both the *pays d'élections* and the *pays d'états*.[3] As a result of this, certain *généralités*—notably Paris, Soissons, Moulins, and Bourges—where intendants had not previously been present without interruption, were to have intendants without a break until the Fronde. On 10 May 1642, the council of finance could refer to the intendants of justice, police, and finance as having been 'establis . . . en chacune province et généralité . . . de ce royaume'.[4] By implication, this meant that they had been introduced into both the *pays d'états* and the *pays d'élections*. In the former, they were usually referred to as the intendants of Languedoc, Provence, Burgundy, or Brittany. In the latter, they were usually referred to as intendants in the *généralités* of Paris, Soissons, Amiens, and so on.

[1] AD + 252.
[2] At Aix [?], Amiens, Caen, Montpellier, and Poitiers—where intendants were already present. At Alençon, Bordeaux, Bourges, Châlons, Dijon, Grenoble, Limoges, Lyon, Moulins, Orléans, Paris, Riom, Rouen, and Tours—where intendants had not been present: Bonney, 'Intendants', pp. 297–9.
[3] There were certainly commissioners at Alençon, Amiens, Châlons, Grenoble, Limoges, Montpellier, Moulins, Orléans, Paris, and Tours: Bonney, 'Intendants', p. 300. K 891 no. 3, instructions for the commissioners, drawn up by Bouthillier, Séguier, and D'Hémery, 1 Feb. 1641. [4] E 170a, fo. 336.

By 1642, therefore, an extremely important rule had come into being: the normal number of intendants in the *pays d'états* should be one per province, while in the *pays d'élections* it should be one per *généralité*. This rule had certainly not existed in a clear form in the 1630s. In 1632, D'Argenson had been given the Limousin, Haute and Basse Marche, and the Auvergne, 'et autres provinces adjacentes et circonvoisines', thus at least two *généralités*.[1] Five years later, Villemontée had been given Poitou, Saintonge, Aunis, and the Angoumois. Although his *généralité* was based on Poitiers by this date, the *élections* of Saintes, Cognac, Angoulême, and Saint-Jean-d'Angély, which he administered, were situated in the *généralités* of Bordeaux and Limoges.[2] In 1636, Mesgrigny was given the Bourbonnais, Haute and Basse Auvergne, 'et pays adjacens', thus at least two *généralités*.[3] Talon was given two provinces in 1634: Provence and the Dauphiné.[4] The situation was simplified and rationalized by the creation of a number of new *généralités*, which were given intendants. The *généralité* of Montauban was created in 1635, thus giving the province of Guyenne its second *généralité*.[5] The *généralité* of Alençon was set up a year later, giving the province of Normandy its third.[6] From 1641 and 1638 respectively, these new *généralités* had their own intendants. There were attempts—between 1634 and 1638 and again between 1646 and 1648—at introducing intendants into Brittany.

The great weakness of the principle of one intendant per province or *généralité* was that the administrative areas, and the populations to be administered, varied greatly in size. The fiscal policies of the crown, whereby new *élections* were continually being created or abolished in these years, makes statements as to the size of these areas rather hazardous. The average number of *élections* per *généralité* was nine.[7] Yet Paris

---

[1] Hanotaux, *Origines*, p. 316. A.G. A1 14, no. 32, 12 Aug. 1632.

[2] A.G. A1 41, no. 257, 30 Mar. 1637. Saintes and Cognac were passed frequently between the *généralités* of Bordeaux and Limoges: cf. E 217b, fo. 354, 24 Nov. 1646.

[3] A.D. L'Allier B 740, fo. 113ᵛ–114ʳ, 10 Jan. 1636.

[4] A.G. A1 49, no. 296, misdated 1638, actually 1634.

[5] L. Desgraves, 'La formation territoriale de la généralité de Guyenne', *Annales du Midi*, lxii (1950), 243–4. A.D. Tarn-et-Garonne C 534, 1635.

[6] M. Foisil, *La révolte des Nu-Pieds et les révoltes normandes de 1639* (1970), p. 59. AD + 242, May 1636.

[7] B.N. 500 Colbert 259, 260, which give 171 *élections* (*élections particulières* omitted) from 19 *généralités*.

had 20, Tours had 16, and Rouen had 13, while Bourges, Lyon, and Riom had half a dozen or less. Moreover, the size of the *élections* varied greatly: Poitiers had 259 parishes, while Châtellerault, within the same *généralité*, had only 55.[1] Clearly, the administrative burden on intendants varied enormously: the intendant of Poitou had 1,009 parishes under his charge, which was about five hundred fewer than average.[2] The intendant of Languedoc had 2,650 parishes,[3] about 1,100 more than the average in the *pays d'élections*.

An attempted solution to this problem before 1648 was to send two intendants to the larger provinces. This was the situation in Languedoc from 1632 until 1647, in Provence from 1630 until 1638, and in the Dauphiné from 1640 to 1643. Among the *pays d'élections*, the *généralité* of Tours had two intendants in 1636–7 and 1642–8, and that of Paris had two from 1644 until 1648. The commission of Bautru de Serrant (8 October 1643) specified that he was being sent to assist De Heere 'considérant que la généralité de Tours est de sy grande estendue qu'il n'est pas possible qu'une seulle personne puisse vacquer...'[4] However, the experiment of joint commissions posed as many problems as it solved. Initially, the overburdened intendant may have asked for an associate.[5] If the intendant's administrative area was reduced in size, however, he became resentful.[6] A separation of Bas and Haut Languedoc, which had taken place in 1618, was rejected as an 'innovation' in 1643–4, despite the bitterness and

[1] A. Bonvallet, 'Le bureau des finances de la généralité de Poitiers', *Mémoires de la Société des Antiquaires de l'Ouest*, 2nd ser., vi (1883), 186.

[2] D. J. Buisseret, *Sully and the growth of centralized government in France, 1598–1610* (1968), p. 58. The figures for Bordeaux, Caen, and Rouen were later affected by the creation of the *généralités* of Montauban and Alençon. Cf. also B.N. 500 Colbert 261, 'rôle des parroisses par généralités et élections', *c.* 1677. No clear estimate of population per *généralité* for the whole of France is possible for the period of Richelieu and Mazarin. For the ten *généralités* in northern France in 1711: J. Dupâquier, 'Essai de cartographie historique: le peuplement du bassin parisien en 1711', *Annales E.S.C.*, xxiv (1969), 993.

[3] B.N. MS.fr. 17384, fo. 17, 24 Apr. 1645.

[4] *L'histoire vue de l'Anjou, 987–1789. Recueil de textes d'histoire locale pour illustrer l'histoire générale*, ed. F. Lebrun (Angers, 1963), i. 129–30.

[5] Lauzon in Provence asked for a colleague: A.G. A1 34, min. 127, 19 Jan. 1637. So too did Bosquet in Languedoc: *Bnutrennyaya politiyka francuzkovo absolutizma. 1633–1649* [= *The internal policy of French absolutism*], ed. A. D. Lublinskaya (Moscow–Leningrad, 1966), p. 36.

[6] *Lettres ... au Chancelier Séguier*, ed. Mousnier, i. 384.

rivalry between the intendants.[1] But the only solution was a geographical one, assuming that the intendants could not co-operate with each other: a functional division of responsibilities failed to work in the Dauphiné in 1640.[2] The difficulties experienced in the Dauphiné and Languedoc may well have warned the government not to repeat the experiment of joint intendants after the Fronde.

The simple fact that one was either an intendant of a province or of a *généralité* demonstrated a continuing distinction between administrative practice in the *pays d'états* and *pays d'élections* after 1641. This was reinforced by the failure of the sales tax, which was suspended in Languedoc, the Dauphiné, Brittany, and Béarn in October 1641. With the exception of Guyenne, it was not abolished in the *pays d'élections* until later, and not formally abolished until 25 February 1643.[3] By the end of 1641, therefore, it had become apparent that the sales tax would never replace the *taille* as a major revenue financing the war.[4] The weight of the *taille* was borne overwhelmingly by the *pays d'élections*, and it was in these areas that the council, by 27 November 1641, had come to consider 'l'établissement de commissaires au lieu desdits officiers [the *élus*]' as permanent administrators of the *taille*.[5]

The reasoning behind this measure was not only the very great importance of this tax, but the fact that, for a variety of reasons, payment by the provinces was greatly in arrears. Bouthillier, on his own as *surintendant des finances* after the death of Bullion in 1640, informed Richelieu: 'ce qui m'afflige est que . . . les [revenus] ordinaires nous manquent tout d'un coup en beaucoup d'endroictz du Royaume que la longueur de la guerre des huit années peu s'en fault a entièrement désolés'.[6] A limited experiment was made of conferring the assessments of the *taille* on two intendants—Fremin at Limoges and Barrin de Rezé at Bourges, both areas in which there were substantial

[1] Lublinskaya, op. cit., pp. 55, 63.

[2] A.G. A1 58, min. 177, 15 Mar. 1640. A.G. A1 61, min. 319, 4 Dec. 1640.

[3] *Lettres . . . de Richelieu*, ed. Avenel, vi. 821-2, 897-8. Ormesson, *Journal*, ed. Chéruel, i. 10.

[4] Chancellor Séguier had hoped this would be the case in 1640: Z1a 161, fo. 29v–30r, 4 Dec. 1640.

[5] Mousnier, *La plume*, p. 190.

[6] A.A.E. France 843, fo. 271v, 24 Aug. 1642.

arrears.[1] On 19 August 1642, the intendants in the *pays d'élections* were ordered by the council of finance to cease all other business and 'tenir la main à l'accélération et levée' of the *taille*.[2] The ruling of 22 August 1642 was issued with the intention of preventing a recurrence of disastrous arrears in the future. It extended without time limit, and throughout the *pays d'élections*, the powers conferred previously only to Fremin and Barrin de Rezé. The ruling made little significant difference to the number of intendants, since they had already been established in all the *pays d'élections* by 1641. In giving the intendants the annual task of the tax assessments, however, the government established them on a permanent basis in the *pays d'élections* and turned them into administrators. Richelieu's death on 4 December 1642 did not interrupt this development, for Louis XIII confirmed the ruling on the *taille* on 16 April 1643.

In 1626–7, the *premiers présidents* of the *Parlements* had asserted that the intendants 'résident . . . plusieurs années', and that they wanted to convert their commissions to life appointments. With the exception of the Lyonnais and Languedoc, this statement was premature in 1626–7. The intendants were commissioners, not office-holders. Thus they could not hold their positions for life.[3] Nevertheless, by the end of Richelieu's ministry, the intendants were certainly staying much longer in the provinces than had previously been the case. François de Villemontée, renowned for his strong-arm tactics against revolts, served as intendant of Poitou for fifteen years (1631–44; 1646–8). Robert Miron served as intendant of Languedoc for eight years (1632–40).[4] Villemontée and Miron, however, were the exceptions and not the rule. A relatively firm three-year rule operated, after which an intendant had to be reappointed, sent to a new province, or recalled.[5] On average, the intendants

---

[1] E 166, fo. 48, 4 Jan. 1642. E 167b, fo. 250, 13 Feb. 1642. E 168b, fo. 442, 29 Mar. 1642. E 172a, fo. 468, 9 July 1642. Perhaps also De Heere at Tours, La Potherie at Caen, and Montescot at Paris were intended to have this role: E 167b, fos. 32, 123, 487; 8, 12, 19 Feb. 1642.   [2] E 173a, fo. 175.

[3] In 1644, there was talk of making the provincial intendants office-holders, but the talk came to nothing: A.A.E. France 849, fo. 25, 9 Jan. 1644.

[4] A.D. Haute-Garonne C 2302, fo. 53, 21 Nov. 1639. Miron talked of having served seven years in Languedoc at this date.

[5] C. Godard, *Les pouvoirs des intendants sous Louis XIV, particulièrement dans les pays d'élections, 1661–1715* (1901, reprinted Geneva 1974), p. 467. Esmonin, *Études*, p. 83. *Lettres . . . au Chancelier Séguier*, ed. Mousnier, i. 46.

stayed less than three years in their posts between 1634 and 1648. A province might expect to receive between five and eight intendants in these years. The average number of appointments each year was between six and ten (Fig. 3).[1] All this was a vast change from the situation in the years before 1624 or even 1630.

The establishment of the Regency of Anne of Austria on 18 May 1643 threatened the new order created by Louis XIII and Richelieu. It raised false hopes among the office-holders that

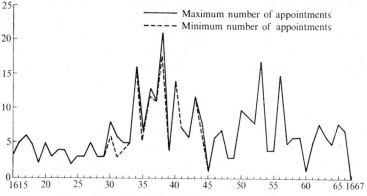

Fig. 3. Annual appointments of provincial intendants, 1615–1667.

the war might be brought to a speedy conclusion and that in the meantime the domestic consequences of the war—the increased taxes and the establishment of the intendants—might be reversed. The office-holders misunderstood the situation in 1643. They thought they had secured, through the action of the *Parlement* of Paris in annulling the last will and testament of Louis XIII, a limitation of the Regent's powers. But Anne of Austria and Mazarin could not afford the luxury of a Regency with limited powers because they were fighting a foreign war which necessitated strong government and domestic political sacrifice. The deputies of the *Parlement* of Paris received a rude awakening in 1645 when Chancellor Séguier reminded them that during a foreign war it was necessary to 'compâtir avec le public, fermer les yeux aux affaires extraordinaires et dans le malheur de la nécessité qui est cognue choisir les moindres maux'.[2] Séguier's

[1] Bonney, 'Intendants', p. 268.   [2] X1a 8388, X1b 8854, 1 Feb. 1645.

words were in answer to protests by the *Parlement* of Paris at an alleged abuse of power by the provincial intendants. Anne of Austria and Mazarin considered themselves bound by Louis XIII's foreign policy. Criticism of the continuation of this policy had begun with the *Cabale des Importants* of 1643–4. The criticism was held in check while the policy appeared to be successful in military terms with the victories in the Low Countries in 1643–6. These campaigns aimed to achieve a quick settlement in the negotiations with the Habsburgs at Münster, but no such settlement emerged. After 1646, there was a deterioration in the French military position, with the failure of the campaign in Italy, the inability to exploit the revolt of Naples against Spanish rule, and the lifting of the siege of Lérida by Spain. The foreign policy of Mazarin could no longer be justified in terms of military success. Nor had the diplomatic victory been achieved. Spain signed a separate treaty with the Dutch, one of France's main allies, on 30 January 1648, and broke off negotiations with France. These events were regarded by the French as a disastrous setback. Many contemporaries were convinced that Mazarin might have had peace if he had acted with more moderation and openness. Peace was signed belatedly with the Emperor on 24 October 1648, but only after two further military victories had been won by France. Rightly or wrongly, Mazarin was regarded as having caused the breakdown with the Spanish and of having patched up a peace with the Emperor only after the Fronde had forced his hand.

Debate over foreign policy was inevitable because the fiscal consequences of the war were extremely serious. In 1642, the last year of Louis XIII and Richelieu's administration, expenditure had reached 88 million. The cost of the war under the Regency was even higher—120 million were spent in 1643 and 136 million in 1645. Because of inefficiency in the system of revenue collection, expenditure on this scale could not be met merely by an increase in direct taxation. Richelieu and Bullion had bridged the budgetary deficit by borrowing money on a significant scale. Mazarin and D'Hémery—the *contrôleur-général des finances* in the years 1643–7 and *surintendant* in 1647–8 —made a bad situation worse. With a gambler's instinct, Mazarin deliberately anticipated as much future revenue as possible in the hope of gaining a conclusive military victory, and thus imposing a decisive peace treaty on the Habsburgs. In 1645, Mazarin and D'Hémery borrowed 115 million *livres*, anticipating the revenues of the French crown up to the end of the fiscal year 1647.[1] When the *Parlement* of Paris claimed in its remonstrances, issued on 21 January 1649, that Mazarin had levied 80 million a year in taxes and had incurred debts of 150 million, it was thus not far from the truth. The *Parlement* failed completely to appreciate Mazarin's motives for acting in this way. It believed that Mazarin wanted the war to continue 'afin de se rendre plus nécessaire et avoir plus de prétextes de lever de grandes sommes de deniers pour s'enrichir'.[2] Mazarin, however, viewed foreign policy in terms of resources: if Philip IV of Spain could be convinced that France possessed the resources and the political will to continue the war for another ten years, he would make peace.[3] The danger of Mazarin's policy was that Philip IV might not come to terms before the financiers of the French monarchy took fright. Expenditure on the scale of the early years of the Regency brought with it an inherent risk of bankruptcy. With luck, bankruptcy could be staved off, provided that enough revenues could be anticipated to maintain financial confidence and provided that peace was signed quickly. Once the peace negotiations appeared to be getting nowhere and the government came under political pressure at home, bankruptcy was inevitable.

By December 1647, the financial situation was desperate.[4] Massive new revenues were needed to stave off bankruptcy. Without new revenues, loans from the financiers would no longer be forthcoming. Without such loans, the war could not be continued. Mazarin's gamble for a quick peace had failed. He was now at the mercy of his critics within France, and chief among these were the office-holders. Certainly there had been an element of miscalculation in Mazarin's dealings with the office-holders.[5] The Fronde of the office-holders did not arise

---

[1] Bonney, 'The secret expenses of Richelieu and Mazarin', p. 830.

[2] B.N. MS.fr. 3854, fo. 23, remonstrances of 21 Jan. 1649.

[3] Talon, *Mémoires*, ed. Michaud and Poujoulat, p. 204.

[4] E 1691, fo. 209, 19 Dec. 1647.

[5] Notably in the arrest of Barillon, a *président* of the *Enquêtes* of the *Parlement* of Paris, in 1645. Barillon died while imprisoned at Pinerolo and was regarded by the office-holders as a martyr.

from miscalculations by the government, however, but from a political impasse. Mazarin could not make concessions to the office-holders in 1648, however desirable such concessions might be in political terms, because concessions cost money—the item which above all the government did not have at its disposal. The office-holders objected to the creation of offices to provide a new source of revenue for the monarchy. The members of the Parisian sovereign courts felt a common bond with the *maîtres des requêtes* and the *parlementaires* at Aix and Rouen whose security of investment was severely threatened by the fall in prices of offices following the establishment of new offices.[1] The office-holders also objected to the use of extraordinary powers to force through fiscal measures. The *lit de justice* of 15 January 1648 was the second occasion when this procedure had been used by the government of Anne of Austria for the enforced registration of fiscal edicts by the *Parlement* of Paris. The crisis of 1648 was also a protest by the office-holders against an increase in the price of the renewal of the *droit annuel*, the annual payment for the privilege of resigning one's office to one's heir. The *arrêt d'union* of 13 May 1648, which has been viewed traditionally as the starting-point of the Fronde, was the result of agitation by the Parisian sovereign courts over the issue of the *droit annuel*.

The Parisian office-holders were united in the summer of 1648 for reasons of self-interest, 'la cause commune de la robe'. They also knew which policies of Mazarin they opposed. Between 13 May and 30 June 1648, the government tried to prevent a joint meeting of the Parisian sovereign courts because it knew that this would lead to criticism of government policies. The political confrontation operated in favour of the office-holders, however. The financiers refused to make further loans to the government until the struggle between the crown and its office-holders was resolved: 'il y a six sepmaines que le commerce de l'argent a cessé'.[2] The government thus capitulated, and delegates from the Parisian sovereign courts met at the *Chambre Saint-Louis* on 30 June 1648. From the outset there was

---

[1] For the fall in prices at Rouen, P. Logié, *La Fronde en Normandie* (3 vols., Amiens, 1951–2), i. 63.

[2] B.L. Harleian 4466, fo. 106ᵛ–107ʳ, 30 June 1648. Cf. Z1a 163, fo. 59ᵛ, 9 July 1648: '... les gens d'affaires avoient pris l'alarme, [tiennent] leurs bourses fermées et ne trouvoient plus d'argent'.

disagreement as to the status of the meeting and whether its proposals were binding on the government. The members of the *Chambre Saint-Louis* made proposals for changes in government, much as the Assemblies of Notables of 1596–7, 1617, and 1626–7 had done. In 1648, however, the Parisian sovereign courts issued these proposals in the form of decrees.[1] Neither the proposals nor the decrees of the Parisian sovereign courts were accepted as binding by the government. The capitulation of the government to the office-holders on 27 June 1648, however, ensured that in the short-term it would have to implement some at least of the proposals.

The *Chambre Saint-Louis* wanted a return to peace-time forms of government. The intendants had been the provincial administrators of France since 1642—yet the members of the *Chambre Saint-Louis* demanded their recall. The *trésoriers* and the *élus* had not administered the *taille* independently since 1642— yet they were to be reinstated. The government had anticipated revenues in the form of loans from financiers regularly since 1639—such loans, it was proposed, should be declared illegal. The cash expenses of the French crown had risen dramatically during the war—a limit was to be placed on such expenditure. The *taille* had been increased three-fold to help pay for the war— a reduction of 25 per cent, equivalent to the alleged interest rate charged by the financiers, was demanded. The *Chambre Saint-Louis* wanted a return to peace-time forms of administration not merely because they felt this was good for France, but because it was also good for the office-holders. The sovereign courts were to regain their former powers, following the abolition of the intendants. The power of the crown to issue commissions was also to be curtailed. There were to be no new judicial offices at all, whether in the sovereign or lesser courts. New financial offices would be allowed, but only after edicts had been registered in the courts 'avec liberté entière des suffrages'. New taxes were to be raised only in accordance with the proper procedure, that is to say after the registration of edicts in the courts, again after a free vote. The salaries of the office-holders and the payment of the *rentes* were to be re-

[1] The *Parlement* of Paris demanded the recall of the intendants in a decree of 4 July 1648: K 117b, no. 36. The *cour des aides* of Paris followed suit on 7 July 1648: Z1a 163, fo. 48.

established progressively. The *droit annuel* was to be renewed on advantageous terms.[1] The effect of these proposals would have been drastically to reduce the profitability of *la vénalité des offices* as a fiscal instrument of the crown.

The immediate consequence of the twenty-seven proposals of the *Chambre Saint-Louis* was the collapse of the government. Bankruptcy was declared in July 1648. The government agreed to reduce the *taille* substantially and to recall most of the intendants.[2] Serious negotiations began on the details of these arrangements. Throughout the negotiations, the ministers insisted that some intendants were necessary even if the actual number was negotiable. The *Chambre Saint-Louis* demanded that such intendants as were to remain should be named and that they should be sent to three provinces only—the Lyonnais, Picardy, and Champagne—and that their commissions should be registered in the *Parlement* of Paris. These demands were not fully accepted by the ministers, however. The royal declaration of 18 July 1648 did not name the intendants, did not mention registration of their commissions, and envisaged sending them to Provence, Burgundy, and Languedoc as well as the three other provinces. Initially, Chancellor Séguier had attempted to preserve the intendants' financial powers, arguing that otherwise it would prove impossible to collect the taxes; but the critics of the government were adamant on this point. As a compromise, therefore, Séguier suggested that in the provinces where the intendants were to be retained they should have the special task of advising the provincial governors and assisting them in military matters but without 'juridiction contentieuse ny cognoissance des finances'.[3] This concession was less far-reaching than might appear at first sight, since fiscal and military affairs were inseparable. The intendants were allowed to organize the payment of *subsistances* to the troops. Where this was carried out—as in Burgundy in December 1648—the intendant was instructed to operate according to the procedure

---

[1] *Nouveau journal contenant tout ce qui s'est fait et passé aux assemblées des compagnies souveraines [et] du Parlement de Paris ès années 1648 et 1649* (1649) [B.N. L37 b 12].

[2] On 10 July, the commissions of all the intendants serving within the jurisdiction of the *Parlement* of Paris were revoked: K 117b, no. 37.

[3] *Recueil des lois*, ed. Isambert et. al., xvii. 84–5. Godard, *Les pouvoirs*, pp. 451–4. For the debates: Talon, *Mémoires*, ed. Michaud and Poujoulat, pp. 244–50, U 28 and Z1a 163 passim.

laid down in the declaration of 16 April 1643, which had given the intendants their financial powers, now at the heart of the conflict.[1]

The royal declaration of 18 July 1648 thus removed the administrative powers of the intendants, and indeed the intendants were recalled from all but six provinces. However, where the intendants remained, it was by no means clear that the limitation on their powers was feasible, since their effectiveness depended on their involvement in financial affairs. This royal declaration remained the legal definition of the powers of the intendants in the six provinces until 22 October 1652, but the government did not adhere strictly to its terms. Yet the intendants could not be re-established throughout France, let alone regain their administrative powers, until the government defeated the Fronde.

[1] K 117b, no. 70, 1 Dec. 1648.

CHAPTER III

The Intendants, 1648–1661

THE OFFICE-HOLDERS regarded the concessions of 1648 as reforms comparable to the three great reforming ordinances of the sixteenth-century.[1] The ordinances of Orléans (1560), Moulins (1566), and Blois (1579), however, were the product of civil war in France and meetings of the Estates-General which had been forced on the government. For this reason, the ministers argued that any clauses in these ordinances could be annulled retrospectively.[2] The declarations extracted from the government during the Fronde were even more clearly *pièces de circonstance*. The declarations of 1648[3] were forced on a weakened government by the unprecedented action of the Parisian office-holders. In the view of the government, the peace of Rueil (11 March 1649), which confirmed these declarations, was the product of armed rebellion by the capital of France, led by the Parisian sovereign courts. The ministers did not accept that these concessions were 'reforms' which had legitimate authority in their own right. They regarded them as temporary expedients, aimed at retrieving the loss of political control by the government. The declarations would be annulled retrospectively once the king's sovereignty was no longer undermined and the king could act in *plenitudo potestatis*. The implicit consequence of the declaration of 18 July 1648 was that instead of the kingdom of France being an absolute monarchy with the king enjoying unlimited sovereignty, France would have been governed by a monarchy limited by the office-holders.[4] Once the implications of the rebellion of 1648–9 were understood,

---

[1] The declarations of 1648 were termed 'règlements nécessaires sur la distribution de la justice et l'ordre de nos finances', which suggests a reforming purpose.

[2] cf. Colbert's argument, quoted by Mousnier, *La plume*, p. 178. This was the position of the ministers during the Fronde, implicit in all their actions.

[3] The declaration of 18 July 1648 was confirmed and to some degree extended on 22 Oct. 1648.

[4] For the unwritten and customary nature of the French consitution, Mousnier, *La plume*, pp. 43–56.

they were rejected by the majority of the office-holders. The concessions were the 'product of extraordinary circumstances'.[1] Once these circumstances had passed, they would be null and void. The office-holders had sought to restrict the king's fiscal powers by dismantling the system of war finance that had operated since 1635. Without independent powers of finance, the king could not conduct an independent foreign policy. The immediate effect on the government was a chronic shortage of funds. Perhaps more than any other factor, the pressure on resources speeded the conclusion of peace with the Emperor on 24 October 1648. Peace with Spain, however, was not forthcoming. Philip IV and Don Luis de Haro had no wish to miss the opportunity presented by the Fonde. They hoped to profit from the weakness of France in order to complete the reconquest of Catalonia. By 1652, not only had this been completed, but conquests in Italy and the Low Countries had been achieved also.[2] Since France was still at war with Spain, the demands of the office-holders during the Fronde allowed only two alternative courses of action for Anne of Austria and Mazarin. Either they could accept the demands, dismantle the system of war finance, and recall the intendants permanently, thus risking the prospect of a humiliating peace; or else the existing foreign policy must be brought to fruition, entailing a commitment to the system of war finance, the re-introduction of the intendants, and the defeat of the office-holders. Since vital aspects of the king's sovereignty—the right to determine his own foreign policy and to interpret and modify the constitution —appeared to be threatened, the defeat of the Fronde of the office-holders was certain to be the course of action chosen by Anne of Austria and Mazarin. Mazarin's reaction was not emotional or unbalanced[3] when he argued that the declarations of 1648, if enacted permanently, would abolish 'la meilleure partie de la monarchie'.[4] Mazarin did not believe that Philip

[1] Moote, *The revolt of the judges*, p. 172.

[2] A.A.E. France 891, fo. 73, anon. memorandum of 1652, which attributed the loss to the Spanish of Barcelona, Casal, Dunkirk, and Gravelines to insufficient government funds.

[3] In contrast, Moote, op. cit., p. 168, asserts that 'Mazarin's emotional reaction to the parlementary Fronde was particularly unbalanced'.

[4] P. A. Chéruel, 'Les carnets de Mazarin pendant la Fronde', *Revue Historique*, iv (1877), 135.

I V of Spain would make peace on terms which were acceptable to France. The war thus had to be continued. The continuance of the war, in Mazarin's view, required the reinstatement of the intendants and the restoration of the system of war finance.

The political and financial weakness of the central government during the Fronde had very serious consequences for the intendants even in the six provinces where they were officially retained by the declaration of 18 July 1648. All six provinces could in some measure be described as 'frontier' areas, thus justifying the retention of intendants for security reasons. Three were, moreover, *pays d'états* whose representative assemblies required close supervision.[1] The main tasks of the intendants were, nevertheless, financial and military. They had responsibility for the organization of the 'staples' (*étapes*), the munition points at which food for the troops was collected and distributed, and which were financed by levies on the local population. (This task was carried out by the *trésoriers de France* within the other *pays d'élections*.)[2] Raising funds for the troops necessitated increased financial powers for the intendants over the civilian population. In Languedoc, Le Tonnelier de Breteuil was ordered to ensure that the grant of 1·2 million *livres* awarded on 9 November 1649 to the crown by the Estates of Languedoc was actually levied.[3] He was also instructed to investigate cases of peculation in the diocese of Uzès.[4] In 1651, the investigation was extended to the whole of Languedoc, and Boucherat was nominated to assist Breteuil in the task.[5]

Although there was clearly a financial aspect to the work of the intendants in the frontier provinces during the Fronde, the judicial aspect seems to have been greatly reduced. At first, Breteuil had thought that it might be possible to 'agir en mon fonction comme je faisois auparavant'.[6] By August 1649,

[1] The council of state thought an intendant of Languedoc was 'autant plus nécessaire qu'en aucune autre [province] pour estre pays d'estatz'. E 1696, no. 302, 24 Oct. 1651.

[2] E 242a, fo. 120 and A.G. A1 122, no. 189, 7 Apr. 1650. Cf. the activities of Le Tonnelier de Breteuil in Languedoc: A.G. A1 119, nos. 250, 449, 6 June and 28 Sept. 1650. E 240, fo. 575, 19 Feb. 1650.

[3] E 240, fo. 24, 5 Feb. 1650.

[4] E 242a, fo. 126, 7 Apr. 1650.

[5] O1 3, fo. 16.   [6] B.N. MS.fr. 17390, fo. 261, 27 Oct. 1648.

however, he admitted that he dared not intervene in judicial questions 'pour ne me commettre pas inutilement avec les juges de la province, en attendant un plus favorable temps'.[1] In November of the same year, he was considering taking upon himself jurisdiction in cases concerning Protestants where decrees of the council had been issued, 'afin de tascher peu à peu à me rendre au mesme estat que j'étois avant les dernières déclarations . . .'[2] The evidence of decrees of the council suggests that matters which were the concern of the intendant before 1648 were sent to the sovereign courts during the Fronde.[3]

The effectiveness of the intendants in the frontier areas during the Fronde depended on the provinces not being left for periods without an intendant, and on the local political situation. In only three provinces—Languedoc, Picardy (until 1651), and Burgundy—was there real continuity. In the Lyonnais there was apparently no intendant at all—instead, there were commissioners drawn from the *cour des aides* of Paris and the *intendants des finances*. In Provence and Champagne there was a break in continuity—after the summer of 1649 and in 1651 respectively, there was no intendant. Provence was a special case, since the interim peace conditions dictated by the *Parlement* of Aix in January 1649 included an article prohibiting intendants.[4] Civil war followed, but the government decided to act cautiously when, in 1650, it sent out a new commissioner, and deliberately avoided calling Jacques de Chaulnes an intendant.[5] The attitude of the *Parlement* of Aix explains in some measure why no intendant was sent to Provence after the Fronde.[6] Where the factions had taken to arms, as in Provence, the intendant was obviously in a weak position. In Provence in 1649, De Sève, the intendant, was caught on the side of the governor in the political conflict between the comte d'Alais and the *Parlement* of Aix. In Languedoc, such polarization did not

[1] B.N. MS.fr. 17394, fo. 111, 2 Aug. 1649.
[2] B.N. MS.fr. 17391, fos. 133ᵛ–134ʳ, 9 Nov. 1649.
[3] For example, V6 230, no. 12, 2 Oct. 1648. V6 236, no. 67, 20 July 1649.
[4] U 29, fo. 62, 24 Jan. 1649.
[5] 'M. le Garde des Sceaux [Châteauneuf] est d'advis qu'on envoye M. de Chaunes en Provence non en qualité d'intendant, bien que le Roy le puisse faire en conformité de la déclaration, mais avec une simple lettre de cachet . . .' A.A.E. France 870, fo. 267ᵛ, 22 Mar. 1650.
[6] cf. the protests of the *Parlement* of Aix against the arrival of Luillier d'Orgeval, a *maître des requêtes*: B.L. Harleian 4490, fo. 133, 8 Jan. 1657.

occur. The troops were exclusively under royal control, and the nobility offered its support to Breteuil, the intendant, and the comte de Bieule, one of the *lieutenants-généraux*.[1] In Picardy, Burgundy, and Languedoc, the continuous or nearly continuous presence of intendants gave the central government much more chance of defeating the local factions.[2]

The intendants were recalled from the fifteen *pays d'élections* in which they were declared illegal on 18 July 1648.[3] In these areas, there was a return to the *status quo ante* 1642, and the *trésoriers* and the *élus* regained the administration of the *taille*. The intentions of Anne of Austria and Mazarin, and the advice given by members of the council, ensured that this would not be a permanent state of affairs. The *Parlement* of Paris was unable to ensure that the letter, let alone the spirit, of the declaration of 18 July 1648 was respected.[4] The evolution of government policy towards the provinces owed much to the advice of former intendants serving in the council during the Fronde, to whose views particular attention was paid.[5] Most important of all, however, was the fact that the reintroduction of the intendants was an integral part of the policy of Anne of Austria and Mazarin and their supporters in the government. The restoration of D'Hémery to the finance ministry in 1649[6] coincided with attempts to reinstate the intendants in various forms in the provinces in which they were officially proscribed. In June 1649, when Aligre and Barillon de Morangis were the *directeurs des finances*, there had already been rumours of a reinstatement of the intendants.[7] D'Hémery translated rumour

---

[1] B.N. MS.fr. 18830, fo. 144ᵛ.

[2] cf. the efforts of La Marguerie in Burgundy, together with D'Épernon, the governor: A.A.E. France 1491, fos. 364, 369, 411; 13 Feb., 5 Mar., 24 July 1652.

[3] For example, Poitou, the Limousin, Guyenne, and the Auvergne, cited by Bercé, *Histoire des croquants*, i. 478.

[4] Moote, *The revolt of the judges*, p. 271.

[5] For example, La Marguerie: E 233a, fo. 176ᵛ, 10 Oct. 1648; Bezons: E 235a, fo. 306ᵛ, 10 July 1649.

[6] As *surintendant des finances*, together with Claude de Mesmes, comte d'Avaux, on 8 Nov. 1649. Cf. the renewal of their powers: B.N. M.S.fr. 4222, fo. 212, 17 Mar. 1650.

[7] Z1a 206, p. 915, 1 June 1649, circular of *syndic* of *élus* to the *élections*. Cf. Mousnier, *La plume*, p. 315. J. P. Charmeil, *Les trésoriers de France à l'époque de la Fronde. Contribution à l'histoire de l'administration financière sous l'ancien régime* (1964), p. 380.

into fact. Commissioners of all types were sent into the *pays d'élections*, including representatives of the sovereign courts; *intendants des finances* and *maîtres des requêtes*; and intendants of the army acted as provincial intendants.

The first expedient was to send out commissioners drawn from the *cour des aides* of Paris. On 22 December 1649, the government announced its intention of doing this. The commissioners would carry out the tax assessments and prosecute cases of tax rebellion—the most important functions of the intendants in the *pays d'élections* before the Fronde. In January 1650, the government nominated eleven commissioners, who sought to introduce 'une manière d'intendance'.[1] There were crucial differences between these officials and the intendants before 1648. They were not permanent administrators,[2] nor did the government have complete control over them. The officials received commissions of the crown: but appeals against their sentences were heard by the *cour des aides* of Paris, not the council of finance, and their first loyalty was to the *cour des aides*.

A second expedient, almost certainly devised by D'Hémery in 1649, although there were precedents in the 1630s, was to send out *intendants des finances*, normally permanently based in the finance ministry,[3] into the provinces. In June 1649, for fiscal reasons, the number of these office-holders had been increased from four to eight, and thus there were *intendants des finances* to spare at the council. Each of these officials had his own area (*département*) comprising certain provinces to which he might be sent for a short visit. The new list of these areas drawn up on 23 June 1649 had given Étienne Foullé responsibility for Bourges, Limoges, and Soissons.[4] Foullé was sent to Limoges in early 1650 to supervise the collection of tax arrears. His efforts aroused the hostility of the local population and the *Parlements* of Bordeaux

---

[1] This was the view of the *trésoriers de France*: Mousnier, *La plume*, pp. 317, 329. The commissioners were: Bragelongne, Guerin, Brissonet, Quatresomme, Roger, Goureau, Poncher, Baussan, Josse, Mareschal, and Brigalier.

[2] Only Baussan stayed any length of time in the provinces, and his two-year stay at Lyon was regarded as illegal: E 252b, fo. 434, 31 Aug. 1652.

[3] cf. the view of the *trésoriers* at Limoges, who claimed that 'la fonction de Messieurs les intendants des finances est dans le Conseil seulement'. Mousnier, *La plume*, p. 316.

[4] *Archives curieuses de l'histoire de France*, 2nd ser., vi (1838), 470–1.

and Toulouse alike.[1] Five *intendants des finances* were sent out and
twelve provinces were affected by the experiment.[2]
A third way of reintroducing the intendants was in the form
of *maîtres des requêtes* on circuit-tour (*chevauchée*), a procedure
which was particularly advantageous to the government in
that it enabled former intendants to be sent into the provinces,
without rendering the government liable to charges of illegal
action.[3] The circuit-tours had good sixteenth-century precedents, and were legitimized by the great reforming ordinances of 1560, 1566, 1579, and 1629.[4] This expedient really got
under way with the sending of Morant to Bordeaux and Montauban in January 1650.[5] Other *maîtres des requêtes* sent out
included Paget at Châlons, Gaulmin at Moulins, Pinon at
Soissons, and Lefèvre d'Ormesson at Paris. The financial
office-holders argued that this was a re-establishment of the
intendants. The *maîtres des requêtes*, they argued, 'sont maintenant autant d'intendants dans les généralités, . . . sans en
prendre la qualité . . .'[6]
A fourth and final way of reintroducing the intendants was in
the guise of intendants of the army serving with the troops in the
provinces. Late in 1648, Villemontée had returned to Poitou in
this role.[7] In February 1649, Foucquet was serving at Pontcarré
as intendant in the army besieging Paris.[8] The following year,

[1] R. Fage, 'Un terroriste au xviie siècle', *Bulletin du Comité des Travaux Historiques*
xxiv (1906), 160. U 29, fo. 233^v, 3 Aug. 1650. E 239, fo. 76, 5 Jan. 1650. E 240, fo. 1,
3 Feb. 1650.
[2] The men were Étienne Foullé, Pierre Gargan, Jacques Le Tillier, Barthélémé
Hervart, and Guillaume de Bordeaux. The provinces were Guyenne, Poitou, the
Saintonge, the Angoumois, Aunis, Berry, the Dauphiné, the Limousin, the
Lyonnais, Languedoc, the Bourbonnais, and the Auvergne. Several *intendants des
finances* held more than one province; some held commissions as intendants of the
army.
[3] cf. the advice of Argenson, a former intendant, to Chancellor Séguier: 'il
faudrait envoyer Mrs. les Mes. des reqtes. soubs d'autres prétextes que pour
estre Intendans' (18 June 1649). *Lettres . . . au Chancelier Séguier*, ed. Mousnier,
ii. 940.
[4] E 1696, fo. 198, 3 June 1650, a decree of the council of state which cited the
ordinances 'et la déclaration de 1553'.
[5] E. Esmonin, 'Un épisode du rétablissement des intendants. La mission de
Morant en Guyenne (1650)', *Revue d'Histoire Moderne* (1954), reprinted in Esmonin,
Études, pp. 53–70.
[6] Mousnier, *La plume*, p. 316; Charmeil, *Trésoriers*, p. 381.
[7] Charmeil, *Trésoriers*, p. 388.
[8] J. Lair, *Nicolas Foucquet. Procureur-général, surintendant des finances, ministre d'état
de Louis XIV* (2 vols., 1890), i. 132–3. U 28, fo. 375, 22 Feb. 1649.

he was serving first in the army in Normandy and then in the army of Burgundy.[1] De Heere is a clear example of a former provincial intendant who returned to his province—the Touraine—as an army intendant and remained there.[2] The army intendants soon had financial powers which extended beyond the army and encompassed the province in which the army was operating. A decree of the council of state of 1 October 1651 empowered the army intendants to countersign ordinances for the payment of troops and to deduct the sums paid by the parishes from the *taille* that was owed for 1647–51.[3]

These moves towards reintroducing the intendants in the *pays d'élections* during the Fronde were of necessity underhand, a partial reintroduction and no more. It was not until after the collapse of the Fronde that complete restoration of the intendants was possible. The great weakness of the Fronde of the office-holders was that the office-holders were not united. The *Parlements* failed to co-operate. Dijon, Rennes, Grenoble, and Metz never joined in political association with Paris. They were reluctant to follow the lead of Paris and to issue decrees against Mazarin. Rouen and Aix, it is true, entered a short-lived 'parfaicte jonction et intelligence' with Paris on 5 February 1649, but there was no political union in the sense of a guarantee of mutual assistance. Neither Rouen nor Aix was prepared to issue decrees against Mazarin.[4] The *Parlement* of Paris acted with considerable caution even during the siege of the capital in 1649. Thereafter, it ended its association with Rouen and Aix, merely issuing remonstrances on the situation outside its own area.[5] Paris wanted to 'conserver l'avantage de sa primo-géniture et de sa dignité' and had no desire to innovate in constitutional matters.[6] The provincial courts rejected a

---

[1] A.G. A1 122, no. 186, 29 Jan. 1650. A.G. A1 120, fo. 177, 15 Mar. 1650.

[2] A.G. A1 125, no. 194, 26 Sept. 1651.   [3] E 249a, fo. 3 (collated copy).

[4] Logié, *La Fronde en Normandie*, ii. 97–9, 102. Talon, *Mémoires*, ed. Michaud and Poujoulat, p. 329. U 28, fo. 337v–339r, 5 Feb. 1649.

[5] In contrast, Moote, *The revolt of the judges*, pp. 15–16, n. 24, emphasizes the attempts of the *Parlements* to overcome 'the problems of separatism and rivalry'.

[6] On 12 Sept. 1650, the *Parlement* of Paris rejected the offer of a political union with its counterpart at Toulouse: Talon, *Mémoires*, ed. Michaud and Poujoulat, p. 397. E. H. Kossmann, *La Fronde* (Leiden, 1954), p. 179. Moote, op. cit., p. 273, minimizes the importance of this offer. But Le Tellier considered the possibility of 'cette jonction . . . très dangereuse': A.A.E. France 872, fo. 33, 6 Sept. 1650.

political union, too, since this would have turned them into mere ciphers of the Parisian office-holders. A close political union with Paris was not wanted in the provinces because this would have restricted the freedom of the courts to bargain with the government and gain local concessions.[1] Almost all the local treaties during the Fronde were negotiated independently. The *Parlement* of Paris had little influence on events in the provinces and took none of the credit for any settlements which emerged. There was little co-operation between the other courts. The *maîtres des requêtes* and the *Parlement* of Paris had enjoyed an informal alliance after January 1648—but by the end of the summer of 1648, the *maîtres des requêtes* were supporting the government once more. The *grand conseil*, too, was incapable of sustained opposition to the government. The relationship between the *Parlements* and the *cours des aides* was strained, sometimes to breaking-point, since the *Parlements* wanted to reduce taxes and the *cours des aides* claimed all fiscal matters as their prerogative.[2] In the summer of 1648, the members of the Parisian sovereign courts had undoubtedly championed the grievances of the lesser courts within their area. This relationship broke down after 22 October 1648, however. The lesser courts had their own, separate, organization.[3] By no means all the lesser courts concerned with finance joined their central agency,[4] or supported its policies.[5] There had been a 'cause commune de la robe' in the spring and summer of 1648. It had been undermined by the separate terms offered to the members

[1] Moote, op. cit., p. 129.
[2] (i) *Parlement* of Toulouse v. *cour des comptes* of Montpellier: P. Serres, *Histoire de la cour des comptes* . . . (Montpellier, 1888), pp. 68–72. E 1696, fo. 406, 28 Mar. 1651. (ii) *Parlement* of Toulouse v. *cour des aides* of Cahors: A.A.E. France 1634, fo. 490, 28 Oct. 1650. (iii) *Parlement* of Bordeaux v. *cour des aides* of Guyenne: C. B. F. Boscheron des Portes, *Histoire du Parlement de Bordeaux depuis sa création jusqu'à sa suppression 1451–1790* (2 vols., Bordeaux, 1877), ii. 15–18, 140–1. E 242a, fos. 19, 21, E 1697, fo. 227, 2, 11 Oct. 1651. (iv) *Parlement* of Grenoble v. *cour des aides* of Vienne: E 245b, fo. 453, 25 Feb. 1651.
[3] Mousnier, *La plume*, pp. 301–33.
[4] In October 1648 only 34 out of 171 *élections* were represented in the *syndicat*: Z1a 206, p. 913. There is clear evidence of opposition by some of the local courts to this agency. Cf. V6 332, no. 190, 30 Sept. 1656 (Tours); V6 229, no. 56, 21 Aug. 1648 (Armagnac); E 331b, fo. 147, 28 Jan. 1660 (Clermont).
[5] The *trésoriers* of Toulouse objected to the policies of their central agency, which were chiefly concerned with the struggle against the *élus* in the *pays d'élections*: B.N. MS.fr. 7686, no. 235, 2 Aug. 1651.

of the sovereign and lesser courts in the declaration of 22 October 1648.[1] It was further weakened by the peace negotiations at Rueil in March 1649, when the *parlementaires* of Paris demonstrated that they were not prepared to delay peace for their area for the sake of their colleagues in the provinces. Thereafter, there was no 'cause commune' at all. Conservatism and traditional rivalry were the twin reasons for this failure. Far from conservatism on constitutional matters being a source of strength to the office-holders and their programme,[2] it was their greatest weakness. The *Parlement* of Paris helped provoke a civil war in January 1649, but had no wish to prolong the breakdown of government. During this crisis, the *Parlement* was prepared to enter a limited political alliance with the nobles, but was reluctant to do so thereafter.[3] Once the nobles had entered the political arena, however—acting ostensibly in support of the *Parlement*—the crisis took on a new momentum. The second and third outbreaks of civil war were the responsibility of the nobles.[4] The failure of the office-holders to co-operate on a permanent basis was an abdication of political responsibility—perhaps this was understandable, yet nevertheless it was an implicit recognition that they had no right to intervene in affairs of state. It undermined the possibility of a 'third party', a *via media*,[5] and left the political struggle to the government and the nobles. In the last resort, most of the office-holders preferred Mazarin and his policies to government of the nobles who acted in alliance with Spain.

The government sought to exploit the regional and social

[1] cf. the speeches of Laisné and Canaye in the *Parlement* of Paris on 20 Feb. and 22 Feb. 1652: 'Journal inédit du Parlement de Paris pendant la Fronde (1 déc. 1651–12 avril 1652)', ed. H. Courteault, *Annuaire-Bulletin de la Société des l'Histoire de France* (1916), 270–3. The government traditionally offered separate terms for the renewal of the *droit annuel*: Mousnier, *La vénalité*, pp. 291–308.

[2] In contrast, Moote, *The revolt of the judges*, pp. 10–11, asserts that 'the danger to the king from his *officiers* actually stemmed more from the legality than the illegality of their actions'.

[3] cf. U 29, fo. 82, 11 Mar. 1649, proposed articles for peace: 'Le Parlement de Paris renoncera à toutes associations qu'il pourroit avoir faictes au dedans du Royaume avec les généraux et autres . . .'

[4] That is to say, the revolt of the supporters of Condé after the imprisonment of their leader in January 1650 and the revolt of Condé after September 1651. This chronology does not take into account the provincial civil wars in Guyenne and Provence.

[5] In contrast, Moote, op. cit., p. 370, asserts that 'the most important factor' in the Fronde was 'the parlementarians' legalistic *via media*'.

differences of France in order to defeat the Fronde. The office-holders could have defeated Mazarin: but they would have needed to move towards constitutional innovation and to have formed permanent political alliances. The negative attitude of the *Parlement* of Paris—its lack of concern for the fate of the provinces, above all the provinces outside its own area—led to the triumph of Mazarin's policy of divide and rule.[1] Once the provinces had fallen to the government, the cause of the Parisian office-holders was hopeless. By the autumn of 1652, Brittany, Languedoc, Provence, the Dauphiné, Burgundy, and most of the central provinces of France were under royal control. The conquest of Guyenne was well under way. Normandy was neutral, but was likely to side with the winning party. Apart from a small area around Bordeaux, only Paris and the north-east of France held out. The resistance at Paris collapsed in October 1652. It was eliminated in north-east France during the winter of 1652–3. Bordeaux, the last bastion of the Fronde, fell on 3 August 1653.

The collapse of the Fronde at Paris was followed by the royal declaration of 22 October 1652. This declaration was extremely significant. It did not have a 'hollow ring'[2] for implicitly it undermined the proposals of the office-holders in 1648 and the subsequent government legislation on those proposals. The declaration disallowed criticism of the ministers by the *Parlement*, forbade its interference in affairs of state and financial questions, and annulled its previous interventions in this area.[3] Thus the ministers were given virtually a free hand with which to direct affairs of state. Chancellor Séguier made it clear that it was not necessary to 'révoqu[er] ouvertement' each item of unpalatable legislation passed during the Fronde. All that was needed was that the king's intentions on a particular issue should be made clear,[4] and this was the reason why the

[1] cf. Moote, op. cit., p. 175.
[2] In contrast, Moote, op. cit., p. 352 argues that the office-holders 'prevent[ed] the royal administration from emerging with the sweeping triumph that Anne and Mazarin wanted'.
[3] U 30, fo. 356: '. . . déclarant dès à présent nul et de nul effect tout ce qui a esté cy devant ou pourroit estre cy après resolu et arresté sir ce subiect dans ladictce compagnie [the *Parlement* of Paris] au préjudice de ladicte déclaration . . .'
[4] A.A.E. France 898, fo. 202, 17 July 1656. Séguier's remarks were on the subject of the declaration in favour of the Protestants (21 May 1652).

royal declaration of 18 July 1648 against the intendants was never officially revoked.[1] Although it is possible that the government acted in this way because it feared that specific reference to the annulling of the declaration of 18 July 1648 would act as a focus for discontent,[2] it is more likely, however, that this step was not necessary since the declaration had not been honoured during the Fronde. Where the royal legislation of 1648 was more effective—notably in the restrictions on government expenditure and the abolition of certain taxes—it was formally abolished in the winter of 1652.[3]

The return of Mazarin to Paris from exile (3 February 1653) and the appointment of Servien and Foucquet as joint *surintendants des finances* five days later[4] further increased the authority of the government. The defeat of the Fronde meant the intensification of the war against Spain. Government expenditure rose from 113 million *livres* in 1653 to 154 million in 1657.[5] The continuation of the war required the restoration of the system of war finance. The new finance ministers had to restore the confidence of the financiers, which had been badly shaken during the Fronde. Both Servien and Foucquet had served as intendants. They regarded the intendants as the means by which the confidence of the financiers could be restored. Without intendants to secure the payment of taxes in the provinces, they argued, the financiers would either not make loans to the government or would demand excessive rates of interest.[6] The intendants were also needed for political reasons.

---

[1] Moote, op. cit., p. 354, interprets this as a sign of weakness on the part of the government.

[2] cf. the view of Gaspard de Fieubet, the *premier président* of the *Parlement* of Toulouse, who told Mazarin that the nobles, the office-holders, and the populace all believed that 'le rétablissement des intendants est un mal qui n'est guères moindre que celuy de la guerre civile': A.A.E. France 1636, fo. 220ᵛ, 15 Nov. 1653.

[3] Lifting of the limit on the secret expenses: E 1698, fo. 183, 16 Nov. 1652. Re-establishment of certain taxes abolished in 1648: Xı b 8857, 31 Dec. 1652. Moote, op. cit., p. 357, regards these measures as no more than 'piecemeal attacks on specific aspects of the reforms of 1648 . . .'

[4] Oı 1, fo. 66, 8 [Feb.] 1653. B.M. Rouen MS. Léber 5767, fo. 9. La Vieuville died on 2 Jan. 1653. Cf. the requests of Foucquet and Servien for appointment as his successor: A.A.E. France 892, fo. 39, 2 Jan. 1653. A.A.E. France 891, fo. 54 and 892, fo. 148, 25 Jan. 1653.

[5] Bonney, 'The secret expenses of Richelieu and Mazarin', p. 832.

[6] A.G. Aı 158, no. 344, 14 July 1654. Cf. A.A.E. France 900, fo. 283, 9 Aug. 1656: '. . . tout [leur] employ estant de finances . . .'

They were an essential aspect of 'l'autorité du Roy que l'on commence d'y restablir'.[1] Mazarin was evidently in agreement. He was informed at various stages when problems concerning the intendants arose, and appears never to have come into conflict with the *surintendants* on this issue. Among the other ministers, Chancellor Séguier supported the reintroduction of the intendants because, having served as an intendant himself, he valued them as an instrument of the central government. Séguier had been the strongest supporter of the intendants during the constitutional negotiations in the summer of 1648. When he had been disgraced during the Fronde, he had retained his close personal ties with the *maitres des requêtes* from whom the intendants were usually recruited. In 1653 and 1656 he accepted their claim to be 'des plus considérables officiers du royaume . . . aussi anciens que la monarchie'[2] in the face of rival claims from the *trésoriers de France* and the *Parlement* of Paris. Given general agreement among the ministers that the intendants should be reintroduced, Séguier was unlikely to oppose the decision. Nor, indeed, was Molé, the Keeper of the Seals, for his eldest son had been an intendant at Châlons in 1648. Molé was in any case 'extraordinairement mesprisé . . . il n'entre du tout point en part du secret'.[3] Le Tellier, the war minister, was strongly in favour of the intendants for the purposes of military administration and reform.[4]

A decree of the council of finance of 26 April 1653 empowered the commissioners sent into the provinces for 'l'accélération du payement et pour la discipline des gens de guerre' to investigate payments forced by the troops.[5] This measure implied a determination on the part of the ministers to transform the army intendants into provincial intendants. On 23 July 1653 a loan of 9 million *livres* was contracted by the government with a consortium of financiers under the name of Richard Richer. This loan was to be repaid from the proceeds of the tax levied

[1] A.A.E. France 892, fo. 322, 8 Sept. 1653.
[2] E. Esmonin, 'Un épisode du rétablissement des intendants après la Fronde. Les maîtres des requêtes envoyés en chevauchée', *Revue d'Histoire Moderne et Contemporaine*, xii (1965), 224. Charmeil, *Trésoriers*, pp. 400–1.
[3] B.L. Harleian 4468, fo. 182ᵛ, 13 Mar. 1652.
[4] A.A.E. France 904, fo. 49, 24 July 1657.
[5] E 255b, fo. 721.

in certain provinces to pay for the troops during the winter
quarter.[1] The chief purpose of the loan was to ensure in advance that the government would be able to pay the troops
during the winter. The provinces were still required to carry the
cost of the winter quarter, but the amount due on the *taille* was
reduced by the same amount. The intendants were required
in the provinces to calculate the reductions in the *taille*. The
intendants were also to carry out the assessments of the *taille*.[2]
Commissions and instructions to this effect were issued to the
intendants within a week of the fall of Bordeaux, the last
bastion of the Fronde (3 August 1653). The office-holders in
the provinces who were affected by this decision—that is, the
trésoriers and the *élus*—regarded it as a return to the royal
declaration of 16 April 1643, which had never been repealed.[3]
With the establishment of an intendancy in the Dauphiné in
1654, and an intendant *per généralité* by this date, for all practical
purposes the intendants had returned as permanent administrators. It is true that in the 1650s, there were intendants in
the *pays d'états*, while there were only *commissaires départis pour
l'exécution des orders de Sa Majesté* in the *pays d'élections*.[4] As soon as
the troops were present in a *généralité*, however, the *commissaire
départi* was given a commission as intendant of justice, police,
and finance.[5] The council, moreover, regarded the two titles
as synonymous.[6] The distinction in title simply reflected the

---

[1] cf. E 261a, fo. 1, 1 Oct. 1653; E 263a, fo. 522, 28 Jan. 1654. The provinces
affected were Alençon, Bourges, Caen, Limoges, Lyon, Moulins, Paris, Poitiers,
Orléans, Riom, Rouen, and Tours.

[2] Instructions to Fortia (Poitiers), 11 Aug. 1653, printed by Boislisle in *Revue des
Sociétés Savantes*, 7th ser., iii (1881), 181–3. Similar instructions (10 Aug. 1653) in
Esmonin, 'Un épisode du rétablissement des intendants après la Fronde. Les
maîtres des requêtes envoyés en chevauchée', 220–1. B.N. MS.fr. 4187, fos. 130ᵛ–
133ᵛ. Commission to Heere for the *élection* of Saumur: B.N. MS.fr. 16218, fo. 279,
17 Aug. 1653. 'Pareilles commissions ont esté envoyés pour les autres eslections et
généralitez.'

[3] Mousnier, *La plume*, p. 319. K 118b, no. 63, 'remonstrances' of the *trésoriers
de France*, 17 Sept. 1653.

[4] Esmonin, *Études*, p. 38. Cf. E 1803, no. 39, an insertion in the decrees of the
council for 1680. The document refers to *généralités* 'des pays d'élections où il n'y
a que des commissaires départis'. On the other hand, it talks of 'pays d'états où il y
a des intendants'.

[5] Mousnier, *La plume*, p. 331. B.L. Harleian 4490, fo. 172, 4 Jan. 1657, Tallemant,
commissaire départi at Bordeaux, thanking Chancellor Séguier for 'la commission
d'intendant de justice dans cette généralité que vous avés eu la bonté de m'accorder'.

[6] E 259a, fo. 1ᵛ, 6 Aug. 1653. E 259b, fo. 269, 23 Aug. 1653. E 260a, fo. 224,
3 Sept. 1653. E 260b, fo. 527ᵛ, 27 Sept. 1653.

difference in fiscal regime between the *pays d'élections* and the *pays d'états*. In the *pays d'élections*, the intendants were responsible for the administration of the *taille* after the Fronde, as they had been in the years 1642–8.[1] In the *pays d'états*, responsibility for the *taille* was not theirs.

After 1654, only Paris among the *pays d'élections* was without an intendant, and then only in the years 1662–5.[2] Among the *pays d'états*, the intendants were not established as permanent administrators in Provence until 1671, in Béarn until 1682, and in Brittany until 1689. In a memorandum to Mazarin, dated *c.* 1658–9, Foucquet wrote that 'les lettres du Roy ont esté envoyées diligemment à MM. les intendants de justice excepté en Bretagne, Provence et Béarn, où elles ont esté adressées à M. le Maréchal de la Meilleraye, M. le duc de Mercœur, M. le Maréchal de Grammont'.[3] The governor was the sole representative of the king in those provinces without intendants. The general characteristics of the intendants after the Fronde were very similar to those before 1648. There were slightly fewer intendants on average; they stayed slightly longer in the provinces.[4] A three-year rule—after which an intendant had to be reappointed, sent to a new province, or recalled—operated after 1653 much as it had done before the Fronde.[5] However, there were important differences between the intendants in the years after the Fronde and their predecessors before 1648. Firstly, in the two *pays d'états* with permanent intendants— Languedoc and Burgundy—the intendants stayed for an unprecedented period of time. Bazin de Bezons stayed in Languedoc for twenty years (1653–73). Bouchu stayed in Burgundy for twenty-seven years (1656–83). Secondly, there

---

[1] Moote's contention (op. cit., p. 356) that the *commissaires départis* were 'not . . . the intendant-administrators of the 1630s and 1640s' exaggerates the purely titular aspect of the problem. The real point was that the royal declaration of 16 Apr. 1643 was implemented once more.

[2] The *généralité* was administered by *trésoriers de France*—Sauteuil and La Barre in 1662–3 and Hachette, Regnault, and Beauchamp in 1662–5. E 359c, fo. 182, 23 Nov. 1662. E 363b, fo. 84, 9 June 1663. E 373a, fo. 227, 8 Aug. 1664. E 377a, fo. 57, 5 Mar. 1665.

[3] A.A.E. France 900, fo. 420.

[4] Bonney, 'Intendants', pp. 268, 316.

[5] Bouchu's opponents in Burgundy tried in vain to assert the three-year rule in order to obtain his recall: A.A.E. France 1492, fos. 284, 294^v, n.d. and 20 Apr. 1660.

were very few cases of joint intendants after the Fronde. Lefèvre de la Barre and Le Tonnelier de Breteuil were joint intendants at Paris in 1653–4; Bazin de Bezons was joined by Boucherat in 1654 and Tubeuf in 1665–7—but these were the only examples of joint intendants. When the intendancy at Tours fell vacant with the death of De Heere in 1656, Foucquet pointed out that 'cette place . . . autrefois a esté occupé par deux',[1] but only one intendant—Hotman de Fontenay—was appointed.

A third important change was the relaxation in 1658–9 of the rule of one intendant *per généralité*, and the *ad hoc* creation of larger administrative units.[2] This was a return to the situation in the 1630s, and the reasoning behind the decision and its proponents in the king's council are not known. It seems doubtful whether the move was a concession to the sovereign courts:[3] the courts would have liked to see fewer intendants, it is true, but they could scarcely have viewed larger administrative units with any enthusiasm. The general political situation may well have dictated an *épuration* of the intendants. The year 1658 was one of acute political and social crisis when, in Servien's words, 'le royaume estoit menacé d'un soulèvement général'.[4] In 1659, the government sought to levy a forced loan on the towns.[5] Colbert argued that certain intendants refused to investigate the noble conspiracies of 1657–9 sufficiently thoroughly and thought that negligent intendants should be sacked.[6] (Although not formally a member of the government, as *intendant de la maison* of Mazarin, Colbert exercised great influence over the Cardinal, and had manœuvred the appointment of several of his friends and relatives as intendants.) For

---

[1] A.A.E. France 900, fo. 283, 9 Aug. 1656.

[2] *Lettres . . . de Colbert*, ed. Clément, i. 410. Colbert wrote that Mazarin 'a couplé toutes les autres généralités du royaume' apart from Guyenne. Fourteen *généralités* were linked into larger units. Usually an intendant was given two *généralités*. Esmonin, *Études*, p. 37.

[3] In contrast, Hamscher [*The Parlement of Paris after the Fronde*, p. 199] argues that Mazarin and Foucquet 'consistently modif[ied] or abandon[ed] their programmes' in the face of the opposition of the *Parlement* of Paris. Yet Hamscher notes (p. 87) that the *Parlement* did not interfere with the re-establishment of the intendants; nor did it criticize their conduct.

[4] A.A.E. France 905, fo. 228ᵛ, 3 July 1658.

[5] A.A.E. France 900, fo. 420. Although the sum demanded was small compared with 1637—only three million *livres*.

[6] *Lettres . . . de Colbert*, ed. Clément, i. 357–8.

his part, Le Tellier argued that the intendants sometimes acted 'avec trop de réserve' when levying new taxes for the simple reason that they had to secure the co-operation of the local notables.[1] From the viewpoint of both Colbert and Le Tellier, therefore, a reorganization of the administrative areas would carry advantages because it would permit the government to retain only the first-class administrators and the most effective and loyal servants. It is of course possible that in reorganizing the administrative areas of the intendants the government took for once a purely administrative decision on its merits and was not influenced by any political considerations. The creation of larger administrative units may be viewed, perhaps, as an attempt, albeit misguided, at reform—the elimination of the great discrepancies in the size of the administrative areas of the intendants.[2] If Claude Pellot, the intendant of the Dauphiné in 1656, could ask for leave of absence, 'n'ayant plus de troupes dans la province et ainsi n'y ayant guères plus d'occupation',[3] how much work did the intendants do in the tiny *généralités*[4] such as Lyon, Bourges, and Riom? Most of the really large *généralités*—Paris, Tours (except in 1663–5), Châlons, and Rouen in particular—were left unaffected by the decision to create large administrative areas. The new areas were almost always smaller than the largest *généralité*, Paris, which had twenty *élections*: Bordeaux and Montauban, which were linked between 1658 and 1669[5] had nineteen; Poitiers and Limoges had sixteen; Orléans and Bourges had fifteen.[6]

Whatever the reasoning behind the creation of larger administrative units, the consequences were clear. Successive

<hr/>

[1] A.A.E. France 907, fo. 264ᵛ, 30 July 1659.

[2] cf. Colbert's comment, 'il faut donner . . . à chacun [intendant] autant de généralités qu'ils en pourront conduire en travaillant toute l'année avec application'. *Lettres . . . de Colbert*, ed. Clément, vii. 177. E. Esmonin, *La taille en Normandie au temps de Colbert, 1661–1683* (1913), p. 49.

[3] B.L. Harleian 4489, fo. 129, 19 July 1656.

[4] In the sense of possessing few *élections*. The intendant in theory had to visit the *chef-lieu* of each *élection* to hold the tax assessments.

[5] With an interval in 1662–3, when Charles Le Jay served as intendant at Bordeaux.

[6] There were exceptions, of course. Pellot held twenty-six *élections* (nominally at least) in 1662–3 and Colbert de Croissy held twenty-five in 1663–5. Pellot nominally held Poitiers, Montauban, and Limoges—but Poitiers was administered by two *trésoriers de France*, Vangueil and La Nabonnière, in the absence and 'soubz les ordres' of Pellot. E 358a, fo. 326, 13 Sept. 1662. Croissy held Tours and Poitiers.

finance ministers encouraged the intendants to enter into the detail of financial administration, especially the administration of the *taille*. Yet this was made very difficult precisely because the administrative units were too large. Hotman de Fontenay was too busy with the troops to visit all the *élections* of Guyenne in 1658.[1] Bochart de Champigny was too busy with affairs in the Lyonnais in 1660 to carry out a prosecution in the Dauphiné.[2] The burden of work on the intendants as a result of the increased size of the administrative areas led them to rely upon subordinates (*subdélégués*)—a development which Colbert came rapidly to regret.

The government needed intendants in the years after the Fronde to restore political order and to reorganize the system of war finance in order to pay for the continuing war against Spain. Mazarin concentrated on foreign policy. He signed the treaty of Westminster with the Cromwellian Protectorate (3 November 1655), an alliance to which Spain had aspired, following this up on 23 March 1657 with a military alliance which committed France to provide 20,000 men in the field and defray half the cost of the English military and naval forces. This expensive alliance achieved its purpose the following year, with the defeat of the Spanish forces at the Battle of the Dunes and the capture of Dunkirk and Gravelines. The struggle for financial resources had been lost by Spain. On 7 January 1659, the Spanish council faced the fact that there was no choice but peace with France if war with Portugal was to be continued. Events moved fast. A truce was signed on 8 May, followed by the treaty of Paris (4 June) and the treaty of the Pyrenees (7 November 1659). The struggle, which had been pursued so single-mindedly by Richelieu and Mazarin since 1630, was thus ended on terms which were advantageous to France. Indeed, Lefèvre d'Ormesson thought that it was the most advantageous peace for 150 years 'car tous les autres traitez de paix la France les a faictz en robbe de deuil et en robbe noire'.[3] The Peace of the Pyrenees permitted a review of

[1] E 319a, fo. 59, 4 Dec. 1658.

[2] E 334a, fo. 176, 15 Apr. 1660.

[3] 144 a.p. 54, Dr. 5, 27 Aug. 1661. Speech of Ormesson, *doyen* of the king's council, to the *cour des aides* of Paris.

the whole of government policy. On 31 December 1659, the council of state—acting on a memorandum from Colbert to Mazarin—concluded that financial reform was not only possible but essential. The need to cut government expenditure to the level of Louis XIII's lifetime was recognized.[1] An attempt was made to reduce the *taille* and to expand the indirect taxes. Nicolas Foucquet, who was the lone *surintendant* after the death of Servien on 17 February 1659,[2] introduced other changes, too, but none of these eliminated the budgetary deficit. The system of war finance therefore continued into the years of peace as Mazarin had predicted it would.[3] The intendants were still needed as the administrators of the *taille*. Foucquet, who had served as an intendant himself, was well aware of the usefulness of these officials, and had no intention of abolishing them or reducing their powers. The office-holders had hoped that after the end of the war, the fiscal powers of the intendants would be removed.[4] They were soon disillusioned by the first actions of Louis XIV after the establishment of his personal rule in 1661.

---

[1] E 1712, fo. 37.
[2] Foucquet was reappointed on 21 Feb. 1659. O1 7, fo. 45.
[3] Chéruel, 'Carnets de Mazarin', p. 132.
[4] Z1a 161, fo. 132ᵛ, 21 July 1643. The *cour des aides* of Paris had requested that the declaration of 16 Apr. 1643 'n'aura lieu que durant la guerre seulement'.

CHAPTER IV

The Intendants: Social Origins

WHO WERE the intendants? Assessment of a new administrative system must take into account its career structure and the social groups from which the administrators were selected. Some contemporaries thought the intendants were men of humble birth. The *Parlement* of Paris asserted in 1645 that 'la pluspart des intendans ne sont pas officiers du Roy, n'ont aucune caractère'.[1]

The great difficulty in analysing the social origins of the intendants appointed by Richelieu and Mazarin arises from the fact that nobility was in the process of redefinition at this time. In the sixteenth century, oral evidence had been accepted as sufficient proof of nobility. A man calling himself 'noble homme', who lived like a noble and was regarded by others as a noble, could enter the ranks of the nobility without difficulty.[2] The edict of March 1600, issued on the subject of the *taille*, had defined by implication two types of nobility. On the one hand, the *noblesse d'épée*, those who earned noble status through the profession of arms, who were 'issus d'un aïeul et père qui aient fait la profession des armes . . . sans avoir fait aucun acte vil et dérogeant à ladite qualité', were exempt from the *taille*. On the other hand, and also exempt, were the *noblesse de robe*,[3] those families who had gradually earned nobility by holding an office over three generations. It was necessary for a grandfather to have held an office for twenty years, or to have died in office, and for the father to have done likewise, for the son to enjoy noble status. This rule applied only to certain offices— chiefly those in the sovereign courts.[4] There were also certain

---

[1] X1a 8388 and X1b 8854, 1 Feb. 1645.

[2] cf. B. Guenée, *Tribunaux et gens de justice dans le bailliage de Senlis à la fin du moyen âge, vers 1380–vers 1550* (Strasbourg–Paris, 1963), pp. 409–11, 440–2.

[3] The expression *noblesse de robe* was not used. The text referred to those who had 'servy au public en quelques charges honorables, de celles qui par les lois et mœurs du royaume peuvent donner commencement de noblesse à la postérité . . .'

[4] R. Mousnier, *Les institutions de la France sous la monarchie absolue. I. Société et état* (1974), pp. 107–8. *Recueil des lois . . .*, ed. Isambert *et al.*, xv. 234 (article 25).

offices which conferred personal nobility on their holders, and subsequently to their heirs—although twenty years' tenure of office was usually required. Chief among these offices was the position of *secrétaire du roi*.[1] During the early years of Mazarin's ministry, this privilege was extended to most of the offices within the Parisian sovereign courts. The *maîtres des requêtes* enjoyed this privilege after 10 August 1644.[2] In addition, there was a third type of nobility recognized in the edict of 1582 on the *taille*: those who had been ennobled by letters patent issued by the king. These letters patent were sold by the crown as a source of revenue, and were also revoked periodically because excessive sales of *lettres d'anoblissement* reduced the number of tax-payers paying the *taille*.[3]

In the early years of Louis XIV's personal rule, the vague definition of nobility was made much more precise. A decree of the king's council, issued on 4 June 1668, ordered that the simple term 'noble homme' was not to be accepted as a proof of nobility.[4] An earlier decree, issued on 19 March 1667, distinguished between 'old' and 'new' nobility—the first having been acquired before 1560.[5] Written evidence was required to prove a claim to either type of nobility, although the *nobles d'ancienne extraction* were regarded as superior to the new nobles. The noble had to demonstrate his title by documents such as marriage contracts, divisions of inheritances (*partages*), acts of guardianship (*actes de tutelle*), and descriptions of fiefs (*aveux et dénombrements*). Moreover, the noble had to prove that he had not committed any deed which was held to be incompatible with noble status (*acte de dérogeance*).[6] In 1669, Colbert revoked many of the grants of personal nobility conferred during the

---

[1] P. Robin, *La compagnie des secrétaires du roi, 1351–1791* (1933). Michaud, *La grande chancellerie*, pp. 90–126, 164–203.

[2] F. Bluche and P. Durye, 'L'anoblissement par charges avant 1789', *Les cahiers nobles*, xxiii, xxiv (1962), especially xxiv. 19–20. B.N. MS.fr. 16218, fo. 375.

[3] J. R. Bloch, *L'anoblissement en France au temps de François Ier. Essai d'une définition de la condition juridique et sociale de la noblesse au début du xvie siècle* (1934). *Dictionnaire des anoblissements* [1788], ed. H. Gourdon de Genouillac (1869). Mousnier, *Les institutions*, p. 106.

[4] Mousnier, *Les institutions*, p. 102.

[5] However, the date of 1559–60 as the dividing line between the *ancien noble* and the *anobli* was not new. It had been used in a ruling of 6 Apr. 1639 concerning the Dauphiné: E 150a, fo. 88.

[6] J. M. Constant, 'L'enquête de noblesse de 1667 et les seigneurs de Beauce', *Revue d'Histoire Moderne et Contemporaine*, xxi (1974), 550.

early years of Mazarin's ministry.[1] The legislation in the first decade of Louis XIV's personal rule was thus an important departure from previous practice and many who claimed noble status had their claims rejected (*débouté*).[2] All the intendants appointed by Richelieu and Mazarin claimed noble status. In the years 1624 to 1661, between 258 and 273 intendants were appointed.[3] However, many intendants were appointed more than once, and the number of individual intendants is thereby reduced to 128. Thirteen families provided two intendants each, and thus the number of families concerned is further reduced to 115. The documentary material on these families varies greatly in quality. Many of the documents which survive were *pièces originales*, produced to demonstrate a claim to nobility.[4] Some may have been forged, and documents which failed to prove a claim to nobility were destroyed for obvious reasons. Genealogies are an additional source, but they are unreliable beyond two generations. Séguier's genealogist claimed that the intendant and Chancellor was descended from Sigar king of Denmark and Sigar king of Saxony living *c.* A.D. 300![5] This 'aveuglement ordinaire à tous les gens eslevées'[6] makes a cautious approach necessary with regard to any claim to nobility dating back beyond 1560. In the case of many families of intendants, it is not possible to state with any certainty how their claim to nobility was derived. Of those families about which there is adequate information, broadly speaking about one-third had been ennobled through the possession of the office of *secrétaire du roi*.[7] Another third

[1] Bluche and Durye, op. cit.

[2] Constant, art. cit., p. 551. J. Meyer, *La noblesse bretonne au xviiie siècle* (2 vols., 1966), i. 51–3.

[3] The higher figure counts joint intendants separately, the lower figure does not. Excluded from these totals are: i. Specialized commissioners without general powers as *intendant de la justice*. ii. Commissioners sent out during the Fronde, but who did not receive commissions between 1624 and 1648 or between 1653 and 1661. iii. Intendants of the army who did not receive commissions as provincial intendants.

[4] See Bibliography, manuscript sources, B.N. pièces originales.

[5] B.L. Harleian 4938.

[6] Ormesson's phrase castigating the alleged Scottish ancestry of the Colbert family: Ormesson, *Journal*, ed. Chéruel, ii. 548–9. Cf. *Le conseil du roi*, ed. Mousnier, pp. 165–6.

[7] Thirty-six families: Aubray, Bénard de Rézé, Besançon, Bordeaux, Bragelongne, Brûlart, Castille, Choisy, Dupré, Foullé, Gallard, Garibal, Imbert, La Guette, Laffemas, Le Camus, Lefèvre de la Barre, Lefèvre d'Ormesson, Le Jay,

had obtained nobility gradually through holding other offices, usually in the sovereign courts,[1] although a few had obtained nobility through appointment to the king's household.[2] About ten had obtained nobility through *lettres d'anoblissement* from the king, of which two were very old (Voyer d'Argenson 1375; Estampes de Valençay 1404).[3] Some intendants themselves obtained nobility during their lifetime by one or other of these means.[4] For 100 intendants, any claim to nobility by office in the sovereign courts or letters patent was reinforced by their having held the office of *maîtres des requêtes* at some time in their career. Twenty-two intendants appointed by Mazarin benefited from the decree of 10 August 1644, which conferred immediate nobility on the holders of this office, to supplement their other claims to nobility.

The distortion in the genealogies and the loss of many family papers makes it impossible to trace the families of the intendants of Richelieu and Mazarin back for more than three generations, except in the case of twenty families. These great-great-grandfathers of intendants were men of greatly differing social backgrounds. Five were *bourgeois*, that is to say they were residents of towns who may or may not have been noble.[5] Seven were already in possession of offices, some more humble than others, but which in general did not confer nobility, while seven others already held offices which did confer this status. In addition, the careers of two great-great-grandfathers

Le Maistre, Le Picard, Le Prévost d'Herbelay, Le Tonnelier, Ligny, Luillier, Méliand, Montescot, Morant, Olier, Phélypeaux, Pinon, Pommereu, Rénouard, Tallemant, Thiersault, Voisin.

[1] Twenty-nine families: Aligre, Bautru, Bochart de Champigny, Boucault, Boucherat, Bouchu, Bretel, Cazet de Vautorte, Chaponay, Charreton, Chaulnes, Dugué de Bagnols, Dyel de Miroménil, Faucon de Ris, Favier de Méry, Fortia, Gamin, Gassion, Gaulmin, Gobelin, Granger, Harouys, Heere, Hotman, Joubert, Lauzon, Le Bret, Lefèvre de Caumartin, Le Gras.

[2] Notably Barrin de la Galisonnière, Coetlogon de Méjusseaume, and Coignet de la Thuillerie.

[3] The others were: Aguesseau, Amelot, Bazin de Bezons, Foucquet, Laisné, Le Roy de La Potherie, Mangot, and Turgot.

[4] Notably Pierre Imbert, who in 1632 was simply a *commis* of La Vrillière, one of the secretaries of state: B.N. p.o. 1556 (Dr. 35,574), 31 May 1632. Imbert was ennobled by the office of *secrétaire du roi*.

[5] cf. Mousnier, *Les institutions*, pp. 103, 106.

of intendants appointed by Richelieu and Mazarin stand out as being of particular importance. The first is Jean Bochart, who was important not because of his social position—he was an *avocat* in the *Parlement* of Paris, although the son of a *conseiller* who had been a candidate for the first presidency of that court —but because of his political standpoint. Jean Bochart was imprisoned by François I for two years because he made 'un plaidoyer hardi touchant la pragmatique sanction'—he made a speech hostile to the Concordat of 1516, and thus ensured great prestige for himself and his descendants in that most Gallican of courts, the *Parlement* of Paris.[1] The second great-great-grandfather whose career is of particular interest is Jean-Jacques I Mesmes de Roissy, who served as a *maître des requêtes* from 1544 to 1559, during which time he received commissions from the king, notably as Ambassador to the Emperor Charles V in 1545. Finally, he became *premier président* of the *Parlement* of Rouen, 'charge qu'il préfère à l'honneur d'être conseiller d'état'.[2]

The third generation of ancestors—the great-grandfathers of the intendants of Richelieu and Mazarin—is a larger group in the sense that it comprises 48 families about whom there is reasonably precise information. The distinctive feature of this generation is the increased incidence of those holding office in the sovereign courts. At least fourteen families held such offices. In addition, Henri Mesmes, seigneur de Roissy, after holding the office of *conseiller* in the *grand conseil*, became a *maître des requêtes* and, unlike his father, a king's councillor: he was reported to be 'pas moins excellent capitaine qu'habile magistrat'.[3] Small offices played a crucial role for twelve families. Among these, the case of James Lauzon is particularly interesting, because as an *avocat* in the *sénéchaussée* of Poitiers, and later *échevin* and mayor there, he used his considerable political authority to help suppress a dangerous revolt against the *gabelle* in 1542.[4]

[1] *Dictionnaire de la noblesse*, ed. Aubert de la Chenaye des Bois and Badier (3rd ed., 19 vols., 1863–76), iii. 365–7.

[2] *Le conseil du roi*, ed. Mousnier, p. 48. *Dictionnaire de la noblesse*, ed. Chenaye, xiii. 753–5. B.N. p.o. 1941 (Dr. 44,633), nos. 3, 4, 1555, 15 July 1558.

[3] *Dictionnaire de la noblesse*, ed. Chenaye, loc. cit. B.N. p.o. 1941 (Dr. 44,633), no. 10, 15 Jan. 1561.

[4] *Dictionnaire, historique, biographique, et généalogique des familles de l'Ancien Poitou*, ed. H. Beauchet-Filleau (2 vols., 1840–54), ii. 283–7. B.N. p.o. 1667 (Dr. 38,764), no. 2, 6 July 1534.

The greatest divergences in social status were still possible in this generation: one family were still, apparently, *laboureurs*; seven termed themselves *bourgeois*; three were *anoblis*; three were household officials of the nobility, while four were themselves nobles.

The 74 grandfathers of intendants appointed by Richelieu and Mazarin about whom there is significant documentary material show a considerable contrast with the previous generation. The new and distinctive feature of the second generation of predecessors was not the four *bourgeois*, or the two grandfathers serving in the households of the great nobility; it was not the number of lesser office-holders either, for at thirteen, this group remained static. What was new were the thirteen *anoblis*, many of whom obtained first generation nobility through municipal office, for example at Lyon or Paris, or through the office of *secrétaire du roi*. A second important new group were the thirteen grandfathers of intendants who bought financial offices of greater or lesser importance. These included various types of *receveurs-généraux*, officials of the *Épargne* and the *extraordinaire des guerres*, and five *trésoriers de France*. The growth of government expenditure and the inflation in the price of offices no doubt accounted for the increased importance of financial offices. Considerable fortunes were needed to buy the important offices held by many of the fathers of the intendants Richelieu and Mazarin: one of the fastest ways to make a fortune was by handling the finances of the state.

Nevertheless, the members of the sovereign courts still predominated in this generation: twenty-seven families of intendants were now firmly established in these courts, chiefly at Paris. Three members of the sovereign courts—Bochart de Champigny, Coignet de La Thuillerie, and Luillier—in addition became *maîtres des requêtes*, Bochart becoming a king's councillor. Three grandfathers had really significant careers. After serving for ten years as *président* in the *Parlement* of Paris, Pierre Séguier was appointed in 1565 as commissioner for the edict of Pacification in Touraine,[1] thus receiving a commission not dissimilar to that enjoyed by his grandson at the

---

[1] E. Maugis, *Histoire du Parlement de Paris dès l'avènement des rois Valois à la mort d'Henri IV* (3 vols., 1913–16), iii. 190, 333. B.N. p.o. 2671 (Dr. 59,402), no. 61, 20 Nov. 1565.

time of Richelieu. François Nesmond, a *président* of the *Parlement* of Bordeaux after 1572, served as intendant in Guyenne 'près Monseigneur de Matignon' in 1594.[1] Jean-Jacques III Mesmes de Roissy, had a truly remarkable career that spanned the reigns of Henri III, Henri IV, and Louis XIII. He became a *maître des requêtes* on 21 November 1594 and was sent to Caen as commissioner for the reform (*régalement*) of the *taille* four years later. On 2 July 1600, he was appointed *conseiller ordinaire*, a position in the king's council that was confirmed on each occasion when a reduction in council membership was proposed —on 31 April 1617, 18 June 1618, and 21 November 1629. On 11 December 1624, he was appointed *conseiller honoraire* 'en considération des 25 années de service dans les conseils du Roy'. By 1630, if not before, he was the longest-serving councillor (*doyen*), and it was in this position that he died in 1642. One of the great career members of the council, Roissy's career foreshadows that of many of the intendants of Richelieu and Mazarin.[2]

Details are known about 104 fathers of intendants appointed by Richelieu and Mazarin. Nineteen fathers served as *maîtres des requêtes*. There was the same participation in financial activity as in the previous generation, eighteen fathers of intendants being involved in this way. (Four were *trésoriers de France*; five were *receveurs-généraux* or *particuliers*; two were involved with military expenditure; a further two were *trésoriers des parties casuelles*; there was also one *trésorier de l'Épargne* and one *trésorier des Ligues Suisses*. Two fathers of intendants were financiers of considerable importance: Pierre Bragelongne was fined 327,275 *livres* for his activities by the *chambre de justice* of 1661.[3] Nicolas Le Camus left a fortune of between 2·7 and 4 million on his death in 1648.)[4] The fathers of the intendants of

[1] F. Vindry, *Les parlementaires français au xvie siècle* (4 vols., 1909–12), ii. pt. i. 44. B.N. p.o. 2097 (Dr. 47,825), no. 20, 4 Sept. 1594.
[2] Maugis, op. cit., iii. 266. B. Barbiche, 'Les commissaires pour le "régalement" des tailles en 1598–99', *Bibliothèque de l'École des Chartes*, cxviii (1960), 63. B.N. MS.fr. 18152, fo. 119. Roissy's uncle, Jean-Jacques Mesmes, sieur des Arches, was intendant in Provence in 1576: Cf. B.N. p.o. 1941 (Dr. 44,633), no. 103, 15 Dec. 1592.
[3] Bragelongne had been a *trésorier de l'ordinaire des guerres*: B.N. p.o. 490 (Dr. 11,005), no. 235, 2 July 1661. B.N. 500 Colbert 233, fo. 39, fine on Louis [*sic*] Bragelongne.
[4] J. L. Bourgeon, *Les Colbert avant Colbert. Destin d'une famille marchande* (1973), pp. 251–4.

Richelieu and Mazarin were even less involved than their predecessors in minor offices (eight families), in the household of the nobility or military service (five families), or in municipal office and *la vie bourgeoise* (eleven families). By contrast, there was a staggering increase in the membership of the sovereign courts—sixty fathers of intendants held such offices at some time in their career. Forty-two fathers of intendants spent a significant part of their careers in the sovereign courts, of whom eighteen served in the *Parlement* of Paris, a further eleven served in other Parisian courts, and thirteen served in the provinces.

The remarkable feature of the careers of the fathers of the intendants of Richelieu and Mazarin is the large number—twenty-one—who had really important careers in the service of the crown. Among these, two had diplomatic careers while ten served in the council. Four more served as intendants—Raoul Favier at le Mans in 1572–3,[1] Bochart in Poitou in 1616–17[2] (he later became a *surintendant des finances*), Morant in Normandy in 1617,[3] and Boucherat in the army of Aunis in 1626.[4] Five fathers of intendants held high ministerial office. Étienne d'Aligre became Keeper of the Seals and then Chancellor in 1624, although he was disgraced two years later following the Chalais conspiracy. Claude Mangot became Keeper of the Seals for the short duration of Concini's ministry (1616–17).[5] Mathieu Molé, the celebrated *premier président* of the *Parlement* of Paris at the time of the Fronde, was Keeper of the Seals on two occasions (3–13 April 1651; 8 September 1651–3 January 1656). Raymond Phélypeaux, seigneur d'Herbault, began his career with financial activities, after which he obtained a secretaryship of state in 1621. His ministerial position enabled him to survive the ignominy of a fine of 300,000 *livres* levied

---

[1] Maugis, op. cit., iii. 241. B.N. p.o. 1111 (Dr. 25,582), no. 6, 11 Mar. 1573.

[2] Maugis, op. cit., iii. 300. F. Bluche, *L'origine des magistrats du Parlement de Paris au xviiie siècle* (1956), pp. 95–6. E 56b, fo. 171, 23 Sept. 1617. Cf. V6 1209, fo. 212 [no. 32], 15 Jan. 1620.

[3] *Dictionnaire de la noblesse*, ed. Chenaye, xiv. 509–14. E 55b, fos. 2, 24, 2 and 7 Mar. 1617.

[4] *Dictionnaire de la noblesse*, ed. Chenaye, iii. 654–8. *Le conseil du roi*, ed. Mousnier, p. 89. B.N. p.o. 436 (Dr. 9820), no. 63, 20 June 1626.

[5] B.L. Harleian 4472b, fo. 297, letters of provision, 25 Nov. 1616. *Serment*, 26 Nov. 1616.

by the *chambre de justice* of 1624–5.[1] In many ways the most significant career, however, was that of Louis Lefèvre de Caumartin, for it illustrated the twin aspect of career as intendant and career as king's councillor that was to become characteristic of the period of Richelieu and Mazarin. A *conseiller* in the *Parlement* of Paris in 1579, *maître des requêtes* in 1585, and *président* of the *Grand Conseil* in 1596, Lefèvre de Caumartin received his first intendancy from Henri III when he was sent to Poitou in 1588. Thereafter, Henri IV sent him twice to Picardy as intendant (1590, 1597), and he received two financial commissions—at Riom, Bourges, and Moulins in 1596–7 and at Rouen in 1598–9. Lefèvre de Caumartin's career in the council began on 10 October 1594. In 1599 he was made a *conseiller ordinaire*. An ambassadorship to Switzerland followed in 1605. Finally, only five months before his death, he was appointed Keeper of the Seals on 23 September 1622.[2] This remarkable career demonstrated not only the interrelationship between service as intendant and in the king's council, but also the importance of length of service in promotions in the council.

Clearly, the majority of the fathers of intendants had already had significant careers in their own right. Very few of the intendants appointed by Richelieu and Mazarin were self-made men. A tradition of family loyalty to Henri IV has been considered an essential prerequisite of future appointment as an intendant at the time of Richelieu and Mazarin.[3] Such a view clearly underestimates the empirical way in which appointments were made in seventeenth-century France. Some fathers of the intendants had supported the Catholic League against Henri IV. Michel Le Tellier was Mayenne's intendant of finance in Champagne in 1591,[4] yet this did not prevent his son from becoming an intendant of the army in Lombardy in 1640 or secretary of state for war in 1643. Nicolas Chaponay was

---

[1] *Dictionnaire de la noblesse*, ed. Chenaye, xv. 781–2. Bluche, *L'origine des magistrats*, pp. 345–6. *Le conseil du roi*, ed. Mousnier, p. 135. B.N. MS.fr. 7583, p. 581, fine of 17 May 1625. B.N. p.o. 2257 (Dr. 51,145), no. 24, 31 Dec. 1616.

[2] Esmonin, *Études*, pp. 41–51. *Lettres . . . au Chancelier Séguier*, ed. Mousnier, ii. 1211. B.L. Harleian 4472b, fo. 293, letters of provision, 23 Sept. 1622. *Serment*, 25 Sept. 1622.

[3] *Lettres . . . au Chancelier Séguier*, ed. Mousnier, i. 171.

[4] B.N. MS.fr. 4004, fo. 53, 9 Aug. 1591. Extract of the registers of the council of the League.

Mayenne's intendant at Lyon in 1591,[1] yet his son could become intendant there forty-three years later. Sir George Carew remarked acidly of Henri IV that 'those who hazarded their lives and fortunes for settling the crown on his head, he neither rewardeth nor payeth; those who were of the league against him, he hath bought to be his friends and given them preferments'.[2] Carew was exaggerating. For every Le Tellier, Chaponay, and Pinon who remained loyal to the League, and whose son became an intendant, there were other fathers of intendants—such as Aguesseau, Amelot, Dyel de Miroménil, Fortia, Harouys, and Séguier[3]—who could demonstrate their loyalty to the king throughout the League. In any case, the political standpoint of a family during the League might be a significant consideration in appointments during the years 1624–30, but scarcely after the Day of Dupes. The ability, social position, and years of service by a potential intendant at the time of Richelieu and Mazarin outweighed any questionable political decisions taken by his father or grandfather. Clear instances of political loyalty reaping its results were rare, and tended to be recent. François Bosquet, the intendant of Languedoc from 1642 to 1646, was the son of Durand Bosquet, a *notaire* at Narbonne. He never held office in a sovereign court or became a *maître des requêtes*. His career began in 1632, when he came to the notice of the government as a result of his loyalty during the revolt of Montmorency. On 2 March 1633 he was rewarded with the office of *juge royal* at Narbonne and 3,000 *livres* towards the cost—24,000 *livres*—of this office.[4] The

---

[1] M. Pallasse, *La sénéchaussée et le siège présidial de Lyon pendant les guerres de religion. Essai sur l'évolution de l'administration royale en province au xvie siècle* (Lyon, 1943), p. 384.

[2] Sir George Carew, 'A relation of the state of France', *An historical view of the negotiations between the courts of England, France and Brussels, 1592–1617*, ed. T. Birch (1749), p. 478.

[3] Jean Séguier followed Henri III in his exile from Paris and then joined Henri IV. Three others (Jean Amelot, Jacques Dyel, and Bernard de Fortia) refused to sign the oath of loyalty to the League and sat in the royalist *Parlements* at Tours and Caen. Charles Harouys refused to join the League at Nantes and his house was attacked as a result. He took refuge at Angers and received an indemnity from the king. François d'Aguesseau was an *échevin* at Amiens and was instrumental in the capitulation of that city to Henri IV in 1597.

[4] P. Henry, *François Bosquet. Intendant de Guyenne et de Languedoc. Evêque de Lodève et de Montpellier. Étude sur une administration civile et ecclésiastique au xviie siècle* (1889), p. 2. J. Tissier, *Documents inédits pour servir à l'histoire de la province de Languedoc et de la ville de Narbonne en particulier, 1596–1632* (Narbonne, 1903), pp. 75, 77–9. E 118b, fo. 70, 20 July 1634. V6 116, no. 85, 29 Sept. 1636.

rewards of loyalty in Bosquet's case were thus not very great, and were no more than a humble starting-point in his career.

The majority of the intendants appointed by Richelieu and Mazarin belonged to a closely-knit social group, the *noblesse de robe*, a group whose characteristics were wealth and inter-marriage. Analysis of fifty-one marriage contracts of intendants[1] —all but eight drawn up before their appointment as intendant —provides an estimate of the wealth of these young office-holders shortly before the most important event of their careers. Nearly always the wealth of the future intendant was immobil-ized in his office. Usually no monetary value was placed on the office simply because the market value fluctuated greatly from year to year. However, in a marriage of equals, the wealth of the future intendant was implicit in the dowry (*dot*) he could command, in the size of the possessions held in common (*communauté*), and in the amount of jointure (*douaire*) he had to pay his wife annually. A *mésalliance* was usually self-evident from the exceptional financial terms of the marriage contract. The great financier, Antoine Feydeau, had to pay 500,000 *livres* to marry his daughter into the nobility in 1622.[2] Among the intendants, Sève had to pay heavily for marrying into the *noblesse d'épée* in 1637.[3] When others—such as Antoine Phély-peaux after his intendancy[4]—married below their status with-out financial compensation, the family boycotted the ceremony. One or two future intendants—notably Baltazar and Laffemas —rose a long way up the social scale in their lifetime, and this fact is revealed by their early marriages, respectively to the daughters of a merchant and a *notaire*.

In general, however, marriages were arranged shortly be-fore or after the future intendant became a *maître des requêtes* or

[1] See Bibliography, manuscript sources, marriage contracts of intendants. For an example of a marriage contract of a member of the Parisian *noblesse de robe*, cf. the marriage of Omer Talon (younger brother of Jacques, the intendant) to Françoise Doujat on 8 Jan. 1626: H. Mailfait, *Un magistrat de l'Ancien Régime. Omer Talon, sa vie et ses oeuvres, 1595–1652* (1902), pp. 349–55. Omer Talon was only an *avocat* at the *Parlement* of Paris at this time.

[2] Minutier Central LI 135, 30 Mar. 1622, marriage of Marye Feydeau to Thimoleon Daillon 'chevalier de l'ordre du Roy, capitaine de 50 hommes d'armes de ses ordonnances', son of the comte de Lude.

[3] *Lettres . . . au Chancelier Séguier*, ed. Mousnier, i. 127. Y 177, fo. 259, 3 Jan. 1637.

[4] *Le conseil du roi*, ed. Mousnier, p. 137. Minutier Central XC 215, 18 Feb. 1652.

bought another major office. Although the office of *maître des requêtes* was much cheaper than a presidency in the Parisian sovereign courts, it was still an enormous capital investment— 150,000 *livres* was the usual figure, although Claude Gobelin had to pay 177,810 *livres* in 1632. The office was officially valued at 200,000 *livres* on 27 October 1674 and reduced to 180,000 *livres* on 18 July 1679.[1] The size of a dowry commanded at marriage was determined by consideration of this capital investment. The average dowry in 37 marriage contracts of intendants was 122,891 *livres*; the average amount of possessions held in common in 41 contracts was 39,975 *livres*; the average amount of jointure paid annually by the husband in 48 contracts was 3,085 *livres* (in capital worth perhaps 43,190 *livres*). The dowry figure of 122,000 *livres* compares with that of 150,000 *livres* recorded in 1647 in a marriage of equals between the children of two of the greatest financiers of the period— Bonneau and Marin—who between them made approximately 10 per cent of all the loans to the government in the 1640s.[2] It compares somewhat less favourably from the intendants' point of view with the average of 173,000 *livres* recorded in 41 marriages of the Parisian *noblesse de robe* in 1660–1.[3] The families of the intendants were not the richest among the *noblesse de robe*: but they were very wealthy indeed compared to the families in the lower levels of office-holding or other sections of society.[4] It is clear from a comparison with 771 marriage contracts from the years 1634–6 that the families of intendants formed the top one per cent of Parisian society.[5]

[1] V. R. Gruder, *The royal provincial intendants. A governing élite in eighteenth-century France* (Ithaca, N.Y., 1969), pp. 61–2. *Lettres . . . au Chancelier Séguier*, ed. Mousnier, i. 171–2. E 1776, fo. 265. E 1798, fo. 25.

[2] Minutier Central XIV 63, 23 June 1647, marriage of Charles Bonneau, sieur du Plessis, son of Thomas Bonneau, to Jacqueline Marin, daughter of Denis Marin. Cf. B.N. 500 Colbert 233, fos. 82–92, fine of 5,196,092 *livres* at the *chambre de justice* of 1661 on Bonneau and Marin, moderated to a fine of 3 million on Bonneau alone. Between 1640 and 1650 Bonneau and Marin loaned about 57 million to the government.

[3] J. P. Labatut, *Les ducs et pairs de France au xviie siècle. Étude sociale* (1972), pp. 323–4.

[4] cf. the analysis of marriage contracts at Amiens: P. Deyon, *Amiens. Capitale provinciale. Étude sur la société urbaine au xviie siècle* (Paris–The Hague, 1967), pp. 548–9.

[5] Only eight dowries of over 100,000 *livres* were recorded: R. Mousnier, *La stratification sociale à Paris aux xviie et xviiie siècles. L'échantillon de 1634, 1635, 1636* (1976), pp. 67–74.

Wealth was important not only in itself but because it implied social connections. Family connections were a feature of all the law-courts and groups of office-holders in seventeenth-century France, and were important politically as well as socially. Two families of intendants—Faucon de Ris and Laisné—had connections with at least six other families. Three families—Bochart de Champigny, Heere, and Mangot—had connections with five others; four families had connections with four others; seven families had connections with three others; eight families had connections with at least two others; twenty families had connections with at least one other family.[1] It can hardly be accidental that most of the Norman families, or families of intendants of Normandy, were connected by marriage. The family of Marc de La Ferté, the intendant of Alençon in 1634–5, was connected by marriage with that of Faucon de Ris, the intendant at Lyon in 1643–7 and *premier président* of the *Parlement* of Rouen after 1647. Despite the disagreement between their respective fathers,[2] Faucon de Ris was connected by marriage with Bretel de Grémonville the intendant of Languedoc in 1642–3. Turgot, the intendant of Normandy in 1630–3, had been connected by marriage since 1619 with the family of Favier de Boullay, which was to provide the intendant at Alençon in 1643–8 and 1653–66. Le Roy de La Potherie, the intendant at Caen in 1639–46, was connected by marriage to the family of Tronchay, which was to provide his successor at Caen in 1646–8.

Emulation of the career of a relative by marriage was an important factor in the decision of a young office-holder to become an intendant. Equally significant in achieving this ambition were the *clientèles* revealed by the marriage contracts of the intendants. Three intendants—Séguier, Servien, and Foucquet—became ministers; but in addition, most of the other ministers had patronage or marriage connections with some of the intendants. Séguier had close connections with at least eight intendants; Bouthillier with at least six; Bullion, Phélypeaux, and Foucquet with at least three each; other

[1] Calculations based on genealogies and lists of witnesses to marriage contracts.
[2] Faucon de Ris, the *premier président* of the *Parlement* of Rouen, refused to join Bretel de Grémonville and others in opposing the establishment of the *semestre* in 1641: Mousnier, *La vénalité*, p. 211. Foisil, *Nu-Pieds*, p. 324.

ministers appear to have had connections too, but on a lesser scale. Nepotism was not unknown. Séguier obtained the intendancy at Riom in 1647–8 for Ligny, his nephew, although he failed to obtain his appointment to the Touraine in 1656.[1] The successful candidate on that occasion was Hotman de Fontenay, who was married to Marguerite Colbert. Paradoxically, Colbert, the great reformer in other respects, was the greatest nepotist in appointments to intendancies, even before his attaining ministerial office in 1661. He gained the appointment of his brother, Colbert de Croissy, as intendant of Alsace in 1655–62. Jean-Baptiste Colbert de Saint-Pouenge was intendant of Lorraine in 1657–61 and of Picardy in 1662–3. Colbert de Terron was intendant of Foix, Bigorre, and the frontier of Guyenne in 1653. Colbert was also related to Hotman and Pellot. Through Hotman, he was connected with Boucherat, Machault, and Morant; through Le Camus, Colbert was connected with Pommereu; and through Machault, he was connected with Aguesseau. Turenne told Olivier Lefèvre d'Ormesson that 'M. Colbert estoit un compère qui ne perdoit aucune occasion d'establir les siens'.[2] Whatever the qualities of Colbert's appointees, the appointments themselves were a good deal less objective than those of his predecessors. It must be remembered, moreover, that this situation was not a consequence of his ministerial position after 1661. Already in 1655 Colbert was thanking Mazarin not only for his own advancement but for that of 'deux de mes frères et un de mes cousins'[3]—in essentials, the Colbert patronage network had been established at least by 1655–6, under the auspices of Mazarin, and as a reward for financial services rendered.[4]

---

[1] A.A.E. France 900, fo. 223, 29 July 1656.

[2] Ormesson, *Journal*, ed. Chéruel, ii. 313. Ormesson had reason to feel aggrieved at Colbert's patronage network. After Ormesson's appointment as *rapporteur* in the trial of Foucquet in 1662, he was replaced as intendant of Picardy by Colbert de Saint-Pouenge.

[3] A.A.E. France, 894, fo. 86, 9 Apr. 1655.

[4] For the working of Colbert's patronage network in financial questions: D. Dessert and J. L. Journet, 'Le lobby Colbert: un royaume ou une affaire de famille?', *Annales E.S.C.*, xxv (1975), 1303–36.

CHAPTER V

The Intendants: Careers

ALMOST ALL the intendants were drawn from the ranks of the office-holders, their training being overwhelmingly legal in character. This state of affairs was entirely predictable: where else could the French monarchy find its servants? As Pierre Gamin, a *président* in the *Parlement* of Paris, remarked in 1640: 'l'occupation des gens d'esglise estoit le prière'. 'Les gens d'espée', Gamin added, 'n'estoient propres que pour l'exécuttion . . . les hommes d'estude bornoient toutte leur cognoissance dans leurs livres.' There was thus no one else but the magistrates who, 'par la nature de leurs emplois et leurs fonctions se rendirent scavants dans les affaires d'estat . . .'[1] Perhaps Gamin overstated the case: certainly, there were members of the church involved in government–most notably, of course, Richelieu and Mazarin. The nobles felt that they should have a greater say in government and resented their exclusion from political responsibility and decision-making. Yet Gamin was broadly speaking correct: the office-holders had one inestimable advantage from the point of view of the government—they had received a reasonably uniform legal training. Entry into the sovereign courts required a *licence ès lois*, usually obtained after three years of legal study,[2] and in theory not until the candidate had attained nineteen years of age. In the provinces, legal studies would take place at one of the great faculties of law— such as Toulouse, Poitiers, or Orléans. Paris had no faculty of civil law until 1679, and thus law studies before that date tended to take place either in the provinces or else under private tuition, some future lawyers receiving their education at the Jesuit *Collège de Clermont*. The curriculum varied according to faculty and tutor, but there was a very heavy diet of Roman

[1] B.N. MS.fr. 16218, fo. 417.
[2] But cf. the protests of Du Prat at Rennes that new *conseillers* were entering the *Parlement* who had no *licence* and had studied law for only six or nine months: B.L. Harleian 4490, fo. 103, 10 Dec. 1656.

law—Justinian's Institutes, the Digest or Code, with a smattering of Canon law, and very little French law.[1] It is easy to dismiss this type of training, yet it must be remembered that in the sixteenth century the study of Roman law had played a formative part in the creation of 'legal humanism' in France and in the development of the political thought of men such as Bodin and Louis Le Roy, both of whom had studied in the faculty of law at Toulouse.[2] The weakness of the judicial training was that it was in a sense non-vocational: Roman law bore almost no relation to the practice of French law, which had evolved under many different influences of which Roman law was but a part.[3] Canon law, if anything, was more influential. Most commentators were in agreement that the real period of vocational training began only after the *licence* had been obtained. Bodin commented that a 'true and sound knowledge of [jurisprudence] lay not in law-college debates but in courtroom battles'. 'Those who know nothing about the art of pleading', he asserted, 'remain in the greatest ignorance of Roman law.'[4] Perceptive commentators and educational reformers recognized the inadequacy of French legal education. In 1642, Le Goux de la Berchère advocated a reduced study of Roman and Canon law, with much greater reference to that which was 'de bon, de solide et qui se peut rapporter à l'usage et aux loys de nostre pays ...' He also wanted to see within the curriculum study of the ordinances, the jurisdictions of the courts, 'l'interprétation des maximes génaralles tirées des coutumes du royaume et autres choses dépendantes du droit français'[5]—things which were

---

[1] J. Portemer, 'Recherches sur l'enseignement du droit public au xviiie siècle', *Revue Historique de Droit Français et Étranger*, 4th ser., xxxvii (1959), 341–97. R. L. Kagan, 'Law students and legal careers in eighteenth-century France', *Past and Present*, lxviii (1975), 40–3.

[2] D. R. Kelley, 'The development and context of Bodin's method', *Jean Bodin. Proceedings of the international conference on Bodin in Munich*, ed. H. Denzer (Munich, 1973), pp. 127–38.

[3] Guy Coquille believed that French law was to be found 'partie ès constitutions des Roys, partie ès coutumes, partie en caballe non écritte qui s'apprent en exerceant et maniant'. Quoted by Portemer, art. cit., p. 344, n. 14.

[4] R. E. Giesey, 'Medieval jurisprudence in Bodin's concept of sovereignty', *Jean Bodin*, ed. Denzer, pp. 178–9.

[5] Quoted by Portemer, art. cit., p. 344, n.18. Colbert recommended to his brother, Colbert de Croissy, 'une estude régulière des ordonnances royales, estant nécessaire de les savoir, particulièrement dans la profession que vous avez em-

learnt only in law practice at the time of Richelieu and Mazarin. Although the concept of 'public law' existed in seventeenth-century France, it was certainly not taught in the universities. Much depended, therefore, on the quality of tuition. A worthy professor, such as Guillaume Maran at Toulouse (died 1621) could produce two brilliant students, François Bosquet and Pierre Marca, both of whom became intendants[1] and bishops. There was nothing to prevent a student from pursuing his studies further. Bosquet's formal training at Toulouse had been the study of Roman law in the tradition of Cujas. He had then studied Canon law under his own auspices, edited the letters of Innocent III, and had written a history of the Gallican church and a treatise on the Concordats. Personal connections could play an important part in intellectual development, too. When he went to Paris in 1632, Bosquet met Mesmes de Roissy, the *doyen* of the king's council. Probably through Roissy, Bosquet was introduced to Peiresc, one of the greatest figures in French intellectual history in the seventeenth century. Nevertheless, although his abilities were recognized by the Assembly of Clergy in 1635, Bosquet's career was due to factors other than intellectual distinction, above all to his friendship with Séguier, which led to his appointment as *procureur-général* in the tribunal over which the Chancellor presided in Normandy in 1640.[2]

Some intendants—notably Besançon and Imbert, whose careers were essentially in military rather than civil administration—may not have received a legal education at all. For the majority, however, the *licence ès lois* led to a period of law practice as experience before buying office. Jean Baltazar, for example, was a 'praticien demeurant à Auxerre' on 24 February 1626, before his twentieth birthday.[3] For the wealthy, however, legal practice was only a short preliminary before office: thirty-seven future intendants spent on average four years in legal practice before purchasing office. The delay was caused

---

brassée . . .' *Lettres . . . de Colbert*, ed. Clément, i. 355. Croissy was intendant in Alsace and *premier président* in the *conseil souverain* at Ensisheim.

[1] Bosquet in Guyenne 1641–2 and Languedoc 1642–6. Marca in Catalonia 1644–5.

[2] Henry, *François Bosquet*, pp. 6–72.

[3] A. D. L'Yonne, Dépôt de Me. André Guimard 33, no. 51, marriage of Jean Baltazar to Barbe Guyon.

chiefly by the legal requirement of 25 years of age for entry into the sovereign courts. Even so, the forty-four future intendants whose age on entry into the sovereign courts is known averaged 23 years of age, well below the prescribed age limit. The *Parlement* of Paris seems to have enforced the age limit, at least in the years 1659–1703,[1] but other courts were much less strict. The situation at the *Parlement* of Rouen was quite different from that at Paris. The establishment of the much hated *semestre*, a second tribunal serving six months a year,[2] in 1641 had led to a lowering of the age of admission from 27 years to 22 years. Moreover, the new offices could be sold only by issuing letters of dispensation from this age limit: Bautru was aged twenty, and Voyer d'Argenson was aged nineteen on becoming *conseillers* at Rouen.[3]

Of the 128 intendants appointed by Richelieu and Mazarin, 56 had spent the earlier part of their career in the *Parlement* of Paris, 34 had served in the *grand conseil*, and 25 had served in the sovereign courts in the provinces.[4] The pattern of earlier careers was almost identical with that of the *maîtres des requêtes* as a whole, despite the fact that 28 intendants had not served previously in this office. Of 205 *maîtres des requêtes* between 1620 and 1659, 102 were drawn from the *Parlement* of Paris, 54 from the *grand conseil*, and 31 from the provincial courts. These proportions did not vary dramatically over the much longer period between 1575 and 1774, the *Parlement* of Paris providing 531 of the 1,000 *maîtres des requêtes* between these dates, the *grand conseil* providing 207, and the provincial courts 138. The pattern of recruitment of the intendants and *maîtres des requêtes* was not new at the time of Richelieu and Mazarin. Moreover, it remained scarcely unaltered until the end of Louis XV's reign, perhaps until the end of the *ancien régime* [Table A].

The predominance of the *Parlement* of Paris requires no explanation. After the *requêtes de l'hôtel*, the *Parlement* was the

[1] F. Bluche, *Les magistrats du Parlement de Paris au xviiie siècle, 1715–1771* (1960), p. 57.
[2] As punishment for the alleged failure of the *Parlement* of Rouen to suppress the revolt of the *Va-Nu-Pieds* in 1639.
[3] E. O'Reilly, *Mémoires sur la vie publique et privée de Claude Pellot, conseiller, maître des requêtes et premier président au Parlement de Normandie, 1619–1683* (2 vols., Paris–Rouen, 1881–2), i. 57–9.
[4] The remaining thirteen served in the lesser courts, or else had unusual earlier careers.

oldest law-court in the land. It claimed precedence over the other courts and denied them status as 'sovereign' courts in their own right. Its judicial practice was regarded as the best in the land. Moreover, while the office of *conseiller* in the *Parlement*

TABLE A.

Recruitment of the maîtres des requêtes, 1620–1659

Date of becoming *maître des requêtes*	i	ii	iii	iv	v	vi	vii	viii
1620–9	46	60·9	15·2	4·3	10·9	2·2	2·2	4·3
1630–9	61	41·0	34·4	3·3	11·5	9·8	—	—
1640–9	53	50·9	24·5	—	20·8	3·8	—	—
1650–9	45	48·9	28·9	2·2	17·8	2·2	—	—
1620–59	205	49·8	26·3	2·4	15·1	4·9	0·5	1·0

Recruitment of the maîtres des requêtes, 1575–1774

	i	ii	iii	iv	v	vi	vii	viii
1575–1619	176	46·0	28·4	4·0	8·0	4·5	3·4	5·7
1620–59	205	49·8	26·3	2·4	15·1	4·9	0·5	1·0
1660–1715	245	54·7	19·2	6·1	12·2	2·4	3·3	2·1
1716–74	374	57·2	15·0	5·1	16·8	3·5	2·4	—
1575–1774	1,000	53·1	20·7	4·6	13·8	3·7	2·4	1·7

Key
i   No. of *maîtres des requêtes*
ii   % recruited from the *Parlement* of Paris
iii   % recruited from the *grand conseil*
iv   % recruited from the *cour des aides* of Paris
v   % recruited from provincial sovereign courts and *cour des comptes* of Paris
vi   % recruited from the lesser courts
vii   % of *avocats, procureurs, maîtres des requêtes* of princes, etc.
viii % of cases without details
Sources: For the years 1575–1715: B.N. MS.fr. 32785, 32786.
         For the years 1716–74: Antoine, *Le conseil du roi*, p. 249 (slightly modified).

of Paris was becoming increasingly expensive, it could still be bought relatively cheaply until the 1630s. Jean Ligny, the father of the intendant appointed by Mazarin, had bought his office for 36,000 *livres* in 1609. Helié Laisné, the future intendant, bought his for 50,000 *livres* in 1610. Heere bought his for 40,000 in 1627. The price rose dramatically in the 1630s, however:

Jeannin paid 100,000 *livres* in 1634. Le Picard paid 70,000 in
1635. Lefèvre d'Ormesson paid 120,000 in 1636.[1] The size of
the *Parlement* increased during the seventeenth century—there
were 498 new members between 1600 and 1649, and 528
between 1650 and 1699—yet the number of *maîtres des requêtes*
produced by the court remained fairly stable (107 in the first
half of the century; 118 in the second). So too did the number of
intendants—51 were produced in the first half of the century
and 56 in the second half [Table B].

The importance of the *grand conseil*, especially in the first half
of the seventeenth century, is more surprising. Of 372 members

TABLE B

Proportion of members of the Parlement *of Paris
who became* maîtres des requêtes *and intendants*

Date of becoming a member of the *Parlement*	No. of members of the *Parlement*	% who became *maîtres des requêtes*	% who became intendants
1600–9	84	14·3	6·0
1610–19	84	29·8	11·9
1620–9	112	21·4	12·5
1630–9	114	23·7	14·0
1640–9	104	18·3	5·8
1650–9	129	24·8	10·9
1660–9	70	21·4	12·9
1670–9	118	20·3	11·0
1680–9	101	23·8	8·9
1690–9	110	20·0	10·0
1600–99	1,026	21·9	10·4

of this court between 1600 and 1699, 105 became *maîtres des
requêtes* and 51 became intendants. Before 1650, 69 members of
the *grand conseil* had become *maîtres des requêtes* and 28 intendants
were produced. After 1650, the number of *maîtres des requêtes* and
intendants produced by this court declined (respectively to 36
and 23) [Table C]. This lower level of activity remained the

[1] These prices are drawn from the marriage contracts of the intendants, plus
Y 149, fo. 168ᵛ, marriage of Jean Ligny to Charlotte Séguier, 21 Nov. 1609. Cf.
Mousnier, *La vénalité*, pp. 361–2, for other price rises. The presentation of office
prices in Hamscher, *The Parlement of Paris after the Fronde*, p. 15, is misleading and
based on a restricted range of sources.

norm for the rest of the *ancien régime*.[1] Part of the decline must be
attributed to the fall in membership of the court—there were
202 new members in the half-century before 1650, yet only 170
in the years between 1650 and 1700. There was a dramatic rise
in the price of offices in this court. Up to 1635, the office of
conseiller had cost 84,000 *livres* or less. The office of *avocat-*

TABLE C

Proportion of members of the grand conseil *who
became* maître des requêtes *and intendants*

Date of becoming a member of the grand conseil	No. of members of the grand conseil	% who became *maîtres des requêtes*	% who became intendants
1600–9	36	41·7	16·7
1610–19	38	31·6	13·6
1620–9	27	44·4	29·6
1630–9	60	30·0	10·0
1640–9	41	29·3	7·3
1650–9	41	14·6	7·3
1660–9	34	23·5	17·6
1670–9	37	21·6	16·2
1680–9	34	26·5	17·6
1690–9	24	20·8	8·3
1600–99	372	28·2	13·7

Sources for Tables B and C: For the *Parlement* of Paris: B.L. Add. MS. 21434,
'Catalogue . . . de tous les conseillers du Parlement de Paris depuis 1600
jusqu'en 1719'.
For the *grand conseil*: B.N. MS.fr. 14015, 'Genuit des conseillers au grand
conseil depuis l'an 1483 jusques à présent [1756]'. In both cases the
comparison with the lists of *maîtres des requêtes* and intendants has been
made by the author.

général had cost 75,000 *livres* in 1625 and 102,000 in 1634. A
further rapid rise in prices occurred thereafter. The office of
conseiller cost Le Jay 108,000 *livres* in 1638—the price of the
more important office of *avocat-général* a few years earlier—and
it cost Pommereu 150,000 *livres* in 1651. The office of *avocat-
général* cost Barrin 200,000 *livres* in 1635, more than the price
of a position as *maître des requêtes*.[2] A further reason for the rela-

[1] Between 1690 and 1791, 23 per cent of the members of the *grand conseil* became
maîtres des requêtes: F. Bluche, *Les magistrats du grand conseil au xviiie siècle, 1690–1791*
(1966), p. 37.
[2] These prices are drawn from the marriage contracts of the intendants.

tive decline of the *grand conseil* was that by the time of Richelieu and Mazarin its jurisdiction was severly limited by the king's council. It had lost all political significance: it dealt with some religious questions; with some appeals and *évocations*; with some distributions of cases between the sovereign courts (*règlements des juges*); with some decrees of the sovereign courts which were contradictory (*contrariétés d'arrêts*)— but only with those cases which the king's council chose to delegate.[1] If the *grand conseil* had any real importance, therefore it was as a training ground for a career in the council. Marillac's view was reported to have been that 'l'instruction estoit très bonne et advantageuse . . . pour ceulx qui aspiroient aux charges de maîtres des requêtes . . .'[2]

The gradual decline of the *grand conseil* coincided with the rise of the provincial courts to importance as a recruiting ground for the *maîtres des requêtes*. Two provincial *Parlements* stand out as particularly significant at the time of Richelieu and Mazarin: Rouen produced seven intendants, while Metz produced six. Rouen was important because of its geographical proximity to Paris, and the establishment of the *semestre* in 1641 led to substantial increase in membership. There were 33 new members of this court between 1630 and 1639, an average of three a year. Yet between 1640 and 1649, there were 106 new members, an average of ten a year, a rate which declined rapidly after 1650 (to six a year).[3] Four future intendants— Bautru, Bernard Fortia, Pellot and René II Voyer d'Argenson —entered this court in the troubled decade of the 1640s, at a time, it must be said, when the price of office was particularly low. The *Parlement* of Metz, which was established in 1633, had a more dubious reputation, being known as a 'pont aux ânes de la robe': it certainly did not insist that office-holders came from the town itself.[4] In Corberon, this court had a distinguished *avocat-général* between 1636 and 1642 who later became in-

---

[1] Bluche, *Les magistrats du grand conseil*, pp. 19–20.
[2] *Lettres . . . au Chancelier Séguier*, ed. Mousnier, i. 334.
[3] H. de Frondeville, *Les conseillers du Parlement de Normandie sous Henri IV et sous Louis XIII, 1594–1640* (Paris–Rouen, 1964). Frondeville, *Les conseillers du Parlement de Normandie de 1641 à 1715* (Rouen, 1970).
[4] Bluche, *Les magistrats du grand conseil*, p. 37. For the placing of sons of the Parisian *noblesse de robe* at Metz: marquis de Roux, *Louis XIV et les provinces conquises. Artois, Alsace, Flandres, Roussillon, Franche-Comté* (1938), pp. 164–5. On the members themselves: E. Michel, *Biographie du Parlement de Metz* (Metz, 1853).

tendant at Limoges. In general, however, the membership was undistinguished and the regulations were particularly lax: Foucquet was a *conseiller* there at eighteen. For the resident office-holders, however, Metz was no more than a temporary exile from Paris: within three years, Foucquet had moved on to become a *maître des requêtes*.[1] The exclusively provincial career was thus unusual at the time of Richelieu and Mazarin. The career of Jean Martin de Laubardemont is the exception that proves the rule. He received a *brevet* as councillor of state in March 1626. He had also been provided with the office of *président* of the *chambre des enquêtes* in the *Parlement* of Bordeaux three years earlier, but he had failed to obtain formal admission to the *Parlement* and had therefore resigned this office on 22 November 1627.[2] In 1631, he became *premier président* in the *cour des aides* of Guyenne. On 8 July of the same year, he received a commission for the demolition of the fortifications of Royan;[3] on 31 November 1633, he received a celebrated commission to prosecute Urbain Grandier.[4] The *cause célèbre* of the devils of Loudun was the making of Laubardemont. Here was Richelieu's *homme sûr*, refusing to listen to witnesses favourable to Grandier, modifying the testimonies to assist the prosecution—assisted of course by local opposition to Grandier.[5] Within three years, Laubardemont received his reward, the position of intendant at Tours.

In social terms, there was little reason why some members of the sovereign courts and not others should become *maîtres des requêtes*. In terms of outlook, however, a vast gulf separated the members of the courts whose aim was to work within the system, and those who left the courts after six years, if not before, to become *maîtres des requêtes* and thus in all probability to follow a career in the council. Was this difference in outlook a question of greater independence of mind? It seems unlikely. Much more important factors were the desire to emulate the career of

---

[1] Lair, *Nicolas Foucquet*, i. 71.
[2] cf. E 102, fo. 153, 6 Mar. 1630.
[3] cf. E 107b, fo. 266, 10 Nov. 1631.
[4] cf. V6 101, no. 4, 12 Dec. 1634.
[5] J. Viard, 'Le procès d'Urbain Grandier. Note critique sur la procédure et sur la culpabilité', *Quelques procès criminels des xviie et xviiie siècles*, ed. J. Imbert (1964), pp. 45–75.

a relative (especially in view of the fact that the office of *maître des requêtes* could be resigned to a relative) and the greater variety of work and opportunities for initiative offered to a *maître des requêtes*.[1] The practice of the *présidents* of the sovereign courts in resigning their offices to members of families who had previously held these positions limited the possibility of a young office-holder ever becoming a *président*. This office was, in any case, extremely expensive—at Paris it could cost up to 350,000 *livres* or even 500,000 *livres* depending on the court and the market conditions at the time of purchase.[2] Moreover, increasingly the *présidents* of the sovereign courts were assuming important powers over the distribution of lawsuits among the office-holders and retaining the important, interesting, and remunerative[3] cases for their relatives, friends, or clients on whom they could rely.[4] The brilliant office-holder, if he was no friend of the important *présidents* in his court, could see his career blocked, his income limited, and his working life restricted to routine tedium. By contrast, the career of *maître des requêtes* was much more open: there was a reasonable probability that ability would be rewarded, though equally incompetence would not pass unnoticed.

The letters patent issued on 5 February 1598 prescribed as the entry qualification for a *maître des requêtes* six years' experience in the sovereign courts or as a *lieutenant-général* in the lesser courts, or, alternatively, twelve years' experience as an *avocat*.[5] The *Parlement* of Paris, in its decrees of 8 June 1596 and 9 March 1602, had proposed an even higher entry qualification— ten years, a rule which was later applied for a short period

---

[1] Antoine, *Le conseil du roi*, pp. 269–72.

[2] René de Longueil de Maisons paid 500,000 *livres* for his office of *président* in the *cour des aides* of Paris in 1630: Ormesson, *Journal*, ed. Chéruel, i. 4. Jacques Le Coigneux paid the same figure for his office as *président* in the *Parlement* of Paris in 1648 (on the resignation of his father): Y 187, fo. 316, marriage of Jacques Le Coigneux to Angelique Le Camus, 11 Jan. 1648. [Also Minutier Central XIV 65.] Nicolas Foucquet paid 450,000 *livres* in 1650 for his office of *procureur-général* in the *Parlement* of Paris: Lair, *Nicolas Foucquet*, i. 142.

[3] Most cases, and certainly the remunerative cases, were accorded in order of seniority: J. J. Hurt, 'Les offices au Parlement de Bretagne sous le règne de Louis XIV: aspects financiers', *Revue d'Histoire Moderne et Contemporaine*, xxiii (1976), 9.

[4] Particularly after the Fronde, when the government encouraged this tendency. e.g. *Parlement* of Dijon: E 1706, no. 3, 13 Jan. 1656. *Parlements* of Bordeaux, Toulouse, and Dijon: E 1716, nos. 25, 31, 126, 23 Feb., 25 Feb., 10 Nov. 1662.

[5] Maugis, *Histoire du Parlement de Paris*, ii. 235.

between 1672 and 1683. Since the *Parlement* of Paris registered the letters of provision of new *maîtres des requêtes*, its attitude was clearly relevant. Without such registration, the new office-holder could not be formally admitted into his office. As Chancellor Séguier pointed out to Mazarin in 1659, there was no point in issuing letters of dispensation if the *Parlement* would not register them.[1] Twelve of the 100 intendants appointed by Richelieu and Mazarin who had served as *maîtres des requêtes* had given less than six years' service in the sovereign courts. Only two, however—Foucquet and Tallemant —had served less than four years. Dispensations probably occurred more frequently in respect of the age limit of 32 than in the years of service. René II Voyer d'Argenson was only twenty-six when he became a *maître des requêtes*, but he had been a *conseiller* in the *Parlement* of Rouen for seven years.

It seems probable that the legal requirements for becoming a *maître des requêtes* were fulfilled more regularly at the time of Richelieu and Mazarin than was later the case in the *ancien régime*.[2] The career of Isaac de Laffemas illustrates the difficulties that a new office-holder might have in obtaining registration of his letters of provision. In 1623 Laffemas had served as *greffier* in a commission to establish new offices in the *élections* of France.[3] By November 1624, he was a *secrétaire du roi*. He had been provided with the office of *premier président* in the *cour des monnaies* at Paris, but this was disallowed.[4] Since 1622 at least, Laffemas had been an *avocat* in the *conseil privé*. On 11 November 1624 he was appointed *avocat-général* and *premier substitut* in the *Chambre de Justice* set up to prosecute cases of fraud in financial administration. His role in this tribunal is open to question, since he had already acted as *avocat* for certain financiers. On 17 October 1625, Laffemas received his letters of provision as *maître des requêtes*. For a combination of reasons—'ayant esté comédien', 'accusé d'estre faussaire', 'recognu turbulent'—the *Parlement* of Paris, on 20 December 1625, refused to admit him formally. On 7 May 1626, the king's council transferred the case to the *Parlement* of Bordeaux, which on 24 March 1627

[1] A.A.E. France 908, fo. 387, 17 Dec. 1659.
[2] cf. Bluche, *Les magistrats du Parlement de Paris*, p. 66.
[3] E 77b, fo. 191, 16 Dec. 1623.
[4] E 80a, fo. 347, 13 Nov. 1624.

agreed to register Laffemas's letters, and finally did so in July of that year.[1] The number of *maîtres des requêtes* increased substantially in the seventeenth century. There were 56 in 1623; 66 in 1640, when there was talk of raising the number to 82; 72 in 1642, 80 in 1674, and 88 in 1689.[2] Just as had the other office-holders of the crown, the *maîtres des requêtes* had suffered from fiscal exploitation by the government. In 1640 and 1648, attempts to establish new offices had brought united opposition from the *maîtres des requêtes* and the *Parlement* of Paris. Richelieu, who had held the view in 1624–5 that 'la multiplication des offices de judicature estoit très préjudiciable à l'estat' had been convinced by his finance ministers that in time of war such creations of offices were 'les moyens les plus innocens et qui estoient le moins à la foule du peuple'.[3] Mazarin and his finance ministers had followed the precedent. It was a curious paradox and evidence of the extreme financial plight of the monarchy that the servants upon whom the crown was most reliant were taxed so heavily. For each creation of offices severely affected the value of the investment and threatened 'la dissipation de soixante et tant de familles . . . des plus illustres de la robe . . .' Barrin bought his office of *maître des requêtes* for 165,000 livres in 1639. The news of the projected establishment of sixteen new offices meant that Choisy could obtain only 150,000 *livres* when he sought to sell his office a year later. Even Richelieu appreciated that 'cela estoit très considérable' and agreed to discuss the matter with the king. The great advantage of the *maîtres des requêtes* over the other office-holders, was—in Richelieu's own words—that 'ils en avoient plus de cognoissance de tous les autres officiers'. Richelieu after some hesitations that such a meeting would be 'contre le service du Roy' agreed to talk to them 'plus franchement' than he would have to any other sectional group in the kingdom.[4] The *maîtres des requêtes* might be required to make a financial sacrifice because the king was fighting a long war against the Habsburgs: but they demanded concessions in return. The privileges obtained by the *maîtres des*

[1] B.N. p.o. 1616 (Dr. 37,580), fos. 37–71, *Factum* against Laffemas.
[2] *Lettres . . . au Chancelier Séguier*, ed. Mousnier, i. 45.
[3] Mousnier, *La vénalité*, pp. 662–3. Cf. Richelieu's own words reported in B.N. MS. fr. 16218, fo. 418, 1640.
[4] B.N. MS.fr. 16218, fos. 411–19.

requêtes at the time of Richelieu and Mazarin were far greater than those enjoyed by their predecessors under Henri IV.

The privileges of the *maîtres des requêtes* were not related to their tribunal at Paris, called the *requêtes de l'hôtel*, because this rarely played a significant political role, unless the king's council transferred important cases to it by the process of *évocation*.[1] The chief privilege of the *maîtres des requêtes* was 'celui de la présidence'.

They were the longest-serving group of royal officials, having carried out 'la justice universelle avant l'establissement du parlement sédentaire'—and they claimed therefore the right to preside in the *grand conseil*, in the *Parlements*, the *bureaux des finances* and the *bailliages*. These privileges were well established, the right of presidency in the *bailliages* having been conferred by edict in 1493, the same right in the *Parlements* having been recognized by the *Parlement* of Paris on 23 January 1521.[2] A second privilege of the *maîtres des requêtes* was that of being sent on circuit-tours (*chevauchées*) in the provinces, which had certainly taken place in the fifteenth century before the edict of 1493.[3] An edict of August 1553 had further defined their responsibilities on circuit-tour.[4] A decree of 23 May 1555 had listed the circuit-tours for the *maîtres des requêtes* then serving.[5] Even if these circuit-tours had become unusual by the time of Henri III, they were at least reaffirmed in all the reforming ordinances and the rulings of the council. These circuit-tours of the *maîtres des requêtes* in the sixteenth century were clearly the origin of the claim by these officials to a monopoly of the intendancies a century later.[6] A third privilege of the *maîtres des requêtes* was that of receiving commissions from the king 'pour faire cesser toutes sortes d'empesch-

[1] *Lettres . . . au Chancelier Séguier*, ed. Mousnier, i. 42–5, describes their functions. For important *évocations* from the council: B.N. MS.fr. 16218, fo. 393ᵛ–394ʳ, V6 1216, fo. 45, no. 21 and V6 49, no. 7, 1 Oct. 1624. Cf. the protests of the *Parlement* of Paris against this tribunal: B.L. Harleian 4466, fos. 150–1, 17 Aug. 1648.

[2] B.N. MS.fr. 16218, fo. 345, 11 Dec. 1493 (copy). B.L. Harleian 4472b, fos. 374–6, remonstrances of the *maîtres des requêtes* to Louis XIV, 20 July 1669.

[3] G. Dupont-Ferrier, 'Le rôle des commissaires royaux dans le gouvernement de la France, spécialement du xivᵉ au xviᵉ siècle', *Mélanges Paul Fournier* (1929) [B.N. 4to F. 2329], 182.

[4] Xıa 8618.

[5] Boislisle, communication in *Revue des sociétés savantes*, 7th ser., iii (1881), 169–71. [B.N. MS.fr. 16218, fo. 347.]

[6] *Inventaire des arrêts du conseil d'état. Règne de Henri IV*, ed. N. Valois (2 vols. 1886, 1893), i. cxviii. B.N. MS.fr. 16218, fo. 357.

emens' on the part of members of the sovereign courts—for example, they received commissions to preside over special tribunals (*Grands Jours*) and political trials. There were good precedents here from the reign of François I, Antoine du Bourg having presided over the *Grands Jours* of Moulins in 1534, and André Guillart having presided over the trial of Guillaume Poyet, the Chancellor, in 1544. François Villemontée, a *maître des requêtes* and intendant, presided over the *Grands Jours* of Poitiers in 1634.[1]

As their name implies, traditionally these officials had heard the requests presented to the king by his subjects. They had therefore become the intermediary between the king's subjects and his council, that is to say the officials who introduced or 'reported' business to the council.[2] Already by 1607, Sully was protesting to Henri IV at 'ce tas de maîtres des requêtes et autres bonnets cornus[3] qui font une cohue du conseil'.[4] By 1610 at the latest the *maîtres des requêtes* enjoyed a monopoly of presenting business to the *conseil privé*. The real increase in responsibility of the *maîtres des requêtes* occurred after the death of Henri IV, however. During the chancellorship of Brûlart de Sillery (10 December 1607–1 January 1624), they were allowed to present their reports to the council of finance, but were then required to leave before the debate. During Guillaume du Vair's keepership of the Seals (16 May 1616–25 November 1616; 25 April 1617–3 August 1621), certainly three and possible all the *maîtres des requêtes* serving in each three-month session (*quartier*) were allowed to enter the council of finance. In the years 1624–30 even those *maîtres des requêtes* not *en quartier* entered the council of finance and participated in debates.[5] Their privileges were confirmed by the ruling of 16 June 1644, which allowed them to introduce 'toutes les affaires de justice, mesmes les procès-verbaux des rébellions faits à l'exécution des édits'. They were also allowed to examine all requests and make reports to the council unless the Chancellor

---

[1] B.L. Harleian 4472b, fos. 359ᵛ–360ʳ.

[2] F. Lot and R. Fawtier, *Histoire des institutions françaises du moyen âge. II. Institutions royales* (1958), pp. 82–4.

[3] A reference to the distinctive pointed hats worn by the *présidents* of the sovereign courts.

[4] *Inventaire des arrêts...*, ed. Valois, i. cvii.

[5] Mousnier, *La plume*, pp. 167–8. B.N. Clairambault 651, fos. 340–1.

for any reason ordered otherwise.[1] By 1648, the *maîtres des requêtes* had become so important that when they went on strike the whole functioning of the council was paralysed.[2] The period of Richelieu and Mazarin offered unprecedented opportunities to a young *maître des requêtes* for a career in the council. This was the only office which in theory was not incompatible with the position of king's councillor (which was not an office but an appointment by letters patent).[3] Between 1585 and *c.* 1610 opinions in the council were taken according to seniority. This procedure proved unworkable as a result of the increase in the size of the council following the death of Henri IV. Chancellor Brûlart de Sillery therefore adopted the procedure whereby the opinions were taken 'tantost par le hault, tantost par le bas, soit de l'un costé, soit de l'autre indifféremment...' A long-lasting reform was thus born from a situation of near chaos in the council.[4] Whereas in the sovereign courts, an office-holder might have to wait several years before being given charge of an important case, a young *maître des requêtes* could make himself known to the Chancellor with a brilliant speech in the council at the first meeting he attended, and within months of buying his office.[5] These possibilities were made more real by the fact that an individual *maître des requêtes*, according to the ruling of 16 June 1644, could make reports on up to six cases every three months. This represented an attempt to distribute equally the *requêtes* and *instances* before the council

---

[1] Mousnier, *La plume*, p. 168. A.A.E. France 849, fo. 284ᵛ–285. E 1688, fo. 111.

[2] *Lettres* . . . *au Chancelier Séguier*, ed. Mousnier, i. 45. Moote, *The revolt of the Judges*, pp. 111–12. E 1693, fo. 59, 17 Mar. 1648.

[3] 'Si les officiers ayans encore leurs offices pourront prendre place dans le conseil. La compagnie jugea que non, hors M. le président Amelot, qui estoit en paisible possession d'un semestre du conseil.' B.M. Rouen MS. Léber 5767, fo. 230, 12 Apr. 1644. However, the same document reveals that certain other exceptions envisaged in the ruling of 8 Jan. 1585 were still occurring. Cf. Mousnier, *La plume*, p. 144.

[4] Mousnier, *La plume*, pp. 145–6. B.L. Egerton 1680, fo. 64: 'D'aultant que ce nombre estant grandement accreu, il estoit difficile de se souvenir du temps de la reception de chacun et que cela formait des contentions entre les seigneurs à cause de différentes prétentions de préséance.'

[5] The ruling of 16 June 1644 required *maîtres des requêtes* to have served ten years before entering the council, but it is doubtful whether it was enforced under Mazarin. Before 1644, there was no such rule. Jean Baltazar was received as a *maître des requêtes* on 20 Mar. 1642. On 11 July, he 'reported' his first decree to the *conseil privé*: V6 168, no. 56. On 26 Aug. he 'reported' his first decree to the council of finance: E 173a, fo. 315.

—a measure, inevitably, which favoured the ambitious young *maître des requêtes.*

At the time of Richelieu and Mazarin, the position of intendant was perhaps not a career in itself but a means to an end. Saint-Simon stated the situation admirably when he wrote of the intendants of Louis XIV:[1]

Le premier but d'un intendant est d'arriver à une des cinq ou six grandes intendances, et le second de parvenir à une place de conseiller d'estat et peut-estre dans le ministère . . . C'est un triste estat pour un intendant de persévérer dans les intendances ordinaires, un plus fascheux de perdre l'espérance d'estre conseiller d'estat; enfin, rien n'égale le mépris et le néant dans lequel un intendant révoqué achève sa vie . . .

The opportunities for achieving these ambitions varied considerably between the reigns of Louis XIII and Louis XIV, however. Under Louis XIII, one Chancellor (Séguier), four Keepers of the Seals (Guillaume du Vair, Méric de Vic, Lefèvre de Caumartin, and Michel de Marillac), three secretaries of state for war (Servien, Sublet des Noyers, and Le Tellier) and three finance ministers (Bochart de Champigny, Marillac, and Bullion)[2] had served as intendants or comparable royal commissioners. Ministerial changes were sufficiently rare, however, for the promotion of intendants to be scarcely a realistic possibility. The opportunities were not much wider after 1661. There was, however, a much greater probability of becoming a councillor of state at the time of Richelieu and Mazarin than thereafter, simply because of the rapid increase in the size of the council. Essentially service as an intendant was a period of preparation for a long career in the council and not vice versa in the period of Richelieu and Mazarin. The rulings on the council in the 1620s, by establishing grades of council membership, and limiting service in the council for most members to only part of the year, gave considerable opportunities to young councillors to gain initial experience in

[1] Louis de Rouvroy, duc de Saint-Simon Vermandois, 'Parallèle des trois premiers rois bourbons' [May 1746], *Écrits inédits de Saint-Simon*, ed. P. Faugère (3 vols., 1880), i. 287.
[2] Six, if three appointees of Mazarin—D'Hémery, Servien, and Foucquet—are included.

council procedure before appointment to their intendancies. Later, as a reward for their service in the provinces, they might be promoted to the position of *conseiller ordinaire*. No complete series of *brevets* of the councillors of state for this period survives, and thus it is impossible to trace the career in the council in detail for more than a few of the intendants appointed by Richelieu and Mazarin.[1] However, ten intendants gained their *brevets* on average at the age of 32. Twelve were appointed to their intendancies on average at the age of 35.[2] Thirteen became *conseillers ordinaires* on average at the age of 48.

For many intendants, less than a third of their career was spent in the provinces as intendant. The major part of their career was spent at Paris and in the council in particular, both before and after the appointment as intendant. This is apparent in the career of the Ormessons, father and son. André Lefèvre d'Ormesson became a *maître des requêtes* on 22 January 1605. On 10 April 1615, he received his *brevet* as councillor of state, replacing his deceased father. Thereupon, he served in various intendancies, especially in Champagne in 1616 and 1625. On 23 January 1625 he was made a *maître des requêtes honoraire* as a recognition of twenty years' service in this office, and despite his having resigned this office to Barillon. The letters recalled his services to Henri IV and Louis XIII 'en plusieurs charges et commissions'. On 15 January 1626, he was made a *conseiller quadrimestre*, a position that was confirmed in 1629 despite the reduction in council membership that occurred at that date. On 4 May 1632, he was issued with instructions to act as royal commissioner to the Estates of Brittany. On his return to Paris, in January 1633, he was made *conseiller semestre*. In July 1634, Chancellor Séguier told him that he could sit as *conseiller ordinaire* since 'les lettres ne faisoient pas les ordinaires mais la

---

[1] B.N. MS.fr. 16218, fos. 330ff., 'mémoire des brevets des conseillers d'estat depuis 1605 jusques en 1643'. B.N. MS.fr. 18152, fos. 119–25.

[2] Two intendants were appointed when particularly young: Bautru (Tours, 1644) was only 22; René II Voyer d'Argenson (Poitiers, 1646) was only 23. These instances provide some evidence for the argument of the *trésoriers de France* that the intendants were 'tirez du conseil auparavant qu'ilz y puissent avoir acquis une grande expérience et venans dans les provinces jeunes et peu informez . . .' B.L. Harleian 4472b, fo. 147ᵛ. However, the average age of 48 intendants at the time of appointment to their first intendancy was a respectable 36 years of age. Some were quite old—Cardin Le Bret was 66; Gilbert Gaulmin was 63; Louis Machault was 52.

capacité'. This position was confirmed on 21 April 1635.[1] By
1661 he was *doyen* in the king's council. André's son, Olivier,
became a *maître des requêtes* on 19 February 1643. Two years
later, he was part of a commission charged with re-establishing
the *semestre* at the *Parlement* of Rouen. In 1650, he was an
intendant at Paris, and later at Amiens and Soissons between
1656 and 1664. On 26 June 1661, he was made a *maître des
requêtes honoraire*, in recognition of his having been 'continuel-
lement employé non seulement en noz conseilz mais encore en
plusieurs commissions importantes . . . et présentement mesme
en nostre province de Picardie en la qualité d'intendant de
justice'. The letters received by Olivier expressed the good will
of the king towards the Ormesson family as a whole, 'la
satisfaction que nous avons des bons et recommendables
services' of Olivier, but chiefly for André, his father, for his
fifty-seven years of service in the council.[2]

The efficiency and effectiveness of the council was improved
as a result of the experience gained by its members having
served in the provinces. When Talon returned from the Dauphiné in 1636[3] and Machault from Burgundy in 1637,[4] they
immediately brought a mass of business to the council and
numerous decrees ensued. The former intendants of a province
were regarded as the most suitable councillors for drawing up
decrees concerning that province: Nesmond, Breteuil, and
Baltazar, for example, all drew up the decrees of the council
relating to the province of Languedoc. The commission of the
council which examined the *cahiers* of the *pays d'états*, which
had been set up by the ruling of 16 June 1627, was packed
with experts on the provinces in question. As La Vrillière
explained to Mazarin, 'M. de Boucherat estant particulièrement informé des affaires de Languedoc, il sera bien à propos
que vous le mettiez du nombre des commissaires que vous
choisiriez pour l'examen dudit cahier . . .'[5]

The opportunities for promotion became increasingly gloomy
during the personal rule of Louis XIV, however. Firstly, the
abolition of the position of *conseiller quadrimestre* in 1657 removed

[1] Mousnier, *La plume*, p. 168. B.M. Rouen MS. Léber 5767, fos. 8–10.
[2] 144 a.p. 58, Dr. 2, 26 June 1661.
[3] E 131b, fo. 2, 25 June 1636.
[4] E 136a, fo. 346ᵛ, 31 Mar. 1637.
[5] A.A.E. France 898, fo. 168, 6 July 1656.

many of the opportunities for gaining council experience at an early stage in a career. Secondly, the council was reduced in 1657 to only a quarter of the size that it had been in 1644. Thirdly, the intendants tended to spend longer periods of residence in their provinces. The proportion of former intendants in the king's council remained fairly stable,[1] but the number of persons involved was greatly reduced. Not surprisingly, it seems that in the later eighteenth century the intendants gradually lost the inclination to become councillors of state.[2] This was a fundamental change from attitudes at the time of Richelieu and Mazarin, however.

The position of intendant was thus no more than the immediate objective of a promising king's councillor with a long career ahead of him. Was the situation described by Saint-Simon— that of five or six *grandes intendances* with the rest no more than *intendances ordinaires*—true of the period of Richelieu and Mazarin? The important provinces after 1661 were the territorial annexations of Louis XIV which, as frontier areas with potentially hostile populations, required close political control. Among the French provinces before 1661, Paris, Orléans, and Lyon of the *pays d'élections* and Languedoc of the *pays d'états* were particularly important. Jean-Étienne Turgot lamented in 1709 that after fourteen years of service he saw himself 'toujours descendre' in the intendancies—he had been at Tours in 1702–9 but was sent to Moulins from 1709 to 1713. Antoine Turgot, his father, had rejected Limoges in 1671 as being of little consequence.[3] Presumably a scale of values is established by the career of Charles Colbert de Croissy, whose brother controlled the nominations to the intendancies and would have ensured that Croissy did not suffer a loss of status. Croissy served first in Alsace (1655–63), then at Poitiers and Tours (1663–5), later at Amiens (1665–8), and finally at Paris (1668–75).[4]

---

[1] Previous intendants, intendants actually serving, and future intendants comprised 30 out of 63 members of the council (14 Dec. 1640), 33 out of 67 members (Feb. 1643), 39 out of 74 members (June 1643), 41 out of 107 members (18 Apr. 1644), 45 out of 122 members (30 Apr. 1644), and 16 out of 30 members (May 1670).

[2] Antoine, *Le conseil du roi*, pp. 188–9, 230.

[3] *Correspondance des contrôleurs-généraux des finances avec les intendants des provinces, 1683–1715*, ed. A. M. de Boislisle (3 vols., 1874–9), iii. no. 530 n.

[4] *Le conseil du roi*, ed. Mousnier, pp. 158–9.

At the time of Richelieu and Mazarin, the province of Languedoc was clearly more important than the *généralité* of Montauban, for Bosquet referred to it as 'plus commode et honorable pour moy'.[1] Languedoc clearly was also more important than Moulins. That Barthélémé Dupré regarded his transfer to Moulins in 1642 as demotion is clear from his anxiety to return to Languedoc the following year.[2] However, many intendants served in a succession of provinces without apparently protesting. The *pays d'états* were clearly preferable since the Estates often granted *gratifications* to the intendants to supplement their income and ensure their good-will. At the time when the new administrative system was being established, the relative importance of the different provinces was far from clear-cut. The longer-term objective of promotion in the king's council might be prejudiced if the intendant showed reluctance to go to the province to which he had been nominated. Loyalty and service were all-important, and were the qualities which were rewarded. Charles Machault followed Condé from Burgundy to Guyenne and finally to Languedoc as his master rose through the governorships in the 1630s. His reward was regular promotion in the king's council: he became a *conseiller semestre* on 17 September 1637 and a *conseiller ordinaire* on 10 January 1643. He also revealed—somewhat ostentatiously—where his loyalties lay by refusing a *gratification* from the Estates of Burgundy.[3] A *maître des requêtes* or king's councillor might apply to the ministers for a particular intendancy—as indeed did Machault in 1629[4]—but there could be no certainty that he would obtain it. That some intendancies were considered more important than others was not the relevant consideration: what mattered was whether the intendant succeeded in his allotted province.

The *maîtres des requêtes* claimed sole right to be appointed to the intendancies, and claimed that the value of their offices would fall if persons others than themselves were appointed. They declared themselves to possess a 'caractère incommunicable à tous autres officiers'. They were moreover, distinguished by a

<hr/>

[1] *Bnutrennyaya*, ed. Lublinskaya, p. 38.
[2] ibid., p. 47.
[3] Ormesson, *Journal*, ed. Chéruel, i. 37.
[4] A.A.E. France 794, fo. 87ᵛ, Marillac to Richelieu, 2 Aug. 1629: 'M. de Machault m'escrit pour la commission d'intendant de justice de Languedoc . . .'

specialized training from other office-holders of the crown: 'nourris dans les conseils, les ordonnances de nos Roys sont leur étude principal et le fondement des décisions soumises à leurs magistratures'. The *maîtres des requêtes* argued that they alone were reliable servants: 'ils ont puisé la science des loix, des maximes de l'état et les veus dud[it] gouvernement'.[1] Thus they argued that the intendancies should be given to them in order of seniority. They opposed the appointment of intendants who had not bought the office of *maître des requêtes* first. At the time of Richelieu and Mazarin they were not entirely successful. They failed to convince the government when they presented remonstrances against the nomination of Lozières to the Dauphiné in 1644 and of Sevin to the Orléanais in 1655.[2] They were rather more succesful after 1661. The ruling of 27 October 1674 specified that the *maîtres des requêtes* would enjoy a monopoly to the intendancies except in cases of importance to the royal service, when other office-holders might be chosen.[3] The *maîtres des requêtes* failed to exclude Boucher from appointment as intendant of the Auvergne in 1717: but their gains are clear from the fact that only 9 of 179 intendants appointed between 1715 and 1790 had not held this office,[4] compared with 28 out of 128 who had not previously served as *maître des requêtes* at the time of Richelieu and Mazarin. The *maîtres des requêtes* could issue remonstrances in support of their sectional interests and this was an obvious factor assisting their claim to a monopoly. Even if a non-*maître des requêtes* was appointed as intendant, it was usual for him to avoid such public scandal by buying up the office as soon as possible. Vincent Hotman de Fontenay did so in 1656 with Colbert's help.[5] Intendants could resign their office of *maître des requêtes* and yet retain their intendancy,

---

[1] *Lettres . . . au Chancelier Séguier*, ed. Mousnier, i. 47–8. B.N. MS.fr. 7013, fo. 558.

[2] ibid., i. 46. A.A.E. France 894, fo. 402, 16 Nov. 1655.

[3] They enjoyed a monopoly 'à moins que Sa Maiesté pour des causes importantes au bien de son service n'en ordonne autrement': E 1776, fo. 265ᵛ.

[4] G. J. de Cusance Mead, 'The administrative *noblesse* of France during the xviiith century, with special reference to the intendants of the *généralités*' (London Univ. Ph.D., 1954), ii. 331.

[5] A.A.E. France 900, fo. 224, 30 July 1656. But cf. A.A.E. France 1707, fo. 206, Cazet de Vautorte to Richelieu, 22 May 1640: 'ayant obtenu du Roy l'intendance de Provence . . . j'y vays en qualité de conseiller d'estat sans charge de maistre des requestes'.

though this was clearly a sensitive issue.[1] If they did so, how-ever, they might well consider that they had prejudiced their chances of future promotion. Jacques Chaulnes, who was forced for financial reasons to sell his office in 1644, lamented four years later that he was 'destitué de toutes les qualitez nécessaires' for promotion.[2] An individual might lobby a minister for a particular intendancy: but unless he was a *maître des requêtes* the odds were against his being appointed.

[1] Barbier, 'Intendants de Poitou', p. 609.
[2] A.G. A1 110, no. 82, 27 June 1648. Chaulnes's comments were somewhat overshadowed by the events of the Fronde.

CHAPTER VI

The Intendants: Political Attitudes

DID THE intendants have common political attitudes? Some historians have regarded them as steeped in the theories of *raison d'état* and Jansenism.[1] Contemporaries of Louis XIV accused the intendants of 'une fureur ambitieuse' which led them to sacrifice 'leur patrie au désir de commander comme ils sacrifie leur conscience à la faveur de la cour . . .'[2] The political attitudes of the intendants clearly had a crucial bearing on their work, yet great caution is required when attempting to define those attitudes. Little is known about a considerable number of the 128 intendants appointed by Richelieu and Mazarin. Moreover, there might be an enormous difference between an intendant's official posture and the private views that he expressed to his relatives and close friends—Basville, the intendant of Languedoc charged with the suppression of the revolt of the *Camisards* after 1702, is a case in point.[3] The intendants rarely used the term *raison d'état*,[4] and when they did, they implied that it was not a secular but an ethical concept.[5] While some intendants were mystics in terms of

---

[1] W. F. Church, 'Louis XIV and reason of state', *Louis XIV and the craft of kingship*, ed. J. C. Rule (Cleveland, Ohio, 1969), p. 374. Y. M. Bercé, 'Aspects de la criminalité au xviie siècle', *Revue Historique*, ccxxxix (1968), 42.

[2] Comte de Boulainvilliers, *État de la France. Extrait des mémoires dressez par les intendans du royaume par ordre du roi Louis XIV à la sollicitation de Monseigneur le Duc de Bourgogne* (1st ed., 3 vols., London, 1727), i. xiii.

[3] J. R. Armogathe and P. Joutard, 'Basville et la guerre des Camisards', *Revue d'Histoire Moderne et Contemporaine*, xix (1972), 44–67.

[4] One example, however, was Baltazar, over a decade after he left his intendancy of Languedoc: 'La raison d'estat . . . semble plustost à accommoder'. A.A.E. France 1492, fo. 194, 22 Nov. 1658.

[5] For example, René I Voyer d'Argenson: 'la raison d'estat qui est la souveraine dans les conseils . . .' Argenson added: 'je ne suis pas de ceux qui croyent que la religion doit servir à l'état.' 'Les lois de Dieu et celles de la raison ne sont qu'une même chose.' *Histoire générale de Languedoc*, ed. C. Devic and J. Vaissette, continued by E. Roschach (Toulouse, 1876), xiv. 152,175. For *raison d'état* as a secular concept: F. Meinecke, *Machiavellism. The doctrine of raison d'état and its place in modern history*, translated D. Scott (1957); Thuau, *Raison d'état et pensée politique*; Church, *Richelieu and reason of state*.

religious conviction, they generally rejected the Jansenist alternative. Had they been Jansenists, the ministers would not have selected them as intendants.[1] This is not to say that there were no common attitudes among the intendants. There were bound to be some, simply because the intendants tended to be drawn from a broadly similar social background and because the majority shared a broadly similar career pattern. Furthermore, the simple fact that a man had to be selected as intendant—unless the ministers made a mistake—presupposed certain qualities and attitudes on the part of the candidate. Some idea of the qualities which Richelieu was looking for may be ascertained from the *Testament politique*. Discussing the qualities needed by a councillor of state, the author emphasized the qualities of *bonté, fermeté d'esprit*, prudence, firmness, foresight, and knowledge—especially of history and comparative institutions. The future councillor of state had to be modest and able to follow good advice. He had to have *solidité de jugement* since the alternative—*légèreté*—was dangerous in government. The candidate for further employment must not have 'une conscience craintive et scrupuleuse' because this might lead to 'beaucoup d'injustices et cruautés'. The author distinguished between rigour and severity: the first was likely to be unjust, the second was sometimes necessary. Above all, it seems, Richelieu demanded a constructive intelligence. 'Il se trouve des gens dont la vertu consiste plus à plaindre les désordres qu'à y remédier par l'établissement d'une bonne discipline. Ce ne sont pas ceux-là que nous cherchons, dont la vertu n'est qu'en apparence . . . La probité d'un conseiller d'état doit être active: elle méprise les plaintes et s'attache aux effets solides, dont le public peut retirer du fruit.'[2] This statement from the *Testament politique* raises the question of the interaction between the ideas and the actions of the intendants. Did they act upon general theories, or did they formulate their theories in response to, and as a result of, their experiences? Richelieu, it seems, was hostile to the first tendency. 'La capacité des conseillers ne requiert pas une capacité

---

[1] The chief exception to this rule was the appointment of members of the Arnauld family to intendancies in the army. However, these were short-lived commissions, and since the armies served abroad, the appointment of Jansenists had no bearing on the domestic political or religious situation.

[2] Richelieu, *Testament politique*, ed. André, pp. 289–96.

pédantesque', the *Testament politique* argued. 'Il n'y a rien de plus dangereux pour l'état que ceux qui veulent gouverner les Royaumes par les maximes qu'ils tirent de leurs livres . . .'[1]

The example of Cardin Le Bret, the greatest political theorist of his generation, although of course an exceptional case, is nevertheless instructive on this point. The future intendant and political theorist had served as an *avocat-général* in the *cour des aides* of Paris, and then in the *Parlement* of Paris (1604–19). He conducted the prosecution of the maréchale d'Ancre, in which he decided that her property and that of her husband— Concini—could be confiscated to the crown. In 1624–5, he served as intendant at Châlons and Metz 'pour informer des usurpations du duc de Lorraine'. In this commission, he invoked the important principle of the inalienability of the royal domain. This was not a new theory, but it was to have great significance in the evolution of Richelieu's foreign policy, since it could be applied to areas of the Carolingian Empire that were no longer part of France, such as Navarre, Naples, Portugal, Flanders, Milan, parts of Savoy and Piedmont. In 1625, Le Bret was sent as commissioner to the Estates of Brittany. The Estates refused to deliberate on the question of voting money to the crown until their privileges had been fully confirmed. Le Bret condemned this attitude. 'C'est capituler, traiter d'égal avec son roi . . .' Privileges, he asserted, were held 'de la pure et grande libéralité de nos rois'. By 1630, Le Bret was fully convinced that the sovereign courts must yield before the supremacy of the council of state, and two years later he was made *premier président* in the *Parlement* of Metz. It was in 1632, at the age of seventy-four, that his *De la souveraineté du roy* first appeared—an attempt, as he put it, to 'recueillir tous les droits et privilèges de la souveraineté royale'. Although Le Bret lived on to the ripe age of ninety-seven, his celebrated political treatise was written in 1625–30, after the most formative influences of his career. It is difficult to imagine the same sort of treatise being written by anyone but Le Bret, with his unique experience in *causes célèbres* involving the king's sovereignty, or a comparable defence of the theory of the royal commissioner coming from someone who had not himself served as intendant. Le Bret is thus a good example of

[1] ibid., p. 289.

Richelieu's principle that councillors of state should not possess 'une capacité pédantesque' but should gain practical experience. Le Bret's political theory came from such experience. From 1630—when *De la souveraineté* was completed—until his death in 1655, Le Bret continued to sit in the king's council, where he became the *doyen*. He was a judge in the trials of the maréchal de Marillac (1632), the duc de la Valette (1639) and the marquis de Cinq-Mars (1642). It was well known that Chancellor Séguier deferred to his advice, notably in the trial of Cinq-Mars. Le Bret's treatise thus became the text-book of government at the time of Richelieu and Mazarin.[1]

The processes of selection presupposed certain qualities and attitudes on the part of the candidates. It is also true to say that the acceptance of a commission presupposed certain theories of government on the part of the intendant. At the time of Richelieu and Mazarin, the most important of these theories was the medieval principle *necessitas legem non habet*, 'necessity knows no law', which had a direct relevance to the problems of government. In the middle ages, this principle had been used to justify almost any measure taken by the king in defence of his kingdom. What it really meant was 'necessity knows no private law': in a national emergency, special immunities, privileges, and exemptions that stood in the way of the public welfare were null and void.[2] At the time of Richelieu and Mazarin, the argument was used to justify increases in taxation and other measures of government which in normal circumstances might seem arbitrary, but which were justified because of the national emergency created by the war against the Habsburgs. The theory is to be found in Le Bret's *De la souveraineté du roy*, where the author argues that the sovereign courts had a duty to register fiscal edicts when there was a 'nécessité pressante pour le bien public'.[3] Similarly, the argument was used in nearly every speech made by an intendant at the time of Richelieu and

[1] G. Picot, *Cardin Le Bret (1558–1655) et la doctrine de la souveraineté* (Nancy, 1948), pp. 35–56. V. I. Comparato, *Cardin Le Bret, 'royauté e 'ordre' nel pensiero di un consigliere del secento* (Florence, 1969). Thuau, *Raison d'état et pensée politique*, pp. 275–8. Church, *Richelieu and reason of state*, pp. 268–76. Le Bret was given the privilege of publishing *De la souveraineté* on 10 Dec. 1630.

[2] cf. G. Post, *Studies in medieval legal thought, public law and the state, 1100–1322* (Princeton, N.J., 1964), pp. 241–309.

[3] Le Bret, *De la souveraineté du roy*, p. 195. Cf. Mousnier, *La plume*, p. 174.

Mazarin. The idea was implicit in the thoughts and actions of the intendants because of the nature of the tasks they had to perform. It was by no means accepted generally in society. In 1640, Paul Scarron, a *conseiller* in the *Parlement* of Paris, argued that the king of France could not be said to be 'in necessity' since his forces were victorious throughout Europe.[1] Four years earlier, the *Croquants* of Saintonge had argued that necessity of state was '[un] beau prétexte . . . une couleur apparente pour ruiner le royaume'. They, too, denied that a real emergency existed.[2] Other, more moderate critics, argued that there was another 'necessity' to be considered—the necessity that the laws of the kingdom be observed.[3] The critics of the government were right to point out that the argument was authoritarian in its implications. René I Voyer d'Argenson argued in 1647 that the king's subjects ought not to enquire whether or not that which was done in the name of necessity was just,[4] and this, it seems, was the position of Richelieu too.[5] Moreover, the intendants eventually came to use the argument to justify measures taken against an internal rather than external enemy of the crown. The principle of *cessante causa, cessat effectus*, 'when necessity ceases what necessity requires should also cease'[6] was not accepted by the government or the intendants. Thus in 1661, the intendants justified the maintenance of troops at war-time levels 'pour empêcher les révoltes et les désordres'.[7] Temporary measures which in 1635–7 had been justified because of a national emergency—entry of France into the Thirty Years War and the invasions of France by Habsburg

---

[1] B.N. MS.fr. 16218, fo. 422. Paul Scarron was arrested and exiled. On 21 Feb. 1641, his office was abolished and it was not re-established until Louis XIII was on his death-bed: Cf. Mailfait, *Un magistrat . . . Omer Talon . . .*, p. 190, n. 1.

[2] *Lettres . . . au Chancelier Séguier*, ed. Mousnier, ii. 1104. Bercé, *Histoire des Croquants*, ii. 736.

[3] *Histoire générale de Languedoc*, ed. Roschach, xiv. 603. Pierre de Marca, archbishop of Toulouse and acting president of the Estates, to the Estates of Languedoc, 30 Dec. 1655.

[4] ibid., xiv. 150.   [5] cf. Church, *Richelieu and reason of state*, pp. 399–400.

[6] For this principle in the middle ages, cf. E. A. R. Brown, 'Cessante causa and the taxes of the last Capetians: the political applications of a philosophical maxim', *Post Scripta. Essays in medieval law and the emergence of the European state in honour of Gaines Post*, ed. J. R. Strayer and D. E. Queller (Rome, 1972), pp. 565–87. The office-holders accepted this principle, however. Cf. remonstrances of the *cour des aides* of Paris (21 July 1643): Z1a 161, fo. 132ᵛ.

[7] *Histoire générale de Languedoc*, ed. Roschach. xiv. 770. Bazin to the Estates of Languedoc, 24 Jan. 1661.

armies—came to be regarded as permanent features of French life. In a sense, France was in a permanent state of emergency between 1635 and 1659: however, such a state of emergency could scarcely be said to have existed in the decade following the Peace of the Pyrenees.

An attempt is made in Table D to categorize the 128 intendants appointed by Richelieu and Mazarin according to generations and dates of appointment. Nearly half the intendants were first appointed between the Day of Dupes (10 November 1630)

TABLE D

Age groups of intendants appointed by Richelieu and Mazarin

Group I	Born 1550–80	3 intendants
Group II	Born 1581–90 or first intendancy before 1624	8 intendants
Group III	Appointed 1624–30	16 intendants
Group IV	Appointed 1631–42	52 intendants
Group V	Appointed 1643–52	26 intendants
Group VI	Appointed 1653–61	22 intendants
		128 intendants

and the death of Richelieu (4 December 1642). However, a significant number of intendants—twenty-seven—were appointed in the first six years of Richelieu's ministry, before the crisis of the Day of Dupes. It is not unreasonable to suppose that there was a great gulf in political attitudes between these men and the twenty-two appointees in Group VI, who were appointed after 1653. For the men appointed before 1630, the great events in recent memory were the wars of religion and the Catholic League. For the intendants at the time of Foucquet, there was one event which overshadowed all others—the Fronde.

The three intendants in Group I were contemporaries of Michel de Marillac, the Keeper of the Seals and—by 1630— the political rival of Richelieu. Marillac, who was born in 1563, was twenty-two years older than Richelieu. Of the three intendants in this group, Le Bret was five years older than Marillac; Lefèvre d'Ormesson was eight years older than Richelieu, and thus the youngest of the group; while Robert Miron was six years younger than Marillac. Miron's career was remarkable, both in itself and in the contrast it provides with that of Le Bret. Miron was first appointed as intendant in the Auvergne in 1599. He served as ambassador negotiating the status of Lorraine in 1601–3 and as ambassador to Switzerland between 1617 and 1627. Between these two embassies, he was appointed mayor (*prévôt des marchands*) of Paris (1614–16) and president of the third estate at the Estates-General of 1614–15. He held the intendancy of Languedoc from 1632 until 1640. Miron was known and trusted by Richelieu. They had certainly met by 5 November 1614, at the Estates-General. They made the closing speeches on behalf of their respective estates on 23 February 1615. When Richelieu was appointed foreign minister on 30 November 1616, he immediately selected Miron as ambassador to Switzerland. Richelieu had confidence in the policy as well as the man: Miron was an advocate of French intervention in the Valtelline.[1] Richelieu's confidence in Miron's powers of negotiation, his ability, and his loyalty was well-founded. The choice of Miron as intendant of Languedoc was a political concession to the province, for by 1639 the septuagenarian Miron must have seemed decidedly old-fashioned.[2] Miron was a believer in sound coinage and low taxation—exactly those principles which were undermined in the 1630s because of the demands of war. Miron and his family were committed to the idea of reform in France. His cousin, Charles Miron, bishop of Angers, had demanded the reform of the king's council and of the king's finances on 30 January 1615.[3] His brother, François Miron, when *prévôt des marchands* at Paris, had vigorously opposed Sully's arbitrary reduction of payments to *rentiers*—this measure appeared more of a fiscal expedient than a genuine reform.[4]

The basic ideas of Robert Miron did not change greatly with

[1] A. Miron de l'Espinay, *Robert Miron et l'administration municipale de Paris de 1614 à 1616* (1922). R. Miron, 'Relation de ce qui s'est passé en Suisse . . .' *Archiv für Schweizerische Geschichte Herausgegeben auf Veranstaltung der allgemeinen geschicht-forschenden Gesellschaft der Schweiz* (Zurich, 1844), 270–321. Cf. R. Pithon, 'La Suisse, théâtre de la guerre froide entre la France et l'Espagne pendant la crise de la Valteline (1621–1626)', *Schweizerische Zeitschrift für Geschichte*, xiii (1963), 40–1.
[2] cf. Miron's reference to his age: A.D. Haute-Garonne C 2302, fo. 55, 21 Nov. 1639.
[3] J. M. Hayden, *France and the Estates-General of 1614* (Cambridge, 1974), p. 152.
[4] A. Miron de l'Espinay, *François Miron et l'administration municipale de Paris sous Henri IV, 1604–1606* (1885). Buisseret, *Sully*, p. 89.

the passing of time. The same themes were included in speeches which he made in 1615 and 1634. Society, he argued, was governed according to the rules of religion and justice. All three estates must reform themselves according to these rules. The way in which Miron developed these ideas changed, however, as political circumstances and Miron's own position dictated. As spokesman of the third estate in 1615, Miron could advocate financial reform, including the reduction of the *taille* to the level of 1576, and the abolition of the sale of offices.[1] As intendant in 1634, Miron argued that Richelieu had already achieved the reform of the state.[2] As intendant, he could not advocate a reduction in taxation: indeed, in 1639, he told the Estates of Languedoc that the state demanded 'absolument' their agreement to extraordinary taxes to pay for the troops during the winter quarter.[3] As intendant, far from abolishing the sale of offices, Miron was instrumental in forcing new offices on the reluctant *Parlement* of Toulouse.[4] Thus Miron's ideas evolved in a similar way to those of Richelieu, who reluctantly came to accept that fiscal reform and the abolition of the sale of offices were not possible in time of war. Miron's view of the role of the intendant accords with certain of Richelieu's statements on this subject: the intendant, in Miron's view, was a temporary investigator rather than a permanent administrator.[5] The difference between them was that whereas Miron considered representative institutions a worthwhile forum for the statement of grievances and proposals for reform,[6] Richelieu did not.

[1] Robert Miron, *Harangue prononcée devant le Roy et la Royne* . . . (23 Feb. 1615), B.L. 12301 aaa 29.
[2] A.D. Haute-Garonne C 2301, fo. 209, 13 Nov. 1634.
[3] Miron de l'Espinay, *Robert Miron*, p. 354. A.D. Haute-Garonne C 2302, fos. 57ᵛ–58ᵛ, 21 Nov. 1639.
[4] J. B. Dubédat, *Histoire du Parlement de Toulouse* (2 vols., 1885), ii. 204–5. B.N. MS.fr. 17371, fo. 36, 15 Sept. 1636.
[5] *Bnutrennyaya*, ed. Lubinskaya, p. 29, 'estant inspecteurs universels de ce qui se passe dans le pais'.
[6] A.D. Haute-Garonne C 2302, fo. 55ᵛ, 21 Nov. 1639: 'l'assemblée des Estats est proprement une conférence des peuples avec le Roy . . . affin d'y exposer les diverses indispositions qui travaillent les subjectz, en chercher le remède et subvenir aux nécessités de l'estat'. Cf. A.A.E. France 1628, fo. 76ᵛ, 12 Dec. 1631: 'une conférence paternelle, paisible et aimable des subjects avec le prince ou avec celuy qui le représente en ce gouvernement pour remédier aux maux par l'advis des malades mêmes'.

Of the eight intendants in Group II—those born in the years between 1581 and 1590 or first appointed to an intendancy before 1624—two stand out as of particular importance. After serving as intendant in Guyenne, Pierre Séguier went on to become Chancellor of France. His servility to Richelieu became notorious. Séguier was generally unpopular by 1643 because he had been appointed by Richelieu, because he had gained a sizeable fortune from office, but above all because as Chancellor he had played a crucial role in selecting suitable judges for the important political trials which took place during Richelieu's ministry. The second intendant of considerable importance in this group—Charles Machault—was one such judge employed by Séguier. Machault was 'surnommé coupteste pour avoir esté emploié par le Cardinal de Richelieu à plusieurs procès criminels'.[1] Machault was an extremely effective intendant who established a climate of political security in the provinces in which he served. Witnesses came forward during his period in office to give evidence against the nobles. Once Machault was recalled, 'il ne se trouve plus de témoins qui osent déposer'.[2] Both Séguier and Machault had entered the service of the crown during the chancellorship of Brûlart de Sillery. Both, however, went on to fulfil their career ambitions under Richelieu. They were almost exact contemporaries of the first minister—Machault was two years younger than Richelieu, Séguier three years younger. Unlike the Cardinal, however, they lived on to a ripe old age. Séguier was eighty-two on his death in 1672 as Chancellor. Machault was eighty on his death in 1667 as *doyen* of the council. Though they owed their political advancement to Richelieu, they showed a considerable capacity for political survival after his death. Essentially, Séguier and Machault were pragmatists, servants of the crown but not initiators. They were inherited by Richelieu from the previous regime, and moulded by the first minister to become instruments of his policy. They do not seem to have made a significant contribution to the formation of that policy or to the political ideas of their time.

Sixteen intendants comprise Group III—those appointed between 1624 and 1630 before the political crisis of the Day of

[1] *Lettres . . . au Chancelier Séguier*, ed. Mousnier, ii. 1217.
[2] B.N. MS.fr. 17380, fo. 137, 14 Sept. 1644.

Dupes. The majority of these were appointed while Michel de Marillac held the Seals, and the appointment of three at least show some influence of the *dévot* party. Jean Lauzon appears to have been a conservative both in matters of politics and religion. He preferred the more limited powers he received as intendant in Normandy in 1626 to the wider powers he exercised as intendant in Guyenne after 1641.[1] He was also conservative on religious questions. It was said that he sought the governorship of Canada in 1651 because the Jesuits had much greater influence in the new colony than they had in France.[2] The careers of two other intendants—René I Voyer d'Argenson and François Villemontée—provide an interesting contrast. Both men entered holy orders and were members of the conservative religious grouping, the *Compagnie de Saint-Sacrament*. Villemontée went on to become bishop of Saint-Malo. Argenson might have followed a similar career, but died shortly after being received into holy orders. Argenson served as intendant for about seventeen years; Villemontée for almost twenty-five. Argenson was essentially an intendant of the army and a diplomat abroad; he served only seven years as an intendant in France. Villemontée in contrast held only two intendancies in the army (1644, 1649) and served for a record number of years in the same province, Poitou. It is sometimes said that Villemontée was much more inclined to use force against rioters than was Argenson, also that Villemontée had a much closer relationship with the financiers.[3] These differences may be explained by the temperaments of the two men, but above all by the difference in the nature of their service. Argenson was in essence a negotiator and a conciliator—this required personal characteristics of calmness and willingness to make concessions in order to obtain a settlement. To negotiate, however, did not imply weakness. Argenson took a firm line when necessary. If the ministers had not believed him capable

---

[1] F. Loirette, 'Un intendant de Guyenne avant la Fronde: Jean de Lauson (1641–1648)', *Bulletin Philologique et Historique jusqu'à 1715 du Comité des Travaux Historiques et Scientifiques [année 1957]* (1958), p. 460. H. Renaud, 'Correspondance relative aux provinces d'Aunis, Saintonge, Angoumois et Poitou . . .', *Archives Historiques de la Saintonge et de l'Aunis*, vii (Saintes, 1880), 347–8.

[2] *Lettres . . . au Chancelier Séguier*, ed. Mousnier, i. 110.

[3] ibid., i. 100. M. de Certeau, 'Politique et mystique. René d'Argenson, 1596–1651', *Revue d'Ascétique et de Mystique*, xxxix (1963), 50, n. 22.

of firm action, they would hardly have sent Argenson as intendant to Languedoc in 1647, for the Estates had refused a money grant to the government in the two previous years. Argenson was also ordered to prosecute the ringleaders of the Montpellier riot of 1645.[1] For his part, Villemontée was intendant in one of the most turbulent provinces in that most unruly area of France, the south-west. He had little choice, therefore, but to resort to coercion and the use of troops. Such actions by the intendants were always interpreted by the taxpayers as beneficial to the financiers. It was said that the financiers preferred Villemontée to Argenson. Certainly, Argenson expressed his distaste for measures 'qui vont à pressurer les peuples',[2] but he was forced to use troops to collect the taxes in the *élection* of Les Sables d'Olonne in 1646.[3] If the financiers preferred Villemontée to Argenson, this was not necessarily because the former was more kindly disposed to the financiers than the latter, but because he had greater experience of financial management in a difficult province.

There is clear evidence—in his religious treatise written in 1640 and in his political speeches—that Argenson sought to relate his political activities to his religious philosophy. In this respect, Argenson's concerns were comparable to those of Richelieu, who tried to justify the active life by a liberal interpretation of the Canons and Decrees of the Council of Trent. Similarly, Argenson saw no conflict between religion and politics. In his view, service to God, service to the king, and service to Richelieu were 'trois fins que j'ai toujours rencontrés par le même chemin et les seules qui règlent mes intentions . . .'[4] Service to the king and service to Richelieu were regarded by Argenson as identical—which was scarcely the *dévot* position in 1630. However, Argenson never said, nor did he believe, that service to God and service to the king were identical. On the contrary, it was pleasing to God to do and to advise what one thought for the best—even if it displeased the king. Although God 'inspire luy-même les secrets de ses volontés aux princes qu'il fait régner souverainement par

---

[1] O1 3, fo. 80ᵛ, 27 Feb. 1647.
[2] *Lettres . . . au Chancelier Séguier*, loc. cit. Certeau, art. cit., p. 79.
[3] E 207b, fo. 539, 31 Jan. 1646.
[4] *Lettres . . . au Chancelier Séguier*, ed. Mousnier, i. 99. Certeau, art. cit., p. 74.

sa grâce', it was axiomatic to Argenson that France was not governed by men alone.[1] Richelieu and Argenson differed as to the ideal religious practice. Richelieu was much more inclined to submit himself to spiritual advisers, notably his confessor Lescot. He thought this 'un des plus souverains rémèdes'. In contrast, Argenson was sceptical of 'ces entretiens des choses spirituelles où il n'y a que de beaux termes'. Richelieu advised the frequent use of the sacraments which 'produisent leur effet par leur propre force'. Argenson, again in contrast, only mentioned one sacrament—that of penance—and then only indirectly. The two men faced similar problems, therefore, but adopted different solutions.[2]

Argenson's absolutist theory came from an intense pessimism about man's nature. It was scarcely accidental that he began his first speech to the Estates of Languedoc in 1647 with the fall of man. The pessimism of his religious treatise, written seven years earlier, was now applied to political society. 'Les hommes sont incapables de se conduire eux-mêmes . . .', he declared. Civil liberty depended on government: 'Dieu nous a donné . . . les roys et les loys civiles pour être les guides de notre liberté.' The abuse of liberty by the king's subjects 'produit . . . les dérèglements dans les états politiques'. According to Argenson, the refusal of the Estates of Languedoc to vote a grant of money in 1645 and 1646 were not 'actes de liberté' but rather 'des acheminemens à la servitude'. The vote of the Estates was needed to help pay for the war effort. The aim of the war was a firm peace. For this reason, it was a just war, and for this reason also the fiscal demands of the crown were just.[3] Argenson was thus a political pragmatist and a religious mystic who saw no incompatibility between the two positions. Politics was an external manifestation of religious 'inspiration' which directed the conduct of the intendant.[4]

Group IV comprises 52 intendants appointed between the Day of Dupes and the death of Richelieu, the majority of whom were appointed after Séguier became Keeper of the Seals (25 February 1633). Three intendants have been chosen

---

[1] Certeau, art. cit., pp. 76–7.

[2] ibid., pp. 54, 55 n. 56. For Richelieu's position: J. Orcibal, 'Richelieu, homme d'église, homme d'état . . .', *Revue d'Histoire de l'Église de France*, xxxiv (1948), 101.

[3] *Histoire générale de Languedoc*, ed. Roschach, xiv. 148–57.

[4] Certeau, art. cit., pp. 59, 75, 81.

as representative of this group. Two—Laubardemont and Laffemas—because they illustrate the rapid extension of the powers of the intendants after the Day of Dupes, and the third—Bosquet—because he provides an important contrast with Baltazar, one of the first appointees of Mazarin. Laubardemont and Laffemas were two of the most hated intendants appointed by Richelieu. Laffemas was called 'le bourreau du Cardinal de Richelieu'[1] and was well aware of his evil reputation by 1636.[2] When he was disgraced in 1643, 'personne le plaignoit, ne s'estant fait aimer . . .'[3] Laubardemont was not employed after 1643 either. Both men were hated because they did not conform to the usual social requirements for intendants, and because they performed highly unpopular tasks. Laffemas was largely a self-made man, an adventurer who profited from his position in the extraordinary financial tribunal (*chambre de justice*) of 1624–5. Up to 1636, Laubardemont's career had been in the provinces: he turned the trial of Urbain Grandier into a national *cause célèbre* and owed his subsequent promotion entirely to the patronage of Richelieu and Séguier. Both Laffemas and Laubardemont were the personification of Richelieu's *homme sûr*—men whose loyalty to the state overrode all other considerations.[4] As intendant, Laffemas interrogated anyone who showed signs of *mauvaise volonté* towards Richelieu. He was careful not to open letters from the Queen Mother—who was in exile—without specific authorization from the ministers.[5] His loyalty to the crown was demonstrated also during the last year of the Fronde. Laffemas was one of those responsible for the royalist *coup* at Paris in the autumn of 1652, and was rehabilitated after this event, serving as *conseiller ordinaire* until his death in 1657.[6] Both Laffemas and Laubarde-

---

[1] G. Mongrédien, *Le bourreau du Cardinal de Richelieu. Isaac de Laffemas* (1929).

[2] *Lettres . . . au Chancelier Séguier*, ed. Mousnier, i. 312. Deyon, *Amiens*, p. 445, n. 26.

[3] Ormesson, *Journal*, ed. Chéruel, i. 15. Ormesson added: 'outre que par sa vanité il s'estoit procuré ce malheur'.

[4] It was precisely because he was one of the 'gens entendus' in whom Séguier had confidence that Laubardemont was chosen for the commission to try Cinq-Mars in 1642: A.A.E. France 843, fos. 140ᵛ, 173, 30 July and 3 Aug. 1642.

[5] *Lettres . . . au Chancelier Séguier*, ed. Mousnier, i. 197, 202–3, 217–18, 224, 319.

[6] Laffemas held the small seal of the chancellery of the *Parlement* of Paris, and had considered joining the royalist *Parlement* at Pontoise. He decided not to leave the capital, and sent the seal instead, because if he went to Pontoise, 'beaucoup de gens qu'il gouvernoit pourroit se raffroidir dans le service du roy . . .' University of London Add. MS. 247, fol. 13ᵛ.

mont owed part of their unpopularity to the fact that they served in political trials. Laffemas was a member of the *Chambre de l'Arsenal* in 1631[1]—which was anathema to the *Parlement* of Paris—while Laubardemont served as *rapporteur* in the trial of Cinq-Mars in 1642. Both displayed extremist tendencies. Laffemas boasted to Louis XIII that he would levy enough money in taxes to pay for two years of the war effort.[2] Laubardemont, though he described his work as intendant in more moderate language, was prepared to extend his authority without prior authorization from the government.[3] He was also prepared to indulge in judicial antiquarianism. Laubardemont contemplated the revival of an ordinance of 22 December 1477, last used in 1569, which purported to be a 'constitution ou loi qui punit de mort les non-révélateurs du crime de lèse-majesté'—a blanket formula for executing the accused in treason trials when there was insufficient evidence of guilt. Both Laffemas and Laubardemont tortured suspects with apparent equanimity, while Laubardemont's moral position in the trials of Urbain Grandier and Cinq-Mars seems to have been very dubious. In the trial of Grandier, he altered the written evidence to make it appear more conclusive, and he refused to listen to statements which were favourable to the accused. In the trial of Cinq-Mars, he offered the accused clemency if he would implicate De Thou. In the event, both Cinq-Mars and De Thou were executed.[4]

The unpopularity of Laffemas and Laubardemont suggests that society as a whole did not accept the government argument that the only successful outcome in a treason trial was a death sentence for the accused. However, their careers illustrate the strength of the prosecution in the French legal system in the seventeenth century. Laffemas and Laubardemont accepted, but did not exceed, contemporary legal attitudes to torture. Death sentences were rarely the decision of one man—Laffemas presided over a commission of thirteen judges in the trial of the chevalier de Jars; the same number of judges participated in the trial of Cinq-Mars. However, the intendant or the *rapporteur*

[1] cf. E 1685, fo. 172, 16 Dec. 1631.

[2] Ormesson, *Journal*, ed. Chéruel, i. 15.

[3] *Lettres . . . au Chancelier Séguier*, ed. Mousnier, i. 289–90, 343.

[4] M. Faucheux, 'Le procès de Cinq-Mars', *Quelques procès criminels*, ed. Imbert, pp. 77–100.

in other judicial commissions had enormous authority as chief prosecutor.[1] Laffemas and Laubardemont dominated the other judges: that was why they had been selected in the first place. They practised Richelieu's theory that in a crisis prompt and effective action must be taken. The ordinary course of justice might require proof and evidence of guilt, but a question of state could not wait for this, since delay in a case of conspiracy or sedition might be disastrous.

The career and personality of François Bosquet was in every way different from that of Laffemas and Laubardemont. It was a contrast also with his colleague as intendant of Languedoc, Jean Baltazar, who was one of the twenty-six intendants appointed between 1643 and 1652 [Table D, Group V]. There was little to choose between Baltazar and Bosquet in age and social origins, but a great deal in previous experience. Baltazar was the son of a member of the *bailliage* of Sens, while Bosquet was the son of a *notaire* and town councillor at Narbonne. Baltazar had served in the *Parlement* of Paris, as *maître des requêtes*, and had been summoned to the council in 1642–3. Bosquet's experience, in contrast, was as *procureur-général* in Séguier's commission in Normandy in 1639–40, then as intendant in Guyenne. He had not bought a major office during his career,[2] although he had been appointed councillor of state. Bosquet, however, dismissed Baltazar's claims to precedence either as *maître des requêtes* or councillor of state. He used his friendship with Séguier to reinforce his argument that since he had arrived first in Languedoc, he should act as senior intendant.[3] Whereas Baltazar was known to Mazarin in 1643, and in correspondence with him, Bosquet was not.[4] If dissimilarities in their earlier careers tended to poison relations between the two men, therefore, the problem was aggravated by the rival patronage support on which they depended. Matters

[1] cf. Imbert's perceptive comments, ibid., pp. 4–7.

[2] Bosquet had bought the office of *lieutenant-général* in the *sénéchaussée* of Narbonne at some date before 1640: F. de Verthamon, *Relation du voyage de Chancelier Séguier en Normandie*, ed. A. M. Floquet (Rouen, 1842), p. 393.

[3] Henry, *François Bosquet*, pp. 157–8. *Bnutrennyaya*, ed. Lublinskaya, pp. 41–2. B.N. MS.fr. 17377, fo. 181, 5 Oct. 1643. Cf. W. H. Beik, 'Two intendants face a popular revolt: social unrest and the structures of absolutism in 1645', *Canadian Journal of History*, ix (1974), 243–62.

[4] cf. A.A.E. France 848, fo. 113, Dec. 1643: Bosquet to Mazarin, 'inconneu que je sois . . .

were made worse by the fact that while Baltazar was paid
promptly by the government, and could afford to wear 'son habit
gay étant de broderie d'argent',[1] Bosquet was paid irregularly
and was in financial difficulties.[2] The real differences between
the men were not personal but political, however, and on 25 May
1644 Bosquet went as far as to demand the recall of his rival.
Bosquet was a political realist, but a moderate. He had
reason to be suspicious of government fiscal initiatives. When
serving as intendant of Guyenne, he was required to levy the
sol pour livre, the 5 per cent sales tax, at Montauban. Bosquet was
forced to flee the city at night and in disguise because of the
ensuing riot; thereafter he always referred to Guyenne as
'une province orageuse'.[3] Bosquet, a Languedocien born and
bred, was thus confirmed in a conciliatory approach which he
had first learnt as a result of the trauma of the Montmorency
rebellion. The archbishop of Narbonne said of Bosquet: 'nous
n'avons jamais eu intendant dans cette province qui aye agy
avec plus de douceur ny avec plus de prudence, ny aye porté
les peuples plus facilement à l'éxécution des ordres du Roy et
du Conseil.'[4] Bosquet said the same of himself: 'je règle les
affaires sans bruit.'[5] All this was an enormous contrast with
Baltazar's administration of Languedoc during Bosquet's absence
in 1643–4. Bosquet believed in conciliation in religious matters
too. His attitude to the Protestants was similar to that of
Richelieu: he believed in their right of coexistence under the
law, and the gradual process of peaceful conversion to Catholicism.[6] Though in later years Bosquet was involved in the
struggle against Jansenism, his role in this respect was much
more moderate than that of his friend and contemporary,
Pierre de Marca, archbishop of Toulouse.[7] Bosquet was a

---

[1] Henry, op. cit., p. 169. B.N. MS.fr. 17379, fo. 129ᵛ, 20 June 1644. This style
of dress was prohibited by the sumptuary ordinance of 31 May 1644.
[2] *Lettres . . . au Chancelier Séguier*, ed. Mousnier, ii. 746.
[3] *Bnutrennyaya*, ed. Lublinskaya, p. 38. E 160c, fo. 704, 27 Apr. 1641.
[4] Henry, op. cit., pp. 148–9. A.A.E. France 848, fo. 101, 17 Nov. 1643.
[5] Henry, op. cit., p. 169. B.N. MS.fr. 17379, fo. 129ᵛ, 20 June 1644.
[6] A.A.E. France 1637, fo. 99, 4 July 1657. For Richelieu's position, cf. P. Blet,
'Le plan de Richelieu pour la réunion des Protestants', *Gregorianum*, xlviii (1967),
100–29.
[7] Henry, op. cit., pp. 405–52. F. Gaquère, *Pierre de Marca (1594–1662). Sa vie, ses
œuvres, son gallicanisme* (1932). P. Jansen, *Le Cardinal Mazarin et le mouvement jan-
séniste français, 1653–1659* (1967).

scholarly and moderate figure, although well capable of bearing a grievance and harbouring personal animosity. As early as 1643 he had sought the bishopric of Pamiers; in 1648 he was rewarded with that of Lodève; in 1655 he was promoted to that of Montpellier.

In contrast, Jean Baltazar was a supreme example of the secular politician. He was described as an 'homme de fortune, dévoué aux puissances, dangereux, et capable de faire toutes choses pour la cour et pour ses interestz'.[1] He went to the commemorative service for Louis XIII on 14 May 1661 at Saint-Denis, not because of any great religious conviction, but to honour the memory of a king for whom he had an 'obligation particulière'—and he took care to inform the Chancellor of the fact.[2] Baltazar was consistent in the defence of his own interests, but less so in his political principles. In the 1640s, Baltazar was an extremist. He entered into conflict with Bosquet; with the *cour des comptes* of Montpellier; with the Estates of Languedoc; with the Protestants; with Gaston d'Orléans, the governor of the province; finally with Schomberg, the lieutenant-general of the province and his own patron. Conflict with the courts seems to have been with Baltazar all his life: he was in conflict with the courts also at La Rochelle in 1651, at Limoges in 1652 and at Dijon in 1658.[3] The key to Baltazar's extremism in the 1640s was a misunderstanding of the nature of the Languedociens, people who 'ne peuvent supporter ni une entière servitude ni une entière liberté'.[4] Baltazar's standpoint was that of the forces of repression: he was reliving the revolt of Montmorency and the royalist victory at Castelnaudary on 1 September 1632.[5] This led him into a number of serious miscalculations. The Estates of Languedoc could not be abolished nearly as easily as he suggested on 9 January 1646. Nor could the *cour des comptes* of Montpellier be broken up without risking serious political

[1] B.N. MS.fr. 14028.
[2] B.L. Harleian 4442, fo. 367.
[3] E 1696, no. 316, 21 Dec. 1651; E 250a, fo. 25, 24 Jan. 1652; E 1708, no. 158, 24 Dec. 1658.
[4] The description is that of Chancellor Aguesseau: *Œuvres de M. le Chancelier d'Aguesseau* (13 vols., 1739), xiii. 26–7.
[5] Baltazar's conspiracy theory is revealed in a memorandum to Mazarin: A.A.E. France 1634, fo. 97, 13 Mar. 1645. Mazarin had warned Baltazar of the dangers of over-reaction in Languedoc as early as 2 Jan. 1644: *Lettres du Cardinal Mazarin pendant son ministère*, ed. P. A. Chéruel and G. d'Avenel (9 vols., 1872–1906), i. 526.

consequences.[1] The Montpellier riot might be punished: but not as vigorously as he wished for this would have led to the 'perte de la ville'.[2] Baltazar left a *damnosa heritas* to his successor as intendant of Languedoc. None of his proposals were implemented. In the 1650s, however, Baltazar seems to have been much more moderate in his advice, and to have learnt the lessons of the Fronde. 'Les divisions civiles se doibvent plustost . . . terminer par accommodent que par victoire', he wrote in 1658, 'parce que l'un persuade les espritz par la raison et l'autre ne les contraignant que par la force leur laisse le déplaisir dans le cœur.'[3] The man who wrote these words was scarcely the same political being who had served as intendant of Languedoc between 1643 and 1647.

A second appointee of Mazarin was Claude Bazin de Bezons, whose career forms a link between the regimes of D'Hémery and Colbert in terms of provincial administration. All commentators agreed that Bazin was an extremely capable intendant, 'rempli d'une grande connaissance des affaires et accredité au point que l'on pourroit désirer'.[4] Even Chancellor Aguesseau, when writing the eulogy of his father (who succeeded Bazin as intendant of Languedoc in 1673), admitted that Bazin was a man 'd'esprit et de talens' though 'plus vif et moins égal que mon père'.[5] Others thought that Bazin enjoyed too much authority in Languedoc and that he had an excessive sense of his own importance.[6] Tallemant des Réaux thought Bazin 'un petit bout d'un homme tout rond, joufflu comme un des quatre vents, et aussy bouffy d'orgueil qu'il y en ayt du monde . . . '[7] Yet there were strong reasons why Bazin should enjoy a certain degree of pomp and circumstance. He had served as intendant in Catalonia and Roussillon: yet the army there had been badly let down by the failure of the Languedociens to support the war effort.[8] He was intendant during the decline of the governorship. The comte de Bieule,

[1] A.A.E. France 1634, fo. 209, 9 Jan. 1646.
[2] *Lettres . . . au Chancelier Séguier*, ed. Mousnier, ii. 738.
[3] A.A.E. France 1492, fo. 194, memorandum of Baltazar, 22 Nov. 1658.
[4] A.A.E. France 1636, fo. 321, Bishop of Lavaur to Mazarin, 20 June 1654.
[5] Aguesseau, *Œuvres*, xiii. 29.
[6] A.A.E. France 1636, fo. 383, 20 Jan. 1655: 'M. de Bezons . . . qui joue icy le plénipotentiaire'.
[7] Tallemant des Réaux, *Historiettes* (3rd ed., Monmerqué and Paulin, 1862), iv. 176.   [8] A.A.E. France 1636, fo. 269ᵛ, 28 Jan. 1654.

who served as lieutenant-general during the 1650s was—in Mazarin's phrase—'bon et facile' whereas Bazin acted 'avec de subtillités et finesses en toutes ses actions'.[1]

Bazin was a political disciple of Mazarin, an exponent of the policy of divide and rule. He advised Mazarin in 1657: 'mon sens seroit, sy j'ose prendre la liberté de la dire, de tenir les choses en suspends et de désunir les compagnies les unes d'avec les autres, ce qui se fera aisément par leurs interests différends'.[2] Bazin was one of only two intendants appointed before 1648 who served under Colbert too. In part, this was a reflection of his immense ability and experience in dealing with a difficult province: at the moment when it seemed he was to retire from the province, in 1670, his presence was required to suppress the revolt of the Vivarais.[3] In part, the continuity of service was accidental. After a long period as intendant, it was extremely difficult to obtain a position which carried adequate status: Bazin sought, but failed to obtain, the *première présidence* at the *Parlements* of Rennes in 1660 and Rouen in 1665. Bazin's career thus ended in the king's council because Colbert wanted to appoint his own clients, such as Pellot, to the offices which Bazin sought.[4]

Twenty-two intendants were appointed between the end of the Fronde and 1661 [Table D, Group VI]. Several were relatives and clients of Colbert. Hotman de Fontenay was appointed by Mazarin to the intendancy of Touraine in 1656 at the request of Colbert. Colbert advised the chief minister that Hotman would prove a loyal servant to him personally. Moreover, Hotman possessed characteristics which were 'peu commun aux hommes de robe': he opposed the extremism of the sovereign courts, which tried to extend their jurisdiction at the expense of the crown.[5] Colbert also secured the appointment of Pellot as intendant of Limoges and Poitiers in 1658.[6]

---

[1] A.A.E. France 1637, fo. 5, 1 Jan. 1657; A.A.E. France 1638, fo. 225, 1 Dec. 1656.

[2] A.A.E. France 1637, fo. 38ᵛ., 22 Jan. 1657.

[3] E. Leroy-Ladurie, *Les paysans de Languedoc* (2 vols., 1966), i. 607–11. E 1758, no. 157, 12 July 1670.

[4] Ormesson, *Journal*, ed. Chéruel, ii. 359. 'M. de Besons . . . on luy destine la première présidence de Rouen.'

[5] *Lettres . . . de Colbert*, ed. Clément, i. 248. A.A.E. France 900, fo. 216, 28 July 1656. Y 194, fo. 253, 7 July 1656.

[6] *Lettres . . . de Colbert*, ed. Clément, i. 314. O'Reilly, *Pellot*, i. 165.

Pellot was renowned as a hard-line intendant, a friend of the financiers,[1] and an advocate of the use of troops in collecting taxes. Pellot, too was a relative of Colbert and their families may well have participated in joint financial ventures earlier in the century.[2] Pellot was the exact contemporary of Colbert—both men were born in 1619. He was also from similar social origins, the world of finance, albeit the lower rather than the upper echelons of finance.

From being opponents of high taxation—as was Miron in his earlier years—the intendants had thus been transformed into sons of financiers who accepted that a large budget was inevitable. Richelieu and Séguier had commenced this trans-formation with the appointment of men such as Antoine Le Camus and Nicolas Jeannin de Castille. Mazarin had continued the process with the appointment of Guillaume Bordeaux and Pierre Gargan. Colbert confirmed these developments, and restricted the area of choice to families which had previously been associated with his own. He appointed Arnoul Marin as intendant of Orléans in 1669. Arnoul was the son of Denis Marin, who had married Marguerite Colbert. Denis Marin served as an *intendant des finances* from 1650 until his death in 1678. Before holding this office, he had been one of the greatest financiers of Mazarin's government. He had escaped relatively unscathed from the extraordinary financial tribunal (*chambre de justice*) of 1661 only because of Colbert's protec-tion.[3] The intendants of the 1650s and 1660s thus had quite different political assumptions from their predecessors before the Fronde. They had experienced civil war resulting from a revolt of the office-holders. They had also experienced, and took for granted, twenty years of vast government expenditure. The intendants of the 1630s and 1640s regarded the growth of government expenditure—and as a result, the growth of taxation—as a necessary, but temporary evil. By the 1650s and

---

[1] B.N. MS.fr. 14028. Pellot was described as 'homme de fortune et d'expédient, amy des partisans'. Pellot married Claude Le Camus. D'Hémery married Marie Le Camus, her sister. Both were daughters of Nicolas Le Camus, the financier. O'Reilly, *Pellot*, i. 331–3. The assets of Pellot and his wife at the time of their mar-riage totalled 800,000 *livres*, which was unusually high: Y 181, fo. 319.

[2] Bourgeon, *Les Colbert avant Colbert*, p. 111. O'Reilly, *Pellot*, i. 229, quoting Colbert: 'vous savez que M. Pellot est nostre parent et tout à nous. . .'

[3] B.N. p.o. 1856 (Dr. 42,786). B.N. Dossiers Bleus 428 (Dr. 11,473)

1660s it was apparent that it was not temporary, and for a number of intendants, it was not an evil either.

A final consideration is the extent to which the expression of independent political attitudes was permissible in an intendant. Most hardliners and moderates could agree on the objectives of royal policy, though they might disagree on the methods by which the policy was put into effect. True independence of character was not encouraged, and was incompatible with a successful career in government.[1] Intendants who stepped out of line saw their careers destroyed. A number of intendants were disgraced—that is to say, they were recalled from their posts because the ministers were dissatisfied with their conduct. However, the government tried to minimize the impact of such dismissals by keeping the details secret. Thus the clearest examples of royal disfavour are provided not by the recall of intendants, but by disgrace resulting from alleged misconduct during a political trial. There are two excellent cases of this—one in the 1630s, and the other in the 1660s, demonstrating that Louis XIII and Richelieu were no more tolerant than Louis XIV and Colbert.

The first example is Paul Hay du Châtelet. He had served as intendant in Burgundy in 1631, where he suppressed all manifestations of rebellion in favour of Gaston d'Orléans and the duc de Bellegarde. The following year, he was appointed as one of the judges in the trial of the maréchal de Marillac. Hay du Châtelet had written a number of political pamphlets on Richelieu's behalf. In one of these, he had written a verse in Latin critical of Marillac: yet when the maréchal objected to Hay acting as one of his judges, the former intendant denied his authorship.[2] Later in the trial, however, it became clear that Hay had committed perjury: he was arrested, ordered to resign his office of *maître des requêtes*, and his political career was

---

[1] Antoine, *Le conseil du roi*, p. 269. Richelieu asked Chancellor Séguier for the names of two judges who did not approve the death penalty for De Thou in 1642: *Lettres . . . de Richelieu*, ed. Avenel, vii. 125. Church, *Richelieu and reason of state*, p. 332 n. 119. Colbert remarked in a letter to Mazarin of 23 May 1657 that promotion for Bénard de Rezé and Lallemant would 'fai[re] connoistre à tous les maistres des requestes que s'ils font bien, ils seront récompensés.' *Lettres . . . de Colbert*, ed. Clément, i. 271.

[2] cf. the rejection of the *récusation* by the council: V6 84 no. 1, 22 Mar. 1632.

terminated. Richelieu had reason to be angry, since Hay's perjury threatened the outcome of the trial—when it came to pass the death sentence on the maréchal de Marillac, there were thirteen votes in favour but ten against. Nevertheless, it appears that Hay du Châtelet's career as a pamphleteer was unaffected by his demise as a servant of the crown.[1]

The second example is Olivier Lefèvre d'Ormesson. In 1661, Ormesson was at the summit of his career, having served as intendant of Picardy since 1656. The following year, he was transferred to the less important intendancy of Soissons, but this was more than compensated by the fact he was appointed as *rapporteur* in the trial of Foucquet. This was the obvious stepping-stone to a brilliant career in the king's council. Yet Ormesson and his family were *dévots* at a time when Louis XIV and Colbert were moving towards the destruction of this religious and quasi-political grouping.[2] Moreover, he was reluctant to accept unpopular royal commissions—in 1645 Ormesson had had grave doubts about accepting a commission for the re-establishment of the *semestre* at the *Parlement* of Rouen.[3] Louis XIV and Colbert pressed for a death sentence against Foucquet. Ormesson's conscience, sense of justice, and distaste for 'coups de haine et d'autorité' convinced him that the evidence was insufficiently clear-cut for a capital sentence.[4] Colbert never forgave Ormesson for this apparent disloyalty: his career was interrupted and he was removed from his position as intendant in 1666. The Ormesson family as a whole was too distinguished to suffer; but the bitterness of Olivier's comments in his journal on the subject of Colbert leave no illusions as to the extent of the disgrace.

Career, character, and political attitudes are inseparable. The intendants were selected because they tended to conform to certain social and career patterns; these patterns tended to induce certain common political attitudes. The period of service as intendant tended to confirm those political attitudes,

[1] G. Hanotaux and duc de la Force, *Histoire du Cardinal de Richelieu* (6 vols., 1893–1947), iv. 240. Church, *Reason of state*, p. 227. B.N. MS.fr. 32785.
[2] Allier, *La cabale des dévots*, pp. 40, 413. B.N. MS.fr. 14028: Ormesson was described as 'd'un esprit poly et de la cabale dévote'.
[3] Ormesson, *Journal*, ed. Chéruel, i. 315. O'Reilly, *Pellot*, i. 97–8.
[4] Ormesson, *Journal*, ed. Chéruel, ii. 289. F. Cherchève, 'Le procès de Nicolas Foucquet', *Quelques procès criminels*, ed. Imbert, p. 120.

especially if the intendant sought promotion—either to a more important intendancy or to the king's council. If the majority of intendants were political conformists, therefore, it was because their career interests dictated that this should be so. In Saint-Simon's words, 'rien n'égale le mépris et le néant dans lequel un intendant révoqué achève sa vie . . . ' At the same time, few intendants saw any incompatibility between service to the crown and loyalty to their consciences. They saw their task as that of advising the ministers of the crown on what action should be taken. Even if their advice was ignored, the duty of the intendants was to implement decisions taken by the ministers.

CHAPTER VII

The Commissions of the Intendants

ADMINISTRATION AND justice were virtually synonymous in *ancien régime* France. In the words of Guyot, the great eighteenth-century jurist, 'il n'y a presque point de matière qui ne soit mêlée de l'un et de l'autre'. The intendant was both a judge and an administrator. He administered by judicial process; in certain circumstances, he could act with 'point de tribunal, point de rapporteurs, point de conseillers, point de partie publique'.[1] The king could accord powers to the intendants in three ways: by commissions; by instructions or other types of letters patent; and by decrees of the council. At the risk of oversimplification, ordinances and commissions can be seen as defining principles of action, while instructions and decrees were the way in which these principles were put into effect.[2] Guyot distinguished two types of authority enjoyed by the intendants. The *attributions ordinaires* of an intendant were those accorded by the commission: 'c'est par la teneur de la commission que l'on juge de la nature et de l'étendue des pouvoirs du commissaire'. There were, in addition, *attributions extraordinaires*: that is to say, powers 'qui ne durent que le prescrivent les règlemens ou ordres du Roi, provoqués par des circonstances momentanées'.[3] Thus it is very difficult to describe the entirety of powers enjoyed by a single intendant at any one moment in time. Commissions, instructions, and decrees were issued on an *ad hoc* basis, which explains something of the dynamism of the intendants under Richelieu and Mazarin. Commissions might confer identical powers on intendants in different provinces, for example at Aix and Limoges

---

[1] G. A. Guyot and P. A. Merlin, *Traité des droits, fonctions, franchises, exemptions, prérogatives, et privilèges annexés en France à chaque dignité, à chaque office, à chaque état, soit civil, soit militaire, soit ecclésiastique* (4 vols., 1786–8), iii. 132, 141.

[2] cf. Picot, *Cardin Le Bret*, p. 89. Le Bret asserted that 'l'autorité des arrêts n'est de guère moindre considération que celle des loix, vu qu'ils sont l'exécution d'icelles'.

[3] Guyot and Merlin, op. cit., iii. 437.

in 1637[1] and at Amiens and Châlons in 1653.[2] Yet those powers might rapidly cease to be identical if the council issued supplementary decrees to the intendants at Aix and Châlons but not to those at Limoges and Amiens.

Commissions might be specific or general in character. Hundreds, possibly thousands of *commissions particulières* were issued each year by the French crown. Some of the commissions received by André Lefèvre d'Ormesson might serve as illustration: on 18 December 1619, he was commissioned to go to Saint-Dizier and investigate complaints against the commander of the garrison; on 23 April 1624 he was commissioned to investigate complaints against Castille, an *intendant des finances*; on 1 June 1626, together with Turpin, he received a commission to draw up a list of payments to be made to the creditors of Antoine Feydeau, a financier who had declared bankruptcy and gone into hiding.[3]

The intendants might receive such *commissions particulières*; but these supplemented their basic commissions much as did decrees of the council. They were no substitute for the *commission générale* which made explicit the nature of the jurisdiction enjoyed by the intendant, particularly with regard to the status of the decrees he issued. Appeals were a vital aspect of the French judicial system which functioned essentially on the principle of cases from lesser courts being subject to appeal in the sovereign courts, which alone could issue definitive sentences. As the supreme court of appeal as well as chief administrative council, the king's council in the last resort could overrule a decision by any other court. Each commission defined the status of ordinances and rulings issued by the commissioner, and most stated whether they were subject to appeal in the sovereign courts, or in the king's council alone. For as Bodin remarked, 'la commission est decernée pour cognoistre et passer outre par dessus l'appel'.[4] If appeals were allowed at an early stage in the judicial proceedings conducted by the intendants, then the effectiveness of the intendants

---

[1] A.G. A1 42, no. 135, 29 May 1637, commission to Bochart de Champigny (Provence) and Le Tonnelier de Conty (Limousin).

[2] A.G. A1 138, no. 268 and A1 140, fo. 189, 30 Aug. 1653, commission to Gargan (Châlons) and Bordeaux (Amiens).

[3] 144 a.p. 54, Dr. 5.

[4] Jean Bodin, *Les six livres de la République* (ed. 1579), p. 380.

would have been undermined. On the other hand, if no opportunity for appeals to the king's council were allowed, then clearly the intendant could act as a petty tyrant without check on his authority, something which was likely to provoke constitutional opposition by the sovereign courts. The way in which the commissions of the intendants developed, therefore, was a practical attempt to resolve this problem of creating an effective administrative institution without undermining the appellate aspect of the French judicial system and the liberties and immunities of Frenchmen that it was supposed to protect.

What was a commission? The original document which was handed over to the intendant was written on parchment, and sealed with the king's great seal.[1] Scarcely any of the originals survive: the intendants guarded them jealously during their lifetime and preserved them among their private papers.[2] The destruction of private papers subsequently has meant the loss, among other things, of the commissions. Minutes and copies of the commissions were kept, however. Firstly, by the various secretaries of state, both as a record of the powers accorded to the intendants and as a guide to the phrasing of any commissions that might be issued subsequently. Secondly, the intendants not infrequently registered their commissions in the provinces, at the local *bailliage* or occasionally in the *Parlement*. There was no obligation on them to do so; but some of the intendants recognized support for Loyseau's claim that no-one was obliged to recognize or obey a commissioner who did not register his powers in the locality.[3]

The wording of the commission began with a formal greeting to the recipient: 'Louis, par la grâce de Dieu, roy de France et de Navarre, à notre amé et féal conseiller ordinaire en nostre conseil d'état, le Sieur . . ., Salut.' General reasons were then produced as to the need for the appointment of an intendant.

---

[1] B.N. p.o. 2789 (Dr. 62,029), no. 421, 6 Sept. 1653, commission of Claude Talon as *intendant des finances* in the army commanded by Turenne. (Original, parchment with seal.)

[2] cf. the collection of commissions and powers kept by Bernard de Besançon, sieur du Plessis, brother of an intendant appointed by Richelieu: B.N. p.o. 320, nos. 40–73, passim.

[3] Charles Loyseau, *Cinq livres du droit des offices* (ed. 1613), p. 569.

The commission of Isaac Laffemas in the Limousin in 1634 was issued because of a threatened 'entreprise au préjudice du repos de noz bons et fidelles subiectz' by the supporters of the Queen Mother and Gaston d'Orléans;[1] that of Claude Vignier in 1636 was issued because of 'les grandes affaires que les entreprises de nos ennemis, qui sont entrez en nostre royaulme de costé de la Picardye, nous ont apportés'.[2] The commission made an obligatory reference to the qualities of the person chosen as intendant. Thus Voyer d'Argenson was commissioned as intendant at Poitiers in 1644 because the king declared himself unable to 'faire un meilleur choix que de vous pour cet employ pour nous avoir fidèllement et dignement servy en plusieurs charges, commissions et négotiations importantes dedans et dehors notre royaume mesmes en Allemagne, Italie et Catalogne dont il nous demeure une entière satisfaction et pour les preuves que vous y avez rendues de votre capacité, expérience au faict de la justice, police et finances, probité, prudence, vigilance, fidélité et affection à notre service . . .'[3]

Thereafter, the formal delegation of authority was explicitly stated: 'nous vous avons commis, ordonné et député, commettons, ordonnons et députons par ces présentes [lettres] signées de notre main, intendant de la justice, police et finances en nostredite province [ou généralité] de . . .' The commission conveyed a remuneration as well as a right of precedence. The intendant was allowed to benefit from the 'honneurs, auctoritez, prérogatives et pré-éminences qui y appartiennent et aux appointemens qui vous seront ordonnez par nos états . . .' The formal powers of the commission then followed. Very great variations were possible here, but they might include the right to preside over the inferior courts, the *bureau des finances*, and the municipal elections; the right of hearing grievances and attempting to remedy these; the power of prosecuting those guilty of conspiracy to commit rebellion or infringement of the ordinances. The commission was then restated: 'vous donnons pouvoir, auctorité, commission et mandement spécial par ces

---

[1] A.G. A1 21, no. 146, 22 July 1634.
[2] H. d'Arbois de Jubainville, *L'administration des intendants d'après les archives de l'Aube* (1880), pp. 203–5.
[3] A.G. A1 86, no. 113, 1 Apr. 1644.

présentes . . .' and a 'derogation clause', sometimes referred to as the *nonobstances*, followed.[1] After this followed a 'mandatory clause': 'mandons à tous nos officiers et subjects qu'il appartiendra de vous recognoistre et obéyr'—sometimes in this context, the governor, the local officials, and tribunals were specified. The commission was then declared to be the express wish of the king, 'car tel est notre plaisir'. The place of issue of the commission—usually the residence of the king, not necessarily the king's council—was specified, as was the date and year of the reign. Finally, the commission was signed 'par le Roy, Louis', and countersigned by a secretary of state.[2]

Over seventy commissions have survived from the period of Richelieu and Mazarin, and over a hundred from the longer period *c*. 1560 to 1690. While certain formulae remained standard throughout the years from 1560 to 1690, important developments nevertheless took place. It is important to recognize that developments in the powers accorded by the commissions were rarely uniform: local circumstances in one province might require much stronger powers for an intendant than was the case elsewhere at the same time; other provinces might lag obstinately and stubbornly behind. The idiosyncrasies may also have resulted from the fact that while some commissions were very carefully prepared by the secretaries of state over a period of months, others were rushed through in a few days and based on earlier commissions.[3] Differences between the commissions may therefore not necessarily reflect a change in government policy. A division into nine chronological periods is possible (before 1589; 1589–1610; 1610–27; 1628–34; 1635–42; 1643–8; 1648–52; 1653–61; after 15 September 1661) and a study of the general characteristics of the commissions in each period repays attention. The essential

[1] 'Nonobstant toutes récusations, prises à parties, édictz, ordonnances et toutes autres choses à ce contraire'—a declaration of the supremacy of the commission over common law practice.
[2] cf. the description of letters patent by Michaud, *La grande chancellerie*, pp. 213–216.
[3] Le Prévost d'Herbelay's commission at Lyon in 1635 was simply a reworking of the commission of Amelot de Chaillou (1629): A.G. A1 26, no. 194. In contrast, there was correspondence between Bullion and Sublet des Noyers and a long delay in drawing up the commission of Laisné for the Dauphiné in 1638: A.G. A1 49, no. 257, 1 Apr. 1638.

aspect of the commissions is their great variety—their flexibility is one reason why the intendants were so important. The first group of commissions cover the years from 1560 to 1588: the commissioners and intendants of Catherine de Médicis and Henri III. The essential characteristic of these is that while an *intendance* or a *surintendance de justice* might be conferred, no mention was made of the three powers of justice, *police*, and finance. This is not to deny that some of the commissioners had financial responsibilities. De Mesmes at Lyon in 1572 was empowered to investigate cases of peculation and issue definitive sentences.[1] The commissioners of 1582 were required to investigate local financial administration back to 1574 (that is to say, when the previous investigation had been terminated) and their decisions were declared equivalent to those of the *conseil privé*.[2] However, an extraordinary financial investigation every decade or so was clearly not a regular *intendance de finance* or an annual presidency in the *bureau des finances*. Nor was there a clearly established *intendance de police*. The commission of Villeneuve and Borvallière in Brittany[3] and that of Jean-Jacques II de Mesmes at Lyon conferred a presidency over the municipality: but it is known that this was bitterly resented at Lyon, and was the reason why Mesmes failed. The major purpose of all the commissions (with the exception of the commissioners sent out in 1582 before the Assembly of Notables) was judicial, the right to preside over the *bailliages* being accorded in all the commissions as also the requirement on the intendants to 'pourveoir aux plainctifz et leur faire bonne et prompte raison [justice] sans exception'. The commissions of Mesmes at Lyon and Villeneuve and Borvallière in Brittany reveal an important difference between the authority of the intendants in prosecutions relating to crimes of rebellion and those concerning peculation. In the first, they could not issue a definitive sentence or pronounce on guilt or innocence; in the second they could. In both types of case, however, they could ignore common-law procedure

---

[1] Pallasse, *Sénéchaussée de Lyon*, pp. 433–5.

[2] Hanotaux, *Origines*, pp. 187–97. For the previous financial investigation, terminated in Dec. 1573: cf. Z1a 157, fo. 49, declaration of 12 Dec. 1573, registered by the *cour des aides* of Paris, 18 Dec. 1573.

[3] S. Canal, *Les origines de l'intendance de Bretagne. Essai sur les relations de la Bretagne avec le pouvoir central* (Rennes, 1911), pp. 207–12.

and overrule appeals in the first instance. In most of the commissions issued at this time, the jurisdiction over appeals was reserved to the king's council. Without exception, any definitive sentence had to be issued by the intendant when presiding at an *ad hoc* tribunal comprising the number of office-holders required by the ordinances (usually a minimum of seven). The intendants could not issue such sentences on their own authority.

The second group of commissions, dating from 1589 to 1610, shows a very uneven development. The powers of the intendants at Lyon were developed most fully, doubtless because of the continuous presence of intendants there after 1597 but not elsewhere. The powers accorded in the other provinces were often weaker than those enjoyed by their predecessors during the Regency of Catherine de Médicis and the reign of Henri III. Again, all the commissioners in question were called *surintendants* or *intendants de justice*—even at Lyon, where their financial powers were developed most fully. Two intendants— Hurault de l'Hôpital at Aix in 1595[1] and Robert Miron in the Auvergne, the Bourbonnais, and the Marche in 1599[2]—clearly could not issue sentences equivalent to those of the sovereign courts; nor was jurisdiction in appeals from their sentences reserved to the council. De l'Hôpital could attempt merely to resolve the 'plainctes en charge de nostre pauvre peuple'; his authority was confined to that of sending reports to the king's council. Miron, a *conseiller* in the *Parlement* of Paris since 14 October 1595, remained essentially a delegate of that court, although he had received a commission from the king: his sentences had the same standing as those of the lesser courts, that is to say, they could be modified by the *Parlement* of Paris. The powers of Pierre d'Amours at Troyes were wider in that he could suspend office-holders accused of peculation; his judgements were declared equivalent to those of a *Parlement* and jurisdiction over appeals was reserved to the king's council.[3] Other commissions, such as that of Camus de Pontcarré in Guyenne, conferred powers chiefly to 'vacquer et entendre au

[1] A.D. Bouches-du-Rhône B 3339, fo. 92ᵛ, 23 Sept. 1595.
[2] X1a 8643, fos. 301, 395, 1 Feb. 1599.
[3] Arbois de Jubainville, op. cit., pp. 194–7.

faict de la justice [soit civile et criminelle]' in close co-operation
with the provincial governor or lieutenant-general.[1]

The commissions of the intendants at Lyon—Méric de Vic
in 1597[2] and Guillaume de Montholon in 1607[3]—were the
only ones to contain a wide range of powers in this period,
including the presidency over the municipality, a defined
relationship with the governor, the authority to discipline
office-holders by suspending them from office and the power to
prosecute those involved in conspiracy to commit rebellion.
In a case of conspiracy, the intendant, as president of an *ad
hoc* tribunal, could issue definitive sentences which were not
subject to appeal in the sovereign courts. In addition, Méric de
Vic had significant financial powers. He was ordered to investigate all levies of taxation over the previous ten years, that is
to say, back to 1587. He was empowered to prosecute those
accused of levying excessive taxes, either issuing a definitive
sentence himself, or else sending the case to the local *cour des
aides* for sentence to be passed. The commission of Vic—the
summit of institutional developments in this direction in the
sixteenth century—was to have a formative influence. Many of
the powers accorded to Vic were to be included in the commissions of the intendants at the time of Richelieu and Mazarin.

The commissions issued in the years between the death of
Henry IV in 1610 and the surrender of La Rochelle (28 October 1628) were in important respects more limited than the
one issued to Méric de Vic in 1597. One tendency was to issue
very short and inexplicit commissions—Lefèvre de Boissy in
1615 was merely given powers similar to those enjoyed by his
father as intendant of Picardy in 1597.[4] As defined in a second
commission, conferred on Boissy in 1623,[5] the task of the intendant of Picardy was essentially to guard the frontier against
Spanish invasion: the provincial intendant could serve also as
intendant of the army. A second tendency in the commissions

[1] A. Petracchi, *Intendenti e prefetti. L'intendente provinciale nella Francia d'Antico Regime. I. 1551–1648* (Milan, 1971), pp. 45–6. B.N. MS.fr. 18752, fo. 1, 18 Apr. 1595.
[2] Pallasse, *Sénéchaussée de Lyon*, pp. 444–8.
[3] B.N. MS.fr. 16218, fo. 459, 22 Feb. 1607. Contrast A.D. Puy-de-Dôme B Clermont 94, fos. 74–7, 12 Sept. 1607, commission of Jacques Mérault (Auvergne).
[4] Esmonin, *Études*, p. 48. A.D. Somme 1B 17, 7 Sept. 1615.
[5] Esmonin, *Études*, pp. 49–50.

during this period was to restrict the powers of the intendant to issuing provisional rulings and sending reports to the Chancellor. This was the case with Gourges in Guyenne and Poitou *c.* 1616;[1] with Bitault de Chizé in Bas Languedoc in 1618:[2] with Pierre Séguier in the Auvergne (27 April 1621);[3] and with Lauzon in Normandy in 1626.[4] Lauzon's commission is especially interesting because it is an example of Richelieu's limited concept of the role of the intendants in the early years of his ministry. Lauzon recalled his experience in Normandy twenty-two years later, arguing that the traditional circuit-tours of the *maîtres des requêtes* had been 'très judicieusement estably'. He had had very limited powers indeed, 'ne faisant nulle action de justice ny nulle fonction sinon de tenir le sceau près du Parlement et tenir souvent les audiences en tous les sièges'. Lauzon reflected on the growth of the powers of the intendants since 1626, on the outbreak of the Fronde and recall of the intendants when he wrote: 'je confesse qu'il seroit à desirer que les intendants n'en fissent pas davantage'.[5]

Three commissions in the years between the death of Henri IV and the surrender of La Rochelle reveal new tendencies which were to be significant later. The first is the commission of Guillaume de Montholon in Poitou in 1617 which included powers to 'cognoistre du faict de noz finances' and a right of presidency in the *bureau des finances*. This was the first commission of an intendant to confer this power outside the *généralité* of Lyon. Apparently Montholon was not called anything more than an *intendant de justice*, however.[6] The commission of Pierre Séguier as intendant of the army in the Limousin, Saintonge, and Aunis (4 July 1621) was important in that for the first time the three powers of justice, *police*, and finance were clearly expressed. Certainly, Séguier's role was chiefly confined to that of intendant in the army, giving advice to the duc d'Épernon much as his uncle had done in 1586. Séguier's chief concern was with the suppression of disorder in the army,

---

[1] Hanotaux, *Origines*, pp. 234–5.
[2] A.D. Haute-Garonne B 1913, fo. 130, 10 July 1618.
[3] Hanotaux, *Origines*, pp. 244–7. B.N. Joly de Fleury 2508, fo. 158.
[4] B.N. MS.fr. 22463, pp. 175–6, 12 July 1626.
[5] Loirette, 'Un intendant', p. 460. Renaud, 'Correspondance', pp. 347–8.
[6] Hanotaux, *Origines*, pp. 237–43. A.G. A1 13, nos. 87, 88 and O1 11, fo. 34
Cf. 115 AP 2, no. 308, 27 Sept. 1617, which confirms the year of the commission.

and his financial powers were essentially restricted to the tasks of military finance. He could, however, give some attention to civil matters in the geographical area in which the army operated, for he had a power to 'cognoistre de tous les délicts, abus et malversations qui seront commises en ladicte armée ou proche des lieux où elle séjournera . . .' It was an important commission, exercising a formative influence on later developments.[1]

The next group of commissions, issued in the years between 1628 and 1635, reveals a strengthening of the powers of the intendants that coincided with the *grand tournant* of Richelieu's ministry. For the first time, a number of provincial intendants were given the three powers of justice, *police*, and finance. The area left open to appeals against the sentences of the intendants was severely restricted. The decrees and sentences issued by the intendants were declared unequivocally to be equivalent to those issued by the sovereign courts and thus subject to appeal in the king's council only. The three powers of justice, *police*, and finance were enjoyed by Turquant d'Aubeterre at Lyon between 1627 and 1629 and by his successor, Amelot de Chaillou. These three powers were given also to Coignet de La Thuillerie, the intendant of Poitou and Saintonge appointed after the fall of La Rochelle to the royalist army in 1628. La Thuillerie enjoyed most of the powers that had been given to Méric de Vic at Lyon in 1597—but in addition, he had clearly defined rights of presidency in the *bureaux des finances* of Poitiers and Limoges. He was also empowered to organize payments to the troops and to negotiate the contracts with entrepreneurs for the demolition of the fortifications of La Rochelle.[2]

The commission of Amelot de Chaillou is particularly interesting. If Lauzon in Normandy in 1626 was the type of intendant Richelieu apparently would have favoured, Amelot was very definitely the type of intendant he disliked. For some reason, Amelot was ordered specifically to 'résider en nostre-dicte ville de Lyon qui est la capitalle de ladicte province'— the very aspect of an intendant's functions that Richelieu

[1] Hanotaux, *Origines*, pp. 248–50. It was repeated virtually word for word in the first commission issued after Richelieu's rise to power on 13 Aug. 1624, which appointed Claude de Bullion as intendant in Lesdiguières's army in the Dauphiné: Petracchi, op. cit., p. 55. B.N. MS. fr. 26477, fo. 53, 13 Aug. 1624.

[2] Hanotaux, *Origines*, pp. 282–9.

considered 'peut plus servir à leur vanité qu'a l'utilité du public . . .' Lyon was a town of exceptional importance, but even so, this clause had not been contained in the commission of Méric de Vic thirty-two years earlier. Amelot's fiscal powers were much more explicitly phrased than those of his predecessor in the reign of Henri IV, and it was probably for this reason that residence in the town was considered necessary. He could preside over the *bureau des finances* 'lorsque nostre service le requérera et principallement à l'assiette des deniers qui se levent sur noz subiectz'.[1]

There were three important differences between Amelot's commission and that conferred on René I Voyer d'Argenson in the Auvergne, the Limousin, and the Marche in 1632.[2] Firstly, there was no clause ordering residence in a capital town, which would in any case scarcely have been practicable since Argenson was given three provinces 'et autres provinces adjacentes et circonvoisines' and a roving commission to find evidence of conspiracy against the crown. Secondly, Argenson's commission contained a specific clause concerning 'homicides, assassinatz, rebellions à justice, malefices, empoissonnements et sorceleries'. Persons accused of such crimes could be prosecuted by an *ad hoc* tribunal under Argenson's presidency, and a definitive sentence issued. This may indicate a witch-scare in south-west France, but in the present state of knowledge it is impossible to state reasons for these unusual powers. Thirdly, a clause in the commission ordered Argenson to continue prosecutions against the financial officials in the *généralité* of Limoges at which he had been working since 1629.[3]

The remaining commissions issued before the French declaration of war against Spain reveal the variety of powers accorded to the intendants at this time. Although they had additional financial tasks, some of the intendants received commissions as *intendants de justice* only, which was scarcely logical. This was the case with Noel Brûlart, who investigated the *ferme des gabelles* in the Lyonnais, the Dauphiné, Provence, and the *douane* of Valence in 1633.[4] It was the case also with regard to

[1] A.G. A1 26, no. 194, 15 Jan. 1629. Cf. Richelieu, *Testament politique*, ed. André, pp. 246–7.
[2] Hanotaux, *Origines*, pp. 316–21. A.G. A1 14, no. 32, 12 Aug. 1632.
[3] cf. E 104, fo. 407, 18 Sept. 1630. V6 73, no. 9, 24 Nov. 1629. V6 76, no. 1, 26 Feb. 1630. [4] E 1684, fo. 536, 27 May 1633.

the commissioners sent out for the *régalement des tailles* in 1634.[1] Their rulings were provisional, and only some of the commissioners received additional powers as intendants of finance, conveying the right to preside over the *bureaux des finances*. In a special category was the commission of Isaac Laffemas in 1633. Laffemas was both a provincial intendant in Champagne and an intendant of the army in Metz, Toul, Verdun, 'et autres lieux en notre obéissance et protection et partout ailleurs où noz armées se pourront estendre'. This was the type of commission which, with variations, was to become a frequent occurrence in northern France during the Thirty Years War. As intendant in the army, Laffemas was in charge of prosecutions for ill-discipline, financial arrangements for the army, and above all, munitions. The concern for *subsistances* led to close contact with the locality: Laffemas was ordered to preside in the town councils and to 'conférer avec eux . . . des moyens qu'il fauldra tenir pour empescher . . . la disette des vivres et procurer l'abondance èz lieux où noz armées passeront . . .' At the same time, however, there was a particular political aspect to Laffemas's intendancy. The French military offensive on the north-east frontier was the result of political factors— the self-imposed exile of Gaston d'Orléans, his secret marriage to Marguerite de Lorraine, and his invasion of France in 1632 with Habsburg support. For this reason, a special place was given in Laffemas's commission to his powers of prosecution, and in order to facilitate his prosecutions, he was accorded the power of nominating subordinates: 'subdéléguer telz de noz juges et officiers que vous adviserez pour continuer les informations que vous aurez commencez ou les faire èz lieux où vous ne pourrez vacquer . . .' That Laffemas was regarded as *le bourreau du Cardinal de Richelieu* is not surprising in view of the powers of prosecution he was given in Champagne in 1633 and in the Limousin a year later—both these commissions conferred wider powers to Laffemas then was the case with the majority of the intendants.[2]

Not surprisingly, the commissions that have survived from the next period, the war years of Richelieu's ministry from 1635 to

---

[1] A.G. A1 21, no. 121, 25 May 1634.
[2] A.G. A1 14, no. 44, 6 Feb. 1633. A.G. A1 21, no. 146, 22 July 1634.

1642, show a much greater involvement with the army than hitherto. Many of the commissions also included powers to verify the debts of the municipalities. It would be anachronistic to expect uniformity in the financial powers of the intendants before 1642. Villemontée's commission in Poitou in 1637, the model for the officials sent out from Paris for the levy of the forced loan on the towns, gave him authority to take 'cognoissance de toutes les affaires générallement quelconques concernant noz finances' and included a presidency over the *bureau des finances* and the *élections*, yet his powers over the troops seem to have been restricted.[1] On the other hand, François Bochart in Provence and Le Tonnelier de Conty in the Limousin in the same year seem to have enjoyed more limited financial powers, yet much wider authority with regard to the troops.[2] Although without exception the intendants were given the three powers of justice, *police*, and finance, it is clear that what was meant by these terms depended greatly on local circumstances and nuances in the wording of the commissions. The title of intendant of finance did not of itself make the commissioner a financial administrator; it might simply confer the power of ascertaining whether the financial administrators were performing their tasks satisfactorily. Nor did it necessarily confer a presidency over the *bureau des finances*. Le Maistre de Bellejambe was an intendant of justice, *police*, and finance at Amiens on 12 March 1636;[3] but the *trésoriers* refused him the presidency over their bureau because his commission contained no reference to this power. The intendant had to obtain a decree of the *conseil privé* on 8 July 1636 to enforce his rights in this respect.[4] The commission of Jeannin de Castille in Champagne (1 August 1642) underlines the importance of the decisions of the king's council in the last year of Richelieu's ministry, when the intendants were transformed into financial administrators. A decree of 14 May 1642 had empowered Jeannin's predecessor, Bretel de Grémonville, together with two *trésoriers*, to draw up lists of the arrears of the *généralité* of Châlons from 1635 to 1640. This task was formally transferred

[1] A.G. A1 41, no. 257, 30 Mar. 1637.   [2] A.G. A1 42, no. 135, 29 May 1637.
[3] C. V. E. Boyer de Sainte-Suzanne, *L'administration sous l'ancien régime. Les intendants de la généralité d'Amiens (Picardie et Artois)* (1865), pp. 572–5. A.D. Somme 1B 21, fo. 172ᵛ, 12 Mar. 1636.
[4] Deyon, *Amiens*, p. 447 n. 35. V6 114 no. 20, 8 July 1636.

to Jeannin on 22 August, the day of the important ruling on the *taille*: but twenty-one days earlier, Jeannin had already been empowered by his commission to 'faire accélérer le recouvrement de noz deniers, tant les tailles que subsistances et autres impositions . . .',[1] powers which were made general throughout the *pays d'élections* on 19 August 1642.

The relationship between the intendants and the sovereign courts was clarified by the fact that the sentences of the intendants were declared subject to appeal in the king's council only, and by the specific clause in their commissions which instructed the intendants to send to the local courts those matters which could safely or usefully be delegated. Few intendants had an automatic right of entry into the local *Parlements* and sovereign courts, except in their capacity as *maîtres des requêtes*. Laisné in the Dauphiné in 1638[2] was the exception to the rule that such powers were conferred by additional letters patent,[3] or else conferred by the local sovereign court as a special mark of esteem of the intendant,[4] rather than as a standard aspect of the commission.

Remarkable, and in many respects unique among the commissions of this period, were the powers accorded to Étienne Foullé in Guyenne on 25 August 1637.[5] He was ordered to levy the forced loan on the towns and to preside over the *bureaux des finances* and *élections* in order to achieve this. The preamble of the commission, however, made it clear that the fundamental purpose of his intendancy was the suppression of the revolt of the *Croquants* of Périgord and Quercy, 'émotions populaires arrivées depuis quelque temps en ça par la sollicitation de noz ennemis . . .' On his own authority, Foullé could prosecute leaders of the revolt, although he had to preside over an *ad hoc* tribunal of seven in order to issue definitive sentences. The tribunal could order the demolition of houses belonging to

---

[1] Arbois de Jubainville, *Intendants de l'Aube*, pp. 208–10. E 173a, fo. 328, 22 Aug. 1642. Cf. the commission for Barrin (Bourges): A.A.E. France 839, fo. 388, 15 Dec. 1641.

[2] A.G. A1 49, no. 257, 1 Apr. 1638.

[3] This power was conferred frequently on the intendants of Provence. Lauzon: A.D. Bouches-du-Rhône B 3351, fo. 6, 27 July 1636; Vautorte: B 3352, fo. 835, 14 May 1640; Champigny: B 3354 fo. 219ᵛ, 3 July 1643.

[4] Miron at Toulouse: A.D. Haute-Garonne B 534, fo. 55, Aug. 1633; Bezons at Toulouse: B.L. Harleian 4442, fo. 107ᵛ, 18 Nov. 1659.

[5] B.N. Joly de Fleury 2508, fo. 162.

persons implicated in the revolt, but such orders could be carried out only with the agreement of duc d'Épernon, the governor. Proceedings against suspects could be commenced by delegates of Foullé: in particular, the intendant chose Helye de la Fon, a *président* in the *présidial* of Cahors, for this purpose.[1] Foullé was ordered to employ a secretary who was to keep secret all papers relating to the prosecutions. Whereas Foullé's sentences in civil cases were subject to appeal in the king's council, those issued in criminal cases were not subject to appeal at all. Clearly, the terms of the commission implied a separate tribunal for the sentencing of crimes of rebellion for the period in which Foullé served as intendant. The nature of the intendant's tasks implied use of the troops: the duc d'Épernon, the governor, his son the duc de la Valette, and D'Espenan, a *maréchal de camp* commanding the troops against the rebels, were all ordered to assist Foullé in his duties. For his personal safety, the intendant was allowed to carry fire-arms.

The most important development in the commissions had already occurred by the time of Richelieu's death on 4 December 1642. The question remains whether or not the death of Louis XIII and the establishment of the Regency on 18 May 1643 seriously affected the powers accorded to the intendants. The crucial issue was the status of the sentences issued by the intendants in their capacity as presidents of *ad hoc* tribunals dealing with cases of conspiracy to commit rebellion. All the commissions that have survived indicate that these sentences were considered to be definitive, equivalent to those issued by the sovereign courts, and subject to appeal in the king's council only.[2] The commission of Henri Gamin at Amiens in 1646 was exceptional in that it distinguished between sentences on charges of conspiracy, and sentences issued by the local *bailliage* under the presidency of the intendant on 'affaires civiles et criminelles qui sy traiteront soit en l'audience ou en la chambre du conseil'. In the first instance, the sentences were definitive,

---

[1] V6 136, no. 23, 25 Feb. 1639.

[2] But cf. below, chapter XI on the implications of the ruling of 16 June 1644: the sovereign courts might be allowed to hear appeals in cases arising from recent legislation, but only if such legislation had been registered without amendments. In practice, this situation did not arise, since the courts modified such legislation, for example on the *taille*.

subject to appeal in the king's council only; in the second, they were not, and appeals could go before the sovereign courts.[1] However, there was no mention of such a clause in the commission of François Bochart as intendant at Lyon in 1647:[2] both Bochart and Gamin were intendants within the geographical area of the *Parlement* of Paris. Nor did the other sovereign courts gain any such concessions, as is evidenced by the commissions of Heere in the Dauphiné in 1647[3] and that of de Sève in Provence in the same year[4]—respectively within the jurisdictions of the *Parlements* of Grenoble and Aix. The sentences of the intendants of Anne of Austria and Mazarin were subject to appeals in the king's council only, as had been the case with the intendants of Louis XIII and Richelieu. The intendants of Provence—François Bochart in 1643 and Sève three years later—were in an even stronger position with regard to the sovereign courts, since their commissions gave them the authority to enter these courts 'pour y conférer et prendre les résolutions utiles au bien de notre service èz choses qui concernent l'administration de la justice, police et direction de noz finances'.

All the commissions issued between 1643 and 1648 conferred authority to the intendants over the troops. The powers enjoyed by Le Picard at Soissons in 1643 were relatively slight;[5] those enjoyed by the intendants at Amiens, Limoges, Lyon, Poitiers, Tours, and in Languedoc and Provence were wider; but the commissions concerning the Dauphiné were exceptional in that Foucquet and Chaulnes in 1643,[6] Yvon de Lozières in 1644,[7] and Heere in 1647 were all called intendants in both the province and the army. Almost all the commissions —the exceptions being Bochart de Champigny in Provence in 1643 and Gamin at Amiens in 1646—conferred on the intendants a right of presidency over the municipalities at the time of elections, and not infrequently powers of investigation over municipal expenditure too. Most of the commissions included powers to verify the debts of the towns.

[1] A.D. Somme 1B 24, fo. 173. A.G. A1 96, no. 152, 2 Dec. 1646.
[2] *Lettres . . . au Chancelier Séguier*, ed. Mousnier, ii. 1079–83.
[3] Esmonin, *Études*, pp. 84–6. O1 11, fo. 38ᵛ. B.N. MS.fr. 4176, fo. 127.
[4] A.A.E. France 1712, fo. 264, 29 Oct. 1647.
[5] *Lettres . . . au Chancelier Séguier*, ed. Mousnier, ii. 1062–5.
[6] ibid., ii. 1065–7.   [7] A.G. A1 86, nos. 218, 219, 26 July 1644.

Almost all the intendants were given powers to preside over
the *bureaux des finances*. The exception was Bautru de Serrant
in 1643:[1] but he was a second intendant in the province, and
it is likely that his colleague, Heere, presided over the *bureau des
finances* at Tours, while Bautru was chiefly concerned with the
élections in Anjou which had no separate *bureau des finances*. A
variety of phrases were used in the commissions to describe the
financial powers accorded to the intendants. François Bochart
in Provence was empowered simply to 'prendre cognoissance
de toutes levées de deniers'; eight commissions included the
longer phrase 'prendre cognoissance de tout ce qui concerne
nos finances et de toutes levées de nos deniers'; Faucon de Ris at
Lyon,[2] and Vautorte at Limoges[3] in 1643 were ordered to 'avoir
l'œil à tout ce qui concerne les levées de nos deniers . . .' It
seems unlikely that such nuances in phraseology carried great
significance. It was more serious, however, when they were
omitted altogether—as was the case with Foucquet and
Chaulnes in the Dauphiné in 1643 and Lozières in the same
province a year later, although on 21 May 1644 Foucquet was
empowered by a decree of the council of finance to investigate
excessive levies of taxation since 1 January 1630.[4] The commission of Le Picard at Soissons (30 June 1643) is of particular
interest since it alluded to the recent rulings on the *taille* less
than a month before the decree of registration was issued by
the *cour des aides* of Paris. It is unlikely that such an explicit
reference to a controversial piece of financial legislation was
made within the commission of an intendant thereafter.
Instead the more neutral phrase 'observer et faire observer
exactement les ordonnances et reiglements sur le faict . . . des
tailles' was used.

The commissions issued between 1643 and 1648 reveal a much
greater uniformity of powers than hitherto and suggest a
clearly established system of administration by intendants.
What of the commissions issued in the years 1648–52, during the
political upheaval of the Fronde? Is a continuity of powers

[1] *L'histoire vue de l'Anjou*, ed. Le Brun, i. 129–32.
[2] *Lettres . . . au Chancelier Séguier*, ed. Mousnier, ii. 1059–62.
[3] A.G. A1 86, no. 28, 26 May 1643.
[4] E 190b, fo. 176, 21 May 1644.

traceable, or were the commissions issued during these years a backward step from developments since 1630? The first and most important point is that the government was extremely reluctant to grant commissions at all during the Fronde. Châteauneuf, the Keeper of the Seals, was of the opinion in March 1650 that it was preferable to issue simply a *lettre de cachet*; in such cases the crown reserved the power to issue a commission 'en cas de besoin',[1] but in the meantime it sought to avoid the odium attaching to the name of intendant during the Fronde.

Nevertheless, a variety of commissions were drawn up by the secretaries of state, and some of these were actually issued. Chaulnes may have been sent to Provence simply with a *lettre de cachet*; but a commission was drawn up to which presumably he could have had recourse had the need arisen. This commission empowered Chaulnes to enter the sovereign courts; to 'prendre cognoissance de toutes levées de deniers'; as president of an *ad hoc* tribunal, to prosecute troops accused of ill-discipline; above all, to continue the *commissions particulières* accorded to François Bochart and Sève, his predecessors, including the task of verification of municipal debts. The judgements issued by Chaulnes were declared equivalent to those of the sovereign courts, and jurisdiction over appeals was reserved to the king's council.[2] Whether or not the commission was used, therefore, it provides important evidence as to the intentions of the ministers during the Fronde. A second type of commission was that issued to Henri Gamin in Picardy probably in April 1650. The main purpose of the commission was to remedy grievances of the local population caused by troop movements along the frontier with the Spanish Netherlands. However, the precise nature of his powers were left equivocal by the commission. He was given authority to 'prendre cognoissance des impositions' including the *taille* and the *subsistances*. He was empowered to investigate municipal expenditure and the accounts of the local *receveurs*. Finally, he was ordered to 'prendre cognoissance des affaires dont les

[1] A.A.E. France 870, fo. 267ᵛ, 22 Mar. 1650. Servien and Le Tellier conveyed to Mazarin Châteauneuf's opinions concerning the projected appointment of De Chaulnes as commissioner in Provence.
[2] A.A.E. France 1713, fo. 353.

153

maistres des requestes . . . peuvent s'entremettre suivant leur ancienne constitution'. The precise nature of these powers were left vague. No mention was made of Gamin's powers of sentencing, or the jurisdiction in appeals from his sentences.[1]

Both Provence and Picardy were provinces excluded from the recall of the intendants on 18 July 1648. Gamin's geographical area included the Soissonnais and the *pays nouvellement reconquis* (the present Pas-de-Calais) as well as Picardy, which explains perhaps why his powers appear to have been those of a *maître des requêtes* on circuit-tour, for the intendants were officially prohibited from the Soissonnais. Even within the six provinces where the intendants were allowed, they seem to have exercised their powers with some circumspection. Additional commissions gave them the control of the frontier areas—Gamin had the *places frontières* of Picardy on 12 November 1648,[2] Le Tonnelier de Breteuil had Roussillon in addition to Languedoc on 5 November 1649,[3] and Tallement had the same areas on 25 September 1651[4]—as the main justification for their activities. What of the provinces where the intendants were officially prohibited? Foullé in the Limousin in January 1650 had a brief *lettre de cachet* empowering him to carry out the functions of an *intendant des finances* and a *maître des requêtes* on circuit-tour.[5] Pierre Gargan had a commission in March 1650 which authorized him in his capacity as an *intendant des finances* to go to Languedoc and Guyenne and 'négotier et traicter en nostre nom avec noz officiers de noz cours souveraines et autres de tout ce qui concerne l'avancement et la levée du payement de noz deniers . . .'[6] The instructions of De Creil, a *maître des requêtes* on circuit-tour in Poitou, in 1652 covered infringements of the ordinances, authority to visit the lesser courts, the *bureau des finances*, and the *élections*, and the power to prosecute cases of ill-discipline among the troops.[7]

The majority of the commissions conferred authority to the

[1] A.G. A1 32, no. 247, misdated 1636, 'la datte est équivoque'. Cf. A.G. A1 122, no. 190, 2 Sept. 1650.
[2] B.N. MS.fr. 4178, fo. 162, 12 Nov. 1648.
[3] *Lettres . . . au Chancelier Séguier*, ed. Mousnier, ii. 1087–9.
[4] A.G. A1 125, no. 193, 25 Sept. 1651.
[5] B.N. MS.fr. 4181, fos. 1–3, 4 Jan. 1650.
[6] A.G. A1 121, no. 288, 3 Mar. 1650.
[7] B.N. MS.fr. 4184, fos. 66-7, Apr. 1652.

intendants within the armies operating in provinces where the intendants were officially prohibited in 1648. Some of the commissions—such as those of Denis Marin in the army of Louis XIV in Guyenne (25 September 1651)[1] and Claude Talon in the army of Saintonge (11 May 1652)[2]—conveyed financial but not judicial powers. Others—notably Heere in the army of Louis XIV in Touraine (26 September 1651),[3] Bazin de Bezons in the army of Berry (25 October 1651),[4] Pontac's first commission in the army of Guyenne (12 April 1652),[5] and Guillaume de Bordeaux in the army of Turenne and Hocquincourt in Guyenne (30 April 1952)[6]—included all three powers. These intendants acted in many respects as had their predecessors in the first years of Mazarin's ministry, and as presidents of *ad hoc* tribunals, they could issue definitive sentences without appeal. The powers of the intendant inevitably spread beyond the army, however, since the troops were needed for political reasons—to suppress the revolt of Condé after 7 September 1651. It was likely therefore that the intendants' powers of prosecution would extend beyond the army to include those whose activities had led to the arrival of the troops in the first place. Although ostensibly an intendant in the army, Heere appeared to be continuing as provincial intendant of the Touraine—the position he had enjoyed before the Fronde. Thus the specific terms of the commissions in the later stages of the Fronde were not necessarily an indication of the true authority enjoyed by the intendants: what mattered were the local political circumstances, the prestige of the intendant, and the commitment of the ministers to a return to the *status quo ante* 1648.

The commissions issued between 1653 and 1661 do not show the same degree of uniformity that had characterized the commissions in the years between 1643 and 1648. Nevertheless, it is clear from the commissions issued in 1653 and after that the

---

[1] A.G. A1 125, no. 192 and A1 126, fo. 471.

[2] A.G. A1 132, no. 302.

[3] A.G. A1 125, no. 194.

[4] A.G. A1 125, no. 196.

[5] A.G. A1 132, no. 300 and A1 135, fo. 183. Cf. his later commission (18 May 1652) as intendant of justice and police only: A.G. A1 132, no. 303.

[6] A.G. A1 132, no. 301 and A1 135, fo. 210[v].

financial powers of the intendants were essentially those conferred by the declaration of 16 April 1643. In August 1653
Bernard Fortia at Poitiers was instructed to go into the *élections*
and 'procéder . . . aux départements desdites impositions sans
attendre attache [des trésoriers]';[1] Lefèvre de la Barre in the
Dauphiné in 1654 was instructed to levy the *taille* assisted by the
trésoriers and the *élus*, and was empowered to preside over the
trésoriers 'toutes et quantes fois qu'il le jugera à propos';[2]
Lefèvre d'Ormesson at Amiens in 1656 was commissioned to
'observer et faire observer exactement les ordonnances et
règlemens sur le faict de nos finances et mesmes ceux concernant la levée de nos tailles . . .'[3] Some of the commissions
emphasized the totality of powers—justice, *police*, and finance,
both civil and military—that had been usual in 1643–8: in
this category were the commissions of François Bochart at
Lyon in 1653,[4] Jean Bochart at Limoges three years later,[5]
Garibal at Riom[6] and Lefèvre d'Ormesson at Amiens, both
also in 1656. Garibal was accorded powers to appoint subdelegates, preside over municipal elections, and intervene in the
conduct of municipal finance. Other commissions were less
explicit with regard to the civil powers enjoyed by the intendant. For example, Lefèvre de la Barre was commissioned as
intendant of the army in the Dauphiné in October 1654;[7] yet
on 19 November supplementary instructions were issued empowering him to levy the *taille*, to investigate the accounts of the
receveurs since 1647, and to mediate in a jurisdictional dispute
between the *Parlement* of Grenoble and the *cour des aides* of
Vienne—all tasks of civil administration. The existence of such
supplementary instructions emphasizes clearly the dangers of
excessive concentration on the terminology in the commissions:
despite the variations in the commissions after the Fronde, the
intendants in the *pays d'élections* appear to have operated
essentially in the same way as their predecessors before 1648.

[1] Boislisle, communication to *Revue des Sociétés Savantes*, 7th ser., iii (1881),
181–3. B.N. MS.fr. 4187, fos. 130–3.
[2] Mousnier, *La plume*, pp. 331–2. K 891, no. 5, 19 Nov. 1654.
[3] A.D. Somme 1B 27, fo. 81 and A.G. A1 32, no. 228, 13 Dec. 1656.
[4] Godard, *Les pouvoirs*, pp. 455–8. A.G. A1 140, fo. 311ᵛ, 15 Oct. 1653.
[5] A.G. A1 147, no. 281, 12 July 1656.
[6] Mousnier, *La plume*, pp. 212–13.
[7] O1 11, fo. 40, 6 Oct. 1654.

Doubtless supplementary instructions and decrees of the council made up for any deficiencies in their commissions. What was certainly noticeable also in the years after the Fronde was a concern for security.[1] Lefèvre de la Barre in the Dauphiné in 1654 was instructed to 'prendre garde qu'il ne se face aucune cabale contre le service de Sa Majesté . . .' and together with the governor, he was to ensure that any such conspiracies did not succeed. At Amiens in 1656 Lefèvre d'Ormesson was empowered to 'tenir la main à ce qu'il ne fasse aucune assemblée illicite, pratiques, monopoles, séditions et esmotions . . .' and if any such disturbances took place, as president of an *ad hoc* judicial tribunal he was to prosecute offenders and issue definitive sentences. In conspiracy cases, there was clearly no concession to the sovereign courts after the Fronde.

The death of Mazarin on 9 March 1661, the abolition of the *surintendance des finances* on 15 September 1661, and the rise to power of Colbert within the *conseil royal des finances*, strengthened existing tendencies towards uniformity in the commissions of the intendants. Colbert de Saint-Pouange, a cousin of the minister, was accorded powers in 1662 as intendant of Amiens comparable to those enjoyed by Lefèvre d'Ormesson, his predecessor; but in addition, he was accorded similar powers to the intendants 'en nos autres provinces'. His commission conferred authority to prosecute cases of disorder among the troops, and of rebellion against taxation, and as president of an *ad hoc* judicial tribunal, to issue definitive sentences in cases of conspiracy and rebellion. He was empowered also to levy the *taille*, to preside over the municpal assemblies, and to verify municipal debts. A right of appointing subdelegates was specifically accorded to Colbert de Saint-Pouange, an important concession in view of Colbert's apparent hostility to intendants' reliance on subordinate officials.[2] The commission of Barillon d'Amon-

---

[1] The concerns of the government are illustrated by a letter from Colbert to Mazarin dated 15 Sept. 1656. Colbert pointed to the threat of the return of Cardinal de Retz to France, and the need to instruct the intendants of the Touraine, the Dauphiné, and elsewhere accordingly. He advised also the appointment of an intendant of Provence: *Lettres . . . de Colbert*, ed. Clément, i. 263.

[2] A.D. Somme 1B 28, fo. 10ᵛ, 9 Jan. 1662. For Colbert's hostility to subdelegates: J. Ricommard, 'Les subdélégués des intendants aux xviiᵉ et xviiiᵉ siècles', *L'Information Historique*, xxiv (1962–3), 144–5.

court, also at Amiens, in 1668 contained a similar power of appointing subordinate officials, and in other respects closely resembled the commission issued six years earlier. The tasks of the intendant with regard to the *taille* were enumerated much more specifically than hitherto, as was also his role with regard to indirect taxation and the reform of the *eaux et forêts*.[1] Moreover, Barillon was ordered to investigate 'des abus au faict de la police [et] tous les crimes qui sont demeurés impunies . . .' and to send reports to the council on such matters. He also had the power to coerce *notaires* to send him necessary documents in their possession, the essential means by which an intendant could judge for himself the size of a person's private fortune.[2]

The powers of Le Tonnelier de Breteuil at Amiens in 1674[3] were almost identical to those of Barillon, and there was henceforth a standardization of the commissions—the commissions of Charron de Ménars at Orléans in 1674 and at Paris in 1681,[4] of Bazin de Bezons at Limoges in 1681,[5] and of Le Vayer de Boutigny at Soissons in 1682[6] were essentially similar. That of Hotman de Fontenay at Paris in 1675 was different only in being an abbreviated form of commission, which nevertheless included the power of appointing subordinate officials.[7] By 1686 the clerks of the secretaries of state could regard the commissions of the intendants of Orléans as sufficiently standardized to avoid any enumeration at all of the powers enjoyed by Barillon de Morangis (appointed 11 March) and Creil de Bournezeau (appointed 26 May).[8]

The commissions were thus far less significant by the last years of Colbert's ministry than the numerous decrees of the council which had extended the area of the intendants' activities and modified in detail powers that had previously been

---

[1] Colbert's achievement in this area is well brought out by M. Devèze, *La grande réformation des forêts sous Colbert, 1661–1683* (1954).

[2] A.D. Somme 1B 29, fo. 16, 2 Jan. 1668. In practice this power of coercion was rarely used, cf. below, chapter IX.

[3] Boyer de Sainte-Suzanne, *Intendants d'Amiens*, pp. 577–83.

[4] O1 18, fo. 75, 28 Feb. 1674. O1 25, fo. 6, 1 Jan. 1681.

[5] O1 25, fo. 11, 1 Jan. 1681.

[6] O1 26, fo. 44[v], 19 Feb. 1682.

[7] O1 19, fo. 301[v], 14 Dec. 1675.

[8] O1 30, fos. 89, 184[v]. In contrast, Esmonin, *La taille*, p. 56, n. 5, considers that differences remained in the standard terminology employed by clerks of different secretaries of state.

accorded. Marle de Versigny, the intendant at Riom between 1671 and 1683, wrote to Colbert in July 1682: 'ayant examiné les commissions dont il a plust au Roy de m'honnorer dans les généralitez d'Alençon et de Riom, il me paroist, Monsieur, que nous pouvons et devons mesme dans l'estendue de nos départemens prendre une connoissance universelle de toutes les choses qui regardent le bien du service du Roy, et le soulage-ment de ses sujets dont la fonction néantmoins se renferme à dresser des mémoires ou procès-verbaux et faire des enquestes et informations pour les envoyer au Conseil . . .' Such limita-tions, declared Marle, conformed to the sixteenth-century ordinances relating to the circuit-tours of the *maîtres des requêtes*. To proceed beyond these restrictions, Marle considered that the intendant had to be empowered either by an ordinance or by a *commission particulière*. 'Nos pouvoirs fondez sur les ordonnances, pour le jugement et instruction des procès, se renferment aux gens de guerre', he declared, an assumption underlying this remark being that conspiracy was no longer a frequent occurrence as at the time of Richelieu and Mazarin, and thus no longer a major area of prosecutions by the inten-dant. Marle listed his *commissions particulières* 'sans parler au département des tailles'—these were sufficiently numerous to suggest that the *commissions particulières* had replaced the *commission générale* in importance in the day to day work of the intendant.[1]

Under Richelieu and Mazarin, the commissions of the inten-dants were developed as a flexible instrument of government. By such means, powers could be transferred to the intendants according to the requirements of a changing political situation. Unlike the other institutions in seventeenth-century France—the sovereign and lesser courts, the governors, and the pro-vincial Estates—the power of the intendants could not become a challenge to the crown. The intendants were allowed to issue ordinances which had equivalent status to the decrees issued by the sovereign courts, but almost invariably, the ordinances of the intendants could be annulled by the king's council. Only occasionally—in criminal prosecutions, when the intendant acted as a president of a special tribunal on the

[1] G7 101, 19 July 1682.

orders of the central government—could the intendant issue definitive sentences which were not subject to appeal in the king's council. The commission was the basis of the power of the intendants in the provinces. Unlike the edicts creating offices, it was a temporary establishment: the commission could be revoked by the crown at will.

PART TWO

THE INTENDANTS AND PROVINCIAL GOVERNMENT

CHAPTER VIII

The Administration of Direct Taxes before the Fronde

CLAUDE LE PELETIER, the *contrôleur-général des finances*, exhorted the intendants in the *pays d'élections* in 1688 to assess the *taille* with the greatest care and exactitude '. . . comme c'est la plus importante de toutes voz fonctions . . .'[1] Such instructions to the intendants would have been inconceivable in 1630: during the ministries of Richelieu and Mazarin, the intendants had become administrators of the *taille*. They became masters of the fate of their *généralités* to the extent that they could advise the council of finance to raise or lower the taxable burden of the area. They also controlled the distribution of taxes between the various regions of the *généralité*—the intendant was 'l'arbitre du sort d'une élection'.[2] Financial administration had become central to the tasks of the intendants on whom, in John Law's phrase, depended 'le bonheur ou le malheur de ces provinces, leur abondance ou leur stérilité'.[3]

Before this vast change occurred in the 1630s and 1640s, the *taille* had been administered by two groups of officials, the *trésoriers* and the *élus*. Each *généralité* had its *bureau des finances* comprising a number of *trésoriers de France*. In theory, every autumn[4] the *trésoriers* went on visits of inspection (*chevauchées*) into each *élection*.[5] The *trésoriers* initialled the registers of the *taille* kept by the *receveurs particuliers* of each *élection*, and ensured that these were kept properly. In addition, they were to ask the *receveurs*, the *élus*, and the local notables a number of questions. What was the state of the harvest? Did the *élus* allow to be present at the assessments any officials whose provisions of

---

[1] G7 4, no. 666, 31 Aug. 1688.
[2] G7 1127, memorandum on the *taille*, 1722.
[3] Frequently quoted, e.g. by Tocqueville, *L'ancien régime*, book II, chapter 2.
[4] Under Richelieu and Mazarin, in Oct.–Dec. After 1678, in July–Sept.: J. Vannier, *Essai sur le bureau des finances de la généralité de Rouen, 1551–1790* (Rouen, 1927), p. 52.
[5] F. Dumont, *Le bureau des finances de la généralité de Moulins* (Moulins, 1923), pp. 144–6. Vannier, op. cit., pp. 47–9. Charmeil, *Trésoriers*, pp. 102–7.

office had not been registered at the *bureau des finances*? Were there any complaints against the *receveurs* of the *taille*? Were there any parish collectors who had been imprisoned because of failure to pay the taxes owed by the parish? Did the *élus* keep a strict control over the registers of the *taille*? Were there any persons enjoying unfair exemption from the *taille*? Were any levies of taxation taking place which had not been ordered by letters patent signed by a secretary of state? These and a number of other standardized questions were asked.[1] In addition, on certain occasions the *trésoriers* carried out the *taxes d'office*,[2] special taxes on privileged persons in the parishes (this was ordered by the ruling of 20 October 1603 and abandoned on 11 September 1608; it was ordered again by the ruling of 6 December 1640[3] and abandoned on 22 August 1642).

After the *trésoriers* had carried out their circuit-tours, they returned to the *bureau des finances* where letters patent fixing the amount of the *taille* for the next fiscal year (called the *brevet de la taille*), sent from the council of finance at Paris, would arrive in late summer. Payment of the *taille* commenced on 1 October in any fiscal year, and thus arrears were inevitable since in some *généralités* the general assessment was not carried out before December. The *trésoriers* of Lyon had a fairly good record, allocating the taxes of 1636 on 5 September 1635 and those for 1637 on 22 September 1636.[4] There were more serious delays in the much larger *généralité* of Rouen.[5] Colbert appreciated that these delays were one of the fundamental reasons for arrears of the *taille*, and sent the *brevet* of the *taille* from Paris in May, instead of in the late summer as in the period of Richelieu and Mazarin. Colbert's reform had one major disadvantage, however. The fiscal year began on 1 October because it was assumed that by late September the true state of the harvest could be ascertained; if the assessments were carried out much earlier in the year, the true wealth of the parishes could not be assessed with any accuracy.[6]

<hr/>

[1] Vannier, op. cit., p. 50 n. 1.
[2] So called not because they were taxes levied on persons holding offices, but because they were levied 'd'office', that is to say officially—i.e. on the authority of the *trésoriers* or whichever official was given this task.
[3] AD + 263, instructions of 6 Dec. 1640.
[4] A.D. Rhône C 561, fol 320. C 562, fo. 304.
[5] Vannier, op. cit., pp. 95–9.   [6] Esmonin, *La taille*, p. 26.

Once the *trésoriers* had decided on the allocation of taxes between the various *élections*, they issued an authorization (*mandement*) to the *élus* to carry out the parish assessments for their respective areas within a week. Both distributions of taxation—on the *généralité* as a whole, and on each *élection*—were called *départements de la taille*,[1] so it is hardly surprising that confusion arose as to whether an individual *trésorier*—usually the one who had previously visited the *élection* on circuit-tour—had the right to preside over the *élus* at this moment or not. In the *élection* of Vire-et-Condé in 1634, Pierre Collardin de Boisollivier, a *trésorier* at Caen, found the *élus* resolved to lower the assessments of parishes 'par eux protégés' and to increase those of parishes that were 'paouvres et non déffendus'. As a result, Boissollivier felt himself obliged to 'procédder de son chef à faire le département . . . fondé sur les raisons et les motifs de la commodité et incommodité des paroisses . . .' He also sought, and obtained, a decree of the council of finance on 23 March 1634 annulling the assessments carried out by the *élus*.[2] Nevertheless, there were exceptional circumstances on this occasion. The *trésoriers* at Caen had harboured suspicion in previous years that the parish assessments of the *élus* of Vire were flagrantly unfair. In cases where the *élus* were accused of irregularities, the council of finance usually commissioned a *trésorier* to investigate. The role of the *trésoriers* was essentially supervisory, however.[3] The rulings on the *taille* in March 1600 and January 1634 both conferred the parish assessments on the *élus*. It was not until 1 March 1640 that in response to the proven negligence and corruption of the *élus* a decree of the council of finance ordered the *trésoriers* to visit each *élection* annually and preside over the parish assessments. This decree operated only until 22 August 1642, however.[4]

There is no doubt that in the years before 1642, the *trésoriers*

---

[1] The commission for the *taille* in Normandy in 1580 distinguished between the *département général* (the assessments carried out by the *trésoriers*) and the *départements particuliers* (the assessments carried out by the *élus* and others). *Cahiers des États de Normandie sous le règne de Henri III*, ed. C. de Robillard de Beaurepaire (2 vols., Rouen, 1887–8), i. 379. Vannier, op. cit., pp. 105–6. In this study, they are called respectively 'the general assessment' and 'the parish assessments'.

[2] E 116b, fo. 60.

[3] cf. the commission to three *trésoriers* of Paris to preside over the parish assessments in the *élection* of Paris: Z1f 192, fo. 82ᵛ, 23 Apr. 1637.

[4] E 154c, fo. 120, 1 Mar. 1640.

were extremely important officials in provincial government. On an individual basis, they acted as advisers to the commissioners for the reform (*régalement*) of the *taille* in 1598–9, 1623–4, and 1634–5. They assisted the intendants in administering the *subsistances* for the troops in 1638–9. Sometimes, they served as intendants.[1] The rapid turnover of intendants in the 1630s and 1640s tended to ensure a continuity of service for the trusted local *trésorier*. Julien Pietre, a *trésorier de France* at Amiens, worked with Bellejambe, the intendant, on the *taille* after 1642. He served as interim intendant in the army of Flanders during the illness of Chaulnes in 1646. Ten years later, Pietre was appointed as interim intendant at Amiens. In 1664 he was serving once more in this position.[2] Jean Desmaretz, a *trésorier de France* at Soissons and father of Nicolas, the future *intendant des finances* (1678–1708) and *contrôleur-général des finances* (1708–1715), was appointed as the assistant of Bazin de Bezons in 1646 and served as interim intendant while Lefèvre d'Ormesson was involved at Paris with the trial of Foucquet in 1663–4: he continued in this position after the disgrace of Ormesson in 1665–6.[3]

Whereas much of the responsibility of the *trésoriers* was concerned with accountancy—whether of the *receveurs des tailles*, the finances of the towns, the royal domain, or the funding of repairs to the public highways—the *élections* were essentially law-courts with jurisdiction in first instance over all matters concerning direct taxation. The *élus* were judges in civil cases for sums up to 30 *livres*; in cases involving sums above that figure, their decisions were subject to appeal in the *cour des aides*. The majority of lawsuits heard by the *élus* were civil cases, of which there were a great variety. Anyone could open an *action en aide ou profit*, that is to say a case seeking to establish that a member of a parish had been omitted without due cause from the local tax-

[1] Charmeil, *Trésoriers*, p. 137, n. 277.

[2] ibid., pp. 138, 458. *Lettres . . . au Chancelier Séguier*, ed. Mousnier, ii. 786. A.G. A1 96, no. 145 and B.N. MS.fr. 4172, fo. 280, 30 May 1646. A.G. A1 147, no. 283, 8 Aug. 1656. E 292c, fo. 250ᵛ, 31 Aug. 1656. E 370a, fo. 252, 6 Mar. 1664. E 373a, fo. 241, 8 Aug. 1664.

[3] Charmeil, *Trésoriers*, pp. 138, 475. E 365a, fo. 179, 3 Aug. 1663. E 382b, fo. 249, 22 Oct. 1665. E 390, fo. 78, 5 Aug. 1666. Desmaretz was married to Marguerite Colbert, sister of Jean-Baptiste Colbert: Bourgeon, *Les Colbert avant Colbert*, p. 223.

roll. When a member of a parish found himself to be too heavily taxed, he could commence an *action en surtaux*, a case against the collector and the members of the parish. A collector who had been appointed against his will, and had no wish to assume such responsibilities because of poverty, old age, ill-health, fear of ostracism or worse from the other inhabitants, could commence an *action en décharge de collecte*. A collector could also bring an *action en validité de saisie*, that is to say, demand authorization from the *élus* for the seizure of the property of parishoners who did not pay their taxes. A collector who owed one quarter of his tax demand could commence an *action en solidité* against the other collectors in his parish, and eventually against the parish as a whole, so that the amount outstanding could be borne by all the collectors and inhabitants and that he alone should not bear the responsibility for negligence. Finally, a privileged person could commence an *action de radiation*, a case against his being included in the tax-rolls on account of his social status. In addition to all these civil procedures, the *élus* also had a criminal jurisdiction: they could issue decrees in cases of rebellion against their orders, those of the *receveurs* or collectors, or against the fiscal police force, the *huissiers* and *sergents des tailles*. These responsibilities taken together comprised the *juridiction contentieuse* of the *élus*.[1]

The *trésoriers* carried out the distribution of taxes between the *élections*; the *élus* carried out the distribution between the parishes; a committee including parishioners and collectors carried out the distribution between the inhabitants of the parishes. The taxes were collected at parish level by nominated collectors.[2]

---

[1] P. de La Barre, *Formulaire des Esleuz auquel sont contenues et déclarées les functions* [*sic*] *et devoirs desdits officiers et sommairement ce qu'ils sont tenus scavoir et faire pour l'acquit de leur charge* ... (Rouen, 1627). P. Pinsseau, *Contribution à l'historire financière du xviiie siècle, 1685–1790. L'élection de Gien, généralité d'Orléans* (1924), pp. 35, 54–61. Cf. Esmonin, *La taille*, p. 123, n. 1, quoting Foucquet's comment that the *trésoriers* 'n'ayant aucune juridiction contentieuse . . . cela dépendoit de la fonction des officiers des eslections'.

[2] A decree of 17 Dec. 1636 [E 134c, fo. 67] fixed the number of collectors in the Touraine at 3 for a parish of 100 hearths; 4 for 150 hearths; 6 for 200 hearths and above. This applied to both the *taille* and the *gabelle*. In 1641, the parishes in the *généralité* of Moulins appointed 'des collecteurs insolvables'. They were ordered to choose the collectors from among the 15 richest inhabitants: E 164a, fo. 285, 7 Sept. 1641. After 1642, the rule was that the collectors should be 'au moins deux des huict plus fortes cottes'—i.e. at least two of the eight parishioners with the heaviest tax burden: *Lettres . . . au Chancelier Séguier*, ed. Mousnier, ii. 804.

The sums were paid over to the *receveurs particuliers* of each *élection* (supervised by the *élus*), who in turn paid the money to the *receveur-général* of the *généralité* (supervised by the *trésoriers*). The system was relatively simple: but it was subject to a number of structural defects. The increased fiscal exploitation of office-holders, especially financial office-holders, by the government in the first quarter of the seventeenth century had a disastrous effect upon the reliability of the *trésoriers* and the *élus* as financial administrators. Many *trésoriers* held their offices *in absentia*; the annual circuit-tours were not performed at all, or else in the most perfunctory manner; on occasions, so few *trésoriers* attended the *bureau des finances* that sessions had to be suspended.[1] Certain groups of *trésoriers*—notably those at Bordeaux[2]—were accused of favouring one area of the *généralité* (in this case the city of Bordeaux) at the expense of the rest. Some *trésoriers* or their families—notably those at Montauban[3] —held the office of *receveur des tailles* and thus the verification of accounts was a meaningless exercise. The abuses of the *trésoriers*, however, were as nothing compared with those of the *élus*, despite the efforts of the *cours des aides* and the council of finance to impose some sort of order. Contemporaries such as Richelieu, Séguier, and Le Bret linked the corruption of the *élus* with the ill-effects of the sale of offices; and it is certain that the *élus* were severely exploited by the government. As early as 4 March 1611, the *cour des aides* of Paris issued remonstrances on 'l'intérêt des officiers des eslections qui crient que depuis 25 ans ils ont été la butte ordinaire des partisans et travaillés de plus de 30 édits tous bursaux . . . ce sont 2000 officiers que vous mécontentés . . . officiers qui ne sont pas les derniers dans les villes et qui peuvent [avoir] beaucoup [de crédit] parmy le peuple'.[4] Yet the taxes paid by the *élus* in the years 1585–1610 were small compared with the 200 million *livres* paid between 1620 and 1648. By 1635 the *élus* claimed that successive new creations of offices had reduced the value of existing offices by half.[5] There

[1] Esmonin, *La taille*, p. 42. Charmeil, *Trésoriers*, pp. 101–2. Cf. the rulings of the *trésoriers* of Paris, dated 3 Oct. 1631 and 4 Jan. 1644, on absenteeism: Z1f 202, fo. 13ᵛ.   [2] E 123b, fo. 46, 9 May 1635.
[3] E 176b, fo. 120, 24 Jan. 1643.   [4] Z1a 159, fo. 90.
[5] E 123b, fo. 33, 9 May 1635. Cf. Esmonin, *La taille*, pp. 108–10, 152. Moote, *The revolt of the judges*, p. 51. Mousnier, *La plume*, p. 304. Z1a 206, pp. 899–905, 'estat au vray des eslections nouvellement créés'.

is a *prima facie* case for supposing that the *élus* sought compensation through peculation.

The *élus* were obliged to go on visits of inspection as a preliminary to their assessments. While on circuit-tour, they were forbidden to incur debts. By a decree of 29 July 1623 they were obliged to stay no longer than one day in a parish of less than 100 hearths, two days in one of 200 hearths and so on.[1] Yet they sometimes abused the hospitality of local inhabitants, exacting 'par violence et contraincte . . . des fraiz extraordinaires qui ruynent entièrement lesdits collecteurs'.[2] They might not go on circuit-tours at all;[3] or if they did, they might ignore the distant parishes. Crancey, Marnay-sur-Seine, and Gélannes were twelve leagues from Troyes and the *élus* refused to go there, thus remaining in ignorance of the poverty of these parishes.[4] They were often non-resident: thus the *élus* of Gascogne resided at Toulouse 'pour leur commodité.[5] The *élus* might refuse to sign the orders of the *receveurs* coercing the inhabitants of parishes which were in arrears. They might charge too much for the lawsuits they heard.[6] Although they were liable to confiscation of their offices if found guilty of peculation,[7] this did not deter the *élus* of Saintes from pocketing 81,143 *livres* in two fiscal years.[8] The *élus* in the *généralité* of Amiens were accused of levying the *taille* themselves 'sans en donner quittance et brouill[a]nt les années les unes avec les autres afin de mettre toutes les levées en confusion et empescher que l'on en puisse faire une exacte vériffication . . .'[9] The *élus* in the *généralité* of Orléans were accused of negligence, including failure to observe the ruling of 27 November 1641, which threatened the appointment of royal commissioners to replace the *élus* if they failed to carry out the assessments fairly during the next fiscal year.[10] Certain groups of *élus* were accused of malevolence towards the government—conniving with revolt by failing to draw up the

[1] E 75b, fo. 317 and Z1a 206, p. 597.
[2] E 163c, fo. 176, 22 Aug. 1641.
[3] Z1a 206, p. 393: 'la pluspart desdsits esleuz ne font lesdites chevauchées . . .'
[4] E 117b, fo. 434, 30 June 1634.
[5] E 173b, fo. 632, 30 Sept. 1642.
[6] E 121b, fo. 128, 9 Dec. 1634.
[7] La Barre, *Formulaire des esleuz*, pp. 166–7.
[8] E 122d, fo. 41, 28 Mar. 1635.
[9] E 175, fo. 417, 17 Dec. 1642.
[10] E 173b, fo. 395, 19 Sept. 1642.

tax-rolls,[1] or failing to assist the levy of the sales tax in 1640–2 because of their private interests as wine growers or wine traders.[2]

The recurring theme, however, was corruption at the assessments. The *élus* were not empowered to intervene in the assessments between the inhabitants of the parishes, yet they frequently did so. The *élus* of le Mans tried to 'pénétrer dans les secretz de toutes les familles' by drawing up the tax-rolls of the town in 1639.[3] The emphasis in the rulings that the parish assessments should be carried out 'en la chambre du conseil'— in plenary session—and 'à la pluralité des voix' was supposed to prevent their being held in 'une maison particulière hors du bureau', as at Vézelay in 1642,[4] and thus subject to cabal. Even if such influence was not brought to bear at parish level—the retaining and altering of the tax-tolls in favour of one's friends and relatives[5]—a similar sort of influence could operate in the distribution of taxes between the various parishes. Certain *élections* had a rule that every year the circuit-tours should be changed.[6] Since the most senior *élus* could choose the parishes they wished to visit, this procedure could not prevent the favouring of some parishes where the *élus* or their relatives had lands, at the expense of others. The family of Christophe Cupif, a *président* in the *élection* of Angers, owned an office of *commissaire des tailles* at Champigné, a parish which they were therefore in a position to tax heavily. However, they had 'des grands biens' at Cheffes, which they taxed lightly.[7] The *élus* at Crépy-en-Valois, because of long-standing lawsuits, bore ill-will towards La Ferté Millon, which they taxed at 14,000 *livres*. Although Crépy was more populous, it paid only 7,000 *livres*.[8] Nineteen per cent of the parishes in the *élection* of Valognes were regularly underassessed.[9] Well might one of the commissioners for the *régalement des tailles* in 1634–5 reflect that the system of *taille*

---

[1] E 171b, fo. 246, 28 June 1642. E 173b, fo. 629, 30 Sept. 1642.
[2] E 172a, fo. 491, 9 July 1642. E 174b, fo. 575, 29 Nov. 1642.
[3] E 151d, fo. 26, 16 July 1639.
[4] E 170b, fo. 164, 24 May 1642.
[5] E 122d, fo. 14, 28 Mar. 1635. E 120a, fo. 20, 6 Sept. 1634.
[6] Z1a 206, p. 749, ruling of the *élus* of Saintes, 19 Dec. 1607.
[7] E 120a, fo. 20, 6 Sept. 1634.
[8] E 173a, fo. 141, 12 Aug. 1642.
[9] A. Lefebvre and F. Tribouillard, 'Fiscalité et population dans l'élection de Valognes de 1540 à 1660', *Annales de Normandie*, xxi (1971), 225.

personnelle was so iniquitous that only basic structural reform—the adoption of the system of *taille réelle*—could produce an equitable system of taxation.[1]

The administration of the *taille* by the *trésoriers* and *élus* was geared essentially to peace-time conditions, when tax-returns could arrive at Paris at a leisurely speed, and when taxes were sufficiently low for inequalities not to be keenly resented. The system broke down under the strain of the war against the Habsburgs. Increased government expenditure inevitably meant higher taxes. Basically, there were three types of revenue: indirect, direct, and 'extraordinary taxes' (*affaires extraordinaires*). The indirect taxes, such as the *gabelle* and the *aides*, were farmed out—that is to say, financiers undertook to administer the revenues themselves and in return agreed to pay the crown a fixed amount each year for the duration of the lease of the tax farm. The direct taxes, primarily the *taille*, were, at least until 1639, administered by treasurers—the *receveurs-généraux* and *receveurs particuliers*—who were in reality financiers as well. The 'extraordinary taxes'—for example, the creation of new offices or new bonds (*rentes*)—were raised by the method of *traités*, that is to say, contracts with financiers who undertook to raise a fixed sum of money in return for a standard rate of interest.[2] The relative importance of the three types of revenue was constantly changing. Each was increased to help pay for the war; but each also suffered from severe disadvantages.

The indirect taxes were essentially taxes on consumption,[3] and as such they became increasingly difficult to administer as the war went on. The interruption of trade between France and

[1] *Lettres . . . au Chancelier Séguier*, ed. Mousnier, i. 248.

[2] Usually a third, a quarter, or one-sixth plus one-tenth (*le sixième denier et le sol pour livre*). The rate depended on the nature of the new tax and the difficulty envisaged in collecting it.

[3] Especially in the case of the *gabelle*: Cf. E. Leroy-Ladurie and J. Récurat, 'L'état des ventes du sel vers 1625', *Annales E.S.C.*, xxiv (1969), 999–1010. Thus consumption of salt fell in northern France from 11,351 *muids* in 1621 to 9,469 *muids* in 1664: J. Récurat and E. Leroy-Ladurie, 'Sur les fluctuations de la consommation taxée du sel dans la France du Nord aux xviie et xviiie siècles', *Revue du Nord*, liv (1972), 385, 398. The *aides* and the *cinq grosses fermes* tended rather to be taxes on commercial circulation—but the general point as to the difficulty in raising these revenues during the war holds firm.

Spain and the devastation of the frontier provinces were important factors in reducing consumption and thus the profitability of the farms. The income enjoyed by the French crown from *traités* was scarcely any more reliable. The contractor stood to forfeit his capital if the tax was revoked[1]—this was one reason why the interest rates on *traités* were so high. Another factor in forcing up interest rates was popular resistance to increased taxation. The contractors had great difficulty in levying the taxes, and for greater security, they insisted on the registration of the *affaires extraordinaires* in the sovereign courts 'sans restriction ni modification'.[2] Such registration was not obligatory on the government, but it helped allay public disquiet and ensure public acquiescence in the taxes.[3] The disadvantage of submitting new fiscal legislation to the courts was that registration was not always forthcoming. The courts tended to oppose increases in taxation generally, and the fiscal exploitation of office-holders in particular. 'Extraordinary taxes' thus became the focus of political controversy, part of the struggle between the crown and its office-holders. The consequences were clear: despite the impressive amounts of money that ought to have been raised from *traités*, much less was actually received and this largely for political reasons. Many of the new taxes were never registered by the courts, and the *traitants* were unable to levy them; others were registered, but with modifications which made them an unprofitable investment to the contractors; still more eventually produced revenues, but intermittently and much less than had been expected. An increase in the number of *traités* could not hope to solve the crown's fiscal problems in time of war unless the courts could be relied upon for support. This was not the case at the time of Richelieu and Mazarin.[4]

---

[1] B.N. MS.fr. 18207, fo. 5ᵛ, *Traité* of Louis Berrier (16 Jan. 1638): a *remise* of 141,866 *livres* 13 *sols* 4 *deniers* was paid because of 'forfaict, advance de deniers, port et voiture et risques et périls d'iceux'. Cf. Foucquet's comment to Mazarin: 'on ne tire de l'argent que d'affaires nouvelles qui sans doute ont des difficultés et des inconvénients . . .' A.A.E. France 900, fo. 158, 12 July 1656.

[2] A. Chauleur, 'Le rôle des traitants dans l'administration financière de la France de 1643 à 1653', *XVIIᵉ Siècle*, lxv (1964), 21–2.

[3] cf. the comment of the *premier président* of the *cour des aides* of Paris on 16 Dec. 1616: '. . . [le] peuple ne croit pas être obligé de se soumettre aux loix que les avis de leurs magistrats n'ont point autorisées'. Z1a 159, fo. 182ᵛ.

[4] cf. below, chapter XI, for the political attitude of the sovereign courts.

The unprofitability of the farms and the uncertainty of the *traités* meant that the government had little choice but to rely on the direct revenues: by 1639 the *taille* accounted for 54 per

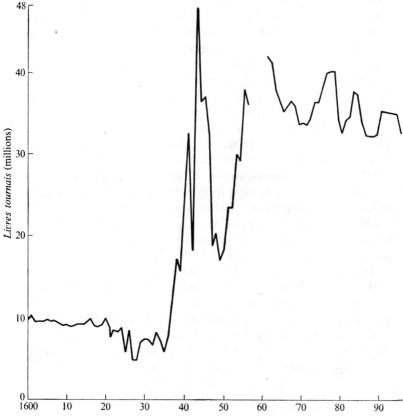

Fɪɢ. 4. Yield from the *taille* in the *pays d'élections, c.* 1600–1695.

Source: J. R. Mallet *Comptes rendus de l'administration des finances du royaume de France* . . . (London, 1789). Mallet gives no figures for 1657–60 or 1696–1700.

cent of estimated total revenues, this proportion reaching 62 per cent in 1648 and falling to 55 per cent in 1661.[1] The estimated revenues from the *taille* rose from 36·6 million in 1635 to 40·7 million in 1636, 43·5 million in 1637[2] and 1639,[3]

[1] Bercé, *Histoire des croquants*, i. 67.
[2] Devèze, *La grande réformation des forêts sous Colbert*, p. 30, n. 1.
[3] B.N. MS.fr. 11138, fo. 1ᵛ–2ʳ.

and 72·6 million in 1643.[1] The Regency government was under considerable political pressure to reduce the *taille*,[2] and did so by sixteen million between 1643 and 1647: in theory, the *taille* stood at 56·6 million on the eve of the Fronde.[3] However, these figures are of estimated revenues, which were out of touch with reality. From the 1630s onwards, arrears of the *taille* had been accumulating: the nominal figures of the 1640s thus contain an element of fantasy. (For this reason, the actual yield from the *taille* in the *pays d'élections*, rather than the projected revenue, is given in Fig. 4.) The highest nominal rate of increase recorded in the *taille* between 1635 and 1648 was 338 per cent.[4] The *Chambre Saint-Louis* demanded a reduction of 25 per cent in 1648. Although the government never acceded wholly to this demand, there is little doubt that revenues from the *taille* fell until 1653. A further rise occurred between that date and 1659, but this seems to have been more of a return to the high levels before the Fronde than a further increase[5] [Fig. 5]. Although there were short-term crises, notably in 1649–52, the war years coincided with a period of relatively stable prices: thus the rise in taxation was not offset by inflation [Fig. 6].

The increase in the *taille* was borne largely by the peasants, and was bitterly resented. The result was 'tax rebellion' on a widespread scale.[6] Enormous arrears of the *taille* built up in certain provinces as a consequence of this tax rebellion. In 1641, the *élection* of Loches owed over one million *livres* from 1632 and subsequent years.[7] By 1643, the *généralité* of Bourges was 2·25 million in arrears over a six-year period.[8] The *élection* of Saintes was 850,000 *livres* in arrears by that date.[9] On

---

[1] B.N. MS.fr. 18510, fo. 7.

[2] X1a 8388, registration by the *Parlement* of Paris on 3 Sept. 1643 of a remission of 10 million on the *taille* and certain other taxes.

[3] B.N. MS.fr. 18510, fo. 7.

[4] 338 per cent at Paris. But other figures were lower. For example, a 204 per cent rise was recorded at Tours and a 301 per cent rise at Bordeaux (1636–48). [References as Fig. 5.] At Caen, there was a rise of 301 per cent between 1631 and 1643: M. Caillard, 'Recherches sur les soulèvements populaires en Basse-Normandie (1620–1640) et spécialement sur la révolte des Nu-Pieds', *À travers la Normandie des xviie et xviiie siècles. Cahiers des Annales de Normandie*, iii (1963), 101, 130–1.

[5] At Tours, the figure in 1660 exceeded that of 1648 (4·5 million against 3·6 million in 1648). At Paris in 1659 it did not (1·2 million against 1·9 million in 1648).

[6] cf. below, chapter X.

[7] E 165b, fo. 205, 9 Nov. 1641.

[8] E 184a, fo. 165, 14 Oct. 1643.

[9] E 176b, fo. 118, 24 Jan. 1643.

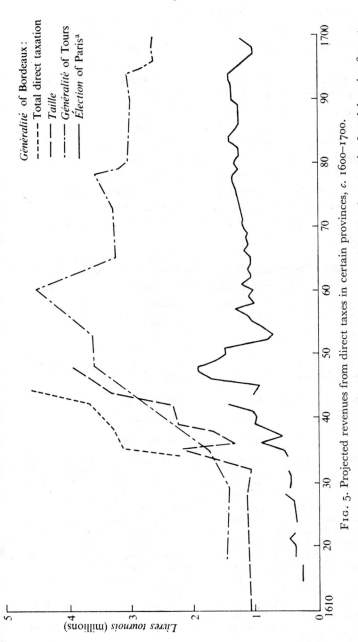

Généralité of Bordeaux:

- - - - - Total direct taxation
— — Taille
— · — Généralité of Tours
———— Élection of Paris[a]

Fig. 5. Projected revenues from direct taxes in certain provinces, *c.* 1600–1700.

[a] In some years the figures for total direct taxation include such items as *substinances*, the *crues*, the forced loan in 1637, etc. The figure for direct taxation in the *élection* of Paris in 1637 was low because troops were present in the province.

Sources: *Généralité* of Bordeaux: Y. M. Bercé 'Recherches sur les soulèvements populaires du sud-ouest pendant la guerre de Trente Ans', unpublished thesis, École des Chartes (1959), pp. 85–6.

Élection of Paris: Z1g 281, 1–3.

Généralité of Tours: *Inventaire sommaire des archives départementales de l'Indre-et-Loire*, ed. C. de Loizeau de Grandmaison (Tours, 1878), pp. 68–83.

23 September 1642, five *élections* in the *généralité* of Montauban owed 1,175,073 *livres* from the years 1639–41.[1] The situation was made worse by the negligence of the *receveurs*, who used the peasant revolts as an excuse for noncooperation with the government.[2] The *receveurs* were not obliged to give collateral security before embarking upon their financial management.[3] Many *receveurs* refused to submit their accounts for auditing after 1635: indeed, they deliberately kept their accounts in confusion so as to preclude an effective investigation of their activities.[4] The turning-point came on 4 July 1641, when the council of finance threatened with summary dismissal *receveurs* who could not account for their management since 1635.[5] The transfer of responsibility over the *taille* to the intendants occurred in 1641–2 as a result of the breakdown of the local fiscal machinery.

The transfer of responsibility in fiscal matters to the intendants could not have occurred without a long period of preparation, when the techniques of management could be tested. The origins of these financial responsibilities were in the sixteenth century. Several of the earlier intendants had been given limited financial

---

[1] E 173b, fo. 504. [2] E 154a, fo. 141, 19 Jan. 1640.
[3] Esmonin, *La taille*, p. 431. E 66a, fo. 215, 6 Feb. 1621. E 178a, fo. 12, 4 Mar. 1643.
[4] E 175, fo. 417, 17 Dec. 1642. [5] E 162c, fo. 173.

FIG. 6. Wheat prices at Paris, 1600–1700.

The prices given are for one *setier* (at Paris this was equivalent to 156 litres) of best quality wheat. The dotted line shows the average figure for the harvest year (August 1600–July 1601 = harvest year 1600), while the continuous line shows the average figure for the calendar year. The half-year difference between the two averages highlights the years in which the harvests failed and the prices rose substantially. No price series can be taken as representative of national trends in the price of the same commodity, let alone national trends in the prices of other commodities. 'Prices varied according to the season of the year. They varied from region to region and market to market and within the same market they varied according to the differing quantities and qualities of the grain being bought.' (C. J. Harrison, 'Grain price analysis and harvest qualities [in England], 1465–1634', *Agricultural History Review*, xix (1971), 146.)
Sources: Harvest years. M. Baulant and J. Meuvret, *Prix des céréales extraits de la Mercuriale de Paris, 1520–1698* (2 vols., 1960, 1962).
    Calendar years. M. Baulant, 'Le prix des grains à Paris de 1431 à 1788', *Annales E.S.C.*, xxiii (1968), 539.

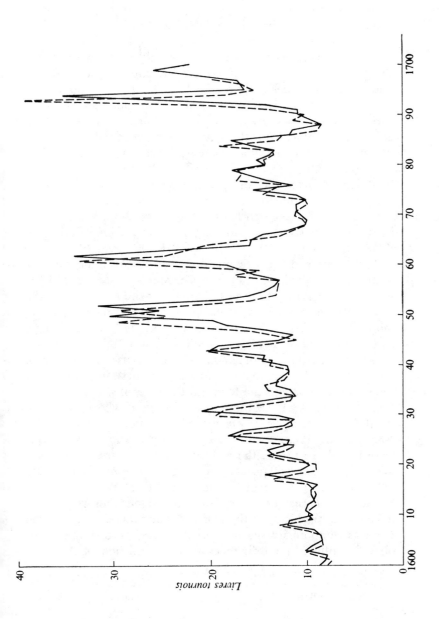

Livres tournois

tasks. In Normandy in 1567, 1570, and 1579, there were commissioners for the reform (*régalement*) of the *taille*.[1] These experiments were to have great importance for the future, and it was not surprising that Normandy should lead the way in the demand for fiscal reform since it contributed between fifteen and twenty-five per cent of the taxes of the kingdom. The Estates of Normandy wanted fiscal reform, but they regarded these commissioners with suspicion. The initiative in this experiment came from the government, in response to complaints about unfair tax assessments. These experiments had a formative influence on Chancellor Cheverny, Sully, and Saldaigne d'Incarville, the *contrôleur-général des finances*. On 23 August 1598 letters patent and instructions were issued to commissioners appointed for the task of re-allocating the *taille* in at least nine *généralités* and possibly in the majority of the *pays d'élections*.

The commissioners were instructed to discover the cause of 'l'abus et ... l'inégalité' in the assessments of the *taille*. They were not necessarily to heed the advice of the *trésoriers* and the *élus*, especially since the latter were suspected of committing most of the abuses. Popular grievances, and in particular, complaints against the *sergents* of the *taille* were to be taken into consideration. The commissioners were to ask a number of questions. Could the area in question pay the sums required by the government? Did the towns in the area pay a fair proportion of the taxes? Were there cases of persons who enjoyed the fiscal privileges of town life yet who actually resided in the countryside? Were there cases of persons who claimed, but were unable to prove, the right of exemption from taxation? Were there cases of peculation by the *receveurs* of the *taille*? Whoever wrote these instructions—whether it was Sully or Saldaigne d'Incarville—was clearly intelligent and well versed in the fiscal problems of the period.[2] The independence of the *élus* was temporarily suspended, since they were required to obey the rulings and ordinances of the commissioners. A decree

---

[1] *Cahiers des États de Normandie sous le règne de Charles IX, 1561–1573*, ed. C. de Robillard de Beaurepaire (Rouen, 1891), pp. 11, 46–7, 235–8. *Cahiers ... Henri III*, ed. Robillard de Beaurepaire, i. 40, 123–5, 149–50; ii. 63. Cf. Esmonin, *La taille*, p. 43.

[2] Barbiche, 'Les commissaires pour le "régalement" des tailles', pp. 65–7. Z1a 206, p. 93, 23 Aug. 1598.

of 23 December 1598 ordered the commissioners and the *élus* to carry out the assessments jointly, except where the commissioners failed to arrive on time in the province.[1] In addition, a thorough investigation into titles of nobility was undertaken in some provinces—for example, by Mesmes de Roissy at Caen.[2] The commissioners concluded their work by drawing up reports and rulings which were the basis of the celebrated edict on the *taille* of March 1600.[3]

A number of doubts about the efficacy of this experiment were raised by contemporaries. It is by no means clear that the *maîtres des requêtes* and councillors of state chosen for the commission possessed sufficient financial ability for the tasks conferred on them. Each was advised by a *trésorier de France* and a *conseiller* in the *cour des aides* chosen usually from outside the *généralité*: but the mere fact that these associate commissioners were appointed at all implies doubt on the part of the government at the ability of its principal servants to grapple with the technicalities of fiscal problems. A second reservation about the experiment was that it was of very short duration—one fiscal year only (1598–9). There was a serious danger that such limited intervention might not only fail to make matters better, but might actually make matters worse. Groulart, a *président* in the *cour des aides* at Rouen thought that '[on] n'a pas beaucoup profité, et au contraire, a plus chargé le pays que jamais . . .'[4] A proposed ruling on the *taille* in 1615 admitted that 'le mal y auroict esté l'année suivante comme au précéddant'.[5] Sully does not seem to have used these commissioners again, except apparently in Normandy in 1604,[6] although he sent out a variety of other types of financial commissioner, especially in 1598–1600. On 24 October 1613, however, the idea was revived. Chancellor Brûlart de Sillery and Gilles de Maupeou, an *intendant des finances*, signed a decree of the council of finance committing the government to send out commissioners the following year 'en ch[ac]une élection de ce Royaume' to

[1] ibid., 76. E 1c, fo. 235.   [2] B.L. Harleian 4567.
[3] Barbiche, art. cit., pp. 84, n. 3, 86–96. La Barre, *Formulaire des esleuz*, pp. 283, 291.
[4] *Cahiers des États de Normandie sous le règne de Henri IV*, ed. C. de Robillard de Beaurepaire (2 vols., Rouen, 1880–2), i. 279. Barbiche, art. cit., p. 83, n. 5.
[5] Z1a 206, p. 479.
[6] La Barre, *Formulaire des esleuz*, p. 202.

investigate contraventions of the edict on the *taille* of March 1600.[1] There were opponents of this policy. In his advice to the council of finance in 1614, a certain M. Gaucher argued that the investigation was likely to prove unsatisfactory since there was no local machinery to ensure that the reforms of the commissioners were implemented after they had returned to Paris. The commissioners were not usually natives of the provinces and did not have time to acquire the necessary detailed knowledge of the relative wealth of the parishes and *élections*. The size of each *généralité* prevented the commissioners from coming to grips with the detail of the problem at parish level.[2] Gaucher's criticisms, together with the revolt of Condé in 1614, seem to have quashed the scheme, except in Normandy, where an investigation into fiscal exemptions was carried out by Jeannin and Arnauld.[3]

In April 1623 a new investigation for the re-allocation of the *taille* was undertaken, and the commission of 1598 was reissued without significant alteration[4] in six *généralités*. In the provinces where the investigation took place, the fundamental weakness was its temporary nature. The *trésoriers* at Rouen conceded the right of Dany de la Faultrière and Dolézy to carry out the allocation of taxes between the *élections* 'sans tirer à conséquence ny préjudicier à la charge et pouvoir des trésoriers de France audit département des tailles'. As soon as the Normandy commissioners had returned to Paris in March 1625, however, there was a general attempt to 'remettre le mesme désordre qui y estoit auparavant et renverser ce qu'ont fait lesdits commissaires'.[5] Moreover in twelve *généralités* the investigation did not take place at all, 'l'estat présent des affaires de Sa Majesté' not permitting an extension of the enquiry into the whole of France. In most of the *pays d'élections*, therefore, the *élus* were merely exhorted by the council of finance on 29 July 1623 to decide on their visits of inspection by 16 August, to compare the parish tax-rolls for 1622 and 1623, to 's'informer des facultez et moyens des cottisez' and to decide upon 'des moyens et remeddes à observer pour corriger les abbus'.[6] Since these were tasks

[1] E 42a, fo. 341, 24 Oct. 1613.   [2] Z1a 206, pp. 467–9.
[3] *Cahiers . . . Louis XIII et Louis XIV*, ed. Robillard de Beaurepaire, i. 75.
[4] B.N. MS.fr. 17311, fo. 33.
[5] Vannier, *Bureau des finances de Rouen*, pp. 96–7, E 81b, fo. 380, 22 Mar. 1625.
[6] Z1a 206, p. 597 and E 75b, fo. 317, 29 July 1623.

which increased rather than diminished the opportunities for corruption of the *élus*, they scarcely suggest a thorough-going fiscal reform.

The investigation in 1634 was much more significant. Whereas ten years earlier a minority of the *généralités* had been affected, on this occasion the enquiry comprised all the *pays d'élections*. The instructions given to the commissioners were clearly based on the model of 1598—the reference to the peace of Vervins was not omitted although France was about to enter the Thirty Years' War.[1] The investigation was greatly assisted by the ruling on the *taille* that was issued in January 1634. This acted as a guide to the commissioners. It also revoked all *lettres d'anoblissement* granted during the previous twenty years which allowed the commissioners to strike at privileges recently gained by the village notables (*coqs de paroisse*)—chiefly *notaires*, lesser office-holders and more prosperous peasants[2]—at the expense of the parish as a whole. During the fiscal years 1635 and 1636, the commissioners exercised the functions of the *trésoriers* and the *élus*. Choisy at Châlons, Dupré at Poitiers, and probably most of the other commissioners were given the power to preside over the *bureaux des finances*.[3] In some cases, as at Tours, the *trésoriers* refused the intendant presidency over, or even entry into, their *bureaux*. A decree of the council of finance of 28 September 1634 ordered them to desist.[4] In addition, the *trésoriers* were prohibited from ordering the *élus* to carry out the parish assessments—unless, that is, that the commissioners failed to arrive on time. The *trésoriers* at Orléans, Moulins, and Rouen disregarded this decree, and consequently it was decided that new assessments should be drawn up in the

---

[1] A.G. A1 21, no. 122, 25 May 1634. However, there were more recent initiatives. Cf. the role of Pierre Bombail, a *commissaire des guerres*, who had worked on proposals for reform since 1628 'de sorte qu'il ne sera plus besoing à l'advenir d'envoyer des commissaires par les provinces pour obvier à telz désordres . . .' E 116b, fo. 333, 27 Mar. 1634.

[2] Bercé, *Histoire des croquants*, i. 77.

[3] A.G. A1 21, no. 160 and A1 96, no. 155, 18 Aug. 1634.

[4] *Lettres . . . au Chancelier Séguier*, ed. Mousnier, i. 248. E 120a, fo. 478, 28 Sept. 1634. This opposition seems to have been traditional. Cf. the opposition of the *trésoriers* of Amiens to Godart, the intendant: E 59b, fo. 259, 22 Sept. 1618. In contrast, the *trésoriers* of Paris registered the commission of Lauzon and Plaine Sevette without difficulty and allowed them to enter the bureau to hold the general assessment: Z1f 189 fos. 180ᵛ, 192, 3 Oct. and 25 Oct. 1634.

presence of the intendants.[1] Certain of the commissioners—
Aligre at Caen, for example—carried out a thorough investigation into claims of nobility and fraudulent exemptions from
taxation.[2] Fines and restitutions were ordered on this question,
and these proved to be exceedingly controversial in Picardy and
the Lyonnais. The *trésoriers* at Lyon used this popular grievance
with some success as an excuse for obstructing the work of the
commissioners.[3] At Amiens there appears to have been corruption on the part of the minor officials employed by the intendants to levy these fines.[4] Wherever possible, however, the
intendants sought to avoid excessive reliance on local officials,
who might be corrupt or prejudiced. Chiefly, they relied on the
objective evidence (or relatively so) of the tax-rolls. Marc de La
Ferté at Alençon checked the tax-rolls back to the previous
investigation of 1624.[5] Verthamon found such confusion in
Guyenne that he checked the tax-rolls back to 1600![6] Above
all, the commissioners in 1634–5 were amazed by the extent of
the corruption of the *élus*.[7] The investigation enjoyed an
exactly similar fate to that ten years earlier. The *trésoriers* of
Rouen and Caen presented a request to the council of finance
to the effect that the allocation of the taxes by the commissioners
should be allowed to stand for 1635 and 1636 only. In 1637 and
thereafter they demanded permission to raise or lower the
amounts paid by the *élections* 'pour le soulagement du peuple et
pour le bien du service de Sadite Majesté'. The council of
finance agreed to the request on 8 March 1636.[8] From this
moment, any benefits that had accrued from the investigation
were likely to be undermined.[9] In one respect, however, the

[1] E 120b, fos. 201–2, 14 Oct. 1634. E 122a, fo. 197, 20 Jan. 1635. At Rouen, the general assessment carried out by the *trésoriers* was eventually allowed to stand: Vannier, *Bureau des finances de Rouen*, pp. 98–9. [2] B.L. Harleian 4568.

[3] *Lettres . . . au Chancelier Séguier*, ed. Mousnier, i. 269–70, 276–7. A.D. Rhône C 561, fos. 152ᵛ, 162ᵛ, 211ᵛ, 8 and 14 June 1635, 16 July 1635. E 124b, fo. 175, 30 June 1635. E 139, fo. 320, 22 Aug. 1637. E 141c, fo. 443, 27 Feb. 1638.

[4] *Lettres . . . au Chancelier Séguier*, ed. Mousnier, i. 273–4. E 124b, fo. 173, 30 June 1635.

[5] M. Baudot, 'La réformation de la taille en Moyenne Normandie en 1634 et la création de l'intendance d'Alençon', *Revue Historique de Droit Français et Étranger*, 4th ser., xxix (1951), 138.

[6] Bercé, *Histoire des croquants*, i. 74. E 123b, fo. 46, 9 May 1635.

[7] A.G. A1 26, no. 144, 23 Jan. 1635. [8] E 129a, n.f.

[9] The uncertainty of the council of finance is revealed by E 128c, fos. 203, 333, 16 Feb. 1636.

investigation in 1634–5 showed a positive achievement particularly as against that of 1598–9. The *maître des requêtes* was accompanied by only one financial official, a *trésorier de France* from outside the province—thus suggesting greater ministerial confidence in the abilities of the intendants, probably as a result of the experience gained in 1623–4. There can be little doubt that the *commissaires pour le régalement des tailles* foreshadowed the transfer of ultimate financial responsibility in the provinces to the intendants. As Guyot observed of the investigation in 1598, 'cette association d'un maître des requêtes aux deux autres commissaires donna par la suite l'idée d'attribuer aux intendans le droit de concourir avec les trésoriers de France dans toutes les opérations relatives au département des tailles'.[1]

The intendants were given new financial responsibilities in 1637, when they had the task of levying the forced loan on the towns, in 1638 when they levied the *subsistances*, in 1639 when they levied a wealth-tax (*taxe des aisés*), and in 1641 when they were charged with the levy of a five per cent sales tax (the *sol pour livre*). On each occasion, the financial officials showed their resentment: the *trésoriers* of Lyon protested in 1637 against the forced loan;[2] the *trésoriers* of Alençon, Lyon, and Limoges and the *élus* of Château-Chinon, Grenoble, Vienne, Romans, Valence, and Montélimar protested in 1638–41 over the *subsistances*;[3] while the *élus* generally were uncooperative with regard to the sales tax. The levy of the *subsistances* in many provinces became an annual activity of the intendants;[4] but this tax brought in much less than the *taille*. The estimated revenues from the *subsistances* were 13·7 million in 1641 and 1642, while the estimated revenues from the *taille* had reached 43·5 million by 1639 and 72·6 million by 1643.

The fundamental problem, therefore, remained the *taille*, upon which the government was forced to rely disproportionately during the war against Spain. By 1642 the revenues of the *taille* had been anticipated at least one year in advance by

[1] Guyot and Merlin, *Traité des droits*, iii. 374.

[2] *Lettres . . . au Chancelier Séguier*, ed. Mousnier, i. 370–1, 385–6, 407–8.

[3] E 146a, fo. 121, 15 Sept. 1638. E 146b, fo. 69, 7 Oct. 1638. E 159b, fo. 58, 17 Jan. 1641.

[4] But not at Paris or Soissons, where the *trésoriers* carried out the levy: Z1f 197, fo. 156ᵛ, 11 Aug. 1640; E 164a, fo. 223ᵛ, 7 Sept. 1641.

the method of loan contracts negotiated with the financiers. The growing arrears of the *taille* were thus extremely serious. Not only did they threaten the credibility of the revenues upon which future loans were to be contracted; they led the financiers to panic about the security of their investment. Throughout 1642 Claude Le Bouthillier, the *surintendant des finances*, warned Richelieu of the need to reduce government expenditure, to improve the collection of the *taille*, and to bolster up financial confidence.[1] A threatened strike by the financiers in the summer of 1642 led to dramatic changes: on 5 June, the council of finance pledged full repayment to the financiers for loans, if necessary by replacement of the revenues upon which repay, ment was assigned;[2] on 22 August 1642, the assessments of the *taille* were conferred on the intendants.

The significance of this decision has long been recognized.[3] The commissions ordering all forms of direct taxation (that is to say, the *taille*, the *subsistances*, the *taillon*, and the *crues*) were henceforth to be directed to the intendants, the *trésoriers*, and the *élus*. The commissions were to be brought to the *bureau des finances*, over which the intendant was to preside and where the distribution of taxes for the *généralité* and all the necessary ordinances and other dispatches were to be drawn up. The intendant was then to visit the *élections* and to carry out the parish assessments. In this task, he was to be assisted by a *trésorier* chosen from the *bureau* by his colleagues and three *élus* nominated by the intendant himself. He was also to be assisted by the *receveur* and various lesser officials. If the *trésoriers* refused the intendant the presidency over their *bureau*, or else to delegate one of their colleagues, the intendant could proceed without them. The same was true for the *élus*, except that the intendant had to replace the absent officials with other local notables. The intendant and his assistants were empowered to carry out the special taxes on privileged persons in the parish (*taxes d'office*) in accordance with the edict of November 1640. In drawing up the assessments, special care was to be taken that the rich contributed in proportion to their wealth. The verifica-

[1] A.A.E. France 842, fo. 44, 17 Feb. 1642.

[2] E 171a, fo. 145.

[3] J. Caillet, *De l'administration en France sous le ministère du Cardinal de Richelieu* (1857), pp. 52–3; Esmonin, *La taille*, p. 45; Mousnier, *La plume*, pp. 190–1. The ruling is in AD + 271.

tion of the tax-rolls was to be carried out by the intendant and his assistants at the parish assessments. They alone could appoint collectors when the parishes failed to do so. The intendant was to investigate all cases of fraud and peculation and to ensure that the *élus* had carried out the decree of 27 November 1641, which had ordered them to ensure that the assessments for the fiscal year 1642 were fair. Illegal interference in the fiscal process by nobles was to be severely punished.

The way in which the ruling worked can be traced in detail, although there were considerable local variations. The *trésoriers* at Bourges registered the commission of Barrin de Rezé, the intendant, on 28 March 1642 and the ruling of 22 August 1642 as well 'pour y estre exécutée et y avoir recours quand besoing sera'. They allowed Barrin to preside over their *bureau* without difficulty in the winter of 1642–3.[1] Elsewhere, the intendants experienced much greater difficulty. The *trésoriers* of Paris resolved on making remonstrances to the council as soon as they received the ruling of 22 August. On 17 October, they decided to refuse Montescot, the intendant, the presidency over their *bureau*. After a delay of over a fortnight (5–23 November 1642), Montescot asked the *trésoriers* for the second time whether they were prepared to 'travailler avec luy dans les termes dudit règlement'. The *trésoriers* refused, whereupon Montescot replied that he would proceed on his own, which is what he did.[2] At Bordeaux, there was little co-operation between Lauzon, the intendant, and the *trésoriers*.[3] Clearly such compliance as at Bourges was rare indeed, although the intendants had the whip-hand: the ruling was implemented throughout the *pays d'élections* regardless of the attitude of the *trésoriers*.[4]

The declaration of 16 April 1643 continued the same system for the next and subsequent fiscal years. It was followed up by decrees on 8 August and 22 August 1643 which ordered that the

[1] A.D. Cher C 916, C 917, *passim*.

[2] G. Delaume *Le bureau des finances de la généralité de Paris* (1966), pp. 35–7. Zif 200, fos. 245, 268, 285, 298, 15 Sept., 17 Oct., 5 and 23 Nov. 1642.

[3] Bercé, *Histoire des croquants*, i. 85. A.D. Gironde C 3879, fo. 36ᵛ, 12 Nov. 1642.

[4] However, the *trésoriers* of Lyon disclaimed all knowledge of the ruling of 22 Aug. 1642 and appeared to regard the declaration of 16 Apr. 1643 as a new departure: *Letters . . . au Chancelier Séguier*, ed. Mousnier, i. 525–8. Mousnier, *La plume*, p. 194.

declaration should be carried out without waiting for full registration by the provincial *cour des aides*.[1] The decree of 8 August empowered the intendants to carry out the assessments 'sans qu'aucuns des trésoriers de France desdits bureaux s'y puissent entremettre'. A subsequent decree—on 23 November 1644—discouraged the *trésoriers* from selecting their own nominees, although the intendant himself, or more usually the council of finance, might do so.[2] The intendants were given the authority to carry out the *taxes d'office* on their own if necessary.[3] The *trésoriers* fought a losing rearguard action against these measures. The *trésoriers* of Paris decided on 18 August 1643 that no member of their *bureau* should co-operate with the intendant during the next fiscal year. However, on 18 December they relented and nominated deputies.[4] The *trésoriers* of Bordeaux issued remonstrances on 'le grand préjudice que nous avons receu depuis 10 ou 12 ans' particularly due to the establishment of the *bureau des finances* at Montauban and 'l'autorité que Messieurs les intendans de justice ont en ceste province qui cognoissent et ordonnent générallem[ent] de tout': but they, too, succumbed.[5] The *trésoriers* of Rouen found themselves divided in their opposition to Miroménil, the intendant.[6]

The council of finance ordered the intendant to nominate three *élus* to assist him at the assessments in each *élection*.[7] By a decree of 10 January 1643 the *élus* who had not been chosen by the intendant were prohibited from interfering with their colleagues on pain of confiscation of their offices.[8] The *cour des*

[1] E 1684, fo. 416 and E 182a, fo. 361, 8 Aug. 1643. E 1684, fos. 427, 429, 22 Aug. 1643.

[2] E 196b, fo. 224, 24 Nov. 1644. Z1f 202, fo. 234ᵛ, 1 Dec. 1644.

[3] E 195b, fo. 362, 19 Oct. 1644. E 217b, fo. 435, 28 Nov. 1646.

[4] Delaume, op. cit., p. 37. Z1f 201, fos. 195, 284, 18 Aug. and 18 Dec. 1643. E 185a, fo. 542, 9 Dec. 1643. E 185b, fo. 278, 19 Dec. 1643.

[5] A.D. Gironde C 3879, fo. 33, 9 Sept. 1643. E 184b, fo. 131, 21 Oct. 1643—four *trésoriers* to assist Lauzon instead of two. Lauzon's position was reinforced by his marriage to Colombe de la Chabanne, sister of Jean de la Chabanne, a *trésorier* at Bordeaux: Bercé, loc cit.

[6] Vannier, *Bureau des finances de Rouen*, p. 101. A.D. Seine-Maritime C 1149, fo. 272ᵛ, 23 Dec. 1643. Cf. also the opposition at Moulins: *Lettres . . . au Chancelier Séguier*, ed. Mousnier, i. 556–7.

[7] Thus on 16 Mar. 1645 Jean Le Camus, the intendant at Châlons, commissioned Boucherat de la Rocatelle as his *subdélégué* in the *élection* of Troyes: Arbois de Jubainville, *Intendants de l'Aube*, pp. 211–12. Commissions 'pour tenir la main à l'accélération et au recouvrement des deniers' were frequently conferred by the intendants on individual *élus* after 1642.   [8] E 176a, fo. 181.

aides of Paris attempted to come to the rescue of the *élus* as a corporate group. On 9 July 1643—and also in the decree of verification of 21 July—it ordered the intendants to be assisted by six *élus* in each *élection* in order of seniority, while at Paris the intendant was to be assisted by all the *élus*.[1] The day after the decree of verification was issued by the *cour des aides*, however, the council of finance ordered the intendants to use only the three *élus* specified in the ruling of 16 April 1643 because of the danger of 'collusion et intelligence avec tous leurs confrères . . . de surcharger les foibles et soulager les parroisses puissantes'.[2] In the *généralité* of Paris, however, Montescot appears to have used six *élus*, though not in order of seniority, and the same *élus subdélégués* were used in successive years.[3]

The intendants certainly carried out the *taxes d'office* affecting privileged persons in the parishes. Miroménil and Pascal gave verdict against a powerful clique at Gisors who had gained exemption from the *taille*.[4] Much depended on the personality of the intendant, however. The intendants of Normandy in general did not have a particularly good record on this subject and were threatened with recall in 1647 since 'se voyants persécuttez par les sollicitations continuelles des gentilzhommes [et] officiers de ladite province . . . [ils] se relaschent d'exécutter lesdits règlements . . .'[5] The intendants verified the tax-rolls[6] and appointed collectors where the parishes had been negligent.[7]

The council of finance sometimes nominated the *receveur-général* to assist the intendant in the assessments.[8] The *receveurs* were instructed to send a copy of their accounts to the intendants month by month, and if they could not account for their financial management since the outbreak of the war they were liable to dismissal by the intendants.[9] There is clear evidence that the intendants examined the registers of the *receveurs* and prosecuted cases of negligence and peculation. In January 1643, the intendants of Riom, Paris, Bourges, Poitiers, Soissons,

[1] Mousnier, *La plume*, p. 192. Z1a 161, fo. 128, 9 July 1643.
[2] E 181c, fo. 112, 22 July 1643.   [3] E 189b, fo. 287, 27 Apr. 1644.
[4] E 206b, fo. 42, 20 Sept. 1645.   [5] E 227c, fo. 647, 19 Dec. 1647.
[6] E 217b, fo. 505, 28 Nov. 1646. E 222a, fo. 590, 13 Apr. 1647. E 228b, fo. 148, 29 Jan. 1648.
[7] E 178a, fo. 143, 11 Mar. 1643.   [8] E 174a, fo. 146, 6 Nov. 1642.
[9] E 162c, fo. 173, 4 July 1641. E 175, fo. 400, 17 Dec. 1642.

and Rouen received identical powers to dismiss the *receveurs* and appoint in their place agents nominated by the financiers.[1] The procedure was simple and effective. The case of Philippes Jacques may be taken as representative. A consortium of financiers under the name of Jacques had made a loan to the government of 1,580,000 *livres* on 14 May 1642, and were to be reimbursed from the receipts of the *généralité* of Rouen.[2] However, the *receveurs* were found to be greatly in arrears. Thus Claude Paris, the intendant, and Pascal, his assistant, were ordered to replace the *receveurs* with agents chosen by Jacques.[3] This was a regular procedure in Normandy and the Lyonnais before the Fronde[4] and it is possible that it occurred widely in the *pays d'élections*. In terms of personnel, the changes may not always have been significant, because the consortium of financiers making the loan to the government may sometimes have included the *receveur-général* of the *généralité*.[5] In institutional terms, however, the change was extremely significant for unlike the *receveurs*, the agents had to give a form of collateral security to the financiers.[6] The measure was intended to prevent substantial arrears on the part of the *receveurs* in future years, and as such it greatly contributed towards the restoration of financial confidence which enabled Mazarin to mortgage the

---

[1] E 176a, fos. 368–77, 17 Jan. 1643.

[2] E 170a, fo. 522, 14 May 1642.

[3] E 176a, fo. 368, 17 Jan. 1643. However, in this case there came to be a conflict of interest between Philippes Jacques and Denis Gedoyn, a temporary *trésorier de l'Épargne*, who had loaned 4 million on five *généralités* including Rouen. Because of this unusual state of affairs, the *receveur-général* was reinstated as a neutral party: E 178b, fo. 352, 28 Mar. 1643.

[4] e.g. Caen: E 177b, fo. 98, 25 Feb. 1643. E 185a, fo. 384, 5 Dec. 1643. E 217a, fo. 150, 7 Nov. 1646. Rouen: E 185a, fo. 382, 5 Dec. 1643. E 186a, fo. 217, 9 Jan. 1644. Alençon: E 214b, fo. 300, 11 Aug. 1646. Lyon: E 204a, fo. 469, 8 July 1645. E 227b, fo. 253, 23 Nov. 1647.

[5] e.g. the loans on the *généralité* of Bordeaux by *prête-noms* for Pierre Puget de Montauron, who was *receveur-général*: P 2358, p. 647, 16 Sept. 1630. Elsewhere, the financiers required the *receveurs* to make loans to them: if they refused, they were dismissed. Bonneau and Marin re-established the *receveurs* of Bourges in 1644–6 in return for loans: cf. E 265b, fo. 115, 20 May 1654.

[6] That is to say, the agents entered private contracts with the financiers 'à forfaict, perilz, risques et fortunes et sans nonvalleurs et de payer dans les temps y mentionnez'. Cf. subcontract between Bonneau and Marin and the *receveurs* of Bourges, 17 Feb. 1645. Cf. E 265b, fo. 114, 20 May 1654. In turn, the financiers agreed that any losses incurred would be borne on the revenues assigned to them, and that the crown would not be obliged to assign further revenues: E 177b, fo. 99, 25 Feb. 1643.

revenues of the kingdom on an unprecedented scale. Certain intendants expressed reservations about these changes,[1] and the changes themselves certainly provided ammunition for those who claimed that it was the financiers who administered the provinces with the intendants reduced to a subservient role[2]— an exaggeration that nevertheless did much to discredit the intendants in 1648.

The intendants also investigated the arrears of taxation from 1636 to 1640,[3] and in cases where this was due to 'malice et rébellion affectée',[4] sent in the troops to restore order. They entered into the detail of fiscal administration in order to speed up the tax-returns. Le Picard de Périgny in the Soissonnais was given permission to 'diminuer et descharger sur lesdits impositions aux parroisses les plus pauvres ou qui sont dans l'impuissance de paier'.[5] At Bourges, Barrin de Rezé was ordered to draw up a detailed list of those parishes most in arrears.[6] The general principle upon which the intendants operated was that of giving favourable treatment to those parishes which at least attempted to pay their arrears. Thus at Caen, Le Roy de La Potherie asked the council of finance to reduce the amount of arrears to be levied lest the parishes in question be left deserted by their inhabitants.[7] The intendants made serious efforts to limit abuses by the *huissiers* and *sergents* of the *taille*: a decree of 10 May 1642 ordered all 'porteurs des quittances, huissiers, sergens et commis' to present their claims to the intendant and obtain his permission before attempting to coerce payment from the parishes.[8] Finally, where large areas of a province refused to pay their taxes, special brigades were set up by the intendant to levy the *taille* on his orders.[9] Thus the government

---

[1] *Lettres . . . au Chancelier Séguier*, ed. Mousnier, i. 133. A.G. A1 110, no. 82, 27 June 1648. Chaulnes was influenced by the projected meeting of the *Chambre Saint-Louis*, however.

[2] Mousnier, *La plume*, pp. 183, 305.

[3] E 171a, fo. 145, 5 June 1642; E 172a, fo. 468, 9 July 1642; E 173b, fo. 324, 16 Sept. 1642.

[4] E 173a, fo. 26, 8 Aug. 1642.

[5] E 193a, fo. 236, 3 Aug. 1644.

[6] E 184a, fo. 165, 14 Oct. 1643.

[7] E 177b, fo. 117, 25 Feb. 1643.

[8] E 170a, fo. 336, 10 May 1642. Cf. E 170b, fo. 217, 24 May 1642. E 173a, fo. 175, 19 Aug. 1642. The preceding system was that the *receveurs des tailles* ordered coercion: E 119b, fo. 2, 23 Aug. 1634.

[9] Bercé, *Histoire des croquants*, i. 108–12. Cf. below, chapter X.

offered the parishes both a positive and a negative incentive to pay their taxes—positive in that a reduction of the amount to be paid was possible if the intendant considered that the parish was doing its best; negative, in that the ultimate recourse for the intendant was to billet troops on the parish if it persisted in its refusal to co-operate.

This extremely controversial financial system, which was introduced in the summer of 1642, lasted initially for six years. The intendants' period of financial administration was a major catalyst in the coalition of forces that began the Fronde. The chronic state of bankruptcy in 1648, the mishandling of the negotiations over the renewal of the *droit annuel*, and the panic reaction to the *arrêt d'union* of 13 May 1648, precipitated the Fronde. It was clear, however, that once the *Chambre Saint-Louis* met, there was likely to be wide-ranging discussion of reform. Once grievances came to the fore, it was probable that the administration of the intendants—because of their role in taxation and their connection with the financiers—would dominate discussion and provide a much-needed unifying factor to the critics of the ministry. The initial attack on the intendants came from those financial officials whose interests had suffered most from their administration since 1642.

CHAPTER IX

The Administration of Direct Taxes
1648–1661

THE ATTACK on the intendants began in earnest in the early summer of 1648. The lesser financial officials attempted direct action and also tried to influence opinion by drawing up remonstrances. On 23 May 1648, the *trésoriers* in their central *bureau* at Paris sent out a circular to their members in the provinces asking for information on 'la mauvaise conduite des intendants sur l'administration des finances, leurs exactions, et celle des traitants'. The only direct consequence of this action, however, was the arrest of six *trésoriers*.[1] Nevertheless, they could seek to influence the much more formidable *Chambre Saint-Louis* by making sure that their views were known. The *élus* issued remonstrances which stated categorically that 'le Roy est mal servy et le peuple ruiné par les traitans, leurs intendans et autres gens à leur dévotion qui font toutes les vexations impunément . . .' The *élus* advised the abrogation of the loan contracts on the *taille*, the recall of the intendants, the abolition of the special brigades, and a substantial remission of taxes to compensate for the interest payments paid to the financiers.[2] A deputation of six *trésoriers* to the *Parlement* of Paris argued that 'ces intendans et partisans' had combined 'non seulement pour la ruine desdicts trésoriers de France, mais de toutes les autres officiers des provinces'. They alleged that the bankruptcy of the state had been caused by the 'concussions, péculats, rançonnemens et autres violences' of the intendants and the financiers.[3]

The proposal of the *Chambre Saint-Louis* for the abolition of the intendants was countered by ministerial objections that 'dans les provinces il étoit fort difficile d'en tirer [de l'argent] sans l'assistance des intendans de justice qui tenoient la main

---

[1] Mousnier, *La plume*, p. 308. Charmeil, *Trésoriers*, pp. 269–70.
[2] Z1a 206, p. 897.
[3] U 28, fos, 188ᵛ–189ʳ, 10 July 1648.

à ce que les deniers du Roy fussent payés par les peuples'. The ministers accepted the principle that the intendants should be abolished, but wished the deputies to consider 'le temps, les momens, et l'importance de ce changement soudaine'. The government stated categorically that the troops could not be paid unless the tax-returns reached Paris promptly; this, it contended, could not be achieved by the *trésoriers* and the *élus*. The ministers considered that a return to financial administration by the *trésoriers* and the *élus* would lead to a collapse of the war effort. Chancellor Séguier fought to retain the intendants' fiscal powers but conceded that they should operate jointly with the *élus* in their *bureaux*.[1] Séguier was not trusted, however, and François-Théodore Nesmond, a former intendant in Languedoc, and a *président à mortier* in the *Parlement* of Paris, tried to obtain a declaration revoking the intendants which began with the words: 'le Roy ayant été informé des abus qui se commettoient dans les provinces par les intendans de justice au fait des tailles . . .'[2] The deputies of the sovereign courts did not succeed in imposing their own wording, but they won the main point, which was the recall of the intendants. The intendants were *personae non gratae* during the Fronde, in part because they were royal commissioners who deprived the financial officials of their tasks; but much more so because they were the administrators of the hated fiscal system - 'ils étoient mal voulus des peuples, lesquels les considéroient comme leurs ennemis, comme les valets des partisans, non pas comme les hommes du Roi . . .'[3] The Fronde was directed both against the fiscal system and its agents.[4]

The fact that the deputies of the Parisian sovereign courts championed the claims of the financial officials secured their reinstatement in the summer of 1648. Return to the *status quo*

[1] Talon, *Mémoires*, ed. Michaud and Poujoulat, pp. 245–6. U 28, fo. 185, 6 July 1648. Z1a 163, fo. 62, 9 July 1648.
[2] Z1a 163, fo. 62ᵛ, 9 July 1648.   [3] Z1a 163, fo. 59, 9 July 1648.
[4] cf. the later manifestos of the Fronde, which proposed that former intendants be debarred from holding public office in France until they had been cleared of all charges against them, either 'en plain Parlement ou en plaine chambre de justice'. Former intendants were also to pay compensation for the sums they were alleged to have stolen during their administration in the provinces. 'Contrat de Mariage du Parlement avec la ville de Paris' (1649). *Choix de Mazarinades*, ed. C. Moreau (2 vols., 1853), i. 46. *Œuvres de Retz*, ed. A. Feillet *et al.* (10 vols., 1870–96), v. 445–6.

ante 1642 there certainly was: but was there to be a return to the system after 1 March 1640, which had given the *trésoriers* the presidency over the *élus* in the parish assessments, or was there to be a return to the rulings of 1600 and 1634 which had allowed the *élus* to enjoy this privilege with only general supervision by the *trésoriers*? The general assessments were clearly held by the *trésoriers* during the Fronde: at Paris, work on the assessment took place on 27 October 1648 and 18 November 1649;[1] at Rouen on 22 September 1648, 6 October 1651, and 25 October 1652;[2] at Lyon on 26 November 1649, on 29 October 1650, and in the autumn of 1651.[3] However, with the possible exception of the Soissonnais,[4] the *élus* succeeded in carrying out the parish assessments and rejecting the presidency of the *trésoriers*.

Clearly, there was great potential for conflict in this ambiguous situation. Numerous local conflicts arose. At various stages of the Fronde, the *élus* of Amiens, Bourges, Dijon, Limoges, Lyon, Roanne, Riom, Troyes, Vire, Vitry, Châteaugontier, Provins, and Melun were involved in conflicts with their respective *bureaux des finances*; most of these conflicts went to the king's council for mediation.[5] In addition, the rival claims of the two groups of officials were proclaimed by their deputies at Paris; attempts to come to a compromise broke down in June 1649. On 14 July 1649, the council of finance exhorted the two groups to 'vivre à l'advenir en bonne intelligence' so that the king's tax-returns would not be delayed.[6] On 25 September 1649, the council of finance appointed a commission to investigate the rival claims.[7] On 7 April 1650 an interim decree was issued whereby 'en attendant qu'il ayt esté pourveu par ung règlement général', the *trésoriers* were to continue 'la fonction et exercisse de leurs charges ainsi qu'ilz ont faict'. The *trésoriers* interpreted this as a weapon both against royal commissioners and against the *élus*; but its practical significance was small, and the success of the *trésoriers* in imposing their interpretation depended greatly on local circumstances. The government maintained an equivocal

[1] Z1f, 207, fo. 189. Z1f 209, fo. 208.
[2] Vannier, *Bureau des finances de Rouen*, pp. 102–3.
[3] A.D. Rhône C 570, fo. 479. C 571, fo. 385. C 572, fo. 233.
[4] Charmeil, *Trésoriers*, pp. 96, 430. E 233a, fo. 171ᵛ, 10 Oct. 1648.
[5] Bonney, 'Intendants', p. 242.
[6] E 235a, fo. 451.   [7] E 236b, fo. 374.

position that was to its own advantage, and avoided a permanent commitment that might have prejudiced the powers of the intendants at a future date.[1]

The dispute between the *trésoriers* and the *élus* would have had a serious effect on the levy of taxation. The *syndics* of the *élus* counselled their colleagues to speed up the recovery of the *taille*. However, there was no effective means of coercing payment, since the special brigades had been disbanded after the recall of the intendants, and in any case the *élus* objected to their use.[2] The council of finance specifically transferred to the *élus* certain of the powers accorded to the intendants in 1642–3. A decree of 18 September 1649 ordered them to carry out the *taxes d'office* in accordance with the ruling of 16 April 1643. They were ordered to verify and sign the tax-rolls without delay. If they refused to do this, the *président* of the *élection* was to sign the tax-rolls on pain of suspension from his office. The *procureur* of the *élection* was to request judicial action against all cases of 'exceds, viollances, rébellions et voyes de faict'.[3] A further decree, dated 8 January 1650, ordered the *président* of the *élection*, assisted by one *élu*, to carry out the *taxes d'office*, subject to appeal in the *cour des aides*. The *président* of the *élection* was to visit any areas that were in revolt and 'décrétter contre les coupables sur le champ'.[4]

The *trésoriers* were chiefly concerned with the suppression of peculation and the supervision of the *receveurs des tailles*, those accountancy aspects of taxation that had been transferred to the intendants in 1642–3. They also had a special role in ensuring that the sums levied were actually transferred to Paris. The evidence of their letters to the central assembly of the *trésoriers* at Paris suggests that they took their role seriously.[5] In addition, the *trésoriers* were given important tasks with regard to the organization of the 'staples' (*étapes*) for the troops.[6] The

[1] Mousnier, *La plume*, p. 328. Charmeil, *Trésoriers*, pp. 431–4. A definitive ruling between the *trésoriers* and the *élus* was still pending in June 1652: E 251b, fo. 267, 20 June 1652.

[2] Bercé, *Histoire des croquants*, i. 481–2. E 235b, fo. 266, 24 July 1649. E 236a, fo. 276, 4 Sept. 1649.   [3] E 236b, fo. 99.

[4] E 239, fo. 138.

[5] Mousnier, *La plume*, p. 312. Cf. E 232a, fo. 39, 5 Aug. 1648.

[6] Delaume, *Bureau des finances de Paris*, pp. 59–61. Bonvallet, 'Bureau des finances de Poitiers', p. 317, n. 1. Dumont, *Bureau des finances de Moulins*, p. 137. Cf. below, chapter XII.

council of finance refused to allow the whole *bureau des finances* in a *généralité* to participate in this activity, and instead nominated individual *trésoriers*. This was a source of contention among the financial officials. The four *trésoriers* of Paris nominated in October 1648 offered to 'se purger par serment de n'avoir recherché ny poursuivy directement ny indirectement lesdits commissions . . .' Their colleagues allowed them to carry out their tasks only with the proviso that such commissions would not 'tirer à conséquence pour l'advenir . . .'[1] All the *trésoriers* wanted to participate in this sort of activity, yet too many commissioners led to inefficiency and delay.[2]

The intentions of the *trésoriers* (except perhaps in the *généralité* of Soissons)[3] seem to have been good. The great weakness of administration by the *trésoriers*, however, was that as local men with property interests in the area they were reluctant to call in the troops to enforce the levy of the *taille*.[4] Without the threat of imminent coercion by the army, the rural taxpayers of France were not prepared to pay their taxes during the Fronde. The quarrel between the *trésoriers* and the *élus* precluded any constructive co-operation between these two groups of officials, and the *élus* were left very much to their own devices. A series of cases concerning alleged corruption on the part of the *élus* was brought to the attention of the council of finance during the Fronde. There were the usual charges of favouritism in the parish assessments—charges made, for example, against the *élus* in the *généralités* of Moulins and Riom,[5] and against the *élus* of Avranches[6] and Loches.[7] When individual *élus* were involved in private lawsuits with parishes in their area, they might exact vengeance at the parish assessments: the *élus* of La Charité overtaxed the parish of Champlency,[8] and the *élus* of Châteaugontier the parish of Saint-Denis d'Anjou,[9] for such reasons. Substantial arrears in taxes might be caused by the *élus*' reducing the burden on the rich parishes and over-

---

[1] Z1f 207, fo. 186, 21 Oct. 1648.   [2] Z1f 210, fo. 280ᵛ, 10 Dec. 1650.

[3] There were serious allegations of misconduct by these officials: Mousnier, *La plume*, p. 321. Charmeil, *Trésoriers*, pp. 95–6, 161, 391.

[4] However, they did consider this at Paris and at Lyon: Z1f 209, fo. 245ᵛ, 31 Dec. 1649. A.D. Rhône C 570, fo. 169, 12 Apr. 1649.

[5] E 254c, fos. 370, 632, 15 and 22 Feb. 1653.

[6] E 248a, fo. 528, 29 July 1651.   [7] E 234c, fo. 365, 19 June 1649.

[8] E 248b, fo. 259, 12 Aug. 1651.   [9] E 256b, fo. 346, 29 May 1653.

taxing the poor parishes, as in the *élection* of Montluçon.[1] Disputes between the *élus* themselves and rival assessments were not uncommon.[2] The *trésoriers* and the *élus* dissipated much of their remaining energies on opposing the re-introduction of the intendants.[3] At the end of the Fronde, the government would draw its own conclusions as to the reliability of the lesser financial officials.

In the spring of 1653, the dispute between the *trésoriers* and the *élus* was still in full momentum. On 27 January, the *élus* accused the *trésoriers* of advising the council to return to the system of war finance, because they had a financial interest in the loan contracts.[4] The appointment of Servien and Foucquet as joint *surintendants* offered both an opportunity and a danger to the financial officials: an opportunity in that they might reverse the drift towards reliance on royal commissioners; a danger in that the new appointees had no commitment to the policies adopted in 1648–9, and were certain to obtain Mazarin's backing for any measures they might consider necessary. The system adopted for the fiscal year commencing in the autumn of 1653[5] was likely to be of crucial importance, therefore. The *élus* issued proposals to the council of finance which would have confirmed their own privileges and salaries. No loans would have been made on the revenues of the *généralités*. Instead, the *élus* undertook to carry out the parish assessments 'si esgalement et justement . . . chascun en son eslection, qu'il n'y aura aucunes non valleurs'. The *élus* contended that they could levy 28 million *livres* net as against 14 million by the system of loans on the *généralités*. They offered as collateral security 6 million *livres* held over from their salaries. They argued that the government would have to pay 16 million in interest to the financiers, who would offer in return much less collateral security: 'tous les presteurs ensemble...n'ont de crédit que par le moyen des deniers de leurs receptes, dont ils

---

[1] E 248b, fo. 284, 23 Aug. 1651.   [2] E 254c, fo. 608, 22 Feb. 1653.

[3] Mousnier, *La plume*, pp. 315–19. Charmeil, *Trésoriers*, pp. 380–9. *Trésoriers* of Moulins: E 242a, fo. 224, 27 Apr. 1650. *Trésoriers* of Paris: Z1f 270, fos. 79ᵛ, 92, 7 and 20 Apr. 1650. *Trésoriers* of Riom: E 254c, fo. 370ᵛ. 15 Feb. 1653.

[4] Z1a 206, p. 1003, 27 Jan. 1653.

[5] Theoretically, the French taxpayers paid in five instalments, viz. 15 Nov., 15 Jan., 15 April, 15 July, 15 Oct.

font les prests et les advances imaginaires'. The *élus* undertook also to levy 30 million in arrears of taxes.[1]

This was not the only advice received by Séguier, Servien, and Foucquet, however. Denis Marin, a former financier who, as an intendant of finance in the army, had visited Guyenne, Poitou, Saintonge, and Aunis in the autumn of 1651, countered the arguments of the *élus* with more realistic figures, contending that the *maîtres des requêtes* in the provinces would save the government at least six million *livres*. Marin did not use the word 'intendant' because of its emotive quality after the debates in the *Chambre Saint-Louis* and sovereign courts in the summer of 1648. It is clear, however, that Marin contemplated the re-introduction of the intendants with financial powers similar to those which they had enjoyed in 1642–8. He argued that the *trésoriers* and the *élus* had committed many abuses in the levy of the *taille* during the Fronde which would be prevented by the presence of *maîtres des requêtes* in the provinces. These commissioners could ensure that any abolition of offices decided upon by the government would in fact be carried out. They could discipline the troops and organize the *étapes*. They could also ensure that the judicial officials performed their duties, or else have them suspended by the council. Above all, the *maîtres des requêtes* would carry out the assessments of the *taille* with great efficiency, and perhaps by their economies prevent recourse to the financiers in future years. They would be able to suppress tax rebellion and investigate any illicit levies of taxes or troops in the provinces.[2]

The two policies—those advocated by the *élus* and Denis Marin respectively—were mutually contradictory. Which would the government choose? Clearly much would depend on the overall direction of foreign policy. A further consideration was the objective assessment by the government of the experience of the Fronde, especially the years 1648 and 1649, when the financial officials had been left more or less to their own devices. The *trésoriers* and the *élus* maintained that they had made the best of a bad job. The admission on the part of the *élus* that there were arrears of 30 million in 1653 cast doubt

---

[1] Z1a 206, p. 1011.

[2] B.N. MS.fr. 16218, fo. 377. 'Mémoire pour monstrer l'utilité de l'employ des maîtres des requêtes dressé par M. Marin', 1653 [?]

on their argument. If the financial officials had failed to levy the relatively light taxes during the Fronde, what chance would there be of their levying the much heavier taxes that would be needed to pay for the war after 1653? Stated in these terms there was no real choice. The loan of 9 million *livres* contracted on 23 July 1653 with a consortium of financiers under the name of Richard Richer marked the decision of Séguier, Servien, and Foucquet to adopt Marin's proposal for the re-introduction of the intendants. The corollary of this decision was the need to eliminate opposition from the financial officials and to require them to day forced loans and other taxes as their contribution towards the war effort.[1]

In the majority of the *pays d'élections*, the intendants held both the general and parish assessments in the fiscal year beginning in the autumn of 1653. The *trésoriers* of Paris issued an ordinance on 29 August 1653 declaring that any 'extraordinary commissioners'—a deliberate slight to Le Tonnelier de Breteuil and Lefèvre de la Barre, the intendants—who sought to hold the assessments were contravening the edicts and rulings concerning the functions of the *trésoriers*.[2] Servien and Foucquet warned Mazarin that it was 'de la dernière importance de leur faire sentir quelque effet signalé de l'indignation du Roy'.[3] In the next few days, however, the situation deteriorated further. The cause was taken up by the *trésoriers* as a corporate group, who presented 'remonstrances' to the council of finance. They recalled that in the fiscal years 1643 and 1644 they had been 'absolument dépouillez de leurs fonctions' by 'divers partisans'—again a deliberately provocative reference to the fiscal powers accorded to the intendants. It now appeared that they were once more to be removed from the general assessment, which was to be transferred to the *maîtres des requêtes* who, in their view, ought to be restricted to the traditional tasks of their circuit-tours and not allowed to interfere in questions of taxation. They argued that royal commissioners were ill-suited to hold the assessments, 'n'en [pouvant] estre informez qu'en

---

[1] e.g. forced loan of 2 million *livres* on the *trésoriers* in 1655. Cf. E 274a, fo. 110, 13 Feb. 1655. Edict of March 1654 abolishing certain offices in the *élections* unless a forced loan was paid: E 1701, fo. 45, 12 Mar. 1654. E 265b, fo. 317, 21 May 1654. E 266b, fo. 428, 27 June 1654.

[2] Charmeil, *Trésoriers*, pp. 398–9. B.N. MS.fr. 16218, fo. 475.

[3] A.A.E. France 892, fo. 322, 8 Sept. 1653.

passant sur le rapport d'autruy'. Moreover, the intendants were interested only in the rapidity of the tax-returns, not in the ability of the parishes to pay: '[ils] n'ont intérest que d'emporter tout le fruict de la vigne pendant leur commission en arrachant le sep ou les branches, au lieu que les trésoriers de France ont intérest de la conserver . . .' The intendants levied the taxes with the aid of troops, while the *trésoriers* did not and thus avoided alienating the populace. Finally, the *trésoriers* blamed the arrears of taxes on the intendants; arrears, they claimed, had never existed before 'cette introduction qui a violé tous les ordres anciens'.[1]

On 17 September 1653, the *trésoriers* were summoned to appear before the council of finance—one of the rare meetings for which an account of the debate survives. Chancellor Séguier informed them that the king was very dissatisfied with their conduct and that they had no right to intervene in affairs of state. He claimed that they had tried to stir up the populace and the other office-holders against the king's orders, that they had held illicit assemblies at Paris, and that they sought to 'mettre...le feu dans toutes les provinces par des lettres circulaires'. The leader of the deputation of *trésoriers* protested the loyalty of his group of officials, and claimed the right to present remonstrances. Séguier brusquely rejected the claim: only sovereign courts enjoyed this privilege. The *trésoriers* could make 'très humbles prières et supplications' but that was all. The 'remonstrances' of the *trésoriers* were thus rejected out of hand. A decree of the council of finance was issued ordering the suspension from office of the *trésoriers* of Paris who had signed the ordinance of 29 August. The ordinance was to be torn from the register and replaced by the decree of the council—the ultimate humiliation. A *maître des requêtes* was ordered to investigate the alleged illicit assemblies held at Paris by the *trésoriers* and the *élus*.[2] The rejection of any power of remonstrance inevitably meant the defeat of the financial officials. On 26 September, the *trésoriers* of Paris sought once more to

[1] K 118b, fo. 63, countersigned by Séguier, Molé, Servien, and Foucquet, 17 Sept. 1653.
[2] Esmonin, 'Un épisode', pp. 223–7. Charmeil, *Trésoriers*, pp. 400–6. Delaume, *Bureau des finances de Paris*, pp. 42–4. B.N. MS.fr. 16218, fo. 484 and E 260b, fo. 158, 17 Sept. 1653. Inserted in the register at 29 Aug. 1653; Z1f 215, fo. 219.

present remonstrances,[1] but the following day another decree
of the council of finance put them in their place.[2]

The financial officials had lost their campaign by the end of
September 1653, but this did not prevent them mounting a
rearguard action. The *trésoriers* of Paris did not become any
more co-operative with Breteuil and Lefèvre de la Barre, and
the council of finance had to issue two decrees on 29 May and
6 June 1654 to prevent them from interference with the intendants' work on the parish assessments.[3] In the autumn of
1655, they tried to place their authorization (*attache*) on the
commissions of the *taille*, but were again prohibited from doing
so by the council of finance, which ordered Breteuil to carry
out the parish assessments.[4] The *trésoriers* of Montauban drew
up a rival general assessment to that prepared by the resident
intendant in October 1653: four members of the *bureau* were
summoned to Paris to account for their actions, while Louis
Machault, the intendant, was empowered to continue his
activities.[5] On 31 June 1655 the *trésoriers* again tried to restrict
Machault's work on the general assessment; this time the
council of finance threatened them with suspension from office
and summoned the two most senior *trésoriers* to Paris.[6] Relations between the *trésoriers* of Poitiers and Bernard Fortia, the
intendant, were particularly strained. In the winter of 1653–4,
the *trésoriers* had tried to annul Fortia's ordinances. In December 1654 an assembly of the *trésoriers* and *élus* at Poitiers
decided on non-co-operation with the intendant in both the
general and parish assessments. According to Fortia's report to
the council, there was also a decision taken to 'semer la révolte
dans les esprits des contribuables et les empescher d'en faire
l'assiette'. Two *trésoriers* and one *élu* were summoned to Paris
to appear before the council. On 15 December 1655 the
trésoriers declared that Fortia's general assessment would be
impossible to implement. In 1657 they were accused of issuing
letters containing 'plusieurs faicts séditieux et supposez' against
the intendant; the council of finance declared that they would

[1] Z1f 216, fo. 11.
[2] B.N. MS.fr. 16218, fo. 490 and E 260b, fo. 552, 27 Sept. 1653.
[3] E 266a, fo. 371 and B.N. MS.fr. 16218, fo. 488. But cf. Delaume, op. cit., p. 44.
[4] E 284a, fo. 263, 2 Dec. 1655.
[5] E 262a, fo. 287, 15 Nov. 1653.   [6] E 280b, fo. 258, 18 Aug. 1655.

be held responsible for any tax rebellions in that province.[1] Elsewhere, there was less continuity in the conflict between the *trésoriers* and the intendants, but it existed nevertheless. The *trésoriers* of Orléans ordered the *élus* to carry out the parish assessments without giving any role to Bénard de Rezé, the intendant, an order which was reversed by a decree of the council of finance.[2] There were less serious conflicts elsewhere.[3]

The intendants dominated the *élus*. An edict of March 1654 ordered the abolition of certain offices in the *élections* unless a forced loan was forthcoming. The intendants were ordered to suspend from office any *élu* who refused to pay these taxes, and to deprive them of any role in the parish assessments. Foullé warned the *élus* of Nevers against attempting 'une caballe et faction' and gave them a fortnight to pay their taxes after which time he would carry out the assessments on his own.[4] If the intendants suspected the *élus* of favouritism or corruption, they simply ignored them. Heere acted independently of the *élus* of Laval in 1656, Tallemant disregarded those of Cognac in 1657 and Le Lièvre disregarded those of Sens and Beauvais in the same year.[5] The intendants asserted the right, in certain circumstances, to hold the parish assessments outside the *élection* concerned. Thus Heere did not go to Laval in 1656, Daniel Voisin did not go to Troyes in 1657, and Hotman de Fontenay was exempted by the council of finance from visiting all the *élections* in Bordeaux and Montauban in 1658.[6] Of course, there were intendants who thought the co-operation of the *élus* worthless, 'une formalité inutille'.[7] But the council of finance must have attached some significance to it, otherwise it would not have troubled to threaten with suspension from office those *élus* who failed to sign the intendant's parish assess-

[1] Bonvallet, 'Bureau des finances de Poitiers', pp. 209–10. E 263a, fo. 522, 28 Jan. 1654. E 272b, fo. 378, 19 Dec. 1654. B.L. Harleian 4490, fo. 137ᵛ, 26 Jan. 1657. E 298a, fo. 348, 17 Feb. 1657.

[2] E 262a, fo. 157 and B.N. MS.fr. 16218, fo. 492, 8 Nov. 1653.

[3] Moulins: E 308b, fo. 211, 20 Dec. 1657, Bourges: E 310b, fo. 533, 27 Feb. 1658. Grenoble: E 320a, fo. 109, 7 Jan. 1659.

[4] E 266b, fo. 270, 20 June 1654.

[5] E 286a, fo. 220, 11 Feb. 1656. E 298a, fo. 296, 17 Feb. 1657. E 308a, fo. 43, 5 Dec. 1657.

[6] E 286a, fo. 230, 11 Feb. 1656. A.A.E. France 904, fo. 49, 24 July 1657. E 319a, fo. 59, 4 Dec. 1658.

[7] cf. the remark of Thoreau, a *trésorier* who assisted Fortia at Poitiers: E 274b, fo. 297, 25 Feb. 1655.

ments.[1] As had been the case before the Fronde, the *élus* who
co-operated with the intendants aroused the hostility of those
who did not.[2]

In the years between 1653 and 1657, the intendants dealt
with all aspects of taxation in the provinces, and the financiers
had to approach them when difficulties arose in the levy of
taxes in which they had a financial interest. This was obviously
inconvenient to the financiers since they were required to be
present in the provinces, and yet they also needed to be at
Paris to renew their contracts and obtain favourable decisions
from the council of finance. Thus on 12 December 1657, a
special commission of the council of finance was set up to deal
with the difficulties faced by the financiers, and this aspect of
financial administration was removed from the care of the
intendants.[3] As had been the case before the Fronde, in some
instances the intendants dismissed the *receveurs* and appointed
in their places the nominees of the financiers.[4] A decree of
20 December 1653 empowered the intendants in eighteen
généralités to investigate whether there were any taxes in their
areas which had been concealed or increased illegally (*deniers
recéllez et surimposez*) since 1630.[5] On 19 September 1654, the
intendants in eighteen *généralités* were ordered to verify any
'deniers demeurez ez mains des collecteurs des tailles'.[6] Daniel
Voisin at Riom and Pellot at Poitiers were empowered to
prosecute *receveurs* of the *taille* who were accused of peculation.[7]
The intendants were ordered to verify the arrears of the *taille*,
and to countersign the orders for the coercion of payment by
the parishes.[8] The special brigades were set up again 'à cause
de la dureté de la pluspart des redevables contre lesquels la
contrainte ordinaire se trouve inutile ... '[9] During the Fronde,

---

[1] E 271, fo. 596, 21 Nov. 1654.

[2] E 297a, fo. 322, 13 Jan. 1657. E 300a, fo. 455, 12 Apr. 1657.

[3] E 308a, fo. 227.

[4] Poitiers: E 274b, fo. 1, 18 Feb. 1655. E 298a, fo. 486, 17 Feb. 1657. Limoges:
E 281b, fo. 492, 23 Sept. 1655. E 288a, fo. 324, 6 Apr. 1656.

[5] E 262c, fo. 484. At Tours and Orléans, the investigation went back to 1642,
and at Bordeaux and Montauban it went back to 1644. In those areas, the intendants before the Fronde had investigated the administration in the years after
1630.

[6] E 269b, fo. 301.

[7] E 272b, fo. 350ᵛ, 17 Dec. 1654. E 323a, fo. 265, 3 Apr. 1659.

[8] E 284b, fo. 284, 18 Dec. 1655. E 304a, fo. 219, 4 Aug. 1659. E 318b, fo. 142,
20 Nov. 1658. E 319a, fo. 57, 4 Dec. 1658.   [9] E 316a, fo. 227, 8 Aug. 1658.

many parishes had obtained letters of remission which discharged them from paying taxes outstanding from the years
between 1647 and 1652. The intendants were ordered to investigate such letters of remission, and parishes which had
obtained such declarations under false pretences were ordered
to pay their taxes in full.[1] The intendants were given powers
to rationalize the structure of taxation and thus to remove
much of the unfairness of the fiscal system, which was regarded
as a major factor in peasant revolts.[2] Favier de Boullay at
Alençon, Morant at Rouen, Miroménil at Caen, Louis Machault at Montauban, Bernard Fortia at Poitiers, and Jean
Bochart at Tours were ordered to carry out the special taxes on
privileged persons in the parishes (*taxes d'office*). A decree of
24 November 1657 reserved this power exclusively to the intendants, and prohibited the *élus* from interference.[3]

The transfer of ultimate financial responsibility to the intendants in the *pays d'élections* was a momentous political change,
breaking down as it did the semi-autonomous administration
of the corporate financial officials. How significant was the
change in financial terms, however? The intendants were
somewhat more successful than the *trésoriers* and the *élus* in
getting in the taxes but this relative success should not be
exaggerated: despite the reliance on the special brigades, the
arrears were still enormous in 1661.[4] The crucial question must
be whether or not the intendants were demonstrably fairer than
the financial officials they replaced.

In theory, of course, the intendants were impartial. The intendants in the *pays d'élections* were not usually natives of the
provinces in which they served, although there were exceptions: Claude Vignier owned lands in Champagne where he
was sent as intendant in 1636;[5] Guillaume de Bautru had a
château in Anjou yet he was intendant in the *généralité* of Tours

---

[1] E 255b, fo. 634, 23 Apr. 1653. E 256a, fo. 95, 7 May 1653. E 257a, fo. 131, 4
June 1653. E 266a, fo. 127, 1 June 1654. E 284b, fo. 177, 18 Dec. 1655.

[2] E 309a, fo. 25, 2 Jan. 1658, request of Christophe Joguet, *receveur des tailles* of
Clamécy, to the council of finance.

[3] E 307b, fo. 377.

[4] cf. the arrears of 1,674,111 *livres* in the *généralité* of Lyon on 9 Dec. 1661: B.N.
Mélanges Colbert 105, fo. 367.

[5] E 162c, fo. 106, 4 July 1641.

between 1644 and 1648.[1] In theory, however, the intendant was
an outsider and thus above the charge of favouritism that could
be levelled against the *élus*, and to some extent, against the
trésoriers. This in itself was a great improvement. However, it
might lead to excessive reliance on subordinates, on the financiers and the *receveurs*: the *trésoriers* contended that since
'tous les anciens officiers leur [étaient] suspectz', the intendants
had no 'lumière des affaires que celle que leur donnent les
personnes intéressées qui les ont souhaitez'.[2]

The rapid turnover of the intendants in the *pays d'élections*—
every three years on average in the years between 1653 and
1666, every five years on average in the years between 1666 and
1716[3]—was generally considered detrimental to their tax collecting activities: 'il faut un certain temps pour acquérir les
connaissances nécessaires d'une généralité...'[4] There is little
evidence, however, that the intendants introduced radical
changes in the general assessment which they took over from
the *trésoriers*; indeed, the intendants and the *trésoriers* shared
similar views as to the relative wealth and poverty of the
élections.[5] The *trésoriers* might claim that the intendants 'n'ont
intérest que d'emporter tout le fruict de la vigne pendant leur
commission', and there was an element of truth in the accusation since an intendant was considered a failure unless he
brought in the tax-returns successfully.[6] However, the ministers occasionally criticized the intendants for acting 'avec trop
de réserve... estant bien aisés de décharger les habitants à cause
qu'ils ont à vivre avec eux'.[7] Nicolas Méliand, the intendant
at Montauban, balanced the rival interests of government and
province nicely when he wrote to Chancellor Séguier in December 1656: 'nous esperons, Monseigneur, quelque petit

[1] Dethan, *Gaston d'Orléans*, p. 171.

[2] B.L. Harleian 4472b, fo. 147ᵛ, 1655 [?].

[3] Bonney, 'Intendants', pp. 316, 334.

[4] G7 1127, memorandum on the *taille*, 1722.

[5] Bercé, *Histoire des croquants*, i. 73. As a result, the variation in the amount of
taxes paid by each 'hearth' (*feu*) could be immense. In 1711 this varied from 10
livres 3 *sols* per hearth to 28 *livres* 10 *sols* per hearth in eleven *élections* in northern
France: Dupâquier, 'Essai de cartographie historique', p. 990.

[6] Bercé *Histoire des croquants*, ii. 805. B.N. MS.fr. 18510, fo. 421.

[7] A.A.E. France 907, fo. 264ᵛ, Le Tellier to Mazarin, 30 July 1659. As an example, Villemontée's request on 26 June 1637 for a tax reduction, which was
accorded by the council of finance on 4 July: *Lettres ... au Chancelier Séguier*, ed.
Mousnier, i. 391. E 138a, fo. 27, 4 July 1637.

soulagement pour cette province affligée. Nous ne laisserons pas de faire nostre possible pour faire exécuter les volontez de Sa Majesté . . .'[1] The council of finance annulled ordinances of the intendants if it did not approve the tax remissions which they had granted.[2]

In 1661, in an attempt to counter the argument that they gave preferential treatment to the parishes in which they held lands, the *élus* argued that the intendants also favoured certain parishes, 'chargeant pour l'ordinaire les bonnes qui payent et font leur devoir, et diminuant les mauvaises, afin d'asseurer les recouvremens qui estoient en party[3] sans se soucier de ceux de l'advenir'.[4] This was in fact the principle upon which the intendants had operated after 1642: the intendants distinguished willingness yet inability to pay (*impuissance*) from deliberate tax rebellion (*endurcissement*).[5] They were also instructed by the council of finance to give favourable treatment to those parishes which at least attempted to pay their taxes.[6] The weakness of this approach was that it rewarded temporization and penalized those parishes which paid their taxes punctually. The ability of a parish to pay its taxes was calculated on the size of its tax arrears: if there were no arrears, it was assumed that a parish could pay heavier taxes. The comte d'Arpajon was not the only person to point out the illogicality and the political danger inherent in this policy, claiming that it would be a 'mauvais exemple de surcharger ceux qui se forcent à payer'.[7] The extent of the difficulties an intendant might face on this subject are well illustrated by the estates of Madame de Pompadour, the widow of the former lieutenant-general in the Limousin. Madame de Pompadour possessed fifty parishes in the *élections* of Limoges, Tulle, and Brive-la-Gaillarde, of which the most important were Treignac and Lubersac. They were

---

[1] B.L. Harleian 4490, fo. 90, 1 Dec. 1656.

[2] e.g. Foullé in Guyenne: E 145a, fo. 249, 10 July 1638.

[3] 'En party' = 'contracted for', a reference to the loan contracts which anticipated the revenues of the *généralités*.

[4] Esmonin, *La taille*, p. 124.

[5] 'L'endurcissement des contribuables' in the *élection* of Les Sables d'Olonne: E 207b, fo. 539, 31 Jan. 1646.

[6] E 177b, fo. 117, 25 Feb. 1643.

[7] E 184c, fo. 382, 12 Nov. 1643. The comte d'Arpajon was lieutentant-general in Languedoc. His request to the council of finance was basically for a tax remission on his parishes in the Rouergue.

the best lands in the *généralité* of Limoges, yet 'les plus soulagés et entièrement exempts de logemens de gens de guerre'. They regularly paid only one-quarter of the *taille*. In 1644 Corberon, the intendant, agreed to discharge them from paying between one-quarter and one-third of their assessments. Such special treatment by the intendant caused 'une extrême jalousie de toute la province'. Indeed, the arrears in the *généralité* since 1640 were blamed on the attitude of Madame de Pompadour, 'chacun prétendant, notamment les gentilzhommes, n'estre pas ... tenu de faire payer [plus] que ladite dame'.

The difficulties of Nicolas de Corberon in the Limousin had a second important feature. Madame de Pompadour would not have dared to 'se mocqu[er] de ses ordonnances' had she not been Séguier's sister-in-law. Corberon's predecessors had let the matter slide 'n'ayant pas osé porter les choses à leurs extrêmes, non pas mesme informer le Conseil à la considération et respect de Monseigneur la Chancelier.'[1] Before the introduction of the intendants, corruption was basically local;[2] after the introduction of the intendants, corruption was centralized to the extent that the ministers—notable Séguier[3] and even Colbert, despite his reputation of incorruptibility[4]—were solicitous for their own estates and those of their relatives and friends.[5] The intendants and former intendants asked for special favours from the ministers. François Laisnier asked Le Tellier for 'le soulagement' of Daumeray, a parish near Durtal in Anjou belonging to his brother.[6] The intendants may well have given each others' lands preferential treatment when they carried out the parish assessments. It was contended in 1670

---

[1] *Lettres ... au Chancelier Séguier*, ed. Mousnier, i. 640–2, ii. 833. Bercé, *Histoire des croquants*, i. 143–4, ii. 804–6. B.N. MS.fr. 18510, fo. 421 (this document must be dated several months after 26 Feb. 1644, the date Corberon was commissioned as intendant).

[2] The Pompadour case illustrates the fact that the financiers, who arguably benefited from central corruption, were unwilling to allow local corruption since it was a threat to their profits.

[3] cf. Séguier's concern for his parish of Sully, which in the three years 1659–61 had its taxes reduced by half. Bernard Fortia, the intendant, remarked sharply: 'je suis certain que si vous avies faict la distribution, vous auries, Monseigneur, eu de la peine à la donner plus grande [modération] ...' B.L. Harleian 4442, fos. 226–7, 15 Feb. 1661.

[4] Colbert's incorruptibility was not consistent: *Lettres ... de Colbert*, ed. Clément, ii. pt. i, 117, 371.

[5] Esmonin, *La taille*, pp. 153–5, 160.   [6] A.G. A1 97, no. 53, 5 Aug. 1645.

that the parishes in the *généralité* of Paris belonging to Favier du Boullay, the intendant at Alençon in the years 1643–8 and 1653–66, 'ont toujours ésté protégés par MM. les maîtres des Requestes ses confrères'.[1] This sort of corruption was standard administrative practice throughout contemporary Europe and its extent, in any case, should not be exaggerated. There was a great difference between the amount of corruption related to half a dozen ministers and nineteen intendants and that resulting from three thousand *trésoriers* and *élus*.

Even assuming that ministerial pressure was not brought to bear on the intendant, his task at the parish assessments was difficult enough. It was a contemporary platitude that the intendants could not '[connaître] par expérience les moyens et les facultez des habitans des paroisses comme les officiers des eslections establis sur les lieux'.[2] Since the visits of inspection by the *trésoriers* and the *élus* were at best intermittent, the intendant had no choice but to visit all the parishes himself if he were to perform his task adequately. The major problem at the parish assessments, apart from the amount of time available, was 'l'incertitude des lumières'—the difficulty of assessing wealth. The evidence provided by the tax-rolls was insufficient.[3] In some areas—such as the area of the *cour des aides* of Rouen following that court's decrees of 28 January 1619 and 4 December 1627—the lessees of property were to pay as their contribution to the *taille* a fixed percentage of their leases, for example 25 per cent.[4] In the *pays de taille personnelle* as a whole, however, the intendants had to rely on exterior signs of wealth. It is true that by the time of Colbert their commissions empowered the intendants to coerce *notaires* to send them any information that they might need.[5] The intendants thus could

---

[1] Eamonin, *La taille*, p. 159, n. 6.

[2] Z1a 206, pp. 468–9, memorandum of M. Gaucher, 1614.

[3] G7 103, Desmaretz de Vaubourg, intendant at Riom, to Le Peletier, 11 Feb. 1688. Desmaretz wanted the implementation of article 16 of the ruling of 1600 and article 45 of the ruling of 1634. The effect of this would have been to record on the tax-rolls all lands owned or leased out, the names of proprietors and lessees, and the number of exempted persons.

[4] Esmonin, *La taille*, p. 322. The lesser nobles disliked this idea, arguing that as a result '[ce] sont lesdictz gentilhommes quy payent la taille, ce quy n'est raisonnable'. R. Mousnier, J. P. Labatut, Y. Durand, *Problèmes de stratification sociale. Deux cahiers de la noblessee pour les États-Généraux de 1649–1651* (1965), p. 151.

[5] Boyer de Sainte-Suzanne, *Intendants d'Amiens*, p. 582.

have obtained from the *notaires* all the information required concerning the extent of a family's wealth. In practice, however, these impressive-sounding powers of coercion were rarely used in questions of taxation. The *cour des aides* of Paris summed up the prevailing attitude on this question in a declaration of 22 January 1664: 'on ne peut admettre cette voye extraordinaire pour en avoir connoissances', it declared, '. . . faire de telles perquisitions . . . estoit contre la liberté publique des français . . .'[1] Without this precise information, the intendant had to rely chiefly on guesswork.

A final consideration is the relationship between the intendants and the financiers, and the remuneration of the intendants. During the constitutional negotiations in the summer of 1648, Chancellor Séguier remarked, 'il se pouvoit faire que quelqu'uns eussent malversé, mais qu'il ne falloit pas les condamner tous, mais épargner leur honneur'. To this the critics of the intendants replied that the intendants were men without honour in any case.[2] The relationship between the intendants and the financiers is complex. Certain intendants—notably Antoine and Jean Le Camus, Nicolas Jeannin de Castille, and Thomas Morant—were the sons of financiers or *trésoriers de l'Épargne*. Others—such as Étienne Foullé, Pierre Gargan, and Jacques Paget—became *intendants des finances* and may be suspected of having considerable financial interests. Certain *maîtres des requêtes* and intendants married the daughters of financiers. Louis Chauvelin, the intendant in the army of Italy in 1644, married a daughter of Thomas Bonneau. The families of Marc de La Ferté and Faucon de Ris were related to Le Tellier de Tourneville, the *commis des gabelles* in Normandy who was attacked by the peasants in 1639.[3]

Certainly the intendants might incur the suspicion of a rioting mob that they had direct financial interests in the taxes they levied. Thus François Pommereu was attacked at Amiens in 1628,[4] Bosquet at Montauban in 1641, Foullé at Ligny-

[1] Esmonin, *La taille*, p. 319.   [2] Z1a 163, fo. 62ᵛ, 9 July 1648.
[3] Foisil, *Nu-Pieds*, p. 237, n. 2.
[4] Deyon, *Amiens*, p. 438. Pagès, 'Richelieu et Marillac', pp. 69–70. V6 67, no. 7, 15 June 1628.

en-Brionnais in 1642,[1] Charreton at Villefranche-en-Rouergue in 1643,[2] Favier du Boullay at Moulins-sur-Orne, also in 1643,[3] and Méliand at Martres-de-Rivière in 1657[4]—excluding such incidents in the *pays d'états*. However, it is by no means clear that the mob was well informed as to the financial interests of the financiers: was Morant's *château* at Le Mesnil-Garnier threatened because he was a former intendant, because he was a former *trésorier de l'Épargne*, or simply because he was successful?[5] Nevertheless, in certain instances the mob was correct: the families of Le Tonnelier de Breteuil, Aligre, and Miroménil possessed some of the *offices de cuirs* at Rouen that were a major factor in the riot of the tanners in 1634.[6] François Le Tonnelier was the intendant charged with suppressing the riot.[7] At the same time, Étienne d'Aligre was the intendant at Caen and within two years Dyel de Miroménil was the intendant at Rouen. Certain of the intendants appear to have been overzealous in the assistance they gave to the financiers. Thiersault permitted the financiers to levy special troops at Alençon without obtaining royal permission first.[8] Colbert was particularly critical of Lefèvre de la Barre, the intendant at Moulins: 'jamais homme n'a esté tant hay des peuples, et n'a donné aux peuples tant de véritables raisons de le hayr, que celuy là par une conduite tout à fait abandonnée', Colbert informed Mazarin.[9]

Much of this evidence is circumstantial, however. A distinction must be made between property interests and investments of the intendants that would be considered normal in persons of their social standing and conscious financial activity on any widespread scale. Few of the intendants died rich, which in popular estimation was the hallmark of a former

---

[1] E 172a, fo. 111, 2 July 1642.

[2] E 179b, fo. 67, 2 May 1643. E 1684, fos. 390, 400, 18 June 1643.

[3] *Lettres . . . au Chancelier Séguier*, ed. Mousnier, i. 538. E 179c, fo. 167, 27 May 1643.

[4] E 302a, fo. 192, 6 June 1657.

[5] Foisil, *Nu-Pieds*, pp. 197, 199, 201–2.

[6] ibid., p. 139.   [7] ibid., p. 142.   [8] ibid., pp. 109–10.

[9] *Lettres . . . de Colbert*, ed. Clément, i. 387–8 (16 Oct. 1659). Mazarin agreed. However, it should be pointed out that Lefèvre de la Barre was a client of Le Tellier's, which may explain part of Colbert's ferocious criticism. Lefèvre de la Barre was described as 'l'esprit souple, accommodant avec les traitans dans son intendance qui par ce moyen a fort augmenté ses biens': B.N. MS.fr. 14028.

financier. Until the structure of finance in seventeenth-century France is revealed in much greater detail, the true extent of the financial dealings of the intendants will remain obscure. There is some evidence that the intendants loaned money both to the financiers and to the government. A good example of a *maître des requêtes* and intendant loaning money to a financier is Jacques Godart de Petit-Marais. He had served as intendant at Amiens in 1618 and in the army of Périgord in 1623: in 1623, he loaned Antoine Feydeau, the farmer-general of both the *aides* and the *gabelles*, the sum of 58,000 *livres*.[1] With regard to loans made to the government, Jean Baltazar[2] and Le Picard de Périgny[3] loaned over 240,000 *livres* to the government during the period when they served as intendant. Admittedly, the loans did not concern the revenues of the provinces they administered, but the receipts of the *droit annuel*. The profits were just as substantial, however.

In itself, participation in financial activities is no indication of corruption on the part of the intendants. For corruption to be proven, there would have to be an evident conflict of interests and fraudulent profiteering: since the whole structure of war finance inevitably led to a high rate of interest being paid to financiers, it would be remarkable indeed if substantial, and legally permissible, profits were not made. In this respect, the absence of financial scandals involving the intendants is significant. There were, it is true, accusations against Talon in the Dauphiné,[4] Fremin in the Limousin,[5] Chaulnes in Picardy,[6] Charreton de La Terrière at Montauban,[7] and Lefèvre de la Barre in the Bourbonnais.[8] If it is accepted that all the members of the council of finance were tainted by corruption,[9] then this in itself might be considered

[1] Minutier Central LI 140, 1 and 4 Aug. 1623.

[2] E 265a, fo. 212, 9 May 1654, E 289b, fo. 336, 20 May 1656. (References to loans of 7 Feb. 1646 and 24 Dec. 1647.)

[3] E 265a, fo. 334, 12 May 1654. (Reference to loan of 26 May 1646.)

[4] Esmonin, *Études*, p. 76. E 135a, fo. 454, 31 Jan. 1637. E 135b, fo. 464, 21 Feb. 1637.

[5] Ormesson, *Journal*, ed. Chéruel, i. 57. E 176b, fo. 398, 29 Jan. 1643.

[6] Deyon, *Amiens*, p. 448, n. 37. B.N. MS.fr. 18510, fo. 447. E 200a, fo. 412, 9 Mar. 1645. E 200c, fo. 260ᵛ, 23 Mar. 1645.

[7] E 265b, fo. 173, 20 May 1654.

[8] E 1720, no. 13, 7 Mar. 1662.

[9] Dent, *Crisis in Finance*, p. 87, talks of 'mass conspiracy' by 'the central administrators'.

proof, in Séguier's words, that 'quelqu'uns eussent malversé'. However, the intendants were doing unpopular tasks in the provinces, and accusations against them could equally well be prejudiced or partisan. On each occasion, the council of finance investigated the evidence, found it to be insufficient, and up-held the intendant's account of the circumstances. There was no attempt by the otherwise thorough *Chambre de Justice* in 1661 to implicate the intendants in any charges of corruption. While the suspicion that cases against the intendants were un-likely to be pursued very far because of family and patronage connections cannot altogether be dispelled, the fact remains that clear proof was lacking. Fraudulent transactions could be proven to have taken place in the case of certain financiers at the *Chambre de Justice* in 1661; this could not be demonstrated of the intendants either at the council of finance before 1661 or in the *Chambre de Justice* thereafter.

There are other reasons that point in the direction of rela-tive integrity on the part of the intendants. Most of the tax contracts they enforced in the provinces were decided upon by the council of finance at Paris. Where they negotiated con-tracts with local financiers and munitions contractors, the con-tracts were sent to the council of finance for approval.[1] Fraud-ulent contracts were difficult to carry through when the council had to be sent full details and when the intendant, an un-popular figure in the province, might be denounced to the ministers or the council. For the sake of quick profiteering it was not worth prejudicing a future career in the council. Of course the intendant would expect favourable treatment for himself and his family. At Lyon, the *échevins* offered Humbert de Chaponay 20 'pieces' of wine, which the intendant con-sidered insufficient 'pour l'usage de sa maison et famille' and required 30 'pieces' instead. In 1642, the intendant at Lyon entered his wine into the city free from the local indirect taxes.[2] None of this proves that the impartiality of the in-tendant as a financial administrator was affected. The critics of the intendants rarely accused them of profiteering, except

[1] E 150a, fo. 80, 6 Apr. 1639. E 154c, fos. 246, 248, 443, 8 and 13 Mar. 1640. E 155a, fo. 13, 5 Apr. 1640.
[2] S. Charléty, 'Lyon sous le ministère de Richelieu', *Revue d'Histoire Moderne et Contemporaine*, iii (1901–2), 503, no. 3.

during the Fronde when they hoped to abolish the position of intendant altogether. They argued instead that they were the ruthless administrators of a hated fiscal system.

If this basic picture of the integrity of the intendants is correct, then their forbearance is remarkable. An intendant earned 1,000 *livres* a month. If there were two intendants, the junior intendant might earn less than this.[1] In addition to his 12,000 *livres* a year as intendant, he might receive 3,000 *livres* a year as councillor of state, and perhaps an additional 1,500 *livres* if he retained his office as *maître des requêtes*.[2] Colbert hinted that he thought the intendants were overpaid,[3] but much depended on the perspective of the observer. Denis Marin advised Chancellor Séguier shrewdly that even 300,000 *livres* in salaries to the intendants was not very much to spend, when they saved perhaps six million in excessive profits to the financiers.[4] The intendants considered themselves underpaid. Jacques Chaulnes was forced to sell his office of *maître des requêtes* in 1644 because his 'appointemens . . . ne peuvent pas fournir à la moityé de [sa] despence'.[5] Income is a meaningless guide to real wealth unless expenditure is taken into account as well. The expenses of the intendants were substantial. To begin with, they had to pay for secretarial assistance,[6] and in most cases travelling costs and rented accommodation. Then, in an emergency, they were expected to provide funds for troop payments and fortifications out of their income. In 1629, La Thuillerie contributed towards an advance payment of 18,887 *livres* for the cavalry used to suppress the popular uprisings in Poitou.[7] In 1632, Mangot de Villarceaux loaned 1,720 *livres* to the town of Carcassonne for military supplies to be used against the Montmorency rebels.[8] In 1637, Verthamon loaned 2,000

[1] In Languedoc, Miron earned 30 *livres* a day, while Dupré earned only 24 *livres* a day: E 150b, fo. 299, 14 May 1639.

[2] *Lettres . . . au Chancelier Séguier*, ed. Mousnier, i. 174. Gruder, *The royal provincial intendants*, pp. 237–9.

[3] *Lettres . . . de Colbert*, ed. Clément, i. 357.

[4] B.N. MS.fr. 16218, fo. 377. The total salary bill was lower than 300,000 *livres* unless payments to councillors of state, etc, are included.

[5] *Lettres . . . au Chancelier Séguier*, ed. Mousnier, i. 624.

[6] After 22 Nov. 1642, clerks employed by the intendants were to be paid 1,200 *livres per annum* from public funds: E 174b, fo. 277. As the direct employer of the clerk, however, the intendant had to assume personal responsibility if the government defaulted on its commitment. All salary payments were in arrears after 1639.

[7] E 116b, fo. 373, 27 Mar. 1634.   [8] E 130a, fo. 256, 10 May 1636.

livres to repair the fortifications at Bayonne, which was threatened by a Spanish invasion.[1] The intendants hoped that they
would be reimbursed for their services. But Verthamon was
still claiming repayment four years later, while the salaries of
the intendants were notoriously in arrears. The government
seems to have treated the intendants better than the office-
holders in that it did not actually cut their salaries. But Villemontée was still claiming 9,000 *livres* of his salary from 1640
nine years later;[2] Villahier waited thirteen years for his salary
as intendant of the Touraine.[3] Even when the government
finally agreed to pay his salary, there was no guarantee that
the intendant would actually receive the sums owed to him:
salaries were frequently assigned on *traités* and revenues that
might or might not pay up at a later date, or were paid through
the *comptables*, the numerous treasurers whose funds might
already have been consumed totally for the year in question.
Clearly, only well-to-do families could contemplate such financial self-sacrifice with equanimity: but they were hardly likely
to get richer in the process. A *président* in a sovereign court who
did not undertake royal commissions was likely to die with
his finances in a much healthier position than a *maître des
requêtes* who also served as an intendant.[4]

---

[1] E 163b, fo. 499, 14 Aug. 1641.   [2] E 235c, fo. 384, 21 Aug. 1649.
[3] E 274b, fo. 360, 25 Feb. 1655.

[4] cf. the concern of the intendants to preserve their offices of *maître des requêtes*,
their chief investment. Choisy: E 129a, fo. 133, 1 Mar. 1636. Baltazar: E 1693,
fo. 54 and E 229a, fo. 233, 11 Mar. 1648.

CHAPTER X

'Tax Rebellion'

THE BURDEN of the increase in the *taille* needed to pay for the war against Spain was carried by the *pays d'élections*, and by the rural parishes within these areas. There can be little doubt that these unprecedented tax demands were the major reason for the 'tax rebellion' which was one of the most important features of the ministries of Richelieu and Mazarin.[1] Already in 1636, the *Croquants* of Saintonge were demanding that the ministers should no longer be allowed the power to 'faire à leur faintaisie des nouvelles taxes sur les peuples . . .'[2] At Lectoure the previous year the rioters threatened the *élus* with death if they attempted to levy 'aultres deniers que ceux qui se lev[ai]ent en l'année 1616'.[3] The intendants were given the task of reforming the fiscal system; it was inevitable that they would also be given the much less enviable task of suppressing revolt.

The *trésoriers* blamed the intendants for the 'tax rebellion'. 'Il est entré dans la pensée du peuple', they wrote, 'que tout leur ministère estoient violent et qu'ils n'estoient emploiez que pour exiger d'eux ce qu'on desiroit au delà des anciennes redevances.'[4] The government insisted on payment of the *taille*, and was prepared to force the peasants to pay their taxes, if need be, by using the troops. Special brigades were set up for this purpose at Poitiers in 1638, at Bordeaux and Caen in 1641, at Limoges in 1642, at Alençon, Riom, and Orléans in 1643, at Amiens, Moulins, Tours, and Montauban in 1644. In all cases, the brigades were controlled by the intendants, their pay being determined by the council of finance. The brigades might be composed simply of a few *archers*; in other cases, they

---

[1] E 307a, fo. 270, 10 Nov. 1657, request of Claude Charmon, the *commis à la recette des tailles* at Tonnerre, to the council of finance.

[2] *Lettres . . . au Chancelier Séguier*, ed. Mousnier, ii. 1104. Bercé, *Histoire des croquants*, ii. 737.

[3] E 124b, fo. 172, 30 June 1635. For the myth of the lost age of fiscal justice: Bercé, op. cit., ii. 636.

[4] B.L. Harleian 4472b, fo. 149, n.d. [1655?].

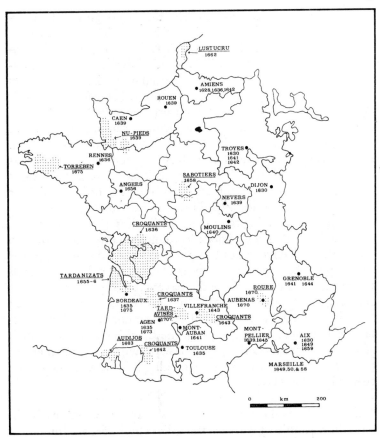

MAP II. Certain peasant revolts and urban riots.

included a substantial number of musketeers and light cavalry.[1]
The special brigades were extremely unpopular—they were
called 'démons déchaînez' by the *Mazarinades*[2]—because they
were ill-disciplined and tended to levy more taxes than were
actually owed by the parish in which they were billeted.

The king's council could determine the law and thus the
action of the intendants in forcing payment of taxation was

---

[1] Bercé, op. cit., i. 108–12. Bonney, 'Intendants', p. 243. In 1648, the total cost
of these brigades was 260,995 *livres*: B.N. n.a.f. 64, fo. 155ᵛ.

[2] They were termed thus in the 'Requeste des trois estats présentée à Messieurs
du Parlement'. *Choix de Mazarinades* (ed. Moreau), i. 30. Doolin, *The Fronde*, p. 153.

perfectly legal. It was contested by the sovereign courts, however, notably by the *cour des aides* of Paris which declared such methods to be 'contraire au droit'. On 30 May 1645, it protested that although the *taille* was administered by the intendants, it had not changed its basic characteristic which was that of a voluntary gift from the king's subjects.[1] Had this principle been accepted by the government, the 'tax rebellion' would undoubtedly have become far more serious, and it might well have become impossible to continue the war against Spain. It was to this principle of voluntary payment of the *taille* that the *trésoriers* referred when they declared that the peasants 'haissent et tiennent pour suspectz tous les ordres qui leur viennent de la part des intendans, ne se persuadant point qu'il eust falu d'autres juges que les ordinaires si ce qu'ilz font estoit de justice'. They added: 'cette imagination est beaucoup accreue par la terreur des troupes que les intendans ont levées exprès pour faire paier les tailles'.[2] The intendants adopted strong-arm tactics to enforce the payment of the *taille*: but their actions were perfectly legal. The growth of government by council resulted in the overriding of common law principles such as the voluntary payment of the *taille*. Instead, the council of finance insisted on the public law principle that payment of taxes to the king was a duty of all subjects, who could be coerced if necessary.[3]

The intendants began to suppress 'tax rebellion' early in Richelieu's ministry. In July 1629, La Thuillerie, the intendant of Poitou, Saintonge, and the Angoumois had to levy two companies of cavalry to suppress the *émotions populaires* in all three of his provinces, which were 'en armes et jusques aux moindres villages barricadez'.[4] There were further significant rebellions in the *élection* of Les Sables d'Olonne in 1632–3,[5] while in Saintonge in 1635 'les peuples sont mutinez et portez à sédition par l'exemple de Bordeaux et province de Guyenne'.[6] The following year there was a general 'tax rebellion' in the

---

[1] Z1a 162, fos. 77ᵛ–79ᵛ. Despite Charles VII in 1439 having 'rendu [la taille] forcée pour le bien de l'état, elle n'a pas laissé de retenir quelque chose de son principe . . .'

[2] B.L. Harleian 4472b, fo. 149, n.d. [1655?]

[3] cf. Bercé, *Histoire des croquants*, i. 117–18.

[4] cf. E 111b, fo. 13, 12 Mar. 1633. E 116b, fo. 373, 27 Mar. 1634.

[5] E 122d, fo. 237, 31 Mar. 1635.   [6] E 125, fo. 242, 18 Aug. 1635.

Limousin: Villemontée ordered the peasants to pay the *taille*, and was assisted by Ventadour, the *lieutenant-général*, in this task; on 23 June 1637 Villemontée was empowered to prosecute those accused of 'rébellions, révoltes et séditions populaires'.[1] A second major area of 'tax rebellion' was Guyenne. Already in 1630 Verthamon, the intendant, had been in action on a limited scale;[2] five years later, a predominantly urban movement spread rapidly to the smaller towns and the countryside.[3] Writing from Périgueux on 18 June 1635, Verthamon feared 'l'humeur des peuples lorsqu'ilz se verront augmentez d'un quart cette année et aujoud'huy la plus part criantz icy vive le Roy sans gabelles, aucuns ont dit sans tailles . . .'[4] On 18 September, Verthamon was ordered to prosecute those accused of 'tax rebellion' at Marcillac.[5] The *élection* of Lomagne fell into substantial arrears after 1635 and the *élus* were frequently attacked at Lectoure: Foullé, Verthamon's successor, was ordered to investigate the 'excès et esmotions popullaires' that had taken place.[6] Foullé's commission as intendant, which was issued on 25 August 1637, was largely a response to the extremely serious revolt of the *Croquants* of Quercy and Périgord. The 'tax rebellion' was so widespread that Foullé had to delegate responsibility in Quercy to Helye de la Fon.[7] Foullé was ordered by the council to prosecute those peasants who had been 'esmeus et assemblées par Léonard de Masures dit Fourniac',[8] and to send the troops under the command of Espenan wherever the *taille* had not been paid.[9] The troops were used extensively in Guyenne to collect the *taille* until November 1638.

The south-west was not the only region of France to be affected by 'tax rebellion', however. In the Auvergne in 1636–7, there was a 'grande ligue entre plusieurs desdites parroisses à main armée' and several tax officials were murdered. Mesgrigny

---

[1] Bercé, op. cit., i. 397–401. E 137d, fo. 63, 27 June 1637. Cf. V6 132, no. 32, 10 Sept. 1638.

[2] E 104, fo. 309, 13 Sept. 1630.

[3] Bercé op. cit., i. 294–363.

[4] *Lettres . . . au Chancelier Séguier*, ed. Mousnier, i. 263.

[5] E 126a, fo. 321, 18 Sept. 1635.

[6] E 152b, fo. 294, 17 Sept. 1639. E 154b, fo. 85, 1 Feb. 1640.

[7] V6 136, no. 23, 25 Feb. 1639. For the revolt of the *Croquants* of Périgord: Bercé, op. cit., i. 403–62.

[8] V6 124, no. 4, 16 Oct. 1637.   [9] E 141c, fo. 27, 4 Feb. 1638.

the intendant, was ordered to levy troops and punish the rebellion, which centred on the *élections* of Saint-Flour and Aurillac.[1] Elsewhere, there is little suggestion of serious difficulty until the great crisis of 1639–40, except in the *élection* of Laon.[2] The first task of Le Roy de La Potherie, the intendant at Caen appointed on 20 October 1639, was to suppress the revolt of the *Va-Nu-Pieds*. La Potherie issued sentences against the rebels while presiding over the *présidiaux* of Caen and Coutances. He was assisted by Gassion, who commanded 1,200 cavalry and 4,000 infantry, and was charged with re-establishing the tax offices, punishing the rebels, and obtaining payment of the winter quarter. On 9 June 1640, 98 per cent of the taxes in the *élection* of Avranches were still outstanding from 1639 and 56 per cent from 1638—the collection of arrears must have become the major preoccupation of La Potherie once the tribunal under the presidency of Chancellor Séguier took over the prosecutions concerning the rebellion.[3]

Thus after 1640, new areas of revolt had been added to the south-west, the chief areas of 'tax rebellion' in France. Apart from Normandy, these included Picardy, where Bellejambe, the intendant, was ordered to investigate rumours of a tax remission and alleged seigneurial protection of the rebels;[4] Berry, where the arrears were mounting up at an alarming rate and where Barrin de Rezé, the intendant, was ordered to suppress the 'rébellions fréquentes' against the *taille*;[5] the Touraine, where Heere was ordered to 'chastier les séditieux et rebelles' who prevented the levy of the *taille*;[6] and the Orléanais, where Bragelongne was unable to quell the continual 'séditions, rébellions et voyes de fait' in the *élections* of Chartres, Châteaudun, Vendôme, and Montargis.[7] At the very moment when

---

[1] Bercé, op. cit., i. 441, 453. *Lettres . . . au Chancelier Séguier*, ed. Mousnier, i. 388–9. Cf. E 163a, fo. 205, 3 Aug. 1641. There were still difficulties in the *élection* of Clermont-Ferrand in 1638: E. 142a, fo. 226, 3 Mar. 1638.

[2] At the end of 1638, Luillier d'Orgeval was carrying out prosecutions there. The riots appear to have been against the *aides*: V6 134, no. 13, 12 Nov. 1638.

[3] Foisil, *Nu-Pieds*, pp. 77, 289–90.

[4] E 155a, fo. 264, 28 Apr. 1640. E 168a, fo. 205, 12 Mar. 1642. E 168b, fo. 445, 29 Mar. 1642.

[5] E 166, fo. 64, 4 Jan. 1642. E 171a, fo. 67, 4 June 1642. A.D. Cher C 916, 29 Oct. 1642. A.D. Cher C 917, 23 Feb. and 20 Apr. 1643.

[6] E 167b, fo. 32, 8 Feb. 1642. E 168a, fo. 282, 12 Mar. 1642.

[7] *Lettres . . . au Chancelier Séguier*, ed. Mousnier, i. 534–6. E 163c, fo. 166, 22 Aug. 1641. E 173b, fos. 613, 615, 617, 30 Sept. 1642. E 174b, fos. 213, 267, 19 Nov. and

there was a profound urban disturbance against the sales tax and when the traditional area of discontent, the south-west, experienced serious trouble again—with Villemontée in Poitou,[1] Fremin in the Limousin,[2] and Lauzon in Guyenne[3] in action once more—new areas of France joined the 'tax rebellion'. Claude Le Bouthillier, the finance minister, did not hide from Richelieu his sense of the impending danger. He wrote to the chief minister on 17 February 1642: 'il ne fault pas estonner si les peuples esloignés s'opposent aux impositions nécessaires pour soubstenir les charges de l'estat, veu mesme que presqu'aux portes de Paris, et au coeur de la France, il y en a qui n'ont poinct imposé la taille, et qui ne la veulent poinct imposer.' He emphasized the urgency of remedial action 'afin que le mal n'augmente pas'.[4]

The solution adopted by Bouthillier and the council of finance was the transfer of ultimate fiscal responsibility to the intendants. A decree of 19 August 1642 ordered the intendants in the *pays d'élections* to cease all other business and 'tenir la main à l'accélération et levée' of the *taille*. The intendants were ordered to prosecute anyone who delayed the king's tax-returns, including nobles who interfered with the process of tax collection.[5] On 10 December 1642 the intendants were ordered to prosecute anyone accused of spreading rumours that the sales tax had been abolished 'affin de fomenter des rébellions et séditions parmi les peuples'.[6] The death of Louis XIII caused a further spate of rumours that taxes had been abolished or remitted—the intendants again were ordered to take whatever action was necessary to halt the spread of such rumours.[7] Finally, on 11 July 1643 'tax rebellion' was declared to be a crime equivalent to that of treason (*lèse-majesté*). The intendants were called upon to prosecute not only those participating in the rebellion, but any judges or magistrates who condoned such activity.[8] Extremely important instructions, which were issued

22 Nov. 1642. E 178a, fo. 309, 14 Mar. 1643. E 1687, fo. 18 and E 180a, fo. 278, 13 June 1643. E 181c, fo. 94, 22 July 1643.
[1] *Lettres . . . au Chancelier Séguier*, ed. Mousnier, ii. 1096–1103. E 173a, fo. 26, 8 Aug. 1642. E 174b, fo. 371, 22 Nov. 1642. E 176b, fo. 118, 24 Jan. 1643.
[2] E 173b, fo. 326, 16 Sept. 1642. [3] E 173b, fo. 138, 2 Sept. 1642.
[4] A.A.E. France 842, fos. 43ᵛ–44ʳ. [5] E 173a, fo. 175.
[6] E 175, fo. 53. [7] E 179b, fo. 502, 20 May 1643.
[8] E 1687, fo. 35 and E 181b, fo. 128.

on the previous day, ordered the intendants to employ all necessary force to suppress 'tax rebellion'. The intendants were instructed to '[faire] le procès aux coupables et auteurs des séditions et rébellions, lesquelz ilz feront punir exemplairement pour réduire le tout dans le debvoir'.[1] The *maréchaussée* was to assist them as a matter of course;[2] but in addition, special brigades were set up in a number of *généralités* to facilitate the collection of the *taille;* if these forces proved insufficient, the army could be called in.

The intendants used their new powers consistently in the uphill task of containing a 'tax rebellion' which spread across nearly two-thirds of France. In Normandy, rumours of tax remissions were particularly rife and a major cause of rebellion.[3] There were also falsified decrees of the council in circulation, which purported to remit the areas of the *taille* from 1638 to 1643: the intendants were ordered to prosecute anyone found in possession of such documents.[4] At Alençon, Thiersault was ordered to use the troops only if absolutely necessary during the winter of 1642–3;[5] but rumours of a tax remission on the death of Louis XIII led to severe problems in the *élections* of Verneuil, Mortagne, and Domfront, with the inhabitants meeting the collectors 'à main armée'.[6] Favier de Boullay, the successor to Thiersault, was convinced that the nobility was behind the rebellion: 'des eslections entières pourroient bien paier ce à quoy elles sont imposées si la protection des gentils-hommes ne les metoient dans une rébellion manifeste pour empescher que leurs fermiers qui haussent leurs fermes ne paient point ou fort peu des tailles.' He added that 'les juges et les gentilshommes gastent tout et ce pays est si fort infecté de rébellion que j'en suis hors de moy . . .'[7] Favier was ordered to prosecute any members of the nobility of Falaise who prevented

[1] K 891, no. 4 [musée AE II 2629]. Cf. Mousnier, *La plume*, p. 194. The intendant, when carrying out such prosecutions, was to be assisted by 'le nombre de gradués portés par les ordonnances', i.e. not less than seven.

[2] E 182a, fo. 361, 8 Aug. 1643.

[3] E 197b, fo. 402, 17 Dec. 1644.

[4] E 201a, fo. 1, 1 Apr. 1645.

[5] A.G. A1 73, mins. 119/2 and 121, 18 Jan. and 22 Jan. 1643. E 177b, fo. 83, 25 Feb. 1643.

[6] *Lettres . . . au Chancelier Séguier*, ed. Mousnier, i. 519–20. E 179b, fo. 496, 20 May 1643.

[7] *Lettres . . . au Chancelier Séguier*, ed. Mousnier, ii. 706–7.

the levy of the *taille*.[1] He was also ordered to prosecute the inhabitants of the *élection* of Domfront who took up arms against the troops and then fled to Brittany and Maine: 'aiant apris . . . qu'ils sont en armes jusques au nombre de deux mil, je n'ay pas voulu hazarder les armes du Roy sans plus grandes forces,' Favier confessed to Séguier, 'veu mesmes que la cavalerie ne peult rien faire en ce pays qui n'est remply que de haies et dans les chemins duquel les mutins ont abatu les arbres . . .'[2] Clearly, the 'tax rebellion' of Domfront was rapidly assuming the character of a guerrilla war, and the situation was serious in several parts of the *généralité* of Alençon until the end of 1646.[3] The breakdown of royal control was less marked in the *généralité* of Caen, although Le Roy de La Potherie could remark that 'les pauvres ont payé partout, il n'y a que les riches et les officiers qui font ces difficultés'.[4] On 1 February 1645, La Potherie was ordered to prosecute any *seigneurs* in the *élections* of Saint-Lo, Vire, Avranches, and Carentan who prevented the levy of the *taille*,[5] while the following year Tronchay, his successor, was forcing payment with the troops.[6]

The situation was equally grave in the south-west of France. The outlying areas of the province of Guyenne—the valleys of Couserans, Pardies, and Luchon—had not paid their taxes in the years between 1638 and 1643, and Lauzon, the intendant at Bordeaux, and Charreton de La Terrière, his colleague at Montauban, were ordered to coerce payment.[7] However, the 'tax rebellion' was also widespread in the more central areas of the province. Throughout much of the *généralité* of Bordeaux, Lauzon was levying the tax arrears by means of the troops.[8] In Périgord, he informed Séguier that 'cette province particulière . . . est fort libertine et mérite que l'on luy tienne la bride haute'.[9] In 1646, Lauzon was ordered to prosecute anyone spreading rumours of a remission of the taxes.[10] Charreton's

---

[1] E 184d, fo. 118, 18 Nov. 1643. E 214b, fo. 283, 11 Aug. 1646.

[2] *Lettres . . . au Chancelier Séguier*, ed. Mousnier, i. 621–2. E 188a, fo. 109, 2 Mar. 1644. E 1692, fo. 72, 3 May 1645.

[3] Foisil, *Nu-Pieds*, p. 182. E 193b, fo. 388, 20 Aug. 1644. E 215a, fo. 531, 15 Sept. 1646. E 217b, fo. 173, 21 Nov. 1646.

[4] *Lettres . . . au Chancelier Séguier*, ed. Mousnier, i. 516.

[5] E 199a, fo. 110, 1 Feb. 1645.   [6] E 217b, fo. 161, 21 Nov. 1646.

[7] E 188a, fo. 323, 9 Mar. 1644.   [8] E 196a, fo. 50, 9 Nov. 1644.

[9] *Lettres . . . au Chancelier Séguier*, ed. Mousnier, i. 639.

[10] E 209a, fo. 185, 7 Mar. 1646.

difficulties in the first year of his intendancy at Montauban were immense, with five *élections* seriously in arrears, and a major urban insurrection with which to contend. Again, Charreton and Louis Laisné, his successor, tried to stamp out rumours of tax remissions, which played an important part in the 'tax rebellion';[1] the intendants also tried to concentrate their attention on parishes which were the traditional centres of discontent, such as Trémouilles in the Rouergue.[2] The situation was tense in the Limousin, with Corberon informing Séguier on 28 October 1644 that he anticipated 'beaucoup de désordre et de rébellion': his fears proved correct in the *élection* of Tulle the following January.[3] The trouble centred on the Pompadour estates, although the peasants put up little resistance when the troops arrived in strength. On 10 March 1645, Corberon noted 'l'abondance des choses qui se sont trouvées en leurs maisons', which in his view was evidence of 'plus de mauvaise volonté que d'impuissance' on the part of the peasants.[4] The situation appears to have been more serious in Poitou, with barricades being set up at Montendre,[5] and rumours of tax remissions proving a constant source of worry to Villemontée in 1643.[6] On 22 March 1644, Villemontée was given general powers to proceed against those parishes which he considered to be 'coupables de rébellion et en demeure affectée'.[7] Villemontée's successor, René I Voyer d'Argenson, was using the troops to collect the taxes in the *élection* of Les Sables d'Olonne in 1646.[8]

The spread of 'tax rebellion' to central France was the reason why the intendants were given stronger powers to deal with the unrest in the years 1642–3. Bragelongne remained in difficulty in the Orléanais at least until 1646, particularly in the *élection* of Montargis.[9] In both the Orléanais and the Touraine

---

[1] E 188c, fo. 116, 19 May 1644. E 220b, fo. 355, 23 Feb. 1647.

[2] E 202a, fo. 631, 13 May 1645.

[3] *Lettres . . . au Chancelier Séguier*, ed. Mousnier, i. 655. B.N. MS.fr. 18510, fo. 423, 11 Jan. 1645.

[4] *Lettres . . . au Chancelier Séguier*, ed. Mousnier, ii. 723. Cf. E 208a, fo. 87, 3 Feb. 1646, ordering Corberon to use troops to obtain payment from Aubeterre-sur-Dronne.   [5] E 179b, fo. 191, 2 May 1643.

[6] E 178b, fo. 153, 26 Mar. 1643. E 181a, fo. 23, 1 July 1643. E 182b, fo. 61, 14 Aug. 1643.   [7] E 188c, fo. 332.

[8] E 207b, fo. 539, 31 Jan. 1646. Rebellions also in the *élections* of Saintes and Cognac: E 199b, fo. 146, 15 Feb. 1645. E 203a, fo. 432, 14 June 1645.

[9] E 209b, fo. 9, 10 Mar. 1646.

there were widespread rumours of tax remissions following the
deaths of Richelieu and Louis XIII. Heere was forced to
publish an ordinance against 'ceux qui font courir semblables
bruicts pour leur estre par [lui] leur procès fait et parfaict'.
On 18 July 1643, Heere was convinced that 'il n'y a que les
plus riches paroisses et celles qui appartiennent aux personnes
de qualité qui sont dans la désobéissance, joint que plusieurs
personnes de condition ont tellement imprimé dans l'esprit des
peuples que l'on remetteroit les tailles qu'ils l'esperent tousjours . . .'[1] The following month, Heere was ordered to prosecute the 'tax rebellions' in the province;[2] and by May 1645, the
situation had stabilized considerably since Heere reported that
'toutes choses sont [en] très bon estat en cette généralité'.[3] In
the neighbouring province of Berry, Barrin de Rezé was trying
to obtain payment of the enormous arrears of the *taille*,[4] while
in the Bourbonnais, and particularly in the *élection* of Nevers,
Phélypeaux was experiencing similar problems.[5] In September
1646, Phélypeaux was empowered to prosecute those guilty of
'tax rebellion' in the province, and troops were to be sent into
the rebellious parishes.[6] In the Auvergne, there were some
parishes which had not paid their taxes for seven or eight
years.[7] There were special problems in the province of geographical inaccessibility and local rivalries: 'les uns ne veulent
payer que les autres n'ayent satisfaict à leurs cottes'.[8] Sève
informed Chancellor Séguier in January 1644: 'je vas tousjours
combattant la désobéissance des parroisses qui se déffendent de
payer la taille et je suis assez fort pour le plat pays. Mais il y a
tant de mauvaise volonté dans les fondz des montagnes . . .
qu'il est bien difficile qu'avec quelques archers que j'ay prez de
moy je puisse les remettre dans le debvoir. D'employer des gens
de guerre, c'est un rémède pire que le mal . . .'[9]

The importance of the work of the intendants with regard to
the suppression of 'tax rebellion' was nowhere demonstrated

[1] *Lettres . . . au Chancelier Séguier*, ed. Mousnier, i. 502, 529.
[2] E 182a, fo. 341, 6 Aug. 1643. Cf. the orders to prosecute those who spread
rumours of tax remissions: E 179b, fo. 93, 2 May 1643. E 183c, fo. 461, 28 Sept.
1643.
[3] *Lettres . . . au Chancelier Séguier*, ed. Mousnier, ii. 731.
[4] E 184a, fo. 165, 14 Oct. 1643. E 206a, fo. 370, 9 Sept. 1645.
[5] E 200c, fo. 558, 31 Mar. 1645.   [6] E 215b, fo. 324, 22 Sept. 1646.
[7] E 181a, fo. 65, 1 July 1643.   [8] E 185a, fo. 591, 9 Dec. 1643.
[9] *Lettres . . . au Chancelier Séguier*, ed. Mousnier, i. 618.

more clearly than in the 'frontier areas' such as Champagne, the Soissonnais, and the Dauphiné, where rebellion on a significant scale took place largely as a result of the almost continuous passage of troops, respectively towards the German, Spanish Netherlands, and Italian fronts. Jeannin de Castille, the intendant of Champagne, was instructed to draw up a list of those parishes which he considered to be the most rebellious and which had built forts to defend themselves against the *archers*.[1] In the Soissonnais, Le Picard de Périgny was ordered to draw up a list of the parishes most in arrears[2] and coerce payment, especially in the rebellious *élection* of Château-Thierry.[3] In the Dauphiné, there were serious riots against taxation in the years between 1644 and 1646, and the intendants regularly used the troops to collect the *taille*. The powers given to the intendants in 1642–3, combined with the reduction of the *taille* by some 16 million *livres* between 1643 and 1647 helped to stabilize the situation in the *pays d'élections*. After the stormy years between 1644 and 1646, the Dauphiné was quiet thereafter until the outbreak of the Fronde;[4] this relative calm seems to have been true also for the rest of France. The administration of Mazarin in the years before the Fronde was stronger than has previously been thought: the intendants played a decisive part in preventing the complete breakdown in law and order in the provinces that might otherwise have occurred from France's failure to win a quick settlement at the Westphalian negotiations in the years between 1644 and 1646. If the *taille* had ceased to be levied in the *pays d'élections*, the financiers would have refused to make loans to the government; without such loans, the war could not have been continued. Once the financiers withdrew their services in 1648, the crown was at the mercy of its domestic critics.

The meeting of the *Chambre Saint-Louis*, and the resulting constitutional negotiations, were accompanied by a breakdown of royal control in the provinces. On 17 July 1648, Gaston d'Orléans, one of the chief representatives of the crown in the negotiations, offered a 12·5 per cent remission of the *taille* and asked in return for an immediate end to the meetings since 'les ennemys se prévalloient supposant . . . que le Royaume estoit divisé et qu'il penchoit à un souslèvement général'.[1] On the previous day, Gaston had demanded immediate agreement to the royal proposals: 'pendant toutes lesdites assemblées, les peuples ne payoient rien et qu'ils se portoient à la sédition; qu'il avoit reçu au Conseil nouvelles des émotions d'Orléans, Forest et Moulins et qu'à toute heure on entendoit de pareilles nouvelles . . .'[2] The 'tax rebellion' during the Fronde was perhaps more widespread than in any other period before 1790. In 1648—as was to be the case nearly 150 years later—the recall of the intendants led the population as a whole to believe that the taxes demanded by the government need no longer be paid. Once the instruments of repression, the intendants, were removed the peasants gave a resounding vote of no confidence in the government. With the best will in the world, the *trésoriers* and the *élus* could not coerce payment from recalcitrant tax-payers without recourse to force: yet the hated special brigades had been disbanded at the moment of the recall of the intend-ants, and the royal troops were fully stretched dealing with the double threat of Spanish invasion and *Frondeur* insurrection.

The 'tax rebellion' during the years of the Fronde was not confined to the traditional areas of discontent, but was wide-spread in the *pays d'élections*. Certainly, the south-west parti-cipated: there were 'fréquentes rébellions' in Guyenne, parti-cularly in the *élection* of Bordeaux[3] and in parts of the *généralité* of Montauban.[4] There were many rumours of tax remissions[5] which were intensified by decrees of the *Parlement* of Toulouse which accorded greater tax remissions than those allowed by the government.[6] In Poitou, rumours of tax remissions caused 'plusieurs rébellions' and the *maréchaussée* was ordered to assist in the collection of taxes.[7] Of all the provinces in the south-west

[1] U 28, fo. 392^v, 17 July 1648.

[2] Z1a 163, fo. 91/2. On the other hand, many of these reports were little more than unsubstantial rumours. There was a report that at Moulins more than 600 men had taken to arms and beseiged Phélypeaux, the intendant. This was untrue: B.N. MS.fr. 18510, fo. 311, declaration to the council by Vincent Cronchot and Gilbert Charbon, 20 July 1648.

[3] E 232b, fo. 176, 10 Sept. 1648. E 233a, fo. 58, 7 Oct. 1648. E 233a, fo. 113 and E 1692, no. 288, 8 Oct. 1648.

[4] E 1696, fo. 363, 14 Oct. 1650.

[5] E 232a, fo. 452, 19 Aug. 1648. E 234c, fo. 357, 19 June 1649.

[6] E 1696, fo. 341, 6 Oct. 1650.   [7] E 237a, fo. 388, 16 Oct. 1649.

of France, however, it appears that the Limousin was most seriously affected: the rumours of tax remissions in 1648[1] were followed the next year by 'meurtres, assassinats, rébellions et voyes de fait', notably in the *élections* of Tulle and Brive-la-Gaillarde.[2] Foullé, the *intendant des finances* sent to the Limousin in 1650, was ordered to prosecute the participants in the 'tax rebellion' and to use the troops to collect the rapidly mounting arrears of taxes.[3] The revolt of Condé in October 1651 led to the complete breakdown of financial administration in parts of the south-west, and the appropriation of royal taxes by the nobility, particularly in the Limousin.[4]

The 'tax rebellion', however, was far from being confined to the south-west of France. In Normandy, there were rumours of tax remissions[5] and seigneurial intimidation of the *archers* was a regular occurrence.[6] In the neighbouring provinces, the problem was just as serious. In the north, in Picardy, there was alleged seigneurial complicity in the rebellion,[7] and even Julien Pietre, the *subdélégué* of successive intendants, was accused of 'entretien[nant] les peuples dans l'opiniâstreté de ne rien payer'.[8] Further south, in the Soissonnais[9] and the Île-de-France,[10] there were rumours of tax remissions, cases of seigneurial complicity in 'tax rebellion', and a general refusal to draw up the tax-rolls. The Touraine was plagued by frequent rebellions, with the parishes refusing to draw up their tax-rolls and some of the *archers* being 'excédez et . . . tuez'; the *maréchaussée* was ordered by the council to 'se transporter dans les paroisses rebelles et désobéissantes'.[11] Finally, a block of provinces in eastern France was affected: Champagne, where

[1] E 233a, fo. 48, 7 Oct. 1648. Spread, among others, by *trésoriers de France* suspended from office by the council: E 242c, fo. 414, 28 June 1650.

[2] E 237b, fo. 453, 27 Nov. 1649.

[3] E 239, fo. 76, 5 Jan. 1650.

[4] E 249a, fo. 518, 27 Oct. 1651.

[5] E 240, fo. 540, 17 Feb. 1650 (rumours spread by Lucas Toustain, *sergent royal* at Bray). E 253c, fo. 47, 4 Dec. 1652.

[6] E 256a, fo. 103, 7 May 1653. E 257a, fo. 129, 4 June 1653.

[7] E 237b, fo. 357, 20 Nov. 1649.

[8] E 243b, fo. 379, 9 Sept. 1650. E 245c, fo. 333, 22 Mar. 1651. E 249a, fo. 218, 11 Oct. 1651.

[9] E 237b, fo. 19, 6 Nov. 1649. E 253c, fo. 78, 4 Dec. 1652.

[10] E 237a, fo. 3, 2 Oct. 1649.

[11] E 235b, fo. 385, 30 July 1649. E 236a, fo. 93, 1 Sept. 1649. E 238, fo. 143, 4 Dec. 1649.

the troops were sent in to suppress the 'grandes rébellions' in November 1649;[1] Burgundy, which although a *pays d'états*, was seeking similar tax remissions to those enjoyed by the *pays d'élections* with the result that there were rebellions in the *élections* of Auxerre and Bar-sur-Seine;[2] the Dauphiné, where in December 1649 it could be said that 'les tailles ne se payent point';[3] the Lyonnais, where as a result of rumours of tax remissions the tax-rolls were not drawn up and 'des grandes rébellions ... se commettent';[4] and finally, the Auvergne, where the troops were being used to coerce payment.[5] The central provinces of the Bourbonnais,[6] Berry,[7] and the Orléanais[8] were similarly affected.

Even if it is conceded that only a small part of each province was affected by the taxpayers' strike, the conclusion is inescapable that a very large part of France was affected by the rebellion, since all the *pays d'élections* were involved. Far from demonstrating a *fureur paysanne*, an undirected manifestation of peasant violence, the 'tax rebellion' of the Fronde demonstrated a certain political consciousness on the part of the French peasantry. The countryside, when given the opportunity to do so, rejected the system of war finance. The 'tax rebellion' of the Fronde had commenced with the meeting of the *Chambre Saint-Louis*, 'une occasion de plaincte et douleur générale pour descrier le gouvernement de l'estat'. It had intensified as a result of the recall of the intendants and the limited tax-remissions granted in the declarations of 18 July and 22 October 1648. Passive resistance had gained, apparently, a great victory: those parishes which had withheld payment of their taxes seemed to have been rewarded in the declarations which accorded a limited remission of tax arrears. Further 'tax rebellion' was therefore encouraged, and spread still further with the news of the peace treaty with the Emperor on 24

---

[1] E 235b, fos. 304, 432, 29 and 31 July 1649. E 237b, fo. 423, 24 Nov. 1649.

[2] E 242a, fo. 188, 21 Apr. 1650. N.B.: there were provincial Estates in Burgundy, yet *élections* had been established too, which accounts for the confusion.

[3] E 237b, fo. 359, 20 Nov. 1649. E 238, fo. 244, 11 Dec. 1649.

[4] E 237b, fo. 170, 13 Nov. 1649. E 242b, fo. 420, 28 May 1650. E 243b, fo. 522, 23 Sept. 1650. E 245a, fo. 271, 21 Jan. 1651. E 252b, fo. 83, 12 Aug. 1652.

[5] E 235c, fo. 257, 12 Aug. 1649. E 236b, fo. 346, 25 Sept. 1649. E 243a, fo. 338, 27 July 1650.

[6] E 235a, fo. 197, 8 July 1649. E 1696, fo. 88 and E 235c, fo. 23, 4 Aug. 1649.

[7] E 240, fo. 447, 16 Feb. 1650.   [8] E 237b, fo. 39, 6 Nov. 1649.

October 1648.[1] To the extent that the actions of the peasantry expressed a political philosophy, it was a vote for peace and the destruction of the system of war finance.[2] There is little doubt that as a result of the 'tax rebellion', the government was reduced to penury, and had the Spanish been in a stronger position to take advantage of the French weakness, serious strategic losses would have occurred. A significant military defeat at a moment of domestic upheaval might well have forced a major reversal in French foreign policy; indeed as late as September 1652, Servien and Le Tellier were well aware of this danger.[3] Had their fears been realized, had such a change in foreign policy occurred, the beneficiaries would have been the taxpayers of the *pays d'élections*.

The scale of the 'tax rebellion' during the Fronde was undoubtedly a major factor in the decision to reintroduce the intendants in 1653. As Denis Marin wrote in his memorandum to Chancellor Séguier, 's'il y a des rébellions dans les provinces . . . lesdits sieurs maîtres des requêtes les pourront empescher'.[4] The intendants were essential to the government in the years after the Fronde: they were needed to contain the resistance of the provinces to the war effort imposed by Mazarin. Any military defeat, as in July 1656, was a threat to the stability of the regime; any resurgence of criticism in the *Parlement* of Paris led to fears of a repetition of the events of 1648;[5] a combination of military disaster and civil unrest might have led to a 'soulèvement général'—Servien felt that this would have happened had the Battle of the Dunes in 1658 been lost by the

[1] B.N. Mélanges Colbert 105, fo. 365. '. . . la remise des restes en [16]48 et la surséance accordée depuis la paix ont flatté les peuples et leur ont fait croire qu'on seroit constrainct de leur remettre leurs tailles, comme on a voit faict, de sorte qu'ils se sont rendus plus mauvais payeurs.' François Bochart de Champigny to Colbert, 9 Dec. 1661. Bochart was referring to the Peace of the Pyrenees, but his basic argument holds true. In 1649–52, many felt that if Mazarin were removed from power, peace with Spain, and further tax remissions, would quickly follow.

[2] Bercé, *Histoire des croquants*, i. 489–94; ii. 612–13.

[3] Servien and Le Tellier advised Mazarin that France could not risk the continuation of both a civil war (the Fronde) and a foreign war (against Spain). Mazarin accepted their argument: *Lettres du Cardinal Mazarin*, ed. Chéruel, v. 251. A.A.E. France 884, fo. 341, 14 Sept. 1652.

[4] B.N. MS.fr. 16218, fo. 377.

[5] cf. B.L. Harleian 4489, fo. 39ᵛ, 22 Aug. 1656. Séguier recalled to Le Tellier 'les fondements sur lequel l'on a eslevé tant d'entreprises en 1648'.

Anglo-French forces. In this context, the role of the intendants was to pinpoint the areas of discontent, to send in the forces needed to contain the unrest, and above all to prevent a repetition of 'tax rebellion' on the scale of the years between 1648 and 1653. The special brigades were set up once again, and the frequency with which the intendants resorted to military force suggests the seriousness of the problem.[1] In 1658, it could be claimed that in Guyenne 'il est absolument nécessaire de se servir desdites brigades à cause de la dureté de la pluspart des redevables contre lesquels la contrainte ordinaire se trouve inutile . . .'[2]

The renewal of hostilities against Spain led once more to higher taxes. As was to be expected, the rebellion against these increased taxes began in the south-west of France, and was well under way by 1655. On 1 September 1655, Tallemant, the intendant at Bordeaux, and Machault, the intendant at Montauban, were ordered to prosecute all persons accused of spreading rumours of a remission of the *taille*.[3] By October, rebellions against the *taille* had taken place at Cadillac, Rions, Lesparre-Médoc, Castillon, Lamarque, Castelnau-de-Médoc, La Teste, Lège, and Podensac.[4] In April 1656, there were further rebellions at Coutras, Cadillac, Rions, Lesparre-Médoc, Castelnau-de-Médoc, and La Teste, and several *archers* were killed. When the troops were billeted on the area to obtain payment of the *taille*, 'tout le pays' took to arms and nineteen soldiers were killed. Saint-Luc, the lieutenant-general in the province, was ordered to attack the rebels.[5] On 1 May 1656, Tallemant had arrived at Coutras with Saint-Luc and the troops: 'nous n'avons trouvé personne . . .', Tallemant informed Chancellor Séguier, 'les innocens aussi bien que les coupables sont en fuitte et n'ont rien laissé dans leurs maisons. Nous n'avons peu prendre aucuns des séditieux . . .'[6] On 21 August, Tallemant informed Séguier 'qu'il a grande subiect d'appréhender un soulèvement général dans Bordeaux et dans la

---

[1] Bercé, *Histoire des croquants*, i. 111, asserts that in 1661 the number of special brigades in the south-west exceeded that of 1648.

[2] E 316a, fo. 227, 8 Aug. 1658.

[3] E 281a, fo. 180, 1 Sept. 1655. E 290b, fo. 148, 28 June 1656. E 292c, fo. 221, 31 Aug. 1656. [4] E 1703, no. 366, 18 Oct. 1655.

[5] E 288a, fo. 371, 29 Apr. 1656. E 289b, fo. 122, 17 May 1656.

[6] B.L. Harleian 4489, fo. 61, 1 May 1656.

province mesme' as a result of projected indirect taxes on the wine trade.[1] Tallemant continued prosecuting those accused of the rebellion centred on Coutras: 'j'espère que la punition que j'ay faitte de ces séditieux', he concluded, 'servira pour contenir les autres dans leur debvoir.'[2] Nevertheless, Mazerus, the *lieutenant* at the *sénéchaussée* of Coutras and a principal leader of the rebellion, was thought to have 'de grande intelligence dans le Périgord et ailleurs avec 3 ou 4000 hommes de faction prest à prendre les armes'.[3] On 11 December 1656, Tallemant informed Séguier that he had made 'ung voyage de près de trois mois dans les élections de Périgord, Saintonge et Angoumois pour faire advancer les recouvrements, y restablir l'ordre et remettre les peuples dans leur debvoir . . .' Although on this occasion he could remark that 'tout est à présent fort calme dans la généralité',[4] trouble began once more around Montguyon in 1657 and in the *élections* of Agen, Saintes, and Cognac the following year.[5]

The intendants in the other provinces of the south-west of France experienced similar difficulties. In the *généralité* of Montauban, Machault was ordered to investigate assemblies held in 1656 to 'éluder le payement de la taille' and to 'exciter les peuples à refuzer l'entière imposition'.[6] On 1 December 1656, Méliand, his successor, was at Rodez with five hundred infantry and a hundred cavalry: 'ce chastiment qui estoit absolument nécessaire pour réprimer les violences qui se rendoient communes', the intendant reported to Séguier, 'a tellement imprimé la crainte dans toute la province qu'il y en viendra de l'argent et de l'obéyssance au Roy et à justice'.[7] On 16 January 1657, the *cour des aides* of Cahors issued a decree prohibiting the levy of the *taille* by 'des brigades et à main armée' within its jurisdictional area. As a result, 'les peuples . . . ont cessé de payer les deniers des tailles' and there were 'soulèvements et émotions populaires' against the brigades. The council of finance annulled the decree of the *cour des aides* and

---

[1] B.L. Harleian 4489, fo. 177, 21 Aug. 1656.
[2] B.L. Harleian 4489, fo. 181, Aug./Sept. 1656.
[3] E 295b, fo. 193, 22 Nov. 1656.   [4] B.L. Harleian 4490, fo. 95.
[5] E 307a, fos. 32, 287, 10 Nov. 1657. E 316a, fo. 227, 8 Aug. 1658.
[6] E 286a, fo. 371, 15 Feb. 1656. E 287c, fo. 210, 23 Mar. 1656. E 290a, fo. 5, 14 June 1656.
[7] B.L. Harleian 4490, fo. 90, 1 Dec. 1656.

ordered Méliand to prosecute the participants in the 'tax rebellion'.[1] The situation deteriorated further in the succeeding months. For three days in May 1657 there was serious rioting at Martres-de-Rivière, with the peasants, 'conduitz par quantité de gentilshommes du pays', besieging a company of cavalry. Méliand arrived with more troops, but his forces were insufficient to lift the siege, and several of his men were killed in the ensuing fighting. Finally the siege was lifted when the rebels panicked at a rumour that more troops were on their way. Méliand was ordered to prosecute the leaders of this insurrection,[2] and to raise forty infantrymen to punish the rebellions in Foix and Comminges.[3] The situation remained tense throughout 1657 and 1658, however.[4] The intendants of the Limousin[5] and Poitou[6] also had to contend with 'tax rebellion' on a serious scale in 1656 and 1657.

The 'tax rebellion' during the last years of the war against Spain was not confined to the south-west of France. There were numerous rumours of tax remissions in Normandy.[7] In the *généralité* of Alençon, twenty-five parishes in a singe *élection*— Bernay—refused to nominate any collectors for the *taille* in the years between 1647 and 1659;[8] while in the *généralité* of Rouen, Miroménil was ordered to take proceedings against more than twenty parishes which had refused to pay any of the *taille* which they owed from the years of the Fronde.[9] The province of Picardy seems to have been relatively quiet in these years,[10] but in the Soissonnais, Villemontée was in serious difficulty in the face of persistent rumours of tax remissions and rebellions, especially in the years between 1654 and 1656.[11] The ministers must have been particularly alarmed at the strength of protest in the area around the capital: the intendants were frequently

---

[1] E 299a, fo. 58, 7 Mar. 1657.   [2] E 302a, fo. 192, 6 June 1657.

[3] E 317a, fo. 708, 26 Sept. 1658.

[4] E 308a, fo. 91, 12 Dec. 1657. E 318b, fo. 296, 27 Nov. 1658.

[5] E 288a, fo. 445, 29 Apr. 1656. E 298a, fo. 111, 17 Feb. 1657.

[6] E 284b, fo. 353, 18 Dec. 1655. E 286a, fo. 351, 15 Feb. 1656. E 290a, fo. 344, 17 June 1656.

[7] E 317a, fo. 247, 5 Sept. 1658. E 290b, fo. 110, 28 June 1656 (rumour spread by a *colporteur* named Pierre du Bois).

[8] E 329a, fo. 8, 8 Oct. 1659.

[9] E 269a, fo. 408, 10 Sept. 1654.

[10] But cf. E 283b, fo. 246, 24 Nov. 1655. E 314a, fo. 9, 1 June 1658.

[11] E 264a, fo. 484, 7 Mar. 1654. E 284a, fo. 346, 11 Dec. 1655. E 285a, fo. 184, 8 Jan. 1656. E 292a, fo. 423, 3 Aug. 1656.

in action in the *élections* of Tonnerre, Dourdan, and Joigny.[1] Much of eastern France was affected by the rebellion, too. In Champagne, Daniel Voisin was ordered to coerce those parishes which 'se sont imaginez estre deschargez des tailles'. In the *élection* of Troyes in particular forts were constructed in the villages to prevent the seizure of cattle and other possessions of the peasants—the seizure of property was the usual procedure of the *receveurs des tailles* when a parish failed to pay its taxes.[2] Further south, in Burgundy, Bouchu did not have such a serious problem, although in 1660 parts of the *élection* of Bar-sur-Seine had not paid the *taille* for twelve or fifteen years and attacked the tax-collectors as a regular event.[3] There were difficulties in levying the *taille* in the Bourbonnais, the Auvergne, and the Lyonnais. In the Bourbonnais, the situation was made worse by the decision to disband the special brigades in September 1655.[4] In 1653 troops were billeted on more than fifteen parishes in the *élection* of Aurillac in the Auvergne.[5] In the *élection* of Thiers, Daniel Voisin was using the troops to collect the taxes; but three-quarters of the taxes outstanding in 1649 were still unpaid in 1655.[6] Thirty-eight parishes in this *élection* had been transferred to the *généralité* of Lyon in 1648, and they had still not paid any taxes from the years of the Fronde in 1654.[7] François Bochart was struggling to contend with the 'rébellions, voyes de fait et esmotions populaires' in the *élection* of Roanne in 1656 and the rumours of tax remissions throughout the *généralité* of Lyon the following year.[8]

Apart from Guyenne, nowhere experienced a more serious 'tax rebellion' in the years after the Fronde than the provinces of Berry and the Orléanais. In May 1658, thirty parishes formed an illegal association and the peasants entered the towns 'où ilz

[1] E 266b, fo. 236, 20 June 1654. E 284a, fo. 215, 2 Dec. 1655. E 288b, fo. 89, 29 Apr. 1656. E 307a, fo. 270, 10 Nov. 1657. E 313a, fo. 403, 9 May 1658. E 318b, fo. 106, 20 Nov. 1658.

[2] E 289c, fo. 290, 31 May 1656. E 303c, fo. 83, 14 July 1657. E 304c, fo. 320, 29 Aug. 1657. E 306a, fo. 31, 4 Oct. 1657.

[3] E 332b, fo. 1, 26 Feb. 1660.

[4] E 281b, fo. 482, 25 Sept. 1655. E 282a, fos. 174, 212, 13 Oct. 1655. E 285b, fos. 31, 33, 20 Jan. 1656.

[5] E 259a, fo. 430, 14 Aug. 1653.

[6] E 274b, fo. 15, 18 Feb. 1655. E 282a, fo. 98, 13 Oct. 1655. E 287a, fo. 320, 8 Mar. 1656. E 298a, fo. 516, 17 Feb. 1657.

[7] E 264a, fo. 56, 5 Mar. 1654.

[8] E 296a, fo. 35, 13 Dec. 1656. E 297a, fo. 7, 4 Jan. 1657.

firent receuz par le menu peuple d'icelles et par la connivence des principaux habitans'. The intendants of Bourges and Orléans were ordered to assemble the *maréchaussée* and to arrest the leaders of this revolt, which soon became known as the *Guerre des Sabotiers*. The intendants were ordered to suppress the revolt by force: 'opposer la force à la force, faire main-basse, particulièrement sur les séditieux attrouppez avec armes'. The revolt spread rapidly—there was talk of 2,000 peasants in arms, and much of the *pays de Sologne*, that is to say basically the *élections* of Gien, Montargis, and Clamécy, was affected. This revolt was extremely difficult to suppress: Sevin, the intendant at Orléans, and Gallard de Poinville, his colleague at Bourges, appeared powerless to deal with the rapidly deteriorating situation. In October 1658, they were recalled and Bernard Fortia was appointed as their successor; Fortia had previously served as intendant of Poitou where he had gained experience in the use of strong-arm tactics. Nevertheless, the failure of the intendants to contain the rebellion in the summer of 1658 had led to military involvement on a hitherto unprecedented scale: in August, Pilloys, the *lieutenant-général* commanding the troops, was ordered to prosecute the rebels by a military court. He was also instructed to disarm the inhabitants and to billet troops in the parishes which had not paid their taxes. Neither Sevin nor Gallard obtained a further intendancy; instead, they were disgraced for allowing a 'tax rebellion' to gain momentum and become a guerrilla war in the heartlands of France.[1]

The Battle of the Dunes and the capture of Dunkirk and Gravelines in 1658 were decisive Anglo-French victories which forced the Spanish council to decide on negotiations with France. The outcome was a truce on 8 May 1659, followed swiftly by the treaty of Paris (4 June) and the treaty of the Pyrenees (7 November). News of these political events was eagerly received in France by a war-weary population, because they held out the prospect of lower taxes. Indeed, the peace of the Pyrenees allowed Foucquet to make a substantial reduction

[1] L. Jarry, *La guerre des Sabotiers de Sologne et les assemblées de la noblesse, 1653–1660* (Orléans, 1880). E 313a, fo. 366, 9 May 1658. E 1707, no. 39 and E 313b, fo. 200, 16 May 1658. E 1708, no. 70, 23 May 1658. E 315a, fo. 182, 3 July 1658. E 315b, fo. 440, 24 July 1658. E 316a, fos. 4, 6, 90, and 414, 7, 8 and 21 Aug. 1658. E 1707, fo. 55, 2 Sept. 1658.

in government expenditure in 1660. This in turn allowed fiscal concessions despite the hesitancy of the council of finance on this subject, fearful as it was of the precedent of 1648. On 5 January 1661, Foucquet made a start at the problem of the huge tax arrears by ordering a remission of 20 million *livres* outstanding from the years between 1647 and 1656.[1] On 5 January 1662, the birth of the Dauphin was chosen as the pretext for remitting all the arrears from these years.[2] The collection of the arrears from the years between 1657 and 1661 was unofficially abandoned during Colbert's ministry.[3] A timid reduction of the *taille* was initiated by Foucquet, and this process was continued in a somewhat more ambitious form by Colbert after 1661.[4]

These were important fiscal concessions by the government, which substantially reduced the tax burden on the *pays d'élections*. Nevertheless, although the government attempted to present these concessions as a magnanimous gesture from a position of strength, they resulted in large measure from the inability of the government to solve the problem of 'tax rebellion' in France. The news of the peace negotiations in 1659 led to a spate of rumours that substantial tax concessions were about to be announced—in Guyenne, Saintonge, and the Angoumois; in much of the *généralité* of Montauban; in Poitou; in parts of the *généralités* of Caen and Paris; in the Soissonnais, in Berry, and the Bourbonnais.[5] On 26 September 1659, before the final peace was signed, Foucquet wrote to Mazarin in a state of considerable anxiety. 'Il y a des rébellions en diverses provinces sur la remise prétendue des tailles', he wrote, 'qu'il est bien nécessaire d'estouffer en leur naissance crainte qu'elles n'ayent des suittes dangereuses . . .' Foucquet cited as evidence to Mazarin the difficulties of Hotman de Fontenay in Guyenne, of Pellot in Poitou and the Limousin, and of Lefèvre de la Barre in the Auvergne: all three intendants were requesting

---

[1] Esmonin, *La taille*, pp. 503–4. E 341a, fo. 12, 5 Jan. 1661.

[2] Esmonin, *La taille*, pp. 505–6. E 350, fo. 14.

[3] Esmonin, *La taille*, pp. 511–12.

[4] ibid., pp. 513–32. E 1714, no. 60, 2 Apr. 1661.

[5] E 328a, fo. 104, 6 Sept. 1659. E 320a, fo. 266, 15 Jan. 1659. E 332a, fo. 290, 21 Feb. 1660. E 324b, fo. 377, 28 May 1659. Mortagne (Caen): E 322a, fo. 430, 12 Mar. 1659. Joigny (Paris): E 324a, fo. 361, 17 May 1659. E 331b, fo. 306, 29 Jan. 1660. E 332a, fo. 294, 21 Feb. 1660. E 333a, fo. 340, 13 Mar. 1660. E 328a, fo. 154, 6 Sept. 1659. E 330, fo. 535, 18 Dec. 1659.

troop reinforcements.[1] On 18 December, Hotman de Fontenay
was ordered to punish those parishes in the *généralités* of Bordeaux and Montauban which rebelled when attempts were
made to levy the *taille*.[2] The situation was particularly serious
in the *élections* of Bordeaux, Condom, Les Lannes, and Cognac.[3]
The one hundred light cavalry at Hotman's disposal in his two
généralités were insufficient for this task, and the intendant was
allowed to levy the number of fusiliers needed 'pour réprimer
les désordres et faciliter la levée des deniers'.[4] The 'tax rebellion'
in Guyenne did not end until after 1661: at that date, the
élection of Figeac in the *généralité* of Montauban still owed much
of the *taille* that should have been paid in the years after 1657.[5]
In 1660, a dozen parishes in the *élection* of Sarlat-la-Canéda
refused to pay any *taille* at all, 'disant que la taille est remise'.[6]
In Poitou and the Limousin, Pellot was still using the troops as
late as 1662,[7] while Le Jay and Aguesseau, his successors in the
Limousin respectively in 1664 and 1667, were combating
rumours of tax remissions and coercing payment of the *taille*.[8]

The 'tax rebellion' in the years after the peace of the Pyrenees
was less serious in Normandy. Nevertheless, there were rebellions in the *élections* of Lisieux and Mortagne in 1659 and as late
as 1662 Favier had to contend with rumours of tax remissions in
the *élection* of Falaise.[9] The problems of Le Lièvre, the intendant
in the *généralité* of Paris, were much greater: on 21 July 1661,
he was empowered by the council to send the troops into over
forty parishes which were implicated in a serious 'tax rebellion'.
Parts of the *élections* of Melun, Tonnerre, Joigny, and Nogent-
sur-Seine were affected: in the last-named area there were
parishes which had not paid any *taille* for ten years.[10] In eastern
France, the *élection* of Troyes in Champagne remained in a
'résolution déterminée . . . de ne rien payer' until 1662.[11] Further
south, the situation in the Orléanais, Berry, and the Bourbonnais calmed down considerably after 1659. There remained

[1] A.A.E. France 908, fo. 135ᵛ, 26 Sept. 1659.
[2] E 330, fo. 659, 18 Dec. 1659.   [3] E 328b, fo. 383, 18 Sept. 1659.
[4] E 1708, no. 148, 7 Dec. 1658. E 320a, fo. 300, 15 Jan. 1659.
[5] E 345b, fo. 362, 25 May 1661.   [6] E 335, fo. 515, 26 Mar. 1660.
[7] E 358b, fo. 161, 28 Sept. 1662.
[8] E 371b, fo. 365, 28 May 1664. E 394b, fo. 98, 10 Feb. 1667.
[9] E 329b, fo. 203, 12 Nov. 1659. E 353, fo. 76, 1 Apr. 1662.
[10] E 335, fo. 576, 26 Mar. 1660. E 1713, fo. 151, 21 July 1661.
[11] E 352b, fo. 297, 23 Mar. 1662.

problems in the Auvergne, where the lesser nobility opposed the
billeting of troops and where there were serious rumours of tax
remissions in 1660. As late as 7 April 1661, the *élection* of Saint-
Flour was in an 'entier refus de payer aucune chose', despite all
the attempts of Lefèvre de la Barre to coerce payment.[1] In the
Dauphiné, François Bochart de Champigny was ordered to
investigate rumours of a tax remission in 1662, while his other
généralité—that of Lyon—owed nearly 1·7 million in tax arrears
on 9 December 1661.[2]

There can be little doubt that the activities of the intendants in
coercing payment of taxes was one of the chief reasons for their
unpopularity during the ministries of Richelieu and Mazarin.
As Corberon, the intendant at Limoges, wrote to Chancellor
Séguier on 28 October 1644, it was 'bien difficile ... d'être
dans l'employ ... et demander de l'argent au peuple, sans
attirer sa haine et exciter ses plaintes'.[3] Prosecutions arising
from cases of 'tax rebellion' were one of the major areas of the
intendants' judicial activities in the *pays d'élections*. In many
cases, the intendants were empowered by decrees of the council
of finance to preside over *ad hoc* judicial tribunals, composed of
law graduates or office-holders, and to issue definitive sentences
without appeal to the sovereign courts or even the king's
council. In other instances, the intendants drew up charges
against those accused of rebellion and presided over the local
bailliage or *présidial* when the sentence was passed. 'Tax rebellion' was endemic in these years: it began with a refusal of
certain parishes in an *élection* to draw up their tax rolls or pay
their *taille*; it led to small-scale rioting or *micro-révoltes* when the
huissiers or *archers* were sent in to coerce payment; if the special
brigades or the army were sent in as a last resort, the rioting
might become more serious, and the size of the area affected
might be increased. The very methods used to suppress the 'tax
rebellion'—summary prosecutions by the intendants and the
enforced levy of taxation by the troops—were likely to intensify
the problem. The alternative, that of letting the 'tax rebellion'
run its course, was worse, however: as the last years of the

[1] E 344, fo. 267, 7 Apr. 1661.
[2] E 355, fo. 216, 14 June 1662. B.N. Mélanges Colbert 105, fo. 367, 9 Dec. 1661.
[3] *Lettres . . . au Chancelier Séguier*, ed. Mousnier, i. 654.

Fronde had demonstrated, a negative policy such as this would have led to rapidly diminishing tax returns and a creeping paralysis of government.

The intendants thus never solved the problem of 'tax rebellion', but they usually managed to contain it within a limited geographical area—usually less than fifty parishes within an 'average' *généralité* of a thousand parishes. This persistent, nagging problem of *l'endurcissement des contribuables*, of politically motivated opposition within part of a *généralité*, was if anything a more serious problem to the government than the great *soulèvements populaires* such as the *Croquants* of Périgord in 1637–41, the *Va-Nu-Pieds* of Normandy in 1639, the *Croquants* of Rouergue in 1643, the *Tardanizats* of Guyenne in 1655–6,[1] and the *Sabotiers* of the Sologne in 1658; these major rebellions were the exception and not the rule. The danger of the major rebellions spreading outside a single province or *pays* was slight —each revolt had its own particular causes, each province had its distinct fiscal regime, and above all, once the peasants assembled in a significant number they could be defeated by the much better equipped and better led (even if numerically inferior) royal troops. By contrast, the 'tax rebellion' within each *généralité* could never be eliminated by force alone. The intendants could not police an entire *généralité* so that rebellion did not occur at all. As the *trésoriers* argued, 'la crainte suit l'intendant partout, mais il ne peut estre qu'en un seul endroit'. They added: 'ainsi pour tenir une province bien réglée par cette méthode, si pourtant elle n'est point trop rude, il y faudroit autant d'intendans qu'il y a d'eslections.'[2] It was not until the fiscal reforms of Colbert, the substitution after 1661 of the *receveurs-généraux* and the *voies ordinaires* for the financiers and coercion by the troops, the greater reliance on indirect revenues and the great agricultural depression after 1670, that 'tax rebellion' ceased to be a fundamental aspect of French life.

---

[1] B.L. Harleian 4489, fo. 61, 1 May 1656. Tallemant used this term, rather than *Tard-Avisés*, the term used by the rebels in 1594, 1636 and 1707.

[2] B.L. Harleian 4472b, fo. 150ᵛ, remonstrances of the *trésoriers*, n.d. [1655?].

CHAPTER XI

The Sovereign Courts

THE POWERS of the intendants were extended during the ministries of Richelieu and Mazarin so that they became the permanent administrators of direct taxation and the officials responsible for the suppression of rebellion arising from the increased fiscal demands of the crown. This extension of the intendants' civil and criminal jurisdiction was inevitably regarded by the sovereign courts as a profound threat. Already at the Assemblies of Notables of 1617 and 1626, the sovereign courts—which were strongly represented in these assemblies—had expressed their anxiety about the intendants, 'un nouvel establissement de justice exécutoire en toutes les provinces du royaume'. Their opposition had several aspects. In part, it was the opposition of permanent office-holders to temporary commissioners. Members of the sovereign courts had to buy their offices. The intendants did not, they were sent into the provinces 'sans édit . . . sans payer finance'.[1] On another level, the opposition was that of the sovereign courts to the extension of government by council. The crown attempted to reserve to the king's council the right to hear appeals against the decisions of the intendants. The sovereign courts saw this as a further extension of the abusive transfer of lawsuits to the king's council (*évocations*) which they had opposed consistently since the reign of François I.[2]

The crucial factor which made conflict inevitable was that the sovereign courts—and the *Parlements* in particular—had their own political aspirations and interests which were quite different from those of the government and its new administrative system, the intendants. These aspirations and interests were expressed most clearly during the Fronde, but they were made manifest in a less acute form throughout the ministries of

[1] Petit, *L'assemblée des notables*, pp. 266–7. B.L. Egerton 1666, fo. 224.

[2] e.g. remonstrances of 10 Apr. 1525: R. Doucet, *Étude sur le gouvernement de François Ier dans ses rapports avec le Parlement de Paris* (2 vols., 1921, 1926), i. 359.

Richelieu and Mazarin. The members of the sovereign courts were dedicated to the maintenance of law and order. Yet on occasions they rebelled in order to protect their authority, privileges, and vested social and economic interests. The provincial *Parlements* in particular claimed to defend the customary constitution of the province—and their own interests at the same time—which they believed were under attack by the crown. Some of the sovereign courts—notably the *Parlement* of Aix-en-Provence—had a tradition of opposition which lasted throughout the ministries of Richelieu and Mazarin. Some members of the *Parlement* of Aix were implicated in murders of political opponents (men who supported the government or who bought new and unpopular offices). A substantial number organized themselves into a loose party opposing the policies of the crown. Most important of all, members of the *Parlement* of Aix—never the whole court, but always a significant section of it—participated in three major revolts in 1630, 1649, and 1659.[1]

Most, though not all, of the opposition occurred at times when controversial royal legislation was presented to the sovereign courts for registration. The *premier président* of the court summoned a joint meeting (usually called the *assemblée des chambres* or the *conseil secret*) at the request of the royal attornies (*gens du roi*) or deputies of the chambers (in the *Parlements*, particularly the *chambre des Enquêtes*, which usually contained the younger and less conservative members of the court). The *procureur-général* presented the edict in question to the court and requested 'pure and simple' registration without protests (*remontrances*) by the court. The *premier président* then asked for opinions by order of seniority in a discussion which was at the same time an oral vote. (Demands for secret ballots were regarded as seditious by the crown and were usually rejected by the courts as innovations which were

---

[1] R. Pillorget, 'Les "Cascaveoux". L'insurrection aixoise de l'automne 1630', *XVIIe Siècle*, lxiv (1964), 3–30, translated in *State and Society in seventeenth-century France*, ed. R. F. Kierstead (New York, 1975), pp. 96–129. Pillorget, 'Vente d'offices et journée de barricades du 20 janvier 1649 à Aix-en-Provence', *Provence Historique*, xv (1965), 25–63. Pillorget, *Les mouvements insurrectionnels de Provence entre 1596 et 1715* (1975), pp. 313–54, 569–602, 791–801. The role of the *parlementaires* is sharply focused by Sharon Kettering, *Judicial politics and urban revolt: the Parlement of Aix, 1629–1659* [forthcoming at Princeton]. I am indebted to Dr. Kettering for allowing me to consult her book in draft form.

unconstitutional.)[1] The exchanges during the debate often became heated and the political divisions within the court were often revealed at such times.[2] The edict could be registered immediately. It could be modified with the effect that the registered legislation lost much of its force and purpose: this amounted to a tacit veto of legislation. Alternatively, the edict might be rejected and the sovereign court might state its objections in the form of oral or written remonstrances which were presented to the king's council.

The edict of February 1641 limited the rights of the *Parlement* of Paris to one remonstrance in the case of judicial legislation and two in the case of financial legislation. In reality, however, the sovereign courts—if they maintained their unity and political resolve—might present remonstrances several times on the same, or related, government measures. The delay in publication and enforcement of new legislation could last years. The crown replied with orders for immediate and unqualified registration of royal legislation (*lettres de jussion*).[3] Sometimes the king himself would send a sealed letter (*lettre de cachet*) informing the court that registration was his express wish ('vous saves que c'est ma volonté).[4] The ultimate sanction of the crown was the suspension of a sovereign court for the failure to register fiscal edicts.[5] In such circumstances, the intendant might be left as the only sovereign judicial or financial authority in the province. Sometimes, as in Languedoc in 1658, the intendant presided over a judicial commission replacing the suspended court.[6] Suspension was an exceptional

---

[1] For example, the *Parlement* of Dijon in 1659–60: A.A.E. France 1492, fo. 261ᵛ. 'L'exemple de cette manière d'opiner par scrutins quy ne se praticque que dans les républicques est de perilleuse conséquence, et c'est donner lieu à ceux qui ne cherchent que le souslèvement.' The innovation was prohibited by a dcree of the council of state: E 1711, no. 89, 5 Mar. 1660.

[2] For the political divisions, e.g. 'Journal inédit du Parlement de Paris pendant la Fronde', ed. Courteault, albeit divisions arising from the political situation rather than registration of edicts.   [3] Mousnier, *La vénalité*, p. 205.

[4] K 105, no. 52/2 [Musée AE II 758], Henri IV to the *chambre des comptes* of Blois, 17 Mar. 1595.

[5] The *Parlement* of Dijon was suspended between Jan. and June 1659 because of its failure to register an edict establishing a *Conseil Souverain* in Bresse: A.A.E. France 1492, fo. 261.

[6] The *cour des comptes* of Montpellier was suspended for its failure to register an edict selling 170,000 *livres* of *terres rurales* in Languedoc. Bazin de Bezons, the intendant, presided the commission which replaced it: E. 1708, no. 88, 23 Sept. 1658. E 322b, fo. 41, 13 Mar. 1659.

occurrence, however. Usually the issue was settled by com-promise. The crown preferred to have the support of the sovereign courts for new legislation because this facilitated its enforce-ment and the compliance of the population as a whole. Such registration was not, however, obligatory: the crown could levy taxes as a result of decrees of the council which were rarely, if ever, presented to the courts for registration. Indeed, the decrees ordering the increase in the *taille*—the major revenue of the French crown—were never presented for registration.

Complete deadlock could be reached when the private political, social or economic interests of members of the sovereign courts were affected by the new legislation presented for registration. The *Parlement* of Aix-en-Provence felt severely threatened by the establishment of a chamber of *requêtes* in 1641 and sent remonstrances to the king's council in defiance of the orders of the crown. On 8 March 1641, the comte d'Alais, the governor, and Vautorte, the intendant, enforced its registra-tion. But the *Parlement* insisted that the new chamber did not exist because the enforced registration was 'illegal': it refused to recognize the new chamber until 25 December 1647, when the quarrel was pacified so that the *Parlement* could present a com-mon front against a new and more serious threat—the edict establishing what amounted to a rival *Parlement* serving six months of the year (the *semestre*).[1] Some of the *parlementaires* at Aix resolved to use force to oppose this measure, which was the crucial issue in the revolt of the *Parlements* of Aix and Rouen in 1649.

Joint meetings of the chambers within a sovereign court could arise at other times than the presentation of legislation for registration, and the courts might decide to intervene in royal policy on their own initiative. The provincial sovereign courts—especially the *Parlements*—wanted local power. They wanted to determine what taxes should and should not be levied. They wanted to decide how and by whom the money should be raised.[2] The complicated motives of a sovereign

---

[1] Pillorget, *Les mouvements insurrectionnels*, pp. 569–77. Kettering, op. cit.

[2] Some members of the *Parlement* of Aix participated in a revolt in 1630 which had as one of its aspects the protest against a proposed establishment of *élections*. Other members of the same court led the revolt of 1659 which had as one of its aspects opposition to an attempt by the crown to billet troops and levy taxes with-out the approval of the representatives of the province, the *procureurs du pays*.

court in opposing the crown are well illustrated by an incident in 1635 involving the *Parlement* of Toulouse. The seriousness of the revolts in Guyenne in that year prompted the *Parlement* (whose jurisdiction extended to parts of Guyenne) to suspend the levy of certain 'extraordinary' taxes and to issue remonstrances for their repeal. Bertier de Montrave, the *premier président* and a client of Richelieu since 1621,[1] justified the conduct of his court on several counts. The taxes were, he claimed, of 'peu d'utillité au Roy'; the officials who levied them, he contended, were corrupt; a decree of the *Parlement* suspending the levy of these taxes was needed, he argued, because this alone would stop the spread of rioting. At the same time, however, there was an element of self-interest in the attitude of the *Parlement*. It is probable that the *parlementaires*, their clients, and their estates had to pay some of these taxes—and the tendency of the *parlementaires* of Toulouse to shirk their fiscal responsibilities was notorious.[2] Moreover, Bertier de Montrave at the same time protested against the actions of Robert Miron and Antoine Le Camus, the intendants, who he claimed 'prennent cognoissance de toutes sortes d'affaires civiles et criminelles et mett[ent] une grande confusion dans l'ordre de la justice . . .' Doubtless this grievance was partly justified: but the real motive, one suspects, was that the intendants lent their authority to the levy of taxes by officials whom the *Parlement* regarded as corrupt. Certainly, the council of state regarded the action of the *Parlement* as potentially seditious ('capable d'esmouvoir les peuples') and ordered the *président* and four of the longest-serving *conseillers* to appear before it to justify the action of the court. Miron and Le Camus were ordered to ensure that the taxes were levied and to receive complaints against alleged corruption on the part of the financial officials. This incident merely demonstrates the willingness of the *parlementaires* to manipulate a situation that was dangerous to the government in order to block measures which harmed their own interests.[3]

---

[1] A.A.E. France 774, fo. 196, 3 Dec. 1621. Bertier was appointed *premier président* at the end of 1631.   [2] A.G. A1 69, min. 596, 4 July 1642.

[3] *Lettres . . . au Chancelier Séguier*, ed. Mousnier, i. 255,271. B.N. MS.fr. 17369, fo. 93, 1 Aug. 1635. E 1684, fo. 158 and E 124a, fo. 81, 16 June 1635. The incident is not fully examined by W. H. Beik, 'Magistrates and popular uprisings in France before the Fronde: the case of Toulouse', *Journal of Modern History*, xlv (1974), 597.

The provincial sovereign courts' concern for local power was a fundamental reason for the absence of a united opposition to the policies of Richelieu and Mazarin. Many of the provincial courts were torn by internal dissension in any case. A small group of dissatisfied *parlementaires* at Aix led the revolt of 1630 to resolve a power struggle which had arisen the previous year when the court left the provincial capital to escape from the plague. In 1659 a group of *parlementaires* at Aix used a revolt begun by the lesser nobles to attack Maynier d'Oppède, the *premier président*, whose authority had recently been increased by powers to act as intendant and governor in the absence of such officials in Provence.[1] The quarrels resulting from the creation of numerous new offices paralysed the *Parlement* of Toulouse in 1639, the *Parlements* of Aix and Rouen between 1641 and 1649, and the *cour des comptes* of Montpellier from 1646 to 1649. While these internal dissensions were dangerous to the crown, they were less dangerous than the alliance of Parisian and provincial courts in opposition to royal policy.

The political, economic, and social grievances of the members of the sovereign courts were focused, sharpened, and concentrated by the tasks of opposition to the intendants. This struggle presented the courts with an opportunity to combine the defence of their own interests (the loss of jurisdiction to the intendants) with defence of the 'constitution' (the intendants being seen as a repressive force threatening the traditional liberties of Frenchmen) and the defence of the interests of the French taxpayers. The sovereign courts demanded that any judicial role given to the intendants should be exercised within the lesser judicial courts (the *présidiaux*, *bailliages*, and *sénéchaussées*) or the lesser financial courts (the *élections*)—in which case appeals would he heard respectively by the *Parlements* or the *cours des aides*. The sovereign courts wanted the right to annul ordinances and sentences issued by the intendants. They sought to register the commissions of the intendants, thus retaining the right to modify the terms of the commissions, particularly where appeals were concerned. Finally, the courts wanted to restrict the area of initiative of the intendants: they wanted to nominate their own examining magistrates; if

[1] cf. the accounts of Pillorget, op. cit., and Kettering, op. cit.

the crown insisted on appointing commissioners, then these
should be chosen, in judicial questions from among the *conseillers* of the *Parlements*,[1] and in fiscal questions from among the
conseillers of the *cours des aides*. Historically, the conflict with the
intendants was begun by the *Parlements*; it was taken up also by
the *cours des aides* once the intendants in the *pays d'élections* were
given fiscal powers; the *chambres des comptes*, being basically
concerned with accountancy, played only a minor part in this
conflict.

The commissions of certain intendants—Hurault de l'Hôpital
in 1595, Robert Miron in 1599, Bitault de Chizé in 1618, and
Jean Lauzon in 1626—were registered in the *Parlements*. This
was extremely unusual, however. The council of state consistently rejected the claims of the *Parlements* to register the
commissions of the intendants. In 1648, Séguier recalled that
twenty-six years earlier Chancellor Brûlart de Sillery had told
him 'qu'il ne falloit point qu'il portât sa commission au
Parlement'.[2] Marillac, the Keeper of the Seals, rejected the
claim of the *Parlement* of Bordeaux in 1628 to register Servien's
commission.[3] Nevertheless, decrees issued by the *Parlements*
ordering the intendants to present their commissions were
common, both before and after the Fronde.[4] Essentially,
however, such decrees issued by the *Parlements* were a meaningless gesture: the *Parlements* could never force the intendants to
register their commissions. The intendant informed the Chancellor of the action taken by the *Parlement*. The Chancellor
might well seek the advice of the chief minister and the other

[1] The *présidents* of the *Parlements* at the Assembly of Notables in 1626–7 wanted
intendants to be chosen from the members of the *Parlements* and elected by them:
Petit, *L'Assemblée des notables*, pp. 266–7. Mousnier, *La vénalité*, p. 648. B.L.
Egerton 1666, fo. 224. Request of the *Parlement* of Aix that if an intendant of the
army was needed 'ceux dudit pays' should be chosen: U 29, fo. 62, 24 Jan. 1649.
Cf. the attitude of the council of state to commissioners appointed by the *Parlement*
of Toulouse during the Fronde: 'ce qui est de plus extraordinaire', since they had
demanded the recall of the intendants 'avec de si grandes instances'. E 1696, no.
211, 23 June 1651.

[2] Z1a 163, fo. 73, 11 July 1648.

[3] Archives Municipales de Bordeaux, Registres Secrets 30, fos. 88–9, 15 Sept.
1628. [I am grateful to Mr. N. Fessenden of Columbia University for this reference.]

[4] A by no means definitive list is: Rouen (1617); Toulouse (1625–6); Bordeaux
(1628); Paris (1629); Rouen (1631–2); Rennes (1638); Metz/Toul (1638);
Pau (1640); Bordeaux (1643), Toulouse (1643); Rennes (1647); Paris (1649,
1652); Toulouse (several times between 1649 and 1653; and in 1657); Aix (1657).

members of the government, but the outcome of their discussions was never in doubt: such decrees of the *Parlements* were always regarded by the ministers as potentially seditious. The government was always anxious to take separate action against each offending court, in order to prevent a common front of the *Parlements* against the intendants.[1] At the instigation of the Chancellor, the king's council thus issued a decree annulling the decree issued by the *Parlement*. After 1661, the *Parlements* displayed a greater sense of realism and rarely demanded that the intendants register their commissions.[2]

The *Parlements* had a second, much more realistic way of voicing their grievances against the intendants. This was by the presentation of remonstrances. Whereas the attempt to enforce the registration of the commissions of the intendants was invariably rejected out of hand by the government, remonstrances could not be annulled by a decree of the king's council except after very careful consideration. In addition, specific complaints against the intendants could form part of a general protest against the *évocations*, the transfer of cases from the sovereign courts to a rival court or the king's council, about which the *Parlements* had a legitimate grievance. The *Parlement* of Paris presented remonstrances against the intendants on 1 February 1645, 10 April 1647, and 29 August 1647.[3] The same court presented remonstrances against the *maîtres des requêtes* on 17 August 1648 and 18 August 1656.[4] On each occasion, the issue of the *évocations* was included in the discussion.

Ministers were prepared to consider seriously the issue of the *évocations*, and to send back to the *Parlements* those cases which had been transferred to the king's council without good reason.[5] On such occasions, the king's council tacitly admitted that it had interfered in the *juridiction contentieuse* of the *Parlements*.

---

[1] A.A.E. France 892, fo. 427, 29 Oct. 1653. Servien and Foucquet suggested that Mazarin order action against the *Parlement* of Toulouse 'pour arrester le cours du mal qui se vast glisser dans la Guienne et dans toutes les provinces voisines'.

[2] A. Thomas, *Une province sous Louis XIV. Situation politique et administrative de la Bourgogne de 1661 à 1715* . . . (Paris–Dijon, 1844), p. 417.

[3] X1a 8388, X1b 8854 and U 2098, 1 Feb. 1645. U 28, fos. 76, 99, 10 Apr. and 29 Aug. 1647.

[4] B.L. Harleian 4466, fo. 150, 17 Aug. 1648. X1a 8390, fo. 418, 18 Aug. 1656.

[5] e.g. E 1705, fo. 5, 11 Jan. 1657. Hamscher [*The Parlement of Paris after the Fronde*, pp. 104–5] perhaps overemphasizes the extent of the government concessions in 1656–7.

A ruling of the king's council, dated 16 June 1644, declared that cases would be sent back to the sovereign courts unless they concerned edicts which the courts had modified in the process of registration.[1] This clause was almost certainly the work of Chancellor Séguier. Its implications were clear. If the sovereign courts, and particularly the *Parlements*, registered new legislation—especially fiscal legislation—which the government thought necessary in time of war, then they would be allowed to consider cases arising from this legislation as part of their *juridiction contentieuse*. However, the *Parlements* rarely registered new legislation without amendments. As a result, cases arising from such new legislation went on appeal to the king's council. The relevance of this issue to the powers of the intendants was pointed out by Chancellor Séguier to members of the *Parlement* of Paris in February 1645. It was not the intention of the Regent, Séguier stated, that the intendants should interfere with the *juridiction contentieuse* of the courts 'ny entreprendre sur les fonctions des premiers juges'. His words were not particularly reassuring to the *Parlement*, however, for Séguier pointed to a crucial area in which this principle did not hold true. The intendants, he said, 'exécutent dans les provinces des eedictz qui n'ont point esté enregistrées au Parlement, eedictz que la nécessité publique de l'estat rend nécessaires . . . ' In this area, the *Parlements* could not be allowed to hear appeals, because they would not uphold decisions taken by the intendants in accordance with legislation which had not been registered in the *Parlements*. Séguier thus admitted that the sixteenth-century ordinances concerning the *juridiction contentieuse* of the courts were not being observed. 'Tous les gens de bien', he stated somewhat piously, hoped for a return to peace conditions which would allow the courts their rights once more.[2]

Séguier remarked also that intendants who held the office of *maître des requêtes* had the right to preside over the lesser courts— the *bailliages*, *présidiaux*, and *sénéchaussées*. Judgements issued by the lesser courts even under the presidency of the intendant nevertheless could go on appeal before the *Parlements*. This

---

[1] Mousnier, *La plume*, p. 177. A.A.E. France 849, fos. 285ᵛ–286. E 1688, fo. 111: 'si ce n'est que lesdites compagnies eussent apporté quelques modifications à l'enregistrement des édits qui auront esté levées par arrest du conseil'.

[2] X1a 8388 and X1b 8854, 1 Feb. 1645.

was an important concession to the *Parlements*, which as early as 1626–7 had lamented the 'grand préjudice' they suffered as a result of the intendants' breaking their control over the lesser courts.[1] The members of the lesser courts, however, resented the appellate jurisdiction of the *Parlements* and the superior social status of the members of the sovereign courts.[2] The lesser courts thus had reason to welcome the intendant: frequently, they registered his commission and offered him the presidency of their court in civil and criminal cases. Of course, there were cases of conflict between an intendant and a *présidial*,[3] not least because the intendant prosecuted members of the lesser courts who were guilty of corruption.[4] Generally, however, relations were harmonious. The intendants usually intervened infrequently with the work of the lesser courts, limiting their interventions to the important cases. In important cases, however, the intendants selected the members of the lesser courts who would take an active role, outlined the procedure to be adopted, and presided over the court for the final judgement.[5] Usually, these were criminal cases, particularly cases of conspiracy and rebellion.

However, the intendants did not confine their activities to presiding over the lesser courts. They also established an independent jurisdiction in both civil and criminal cases. Many cases of conspiracy and rebellion[6] were heard by the

[1] Petit, *L'assemblé des notables*, pp. 266–7. B.L. Egerton 1666, fo. 224.

[2] R. Giffard, *Essai sur les présidiaux bretons* (1904), pp. 21, 49, 52–3. P. Goubert, 'Les officiers royaux des présidiaux, bailliages et élections dans la société française au xviie siècle', *XVIIe Siècle*, xlii–xliii (1959), 54–75.

[3] *Présidial* of Soissons v. Luillier: V6 139, no. 3, 3 June 1639. *Présidial* of Angers v. Laisnier: V6 143, no. 41, 27 Sept. 1639. *Présidial* of La Rochelle v. Baltazar: E 1696, no. 316, 21 Dec. 1651. For a conflict between Auguste-Robert Pommereu, the intendant, and the *présidial* of Moulins over the control of troops: B.L. Harleian 4442, fo. 205, 20 June 1660.

[4] François Bochart prosecuted Arnault de Monier, *lieutenant civil et criminel* at Draguignan. V6 128, no. 29, 16 Apr. 1638.

[5] For one such judgement, Laubardemont with the *présidial* of Tours (29 Mar. 1636): *Lettres . . . au Chancelier Séguier*, ed. Mousnier, i. 288–9. For the process of selecting judges, cf. Hotman de Fontenay at Angers: B.L. Harleian 4490, fo. 91, 3 Dec. 1656.

[6] For example, sentence of Le Maistre de Bellejambe, intendant of Picardy, against those accused of surrendering La Capelle to the Spanish in 1636: B.N. MS.fr. 18431, fo. 81. Interrogation by Chazé, intendant of the Dauphiné, of accomplices in the Cinq-Mars conspiracy: B.N. MS.fr. 18431, fos. 340–73, 377–88, 8, 12, and 13 July 1642.

intendant not as president of a local *présidial* but as president of an *ad hoc* tribunal, usually with seven or thirteen members drawn from the lesser courts or with other law graduates.[1] Thus Laffemas presided over a tribunal of thirteen at Troyes in November 1633.[2] In October 1636, however, the members of the *bailliage* of Amiens refused to assist Le Maistre de Belle-jambe in a trial at Roye.[3] In the summer of 1656, Tallemant was obliged to seek judges at Bergerac, 'n'ayant peu trouver dans Bordeaux aucun officier ny aucun advocat qui ayt voulu estre juge avec moy, Messieurs du Parlement leur ont faict cognoistre qu'ils ne le trouveroient pas bon'.[4] The activity of the intendants in criminal cases was a frequent source of conflict with the sovereign courts. This was the reason why the intendants sent into Languedoc to suppress the Montmorency rebellion came into conflict with the sovereign courts.[5] Similarly, Étienne Foullé, the intendant sent to suppress the revolt of the *Croquants* of Périgord and Quercy in 1637, came into conflict with the *Parlement* of Toulouse.[6] The intendants became involved in civil cases too. Jean Baltazar, the intendant of Languedoc, presided over a commission of six judges in session for six or seven hours a day for a month in a case concerning the debts of the town of Cordes in Languedoc. There were thirty bundles of evidence and two hundred specific points to be dealt with. The final verdict was made on the basis of a synopsis of the evidence drawn up by a councillor in the *présidial* of Montpellier under Baltazar's direction. No legal fees were charged.[7] There was conflict between the

[1] Above, chapter VII.

[2] *Lettres . . . au Chancelier Séguier*, ed. Mousnier, i. 207.

[3] ibid., i. 315.

[4] B.L. Harleian 4489, fo. 181.

[5] Mangot de Villarceaux v. *cour des comptes* of Montpellier: V6 89, no. 48, 18 Mar. 1633. Bellejambe v. *Parlement* of Toulouse: V6 92, no. 3, 30 Sept. 1633. Charles Machault v. sovereign courts of Languedoc: E 1684, fo. 98, 1 June 1633. V6 92, no. 21, 20 Nov. 1633.

[6] V6 136, no. 23, 25 Feb. 1639.

[7] A.A.E. France 1634, fo. 166, 1 Oct. 1645. But cf. V6 235, no. 54, 30 June 1649, a plea of the inhabitants of Cordes to the *conseil privé* to the effect that Baltazar 's'est tellement emporté contre leadits habitans'. This aspect of free or cheap justice remained true throughout the *ancien régime*. Cf. the analysis of 350 judge-ments and ordinances issued by the intendant of Paris between 1780 and 1790: H. Spitteri, 'Les jugements de l'intendant de Paris en tant que commissaire du conseil', J. Phytilis, N. Kisliakoff, H. Spitteri, G. Frêche, *Questions administratives dans la France du xviii*e *siècle* (1965), p. 200.

intendants and the *Parlements* over the issue of the verification of debts at Dijon in 1634,[1] Aix in 1645,[2] and Metz[3] in the same year.

The establishment of independent jurisdiction by the intendants was a serious threat to the *Parlements*. Even worse was the fact that the intendant chose members of the lesser courts to act as his assistants.[4] The origins of the local bureaucracy employed by later intendants in the provinces are to be found in these assistants appointed at the time of Richelieu and Mazarin.[5] The assistants could serve a number of intendants over a period of years. Barbier, an *avocat* in the *présidial* of Béziers, served four successive intendants of Languedoc.[6] Jean Anoul, a *juge royal* at Uzès, was a faithful servant of the intendants from 1630 to 1661.[7] Both Anoul and his colleague Jacques Cassaignes, a member of the *présidial* of Nîmes who assisted the intendants, were Protestants—a fact which only increased the hostility of the ultra-Catholic *Parlement* of Toulouse.[8] A member of the lesser courts who served the intendants thus acquired the hatred of the members of the sovereign courts, and sometimes of his own colleagues as well.[9] The threat to the *Parlements* was limited in that the intendant could not transfer to his assistants cases of rebellion or the power to issue definitive sentences—although this authority could be granted by the king's council.[10] Nevertheless, there is a possibility that some of the intendants exceeded their powers

---

[1] V6 94, no. 56, 29 Mar. 1634.

[2] *Lettres . . . au Chancelier Séguier*, ed. Mousnier, ii. 713–15. E 1689, fo. 109, 12 July 1645. E 220a, fo. 447, 13 Feb. 1647.

[3] Guyot and Merlin, *Traité des droits*, iii. 141. *Lettres . . . au Chancelier Séguier*, ed. Mousnier, ii, 710–11, 751–2.

[4] Pierre Commeau, *lieutenant-criminel* in the *bailliage* of Dijon employed by Mangot d'Orgères: V6 141, no. 24, 29 July 1639. Lamy, *conseiller* in the *présidial* of Villefranche, employed by Méliand: E 297a, fo. 21, 4 Jan. 1657. Le Doulx, *président* in the *présidial* of Évreux, employed by Voisin de la Noiraye: E 1734, no. 1, 11 Jan. 1666.

[5] Ricommard, 'Les subdélégués des intendants', pp. 139–42, which summarizes earlier articles by the same author.

[6] *Bnutrennyaya*, ed. Lublinskaya, p. 68.

[7] ibid., p. 28. O1 1, fo. 134, n.d. A.A.E. France 1628, fo. 392^v, 1 Mar. 1637. B.L. Harleian 4442, fos. 361^v–362, 9 Sept. 1661.

[8] V6 116, no. 22, 3 Dec. 1636. E 1696, no. 282, 17 Oct. 1651. Antoine Le Camus, one of the intendants, had his doubts too: B.N. MS.fr. 17369, fo. 5^v, 7 June 1633.

[9] V6 162, no. 36, 10 Jan. 1642.

[10] E 199b, fo. 146, 15 Feb. 1645.

in this respect, and that some of the assistants of the intendants did in fact carry out such judicial prosecutions.[1]

The intendants sought to avoid confrontation with the *Parlements*, rarely visiting them unless there was reason to do so. As a *maître des requêtes*, the intendant had the right to enter a *Parlement* and was next in standing after the *présidents*. This right of entry might be refused—Claude Pellot, the intendant of the Dauphiné, was denied entry to the *Parlement* of Grenoble on 21 July 1657; Jean Baltazar, a *maître des requêtes* sent to Burgundy by the Chancellor, was denied entry to the *Parlement* of Dijon on 22 November 1658.[2] Such action was regarded as illegal, however. Claude Pellot remarked that 'le refus . . . ne s'arrestoit pas à sa personne [mais] intéressoit tout le corps de Messieurs les Maistres des Requestes . . .'[3] In such circumstances, the council of state ordered the members of the offending *Parlement* to allow the *maître des requêtes* or intendant entry into their court. The hostility of the *Parlements* was partly due to the fact that the intendant was sometimes ordered to enforce the registration of fiscal edicts, much as the king would do by the procedure of extraordinary sessions (*lit de justice*). Charles Machault, the intendant of Burgundy, was required to do this in 1637. The *Parlement* of Dijon objected to 'la publication et enregistrement par la bouche du sieur Me. des Requestes de Machault' and refused to co-operate in an extraordinary session which they thought 'préjudiciable à l'aucthorité royalle et tendante à l'anéantissement de l'honneur et des prérogatives des Parlements'. Because of this refusal, the council of state— acting on the advice of Condé, the governor—suspended the sessions of the *Parlement*.[4] A degree of conflict between the intendants and the *Parlements* was therefore inevitable during wartime because of the opposition of the *Parlements* to new fiscal edicts.[5]

---

[1] cf. the remark of Barthélémé Dupré. E 165b, fo. 229, 9 Nov. 1641.

[2] A.A.E. France 1492, fos. 196–9. E 1708, no. 158, 24 Dec. 1658.

[3] O'Reilly, *Pellot*, i. 185–6. B.L. Harleian 4489, fo. 231ᵛ.

[4] A.A.E. France 1491, fo. 47, remonstrances of the *Parlement* of Dijon to Richelieu, Apr. 1637. Machault, they claimed, had acted 'de mesme qu'eust peu[t] faire le Roy en sa personne par le ministère de son Chancelier'.

[5] In this respect, it was merely an extension of the conflict between the council and the *Parlements*. The *Parlement* of Paris admitted in 1661 that such conflict had been due chiefly to war taxes which the *Parlement* had felt obliged to resist: X1a 8392, fo. 401ᵛ, 5 Aug. 1661. For this opposition in the 1650s, cf. Hamscher, *The*

The conflict could be minimized by good personal relations between the intendant and the *premiers présidents* of the *Parlements*. The *premiers présidents* were political appointees of the crown: several former intendants attained this position,[1] although conflict between the *Parlement* and the intendant was still possible even in these auspicious circumstances.[2] The conflict could be made much worse, however, by an inappropriate choice of intendant. The intendants were rarely local men: but in instances when they were natives of the province, this was almost invariably a source of conflict with the *Parlement*.[3] The Bouchu and Brûlart families had begun feuding in Burgundy by 1637.[4] Both families had provided *présidents* in the *Parlement* of Dijon, and on 27 February 1638, after Condé had forced the resignation of Le Goux de la Berchère, Jean Bouchu became *premier président*.[5] On 17 April 1657, Nicolas Brûlart became *premier président*; Bouchu's son Claude was now intendant. Conflict between the intendant and the *premier président* began almost at once. On 20 April 1660, Brûlart demanded the recall of Bouchu: 'il est dans un mépris et j'ose dire dans un opprobre', Brûlart wrote, '. . . cela ne va que contre sa personne et non pas contre son employ . . .'[6] The conflict between the two men endured at least until 1671.[7] Bouchu's private lawsuits had to be transferred by the king's council from the

---

Parlement of Paris after the Fronde, pp. 88–98, who exaggerates when he asserts (p. 118) that the *Parlement* 'modified, if not totally dismantled, the government's programmes . . .'

[1] Faucon de Ris, and later Pellot, at Rouen; Louis Laisné at Dijon. At Aix between 1631 and 1655, two out of the three *premier présidents* (Laisné and Mesgrigny) were former intendants: Pillorget, *Les mouvements insurrectionnels*, p. 127. After *c.* 1657, D'Oppède, the *premier président*, was an acting intendant without a commission.

[2] e.g. Mesgrigny v. François Bochart at Aix in 1645: *Lettres . . . au Chancelier Séguier*, ed. Mousnier, ii. 715. Mesgrigny noted 'l'antienne amitié que j'ay avec luy'—they had been received as *maîtres des requêtes* in the same month (Jan. 1634).

[3] e.g. Boucault (1625); Gassion (1640); Coetlogon de Méjusseaume (1647–8); Bouchu (after 1656); D'Oppède in a sense in 1659.

[4] Thomas, *Une province*, p. 411.

[5] A.A.E. France 1491, fo. 49.

[6] A.A.E. France 1492, fo. 294ᵛ.

[7] Thomas, *Une province*, pp. 408–18, using the Brûlart correspondence at Dijon. The conflict was certainly made worse by the *cause célèbre* of the Auxonne witchcraft trial. The *Parlement* resented the powers granted to Bouchu on 14 Oct. 1662 to prosecute Barbe Buvée, who was accused of witchcraft, and on 3 Aug. 1663 to investigate the situation at Auxonne: R. Mandrou, *Magistrats et sorciers en France au xviiᵉ siècle. Une analyse de psychologie historique* (1968), pp. 404–23.

Parlement of Dijon because it was assumed that he would not obtain a fair hearing.[1]

In contrast to the *Parlements*, the *cours des aides* rarely demanded the registration of the commissions of the intendants.[2] The question of appeals, however, was just as contentious an issue between the *cours des aides* and the intendants as it was between the *Parlements* and the intendants. Historically, this conflict had its origin in the conflict between the *cours des aides* and the commissioners sent out for the reallocation (*régalement*) of the *taille* in 1598–9, 1623–4, and 1634–5. The *cour des aides* of Paris registered the instructions given to the commissioners in 1598 only on condition that it would hear appeals from their sentences, and there is evidence that it annulled at least three sentences issued by the commissioners.[3] In 1623, the Estates of Normandy demanded the recall of the commissioners sent out in that year, or at least a modification of their powers so that appeals from their judgements were heard by the *cour des aides* of Rouen. Initially, the government refused any modification of their powers, and appeals were to be heard by the king's council, with the *cour des aides* and *Parlement* of Rouen specifically excluded from jurisdiction.[4] Later, the council decided that the sentences of the commissioners were to be without appeal if they involved sums under 100 *livres*, but above that figure, their sentences were provisional only.[5] On 5 September 1624, however, the *cour des aides* of Rouen prohibited all persons from taking their cases before the commisssioners in Normandy.[6] Five days later, the council decided to allow the *maîtres des requêtes* at Paris to hear appeals.[7] The *maîtres des requêtes* usually upheld the decision of the commissioners, rejecting appeals,

[1] Godard, *Les pouvoirs*, pp. 476–8. E 1723, 31 Dec. 1664.

[2] But cf. Z1a 161, fos. 95–7, 3 Feb. 1643. The *cour des aides* of Paris on this occasion upheld an appeal against a sentence issued by Bragelongne, the intendant at Orléans, on the grounds that his commission had not been registered by the court.

[3] Barbiche, 'Les commissaires', pp. 79–81.

[4] *Cahiers . . . Louis XIII et Louis XIV*, ed. Robillard de Beaurepaire, ii. 67. E 77a, fo. 268, 14 Nov. 1623. E 78c, fo. 72, 22 Apr. 1624. E 79b, fo. 224, 7 Aug. 1624.

[5] E 80a, fo. 241, 26 Oct. 1624.

[6] This decree was annulled by the council: V6 1216, fo. 58ᵛ, no. 4 and V6 49, no. 1, 15 Oct. 1624.

[7] B.N. MS.fr. 16218, fos. 393ᵛ–394ʳ. The first cases were transferred on 1 Oct. 1624: V6 1216, fo. 45, no. 21 and V6 49, no. 7.

dismissing *élus* from their offices, and even ordering their imprisonment.[1] Not suprisingly, these activities were regarded by the *cour des aides of* Rouen as extremely prejudicial to its authority. The council of finance, under the presidency of Chancellor Étienne II d'Aligre and Jean V Bochart de Champigny, the *surintendant des finances*, accepted its arguments. The *cour des aides* was empowered to hear appeals against the provisional sentences of the commissioners, and to prosecute those *élus* who were accused of peculation.[2] However, the prohibition on the *cours des aides* of Rouen and Paris from hearing appeals in cases involving sums under 100 *livres* remained.[3] Thus the government did not capitulate entirely on the question, although it is clear that the most important cases were precisely those which were subject to appeal, and where the dangers of collusion within the local court were most likely to be detrimental to the course of justice. In 1634, the commissioners were empowered to pass judgement without appeal in cases involving sums of less than 100 *livres*. Above that figure, appeals were to be heard by the council, a significant improvement on the compromise ten years earlier.[4] The *cour des aides* of Paris was prohibited from interfering with the work of the commissioners, although in at least four cases, the court received appeals against their sentences.[5]

The *cour des aides* of Paris reacted unfavourably to the new fiscal powers which were conferred on the intendants in 1642–3. In a conciliatory gesture, the new Regency government presented the declaration of 16 April 1643, which confirmed these powers, to the *cour des aides* of Paris for registration. The process was likely to be a lengthy one: the court had demonstrated its hostility to the intendants consistently after 1639.[6]

---

[1] V4 63, 26 Oct., 14 Nov., 17 Dec. 1624.

[2] E 80b, fo. 115, 5 Dec. 1624.

[3] E 81b, fo. 380, 22 Mar. 1625. E 83a, fo. 245, 24 July 1625.

[4] A.G. AI 21, no. 120, 25 May 1634. Improvement, that is, from the point of view of the government not the *cour des aides*.

[5] Z1a 84–5. Appeals were upheld against sentences issued by Le Maistre de Bellejambe: 29 Dec. 1634; Estampes de Valençay: 9 Jan. 1635 and 16 Feb. 1637; Lauzon: 18 July 1640.

[6] Between 1639 and 1645, it received at least 13 appeals against sentences issued by the intendants and upheld the appeals in at least eight cases: Z1a 85–8, *passim*. In July 1643, the *premier président* protested gainst the activities of Montescot, the intendant at Paris: Z1a 161, fo. 135, 7 July 1643.

By the first days of July 1643, the *cour des aides* had not even begun to deliberate on the declaration of 16 April. A further six months' delay was confidently predicted, 'ce que les affaires du Roy ne pouvoient permettre . . .'[1] The Regency government feared that any delay in registration of this legislation would lead to difficulties in tax-collection and would increase the problem of arrears. On 11 July, the council of finance, with Séguier, Condé, De Bailleul, and D'Hémery presiding, ordered the declaration of 16 April to be carried out 'sans attendre l'enregistrement de la Cour des Aides'.[2] When it discovered the contents of the decree of 11 July, the *cour des aides* of Paris immediately decided on remonstrances, and sent a deputation to negotiate with the ministers.[3] Chancellor Séguier declared that a majority of the council had decided on the decree, and was evasive about a meeting of the deputies with the Regent. In a second interview, he positively refused to revoke the decree; the most he was prepared to concede was that it could be suspended if acceptable modifications could be agreed on by 20 July.[4] De Bailleul, the *surintendant des finances*, took a somewhat different line, but agreed that there could be no question of revoking the decree of 11 July since 'l'autorité du Roy y étoit engagée'. However, a decree of the council could order agreed modifications to be carried out, and this would amount to a tacit revocation of the decree of 11 July.[5]

In the meantime, the *cour des aides* had set to work on the declaration of 16 April 1643. It decided on substantial changes. The intendants were to be required to register their commissions. The intendants were to work with six *élus* at the parish assessments, and these were to be chosen in order of seniority. In the *élection* of Paris, all the *élus* were to work with the intendants at the parish assessments. The prosecution of *seigneurs* and others who incited the peasants to refuse payment of their taxes was not be carried out by the intendants alone, but by the intendants and the *élus* with appeal to the *cour des aides*. All cases of peculation investigated by the intendants and the *élus* were to be sent to the *cour des aides* and not the council. In

---

[1] Z1a 161, fo. 145, 17 July 1643.   [2] E 181b, fo. 146.
[3] Z1a 161, fo. 138, 14 July 1643.
[4] Z1a 161, fos. 139ᵛ, 142ᵛ, 15 and 16 July 1643.
[5] Z1a 161, fo. 147, 18 July 1643.

its remonstrances of 18 July 1643, the court summarized its objections to the declaration of 16 April: 'par cette déclaration, toutes nos maximes sont perverties, les officiers privés de l'exercice de leurs charges, et il s'agit de faire un règlement qui doit estre de durée et duquel la conséquence est infinie puisqu'il regarde tout le peuple'.[1] The final amendment to the declaration—'que le présent édit n'aura lieu que durant la guerre seulement'[2]—was intended to remove this fundamental objection, and to place a time-limit on administrative innovation. These objections were assembled in the decree of verification of 21 July 1643, which was then printed and circulated. The court appeared to have won a great victory: a victory of the permanent financial officials over the administrative changes imposed by Louis XIII and Richelieu, a victory, too, of the sovereign courts on the question of appeals from the sentences of the intendants.[3]

However, the ministers regarded the modifications of the *cour des aides* as unacceptable, and thus treated the declaration of 16 April 1643 as unregistered. The day after the decree of the *cour des aides* was issued, the council of finance ordered the intendants to use only the three *élus* specified in the declaration of 16 April.[4] On 20 February 1644, the court admitted that its decree of registration was not being observed, and complained to Chancellor Séguier about the situation.[5] The ruling issued on 16 June 1644 provided the government answer. Appeals would be allowed to the *cours des aides*, as to the *Parlements*, only in cases where the relevant legislation had been registered without amendments. The problem, of course, was that the declaration of 16 April 1643 had been modified by the *cour des aides* of Paris. A similar situation prevailed in the provinces.[6] Lauzon in Guyenne was empowered to observe the declaration of 16 April 1643 and the *cour des aides* of Bordeaux was prohibited 'd'y apporter aucun empeschement ny de cognoistre de

---

[1] Z1a 161, fo. 149ᵛ.
[2] Z1a 161, fo. 132ᵛ, 21 July 1643.
[3] Mousnier, *La plume*, p. 192.
[4] E 181c, fo. 112, 22 July 1643.
[5] Z1a 161, fo. 180ᵛ, 20 Feb. 1644.
[6] *Cour des aides* of Rouen: E 1684, fo. 416, 8 Aug. 1643. *Cour des aides* of Clermont-Ferrand: E 1684, fo. 427, 22 Aug. 1643. *Cour des aides* of Bordeaux: E 1684, fo. 429, 22 Aug. 1643.

l'exécution de ladite déclaration'.[1] The intendants of Normandy
were commanded to carry out the declaration 'sans attendre
l'enregistrement' of the *cour des aides* of Rouen.[2] Similarly,
Chaulnes, the intendant in the Auvergne, was freed from the
constraints imposed by the *cour des aides* of Clermont-Ferrand,
which did not register the declaration until 1662.[3] The *cour des
aides* of Paris later won certain concessions which were not
obtained by the provincial courts.[4]

The position of the *cour des aides* with regard to the intendants
was strengthened somewhat during the Fronde. On 11 July
1648, Jacques Le Coigneux, a *président à mortier* in the *Parlement*
of Paris, argued in a meeting with ministers that *conseillers* of the
cour des aides could perform the intendants' tasks with regard to
taxation.[5] In 1650, commissioners from the *cour des aides* of
Paris were sent out by the government to hold the assessments,
and to decide all questions of taxation subject to appeal in that
court.[6] After the Fronde, measures were taken to avoid interference by the intendants in the jurisdiction of the *cour des
aides*. In 1654, Daniel Voisin, the intendant of the Auvergne, was
given jurisdiction in cases of tax rebellion. But a significant
alteration to the decree of the council of finance in the hand of
Étienne Foullé, an *intendant des finances* and former provincial
intendant, empowered Voisin merely to commence proceedings
in such cases: the cases were then to be taken to the *cour des
aides* of Clermont-Ferrand, where they would be judged.[7]
Similarly, a decree of 18 April 1657 gave the *cour des aides* of
Paris jurisdiction over 'tous les procès et différentz d'assiettes et

---

[1] E 191b, fo. 251, 22 June 1644.
[2] E 182a, fo. 385, 8 Aug. 1643. E 184a, fo. 102. 14 Oct. 1643.
[3] E 185a, fo. 585, 9 Dec. 1643. E 352b, fo. 283, 23 Mar. 1662.
[4] Appeals against the sentences of the intendants issued in cases where *receveurs
des tailles* were found guilty of peculation were heard by the *cour des aides* of Paris
after 9 Sept. 1643: E 183a, fo. 370. Similarly, it was allowed to hear appeals against
the intendants' special taxes on privileged persons (*taxes d'office*). On 23 Feb. 1647,
the *cour des aides* of Paris obtained further concessions: E 199b, fo. 169, 16 Feb.
1645. AD IX 10, 23 Feb. 1647.
None of these concessions applied in the areas of the provincial courts. Indeed,
outside the jurisdiction of the *cour des aides* of Paris appeals from the intendants'
taxes d'office were heard by a commission comprising the intendant and seven *élus*:
Lettres . . . au Chancelier Séguier, ed. Mousnier, ii. 805–6.
[5] Z1a 163, fo. 72ᵛ, 11 July 1648.
[6] Above, chapter III.
[7] E 263b, fo. 301, 5 Feb. 1654.

collectes, émotions popullaires et rébellions arrivées au subiect de la levée des deniers de Sa Majesté.'[1]

An important struggle for influence took place between the *cour des aides* of Paris and the intendants later in 1657. In that year, Daniel Voisin, who had become intendant of Champagne, held the parish assessments for the *élection* of Troyes on his own and outside the *élection* itself. On 17 July, the *cour des aides* of Paris sent deputies to protest to the king's council that 'l'intérest public sembloit estre abandonné' by this action. They wanted a 'règlement général . . . pour faire cesser les entreprises journalliers de Messieurs les Maistres des Requêtes commissaires députés dans les provinces tant au sujet des départemens des quartiers d'hyver et autres impositions qu'aucuns d'eux ont fait de leur autorité seul et hors les sièges des élections, que pour une prétendue juridiction qu'ils s'attribuent et un pouvoir de rendre des ordonnances'. Foucquet made conciliatory remarks to the deputies but did not commit himself. Le Tellier protested to Mazarin that the assessments had to be carried out by the intendants, and thus a fundamental limitation on the powers of the intendants was ruled out from the start. Chancellor Séguier told the deputies on 23 August 1657 that the king would receive verbal, but not written, remonstrances on the grounds that 'ces sortes d'écritures étoient fort souvent composées des choses dont le public ne devoit pas estre informé et que la seule nécessité des guerres produisoit . . .' On the other hand, Séguier made a major statement of principle that was favourable to the *cour des aides*: 'l'on n'étoit en aucune intention de toucher aux affaires qui étoient de sa juridiction, au contraire de luy laisser une entière connaissance avec toute liberté'.[2] This situation applied to the provincial courts too. In 1661, the *cour des aides* of Rouen protested against *évocations* to the council and interference by the intendants. A decree of the council, issued on 28 May 1661, ordered all financial lawsuits, whether civil or criminal, and including cases of tax rebellion, to be adjudged by the *élus* with appeal to the *cour des aides*. The *évocations* to the council were revoked, and the

---

[1] E 1705, fo. 28, 18 Apr. 1657. Cf. E 320a, fo. 76, 4 Jan. 1659 (*cour des aides* of Guyenne).

[2] Z1a 164, fos. 191^v–196^v, 17 July–23 Aug. 1657. A.A.E. France 904, fo. 49, 24 July 1657.

intendants were ordered not to interfere with the court's *juridiction contentieuse*.[1] Thus, by the time of Colbert, the interference of the intendants in the work of the sovereign courts, except where they had been empowered to do so by a specific decree of the council, had become rare.

Between 1624 and 1661 the conflict between the central government and the sovereign courts had been intensified by unprecedented fiscal demands. The war had required new fiscal edicts, which the courts opposed. The war has required that the office-holders should contribute towards the national effort: the fiscal exploitation of office-holders was a major source of conflict. Finally, the war had required an extension of public law, particularly noticeable in cases of conspiracy and tax rebellion. The safety of the state required that royal commissioners, including intendants, should conduct the trials in such cases. Conversely, peace reduced the necessity for these measures and created conditions in which the government and the sovereign courts could co-operate. The sovereign courts lost the struggle to dictate policy to the crown: but they had always been divided on this issue, and most members of the courts were ultra-conservative and disinclined to force constitutional changes. During the 1660s, the office-holders broadly supported government fiscal policies, for the first time in a generation. After 1661, the ministers discouraged the intendants from assuming jurisdiction in any area in which they had not been given precise authority by the king's council.[2] The privileges of the sovereign courts were thus to a certain extent protected by the ministers themselves. The interests of the courts were better protected by the legitimate and guaranteed right to present remonstrances against any threat to their *juridiction contentieuse* than by the issuing of decrees against the intendants which could never be enforced. After 1661, the privileges of the courts may have been limited, but they were guaranteed by the king and his council.

[1] E 1714, no. 79, 28 May 1661.

[2] *Lettres . . . de Colbert*, ed. Clément, ii. pt. i 210. Colbert to Le Vayer de Boutigny, intendant of Soissons, 22 Oct. 1682.

CHAPTER XII

The Army

THE ARMY was a microcosm of the problems of French society, a combination of many of the political, economic and social ills which, in civil administration, required action by the intendants. The principle of Richelieu's *guerre couverte* after 1630 had been to delay the declaration of war for as long as possible, both to facilitate military preparations in France and to keep the field of battle away from the French frontier. By the time that war was declared, Richelieu had hoped to be in a position to attack the Habsburgs 'fortement dans leur pays', and to make the Spanish dependencies 'le champ de la bataille . . .'[1] The first years of war after 1635 did not live up to Richelieu's hopes. The offshore islands of Provence were invaded in 1635; northern and eastern France followed in 1636; the Spanish raided Languedoc in 1637. After the capture of Breisach in 1638, the French armies went on to the offensive, and the field of battle was taken to Artois, Italy, and Catalonia within two years. Nevertheless, with the collapse of royal control during the Fronde, many of the French strategic gains were reversed: in 1650 a Spanish army under Turenne invaded Champagne and Picardy and in 1652 the armies of Spain and the duke of Lorraine invaded northern France. In the 1650s it was rarely possible to station French troops abroad: most of the fighting was near the frontiers of France, and the troops had to be assembled quickly for the next campaign.

Thus there was a continual movement of troops along the route marches within France at the beginning and end of the campaigning season. The fighting usually lasted from early April until late October; the worst effects of the route marches were therefore experienced in March–April, when many of the crops were being sown, and in late September, October, and November, when they might still be being harvested. For four months in most of the war years the troops were billeted

[1] *Acta Pacis Westphalicae. Serie I. Instruktionen. Frankreich. Schweden. Kaiser*, ed. F. Dickmann *et al.* (Münster, 1962), p. 20.

within France. Provence was one of the most privileged provinces in the kingdom. Yet at the lowest point of its commitment in the war—1640—it had 4,100 troops in billets. At the highest points—1629 and 1631—it had respectively 18,000 and 16,400 troops in transit and billets. The annual average was about 9,000 or 10,000 men.[1] Thus provincial France experienced something of the devastation which was suffered by Germany during the Thirty Years War, when Swedish and Imperial armies roamed at will, supported by the system of 'contributions' which was little more than legalized pillaging of the countryside.[2] *La terreur des troupes* was a contemporary aphorism which well described the effect of the arrival of the army on the local population, for the troops wreaked havoc not only in the frontier provinces of France but along their route marches into the heartlands of the country. Nevertheless, there are strong reasons for supposing that the French peasant was relatively better off than his German counterpart when the troops arrived. In Germany, the entrepreneurial organization of the army and the absence of any *Kriegskommissariat* before 1655–60 left the military commander great independence: when it was exercised in an arbitrary manner, such independence could maximize the devastation caused by the army.[3] In contrast, in France the royal control over the military commanders was relatively greater and the powers of the intendants were strengthened as a conscious act of policy in order to mitigate the worst effects of occupation by the troops.

Why was the army such an administrative problem? Why was it so difficult to secure control over the troops? The basic reasons were financial and logistical: insufficient resources combined with administrative incompetence to produce a terrifyingly large number of men with a grievance—and weapons. The French army had to be large to defeat the Habsburg forces—the victorious Habsburg armies at Nördlingen in 1634 numbered perhaps 35,000 men.[4] As a result,

[1] Kettering, *Judicial politics.*

[2] F. Redlich, 'Contributions in the Thirty Years War', *Economic History Review*, 2nd ser., xii (1959), 247–54.

[3] F. Redlich, 'The German military enterpriser and his work force. A study in European economic and social history', *Vierteljahrschrift für sozial- und wirtschaftsgeschichte*, xlvii and xlviii (1964).

[4] C. V. Wedgewood, *The Thirty Years War* (repr. 1962), pp. 369–70.

military expenditure rose substantially; but the overall cost of the war was much greater than the amounts spent on the army might indicate, because the insufficiency of the revenues led to an increasing burden of debt as the war proceeded. As the debts of the French crown mounted, so it became progressively more difficult to pay the troops. The system of assigning payments upon specific revenues worked reasonably well in peacetime, when the revenues could be collected without difficulty. It worked very inefficiently in time of war, when there were major problems in collecting the taxes. The army was the first—and most serious—casualty of cheques signed willingly by the finance ministers which 'bounced' when attempts were made to cash them.[1] The failure of the Valtelline expedition in 1637, for example, was directly linked to the delay in levying the forced loan on the French towns.[2] Army pay, army rations, and army equipment were thus subjected to the vagaries of the French fiscal system: one or all of these might be delayed if a much needed tax was sabotaged in the provinces of France.[3] This was the chief cause of the permanent ill-discipline of the troops. That there were no major mutinies on the scale of the Spanish armies between 1589 and 1607[4] and of the Parliamentary armies in England and Wales in 1646–7[5] suggests that the French troops were eventually paid, fed, and equipped, albeit after varying delays and with glaring deficiencies and administrative abuses. Mutinies did occur, however, notably in Catalonia in 1652.[6]

Administrative corruption existed at all levels in the army. The recruiting officers rarely levied the number of recruits which they declared; they pocketed the pay set aside for the troops who had not been recruited; the real rate of desertion was

---

[1] For one such *assignation*: E 134c, fo. 201, 20 Dec. 1636. Payment of the army in Italy and the Valtelline was assigned in part on future revenues from the tax-farms.

[2] Above, chapter II.

[3] cf. E 151b, fo. 309, 28 June 1639. The payment of the army in Italy was affected by difficulties in recovering taxes on the *élus*.

[4] G. Parker, 'Mutiny and discontent in the Spanish army of Flanders, 1572–1607', *Past and Present*, lviii (1973), 38–52.

[5] J. S. Morrill, 'Mutiny and discontent in English provincial armies, 1645–1647', *Past and Present*, lvi (1972), 49–74.

[6] A.A.E. France, 885 fo. 73, 5 Oct. 1652. For local mutinies on a small scale: Pillorget, *Les mouvements insurrectionnels*, pp. 505, 848–9.

never declared for the same reason.[1] Thus the army was permanently below the target strength set by the ministers. When the troops operated beyond the French frontiers the generals proved insatiable in their demands for 'contributions';[2] even within France, the generals and the provincial governors seem to have altered the route marches and billets at whim which had devastating effects upon the countryside.[3] The company captains not infrequently took their billets where they pleased instead of in the areas assigned to them; in any case, the commanders issued their billets in a discriminatory manner, treating savagely those parishes which were foolish enough not to purchase exemption.[4] When billeted, the troops tended to force more payment from the local population than that to which they were legally entitled. The supply system of the army was left largely to private enterprise. The munitions contractors were assured of huge profits, since they ran few risks and there was little chance of their corrupt practices being revealed. The ill-fed and ill-clothed troops vented their resentment on the local population. Not surprisingly, the peasants and townsmen reacted in kind. The army was not only a threat to political order in the provinces; it was also a political threat to the government. As Le Tellier commented on 16 October 1650, 'l'armée estoit une véritable république et . . . les lieutenants généraux considéroient leurs brigades comme autant de cantons.'[5] Military commands were of great importance to the *Frondeur* nobles. The comte de Marsin served as lieutenant-general in Catalonia in 1649 before joining the Fronde; after Condé's release from prison in January 1651, he returned to his command; on 28 September 1651, he once again deserted to join Condé, taking with him two brigadier-generals and four regiments.[6] The attempt of the war ministers to achieve the reform of this mass of problems is witnessed by a

[1] André, *Michel Le Tellier et l'organisation*, pp. 256, 260.

[2] cf. Cazet de Vautorte's criticisms of D'Espenan's demands for 'contributions' between the rivers Rhine and Necker: A.G. A1 98, no. 158, 16 Aug. 1645.

[3] Picardy, Champagne and the Soissonnais: E 1684, fo. 418, 8 Aug. 1643. Languedoc: A.A.E. France 1637, fo. 25ᵛ, 15 Jan. 1657. Provence: Pillorget, op. cit., pp. 753–5, 761–7.

[4] A.A.E. France 1637, fo. 18, 8 Jan. 1657.

[5] André, op. cit., p. 117, no. 2.

[6] cf. Mazarin's fears in May 1651 of Marsin's possible defection: *Lettres du Cardinal Mazarin à la Reine, à la princesse Palatine . . .*, ed. J. Ravenel (1836), p. 71.

remarkable series of ordinances;[1] but to be successful, reforms had to be enforced. The transfer of increasing authority to the intendants was seen by the war ministers—by Sublet des Noyers between 1636 and 1643, and by Le Tellier after that date—as the essential means of implementing reform in the army. The intendant was to act as a 'contrôleur ... exact' of the actions of the general; he was to provide for the needs of the army 'avec ordre et police' to prevent the troops from taking what they wanted 'par nécessité ... avec violence'; finally, he was to act as a judicial authority, 'pour y restablir la justice autant que la violence de la guerre pourra souffrir la douceur de la paix ...'[2]

There were two main types of intendant with responsibilities in military matters. The provincial intendants came to assume complete control over the army between early November and late March, the period of the winter quarter; they also had a considerable importance during the rest of the year in ensuring the movement of supplies and troop reinforcements. In addition each army—at least from the 1620s and probably from the reign of Henri IV—had its own intendant. These intendants of the army were often, but not necessarily, entitled *intendants de justice, police, et finances*, but an additional clause in their title specified the army, the military commander, and often the area of operations. Both army intendants and provincial intendants received a commission from the king which delimited their powers; the powers of both ceased when the commission was revoked. The most obvious differences between the two types of official was in the duration and terminology of the commissions.

There was a fundamental difference in the periods of service of the two types of intendant. The provincial intendants served on average for less than three years, but it was usual for them to serve for longer than a year. By contrast, the intendants of the army usually operated during the campaigning season only, thus for seven or eight months in a year; their commissions were renewed annually. Some of the army intendants were specialists, who rarely—if ever—served in the provinces.

---

[1] These form the basis of André's study. André, op. cit., *passim*.
[2] Livet, *L'intendance d'Alsace*, p. 100, no. 4.

Claude Gobelin, for example, was appointed as intendant in the army in Germany in 1634,[1] and in the army of Gaston d'Orléans on 10 August 1636.[2] A brief period as provincial intendant followed—at Orléans in 1637.[3] Then he returned once more to the armies: the army of La Meilleraye on 12 April 1639[4] and 18 April 1640,[5] and that of Roussillon on 26 January 1642.[6] Finally, he seems to have spent a short time as intendant of the army in Brittany in 1643.[7] In other cases, there was a more equal balance between the two types of service. The balance between service in the army and service in the provinces probably varied according to personal inclination, experience, and the elements of chance. It seems certain, however, that the majority of army intendants—men such as Philibert de Baussan, De Girolles, Goury, Jacques Brachet, De la Court, Osny, Croisilles, Brethe de Clermont and Arnaud d'Andilly—never served in the provinces at all. The number of appointments of army intendants increased at about the time that the provincial intendants became permanent administrators within France: the development of both was closely related to the entry of France into the Thirty Years War. One hundred and eleven commissions for service in the army survive from the years between 1627 and 1657, of which 77 were issued in the twelve years between 1637 and 1649 [Fig. 7].[8] Although the intendants of the army provided an element of administrative continuity within France during the Fronde,[9] they went into decline thereafter: only 16 commissions have survived from the years between 1650 and 1657; there were only two intendants of the army in active service in 1659—Jacques Brachet in Italy and Claude Talon in the army of Flanders.[10] The strategic gains of the Spanish during the Fronde—Barcelona, Casale, Dunkirk, and Gravelines—had pushed the French armies onto the defensive. This strategic change, combined with the effects of Le Tellier's

---

[1] ibid., pp. 40–3. [2] *Lettres . . . au Chancelier Séguier*, ed. Mousnier, ii. 1047.
[3] ibid., i. 401–2. E 137c, fo. 362, 17 June 1637. E 138b, fo. 233, 23 July 1637.
[4] A.G. A1 56, no. 82. [5] A.G. A1 62, no. 121.
[6] A.G. A1 71, no. 49. [7] E 185b, fo. 309, 19 Dec. 1643.
[8] A.G. A1 14–151, *passim* (volumes of *expéditions*). D. C. Baxter, *Servants of the sword. French intendants of the army, 1630–1670* (Urbana, Illinois, 1976), pp. 209–27, lists many of these. Baxter's list differs from that of Bonney, 'Intendants', pp. 286–94, in that it includes some provincial intendants.
[9] Above, chapter III.
[10] Baxter, *Servants of the sword*, pp. 138–9.

reforms, left control of the army increasingly in the hands of the provincial intendants, while in the 'new provinces', such as Roussillon, Artois, and Alsace, the army intendants came gradually to assume the characteristics of provincial intendants.[1]

The majority of the commissions of the army intendants which have survived were issued in a similar form. The commission of Jacques Dyel, sieur de Miroménil, as *intendant de justice, police, et finances en* [*l'*]*armée*, which was conferred on 14 April 1635, was typical. He was ordered to keep in close

FIG. 7. Annual appointments of intendants of the army, 1628–1657.

contact with the maréchaux de Châtillon and de Brézé, the commanders of the army, and to 'leur y donner votre bon advis'. His major task was to maintain the rule of law in the army, to ensure that the ordinances were observed and that all crimes and *délits* were punished. He was empowered to investigate 'toutes entreprises, practiques et menées' against the king's service, and to prosecute offenders, issuing a definitive sentence as president of an *ad hoc* judicial tribunal. The ordinances issued by the intendant of the army were declared to have the same authority as decrees issued by the sovereign courts. Miroménil was given wide-ranging investigative functions, with important financial powers, including a specific rôle in accountancy.[2] Dozens of commissions for the army intendants were based on this formula, with relatively minor stylistic variations. On many occasions, the clerks in the ministry of war did not feel that it was necessary to specify the details of powers that were already well known.[3] Nevertheless, while the powers that were conferred

---

[1] Below, chapter XVII. [2] A.G. A1 26, no. 43.
[3] A.G. A1 32, no. 178, 12 Sept. 1636. A1 62, no. 121, 18 Apr. 1640. A1 67, nos. 136, 158, 25 Apr., 21 June 1641. A1 71, no. 49, 26 Jan. 1642. A1 114, fos. 26ᵛ, 28ᵛ, 15 Jan. 1649. A1 139, fo. 217, 21 May 1653.

on Miroménil were undoubtedly the most common, it would be a mistake to regard them as the only type of commission. Other, less extensive, powers were accorded. Commissions as an *intendant des finances* serving in an army,[1] or in a frontier town;[2] as an *intendant des vivres* serving in an army;[3] as an *intendant des finances et vivres*,[4] or as an *intendant des nos finances, fortifications, et vivres*[5]—all these types of commission were relatively common. Behind these variations in title lies the essential fact that some army intendants were specialists in questions of munitions, logistics, and finance and lacked the fundamental judicial powers possessed by virtually all the provincial intendants at the time of Richelieu and Mazarin.[6]

The intendants of the army were required to give advice to the military commanders in the council of war. Far too little is known about the councils of war to ascertain with certainty the influence of the army intendants.[7] There were twelve members of Condé's council of war for the Roussillon front, which was held at Narbonne on 8 November 1639. Charles Machault and Dupré, the intendants, signed the *résultat* of the council, together with the commanders—Condé, Schomberg, Arpajon, Argencour, and others—and Rebé, the archbishop of Narbonne and president of the Estates of Languedoc.[8] It seems evident from this document that the principles upon which the king's council acted were applied to the council of war held by the military commanders: decisions were taken by a majority vote, but were thereafter binding on all who had been present at the meeting. It is likely that the military commanders had the dominant say when it came to strategy,[9] but since almost all military decisions had consequences in the realm of finance and logistics, a sensible commander would have at least to take into consideration the views of the intendant. Just as with the governors and the provincial intendants, however, there were

---

[1] A.G. AI 125, no. 192, 25 Sept. 1651. AI 141, no. 180, 6 Sept. 1653.

[2] Livet, *L'intendance d'Alsace*, p. 92. B.N. MS.fr. 4171, fo. 65, 23 Jan. 1645.

[3] A.G. AI 56, no. 47, 12 Feb. 1639. AI 67, no. 100, 14 Mar. 1641. AI 67, no. 144, 12 May 1641.   [4] A.G. AI 71, no. 51, 27 Jan. 1642.

[5] A.G. AI 79/2, no. 24, 7 June 1643.   [6] cf. Livet, op. cit., p. 85, n. 3.

[7] André, *Michel Le Tellier et l'organisation*, p. 592, notes that the ruling of 4 May 1646 envisaged fortnightly meetings with the officers and the intendants both making reports.   [8] A.A.E. France 1631, fo. 227.

[9] Even so, Arnaud d'Andilly advised Feuquières and the Cardinal de la Valette not to relieve Mannheim in 1635: Baxter, *Servants of the sword*, p. 65.

disputes between the generals and the army intendants. Arnauld d'Andilly in Germany in 1634 co-operated well with the maréchal de Brézé, Richelieu's son-in-law, but less well with the maréchal de la Force;[1] at Philipsbourg in 1645, Vautorte was in conflict with D'Espenan, the local commander, and his relations with Turenne were threatened;[2] at Breisach in the same year, Girolles was in conflict with D'Erlach.[3] There were conflicts between Vignier, the intendant of Lorraine, and La Ferté Seneterre in 1645,[4] and between Beaubourg, Vignier's successor, and La Ferté Seneterre in 1649; between Ennemond Servien, the intendant in the army of Italy, and Prince Thomas of Savoy two years later; while in 1652, D'Elbeuf demanded the recall of Luillier d'Orgeval from the intendancy of the army on the frontier of Picardy calling him a person without brains.[5]

None of this denies that certain generals picked their own intendants, with whom they developed a close relationship—the elder Condé preferred Machault; his son co-operated well with Molé de Champlâtreaux; Gaston d'Orléans preferred Choisy, who later became his chancellor; Harcourt wanted Baltazar to serve with him in Catalonia in 1645.[6] Yet there were clearly areas of potential conflict between the general and the army intendant, notably in financial questions. The general could usually order expenses, but all his ordinances had to be countersigned by the intendant. The intendant could always report to the war minister—if need be, in code—on the unsatisfactory conduct of the commander.[7] D'Erlach, the governor of Breisach, the key fortress in Alsace, was a firm believer in the independence of action of the military: 'il est bien difficile', he wrote to Mazarin, 'que les différends qui sont à cause des contributions puissent être réglées à la cour, parce qu'il est nécessaire d'avoir la connaissance du pays . . .'[8] The claim of the commander to a monopoly of local knowledge was less convincing when Girolles, the intendant, informed Le

---

[1] ibid., p. 82. [2] A.G. A1 98, no. 158, 16 Aug. 1645.

[3] Livet, op. cit., pp. 93–4. A.G. A1 98, no. 182, 22 Aug. 1645.

[4] *Lettres . . . au Chancelier Séguier*, ed. Mousnier, ii. 722, 756–7.

[5] Baxter, *Servants of the sword*, pp. 133–4, 136–7.

[6] At least, Baltazar alleged that Harcourt wanted him: A.A.E. France 1634, fo. 133, 14 June 1645.

[7] As did Cazet de Vautorte on 16 Aug. 1645, when reporting the unsatisfactory conduct of D'Espenan over the 'contributions' between the Rhine and Necker rivers. [8] Livet, op. cit., p. 108.

Tellier in a coded letter that he could detail 'des revenus que l'on tire sur les moulins de cette ville et des villages entiers que l'on donne à des particuliers, ce qui ne se faict point à l'inceu de M. d'Erlac . . .'[1] The criticisms of the intendants were often especially sharp because they made covering loans to the troops when the government failed to fulfil its obligations. Pierre Imbert, the intendant in Roussillon in the 1640s, sank all his silver and cash into loans for the troops. 'Ces emprunts . . . ne sont pas des fables ny des chymeres . . .' he lamented to Le Tellier.[2] Le Tellier needed little convincing in such matters; as intendant in the army of Italy he had seen for himself the abuses committed by the generals.[3]

The army intendants thus tried to ensure a rough justice in the 'contributions' exacted by the troops abroad and in the frontier areas. Acting on the instructions of the war minister, they tried to ensure that the 'contributions' were levied in the correct area. On 1 December 1645, Vignier reported that he had 'empesché les officiers de ladite garnison de Metz de lever des contributions dans la Lorraine suivant et conformément aux ordres du Roy que j'en avais receus . . .'[4] If the intendant failed in this fundamental task, then the success of his intendancy was in doubt: as Cazet de Vautorte remarked to Le Tellier in the same year, 'si [les] troupes . . . occupent le Palatinat, et consomment les contributions, il n'y aura nulle utilité pour le Roy dans mon seiour ny aucune occupation pour moy . . .'[5] Not infrequently, the 'contributions' did not meet the real expenses of the army: this was the case in Lorraine in 1643[6] and in Artois in 1648.[7] In this situation, it was of great importance that the army intendant had a small reserve fund—Arnaud d'Andilly had 10,000 *livres* a month in Germany in 1634—over which he had absolute control, without reference to the generals. This reserve fund allowed at least a week's grace, perhaps longer, depending on the size of the army and the availa-

[1] Livet., p. 93. A.G. A1 98, no. 182, 22 Aug. 1645.

[2] A.G. A1 106, no. 41, 15 June 1648.

[3] André, *Michel Le Tellier et l'organisation*, p. 260. 'C'est une chose que j'ay aprise tandis que j'ay esté intendant en Piedmont.' Le Tellier to Lauzon, 30 Nov. 1647.

[4] *Lettres . . . au Chancelier Séguier*, ed. Mousnier, ii. 773.

[5] A.G. A1 98, no. 158, 16 Aug. 1645.

[6] *Lettres . . . au Chancelier Séguier*, ed. Mousnier, i. 571–3.

[7] Baxter, *Servants of the sword*, p. 109.

bility of supplies. As Bazin de Bezons, the intendant at Barcelona, remarked in December 1649, 'j'espère que nous empescherons qu'il n'arrive aucun désordre aux quartiers, dans l'espérance d'avoir de l'argent dans ce mois'.[1] When Barcelona fell on 13 October 1652, the garrison had been without food for six days: a mere 92,150 *livres* could have kept it going for a month longer.[2] The emergency fund of the intendant was usually enough to keep the latent discontent of the troops from breaking out into open mutiny; beyond this the intendant tried to secure covering loans on his own credit. In the last resort, if funds did not arrive from Paris to supplement the 'contributions', the intendant was powerless.

The army intendants also had an important role with regard to recruiting for the army. Barthélémé Hervart, an *intendant des finances*, and Philibert Baussan, the intendant of Alsace, signed a contract on 17 May 1650 with Klüge, a German colonel who was to raise a regiment of 250 infantry.[3] In the 1630s, specialized commissioners such as Colbert de Saint-Pouange in the Touraine and the Orléanais[4] and Pierre Imbert in the Dauphiné, the Lyonnais, and Provence[5] had been sent out on recruiting missions. Imbert rose to the position of army intendant in the 1640s, largely as a result of this experience, yet still carried out recruiting missions as at Narbonne in December 1647.[6] Essentially the intendants concluded contracts with recruiting officers. These officers had to be paid—the usual rate was 24 *livres* per soldier for each company of 20 men (18 *livres* to the officer for recruiting the soldier; 6 *livres* for the recruit's subsistence).[7] Thereafter, the intendant had to supervise the military reviews to ensure that the number of recruits for which the officer had contracted were in fact levied.

The military reviews gave the intendants the essential knowledge of the size of the army upon which they could base their calculations for uniforms and grain supplies. In some instances, the intendants purchased the necessary grain for the army: in 1629-30, the French army intervening in Italy

[1] A.G. A1 116, no. 475, 15 Dec. 1649.
[2] A.G. A1 137/2, nos. 353, 451, 16 Aug., 16 Oct. 1652.
[3] D. C. Baxter, 'French intendants of the army, 1630-1670', (University of Minnesota Ph.D., 1971), p. 171.   [4] A.G. A1 51, min. 392, 9 Apr. 1639.
[5] A.G. A1 48, nos. 425, 426, 1 Nov. 1638.
[6] Baxter, 'French intendants of the army', p. 172.   [7] ibid., pp. 172-3.

was supplied by Maupeou d'Ableiges and Dugué, the intendants, from Burgundy, the Lyonnais, and the surrounding provinces;[1] in 1648, Jacques Brachet purchased grain supplies in Languedoc for use by the army in Lombardy.[2] Much of the provisioning, however, was left to private enterprise, although the intendants came to exercise an increasing control over the activities of the entrepreneurs. They certainly negotiated the contracts—Bazin de Bezons, the intendant in the army of Catalonia, signed a contract with Pierre Augé of Narbonne on 19 July 1654 for the transport of 1,650 wagon-loads of oats to the army at a fixed price. The instructions issued to the intendants emphasized the need to prevent fraud in such contracts.[3] Large contracts were more convenient, but were regarded with justified suspicion by the army intendants. The entrepreneurs were willing to accept the lucrative task of supplying the large land armies; but the small contracts concerning specific garrisons were more onerous and less profitable. If the munitions contractors failed in their obligations, the intendant might allow the troops to take what they needed from the stores; if he did not allow this, unauthorized pillaging would take place in any case. In 1650, Clausel and the other Languedoc contractors refused to supply double rations to the garrisons of Perpignan and Collioure. Imbert, the intendant, allowed the troops to break into the stores; the contractors demanded 20,000 *livres* compensation for the ensuing damage.[4] Breteuil, the intendant of Roussillon, commented: 'voilà le désordre que produit de faire un mesme traité des places de Roussillon avec la fourniture de l'armée, qui n'[a] point [été] fait auparavant l'année 1649.' And he advised Le Tellier to 'remettre les choses dans leur premier estat et de faire un traité séparé et distinct . . .'[5]

The loss of Barcelona in 1652 was due in part to the collapse of the supply system. Michel d'Aligre de Saint-Lié, the intendant, remarked on the 'horrible peine' he suffered to 'entretenir une armée sans quoy que ce soit'. Later in July 1652, he commented that the army had become 'si insolente par la

---

[1] A.G. AI 13, no. 149, 21 Nov. 1629. AI 12, no. 131, 3 Feb. 1630.
[2] A.A.E. France 861, fo. 474 and A.A.E. France 1634, fo. 350, 9 Nov. 1648.
[3] Baxter, 'French intendants of the army', pp. 197, 199.
[4] A.G. AI 119, no. 328, 28 June 1650.
[5] A.G. AI 119, no. 449, 28 Sept. 1650.

nécessité' that he was under constant threat of assassination.[1]
The failure of the supply system in Catalonia in 1652 resulted
from the financial embarrassment of the French government,
whose attentions were distracted by the revolt of Condé. In such
circumstances, the intendant was powerless to provide for the
needs of the army. In more favourable circumstances, the army
intendants acted as efficient, objective administrators, balancing
the strategic aims of the generals against the financial interests
of the contractors and the material needs of the troops.[2] They
came to dominate the existing administrative structure in the
army—the *commissaires des guerres*, who had bought their offices[3]
—just as the provincial intendants came to dominate the *élus* in
financial administration.

The provincial intendants were frequently given control of the
troops—by their general commissions, or by a second, more
specialized commission as intendant of the army. Certain
intendants—Le Maistre de Bellejambe at Amiens (1636),[4]
Étienne III d' Aligre and Dreux d'Aubray in Provence
(1635, 1637),[5] Mesgrigny in Champagne (1638),[6] and Cazet de
Vautorte in Provence (1640)[7]—were specifically called intendants of the army as well as intendants of the provinces in
question. In other cases, an additional commission as intendant
of the army was sent to the intendant who was already serving
in the province: the commissions received by Choisy on 28
April 1635,[8] by Verthamon on 15 November 1636,[9] by Le
Maistre de Bellejambe on 16 August 1638,[10] by Bretel de
Grémonville on 23 November 1640,[11] and by Jeannin de
Castille on 28 April 1643[12] are examples of this tendency.
Very few intendants were denied powers to deal with the troops.

[1] A.G. A1 137/2, nos. 258, 281, 9 and 15 July 1652.

[2] cf. Vautorte's comment, quoted by Livet, *L'intendance d'Alsace*, p. 100.

[3] A.G. A1 137/2, no. 367, 22 Aug. 1652. 'M. Douarel commissaire des guerres a
travaillé toute l'année . . . près M. Breteuil' [the intendant].

[4] Boyer de Sainte-Suzanne, *Intendants d'Amiens*, pp. 572–5. A.D. Somme 1B 21,
fo. 172v, 12 Mar. 1636.

[5] A.G. A1 26, no. 199, 30 Aug. 1635. A1 41, fo. 288, 12 Oct. 1637 [?]. Were they
sent to the province, however? Cf. Pillorget, *Les mouvements insurrectionnels*, p. 133,
n. 459.

[6] Arbois de Jubainville, *Intendants de l'Aube*, pp. 206–8.

[7] A.G. A1 62, no. 139, 12 May 1640.   [8] A.G. A1 26, no. 49.

[9] B.N. Joly de Fleury 2508, fo. 160.   [10] A.D. Somme 1B 21, fo. 294.

[11] A.G. A1 62, no. 236.   [12] A.G. A1 79/2, no. 7.

Foullé in Guyenne in 1637 and Moric and Chazé in the Dauphiné in 1640 had no such powers, but then Verthamon[1] and Lauzon[2] had remained in the respective provinces exclusively for this purpose. When they left, their successors took over their military responsibilities as well. When the provincial intendant received a more specialized commission as intendant of the army, the powers conferred were usually similar to those granted to Dyel de Miroménil on 14 April 1635.

During the secretaryship of state for war of Sublet des Noyers (16 February 1636–13 April 1643), the provincial intendants were given increasingly important tasks with regard to the troops. Before 1641, the governors still controlled the route marches of the troops, it is true. But the intendants had a major role in maintaining the discipline of the troops. On 1 May 1636, Louis XIII ordered Séguier to 'n'obmettre aucune diligence possible pour arrester le cours des désordres des gens de guerre' and it seems certain that the Chancellor issued instructions to the intendants on this subject.[3] When the troops deserted, the intendants carried out the necessary prosecutions. Miron and Dupré in Languedoc were empowered on 19 January 1638 to prosecute Gastigues, the captain of a company of dragoons destined for the army of Italy, who had stayed eight months during the winter quarter instead of the statutory four, and whose regiment had been composed of twelve or fifteen 'mauvais soldats' when it eventually arrived. Gastigues and Vestric, a captain in the regiment of Cauvisson, were noted as much for 'mespris pour leur charge que d'avidité à en profficter . . .'[4] When accusations were levelled against the troops quartered in Picardy, to the effect that they participated in the organized smuggling in salt, it was the intendant— Bellejambe—who was ordered to investigate and prosecute offenders.[5] In Burgundy in 1642 Mangot d'Orgères and his *subdélégués* were ordered to issue definitive sentences against those soldiers found guilty of disorderly conduct.[6] The provin-

---

[1] Verthamon's continued presence is made clear in Foullé's commission: B.N. Joly de Fleury 2508, fo. 162, 25 Aug. 1637.

[2] A.G. A1 58, min. 177, 15 Mar. 1640. A1 61, min. 319, 4 Dec. 1640.

[3] *Lettres . . . de Richelieu*, ed. Avenel, v. 455. B.N. MS.fr. 3843, fo. 36. Séguier's instructions are mentioned in *Lettres . . . au Chancelier Séguier*, ed. Mousnier, i. 290.

[4] A.G. A1 43, min. 148, 19 Jan. 1638.

[5] A.G. A1 48, no. 285, 19 Aug. 1638.   [6] E 175, fo. 467, 18 Dec. 1642.

cial intendants also assisted in the recruiting of troops. Miron and Dupré in Languedoc, Lauzon in the Dauphiné, and François Bochart in the Lyonnais were all ordered to assist Imbert in his various recruiting missions between 1639 and 1641.[1] By 1639–40, the provincial intendants were receiving regular instructions from Sublet des Noyers to investigate abuses in the *congés* granted to the troops, to prevent unruly behaviour of the troops, and to prosecute officers who disbanded their troops without royal permission.[2]

The billeting of troops was a major cause of social discontent,[3] and the repression of such disorder became a function of the intendants. In 1637 Choisy was investigating riots at Neufchâtel;[4] Laubardemont was similarly involved in the provinces of Maine and the Perche,[5] as were Fremin at Usarche in the Limousin[6] and Verthamon at Savignac in Guyenne.[7] The following year, Foullé at Saint-Geniez in the Rouergue,[8] Moric at Vire,[9] and Villemontée at Monterol in Poitou[10] were all involved in similar prosecutions. There were other cases in 1639 and 1641—involving Villemontée at Montmorillon in Poitou[11] and François Bochart and Imbert at Saligny in the Lyonnais.[12] In some of these cases, the intendant carried out the investigations, and sentences were issued by the local *présidial* or by the *maîtres des requêtes* at Paris. In the most serious cases—as at Abiat in the Périgord in 1640—the intendant was ordered to carry out the prosecutions 'souverainement et en dernier ressort'. In this incident, three or four hundred rioters, armed with muskets, had killed the sieur de Vancour, the captain of a company of cavalry that had been seeking billets in the town. Several soldiers had been wounded; the horses of the company had been stolen and their baggage pillaged; 460 *pistolles*—payment for the transportation costs of

---

[1] A.G. A1 50/2, min. 82, 7 Feb. 1639. A1 55, min. 378, 29 Dec. 1639. A1 63, no. 111, 15 Jan. 1641.

[2] A.G. A1 51, min. 384, 7 Apr. 1639. A1 58, min. 79, 7 Mar. 1640. A1 62, fo. 211, 21 Sept. 1640.

[3] Bercé, *Histoire des croquants*, i. 57–66, ii. 858. Pillorget, *Les mouvements insurrectionnels*, pp. 505–7.

[4] V6 120, no. 27, 22 May 1637.

[5] V6 121, no. 6, 3 July 1637.

[6] cf. V6 145, no. 20, Feb. 1640.

[7] V6 123, no. 29, 1 Sept. 1637.

[8] V6 128, no. 26, 13 Apr. 1638.

[9] V6 130, no. 57, 4 June 1638.

[10] V6 130, no. 35, 28 June 1638.

[11] V6 141, no. 15, 2 Aug. 1639.

[12] V6 158, no. 41, 2 Aug. 1641.

the company to Lyon—had been stolen.[1] The lodging of troops
was always likely to cause rioting because the army was collecting what amounted to an additional tax paid by the local
inhabitants; but the period when the troops were enrolled
(a virtual tax paid in men, since recruits were often forced to
join up) was equally dangerous. Villemontée prosecuted the
leaders of a riot against army recruiting at Saint-Hilaire-du-
Bois in Poitou in 1640.[2]

Since the riots caused by the presence of troops were a
consequence of financial stringency—the troops were underpaid and thus they took what they wanted from the civilian
population—it was inevitable that the provincial intendants
would be given the task of supervising the payment of the army
during the winter quarter. In 1637–8, 8·5 million *livres* were
spent on the *subsistances* of the troops;[3] the amount was raised
to 9·6 million in 1638–9[4] and reached 13·6 million in 1640–1
and 1641–2.[5] The increasing cost of the winter quarter and its
adverse effect on the returns of other taxes such as the *taille*[6]
made imperative the close control of such expenditure by the
intendants. A ruling of 24 July 1638 gave the intendant the
assessments of the *subsistances* for six armies seeking winter
quarter within France. The provincial intendants were to have
'la direction principale des impositions et levées, distribution
d'icelles et police des troupes sous les généraux d'armées
avec la mesme authorité qu'ils ont estans dans les corps
d'icelles'. The ruling committed the government to appoint
'des commissaires en chacune des provinces', one of whom
would be the provincial intendant, the other a financial office-
holder such as a *maître des comptes*, or more frequently, a
trésorier de France.[7]

These commissioners—and the task was carried out in 19
généralités excluding 'new provinces' such as Alsace—were
ordered to levy the *subsistances* either in money or in kind. They
were to use the rolls of the *taille* as the basis for their calculations, but if the town or village had suffered devastation since
the tax rolls had been drawn up, they could moderate the

---

[1] V6 152, no. 37, 4 Dec. 1640.   [2] V6 151, no. 52, 16 Oct. 1640.
[3] cf. E 146a, fo. 349, 18 Sept. 1638.   [4] AD + 252, 24 July 1638.
[5] E 156a, fo. 57, 5 July 1640. E 163a, fo. 116, 1 Aug. 1641.
[6] A.A.E. France 830, fo. 266, 21 July 1638. E 150a, fo. 428, 20 Apr. 1639.
[7] AD + 252.

amounts as necessary and increase the contributions of other towns and villages accordingly. The levy was to be carried out in six payments—instead of five payments, as was the case with the *taille*—and the commissioners were empowered to nominate *receveurs des tailles* to organize the collection of the payments in money and kind. The commissioners were to inspect the stock-piles of grain and forage and for these and other tasks they had the power to appoint *subdélégués*. Essentially, the troops were to be billeted on the towns and the number of troops to be borne by a particular town was decided by the crown: such decisions could not be altered by the commanding officers, although they could make proposals for change. The *subsistances* were to be given to the troops only after the most exacting review of numbers by the intendant and the *commissaire des guerres*. The intendants, together with the commanding officers and the *prévôts*, were to remain in the province during the winter quarter to maintain the discipline of the troops, to deal with the complaints of the civilian population and to take any necessary action on 'manquemens, abus, désordres, excez et violences arrivez au sujet des gens de guerre'. The council of finance insisted on the levy being carried out by the *voies ordinaires* rather than *à main armée*.[1] But this decision inevitably caused delays in payment. The king need not, therefore, have been 'fort estonné d'apprendre le peu d'advance qu'il y a en la levée de la subsistance de Dauphiné . . .'[2] Moreover, as an instrument of fiscal policy, the levy of the *subsistances* left much to be desired. It was not redistributive, since the wealthy were exempt from payment by poll-tax, and contributed only if the levy took place by sales tax, which was unusual.[3] Thus the tax hit hardest those who were already crippled by the increase in the *taille*, and it is not surprising that the returns of the other direct taxes were adversely affected.

Nevertheless, the ruling of 24 July 1638 was part of an overall reform of considerable significance, being drawn up as it was at about the same time as the financial ruling of 19 July.[4] In both measures the influence of Claude de Bullion, the *surintendant*

---

[1] Foisil, *Nu-Pieds*, pp. 109–10. E 151a, fos. 152, 208, 4 and 8 June 1639.

[2] A.G. A1 50, min. 210, 23 Jan. 1639.

[3] E 146b, fo. 66, 7 Oct. 1638.

[4] Ranum, *Richelieu and the councillors of Louis XIII*, pp. 197–8. A.A.E. France 830, fo. 261.

des finances, can be perceived—Bullion sponsored these rulings in a desperate attempt to avoid dismissal in the aftermath of the Valtelline débâcle and the subsequent charges of corruption and inefficiency. As early as 1635 Bullion had favoured the billeting of the troops on the towns during the winter quarter, since the burden of the *taille* was borne chiefly by the countryside. He had envisaged resident intendants in the towns, especially 'dans celles où les généralités sont établies', whose task it would be to maintain the discipline among the troops.[1] None of this suggests that Sublet des Noyers, the war minister, did not have a major say in the formulation of the ruling of 24 July 1638: Bullion and Sublet seem to have co-operated much better than Bullion and Servien had done.[2] The experiment of 1638–9 was followed up. On 26 August 1639, the same task was assigned to the intendants in twelve *généralités* during the winter quarter of 1639–40.[3] The levy of the *subsistances* was carried out each year until the Fronde—whether the troops sought their winter quarter in France, or in Germany, Italy, and Catalonia—and thus required continuity of provincial intendants where there had been none previously. The financial management of the troops, closely allied as it was with the levy of the *taille*, was thus the essential link in the evolution of the powers of the intendants between 1634 and 1642. After 22 August 1642, the intendants levied the *subsistances* jointly with the *taille*.

The establishment of the provincial intendants as the paymasters of the army for four months of every year was only one of the achievements of Bullion and Sublet des Noyers. The role of the intendants in negotiating contracts with financiers for advance payments of the *subsistances* was clearly defined in 1639–40.[4] So too were the activities of the provincial intendants in negotiating advance payments for recruiting activities.[5] When the intendants negotiated such contracts they were usually ratified by the ministers or by the council of finance. The intendants also supervised the activities of the munitions

---

[1] A.A.E. France 819, fos. 98^v–99^r, mémoire du Sr. Bullion sur les quartiers d'hiver'.

[2] For example, Ranum, op. cit., p. 130, no. 3 (co-operation in Apr. 1638).

[3] cf. E 152b, fo. 365, 17 Sept. 1639.

[4] Foisil, *Nu-Pieds*, pp. 80–1. E 150a, fo. 80, 6 Apr. 1639. E 154c, fos. 246, 248, 8 Mar. 1640. E 155a, fo. 13, 5 Apr. 1640.

[5] E 154c, fo. 443, 13 Mar. 1640.

contractors—Dupré in Languedoc in 1640 investigated allegations that poor quality rations had been issued to the troops.[1] When there were allegations that the contractors had made troop payments in debased coin, again it was the intendant who was ordered to investigate.[2] After Bullion's death in December 1640, Bouthillier, his colleague and successor, continued to cooperate with Sublet des Noyers, this time in fundamental reform of the route marches and the *étapes*—the 'staples' where troops were bivouaced *en route* and where munitions were assembled. By April 1641, a general *étape*—a list of stopping points—had been established in the Dauphiné and the Lyonnais; it was set up in Languedoc during that month;[3] Schomberg, the governor and Lauzon, the intendant, were ordered to advise on the reform of the route marches in Guyenne in June 1641.[4] On 16 February 1643, during a military offensive on the Boulonnais— Artois front, the intendants in eight *généralités* were ordered to organize the *étapes* for reinforcements travelling north.[5] This task was an extension of their control of the *subsistances*: the costs of the *étapes*, indeed, were deducted from this tax.

The appointment of Michel Le Tellier as secretary of state for war on 13 April 1643 could scarcely have led to a dramatic strengthening of the military powers of the provincial intendants —these powers had already been fully developed by Sublet des Noyers in close association with Bullion and Bouthillier. Some changes did occur between 1643 and 1648, but these were essentially in the nature of codification and extension of existing administrative practice. A decree of the council of state issued on 15 July 1643 extended the reform of the *étapes* by setting up 'un fondz asseuré en chacune desdites provinces' and appointing the intendant and a *trésorier de France* as the commissioners for this task.[6] The same function was carried out the following year by the provincial intendants in twelve *généralités*.[7] On 10 November 1643 instructions were issued to the intendants of fourteen *généralités*, confirming their powers over the troops. They were to have the 'soin général de leur paye-

[1] A.G. A1 57, min. 376, 13 Feb. 1640.   [2] A.G. A1 69, min. 46, 9 Apr. 1642.
[3] E 1684, fo. 291 and E 160c, fo. 726, 30 Apr. 1641.
[4] E 162a, fo. 259, 8 June 1641.   [5] A.G. A1 73, min. 296, 16 Feb. 1643.
[6] E 181b, fo. 200 (collated copy countersigned by Le Tellier).
[7] A.G. A1 81, min. 653, 30 Mar. 1644.

ment'. Payments were to be made only after the reviews had been held, and the intendants were to ensure that only those present and effective were paid. The troops were to receive their money as soon as possible 'afin qu'ils n'ayent aucun prétexte d'exiger leur subsistance du peuple'. The intendants were to supervise the bread rations of the infantry and the hay and straw rations of the cavalry. They were to negotiate the contracts with the entrepreneurs at the best possible price, ensuring that there was no collusion between the troops and the entrepreneurs to defraud the government. Copies of the reviews, the payments made to each company, and fortnightly reports on the state of the troops were to be sent by the intendants to Le Tellier, as was also news of any abuses and disorders.[1]

The instructions of 10 November 1643 were not particularly original, though they illustrate very clearly Le Tellier's ability to summarize all the preceding legislation, his grasp of administrative detail—the result of his experience as intendant of the army in Italy—and his desire for new information. He firmly believed that the elimination of abuses in the army could best be achieved during the winter quarter—and thus by the provincial intendants—rather than during the campaign when it was essential to retain the good will of the troop commanders.[2] Thus the intendants' supervision of recruiting activities was intensified. On 9 January 1644 the intendants were ordered to punish the recruiting officers who had not provided the number of troops for which they had contracted;[3] on 14 March the intendants in twelve *généralités* were instructed to reward captains who had provided the minimum number of 40 recruits.[4] Le Tellier used the provincial intendants as the co-ordinators of the war effort. They were to advise him on matters needing decisions by the central government,[5] but in all matters where local decisions could safely be taken, the intendants had supreme authority.

The 'constitutional' Fronde in the summer of 1648 under-

---

[1] A.G. A1 77, fo. 135, 10 Nov. 1643. A1 76, min. 327, 30 Nov. 1643. A1 79, fo. 143, 14 Nov. 1643.

[2] André, op. cit., p. 249. Le Tellier to Villemontée, 23 June 1644.

[3] A.G. A1 80, min. 57.   [4] A.G. A1 81, min. 558.

[5] A.G. A1 77, fo. 136ᵛ, 10 Nov. 1643: 'vous m'en donniez advis pour y employer mon autorité'.

mined the reforms of Sublet des Noyers and Le Tellier over the previous twelve years. There was, of course, no systematic attack on the army reforms because the ministers and their critics alike were in agreement that the army should be closely controlled and that the social cost of letting the army loose in France, unpaid and ill-fed, was too high. Nevertheless, the members of the *Chambre Saint-Louis* undermined the reforms indirectly; firstly, by the attack on the system of war finance as it had operated under Richelieu and Mazarin. Most of the problems of the army arose from the fact that it was never completely paid; the abolition of the loans, the reduction of the levels of expenditure and income could only intensify these problems. On 5 July, the ministers pointed out the serious consequences in the next few months: Condé's army would be left without bread rations, a Spanish invasion of Picardy comparable to that of 1636 might occur, and Sweden might be prompted to make a separate peace with the Emperor.[1] The army reforms were undermined in a second way: the recall of the intendants from all but six provinces on 18 July removed the local administrators of the army, the essential instruments by which reform could be achieved. It is true that the Lyonnais, Picardy, Champagne, Provence, Burgundy, and Languedoc were considered 'frontier' provinces, and the intendants were retained in these areas primarily because of their military responsibilities.[2] Yet the distinction between the 'frontier provinces', in which the intendants were retained, and the rest of France was arbitrary: the Dauphiné, which had played a major part in the recruiting and movement of troops for the Italian front in the 1640s, was not allowed to retain an intendant. There, and elsewhere, the financial control of the troops was left to the *trésoriers de France*.

The revolt of Condé in the autumn of 1651 led the government to reaffirm the military responsibilities of the intendants. A ruling to this effect was issued on 4 November 1651. The negotiations with the munitions contractors, the supervision of

---

[1] Talon, *Mémoires*, ed. Michaud and Poujoulat, p. 246. U 28, fo. 185, 6 July 1648. The reasoning of the government was perfectly clear. The Dutch had already made a separate peace, which might act as an example to Sweden. Condé's army had only twelve days' bread rations [A.G. A1 110, no. 97, 2 July 1648] while the Spanish had already made a preliminary incursion into the Soissonnais [A.G. A1 106, no. 64, 20 June 1648].   [2] cf. E 1696, fo. 90, 23 Aug. 1649.

the reviews and billets, were conferred on the intendants in the six provinces reserved from the declaration of 18 July 1648 and on the *maîtres des requêtes* 'faisans leurs visites' elsewhere.[1] The *Parlement* of Paris responded to the threat by proscribing all intendancies and extraordinary commissions and prohibiting the *maîtres des requêtes* 'et autres personnes' from carrying them out.[2] The decree of the *Parlement* was unenforced, however, and unenforceable: during the winter quarter of 1652–3 there were once more 'commissaires départys ès généralitez du royaume pour l'accélération du payement et pour la discipline des gens de guerre'. The ruling of 12 February 1653 empowered these intendants to pay the troops and organize the bread rations; on 26 April, their powers were broadened to allow an investigation into abuses in the levy of the *taille*.[3]

The rulings of 4 November 1651 and 12 February 1653 provided the framework within which intendants of the army such as Colbert de Terron in Foix, Bigorre, and the frontier of Guyenne in 1653–4 might operate.[4] This was true also of the provincial intendants, who were re-established—it was to prove, on a permanent basis—in 1653–4. Certain intendants— Gargan at Châlons, Guillaume de Bordeaux at Amiens in 1653, Pietre also at Amiens in 1656—lacked effective judicial powers over the troops: they had to hand over offenders to the local judiciary, which meant delay and in all probability a light sentence for the culprits.[5] It is clear, however, that most of the intendants had sufficient authority. Tallemant at Bordeaux and Louis Machault at Montauban were criticized by Servien and Foucquet, the *surintendants des finances*, in 1654 because they had been given all the powers that were necessary, but had abne- gated their responsibilities. Servien and Foucquet considered that the administration of the army by the intendants was 'le principal sujet de leur envoy'.[6]

The major concern of the intendants during the winter quarter was to levy the *subsistances* for the troops. During the winter of 1655–6, the maréchal de Fabert and Daniel Voisin,

---

[1] André, op. cit., pp. 667–82.   [2] U 30, fo. 61, 8 Feb. 1652.
[3] André, op. cit., p. 689. E 255b, fo. 721, 26 Apr. 1653.
[4] A.G. A1 141, no. 183, 18 Nov. 1653.
[5] A.G. A1 138, no. 268 and A1 140, fo. 189, 30 Aug. 1653. A1 147, no. 283, 8 Aug. 1656.
[6] A.A.E. France 893/2, fo. 150, 8 July 1654. A.G. A1 158, no. 344, 14 July 1654.

the intendant of Champagne, billeted the troops on the rural parishes as well as on the towns. The system proved successful— by the ruling of 25 October 1656, it was applied to Champagne, the Soissonnais, the Île de France, the Orléanais, Normandy, and doubtless the rest of France, too.[1] The principle behind the scheme was the joint control of the *taille* and the *subsistances* by the intendant. The intendant carried out the levy of the *subsistances* during the winter and compensated the village in question for any damage caused by the troops at the next assessments of the *taille*. In essentials, the system was the same as that in the years between 1642 and 1648, with the troops billeted on the rural parishes instead of the towns. The provincial intendants also carried out the usual more specialized tasks concerning the army. On 3 March 1656, the intendants of thirteen *généralités* were ordered to prepare the *étapes* for the troops, and to take any money that was needed from the *receveurs généraux*.[2] They were also ordered to investigate abuses in the levy of the *étapes*.[3] When the disorders of the troops in a particular province assumed serious proportions, the intendants were ordered to carry out the necessary prosecutions. This was the case in the *généralités* of Bordeaux and Montauban in 1656,[4] in Berry in 1659,[5] and in the Île-de-France, the Soissonnais, Berry, Champagne, Picardy, the Bourbonnais, and the Auvergne in 1660.[6] Servien and Foucquet seem to have co-operated well with Le Tellier in re-organizing the military functions of the intendants after the Fronde: military tasks were assigned to the provincial intendants by ministerial dispatches from Le Tellier, and by decrees of the council of finance and commissions which were countersigned by Servien, Foucquet, and the *intendants des finances*.

Yet the return of the provincial intendants as the administrators of the army was not achieved without some resistance. The nobles in Normandy demanded in 1658 that the governor should supervise the billeting of troops 'sans y souffrir le mesle

---

[1] André, op. cit., pp. 394–5, 397. Baxter, 'French intendants of the army', p. 187 (who argues for a limited application of the ruling). A.G. A1 146, nos. 315, 316, 321, 322, 8–22 Nov. 1656. A.A.E. France 904, fo. 49, 24 July 1657. For the ruling itself: M 638 [Musée AE II 2581].   [2] A.G. A1 146, no. 271.

[3] E 263b, fo. 297, 5 Feb. 1654. E 306b, fo. 288, 24 Oct. 1657.

[4] E 287a, fo. 314, 8 Mar. 1656.

[5] E 322a, fo. 478, 13 Mar. 1659.   [6] E 331a, fo. 205, 8 Jan. 1660.

d'aucun intendant'.[1] The duc de Longueville followed up
their demand by asking for the recall of Morant, the intendant,
whom he may have arrested.[2] Mazarin was faced with a
dilemma: the governors could not be trusted to carry out the
billets fairly; their power could not be increased dramatically
at a time when the lesser nobles in part of France were in
rebellion and when the loyalty of certain of the provincial
governors was suspect. However, it was impolitic not to concede
something of the demand. Mazarin declared that he thought it
wrong to 'donne[r] aux intendants toute l'autorité et [de
l'oster] entièrement aux gouverneurs . . .'[3] Morant was
retained as intendant in the *généralité* of Rouen, but he—and
probably the other provincial intendants as well—received a
ministerial dispatch which empowered the governors and the
lieutenants-general to carry out the billeting of the troops
'selon qu'ilz en seront informez par las intendantz'. The
result was therefore a compromise. The commissions of the
winter quarter were to be delivered to the intendants, who
would be given the other 'soins concerning le payement, la
police et le restablissement de[s] troupes'.[4] Mazarin's art of
government was to allow concessions that were of form rather
than substance. The intendant remained the master of the
fiscal process, he alone had the essential knowledge of the
'proportion de ce que chaque lieu contribuable aux tailles
porte de l'imposition du quartier d'hyver': the governor was
thus dependent on his advice. It would be a mistake to under-
estimate the local power of a governor such as the duc de
Longueville: but the intendants' control of the army had gone
too far by 1658 to be reversed at a stroke.

The military functions of the intendants continued even
after the Peace of the Pyrenees, because substantial numbers of
men remained under arms. Bazin de Bezons, the intendant of
Languedoc, told the provincial Estates that 'la paix ne peut

[1] A. Legrelle, 'Les assemblées de la noblesse en Normandie (1658–1659)',
Société de l'histoire de Normandie. Mélanges, 4th ser. (1898), p. 327.
[2] Logié, *La Fronde en Normandie*, iii. 145. Cf. protests of the *maîtres des requêtes* on
behalf of Morant: B.L. Harleian 4442, fos. 113, 115, 14 and 15 Dec. 1658. Longueville had been hostile to the reintroduction of intendants in 1653: Esmonin,
Études, p. 35.
[3] *Lettres . . . de Mazarin*, ed. Chéruel and d'Avenel, ix. 115–16.
[4] A.G. A1 151, no. 368, 8 Dec. 1658.

être entretenue que par la subsistance des troupes'.[1] In 1661
France remained on a war footing. In 1666 Louvois carried out
military reviews on such a scale that Colbert claimed that the
généralités of Paris, Amiens, Châlons, and Soissons had suffered
more than in the last six years of the war against Spain.[2]
From being the military arm of Richelieu's foreign policy aimed
at the 'collective security' of Europe against the Habsburg
menace, the army became the instrument of Louis XIV's
struggle with the Netherlands, the Emperor, and William III.
The purpose to which the army was put made no difference to
the authority of the provincial intendants; nor did the billeting
of the troops on the towns (as in the years 1661–6) or the
countryside (as in the years 1666–75).[3] The long wars of Louis
XIV merely confirmed that under Richelieu and Mazarin the
provincial intendants had been made the administrators of the
army during the winter quarter, and the co-ordinators of the
war effort during the rest of the year. Without the intendants,
the army reforms of Le Tellier and Louvois could not have been
implemented.

[1] *Histoire générale de Languedoc*, ed. Roschach, xiv. 781.
[2] Quoted by A. Navereau, *Le logement et les ustensiles des gens de guerre de 1439 à
1789* (Poitiers, 1924), pp. 71–2. L. André, *Louis XIV et l'Europe* (1950), p. 103.
[3] André, *Michel Le Tellier et l'organisation*, p. 404. Baxter, 'French intendants of
the army', pp. 189–90.

CHAPTER XIII

The Provincial Governors and the Nobles

BETWEEN THE conspiracy of Biron in 1602 and that of Rohan in 1674 there were approximately twenty conspiracies and revolts of the nobles in France. There is little doubt that the nobles were the most consistent opponents of political change under Richelieu and Mazarin. There was a close connection in issues and personalities between these aristocratic conspiracies. The ducs de Bouillon were involved in conspiracy or revolt in 1605–6, 1641–2, and 1649–50. Gaston d'Orléans was similarly involved in conspiracy or revolt in 1629–30, 1631–4, 1642, and 1652. So too were the Bourbon princes of Condé in 1610, 1614–16, and 1651–9. Certain of the lesser nobles were similarly involved in more than one conspiracy. Louis d'Astarac, marquis de Fontrailles, was a *Frondeur* noble in 1649–50; yet he had also taken the Cinq-Mars treaty to Spain for Philip IV's signature seven years earlier.[1] It is commonly assumed that the nobles lacked clearly defined political objectives and that their actions were merely 'feudal', reactionary, and illegal. It is also assumed that the nobles were motivated exclusively by self-interest and thus could not form a credible alternative government.[2]

The first assumption, that the nobles lacked clearly defined political objectives, is not borne out by the evidence. The nobles opposed the foreign policy of the crown. In the case of Condé's revolt in 1615–16, it was the policy of the Spanish marriages which was opposed.[3] After 1630, the great political issue for the nobles was the war against Spain. Almost all the noble conspiracies after this date were concerned with bringing about a peace settlement between France and Spain. This was the clear link between the revolts of Gaston d'Orléans in the

---

[1] Dethan, *Gaston d'Orléans*, p. 268. *Lettres du Cardinal Mazarin . . .*, ed. Ravenel, p. 26. Talon, *Mémoires*, ed. Michaud and Poujoulat, pp. 389–90.

[2] For example, A. Thierry, 'Essai sur l'histoire de la formation et des progrès du Tiers État', *Recueil des monuments inédits sur l'histoire de France* (3 vols. 1850), i. ccviii. Kossmann, *La Fronde*, pp. 239–41. Moote, *The revolt of the judges*, p. 223.

[3] Hayden, *France and the Estates-General of 1614*, p. 169.

1630s, the Soissons conspiracy of 1641, the Cinq-Mars conspiracy of 1642, and the three aristocratic revolts during the Fronde. The nobles also objected to the *ministériat*. They would have purged the government of unpopular ministers—chiefly, of course, Richelieu and Mazarin, but also their clients—to ensure the reversal of their policies. They would also have attempted to impose a new form of conciliar government, which would have allowed the nobles political power. Finally, they would have reversed the political changes which had occurred under Richelieu and Mazarin, and mitigated the domestic consequences of the war. They wanted to abolish the intendants, dismantle the system of war finance, and reduce government expenditure and taxation. Ultimately, they wanted a dramatic reduction in the price of offices.[1] The crucial demands of the nobles—particularly during the Fronde—were the removal of Mazarin and the signing of peace with Spain. Without peace, the nobles assumed that there could be no end to administrative change. Without Mazarin's removal from office, it was assumed that there could be no peace with Spain.[2] The demands of the nobles were thus in a sense perfectly realistic: personalities and policies were inseparable. Intrigue and conspiracy were not 'de pures questions de personnes.' They had fundamental implications for the future policies of government.

Many of the nobles who participated in conspiracies against the government were *Malcontents*: but they were not motivated

---

[1] For the ideas of lesser nobles in the Angoumois in 1649 and the *bailliage* of Troyes in 1651: Mousnier, Labatut, Durand, *Problèmes de stratification sociale*. For the ideas of Condé's supporters: 'Concordat de l'union fait entre le Parlement et la ville de Bordeaux avec Nosseigneurs les princes contre les Ennemis de l'Estat' A.D. Gironde 4J 127, 3 Jan. 1652. [Excerpts from this document in *Histoire de l'Aquitaine. Documents*, ed, Higounet, p. 219.] For the ideas of supporters of Gaston and Condé: 'Les articles de la dernière délibération de Messieurs les princes avec les bourgeois de la ville de Paris faite en Parlement et en la maison de ville les 6 et 8 juillet 1652', B.N. Lb 37 2756 in 4to.

[2] Without this, the nobles maintained that 'toutes ces bonnes choses' contained in their manifestos could not be achieved. e.g. 'Contrat du Mariage du Parlement avec la ville de Paris' (1649), *Choix de Mazarinades*, ed. Moreau, i. 39–50. *Oeuvres de Retz*, ed. Feillet *et al.* v. 438–50. The document may have been written by Retz, one of the *Frondeur* nobles, in January 1649, but neither the authorship nor the dating is certain. It was clearly the source for 'l'union ou l'association des princes sur l'injuste détention des princes de Condé, Conty et duc de Longueville' of 1650 [*Choix de Mazarinades*, ed. Moreau, ii. 63–8] and the manifestos of Jan. 1652 and July 1652.

exclusively by self-interest. The government publicized the *demandes particulières* of the nobles in a deliberate attempt to discredit them; but, for reasons of political prudence, the government kept secret their *demandes générales*.[1] Essentially, the nobles championed issues because they wanted to gain political power. Their best hopes lay in the periods of royal minority (1610–14, 1643–51). The Regency could become a political issue at such a time. So too could the age of majority of the king, the education of the king, and the size and composition of the governing council. In the last resort, however, everything depended on the determination of the nobility. Were they prepared to seize the person of the Regent, coerce her, perhaps even depose her? Were they prepared to seize the boy king and indoctrinate him with their values? The events of the Fronde suggest that very few nobles were prepared to press their resistance to change this far.

Against this background of noble conspiracy and revolt, the provincial governorships assumed immense political significance. The provincial governor, especially if he resided in his province, controlled military affairs. He had a major, indeed often a decisive say in local appointments, whether to offices, the governorship of fortresses, or to municipal administration. This military power and patronage gave the governors overwhelming authority in their provinces before the establishment of the intendants, subject only to the competing influence of the sovereign courts.[2] Marc-Antoine Millotet, the *avocat-général* at the *Parlement* of Dijon, confirmed the fact that the Bourbon princes of Condé exercised absolute control of patronage as the governors of Burgundy between 1631 and 1651.[3] Such political power carried great advantages to the government when the governor was a loyal supporter. However, even a loyal supporter over many years could turn

---

[1] e.g. Molé's release of the *demandes particulières* of the *Frondeur* nobles in 1649: Talon, *Mémoires*, ed. Michaud and Poujoulat, p. 350. *Oeuvres de Retz*, ed. Feillet *et al.*, ii. 454. *Choix de Mazarinades*, ed. Moreau, i. 431–6. Cf. also Mazarin's comment to Le Tellier on 11 Sept. 1652: *Lettres du Cardinal Mazarin*, ed. Chéruel, v. 228.

[2] G. Zeller, 'L'administration monarchique avant les intendants. Parlements et gouverneurs', *Revue Historique*, cxcvii (1947), 180–215. J. R. Major, 'The crown and the aristocracy in Renaissance France', *American Historical Review*, lxix (1964), 631–45. [3] Thomas, *Une province*, p. 25.

against the government on an issue of pride, principle, or self-interest. In such circumstances, the government was threatened with the complete loss of control of the province: the duc de Longueville had little difficulty in raising Normandy in January 1649.[1]

The events of the Chalais conspiracy and the Day of Dupes taught Richelieu to distrust certain noble families, whom he suspected of excessive independence, criticism of himself or the king, and opposition to royal policy. He believed that the stability of the governorships was of itself a bad thing—'l'assurance de sa charge lui donne beaucoup de licence'—and that the abolition of the *droit de survivance* and the creation of triennial governorships was preferable.[2] Richelieu put his ideas into practice. A remarkable number of governors were removed from their posts, disgraced, exiled, or imprisoned during Richelieu's ministry: Vendôme (Brittany, 1626); Bellegarde (Burgundy, 1631); Guise (Provence, 1631); Marie de Médicis, the Queen Mother (Anjou, 1631); Gaston d'Orléans (the Orléanais, 1631); Montmorency (Languedoc, 1632); D'Elbeuf (Picardy, 1633); Châteauneuf (the Touraine, 1633); Vitry (Provence, 1637); D'Épernon (Guyenne, 1638); the comte de Soissons (the Dauphiné, 1641); and Gaston d'Orléans (the Auvergne, 1642).[3] Even this list may not be exhaustive. Very few provinces—Normandy,[4] Poitou,[5] the Lyonnais,[6] the Dauphiné,[7] and the Boulonnais[8] being the most important—were unaffected by change.

---

[1] Logié, *La Fronde en Normandie*, ii. 47–162.

[2] *Lettres . . . de Richelieu*, ed. Avenel, ii. 161. Richelieu, *Testament politique*, ed. André, p. 258. Richelieu was not alone in wanting triennial governorships. The lesser nobles in the *bailliage* of Troyes in 1651 wanted this as a means of opening up the governorships to themselves: Mousnier, Labatut, Durand, *Problèmes de stratification sociale*, p. 142.

[3] With two exceptions, the dates cited are those when a new governor was appointed. Sometimes this occurred within a few days or weeks of the dismissal. On other occasions, the position was left vacant for several years. These events are established from, among other sources: B.N. MS.fr. 18147, 18148, 21542, 22626. Cf. the list of governors in 1621: B.N. n.a.f. 7228, fos. 175–203.

[4] In Normandy, Longueville retained control from 1619 until his death in 1663, and obtained the *survivance* for his heir.

[5] In Poitou, the La Rochefoucauld dynasty retained control after 1622.

[6] In the Lyonnais, the Neufville de Villeroy dynasty retained control from 1612 until the eighteenth century.

[7] The Dauphiné lost its governor in 1641 when the comte de Soissons was killed leading a rebel army at the battle of La Marfée. As an outstanding military

Most of these dismissals were *causes célèbres* at the time. They resulted in a severe threat to the fortunes of some of the leading noble families during the reigns of Henri III, Henri IV, and the minority of Louis XIII. The house of Lorraine, the clientage network behind the Catholic League of which Richelieu was so wary,[1] was decimiated. Henri de Lorraine, duc de Mayenne, the governor of Guyenne, was killed while serving in the king's army at the siege of Montauban, and with him died the Mayenne line. The line of Mercœur was continued only indirectly, by César de Vendôme, the bastard of Henri IV: but Vendôme was arrested in 1626 after the Chalais conspiracy, and the governorship of Brittany was taken from him. Charles de Lorraine, duc de Guise, who had held the governorship of Provence since 17 October 1594, was forced into exile on 6 August 1631 because he had sided with the Queen Mother against Richelieu during the Day of Dupes, and because he had failed to suppress the revolt of the *Cascaveoux* the previous year. Charles de Lorraine, duc d'Elbeuf, who received the governorship of Picardy after the death of Lesdiguières in 1626, was forced into exile because he joined the revolt of Gaston d'Orléans in 1631. His governorship was transferred on a temporary basis to Claude de Lorraine, duc de Chevreuse: but Chevreuse was a political nonentity who had resigned his governorship of the Auvergne earlier in the same year.[2] In 1633 the governorship of Picardy was transferred to Henri d'Albert, duc de Chaulnes. The only member of the house of Lorraine to retain a governorship at the end of Richelieu's ministry was D'Elbeuf's son, Henri de Lorraine, comte d'Harcourt, who was appointed to the Touraine in 1637. Another great noble family, the Montmorency, was destroyed during Richelieu's ministry: the dynasty had held the governorship of Languedoc since 23 March 1525; but the rebellion

---

commander, however, the comte de Soissons had been an absentee governor. Real control was exercised after 3 Feb. 1597 by the Bonne de Lesdiguières dynasty, first as lieutenants-general and then, after 3 July 1642, as governors.

[8] The D'Aumont dynasty retained control in the Boulonnais after 1622.

[1] Richelieu, *Testament politique*, ed. André, pp. 233–4. For the basic unity of the house of Lorraine, cf. F. des Robert, *Charles IV et Mazarin, 1643–1661* (Paris–Nancy, 1899), p. 739: dukes of Guise, Chevreuse, D'Elbeuf, and Harcourt, 'tous ceux du beau sang de Lorraine qui de présent sont à Paris'.

[2] Richelieu, *Testament politique*, ed. André, p. 121. E 65b, fo. 382, 30 Dec. 1620. E 107b, fo. 178, 15 Oct. 1631.

of Henri, duc de Montmorency, in 1632 led to his execution and the confiscation of his lands, some of which were awarded to his rivals such as Condé.[1] Other families were threatened to a greater or lesser extent. Roger de Saint-Lary, duc de Bellegarde, was Henri IV's trusted appointee as lieutenant-general in Burgundy on 3 August 1602, after the arrest and execution of Biron for treason. On 20 May 1610, shortly after the assassination of Henri IV, Marie de Médicis demonstrated her confidence in him by appointing him as governor, a position he held until 1631, when he was dismissed as one of Richelieu's 'gouverneurs ingrats et infidèles': he supported the rebellion of Gaston d'Orléans.[2] The family of Nogaret de la Valette barely escaped destruction in the last years of Richelieu's ministry. Richelieu had every reason to fear Jean-Louis de Nogaret, duc d'Épernon, the favourite of Henri III and former governor of Provence, who had held the governorship of Guyenne since 28 August 1622. Épernon had been a major force in the rebellions of the Queen Mother in 1619 and 1620, which Richelieu had helped to settle; his son Bernard had been implicated in the conspiracies of Gaston d'Orléans and the comte de Soissons in 1636. In the autumn of 1638, Richelieu was given a unique opportunity to strike against the family. On 7 September 1638, the French forces besieging Fuenterrabía, a Spanish frontier fortress near San Sebastien, were defeated. A scapegoat had to be found, and Bernard de Nogaret was chosen by Richelieu: on 19 October, he fled to England, thus damning himself in Richelieu's eyes. Thirteen days previously, the governorship of Guyenne had been transferred to Condé. On 8 December 1638, the octogenarian paterfamilias wrote what was for him a beseeching letter to Richelieu, asking for clemency because of 'le malheur de ma maison'. On 24 May 1639 Bernard was declared guilty of treason (*lèse-majesté*) and his property confiscated to the crown; on 13 June 1641,

---

[1] D. Roche, 'Aperçus sur la fortune et les revenus des princes de Condé à l'aube du xviiie siècle', *Revue d'Histoire Moderne et Contemporaine*, xiv (1967), 231, n. 5. For other confiscations awarded to Condé: D. Gallet-Guerne, 'Une conséquence des troubles féodaux sous Louis XIII: les confiscations royales de 1629 à 1641', *Bibliothèque de l'École des Chartes*, cxxvii (1969), 337–8. E 107b, fos. 323, 336, 18 Nov. 1631.

[2] Richelieu, *Testament politique*, ed. André, p. 120. A.A.E. France 1490, fo. 254, Bellegarde to Louis XIII, May 1631, asking for a royal pardon.

during the Soissons conspiracy, his father was exiled from his lands in Guyenne to the fortress of Loches.[1] The disgrace of the family continued until Richelieu's death, the governorship being transferred from Condé to Schomberg in 1641.

Richelieu dismissed many governors, but he did not undertake a generalized attack on the upper nobility as such, or attempt to undermine the importance of the governorships. If certain nobles were threatened during his ministry, others— Richelieu (a peer of the realm after 1631), his family, and clients—were the beneficiaries of political change. Richelieu appointed himself governor of Brittany on 18 February 1631. It was evident that as chief minister Richelieu would be an absentee governor. The real power in the province was enjoyed after 18 March 1632 by the lieutenant-general, who was none other than Charles de la Porte, sieur—and later duc—de La Meilleraye, Richelieu's cousin. When the Queen Mother fled to the Spanish Netherlands in 1631, the governorship of Anjou was conferred first on Antoine Coiffier de Ruzé, marquis d'Effiat, and then on the Cardinal de la Valette (14 October 1631)—both were trusted supporters of Richelieu. Finally, the position was held by Urbain de Maillé, marquis de Brézé, Richelieu's son-in-law (4 October 1636). A number of other governorships were filled by Richelieu's clients, who owed their careers chiefly[2] to the principal minister of Louis XIII: Pons de Lausières, maréchal de Thémines (Brittany, 23 June 1626); Nicolas de l'Hôpital, marquis de Vitry (Provence, 7 August 1631); Charles de Schomberg (Languedoc, 22 October 1632); and Jean du Caylar, maréchal de Toiras (the Auvergne, 30 October 1632).

Finally, there were certain magnates, whose loyalty to the French king had been questionable before 1624, but whom Richelieu was able to trust. Chief among these was Henri de Bourbon, prince de Condé. Condé had spent a considerable

---

[1] L. Mouton, *Le duc et le roi. D'Épernon, Henri IV, Louis XIII* (1924).

[2] It is rarely possible to say that a governor's career was *entirely* the result of Richelieu's patronage. For example, Richelieu granted Charles de Schomberg the *survivance* to the governorship of Languedoc. Yet his father, Henri de Schomberg, had been a *maréchal de France* and *surintendant des finances* before Richelieu became chief minister. His grandfather, Gaspard de Schomberg, comte de Nanteuil, had contracted great debts in the service of Henri IV: Mousnier, *La vénalité*, p. 372. E 96b, fo. 21, 28 June 1628.

part of the minority of Louis XIII in revolt: by the treaty of
Sainte Menehould (15 May 1614), he had forced the summoning
of an Estates-General on the government; in his next revolt,
after 27 November 1615, he was in alliance with the Protestants; by the treaty of Loudun (3 May 1616), Condé imposed
himself on the government as one of the chief ministers; the
arrest of Condé on 1 September 1616 had led to the rebellion
of the ducs de Mayenne, Nevers, and Bouillon; after the
murder of Concini (24 April 1617), Condé had an important
influence on the king's council until the peace of Montpellier
(19 October 1622), which he regarded as the defeat of his aim
of eliminating the Huguenot party by political means. The
dismissal of his ally, Henri de Schomberg, in January 1623
ended Condé's last ties with the government. However, following the arrest of the maréchal d'Ornano—the nobleman
charged with Gaston's education[1]—on 4 May 1626, which
precipitated a crisis at court, Louis XIII and Richelieu sought,
—and achieved,—an alliance with Condé which was to last
throughout the reign. Condé seized the opportunity of reconciliation presented by Richelieu on 30 May 1626 and consolidated in the form of a lieutenant-generalship in the army
of Languedoc, Guyenne, the Dauphiné, and the Lyonnais
(10 October 1627) and the governorship of Berry.[2] The renewal
of the war against the Protestants was the great issue on which
reconciliation could take place, but Condé rapidly began to
understand Richelieu's suspicions of the governors. On 16
June 1628, in a reference to Épernon in Guyenne and Montmorency in Languedoc, he complained to Richelieu of 'les
artifices des gouverneurs pour me rendre inutile'.[3] Condé's
first great opportunity to demonstrate his loyalty to Richelieu
came in December 1630, when he led five thousand men to
Aix to suppress the revolt of the *Cascaveoux*. When he met the
governor of Provence at Avignon in February 1631, Guise
arrived with a large armed retinue to forestall any attempt to
arrest him. When the duc de Bellegarde sided with the revolt
of Gaston in March 1631, Condé led the royal army into
Burgundy. These services to Richelieu coincided with Condé's

[1] cf. E 62c, fo. 123, 23 Dec. 1619.
[2] *Les papiers de Richelieu*, ed. Grillon, i. 339–43. B.N. MS.fr. 18147, fo. 223ᵛ.
[3] A.A.E. France 790, fo. 201ᵛ.

promotion in the governorships: to the province of Berry, which he had held since 1627, he added Burgundy on 10 September 1631. Similarly, Condé was the beneficiary in 1638 of the disgrace of Bernard d'Épernon: he received the vacant governorship of Guyenne (6 October 1638);[1] his son, Louis de Bourbon, duc d'Anguien, had already been given the governorship of Burgundy during his absence (11 March 1638). Finally, in 1641–2, Condé was made virtually the king of southern France, combining the governorship of Languedoc with the military command of the French frontier and the Roussillon campaign.[2]

The deaths of Richelieu and Louis XIII led to a reappraisal of royal policy towards the magnates. On his deathbed, Louis XIII pardoned all the governors dismissed by Richelieu with only one exception—Châteauneuf, the former Keeper of the Seals and governor of the Touraine.[3] The new Regency government could not afford to deal out its patronage in the high-handed manner of Richelieu. A number of the politically pro-scribed under Richelieu regained their positions during the first years of Mazarin's ministry. Chief among these was Gaston d'Orléans. As late as 1 December 1642, Louis XIII had debarred Gaston from holding public office in France because of his complicity in the Cinq-Mars conspiracy;[4] although this decision had been reversed in Louis's last will and testament, dated 20 April 1643, Gaston remained without a governorship. On 1 February 1644, this situation was remedied, when Schomberg—who had returned to Languedoc in 1643—was demoted to the status of lieutenant-general. In 1646, Schomberg left the province to take up the governorship of Metz, Toul, and Verdun, but Gaston remained the absentee governor of

[1] Bercé, *Histoire des croquants*, i. 452–3.

[2] A.A.E. France 1631, fo. 87, instructions to Condé 's'en allant en Guyenne et Languedoc', 22 Mar. 1639. A.A.E. France 1631, fos. 420–8, memorandum of Condé against Schomberg, 1639 [?].

[3] This exception was recalled by Anne of Austria during the Fronde: A.A.E. France 888, fo. 38. Louis XIII also failed to pardon Madame de Chevreuse: cf, Mailfait, *Un magistrat . . . Omer Talon*, p. 211, n. 2.

[4] B.L. Harleian 4472b, fos. 159–61, 1 Dec. 1642. This decision is usually re-garded as the last act of Richelieu before his death [e.g. Dethan, *Gaston d'Orléans*, p. 284]. However, Louis XIII made it clear to Séguier that the decision, taken on 30 November, was his personal responsibility ('com[m]e estant ma volonté').

Languedoc. Both Gaston and Condé were rewarded with important military commands and sat in the council of state. Although Condé's support for the Regency was somewhat less firm than Gaston's, his elder son, Louis duc d'Anguien, retained the governorship of Burgundy, while his younger son, Armand prince de Conty, obtained that of Champagne on 16 May 1644. Condé himself retained Berry in the years before his death in 1646, but Bernard d'Épernon was reinstated in Guyenne after the *Parlement* of Paris cleared him of the charge of treason on 16 July 1643. Charles de Lorraine, duc d'Elbeuf, was restored to his governorship of Picardy in 1644, doubtless because of the influence of Gaston d'Orléans on the Regent.

It is questionable whether this policy of reconciliation after 1643 was successful. Firstly, there was a serious danger that men such as Schomberg,[1] and Chaulnes, who had served Richelieu loyally after 1633 respectively in Languedoc and Picardy, would be alienated. More recent appointees, such as the comte d'Alais in Provence, might well fear for their positions and move increasingly towards a policy of opposition to Mazarin. Moreover, Richelieu had proscribed so many nobles that all the demands could not possibly be met. Vendôme and Châteauneuf hoped to be restored to their governorships of Brittany and the Touraine:[2] but La Meilleraye especially could not be removed without a complete renunciation by the Regency government of the political legacy of Richelieu. When the excluded realized they were doomed to failure, they organized the *cabale des importants* in an attempt to overthrow Mazarin. Even where an exiled governor was restored—Guyenne and Picardy were clear illustrations of this problem—this did not produce the desired effect of political reconciliation. Bernard d'Épernon in Guyenne was a governor with no time to spare: for almost five years, his family had been threatened with ruin. His intransigence during the Fronde, and the animosity of the *Parlement* of Bordeaux towards him, were in large measure the result of his humiliation and years in

---

[1] In Schomberg's case, cf. his hopes that Gaston would be transferred to Brittany and that Schomberg would once more be governor: A.A.E. France 1634, fos. 229, 231, 233, 10 Apr., 10 May 1646.

[2] Châteauneuf was released on 24 May 1643 and restored to his governorship, but exiled there after the failure of the *importants*. Vendôme, too, was exiled after this event. His son, the duc de Beaufort, was arrested on 2–3 Sept. 1643.

exile.[1] Similarly in Picardy, Elbeuf came up against the entrenched resistance of the Albert de Chaulnes family, who had held the lieutenant-generalship since 1621 and the governorship since 3 January 1633. The Fronde in Picardy was essentially the result of the struggle for power between these two families.[2]

By 1648, it was clear that Mazarin had undone some of Richelieu's achievements in quelling the unreliable magnates while failing to substitute any coherent alternative policy.[3] The constitutional breakdown in the summer and autumn of 1648, leading to the siege of Paris in January 1649, created a political vacuum which brought the governors to the fore. They were clearly divided. Conty, the governor of Champagne; Longueville, the governor of Normandy; the prince de Marsillac, who held the *survivance* on the governorship of Poitou; and Elbeuf, the governor of Picardy, all lined up against the government.[4] So too did most of the claimants—the duc de Beaufort, who wanted the governorship of Brittany for Vendôme, his father; the duc de Bouillon, who wanted the governorship of the Auvergne; the vicomte de Turenne, the younger brother of Bouillon, who wanted the governorship of Alsace; and the duc de Luynes, who wanted the governorship of the Touraine.[5] Other governors—notably Épernon in Guyenne and the comte d'Alais in Provence—took a highly equivocal stand, pursuing their own feuds in the provinces. La Meilleraye, the *surintendant des finances* and lieutenant-general of Brittany,

---

[1] cf. René I Voyer d'Argenson's comment that Épernon 'ne respirait que la vengeance . . . son humeur implacable et trop altière a causé une grande partie des désordres qui ont affligé la Guyenne'. *Lettres . . . au Chancelier Séguier*, ed. Mousnier, i. 102–3. Certeau, 'Politique et mystique', p. 79.

[2] Deyon, *Amiens*, pp. 452–60.

[3] In particular, the power of Condé had been increased to a dangerous extent, as Lionne was warned in 1646. Des Robert, *Charles IV*, p. 219, n. 1.

[4] Conty wanted a place in the council of state, a fortress in Champagne, and certain gifts for his supporters. Longueville wanted a major position of the crown (e.g. the Admiralty), a fortress in Normandy, and the *survivance* of his positions for his sons. Elbeuf wanted the governorship of Montreuil and a suitable position in the army for his two sons.

[5] One might add that La Trémouille hoped for the governorship of Anjou, although in March 1649 he was claiming Roussillon and Cerdagne as a result of marriage contracts dating from 11 Feb. 1481 and 19 June 1492! The *demandes particulières* of the *Frondeur* nobles at Rueil are in B.N. 500 Colbert 3, fos. 157–89. Some of the requests, notably Conty's, are originals. Others are copies. They are in a collection belonging to Molé, the *premier président* of the *Parlement* of Paris and one of the negotiators at Rueil.

Gaston d'Orléans, the governor of Languedoc, Condé, the governor of Berry and Burgundy, Gramont, the governor of Béarn, and Harcourt, who hoped to regain an important governorship for himself, were active in opposing the first Fronde. The treaty of Rueil (11 March 1649), and subsequent local settlements, did not solve the issue of the governorships. The power of the leading *Frondeur* nobles—Conty in Champagne, Longueville in Normandy, and Elbeuf in Picardy—had probably increased. Yet the governors who had sided with Mazarin had undergone a revolution in expectations. Harcourt had hoped for nothing less than the governorship of Normandy yet was given the far smaller prize of Alsace (26 April 1649). Condé's demands became exorbitant in the second half of the year: on 2 October 1649 and 16 January 1650, Condé virtually made himself chief minister. On 18 January 1650, Mazarin—almost certainly with the agreement of Gaston d'Orléans—decided on the arrest of Condé, Conty, and Longueville. Mazarin appointed his own supporters to the vacant governorships in the provinces—the maréchal de l'Hôpital to Champagne, the comte de Saint-Aignan to Berry, and the duc de Vendôme to Burgundy.[1] These decisions led to a further round of fighting, and the release of the princes became imperative with the signing on 30 January 1651 of the so-called 'union of the two Frondes', an alliance between Condé's supporters and former *Frondeur* nobles such as Retz and Beaufort. On 10 February 1651, Anne of Austria and Gaston d'Orléans agreed on terms for the release of the princes. They were to be prohibited from entering any 'ligue, traité ni association, soit au dedans, soit au dehors du royaume'. Condé and Conty were not to enter their governorships of Berry, Burgundy, and Champagne until two years after the majority of the king (i.e. after 7 September 1653). They were not allowed to hold fortresses within their governorships for a further two years (i.e. not until 7 September 1655). Longueville was not to be allowed to return to Normandy: instead he should hold either Guyenne or Provence 'au choix et option de Sa Majesté', although he would be allowed to retain the *survivance* on his governorship.[2] In the event, Mazarin released the princes after

---

[1] Des Robert, *Charles IV*, pp. 356–7. Moote, *Revolt of the judges*, pp. 260–1, 283.

[2] A. Feillet, *La misère au temps de la Fronde et Saint-Vincent de Paul* (5th ed. 1886),

meaningless verbal assurances and went into self-imposed exile: the result was that Longueville, Condé, and Conty were stronger than before, while Gaston had been alienated. These miscalculations were compounded on 16 April 1651 when Condé succeeded in exchanging governorships with the duc d'Épernon. The removal of Épernon had been the price of any settlement in Guyenne: but the settlement was doomed to failure in any case in view of the rise to power of a radical party, the *Ormée*, at Bordeaux in the summer of 1651. Instead of securing a settlement, the transfer of the governorship of Guyenne gave Condé a new and much more dangerous power base. Mazarin, who viewed the governorships in strategic terms, appreciated the situation, but was powerless to stop the Regent from committing this error.[1] The failure of the government's policy towards the governors was made evident in Condé's revolt after 7 September 1651. Mazarin, who had refused to cede his governorship of the Auvergne during this first exile,[2] returned with a force of six thousand German mercenaries to pursue the campaign in south-west France in January 1652. Nevertheless, Condé was able to reside in Guyenne from September 1651 until March 1652, and to use the province as the base for his seizure of control at Paris (11 April–13 October 1652). Conty and La Rochefoucault joined the revolt and brought in their provinces of Champagne and Poitou. The new governor of Anjou, Henri Chabot, duc de Rohan, brought his province into the revolt, too, and was in contact with the radical *Loricard* party at Angers. Elswhere, for example in Provence, royal control was faltering. In Normandy, the wily Longueville was earning his epithet—'le vieux renard'—by his neutrality, extracting the maximum concessions from both sides for any future alliance. Nevertheless, the royalist governors had regained control of their provinces in most cases by the end of 1652. In Provence, Louis de Vendôme, duc de Mercœur, who was appointed temporary governor on 18 April 1652, had brought about peace by October of the same year. Finally, on 30 July 1653, Conty at

---

p. 276, n. 1. B.N. n.a.f. 7806, fo. 184 (eighteenth-century copy for Fontanieu).

[1] *Lettres du Cardinal Mazarin*, ed. Ravenel, pp. 69–70.

[2] ibid., p. 63. Mazarin had obtained the governorship of the Auvergne in 1650: cf. A.A.E. France 870, fo. 423, 15 Apr. 1650.

Bordeaux began negotiations with the royalist generals and the city surrendered on 3 August.

The political settlement of the governorships after the Fronde rewarded those Mazarinists and *Frondeurs* who had come to terms with the government. Gaston d'Orléans, who had made his peace with the government on 28 October 1652, retained Languedoc until his death in 1660, although he never visited the province. Longueville retained Normandy until his death in 1663, and was succeeded by his son, Jean-Louis-Charles d'Orléans, duc de Longueville. The royalist generals were richly rewarded, notably the Épernon family, who were at least partly responsible for the Fronde in Guyenne: Bernard retained Burgundy until 1660; his son, Louis-Charles-Gaston, duc de Candalle, who had received the surrender of Bordeaux, held the Auvergne until his death on 28 January 1658. Mercoeur was rewarded with the permanent governorship of Provence on 24 February 1653, after the death of the comte d'Alais.[1] The *Frondeurs* who had negotiated with the government also received satisfaction: Turenne, who had become a royalist commander in March 1652, was appointed governor of the Limousin on 16 June 1653; La Rochefoucault retained his governorship of Poitou; Conty was rewarded with military commands and—on 28 March 1656—with the governorship of Guyenne that was vacant because of Condé's exile in the Spanish Netherlands. Conty was absent from the province for most of the time on military service, and thus real local power was left to François d'Espinay, marquis de Saint-Luc, the lieutenant-general. At the Peace of the Pyrenees in 1659, it was agreed that Condé should return from exile before 10 January 1660. Thus Épernon was moved from Burgundy back to Guyenne, where he died on 25 July 1661, without heir. Condé returned to Burgundy, the province his family had held between 1631 and 1651. Conty was recompensed by Champagne and Brie, the provinces which he had held in 1644: after the death of Gaston d'Orléans in 1660, Conty received the governorship of Languedoc.[2] The Peace of the Pyrenees thus

---

[1] On 10 Sept. 1653, Mazarin was made governor of Provence and paid 400,000 *livres* for this office. He was allowed to sell the position for 600,000 *livres* and presumably did so to his son-in-law, Mercœur: A.A.E. France 890, fos. 289, 297, 10 and 15 Sept. 1653.

[2] A.A.E. France 908, fo. 425. A.A.E. France 909, fos. 27, 28, 1 Feb. 1660.

provided a final solution to the Fronde. Mazarin and Condé
were reconciled, yet on terms which were an outright victory
for the chief minister: Condé had to abandon his alliance with
Spain before he received a royal pardon.[1]

The Peace of the Pyrenees confirmed a new attitude of political realism on the part of the French nobles. The transfer
of Artois and Roussillon to France by this treaty removed two
potential territorial bases for invasion by Spanish forces in
support of an aristocratic conspiracy. Louis XIV was to remove
two others, by invading Lorraine in 1670 and annexing Franche-
Comté in 1674. Far from being in a position to invade France,
Spain was unable to protect her possessions in the Netherlands
against French attack in 1667–8. On the whole, the French
nobles benefited from these changes. They had suffered from
the accusation of Mazarin and others that their agreements
with Philip IV of Spain were partition treaties and therefore
treasonable acts.[2] The nobles could no longer go into rebellion
against the king and hope to be successful. But they had no
reason to go into rebellion: on his deathbed in 1661, Mazarin
advised Louis XIV to preserve the privileges of the nobility[3]
and the king did so. They obtained handsome pensions as a
matter of course; they received military commands; and they
profited from marriage alliances which the ministers were
anxious to secure between their relatives and the nobles.
Mazarin had led the way, marrying his nieces off to future
governors such as Mercœur in 1651 and Charles Armand de la
Porte—the duc Mazarin as he became—in 1661.[4] The emphasis
on court activities and the importance of military commands
meant that after 1661 few governors resided permanently
in their provinces.[5] As such, they were far less dangerous to
the government.

The governor was a member of the upper aristocracy, appointed
by the crown for political reasons, but nevertheless he bought

[1] J 930, nos. 2, 4, 5 [Musée, AE II 852], 7 Nov. 1659.
[2] *Lettres du Cardinal Mazarin*, ed. Ravenel, p. 26. E 1698, no. 120, 23 July 1652.
[3] G. Lacour-Gayet, *L'éducation politique de Louis XIV* (2nd ed, 1923), p. 131.
[4] G. Livet, *Le duc Mazarin. Gouverneur d'Alsace, 1661–1713* (Strasbourg–Paris,
1954). Mercœur's career is brought out by Kettering, *Judicial politics*.
[5] For example, the duc de Verneuil in Languedoc and the duc de Penthièvre in
Provence were both absentee governors.

his position. No limit was placed on the length of time served by governors at the beginning of Richelieu's ministry, although Richelieu may have tried to review appointments triennially and Louis XIV almost certainly did so. In contrast, the intendant was usually a member of the *noblesse de robe*, appointed by the crown on merit to a position which could not be bought and sold, and from which he was usually recalled within three years of his appointment. There must inevitably have been a basis for tension, and sometimes conflict, between the two types of official even if it is accepted that the intendants were not introduced deliberately as a means of weakening or destroying the authority of the governors.[1] Several of the earliest intendants—Sade de Maxan in Languedoc in 1577, Camus de Pontcarré in Guyenne in 1595, and Séguier in the Auvergne and the Limousin in 1621—were chosen primarily as the assistants of the governors. From the beginning, however, the 'assistance' given to the governor was double-edged. The intendant was commissioned to 'reside near' to the governor and to assist him with advice and counsel; if that advice and counsel was ignored, the intendant wrote directly to Paris to inform the ministers. As early as 1615, François du Faure, the intendant of Languedoc, was reporting on the disputes between Montmorency, the governor, and the *Parlement* of Toulouse, as also on the 'mauvaise intelligence' between Montmorency and Ventadour, one of the lieutenants-general. Faure had instructions to report to Brûlart de Sillery, the Chancellor, on Montmorency's 'desseins ou intérests présents'.[2] Of course, when a governor went into revolt, there was very little that an intendant or a royal commissioner could do. Sève asked to be recalled from Provence in 1649 when it became clear that the comte d'Alais was bent on pursuing his feud with the *Parlement* of Aix to the point of civil war.[3] When Montmorency went into revolt in 1632, he held D'Hémery, one of the royal

---

[1] Mousnier, *La plume*, pp. 201–9, disputes Zeller's argument that the intendants were introduced primarily to destroy the power of the governors. Nevertheless, a potentially rebellious governor such as Vendôme in Brittany might consider the appointment of an intendant 'une marque de meffiance' because the man appointed would be Richelieu's client: A.A.E. France 782, fos. 131, 132ᵛ, 8 Aug. 1624 and 28 Mar. 1626.

[2] A.A.E. France 1627, fos. 107, 110, 7 Mar. and 8 May 1615.

[3] *Lettres . . . au Chancelier Séguier*, ed. Mousnier, ii. 914.

commissioners to the Estates of Languedoc, captive for nearly
ten days, only releasing him after a ransom of 36,000 *livres* had
been paid.[1] In such circumstances, the intendants were powerless: a governor rarely went into revolt unless he was certain
that his clientage network could be rallied and thus initial
military advantage secured. The real value of the intendants
was pre-emptive, however—to prevent the governors changing
allegiance or declaring their rebellion when their demands
could still be met by the government.

The governors appreciated the advantages of securing their
own nominees as intendants. They were usually consulted
about the choice of candidates and might well veto the nominee
of the ministers. The *Code Michaud* of 1629 stated clearly in
article 81 that no intendant was to be chosen who served as a
'domestique, conseiller ou employé aux affaires ou proche
parent des généraux desdites armées ou gouverneurs desdites
provinces . . .'[2] But this ordinance was clearly ignored in the
case of Baltazar's appointment to Languedoc in 1643, for
Baltazar had been in the service of the Schomberg family since
at least 1632.[3] The intervention of the governors in the selection process was extremely common. The duc d'Epernon chose
Séguier to assist him in Guyenne in 1622, and chose Verthamon nine years later.[4] Condé chose La Potherie to assist
him in Province in 1630,[5] and it was well known that he
was the patron of Machault.[6] Ventadour chose Le Tonnelier
for the Limousin in 1637,[7] and La Meilleraye chose Cœtlogon
de Méjusseaume for Brittany in 1645.[8] The comte d'Alais
bitterly regretted the transfer of François Bochart from Provence to the Lyonnais in 1640, and obtained his return in
1643.[9] The demands of the governors were not always suc-

[1] E 109b, fo. 3, 1 Oct. 1632.
[2] Frequently quoted, e.g. by P. Viollet, *Histoire des institutions politiques et administratives de la France* . . . (3 vols., repr. 1912), iii. 661, n. 1. Mousnier, *La vénalité*,
p. 650.
[3] A.A.E. France 805, fo. 158, 16 Dec. 1632.
[4] Girard, *Histoire de la vie du duc d'Épernon* (1655), pp. 368, 449–50.
[5] *Lettres . . . au Chancelier Séguier*, ed. Mousnier, i. 60, n. 60.
[6] *Lettres . . . de Richelieu*, ed. Avenel, vi. 897–8.
[7] Mousnier, *La plume*, p. 207.
[8] Canal, *Origines de l'intendance de Bretagne*, p. 99. *Lettres . . . au Chancelier Séguier*, ed.
Mousnier, ii. 724–5.
[9] *Lettres . . . au Chancelier Séguier*, ed. Mousnier, i. 587. A.A.E. France 1707, fo. 5,
2 Jan. 1640.

cessful of course: Villeroy did not obtain his choice of intendant for the Lyonnais in 1665–6.[1] But in general, the governors were of sufficient political importance, and the need for future co-operation between the governors and the intendants so pressing, that the government heeded their requests.

The ministers valued loyal governors because they could perform tasks which the intendants could not. It could not be said of an intendant, as Louis XIII said of the duc de Longueville in 1636, 'je sçay combien ma noblesse de Normandie a de créance en vous . . .' The intendant could not act as the military leader of a vast patronage network. As Louis XIII told the duc de Longueville, 'plusieurs vous suivront qui ne voudroyent pas marcher soubz un autre . . .'[2] Thus co-operation within the council of the governor was regarded as a desirable and an attainable objective. But it was based on an assumption of the superiority of the governor, the representative of the king in the province, the mediator between the king and his subjects. What if the social superiority of the governor was insufficient, if co-operation was not forthcoming, if there was a difference of opinion between the governor and the intendant? The governor, of course, would insist that his view should prevail. Schomberg declared to Richelieu that he respected the characters of Miron and Dupré, the intendants of Languedoc, 'mais qu'ils ayent confiance de se détacher de moy, et d'opprimer mon autorité pour establir la leur, c'est ce que je ne croy pas juste, et je me donneray bien garde de souffrir . . .'[3] 'Je n'ai jamais ouy dire', he told Richelieu on another occasion, 'que leurs commissions nous rendissent exclus de nos autres fonctions . . .'[4]

In cases of conflict between the governors and the intendants, it is not always clear who was responsible, and how far it was a question of personalities or a genuine power struggle. In 1635, Schomberg was in conflict with Antoine Le Camus over the nomination of the *consuls* of Montpellier and the fortifications payments at Narbonne[5]. In 1637, he was in conflict with Miron

[1] Ormesson, *Journal*, ed. Chéruel, ii. 421–2.
[2] B.N. MS.fr. 3843, fo. 60, 25 July 1636.
[3] A.A.E. France 1628, fo. 392ᵛ, 1 Mar. 1637.
[4] A.A.E. France 1629, fo. 135ᵛ, 22 Mar. 1635.
[5] P. Gachon, *Les États de Languedoc et l'édit de Béziers, 1632* (1887), pp. 296–7. A.A.E. France 1629, fo. 135ᵛ, 22 Mar. 1635.

and Dupré over the nomination of the *consuls* at Uzès.[1] His relations were poor with Dupré in 1639[2] and with Charles Machault in 1641.[3] (He disliked Machault chiefly because he was the client of Condé, Schomberg's enemy after 1639.) Early in 1643, while Schomberg was in Guyenne, the marquis d'Ambres, the lieutenant-general, was in conflict with Bretel de Grémonville and Bosquet.[4] By 1646, Schomberg had even turned against his own nominee, Baltazar.[5] Plessis Praslin, the chief commissioner to the Estates of Languedoc in 1647, did not co-operate much better with René I Voyer d'Argenson, the intendant.[6]

The Languedoc evidence suggests a tension between the governor and the intendants that was more than a clash of personalities. Baltazar, the client of the Schomberg family, co-operated no more successfully with the governor than the ageing and independent Robert Miron. Moreover, Schomberg was one of the least intractable of the provincial governors. Elsewhere, the governors were less inclined to follow the line advocated by Richelieu and Mazarin, and conflict between the governors and the intendants resulted.[7] The tension between the governors and the intendants was not a permanent struggle for power—the attitude of the ministers precluded this—but rather a short-term conflict over specific issues. The first of these issues was the relationship between the representatives of the crown and the sovereign courts. The governor and the intendant were often ordered to carry out decrees of the council jointly. If the intendant was ordered to solve a particular administrative problem, it was usual for the governor to be ordered to 'tenir la main', that is to say, ensure that the intendant's decision, in the form of an ordinance, was put into effect. Alternatively, the govenor might issue an ordinance which was then countersigned by the intendant.[8] Joint action by the governor

---

[1] A.A.E. France 1628, fo. 392ᵛ, 1 Mar. 1637.
[2] A.A.E. France 1631, fo. 279, 27 Aug. 1639.
[3] A.A.E. France 1633, fo. 85, 28 Mar. 1641.
[4] A.G. A1 73, min. 443, 4 Mar. 1643.
[5] A.A.E. France 1634, fo. 251, 16 Oct. 1646.
[6] A.A.E. France 1634, fo. 288ᵛ, May 1647.
[7] For example in Provence in the 1630s and 1640s.
[8] Examples of a governor's ordinances being countersigned by an intendant: A.A.E. France 1629, fo. 370, 28 Sept. 1635. A.A.E. France 1630, fo. 215, 30 Mar. 1636.

and the intendant is most evident in the area of registration of
royal edicts by the local sovereign courts: in Provence, Vitry
and Jacques Talon were ordered to secure the registration of
certain fiscal edicts by the *cour des comptes* at Aix on 13 October
1632.[1] The comte d'Alais and Cazet de Vautorte were ordered
to perform a similar task on 26 May 1641.[2] Many of the decrees
of the council were sent directly to the intendants in the first
instance, but with the provision that the governors should
ensure the implementation of the decision of the intendant. In
1643, Schomberg demonstrated the importance of the intendants' role as technical advisers to the governors: if the
governor was to be 'destitué d'intendans', Schomberg argued,
his ordinances 'ne seront pas visées . . .'[3] On another occasion,
Schomberg had argued that the function of the intendant was
to ensure that the decrees of the council were implemented if
the governor was disinclined to take action.[4] The ministers
agreed: the intendants, Schomberg was informed, 'sont principallement ordonnées pour vous assister d'advis et conseils en
semblables natures d'affaires'.[5] The implementation of new
legislation, with or without the consent of the local sovereign
courts, was clearly an issue of the greatest political sensitivity.
The ministers hoped that the intendants' advice would prevent
unnecessary political conflict between the governors and the
local courts. However, both the governors and the *Parlements*
wanted undisputed local power and acceptance of their claims
to intervene in municipal administration: in addition, the
Parlements resented any infringement of their judicial powers
by the governors, while the governors resisted any infringement
of their military powers by the *Parlements*.[6] The legacy of previous conflicts and the march of events tended to lead the
governors into personal vendettas with the local courts, which
clouded their political judgement. For this reason, they were
usually more uncompromising then the intendants when it
came to the enforced registration of fiscal edicts, and the conclusions to be drawn from the resistance of the courts. The most

---

[1] K 113b, no. 70.
[2] A.G. A1 64, mins. 548, 549. A1 67, no. 149, 27 May 1641.
[3] *Bnutrennyaya*, ed. Lublinskaya, p. 55. Mousnier, *La plume*, p. 204.
[4] A.A.E. France 1630, fo. 380ᵛ, 14 June 1638.   [5] O1 2, fo. 110, 1638 [?]
[6] cf. A.A.E. France 1703, fo. 83, ruling of 8 Mar. 1635 attempting a reconciliation between Vitry and the *Parlement* of Provence.

extreme examples of this tendency were in 1649, when René I Voyer d'Argenson in Guyenne and Sève in Provence tried—and failed—to contain Épernon and the comte d'Alais in their armed conflicts with the *Parlements* of Bordeaux and Aix. But there were earlier, and less extreme instances: on 21 July 1645, François Bochart advised against the comte d'Alais's proposal that the *cour des comptes* at Aix should be suspended.[1] The more moderate advice of the intendants usually prevailed at Paris. On 14 June 1638, Schomberg declared to Richelieu that the registration of certain fiscal edicts was refused by the *cour des comptes* of Montpellier because of 'la hardiesse [que]MM. les intendants en cette province luy ont donnée'; but his desire to push matters 'jusques à la dernière extremité'[2] was rejected and he was rebuked for ignoring the advice of the intendants. The difficulty lay in enforcing moderate counsels in the province.

The intendants and the governors also needed to co-operate when it came to military administration, the control of the towns and the raising of taxes. Yet in all these areas, there was room for conflict. The nobles in Normandy in 1658 wanted the governor to order the billeting of troops 'sans y souffrir le mesle d'aucun intendant', and the governors certainly demanded freedom of action on this question. In 1636, the duc de Chaulnes demanded the recall of Laffemas from Picardy after a disagreement on this issue;[3] the duc de Longueville demanded the recall of Morant from Normandy after a similar disagreement in 1658 and may have arrested the intendant.[4] But the governors simply could not be left to their own devices on this question. They used the billeting of troops as a weapon against their political opponents who were not necessarily the political opponents of Richelieu and Mazarin. In 1638, Schomberg was accused of having sent troops into the lands of the bishop of Nîmes; he denied the charge and claimed to have acted with moderation since the bishop had declared himself 'mon ennemi juré sans nul sujet légitime . . .[5]' Whatever the rights and wrongs in Languedoc in the 1630s, there is little doubt that in

---

[1] Kettering, *Judicial politics.*
[2] A.A.E. France 1630, fos. 380ᵛ, 382, 14 and 28 June 1638.
[3] Deyon, *Amiens*, p. 444.   [4] Above, chapter XII.
[5] A.A.E. France 1630, fo. 386, 13 July 1638.

Provence in 1649 the comte d'Alais did his best to destroy the lands of his *parlementaire* opponents by allowing his troops free rein.[1] Nor was the governor's interest in controlling the towns necessarily identical with the aim of increased royal control. The intendants were against all factions, all disorder, regardless of who was responsible. The governors took a strong line in disputed elections that had been won by their political opponents, and especially when rioting had taken place; they were much less inclined to take action in such cases when the outcome was favourable to their supporters. The *Parlement* of Aix accused the comte d'Alais of causing riots at Brignoles when the election went against his supporters: 'il a faict exciter une sédition par laquelle on a esté contraint de faire d'autres consuls . . . dans touttes les villes il a foumanté sa faction . . .'[2] The frequent election disputes and rioting at Béziers in the 1640s were at least partly caused by Schomberg's private political interests in the town.[3]

When it came to the raising of taxes, particularly by force, the active participation of the governor was often essential, as the intendants of Languedoc discovered in 1639–40. Nevertheless, the governor could not be trusted to exercise such authority without the strictest control from above: a decree of the council of finance issued on 5 September 1640 prohibited the governor and the lieutenants-general of Languedoc from ordering the levy of taxes without previous royal permission.[4] The ministers were well aware that one of the first acts of a rebellious governor—during the minority of Louis XIII and during the Fronde—was to appropriate the receipts of taxation.[5] The task of the intendants was to prevent any form of peculation. In addition, they were to ensure that the governors did not use their political authority for corrupt purposes—the defence of the fiscal privileges enjoyed by their lands. They made a start at tackling this problem, but no more, as is suggested by Corberon's difficulties with the Pompadour estates

---

[1] Pillorget, *Les mouvements insurrectionnels*, pp. 612–13. A.A.E. France 1714, fos. 330, 338, 18 and 25 May 1649.

[2] Pillorget, op. cit., p. 618. A.A.E. France 1716, fo. 215, 1 Feb. 1650.

[3] A.A.E. France 1634, fo. 212, 15 Jan. 1646.   [4] E 157a, fo. 4.

[5] For example, the revolt of Condé: E 51, fo. 228, 3 Nov. 1615. Revolt of Condé and Gaston: E 249a, fo. 1, 1 Oct. 1651. E 1698, nos. 58, 83, 86, 1 Mar., 2 May, and 12 May 1652.

in the Limousin.[1] The intendants of Guyenne scarcely fared
any better with the Épernon estates.[2] Tallemant confessed to
Séguier in 1656 that the troops had not been sent into 'les
terres de Bénauge, qui appartiennent à M. d'Espernon . . . de
craincte d'avoir trop de gens sur les bras . . .'[3] On 31 August
1659, Colbert informed Mazarin that the lands of the duc
d'Épernon had not drawn up the tax rolls or paid any *taille* for
seven or eight years; 'toutes les personnes de qualité dans
l'estendue de Guyenne', he declared, 'suivent cet exemple'.[4]

With leadership such as that provided by Épernon in Guyenne
and Pompadour in the Limousin, it was scarcely surprising that
the lesser nobility were reluctant to suppress 'tax rebellion' and
often actively encouraged it. The gulf between the provincial
governors and the lesser nobles in terms of wealth and social
position precluded a frequent rallying of the patronage network. The nobles were virtually incapable of raising an army
for service against Spain, as the failure of the *arrière-ban* in the
Thirty Years War demonstrated.[5] The nobles of Poitou turned
out, under the leadership of La Rochefoucauld, to resist the
English invasion in 1627.[6] Under Schomberg's leadership, the
nobles of Languedoc turned out to resist the Spanish invasion
ten years later, and defeated it at Leucate.[7] Elsewhere, the
military service owed by the nobles was commuted into a
money payment. The nobles would not fight for the king if they
could avoid it (unless they had chosen the army as a career);

[1] Above, chapter IX.
[2] The situation was complicated by the transfer of Épernon to the governorship
of Burgundy in 1651. During his absence, his lands in Guyenne were not to be
burdened by billeting of troops, and taxes were not to be increased: E 1696, no.
254, 3 Sept. 1651.   [3] B.L. Harleian 4489, fos. 180–1.
[4] *Lettres . . . de Colbert*, ed. Clément, i. 360.
[5] At the beginning of the war it was hoped to raise a 'puissante armée' in this
way [A.G. A1 26, no. 64, 11 July 1635. A.A.E. France 819, fo. 114, 30 July 1635],
but the invasions of 1636–7 put paid to such hopes, especially in northern France.
In 1658 Colbert de Terron noted to Colbert that 'toute la noblesse de la province
[d'Aunis] . . . est naturellement inquiète, attachée à ses affaires domestiques et
nullement portée à la guerre, et outre cela aimant fort l'abaissement de l'autorité
du roy . . .' *Lettres . . . de Colbert*, ed. Clément, i. 293, n. 2. Cf. P. Deyon, 'À propos
des rapports entre la la noblesse française et la monarchie absolue pendant la
première moitié du xviie siècle', *Revue Historique* lxxxviii (1964), 341–56, translated
in *State and society*, ed. Kierstead, esp. pp. 30, 32–5.
[6] E 105b, fo. 152, 8 Mar. 1631.
[7] Schomberg noted their poverty: A.A.E. France 1630, fo. 152, 27 July 1637.

they would not fight for the governor except when—as in Languedoc in 1632 and Normandy in 1649—the governor, the lieutenants-general, and the lesser nobles shared common interests. The French nobles at the time of Richelieu and Mazarin did not fear social revolution and almost never took up arms against the peasants. Local associations of the nobles certainly existed in France: the union of 'plusieurs gentilshommes de la Beauce contre les désordres des gens de guerre' —which was probably signed in 1652—is a case in point.[1] This league of nobles had its own military organization—a captain, lieutenant, ensign, and *maréchal des logis* were selected, and the objective of the league was to 'secourir ceux qui se trouveront attaqués par lesdits gens de guerre'. The league intended to gain support outside the Beauce, and ultimately to create a union of *bailliages*: 'nous unir aux autres bailliages et les faire venir à notre union'. At first sight, this political union appears purely defensive and limited in character. In reality, however, it was much broader and more dangerous than its avowed purpose might indicate. The troops were used by the government to enforce the collection of taxes; those who were 'attacked' by the troops were essentially the taxpayers, that is to say, the peasants. Far from defending the monarchy, therefore, the nobles were lining up with the peasants and supporting them in their 'tax rebellion'. A similar situation existed elsewhere in France. Méliand, the intendant at Montauban, noted in 1657 the existence of a league of nobles in the mountainous areas of his province which had been in existence for over two years, 'à dessein d'abord de faire vivre dans l'ordre les trouppes...mais qui depuis s'est estendue à tout ce qui vient de la part du roy soit pour le fait des tailles, trouppes ou autre chose'.[2] In the previous year, Heere had reported the existence of a league of nobles in Haute Touraine, whose list of grievances 'estoit un vray cahier d'Estats'. Essentially, the grievances of the nobles in the Touraine were fiscal: they demanded that the *taxes d'office*, special taxes levied by the intendants, should no longer be paid by their wealthier peasant farmers.[3] The nobles in the Angoumois in 1649 and Champagne in 1651 had ex-

---

[1] Jarry, *La guerre des Sabotiers*, pp. 48, 129–30.
[2] B.L. Harleian 4490, fo. 204, 24 Mar. 1657.
[3] B.L. Harleian 4489, fo. 59, 25 May 1656.

pressed similar views.[1] The nobles tended to support the peasants in their protests against the *taille*; the *seigneur* could not expect his peasant farmer to pay both higher rents and higher taxes to the crown. The nobles wanted a reduction of taxation: this would mean that existing rents could be paid, perhaps even that they could be raised.

The governors did little to discourage local leagues and associations of the nobles; they rarely showed any enthusiasm in rallying the nobles to suppress revolts. Bernard d'Épernon defeated the *Croquants* at La Sauvetat-du-Drop on 1 June 1637, but his army was composed of royal troops, not nobles.[2] Lesdiguières certainly summoned the nobles to suppress the revolts in the Dauphiné in 1644, but this appears to have been wholly exceptional, and he was backed up by the regiment of Sully.[3] Mercœur summoned the nobles of Provence to suppress the revolt at Aix in 1659, but they were not enthusiastic about turning out, were only mobilized for a fortnight, and when he sent them home, Mercœur felt obliged to offer as concession his hope that the provincial Estates would be summoned.[4] Condé criticized Saint-Géran, the governor of the Bourbonnais, for failing to summon the nobles to suppress the rioting at Moulins in 1640:[5] but Saint-Géran's policy of negotiation with the rebels typified the attitude of several governors. It was extremely unusual for a governor to lead the repression of a revolt in his province. The maréchal de Gassion, not the duc de Longueville, led 5,200 troops into Normandy after the revolt of the *Va-Nu-Pieds* in 1639. Longueville was conveniently absent, serving in the royal armies on the frontier, but it is unlikely that the punishment meeted out to the rebels would have been so severe had he been present. When a governor advocated a strong line against the rebels, or warned of the outbreak of a new revolt, there was usually an element of special pleading:

---

[1] Mousnier, Labatut, Durand, *Problèmes de stratification sociale*, pp. 88, 151. Cf. *Lettres . . . au Chancelier Séguier*, ed. Mousnier, ii. 706.

[2] Bercé, *Histoire des croquants*, i. 426–30, ii. 771. An anonymous account of the battle asserts that fewer than six nobles of the Périgord assisted La Valette: after the battle, when a government victory over the *Croquants* was certain, more than 200 nobles joined him in three days.

[3] B. F. Porchnev, *Les soulèvements populaires en France de 1623 à 1648* (1963), p. 633. Mousnier, *La plume*, p. 359. A.G. A1 83, min. 441, 21 Aug. 1644.

[4] Pillorget, *Les mouvements insurrectionnels*, pp. 796–9.

[5] Mousnier, *La plume*, p. 359. *Lettres . . . au Chancelier Séguier*, ed. Mousnier, i. 460.

the governor wanted to make himself appear indispensable to the ministers, the sole guardian of public order in the province. The governors assembled the nobles when it was in their interests to do so, as in Provence, Guyenne, and Normandy in 1649; when it was not in their interests, they did not bother.[1]

The unwillingness of the governors to take action against crimes committed by the lesser nobles, against the support given by the lesser nobles to the peasants, and against political assemblies of the lesser nobles left the intendants as the sole agents upon whom the government could rely in such matters. The role of the intendants in suppressing noble rebellions had begun as early as 1617 during Richelieu's first brief period in government.[2] From 1629, the intendants were policing the activities of the lesser nobles as a matter of course. In that year, La Thuillerie, the intendant of Poitou, was ordered to prosecute the marquis d'Obeterre, who it was alleged, 'exerce nombre de tirannies et cruaultés sur les sujets de Sa Majesté, les taxe à diverses sommes de deniers, pour avoir lesquels [il] les faict emprisonner et mettre en cachots'.[3] The following year, Verthamon, his colleague in Guyenne, was ordered to investigate the activities of the sieur de Montbreton. It was alleged that Montbreton had attacked the guards of the *gabelle*, with the assistance of five other nobles, armed with curasses, swords, and pistols, and with a force of twenty-five musketeers and sixty peasants armed with long-bows.[4] In the Limousin in 1633, René I Voyer d'Argenson was ordered to prosecute the sieur du Courbier who, accompanied by ten of his clients armed with swords, pistols, and arquebuses, had broken into the coffers of the tax collectors at Benais and torn up the tax rolls.[5] The increase in taxes during the 1630s led to far greater illegal interference by the lesser nobles in the fiscal process. In the Auvergne in 1641, Chaulnes was ordered to investigate accusations that the marquis de Langeat had threatened to 'assommer... tous les esleuz qu'il rencontreroit'.[6] In Picardy, the *seigneurs* were notorious for the protection which they accorded to the property of their peasant farmers when attempts

---

[1] cf. Molé's criticism of the governors in 1627: Porchnev, *Les soulèvements*, p. 80. *Lettres ... de Richelieu*, ed. Avenel, viii. 41. [2] Bonney, 'Intendants', p. 39.
[3] V6 70, no. 15, 6 Feb. 1629. [4] E 101a, fo. 65, 10 Jan. 1630.
[5] E 114b, fo. 191, 15 Dec. 1633. [6] E 162c, fo. 514. 10 July 1641.

were made to seize it by the tax collectors.[1] The same was true in the south-west, especially in the *élection* of Les Sables d'Ollonne, where Villemontée was ordered to prosecute such cases of seigneurial interference.[2]

The strength of the alliance between the lesser nobles and the peasants was recognized in a decree issued by the council of finance on 19 August 1642. The intendants were ordered to prosecute anyone who delayed the king's tax returns, and this included the *seigneur* of the parish. The ruling of 22 August prohibited interference in the fiscal process by the lesser nobles. If they did so, they were to be declared commoners (*roturiers*) and would be forced to pay the taxes owed by the parishes they were protecting. Their estates would be confiscated for this purpose. The intendants were instructed to 'informer exactement, faire et parfaire le procez à ceux qui se trouveront coulpables desdits empeschemens'. The sentences of the intendants in such cases were without appeal provided that the requisite number of law graduates had assisted in the trial. The instructions issued to the intendants on 10 July 1643 confirmed these duties and proclaimed seigneurial interference in the fiscal process as 'l'un des plus importans subjectz du retardement desdits impositions'.[3]

The effect of these administrative measures was to increase greatly the disciplinary role of the intendants with regard to the lesser nobles. Villemontée was active in the Saintonge in 1642–3, prosecuting the sieur Dauguitard who had 'gourmandé et maltraité' the *vissenechal*, and other *seigneurs* who were accused of conniving at the 'tax rebellion'.[4] In the Touraine in 1644, Heere was prosecuting nobles who prevented payment of the *taille*.[5] In the Dauphiné the following year, Lozières issued a decree against the baron de la Salle, whom he accused of trying to prevent the troops from levying the *taille* at Jons.[6] In Berry in the same year, Barrin de la Galisonnière was ordered to prosecute the sieurs Imbert, Brouilly, and Clanière, who

---

[1] E 168a, fo. 205, 12 Mar. 1642.   [2] E 174b, fo. 371, 22 Nov. 1642.

[3] E 173a, fo. 175, 19 Aug. 1642. K 891, no. 4 [Musée AE II 2629], 10 July 1643.   [4] E 173b, fo. 627, 30 Sept. 1642. E 176b, fo. 118, 24 Jan. 1643.

[5] E 187b, fo. 276ᵛ, 23 Feb. 1644.

[6] *Lettres . . . au Chancelier Séguier*, ed. Mousnier, ii. 726–7. Porchnev, *Les soulèvements*, pp. 123, 646–7. E 201b, fo. 342, 29 Apr. 1645. Moote, *The revolt of the judges*, p. 79, exaggerates the significance of the incident.

were accused of responsibility for the failure of the parish of Villegermain to pay its taxes.[1] The intendants were active in policing the nobles of Normandy in the years before the Fronde. Le Roy de La Potherie was ordered to prosecute those *seigneurs* in the *élections* of Saint-Lo, Vire, Avranches, and Carentan who prevented the levy of the *taille*;[2] Favier had a similar role in the *élection* of Falaise.[3]

The recall of the intendants in 1648 naturally reversed this trend towards increasing royal control over the lesser nobles. The 'tax rebellions' in Champagne in 1649 were 'appuyez et favorisez d'aucuns gentilshommes et seigneurs des parroisses ... lesquels souffrent qu'ils facent des fortz dans les villages'.[4] The *seigneurs* in Picardy took similar advantage of the weakness of the government.[5] The arrest of the princes in 1650 led to a further deterioration, with the lesser nobles encouraging 'tax rebellion' in Guyenne,[6] Burgundy,[7] and Berry.[8] Their activities were not simply a reaction to political events, however: the nobles of Normandy and Languedoc were supposedly loyal to the government in 1653, yet they still intimidated the tax collectors.[9] The scale of the 'tax rebellion' during the Fronde made a return to intensive policing of the nobles by the intendants inevitable after 1653. The nobles in the years after the Fronde were just as inclined as ever to resort to violence when their own interests were affected—for example, by the investigation into false titles of nobility in Normandy;[10] by the tax on seigneurial monopolies such as forges in Normandy;[11] and by the fen drainage scheme at Niort and Fontenay-le-Comte.[12] There was also the residual problem of recourse to violence by the lesser nobles, particularly in south-west France, in order to secure the implementation of victories won in private law-suits.[13] The fundamental problem, however, remained the

[1] E 206a, fo. 397, 9 Sept. 1645. [2] E 199a, fo. 110, 1 Feb. 1645.
[3] E 184d, fo. 118, 18 Nov. 1643. E 214b, fo. 283, 11 Aug. 1646.
[4] E 235b, fos. 304, 432, 29 and 31 July 1649.
[5] E 237b, fo. 357, 20 Nov. 1649. [6] E 1696, fo. 230, 18 Aug. 1650.
[7] E 242a, fo. 188, 21 Apr. 1650. [8] E 240, fo. 447, 16 Feb. 1650.
[9] E 257a, fo. 129, 4 June 1653. E 256b, fo. 195, 24 May 1653.
[10] E 304a, fo. 229, 4 Aug. 1657. E 305b, fo. 296, 20 Sept. 1657.
[11] E 329b, fo. 285, 20 Nov. 1659. [12] E 297a, fo. 35, 4 Jan. 1657.
[13] Y. M. Bercé, 'De la criminalité aux troubles sociaux. La noblesse rurale du sud-ouest de la France sous Louis XIII', *Annales du Midi*, lxxvi (1964), 41–59. E 1708, no. 152 and E 319a, fo. 272, 11 Dec. 1658. E 1711, no. 4, 3 Jan. 1659.

seigneurial assistance to 'tax rebellion' and the related danger
of assemblies of the nobles. This seigneurial interference was
not a figment of the imagination of the ministers and the intendants: the names of the recalcitrant nobles were recorded.
In the Auvergne in 1654, the sieur du Castel Dauze conducted
forays from his *château* at Sénergues in order to protect his
clients from the tax collectors.[1] The *bailli* of Jailly in the *élection*
of Nevers tried to cover up the rébellion of the sieur du Verve
de Varennes in the same year.[2] In the *élection* of Brives in 1655,
the sieur de Boisseuil threatened to 'esgorger et faire périr' any
huissiers who returned to collect the taxes.[3] At Chizé in Poitou
the following year, the sieurs de La Thibaudière, Châteaurouet,
and Des Ayeux were guilty of 'rébellions et voyes de fait'.[4] The
sieur de Gadmoulins was largely responsible for the refusal of
the *élection* of Cognac to pay its taxes in 1658.[5] Between that
year and 1660, the sieur de Mazottes hid away over 160 crates
of possessions belonging to the peasants at Segonzac, possessions
which would otherwise have been seized because of non-pay-
ment of the *taille*.[6] In 1658, the sieur de Château-Thierry tried
to cover up the rebellion of the parish of Chénas in the Lyonnais;[7] the following year, in Normandy, the sieur Turin imprisoned the collectors of the *taille* at his *château* of Ceton.[8] In
Guyenne in 1659, the sieurs de Jarnac and de Roissot were
accused of protecting the inhabitants 'pour les empescher de
payer leurs tailles.'[9] In the Lyonnais in 1660, the marquis de
Saint-André was among those accused of 'violences, outrages
et battemens' against the guards of the *gabelle*.[10] As late as 1663
in Berry, the marquis de Chastrenancy was cutting off the ears
and noses of the *huissiers* of the *taille* when he could catch
them![11]

Most of these cases resulted in successful judicial prosecution
by the intendants, even if sufficient evidence was not always
available,[12] doubtless because the accused noble had tried to

---

[1] E 266a, fo. 533, 10 June 1654.   [2] E 271, fo. 93, 7 Nov. 1654.
[3] E 283a, fo. 40, 6 Nov. 1655.   [4] E 292b, fo. 58, 9 Aug. 1656.
[5] E 318b, fo. 74, 20 Nov. 1658.
[6] E 333a, fo. 255, 11 Mar. 1660. E 334a, fo. 76, 14 Apr. 1660.
[7] E 315b, fo. 329, 18 July 1658.   [8] E 322a, fo. 441, 12 Mar. 1659.
[9] E 328b, fo. 383, 18 Sept. 1659.   [10] E 338a, fo. 423, 9 Sept. 1660.
[11] E 362a, fo. 142, 10 Mar. 1663. E 362b, fo. 108, 3 Apr. 1663.
[12] E 359c, fo. 192, 23 Nov. 1662.

prevent the course of justice and to procure witnesses who 'ont faict telles dépositions qu'il a voulu'.[1] The successful intendant —such as Charles Machault in Languedoc in 1632–3—was first and foremost the one who could secure the testimony of a sufficient number of witnesses.[2] Even then, however, the sentence had to be carried out. As late as 1675, the nobles of Couserans formed a union to 'se soustraire tant de la justice ordinaire que de la juridiction du . . . sieur intendant'.[3] And there was always the danger—as in the Orléanais in 1665—that the nobles would try to assassinate an unpopular intendant.[4] The nobles often mobilized considerable numbers in support of their local objectives. Méliand's defeat at Martres-de-Rivière in 1657 is a clear illustration: the intendant arrived with insufficient troops to quell a disturbance led by 'quantité de gentilshommes'.[5] Hotman de Fontenay had similar difficulties the following year when the sieur de Montranue [?] led two hundred 'nobles et gentilshommes' in a military campaign to drive the royal troops out of 'les maisons et métairies des gentilshommes' in the *généralité* of Montauban.[6] In the *élection* of Aurillac in 1659, Lefèvre de la Barre had to combat a band of three hundred peasants led by four barons and the brother of an *élu*.[7] The obvious answer to this problem of numerical inferiority was for the intendant to increase the strength of his special brigades. In the south-west of France, however, the nobles resisted such attempts. As soon as the nobles of Armagnac heard rumours of an increase in the forces of order in 1657 they assembled at Nogaro to decide on measures to prevent the decision being put into effect.[8]

The political role of the intendants is brought out most clearly by the way in which the government relied on them to suppress the assemblies of the nobles in 1657–9. The pretext of these assemblies was the demand for a meeting of the Estates-General. The Estates-General had been summoned twice during the Fronde, but the date of the meeting had been delayed successively. After 13 May 1653, when Louis XIV informed

[1] E 334a, fo. 76, 14 Apr. 1660.
[2] cf. B.N. MS.fr. 17380, fo. 137, 14 Sept. 1644.
[3] E 1781, no. 225, 15 Nov. 1675.   [4] E 1728, no. 80, 5 May 1665.
[5] E 302a, fo. 192, 6 June 1657.   [6] E 318b, fo. 298, 27 Nov. 1658.
[7] E 328a, fo. 366, 10 Sept. 1659.   [8] E 1706, no. 233, 24 Oct. 1657.

Gaston d'Orléans of his intention not to call the meeting,[1] no further mention of the Estates-General was made by the government. The nobles in Normandy began their assemblies in 1657. Further meetings were held at Trun on 29 March 1658; in the forest of Conches on 20 July; later in the year, at Lieurey and near Laval; in January 1659 at Montmirail and at Authon in the Perche; in April and May 1659 near Brestot; finally at Les Tesnières, Cloyes, Villequoy, and Les Tourailles in the Orléanais.[2] The ministers were seized by panic at these meetings. There was talk of a 'union' of the nobles in eight or even fourteen provinces. Nine major provinces were affected: Normandy, Berry, Burgundy, Maine, Poitou, the Orléanais, the Touraine, Anjou, and—in the view of Colbert at least—the Auvergne. In addition, the minor provinces of the Vexin, pays Dunois, pays Chartrain, and the Perche were also involved.[3] Colbert expressed his anxiety to Mazarin on 8 August 1658 that this league of lesser nobles might 'gagne[r] toutes les provinces du royaume et . . . [faire] une fascheuse affaire'.[4] On 9 August 1659 Mazarin feared that the nobles of the Nivernais, Picardy, the Marche, the Bourbonnais, and the Limousin might also be implicated. He was reliably informed 'que l'union est plus considérable qu'on ne croit'.[5] Servien thought it 'absolument nécessaire de déraciner par quelque grand exemple les erreurs qui se sont glissés dans l'esprit de la noblesse'.[6] Foucquet was convinced that the revolt of the peasants in the Orléanais and Berry—the *Sabotiers* of the Sologne—was assisted by the lesser nobles.[7] All the ministers would have agreed with Servien's judgement that the aims of the nobles were to 'renverser la royauté'.[8]

The ministers were correct to view the assemblies of the lesser nobles as a serious threat to the war effort and to the direction of royal policy in general. The Spanish government did not make the decision for peace with France until 7 January 1659,

[1] Dethan, *Gaston d'Orleans*, p. 415, n. 1.

[2] Logié, *La Fronde en Normandie*, iii. 149–60.

[3] Jarry, *La guerre des Sabotiers*, pp. 149–53. A.A.E. France 905, fo. 239, 7 July 1658.

[4] *Lettres . . . de Colbert*, ed. Clément, i. 308. A.A.E. France 905, fo. 357.

[5] Jarry, op. cit., p. 133.   [6] A.A.E. France 905, fo. 228ᵛ, 3 July 1658.

[7] A.A.E. France 905, fo. 350ᵛ, 8 Aug. 1658.

[8] A.A.E. France 905, fo. 388ᵛ, 17 Aug. 1658. Not that the nobles were republicans: they opposed monarchical government exercised in reality by Mazarin.

and the relative ease with which peace was concluded could not have been foreseen after over a decade of Spanish inflexibility. Condé, who was in exile in these years, hoped to harness the assemblies of the nobles as a means of forcing his return and the overthrow of Mazarin. The delegates of the nobles certainly negotiated with the Spanish government. They also visited Gaston d'Orléans in his apanage at Blois to ask him to keep his promise, made to the lesser nobles in 1651, that he would support a meeting of the Estates-General. But Gaston d'Orléans in 1658 was a very different man from the reluctant *Frondeur* of 1651–2. He had recently been alarmed by the apparent threat to the social order posed by the *guerre des Sabotiers* which he had helped suppress:[1] he thus refused to lend assistance to the nobles. In June 1658, Servien had regarded the governors as the essential means of suppressing the noble assemblies, provided that the governors were given the necessary troops.[2] The attitude of the duc de Longueville prevented Servien's advice from being put into effect. Colbert was convinced that Longueville secretly supported the noble assemblies.[3] Certainly Longueville was hostile to the intendants and sided with the demand of the lesser nobles that the governors, not the intendants, should control the *subsistances* of the troops. Mazarin was extremely reluctant to give the governors any extra authority at such a critical juncture, and he rejected Colbert's advice that additional troops should be sent to Normandy.[4] The sending of troops might well have galvanized the lesser nobles into more extreme action, and strengthened the position of the duc de Longueville had he declared for the Estates-General and Condé. Mazarin's decision was therefore in part correct. The disadvantage was that without troops the intendants—who were left as the only agents upon whom the crown could rely—were unable to arrest the nobles who participated in the assemblies.

A council of war comprising Séguier, Villeroy, Servien, Foucquet, and Le Tellier, with Colbert acting as Mazarin's representative, was set up in August 1658 to direct operations

---

[1] Dethan, *Gaston d'Orléans*, p. 425.

[2] A.A.E. France 905, fo. 200ᵛ, 22 June 1658.

[3] *Lettres . . . de Colbert*, ed. Clément, i. 308, 376. Logié, *La Fronde en Normandie*, iii. 159. A.A.E. France 905, fo. 357, 8 Aug. 1658.

[4] Jarry, *La guerre des Sabotiers*, p. 72.

against the conspiracy. From April 1659, Pommereu de la Bretesche, a *maître des requêtes* and *président* of the *grand conseil*, directed the interrogation of suspects, the issuing of decrees, and liaison between the ministers and the intendants on the question of the assemblies of the nobles. The results were not encouraging: on 29 July 1659, Mazarin demanded a 'résolution vigoreuse'.[1] Only thirty-five nobles were named in the conspiracy; only one—the marquis de Bonneson on 13 December 1659—was executed. Colbert was highly critical of the intendants, informing Mazarin that if his own brother had been an intendant in Normandy he would have demanded his recall.[2] Colbert's criticism of the intendants was unjust. Pommereu de la Bretesche, who was in close touch with the intendants on this question, praised Bernard Fortia's 'grande activité' in elucidating the role of the marquis de Bonneson in 'l'affaire des Sabotiers de Sologne'.[3] If the intendants in Normandy were relatively less successful than Fortia in the Orléanais and Berry, this was because they had far fewer troops at their disposal and had to act independently from a governor whose loyalty was questionable. The real problem for the intendants was that the decree of 23 June 1658, which had declared the assemblies of the nobles to be seditious, and had threatened any culprits with the death sentence, had forced the conspirators to take much greater precautions against arrest.[4] The intendants needed a greatly improved intelligence network. Colbert drew the correct conclusion from the events of 1657–9 when he drew up his instructions to the *maîtres des requêtes* in the autumn of 1663: they were to investigate the 'bonne et mauvaise conduite' of the governors, and particularly their past conduct 'pour juger ce qu[e Sa Majesté] en doit et peut attendre à l'advenir'. The intendants were instructed to investigate also the size and composition of the clientage network of the governors: 'quel crédit ils ont parmi la noblesse et les peuples'. The intendants were also ordered to investigate the lesser nobles, 'leurs alliances, leurs biens et l'estendue de leurs terres et seigneuries, leurs mœurs et bonne conduite'. They were to pay particular attention to their

---

[1] Logié, *La Fronde en Normandie*, iii. 157, n. 73.
[2] *Lettres . . . de Colbert*, ed. Clément, i. 357–8.
[3] Jarry, *La guerre des Sabotiers*, p. 141.   [4] ibid., pp. 57, 88.

wealth and their political attitudes.[1] These measures were essentially long-term. Their implementation would be greatly facilitated by the appointment of men such as Pommereu de la Bretesche, who was rewarded for his services in 1659 with the intendancy of the Bourbonnais the following year. In the short term, the signing of the Peace of the Pyrenees, the ending of the war effort, and the reconciliation between Mazarin and Condé removed the pretext for agitation.

[1] *Lettres . . . de Colbert*, ed. Clément, iv. 30–1.

CHAPTER XIV

The Towns

THE MAJORITY of Frenchmen lived in relatively isolated rural parishes, and many of the so-called towns, particularly in the Midi, were little more than large villages. Towns were important less because of the size of their population than because they were centres of communications and administration. They each also had their own constitution, an endless variation on the basic theme of a mayor, a small governing council (*échevins* in northern France, *consuls* in the Midi, *jurats* at Bordeaux, *capitouls* at Toulouse) and a larger, general assembly. Most of these constitutions had been conceded by a royal charter[1] and had been modified subsequently by decrees of the king's council[2] or decrees of the local *Parlement*. Traditionally, the French crown had appreciated that large assemblies representing small traders and artisans were potentially seditious and predictably hostile to any increase in taxation. Rule by the few, 'les gros de la ville', might ensure not only the rule of law, but a strengthening of royal power through acceptance of the crown's fiscal demands. The oligarchies varied greatly in strength and self-confidence from one town to another. In many of the towns of the Midi, even during Mazarin's ministry, the general assemblies were still summoned regularly and had a semi-popular character. At Béziers, perhaps the most extreme example, a general council of 120 persons possessing at least four *livres* of property on the land register (*compoix*) was supposed to control the general business of the town, the nomination of municipal officials, and the contracts for collecting the taxes. Yet two thousand persons, 'la pluspart d'entr'eux armez et dont les paroles tendoient à esmotion et sédition' flocked to the municipal election of 1647.[3] The meetings of the general council were

---

[1] For example, the privileges of Beauvais cited in a case at the council of finance to justify its fiscal exemption: E 124a, fo. 211, 23 June 1635. Similarly, Bourges: E 121b, fo. 206, 13 Dec. 1634.

[2] For example, the decree confirming the privileges of Sainte-Menehould: E 111a, fo. 247, 9 Mar. 1633.   [3] E 1692, no. 220, 22 Nov. 1647.

disrupted frequently during the Fronde by the presence of 'tous les artisans . . . en si grand nombre'.[1] In most towns, an oligarchy was firmly in control; but this could cause problems too. At Aix-en-Provence, nominees for the elections were recorded by the *consulaires*, former *consuls* who had the right to advise, but not to nominate. Oppède, the first president of the *Parlement* of Aix, noted in 1659 that the *consulaires* 'ne sortent de toute leur vie du conseil de la maison de ville'. 'Par cette perpétuité', he added, 'on peut aisément juger du crédit qu'ils acquierent dans l'administration des affaires publiques . . . il n'y a rien de si pernicieux . . . cette perpétuité dans les fonctions les rend habiles, plus cognoissants des affaires et plus hardis à choquer celles du Roy . . .'[2] At Tours, it was declared that 'les eschevins sont en trop grand nombre et possédent leurs charges leur vie durant, ce qui donne jalousie aux autres.'[3] Thus even when an oligarchy was firmly in control, this was no guarantee that the municipality would be subservient to the wishes of the government. An oligarchy could easily dissolve into faction fighting, which was the cause of much of the urban rioting in Provence.[4]

However strong its hold on power, an oligarchy needed to tread warily: the neutrality of other social groups regarding its monopoly of power had to be secured. At Angers, the oligarchy was too restricted, being drawn almost exclusively from the office-holders in the local *présidial*: the opposition party, the *Loricards*, drew its support from a wide range of the excluded, 'les bourgeois, marchands, artisans et battéliers'.[5] The main way for an oligarchy to secure its position was by the ardent defence of the liberties and immunities of the town, privileges which were usually fiscal in character. A municipality which failed to defend these privileges could expect nothing but trouble. François Vivart, the mayor of Noyon in 1636–7 and 1640–1, lamented to the council of finance that he had been obliged from 'nécessité pour le service de Sa Majesté de faire

[1] E 1706, no. 67, 4 Sept. 1656.

[2] B.L. Harleian 4493, fo. 80, advice of Maynier d'Oppède to Séguier, n.d. [1659].

[3] E 1692, no. 273, 19 June 1648.

[4] Pillorget, *Les mouvements insurrectionnels, passim.*

[5] A. Débidour, *La Fronde angevine. Tableau de la vie municipale au xviie siècle* (1877), pp. 8, 74, 104, 139–40, 272, 280–1. F. Lebrun, 'Les soulèvements populaires à Angers aux xviie et xviiie siècles', *Actes du 90e congrès national des sociétés savantes* [1965] (1966), 130–2. B.L. Harleian 4468, fo. 183, 'relation du siège d'Angers'.

plusieurs choses qui luy ont causé la haine et inimitié (quoyqu'
injustement) de plusieurs de ladite ville . . .' The mayor had
committed an unforgiveable sin: he had billeted two thousand
troops on the town, including the houses of the office-holders![1]
In every town, there was a bourgeois militia of sorts which
could be used to suppress riots. Yet the militia was rarely mobilized: often this was because the oligarchy hoped to utilize the
mob in order to secure the abolition of new and unpopular
taxes. In some towns in any case the militia was relatively small
and insufficient to cope with a serious riot. In these areas, the
oligarchy could not defer exclusively to the wishes of the central
government and survive.[2] The widow of the *receveur des aides* at
Neufchâtel protested to the *conseil privé*: 'dans toute la province
de Normandie . . . il n'y auroit plus aucuns eschevins ny autres
officiers des villes quy osassent entreprendre d'exécuter les
volontez du Roy s'il estoit permis à ceux qui se trouvent taxez . . .
d'assassiner . . .'[3] Negligence in implementing the decisions of
the government, even vocal opposition to the crown's fiscal
demands, were thus the answer of many municipalities which
feared provoking the fury of the mob against themselves. The
members of the oligarchy neither wished, nor dared, to re-
linquish power to the populace, however, and were evidently
reliant on the government which alone could limit the franchise
and preserve them in power. The dilemma of the oligarchy is
well illustrated by the experience of the mayor and *échevins* of
Orléans in 1642. When they attempted to levy the *subsistances*
by poll tax, this caused 'divisions et désordres dans ladite ville'.
When they suspended the levy, they were 'si rigoreusement
poursuivis par les contrainctes solidaires . . . qu'ilz sont réduitz
à demeurer renfermez dans ladite ville et privez de la liberté
d'aller et venir à leurs affaires'.[4] Too great an independence,
too vocal an opposition to the fiscal demands of the government,
and the members of the town council might be arrested and the
troops sent into the town. Claude Roy, one of the leading
citizens in Moulins, was arrested and imprisoned at Fort

---

[1] E 167c, fo. 320, 26 Feb. 1642.
[2] For the bourgeois militia: Bercé, *Histoire des croquants*, i. 193–5. Pillorget, *Les
mouvements insurrectionnels*, pp. 64–5. For its failure to suppress riots: Mousnier, *La
plume*, pp. 356–7. Criticism of the inadequacy of the militia by the council of
state: E 1685, fo. 132 and E 106a, fo. 26, 15 May 1631.
[3] V6 123 no. 32, 11 Sept. 1637.   [4] E 170b, fo. 219, 24 May 1642.

Levesque because the town owed 60,000 *livres* of its forced loan in 1637.[1]

The situation in the towns of France was complicated further by the existence of large numbers of office-holders, grouped together in courts dealing with both judicial and fiscal questions, courts that were quite independent of municipal control. In some towns—Toulouse, Bordeaux, Rouen, Aix-en-Provence —the municipality was in a position of political dependence on the local *Parlement*. In towns without sovereign courts, the predominance of the office-holders was usually less clear-cut, the balance of political power more fluid. On two occasions in July 1636, a dispute between the *présidial* and the municipality of Saint-Maixant led to rioting.[2] The conflict between the *présidial* of Carcassonne and the municipality led to rioting on 10 September 1630, 27 June 1633, and 5 March 1656.[3] There was obviously no identity of interests between the urban notables and the office-holders. The office-holders were stout champions of oligarchy in principle, but support was not always extended to the oligarchy in power. The courts, and particularly the *Parlements*, wanted local power for themselves. They wanted to intervene in the politics of other municipalities, using their appellate jurisdiction in election disputes in order to secure the nomination of their friends and relatives. Faction fighting within a sovereign court might have a profound effect on urban politics in general. The faction within the *Parlement* of Aix that was opposed to the policies of the crown was largely responsible for the urban revolts of 1630, 1649, and 1659.[4] The office-holders stirred up riots to protect their own interests.[5] In 1638, the *élus* of Armagnac refused to allow an investigation of their salaries. Instead they caused a rumour at Rodez that the *trésoriers* had arrived from Montauban to 'establir la gabelle et faire de nouvelles impositions'. L'Espinette and De Thuillier, the *trésoriers* in question, were forced to flee the town because of 'une grande rumeur et esmotion

---

[1] V6 136, no. 10, 11 Feb. 1639. E 172a, fo. 477, 9 July 1642.

[2] V6 115, 1 Aug. 1636. Cf. V6 120, no. 8, 19 May 1637.

[3] V6 333, no. 31, 17 Oct. 1656.

[4] The role of this faction is sharply focused by Kettering, *Judicial politics*. Pilorget, *Les mouvements insurrectionnels*, pp. 313–54, 569–602, 791–5, discusses the riots.

[5] Bercé, *Histoire des croquants*, i. 172–84, ii. 855–7.

du peuple, criant dans les rues il faut tuer tous les gabelleurs'.[1]

Financial and economic considerations also pointed to the desirability of closer control over the towns. Many of the towns were in debt. War, famine, and plague might involve a town in unforseen expenditure that could only be paid by contracting debts, as the town of Bar-sur-Aube in Champagne discovered in 1631–3.[2] At Narbonne, the plague of 1629 caused the town to contract debts of 8,930 *livres*.[3] In general, however, the debts of the towns resulted from the deliberate policy of the municipal officials. During the ministries of Richelieu and Mazarin, the policy of many municipalities was to spread payment of taxation over a number of years by means of covering loans instead of paying the amount immediately. Toulouse owed 883,315 *livres* in 1636 and 1,897,291 *livres* in 1659. Eighty-five per cent of the debts in 1659 resulted from deferred payment of the *taille*.[4] There were many rich office-holders and bourgeois who were only too anxious to offer their services in this profitable form of investment.[5] There were also cases of fraud and mismanagement. 100,000 *livres* had been embezzled by Devaulx, a financial official at Toulouse in 1641,[6] and there was an important charge against the mayor and *échevins* of Moulins in 1640.[7] Financial and political considerations tended to overlap, because charges of fiscal mismanagement played an important, and often decisive, part in the development of factions in the towns.[8] At Lavaur, it was claimed that in the years before 1648 the general council had been reduced from 80 to 24 members at the instigation of the *consuls*, who wished to make themselves the absolute rulers of the town. Such supreme power, it was alleged, was a cover for 'de très grandes désordres aux impositions desdites tailles et subsistances d'autant que l'esgalité ny les facultez desd[its] habitans ne sont poinct

---

[1] E 146b, fo. 176, 16 Oct. 1638.   [2] E 115a, fo. 408, 28 Jan. 1634.

[3] E 118b, fo. 66, 20 July 1634.

[4] A.A.E. France 1634, fo. 23, n.d. [1659].

[5] A.A.E. France 1634, fo. 216ᵛ, 5 Feb. 1646.

[6] *Histoire générale de Languedoc*, ed. Roschach, xiii. 218. *Bnutrennyaya*, ed. Lublinskaya, p. 138. V6 230, no. 12, 2 Oct. 1648.

[7] V6 149, no. 73, 27 July 1640.

[8] cf. R. Pillorget, 'Les luttes de factions à Salon de 1608 à 1615', *Provence Historique*, xviii (1968), 293–311. Pillorget, 'Luttes de factions et intérêts économiques à Marseille de 1598 à 1618', *Annales E.S.C.*, xxvii (1972), 705–30. Pillorget, *Les mouvements insurrectionnels*, pp. 190–236, 539–41.

gardées et observées . . .'[1] Similarly, the oligarchy at Angers was accused of having 'mal usé du revenu dudit hostel de ville, c'est ce qui a faict ces deux partys'.[2]

Between 1624 and 1648 there were several hundred urban riots of greatly varying importance.[3] There were perhaps as many again in the years of the Fronde and the turbulent 1650s —no accurate total is as yet possible. Some were grain riots, and some were riots of the 'pre-industrial action' type by arti-sans, aimed at securing an improvement in their standard of living. Predominantly, however, the urban riots were about taxation, because it was an age of unprecedented fiscal de-mands by the government and because the towns had im-portant fiscal privileges which the crown was attempting to undermine. Faction fighting within the towns, election disputes, and the suspension of elections intensified the problem of urban rioting. It is probable that rural discontent was more frequent, chiefly because the countryside was taxed more heavily than the towns. Urban disturbances were more serious, however, because many towns were fortified[4] and loss of control in a town implied loss of the surrounding area too.[5] For these reasons, it was unacceptable that a town should shut its gates on the governor, the intendant, or the commissioner of a local *Parlement*—as did Béziers on 10 December 1652,[6] Le Puy on 12 August 1656,[7] and Nîmes on 31 December 1657.[8] The in-dependence of the towns had to be undermined.

One way in which this independence was undermined was by the granting of powers to the intendants to investigate urban riots and prosecute the ringleaders when sufficient evidence was

---

[1] V6 229, no. 2, 4 Sept. 1648.

[2] B.L. Harleian 4468, fo. 183.

[3] Approximately two hundred according to Porchnev, *Les soulèvements*, pp. 133–4, 661–4. However, the inadequacy of Porchnev's documentary material is clear. Professor Pillorget has found this number in Provence alone!

[4] For example, Lyon: E 139c, fo. 1, 23 Sept. 1637. The small number of 'villes et bourgs fermez' in Normandy—some 25 or 30—was regarded as exceptional: E 179a, fo. 68, 15 Apr. 1643.

[5] 'Les villes maistres de la campagne comme ils sont.' D'Hémery to Richelieu, *c.* 1 Aug. 1632, during the Montmorency revolt. Gachon, *États de Languedoc*, p. 286. A.A.E. France 1628, fo. 194ᵛ.

[6] E 1700, no. 126, 17 Jan. 1653. Cf. E 1706, no. 67, 4 Sept. 1656.

[7] E 1706, no. 209, 11 Aug. 1657.

[8] E 1708, no. 55, 11 Apr. 1658.

available. Maximilien Granger investigated the riot at Lyon on 6 October 1624.[1] Four years later, Pommereu prosecuted the leaders of the riots at Amiens,[2] while in 1629 Moric and La Thuillerie did the same, respectively at Moulins[3] and Angoulême.[4] The role of the intendants assumed even greater importance in 1630, the *grand tournant* of Richelieu's ministry: in that year, Turgot helped suppress a riot at Caen,[5] La Thuillerie, Estampes de Valençay (together with Villemontée) and Le Maistre de Bellejambe were similarly active at Fontenay-le-Comte,[6] Troyes,[7] and Angers.[8] At Aix-en-Provence on 19 September 1630, the carriage of Dreux d'Aubray, the intendant, was stopped, and his possessions burnt unceremoniously on the public highway. The rioting against the intendant had been started by a faction in the *Parlement* of Aix led by Laurent de Coriolis and Paul de Joannis de Châteauneuf. The intendant was forced to leave the town to the mercy of the *Cascaveoux*: when he returned it was with 5,000 troops under the command of Condé and a colleague—Le Roy de La Potherie —as intendant.[9] It was doubtless as a result of the investigations by the two intendants that Condé was in a position on 30 March 1631 to proscribe forty-two alleged leaders of the riots at Aix and elsewhere.[10] The concern of the government at the extent of urban rioting emerges clearly from the correspondence between Marillac and Richelieu.[11] It is also well illustrated by the decree issued by the council of state on 15 May 1631, which strengthened the police force in the towns: whatever its deficiencies, the urban police force was henceforth better organized and more numerous than that of the countryside.

[1] Pagès, 'Richelieu et Marillac', p. 68 (riot at Montélimar). E 81a, fo. 189, 30 Jan. 1625.
[2] Pagès, art. cit., pp. 69–70. Deyon, *Amiens*, pp. 437–9. V6 67, no. 7, 15 June 1628.   [3] cf. V6 75, no. 50, 19 Feb. 1630.
[4] E 100c, fo. 90, 19 Sept. 1629. V6 77, no. 20, 11 June 1630.
[5] Pagès, 'Richelieu et Marillac', pp. 70–1.
[6] V6 79, no. 4, 28 Nov. 1630.   [7] E 103b, fo. 476, 20 July 1630.
[8] Lebrun, 'Les soulèvements populaires à Angers', pp. 123–6. E 105a, fo. 77, 9 Jan. 1631. V6 82, no. 51, 17 June 1631.
[9] Pillorget, 'Les cascaveoux' [translated in *State and society*, ed. Kierstead, pp. 96–129], and Pillorget, *Les mouvements insurrectionnels*, pp. 313–54. Kettering, *Judicial politics*. V6 79, no. 1, 5 Dec. 1630.
[10] B.N. MS. Dupuy 94, fo. 217.
[11] Marillac to Richelieu, 15 July 1630, quoted by Pagès, 'Richelieu et Marillac', p. 73 and Mousnier, *La plume*, p. 383.

The collapse of the Heilbrönn League in Germany in 1634, the alliance with Sweden and the Netherlands, and the declaration of war against Spain in 1635, naturally led to increased fiscal demands on the part of the government. These in turn worked their way through to the towns, notably in the form of a tax on taverners (*cabaretiers*).[1] Villemontée was prosecuting riots at Niort in April 1634 and at Fontenay-Le-Comte and elsewhere later in the year;[2] Le Camus was investigating riots at Laujeac (31 May) and Villefranche-en-Rouergue (26 July);[3] so too was Le Tonnelier de Conty at Rouen.[4] The riots in the year of Nördlingen were as nothing compared with those the following year: 1635 saw more urban disturbances than in any other year before the Fronde with the possible exception of 1639. Urban discontent was so widespread in Guyenne that Verthamon, who was trying to contain the rioting at Périgueux, lost control of the situation. Both Verthamon and Villemontée, his colleague in Poitou, appear to have carried out prosecutions but they were unable to contain the unrest.[5] By contrast, the urban riots in 1636 were not only less numerous, they also lacked geographical coherence. Prosecutions were certainly carried out by Villemontée at Saint-Maixant and Saint-Jean-d'Angély,[6] by Laubardemont at Alençon (in the absence of Le Tonnelier de Conty);[7] at Rennes, on the other hand, the riot was directed essentially against Estampes de Valençay, the intendant, who was not allowed to carry out prosecutions.[8]

A new focus for urban discontent was provided by the attempt to levy a forced loan on the towns, which was ordered on 18 December 1636, although not implemented effectively until after 28 March 1637. Almost everywhere the oligarchies stalled for time. The debates on how much to pay and how to levy the forced loan intensified faction fighting within the

[1] The importance of this tax is emphasized by Bercé, *Histoire des croquants*, i. 296-8.

[2] E 117b, fos. 95, 187, 1 and 3 June 1634.

[3] E 120a, fo. 229, 23 Sept. 1634.

[4] Foisil, *Nu-Pieds*, p. 142. E 123b, fo. 265, 19 May 1635.

[5] Bercé, op. cit., i. 294-363. E 1684, fo. 164, 15 Sept. 1635 (Villemontée). E 126a, fo. 321, 18 Sept. 1635 (Verthamon).

[6] V6 121, no. 53, 12 June 1637. [7] E 129b, fo. 340, 29 Mar. 1636.

[8] *Lettres . . . au Chancelier Séguier*, ed. Mousnier, i. 312-13, 349. Porchnev, *Les soulèvements*, pp. 188-90.

towns. The faction opposing payment of the forced loan usually emerged victorious. The towns showed determined 'constitutional' resistance to this forced loan, despite the presence of intendants whose forceful personalities were matched by explicit instructions, and who were supported by the council of finance which issued additional powers at their request. The extent to which the faction fighting in the towns turned into urban rioting against the forced loan is an open question. At Neufchâtel, Talon, the intendant, prosecuted rioters against the forced loan;[1] there were riots at Ponthieu[2] and Coutances,[3] too. At Clermont-Ferrand, Mesgrigny was convinced that the third *consul* was responsible for the 'séditions et rébellions' which he claimed had taken place. The issue was complicated by the question of the legitimacy or otherwise of the Estates of the Bas Auvergne, and the right of the *consuls* of Clermont-Ferrand to call themselves the representatives of the third estate of the Auvergne. The council of finance eventually accepted that there had been no serious rioting. Nevertheless, it clearly anticipated further resistance: Polignac, the governor, and Navailles, the lieutenant-general, were ordered to billet troops on the towns in the Auvergne, and the *cour des aides* of Clermont-Ferrand was instructed to 'procéder extraordinairement' against any rioters.[4] Most of the towns submitted formally to the forced loan: the problem was to obtain payment from individuals. One intendant confessed that he had to use 'de menaces . . . pour les réduire . . . par la terreur . . . car d'en venir aux exécutions et contraintes effectives, je ne le feray qu'en toute extrémité . . .'[5] The commissioners were not in the provinces long enough to ensure that the sums were levied as they had envisaged. 'Aussy tost que les . . . commissaires ont esté hors des provinces', it was said, 'la pluspart des habitants des . . . villes et bourgz ont esté reffusans de payer.' In January 1638, Paris, Troyes, Reims, Châlons, and Moulins still had not paid the sums which they had agreed.[6] In July 1637, the intendants had been allowed to send troops into the towns 'pour y tenir garnison et vivre jusques à ce qu'elles ayent rendu l'entière obéis-

---

[1] V6 123, no. 32, 11 Sept. 1637.
[2] E 139a, fo. 185, 20 Aug. 1637.   [3] E 142a, fo. 348, 6 Mar. 1638.
[4] E 139a, fo. 102, 19 Aug. 1637. E 140a, fos. 507, 508, 24 Oct. 1637.
[5] *Lettres . . . au Chancelier Séguier*, ed. Mousnier, i. 412. Foisil, *Nu-Pieds*, p. 65.
[6] E 1685, fo. 372, 15 Jan. 1638.

sance'. The threat does not seem to have been carried out systematically. In March 1639, however, Bourges still had not paid its forced loan, and this time Heere, the intendant, was ordered to send in the troops. In case of resistance or rebellion, he was empowered to 'procéder extraordinairement contre eux, tant par interdiction de leurs charges, que saisie de leurs biens . . .'[1]

The revolt of the *Va-Nu-Pieds* in Normandy in 1639, although predominantly an agrarian movement, coincided with serious riots in towns such as Rouen, Caen, Coutances, Vire, Mortain, Mantilly, Domfront, and Avranches. In the last-named town, Le Roy de La Potherie, the intendant, carried out the resulting prosecutions.[2] The presence of an intendant was in itself no guarantee against the outbreak of rioting. There were riots at Nevers in February 1639[3] and Montpellier in September 1639[4] despite the presence of Miroménil and Dupré in the towns in question. The levy of the *taxe des aisés* in 1639–40, provided additional momentum to urban disturbance. This tax, which was ordered on 22 January 1639, was in reality a forced distribution of 600,000 *livres* in *rentes* on the *taille* which remained from an original creation of *rentes* in 1634.[5] The intendants themselves drew up the distribution of the *rentes*, as one intendant put it, 'avec une cognoissance très exacte des biens et facultez des particuliers'.[6] François Bochart acted in this way at Lyon, as did Le Prévôt d'Herbelay at Orléans, Claude de Paris at Rouen, and Lefèvre de Caumartin at Soissons.[7] It seems likely that this tax was levied throughout the *pays d'élections*. The creation of *rentes* was in general a bad investment for the government, but in this case, it was a form of taxation that was genuinely redistributive—it was a *taxe des aisés*, a tax on the well-to-do. As such, it was political dynamite. There were riots against the tax at Lyon in 1640–1;[8] there were certainly 'rebellions' by some of those taxed in the *généralité* of Soissons.[9] However, the most dangerous rioting against the tax

---

[1] E 149a, fo. 69, 2 Mar. 1639.

[2] Foisil, *Nu-Pieds*, pp. 163–8, 287–90. V6 153, no. 29, 18 Jan. 1641.

[3] E 153c, fo. 173, 10 Dec. 1639. [4] E 153a, fo. 96, 5 Oct. 1639.

[5] Foisil, *Nu-Pieds*, p. 67. AD + 226. [6] E 161a, fo. 440, 11 May 1641.

[7] E 155b, fo. 344, 10 May 1640. E 156b, fo. 378, 18 Aug. 1640. E 157a, fo. 156, 19 Sept. 1640. E 157b, fo. 144, 27 Oct. 1640.

[8] E 159b, fo. 385, 31 Jan. 1641. [9] E 157b, fo. 144, 27 Oct. 1640.

was at Moulins, where the disturbances lasted off and on from 23 June until 25 August 1640. Jacques Puesche, the agent collecting the tax, was murdered. Claude Roy, who was by now the mayor of the town, played a highly equivocal role, shutting himself up in the citadel for more than a month, writing letters to the ministers in which he criticized the great abuses which allegedly had taken place in the levy of the tax. Saint-Géran, the governor, criticized Roy for abandoning him during the revolt; Roy criticized Saint-Géran for inactivity. Three rioters were executed on the orders of Saint-Géran before Humbert de Chaponay and Barthélémé Dupré, the intendants, arrived with the troops. The intendants carried out further prosecutions, issuing punishments such as galley service, exile, and heavy fines. In carrying out these prosecutions, Dupré was accused by Roy and Antoine Vauvillon, the *lieutenant-criminel* in the *présidial*, of favouring Saint-Géran's interpretation of the events during the riot.[1]

The widespread hostility to the *taxe des aisés*—and the relatively minor sums involved—convinced the ministers that it was unrealistic to view it as a major alternative source of revenue to the *taille*. Other forms of taxation on the towns had to be considered. Thus in November 1640, in return for a pledge not to levy taxes 'par capitation, comme aysez . . .', the government came to one of the most enterprising of its fiscal experiments, the *sol pour livre*, a 5 per cent sales tax.[2] Despite the hopes of the ministers, this tax was not wholly redistributive, yet it appeared to threaten the interests of merchants and officeholders alike, who stirred up popular agitation for the withdrawal of the tax. Bosquet, the intendant at Montauban, was forced to flee the city at night and in disguise because of the 'émotions et séditions' caused by the sales tax.[3] Ollier was ordered to prosecute those accused of leading the riots at Troyes on 14 August 1641 and the following days; there were also riots at Troyes in 1642. The butchers were accused of responsibility for these riots, since they had to pay the tax on cattle brought

[1] Porchnev, *Les soulèvements*, pp. 186–213. *Lettres . . . au Chancelier Séguier*, ed. Mousnier, i. 438–62, 465–6, 468–9. A. Leguai, 'Les "émotions" et séditions populaires dans la généralité de Moulins au xviie et xviiie siècles', *Revue d'Histoire Économique et Sociale*, xliii (1965), 49–63. V6 158, no. 37, 2 July 1641.

[2] AD IX 8.

[3] E 160c, fo. 704, 27 Apr. 1641.

into the town for slaughter.[1] Montescot was ordered to prosecute those guilty of rioting at Chéroy, Nemours, and Aigne-
ville in the *généralité* of Paris.[2] In 1642, Mangot de Villarceaux
was ordered to carry out investigations and prosecutions after
rioting had taken place at Château-Thierry against the sales
tax: again, the butchers seem to have played a major part in
the riots.[3] In the same year, Le Maistre de Bellejambe was
ordered to carry out prosecutions at Amiens, where the mob
had pillaged the office established for collecting the sales tax.[4]
At Ligny-en-Brionnais, Foullé found most of the inhabitants in
arms, and he and his entourage had to flee the town under a
hail of stones.[5] At Orléans, Bragelongne was trying to control
'les esmotions et séditions continuelles' against the tax,[6] while
in Guyenne—as Bouthillier confessed to Richelieu—'l'affaire
va très mal . . . personne n'oze parler de la subvention genérale
en la ville de Bordeaux'.[7] For his part, Richelieu feared a
general insurrection comparable to the revolt of the Catalans
in Spain,[8] and not without reason: the protest against the sales
tax stiffened resistance to the other taxes as well. At Grenoble
in 1641[9] and Chartres in 1642 there were riots against the
subsistances.[10] At Tours, Besançon found it impossible to levy any
taxes at all in 1642–3.[11] There were riots against the *convoy* of
Bordeaux at Soulac-sur-Mer;[12] against the investigation into
the *rentes* on the *taille* at Limoges;[13] against the taxes on the
notaries at Sainte-Suzanne;[14] against the taxes on the *élus* at
Argentan[15] and Rodez in 1641[16] and at Mortagne, Bernay,[17] and
Langres[18] in the following year.

The *sol pour livre* was withdrawn on 25 February 1643, an act

[1] E 163c, fo. 443, 31 Aug. 1641. E 165a, fo. 259, 16 Oct. 1641. E 172a, fo. 286,
5 July 1642. E 173a, fo. 81, 12 Aug. 1642.
[2] E 164b, fo. 89, 18 Sept. 1641.   [3] E 167a, fo. 49, 1 Feb. 1642.
[4] E 168b, fo. 451, 29 Mar. 1642.   [6] E 172a, fo. 111, 2 July 1642.
[5] E 173a, fo. 104, 12 Aug. 1642.
[7] A.A.E. France 842, fo. 43, 17 Feb. 1642.
[8] *Lettres . . . de Richelieu*, ed. Avenel, vi. 881.
[9] E 163b, fo. 372, 10 Aug. 1641. E 165a, fo. 253, 16 Oct. 1641.
[10] E 173b, fo. 613, 30 Sept. 1642.
[11] E 172a, fo. 87, 2 July 1642. E 178b, fo. 509, 31 Mar. 1643. For riots at Angers
in 1641 and 1643: Lebrun, 'Les soulèvements populaires à Angers', pp. 126–9.
[12] E 173b, fo. 138, 2 Sept. 1642.   [13] E 173b, fo. 337, 16 Sept. 1642.
[14] E 176b, fo. 350, 29 Jan. 1643.   [15] E 163b, fo. 495, 14 Aug. 1641.
[16] E 173a, fo. 275, 22 Aug. 1642.   [17] E 173b, fo. 146, 2 Sept. 1642.
[18] V6 168, no. 35, 15 July 1642.

which demonstrated the weakness of the government in the face of urban insurrection. The death of Louis XIII on 14 May 1643 led to the introduction of a traditional tax, the *droit de confirmation*, a tax payable for the confirmation of privileges on the accession of Louis XIV. Opposition to this tax was a common feature of urban riots in 1644 and 1645. On 28 June 1645, D'Hémery ordered a second *taxe des aisés*,[1] which despite the opposition of the *Parlement* of Paris, raised 2,388,678 *livres* in the capital alone.[2] It was extremely unpopular, however, and caused several urban riots in 1646. Throughout the years 1643 to 1648, the intendants acted in the manner of their predecessors in the reign of Louis XIII. After each urban disturbance, they were ordered to carry out preliminary investigations, and—if there was sufficient evidence—summary prosecutions. They were relatively successful: despite the increasing foreign and domestic political difficulties of the Regency government, urban rioting was held in check. There were fewer urban riots in 1647 than in any year since 1635. The urban riots before the Fronde were limited in character, directed against a specific tax, and isolated geographically. There was no pattern to urban revolt, the rioters had no common programme. The extent of the rioting sometimes forced the government to withdraw, or modify, unpopular taxes; once the tax in question was withdrawn, however, the rioting stopped. Few of the riots lasted longer than a day. If the riot lasted longer than this, it was usually because factors other than taxation were involved, such as a stuggle for power in the municipal government, or the special interests of the office-holders.

The urban riots during the Fronde were different in character from those of the preceding years, for between 1648 and 1652 the government was forced to abandon its attack on the fiscal privileges of the towns. By the declarations of 18 July and 22 October 1648, the government renounced the levy of taxes which had not been registered in the sovereign courts and in addition a number of recent taxes were cancelled. Before 1648, the intendants had been used to enforce fiscal edicts which had not been registered in the courts. With the recall of the intendants, those taxes which had not been reduced or abolished became unenforceable. There was thus little reason for rioting

---

[1] Dating established from E 216b, fo. 308, 27 Oct. 1646.   [2] P 3474.

on a widespread scale against taxation during the Fronde.[1]
Most of the riots in these years had a political rather than an
anti-fiscal character. They were the product of national and
regional political divisions, local faction fighting, and election
struggles.[2] In the aftermath of the Fronde, the government
declared its intention of resuming the struggle against the
fiscal privileges of the towns. The *lit de justice* of 31 December
1652 re-established the taxes that had been abolished on 22
October 1648.[3] The tax on wine sales was reintroduced and
produced a number of urban disturbances in 1654–6.[4] The
appropriation by the government of the municipal revenues,
the *octrois*, which had been ordered in 1647, was put into effect
and was a major cause of urban discontent.[5] So too were the
forced loans exacted from the towns in 1656 and 1659, the first
to help pay for the military campaigns during the war against
Spain, the second to help pay for the costs of the Peace of the
Pyrenees and the marriage alliance with Spain.[6] The number
of urban riots was related essentially to the fiscal burden on the
towns—as expenditure on the war rose, the burden on the
towns became heavier. The result was a serious outburst of
urban rioting in 1656 and 1657. However, the intendants had
already returned to the provinces and their authority was well
established by the time that this outbreak of rioting occurred.
Their task was essentially the same as in the years before the
Fronde: to enforce the levy of new and unpopular taxes, and
to carry out investigations and prosecutions if riots took place.[7]

From the scale of urban rioting under Richelieu and Mazarin,
it was clear that royal control over the towns was insufficient.

[1] Though there could be riots resulting from rumours of tax increases as at
Limoges on 16 and 24 May 1650: E 242c, fo. 414, 28 June 1650.
[2] As in Provence: Pillorget, *Les mouvements insurrectionnels*, pp. 603–705.
[3] X1b 8857. Cf. E 254c, fo. 132, 5 Feb. 1653.
[4] B.L. Harleian 4489, fo. 177, 21 Aug. 1656 (Bordeaux). There were also riots at
Carentan, Tonnerre, Montargis, Chablis, Vendôme, and Argentueil.
[5] Riots at Vitry: E 302a, fo. 36, 6 June 1657. Le Mans: E 338a, fo. 73, 1 Sept.
1660.
[6] A.A.E. France 900, fo. 287, 11 Aug. 1656. A.A.E. France 907, fo. 289, 10
Aug. 1659.
[7] Examples of prosecutions by the intendants after the Fronde—Joubert de
Bouville (Bourges): E 285a, fo. 11, 8 Jan. 1656. Lefèvre de la Barre (Château-
Chinon): E 285b, fo. 31, 20 Jan. 1656. Fortia (La Rochelle, Marenne, and Chizé):
E 290a, fo. 373, 17 June 1656. E 292b, fo. 58, 9 Aug. 1656. B.L. Harleian 4489, fo.

In their reports to the ministers, the provincial governors and the intendants passed judgement on the constitutions of the towns and on the reliability of the municipal officials—and they suggested changes. At Aix-en-Provence, for example, the *Parlement* had done very little to suppress the revolt of the *Cascaveoux* which lasted from 19 September 1630 until 19 March 1631. The municipality had done very little either. The *Parlement* was transferred (temporarily) to Brignoles; the *consuls* and the assessor were suspended for complicity. On 17 March 1631, Condé revoked the right to hold municipal elections, and Dreux d'Aubray and La Potherie, the intendants, presented *lettres de cachet* appointing new officials. Aix did not regain its privilege of municipal elections until 1638. Vitry, the new governor, was responsible for suspending elections at Aix in 1632, 1633, 1634 and 1636. The elections were suspended in 1635 because of the emergency created by the Spanish invasion. The archbishop of Bordeaux suspended the elections in 1637 after a dispute over the payment of garrisons on the recently recaptured Lérins islands.[1] This reaction of the government—basically to a serious urban riot in 1630–1—was understandable and perhaps inevitable. There was a similar response when a town threatened to join a noble conspiracy or insurrection. In 1632, Narbonne had appeared likely to join the rebellion of Montmorency, although in the event the royalist party—including Bosquet, a future intendant—held the town firm. Nevertheless, the town lost its privileges between 1632 and 1640. When Condé restored its privileges in the autumn of 1640, he modified the constitution.[2] It seems doubtful whether Condé's measures achieved their purpose[3]—the fact remains that a town which had appeared to act treasonably forfeited all its political privileges. Some of its political rights might be restored at a later date, but it was up to the govern-

---

99, 8 June 1656. Le Tonnelier de Breteuil (Sens): E 298b, fo. 237, 28 Feb. 1657. Lefèvre de la Barre (Moulins): E 302b, fos. 442, 587, 23 June 1657. Hotman de Fontenay (Mirande): E 318b, fo. 296, 27 Nov. 1658. Le Lièvre (Joigny, Pont Sainte-Maxence): E 324a, fo. 361, 17 May 1659. E 326b, fo. 424, 23 July 1659. Lefèvre d'Ormesson (Saint-Quentin): E 328b, fo. 491, 24 Sept. 1659. Pellot (Tulle): E 340, fo. 619, 23 Dec. 1660. Bochart de Champigny (le Havre): B.L. Harleian 4442, fo. 135, 7 Nov. 1660. Aligre (Coutances): E 343b, fo. 33, 24 Mar. 1661.   [1] Kettering, *Judicial politics*.   [2] E 1684, fo. 235, 25 Sept. 1640.
[3] In 1648 there were still thought to be abuses in the municipal elections at Narbonne: E 1692, no. 298, 10 Dec. 1648.

ment and its advisers to determine which of those rights could be allowed without threatening the security of the state.

During Richelieu's ministry, the governors and the intendants usually acted jointly in matters affecting urban politics. When an illegal election was held at Nîmes on 1 December 1640, Condé reacted by issuing an ordinance which summoned the faction which had acted illegally to appear before Charles Machault and Yvetaux, the intendants.[1] However, it was essential that the governor and the intendant should agree upon a choice of candidates in elections. At Montpellier in 1635 Schomberg and Le Camus came into conflict on this issue.[2] So too did Schomberg and the intendants of Languedoc over the municipal election at Uzès.[3] During Mazarin's ministry, the intendants were given increasing authority to nominate town councillors—sometimes acting with the governors, on other occasions acting in their own right. In Provence, the comte d'Alais, the governor, and François Bochart, the intendant, suspended the elections and appointed municipal officials at Aix in 1643–4 and 1647–8. The elections at Marseille were suspended annually from 1643 to 1650. On 25 February 1644, the comte d'Alais and Champigny named the *consuls* at Arles and modified the city's electoral procedure. By 1646, Bochart was suspending elections and suggesting appointees on his own initiative.[4] Provence was by no means exceptional. The intendants were acting in a similar manner in other provinces too. A decree of the council of finance, issued on 14 July 1644, empowered Charreton de La Terrière to appoint new *consuls* at Cahors. In this case, the previous *consuls* had refused to collect the *taille*.[5] The town of Saint-Geniez in the Rouergue refused to allow a company of light cavalry under the command of the sieur de Sailhan to be billeted. A riot ensued, in which a number of soldiers were wounded, their horses killed, and their baggage stolen. Louis Laisné, the intendant, carried out the prosecutions arising from this incident.

[1] E 1684, fo. 249, 21 Dec. 1640. The leaders of the faction refused to do so, and were summoned to appear before the king's council.
[2] Gachon, *États de Languedoc*, pp. 296–7. A.A.E. France 1629, fo. 136, 22 Mar. 1635.
[3] A.A.E. France 1628, fo. 392v, 1 Mar. 1637. E 1684, fos. 211, 213, 28 Nov. 1636 and 16 Feb. 1637.
[4] Kettering, *Judicial politics*.   [5] E 192b, fo. 88, 14 July 1644.

He discovered that three of the *consuls* were implicated in the riot and sentenced them to death. New *consuls* were nominated by the intendant in their place.[1] In Languedoc, too, the intendants attempted to control municipal elections, in this case in order to secure compliant delegates to the Estates of Languedoc. They were not entirely successful at Béziers,[2] Albi,[3] and Mende[4] in the last years before the Fronde, however.

Such support as was given to the Fronde in the French towns was in large measure a reaction to the attempts by the king's council, the provincial governors, and the intendants to control elections in the years before 1648. The *Parlement* of Toulouse, in its remonstrances of 10 September 1648, demanded that *lettres de cachet* should no longer be issued on the subject of municipal elections, since these were solicited 'plutost pour [l']intérest particulier que pour l'utilité publique'.[5] The *Parlement* of Aix made similar political demands on 24 January 1649.[6] In general, the years of the Fronde saw a bitter struggle between the factions, both national and local, for control of the towns. In some provinces, such as Provence up to 1651, the struggle was between a provincial governor and the local *Parlement*, each seeking to win the support of the towns.[7] In Languedoc after 1651 there was a conflict between the provincial Estates, the lieutenants-general of the province, and the intendant in one camp, and the *Parlement* of Toulouse in the other: the *Parlement* offered towns which followed its lead the prospect of free municipal elections and free votes at the meetings of the Estates. Commissioners of the *Parlement* tried to seize control of the towns, ostensibly in order to investigate alleged financial abuses committed by the Estates.[8] Elsewhere in France, when provincial governors sided either for or against

[1] E 1692, nos. 154, 167, 7 July and [?] Oct. 1646.

[2] E 1692, nos. 111, 176, 220, 6 Dec. 1645, 19 Nov. 1646, 22 Nov. 1647. E 211b, fo. 51, 16 May 1646.

[3] E.A. Rossignol, *Petits États d'Albigeois ou assemblées du diocèse d'Albi* (Paris–Albi 1875), pp. 19–23. E 1692, nos. 206, 209, 281, 4 July 1647, 23 July 1647, 31 Aug. 1648.

[4] E 1692, nos. 145, 149, 160, 19 Apr., 16 May, 30 Aug. 1646. E 214c, fos. 12 454, 22 and 30 Aug. 1646. E 215b, fo. 222, 22 Sept. 1646.

[5] B.N. MS. fr. 18830, fo. 120ᵛ–121ʳ.   [7] U 29, fo. 62.

[6] Pillorget, *Les mouvements insurrectionnels*, pp. 619–31.

[8] B.N. MS.fr. 18830, fo. 158. E 1696, *passim*: numerous decrees from 1651 on this conflict.

Mazarin, they naturally tried to mobilize the towns behind them. The issues in the struggle, therefore, differed from province to province: but almost everywhere control of the towns was a vital issue. The Fronde thus demonstrated that when the central government was weak the nobles and the sovereign courts would seek to control the towns in their own interests. Recovery from the Fronde meant tighter oligarchical control, restricted electoral bodies and a narrow franchise. The intendants were needed to intervene in municipal politics on a hitherto unprecedented scale.

The history of Angers in the years after the Fronde provides an excellent illustration of this trend towards tighter oligarchical control. After the capitulation of the 'popular' party, the *Loricards*, at Angers on 28 February 1652, De Heere, the intendant, extracted an oath of loyalty from the various corporations of the town, including the clergy. The intendant removed the mayor and four *échevins* from office, and dismissed the captains, lieutenants, and ensigns of the militia.[1] Despite these measures Angers was still not quiet, and there was a strong party of *Malcontents* dedicated to continuing the Fronde. On 18 March 1652, there was a further riot. La Meilleraye, the military commander in Poitou and Anjou, arrived with troops and on 2 August exiled forty-two *Malcontents*. Although an amnesty was accorded in November, the *Malcontents* were allowed back to Angers only after taking a further oath of loyalty.[2] On 17 April 1653, in consideration of 'les cabales et monopolles qui se pratiquent ordinairement', Heere was authorized by a decree of the council of state to visit Angers and nominate the *échevins*.[3] Nomination to the municipality was practised in 1654 and 1655 also. Probably as a result of Servien's influence—the finance minister had lands in Anjou—the town was allowed to elect its representatives once more after 22 April 1656. The election of that year nevertheless resulted in 'monopoles, caballes et viollences'.[4] Worse still, there were two riots, on 2 and 22 October, against a new indirect tax. Hotman de Fontenay, the new intendant, arrived at the town with

[1] Débidour, *La Fronde angevine*, pp. 268–72. E 1700, no. 32, 5 Mar. 1652.
[2] Débidour, op. cit., pp. 289, 295, 399–400. X1b 8857, 11 Dec. 1652.
[3] Débidour, op. cit., p. 298. E 1700, no. 147.
[4] Débidour, op. cit., p. 305. E 1706, no. 51, 15 June 1656.

troops at the end of November. He immediately proposed a
new constitution for the town to Chancellor Séguier. Hotman's
views were accepted by the government. A decree of 21 April
1657 imposed the mayor and *échevins* of Angers for the next
two years.[1]

Elsewhere, events followed a similar pattern. The disturbances
at Béziers during the Fronde had been notorious. In 1655, the
consuls were named in a decree of the council of state, and
Bazin de Bezons, the intendant, was ordered to receive their
oaths of loyalty. The same procedure was followed in 1656,
although an illegal election was held on 12 November. In
1657, the same *consuls* were continued in office, but the political
divisions in the town continued. Finally, on 11 April 1658, the
council of state modified the constitution of Béziers. The
electors had to be twenty-five years of age and possess eight
livres of property on the land register (*compoix*). This was a
doubling of the traditional property qualification. The government sought by these means to restrict the artisans from participation in urban government at Béziers.[2] At Dijon, political
conflicts in 1654 and 1656 forced the king's council to reduce
the size of the municipal government from twenty to seven
échevins: on 4 August 1656, Bouchu, the intendant, was ordered
to investigate the 'factions et désobéissances' and ensure that
the small, nominated town council was established.[3] At Limoges
in September 1659, Claude Pellot nominated three of the 'plus
considérables et mieux intentionnez' as *consuls*. He confidently
predicted that 'ce nouvel ordre donnera le repos à cette ville qui
estoit en division et en confusion il y avoit trois ans pour ce sujet
du consulat'.[4]

At Aix-en-Provence, the royalist triumph was complete by
the end of 1659. A riot had broken out in this town in February
of that year, which had been led by a small group of *parlementaires* against Maynier d'Oppède, the *premier président* of the
Parlement of Aix. The majority of the *Parlement* was neutral
in the conflict, however, and after 3 March, a commission

<hr/>

[1] Débidour, op. cit., p. 322. Lebrun, 'Les soulèvements populaires à Angers',
pp. 132–3. B.L. Harleian 4490, fo. 98, 10 Dec. 1656. E 1706, no. 107, 8 Jan. 1657.
[2] Numerous decrees in E 1700, E 1706, and E 1708. Also E 1703, no. 368, 18
Oct. 1655. E 1711, no. 44, 18 June 1659. B.L. Harleian 4490, fo. 421, 4 Nov. 1657.
[3] E 1703, fo. 225, 19 Mar. 1654. E 1706, nos. 49, 58, 59, 8 June and 4 Aug. 1656.
[4] B.L. Harleian 4442, fo. 89, 22 Sept. 1659.

was set up by the *Parlement* to investigate the revolt. This did not satisfy the government. Bazin de Bezons, the intendant of Languedoc, and Verthamon, a *maître des requêtes*, were commissioned, together with six judges from the towns of Languedoc, to prosecute the rebels at Aix. They began their investigations on 23 April. About fifty or sixty rebels were prosecuted, and sentenced to be hanged, broken on the wheel, beheaded, sent to the galleys, or exiled.[1] Even Maynier d'Oppède thought the sentences unjust and considered that there was 'trop de vigueur et de sévérité' in the conduct of the commissioners:[2] his attitude was understandable, since the revolt seems to have been something of a damp squib. Unlike the revolts in 1630 and 1649, the first of which had been partially, the second completely, amnestied, that of 1659 at Aix was punished severely. The revolt provided a pretext for the removal of the political privileges of Aix. Maynier d'Oppède thought this 'essentiel au repos et à la paix de cette province',[3] and sent Séguier a memorandum on the subject. The result was that in August 1659, the *consulaires* were removed from participation in the municipal government. A system of co-option, subject to the approval of the election assembly, was adopted for the *consuls*. An interim executive committee of up to twelve councillors was created to check the power of the *consuls*, and assist them in the handling of day-to-day business concerning the town. The reforms thus had a number of checks and balances to prevent one sectional group from obtaining too much power; they were also intended to make elections peaceful affairs instead of opportunities for political and social conflict to come into the open.[4] Similarly, the riots at Marseille in 1659 and previous years were punished extremely severely (this time by a commission of the *Parlement* of Aix) and a completely new form of municipal government established after 5 March 1660.[5]

By interference in the electoral process, the nomination of compliant candidates for municipal office and modification of

---

[1] cf. the *jugements souverains*: B.L. Harleian 4442, fos. 12, 42–4, 67–8, 29 Apr., 4 Aug. 1659, 21 July 1660.
[2] B.L. Harleian 4493, fo. 70, 3 June 1659.
[3] B.L. Harleian 4493, fo. 78, 22 July 1659.
[4] Kettering, *Judicial politics*. Pillorget, *Les mouvements insurrectionnels*, p. 811.
[5] Pillorget, op. cit., pp. 820–7.

the urban constitutions, the intendants gained political control over the towns. This control was consolidated by their intervention in the realm of municipal finance. It is sometimes asserted that Colbert was the first minister of the French crown to do something about the reform of municipal finance.[1] In reality, as with many of Colbert's reforms, that minister did no more than apply himself with great tenacity to a problem which had long been recognized as serious: already by the time of Sully, the problem had been identified[2] and important liquidations of municipal debts were carried out in Provence[3] and the Dauphiné.[4] The verification of debts was continued under Richelieu, but on a much wider scale. The driving force behind the reform appears to have been D'Effiat, the capable and energetic *surintendant* between 1626 and 1632. D'Effiat chose Languedoc for a controlled experiment, since this province had experienced the military campaigns of Rohan in the 1620s, which resulted in enormous debts for the towns.[5] On 27 June 1631, a commission for the verification of debts was issued, which specified 'une exacte recherche en vérification de l'origine de toutes lesdites debtes en parfaite cognoissance'. The crown wished to select for this task 'quelques personnes dont la prud'homme, suffisance et capacité . . . soit cognue'. Their decisions would be subject to appeal, but this process would not be allowed to hinder the enquiry. On 16 October, instructions were issued to Le Maistre de Bellejambe, Mangot de Villarceaux, and Turpin de Verderonne, who together with Collet and Comihan, two *trésoriers* at Toulouse, were entitled 'commissaires députés par le Roy pour la vérification des debtes de Hault Languedoc'. They were empowered to verify the debts of the dioceses, towns, and communities, whether or not the king's council or the provincial Estates had already done so. Creditors were ordered to show their title-deeds to the commissioners, or else they stood to forfeit their claims. A copy of the municipal

---

[1] N. Temple, 'The control and exploitation of French towns during the *ancien regime*', *History*, clxxi (1966), 16, reprinted in *State and Society*, ed. Kierstead, p. 67.

[2] 120 a.p. 31, fo. 41, n.d., memorandum to Sully.

[3] By Guillaume du Vair. V6 1222, no. 20 (4), 1 Dec. 1603.

[4] By a commission headed by Méric de Vic: Esmonin, *Études*, p. 72. E 28b, fo. 309, 30 Dec. 1610. E 33a, fos. 149, 214, 25 and 27 Oct. 1611.

[5] In 1630, Charles Machault, the intendant, was examining the debts in the dioceses of Saint-Papoul, Carcassonne, Narbonne, and Anduze: E 103a, fos. 410, 413, 29 May 1630. V6 77, no. 6, 25 June 1630. V6 77, no. 2, 15 June 1630.

accounts was to be brought before the commissioners for them to ascertain whether a debt could be paid off without a new tax being levied. All coercion of payment of municipal debts was suspended while the investigation proceeded. The commissioners were to ensure that interest charged on the debts did not exceed 6·25 per cent. They were to determine whether or not the *consuls* had ordered payments legitimately, and whether any of the debts could be written off. In order to ensure that the same debt was not acquitted more than once, the commissioners were to extend their enquiry back to 1620. Finally, they were to draw up a report of their proceedings.[1] The work of the Languedoc commissioners was halted by the outbreak of the Montmorency rebellion, when they received powers to prosecute the rebels and to demolish private fortresses in the province. After the edict of Béziers was imposed on Languedoc in October 1632, the task of verifying the debts—including new ones contracted during the rebellion—was begun once more. This time, the work was carried out by Robert Miron and Antoine Le Camus, the new intendants.[2] They made considerable progress. On 21 July 1636 it was stated that all debts of the dioceses had been verified, while relatively few of the municipal debts still had to be checked. The work was considered sufficiently far advanced for it to be carried out during the sessions of the provincial Estates, by the intendants in their capacity as royal commissioners to the Estates.[3]

The verification of the debts of Languedoc had been conceived by D'Effiat as a once and for all task, capable of prompt solution. It proved to be nothing of the kind. New debts were continually being added to the old. On 30 June 1638, Schomberg, Miron, and Dupré were ordered by the council of finance to report within three months 'de ce qu'ilz estiment estre plus utile au bien et soulagement de ladite province pour le payement des debtes . . .'[4] The following year, the council of finance levied a tax of 1·2 million *livres*, equivalent to a half yearly payment of interest on the debt. The creditors of the Languedoc towns were thus forced by the intendants—who had to levy this tax—to contribute something towards the cost of the

[1] A.A.E. France 1629, fo. 32. A.G. A1 41, fos. 4, 5.
[2] E 132a, fo. 236, 10 July 1636. E 137a, fo. 54, 6 May 1637 (Miron and Dupré).
[3] E 1684, fo. 197.   [4] E 144b, fo. 391.

war.[1] Yet the government did very little to liquidate the debt
of Languedoc, which may be estimated at 12 million *livres* in
1639. Rather than regarding the municipal debts as a sign of
poverty, the finance ministers appear to have viewed them as
an indication of hidden, untaxed, urban wealth.[2] It was in
the financial interests of the government to verify the debts of
the towns. Whether or not anything was done to redeem the
debts depended on whether the short-term gain—a tax on the
creditors—outweighed the long-term financial interest of the
monarchy—a redemption of municipal debts in order to facilitate payment of the *taille*. Under Bullion, Bouthillier, and
D'Hémery, short-term gain was paramount.

The investigation into the debts of the towns was carried
out in other provinces apart from Languedoc. The council of
state ordered a general verification of the debts of Provence
on 16 November 1634.[3] In the following January, a commission was drawn up for Le Roy de La Potherie, Le Prévost
d'Herbelay, and Hubert, an *auditeur des comptes* at Paris.[4] The
Estates of Provence protested to the council against the activities of the commissioners. They claimed that Le Roy de La
Potherie and his colleagues were not 'informez des facultez
desdits communaultez et des us et coustumes du pais'. The
process of verification, they argued, would therefore be extremely lengthy and costly. The Estates offered to verify the
debts 'pardevant les juges des lieux'. The council rejected this
idea but suspended the work of the commissioners.[5] The investigation was resumed on 30 August. Étienne III d'Aligre and
Dreux d'Aubray were to act as intendants and commissioners
for the debt. In the technical aspects of their work, the intendants were to be assisted by Mallier, an *intendant des turcies*,
and Particelli, a *trésorier* at Lyon. In this investigation, the
commissioners were to pay careful attention to fraudulent
transactions, 'en retranchant d'icelles les parties uzuraires et

[1] E 148b, fo. 48, 9 Feb. 1639. E 179a, fo. 158, 15 Apr. 1643 (reduction of the
tax to 810,000 *livres*).
[2] cf. the speech of Charles Machault, the intendant, to the Estates at Pézénas in
1640: 'c'est louer sa richesse et son abondance pour ce qu'estant presque toutes
contractées au profit de ceux de la province eux-mesmes . . .'
[3] cf. E 122d, fo. 105, 31 Mar. 1635.
[4] A.G. A1 26, no. 147, 28 Jan. 1635.
[5] E 122d, fo. 105, 31 Mar. 1635 (collated copy).

illegitimes soit en principal ou intérest'. Interests were to be levied at five per cent on towns which could afford to pay this amount, and at four per cent on towns which could not. The commissioners were allowed two secretaries and appeals from their sentences were to be heard by the king's council only. On 23 April 1636, a new intendant—Jacques II Danès de Marly, a councillor of state—was appointed and this necessitated a reorganization of the procedure concerning the debt. Marly, Dubernet, the *premier président* of the *Parlement* of Aix, and Séguiran, the *premier président* of the *cour des comptes* of Aix, were given a joint presidency over a commission drawn from members of the *Parlement*. The commissioners could issue definitive sentences in all cases concerning the eighty-four indebted communities of Provence.[1] Again the experiment was short-lived. Marly was nominated bishop of Toulon and was replaced by Jean de Lauzon. On 29 August, Lauzon was given joint presidency with Dubernet and Séguiran in a commission which also included Perier and Peiresc, two councillors of the *Parlement*.[2] By February 1637, however, it appears that Lauzon and François Bochart, the two intendants, were acting on their own on the question of the debt.[3] As in the case of Languedoc, the verification of the debts in Provence had a fiscal purpose too. On 3 March 1638, Lauzon and Bochart were ordered to levy 690,000 *livres* on the creditors, which was to be paid directly to the crown.[4] The work on the debt was still not completed in 1647.[5]

There was also an investigation into the debts of the Dauphiné in the 1630s. In this case, the impetus came from the Third Estate of the province, which presented a request for verification to the council of finance on 17 August 1634. Jacques Talon, the intendant of the Dauphiné, was given the task.[6] Successively from 1635 to 1639, interest payments on the debts were suspended. Then on 26 March 1639, Lauzon was empowered to liquidate the debts, a task which was continued by his successors De Chazé and Sève. It was still not completed

---

[1] A.G. A1 32, no. 62, 23 Apr. 1636. E 130b, n.f., 31 May 1636.
[2] A.G. A1 32, no. 313.
[3] E 135b, fo. 459, 21 Feb. 1637.
[4] E 142a, fo. 71, 3 Mar. 1638. E 146a, fo. 429, 22 Sept. 1638
[5] E 170b, fo. 315, 24 May 1642. E 220a, fo. 447, 13 Feb. 1647.
[6] E 119a, fo. 254.

in 1648.[1] Burgundy experienced a thoroughgoing investigation into the debts. Work commenced on 5 March 1635, and
later Charles Machault, the intendant, presided over a commission which also included De Montjay, a *conseiller* in the
Parlement of Dijon, De Figen, a *maître des comptes* at Dijon, and
Catin, a *trésorier*. When this commission was increased to seven
by the inclusion of other judges or law graduates, it could issue
sentences without appeal.[2] There was work on the debt in other
provinces also—Verthamon in Guyenne,[3] Mesgrigny in the
Auvergne,[4] Laffemas and Choisy in Champagne,[5] and Montescot in the Île-de-France[6] were all active on this subject—but
on a smaller scale. There were also verifications of the debts in
the 'new' provinces such as Bresse,[7] Pignerola,[8] and Lorraine.[9]

It is clear that in the years after the Fronde there was no
comparable investigation into municipal finance. The problems
of financial administration were even greater in the 1650s than
they had been in the 1630s and 1640s. Servien and Foucquet
thus had other, more pressing, problems than the reform of
municipal finance. In December 1647, D'Hémery had decided
to divert the municipal *octrois*—the chief source of urban
revenue—to the treasury, and this decision was enforced by
Servien and Foucquet after 1654. With the loss of these revenues, the towns had no chance of balancing their accounts.
The debts of the towns thus grew substantially, quite apart
from additional costs that had been incurred during the
Fronde. The reform of municipal finance was meaningless unless
the towns had some chance in the future of becoming self-
sufficient financially.[10] The liquidation of the debts, therefore,
had to await the Peace of the Pyrenees and the restitution of
the *octrois*.[11] Foucquet recommenced the work when he ordered

---

[1] E 149b, fo. 155, 26 Mar. 1639. E 178a, fo. 282, 14 Mar. 1643. E 223a, fo. 197,
5 June 1647. E 229a, fo. 223, 11 Mar. 1648.

[2] E 151b, fo. 95, 18 June 1639.

[3] E 118b, fo. 134, 20 July 1634. E 119a, fo. 149, 12 Aug. 1634. E 120a, fo. 146,
20 Sept. 1634. E 120b, fo. 291, 25 Oct. 1634. E 125, fo. 540, 25 Aug. 1635.

[4] E 130b, n.f., 31 May 1636. E 136b, fo. 33, 1 Apr. 1637.

[5] E 121b, fo. 58, 2 Dec. 1634. E 129b, fo. 87, 20 Mar. 1636.

[6] E 215a, fo. 103, 5 Sept. 1646.   [7] E 119a, fo. 269, 17 Aug. 1634.

[8] E 119a, fo. 10, 2 Aug. 1634.   [9] E 122c, fo. 322, 8 Mar. 1635.

[10] For the loss of the *octrois* at Amiens: Deyon, *Amiens*, pp. 451–2, 461, 567
(Graph 56).

[11] Except in the Dauphiné, where Lefèvre de la Barre was charged with this
task: E 276a, fo. 1, 1 Apr. 1655.

the verification of debts in the province of Burgundy[1] and also at Toulouse[2] and Moulins.[3] Colbert, however, broadened the scope of the investigation: a verification of debts had not taken place in Brittany under Richelieu and Mazarin, but one took place in the 1660s. Other provinces, such as Languedoc, Burgundy, Provence, and the Dauphiné, which had experienced such investigations in the 1630s and 1640s, were not excluded from the verification of the debts under Colbert. The task of liquidating the debt took a long time, however: the process was interrupted during the Dutch war of 1672–84[4] and was still not complete by the time of Colbert's death.[5]

Thus if it is premature to talk of a *tutelle administrative* having been established by the intendants over the towns by 1661, it is clear that in the suppression of revolt, the modification of urban institutions, and the intervention in municipal finance, the intendants appointed by Richelieu and Mazarin had made substantial progress in undermining the autonomy of the towns. After 1661, there was little prospect of the nobles or the sovereign courts gaining control over the French towns, even assuming they possessed the political will to attempt such a seizure of power. The towns were never totally quiescent, their privileges were never totally removed: but the opportunities for rebellion and the assertion of fiscal independence had passed by the time that Louis XIV assumed personal rule in 1661.

[1] E 1714, no. 1, 2 Jan. 1661. The first date mentioned by P. de Saint-Jacob [*Documents relatifs à la communauté villageoise en Bourgogne du milieu du xviie siècle à la Révolution* (1962), p. 3] was 14 Mar. 1662.

[2] A.A.E. France 1634, fo. 23. B.L. Harleian 4442, fo. 194, 6 Mar. 1660. E 1711, no. 154, 15 Nov. 1660.

[3] Temple, 'Control of French towns', p. 19, reprinted in *State and society*, ed. Kierstead, p. 70.

[4] E 1795, fos. 299, 305. E 1800, nos. 103–12, 6 May 1679. E 1795, fo. 379, 17 Oct. 1679.

[5] For example, Languedoc: E 1832, no. 147, 6 Nov. 1685. E 1893, no. 19, 29 Mar. 1695.

CHAPTER XV

The Provincial Estates

THE ADMINISTRATIVE problems of seventeenth-century France were made more complex by the fact that certain provinces were in a privileged position. Most of these privileges were specific concessions of individual kings. The *Chartre aux Normands*, dating from the baronial rebellion of 1314–15, sought to guarantee the fundamental privileges of Normandy. It was confirmed in 1339, 1381, 1428 (by the English Regent, the duke of Bedford), 1462, and 1579. During the seventeenth century, the charter was frequently invoked, but never confirmed by the crown.[1] The Estates of Languedoc recalled the privileges granted by Charles VIII in March 1483 and May 1488, by François I in May 1522 (subsequently called the *Grande Chartre de Languedoc*), and by Henri II in May 1549.[2] The provinces that had become linked with France in the fifteenth century had done so on terms. The Dauphiné was not fully united with the kingdom until 1457, and with a guarantee of its privileges.[3] Louis XI took the duchy of Burgundy by force of arms in 1477, yet its privileges, too, were confirmed on the accession of Charles VIII.[4] The county of Provence was left to Louis XI in the last will and testament of Charles III of Anjou (10 December 1481). The will provided that the liberties of the county should be preserved by its new ruler.[5] The duchy of Brittany was linked to France by the marriage of

[1] H. Prentout, 'Les États provinciaux de Normandie', *Mémoires de l'Académie Nationale des Sciences, Arts et Belles-lettres de Caen*, ii (1926), 338–46. *Cahiers . . . Louis XIII et Louis XIV*, ed. Robillard de Beaurepaire, iii. 129–30.

[2] H. Gilles, *Les États de Languedoc au xve siècle* (Toulouse, 1965), p. 73. Gachon, *États de Languedoc*, pp. 21, n. 1, 44.

[3] A. Dussert, *Les États du Dauphiné aux xive et xve siècles* (Grenoble, 1915), p. 286. A. Dussert, 'Catherine de Médicis et les États du Dauphiné. Préludes du procès des tailles et arbitrage de la Reine Mère en 1579', *Bulletin de l'académie delphinale*, 6th ser., ii (1931), 141, 166–7.

[4] For the importance of 1477: H. Drouot, *Mayenne et la Bourgogne. Étude sur la Ligue, 1587–1596* (2 vols., Dijon, 1937), i. 100.

[5] The importance of the last will and testament to Provence in the seventeenth century is emphasized by Kettering, *Judicial politics*.

MAP. III. The provinces of France.

Stippled areas are those with provincial estates in 1661 and after.

Anne, the daughter of François II, the last duke, to Charles VIII (6 December 1491) and later to Louis XII (January 1498). The second of these marriage contracts was recalled by the Estates, together with the edict of union with France (August 1532) and the edict of July 1579 as the charters guaranteeing Breton privileges.[1]

Provincial privilege, enshrined in the form of charters, was clearly exercised at the expense of the rest of the kingdom. The

[1] A. Rébillon, *Les États de Bretagne de 1661 à 1789. Leur organisation. L'évolution de leurs pouvoirs. Leur administration financière* (Paris–Rennes, 1932), pp. 197–9.

privileged might well be exempted from the common law;[1] they certainly enjoyed the right to 'traiter avec le Roy soubs des conditions'.[2] Were these privileges inviolable? Even Caseneuve, the historian of the privileges of Languedoc, argued that they could be abrogated when this was required by the common good, but that in practice kings rarely did so.[3] The Estates agreed that sometimes their privileges had been abrogated. In August 1649, the Estates of Languedoc declared the edict of Béziers of October 1632 'contraire aux conditions sous lesquelles la province a esté unie à la couronne'. They demanded the return of Languedoc's 'anciens prérogatives, droits et libertés ...'[4] If provincial privilege was sometimes violated by kings, this only went to show that the continuance of privilege required that it be exercised with prudence and circumspection.[5] The intendants, as representatives of the government, were prepared to argue that special privileges were no longer allowable when there were 'nécessités pressantes pour le bien de l'état'. The argument that 'necessity knows no law' was bound to produce a degree of political conflict with the provincial Estates in time of war. The extent of that conflict depended very much on the strength of the regional assembly and the objectives of the government in the province concerned.

The essential privilege to be defended was the right of assembly, something which was not enjoyed generally in seventeenth-century France. The danger of assemblies from the point of view of the king, their desirability from the point of view of his subjects, were of course well known in the later middle ages. Jean Bodin had pointed out the importance of the right of assembly in the sixteenth century. In 1576, Bodin argued that this was the most important privilege of Normandy, Languedoc, Brittany, Burgundy, the Dauphiné, and Provence. 'Jamais les plaintes et doléances des pais gouvernez par élection-[s] ne sont veues, leues, ni presentées', he wrote, 'ou quoy que ce

---

[1] A.A.E. France 1634, fo. 245ᵛ, 12 Sept. 1646.

[2] A.A.E. France 1636, fo. 479, 13 Feb. 1656.

[3] Caseneuve, *Le franc-alleu et la province de Languedoc establi et défendu* (2nd ed., Toulouse, 1645), p. 75. This work was an elaborate reply to A. Galland, *Du franc-alleu et origines des droits seigneuriaux avec les loix données au pays d'Albigeois par Simon Comte Montfort l'an 1212* (1637).

[4] A.A.E. France 1634, fo. 409, 12 Aug. 1649.

[5] *Histoire générale de Languedoc*, ed. Roschach, xiv. 151.

soit, on n'y a jamais d'esgard, comme estant particulières . . .'
In contrast, he added, 'quand les collèges, les communautez,
les estats d'un pais, d'un peuple, d'un royaume font leur
plainte au Roy, il luy est malaisé de les refuser'.[1] Regional
assemblies were historically an alternative to the Estates-
General, a fact of which some assemblies were well aware. At
their meeting at Pézenas in 1650, the Estates of Languedoc
argued that they had 'sur cette province le mesme droit que les
États-Généraux du Royaume sur toute la France, pour
supplier le Roy de corriger et réformer les abus qui se glissent
et s'introduisent dans tous les corps de ladite province'.[2]

The comparison with the Estates-General was not without
paradox, however. The nature of representation in the Estates-
General had never been clearly defined. Kings summoned them
when they were weak, and neglected to do so when they were
strong. The Estates-General of 1614 had been forced on the
government by a rebellion of the nobles; the projected sessions in 1649 and 1651 arose from similar circumstances. The
Estates-General was summoned at will: it could not appropriate
a permanent position in the constitution for precisely this
reason. But the regional Estates sought to achieve a permanent
position in provincial political life. The Estates of Normandy,
for example, cited the *Chartre aux Normands* as late as 1655 in
order to justify the claim that they should meet annually. Their
hopes for 'la liberté d' . . . assemblée, interrompue depuis unze
ans' were dashed however, when the ministers replied that
letters of summons would be issued only when the king judged
it appropriate.[3] The comparison with the Estates-General was
equally dubious when it came to the right of consent to
taxation. The Estates of Languedoc in 1650, although they
referred to themselves as a regional Estates-General, nevertheless emphasized that 'sur le fait des impositions' their assembly
'est en droit'.[4] The point was clear: the Estates-General had
never enjoyed the right of consent to all taxes, despite the myths
of the sixteenth-century political theorists. Nor had by any
means all the regional assemblies enjoyed this right. The third

[1] Bodin, *Les six livres de la République* (ed. 1583), p. 501.
[2] A.A.E. France 1634, fo. 493, Oct. 1650.
[3] *Cahiers . . . Louis XIII et Louis XIV*, ed. Robillard de Beaurepaire, iii. 129–30.
[4] A.A.E. France 1634, fos. 493, 505, Oct. and 21 Nov. 1650.

paradox was in the right of legislation. The Estates-General could not make laws. It could draw up general *doléances*, based on a number of regional *cahiers*. These might then be enacted by the king's council. General assemblies had few powers of ratification—this was the task of the sovereign courts. The ratifying powers of the regional assemblies were perhaps greater, but then so too were the opportunities for conflict with the sovereign courts. The crucial aspect of legislation, however, was the extent to which the *cahiers* of the regional assemblies influenced the ministers. The Estates of Normandy met at Rouen in 1631 without having received a reply to their *cahier* from the previous session. When the ministers finally replied, on 1 June 1633, they gave similarly negative answers to two sets of remonstrances.[1] The delay of the government in answering the *cahiers* was one ominous indication that the future of the regional assembly was in doubt. Many of the answers were evasive. The king always hoped to 'donner ce contentement' to his subjects, but only after a peace treaty which appeared yearly more distant.[2] Those assemblies whose existence was threatened doubted whether the king's word could be trusted. The Estates of Normandy in 1655 wanted registration of the replies to their *cahiers* by the sovereign courts.[3] On an earlier occasion, they lamented that they were 'la risée des partisans' because the financiers obtained decrees of the council reversing ministerial replies to the *cahiers*. The ministers did not deny that this had happened; they merely conceded that this would occur in future only after an examination of the merits of the case.[4]

The ministers found provincial Estates a nuisance. They had to be dealt with separately; the taxes raised from these provinces were usually subject to negotiation and could not be increased at will. By the time of Richelieu and Mazarin, most members of the government would have preferred France to have been governed without the provincial Estates. The ideal and the fulfilment of the ideal were two quite different matters, however. The deliberate assault on provincial privilege was a risky business and might cause more trouble than it was worth. Henri IV and Sully certainly commenced the work in some—

---

[1] *Cahiers . . . Louis XIII et Louis XIV*, ed. Robillard de Beaurepaire, ii. 191, 194, 212.   [2] ibid., iii. 2–3.   [3] ibid., iii. 131.   [4] ibid., iii. 3–4.

but by no means all—of the provinces.[1] It has been argued
that 'the assault on the provincial Estates was renewed with
unparalleled vigour between 1628 and 1630 when orders were
issued creating *élections* in the Dauphiné, Burgundy, Languedoc,
and Provence'.[2] Who was responsible for this apparent royal
policy of undermining the provincial Estates? The work may
well have been continued by Michel de Marillac, who was
surintendant des finances between 1624 and 1626 and Keeper of the
Seals between 1626 and 1630. Marillac was dismissed on the
Day of Dupes (10 November 1630) and after this event,
Richelieu, his victorious rival, is alleged to have 'abandoned
the effort to create an absolute monarchy' through the destruction of the provincial Estates.[3]

Great caution is needed, however, before the responsibility
for royal policy is assigned to one man (Marillac)—a man,
moreover, who was not the chief minister of the king. The
chronology of the attack on the provincial Estates does not
accord conclusively with the theory that Marillac was the
primum mobile.[4] Nor is it conclusively demonstrated that Marillac
and the *dévot* party he led implied by their commitment to
'réforme au dedans du royaume' the destruction of provincial
autonomy.[5] Finally, it is by no means certain that the creation
of *élections* necessarily and inevitably meant the destruction of
the provincial estates.[6] The creation of *élections* was in any case a
fiscal device, one of the numerous *traités* prepared by the *surintendant* and *intendants des finances*. It could be prevented by a
province if satisfactory compensation were offered to the
financiers who had contracted with the government.[7] The

[1] J. R. Major, 'Henry IV and Guyenne. A study concerning origins of royal
absolutism', *French Historical Studies*, iv (1966), 376–81, reprinted in *State and society*,
ed. Kierstead, pp. 12–16. Buisseret, *Sully*, pp. 97–8.

[2] Major, 'Henry IV and Guyenne', p. 383, reprinted in *State and society*, ed.
Kierstead, p. 17.   [3] ibid.

[4] Thus although *élections* were introduced in Provence in 1629–31, and then
abolished, the Estates disappeared after 1639. The creation of *élections* in Basse-
Navarre and Béarn did not occur until May 1632: A. D'Estrée, *La Basse Navarre et
ses institutions de 1620 à la Révolution* (Zaragoza, 1955), p. 156.

[5] But cf. Mongrédien, *La journée des dupes*, p. 36.

[6] They coexisted in Normandy for many years before the demise of the Estates
in 1655. They coexisted in Burgundy although the new creation of *élections* was
bought off by the Estates in 1631.

[7] The Estates of Provence, meeting at Tarascon, offered 1·5 million *livres* payable over eight years: E 105b, fo. 297, 29 Mar. 1631. The Estates of Burgundy

threat to the privileges of the local Estates became a serious political problem only when the province failed to offer sufficient compensation. As a former finance minister, and président of the council of finance between 1626 and 1630, Marillac was well acquainted with these facts of life. It is hardly necessary to view Marillac as the proponent of such measures, moreover. In normal circumstances, they would have been the concern of D'Effiat, the *surintendant des finances* between 1626 and 1632, who was an appointee of Richelieu. In general, Marillac favoured temporization and conciliation, while D'Effiat was more authoritarian. Such fragmentary evidence as exists suggest that it was D'Effiat not Marillac who insisted on high rates of compensation by the provinces affected by the creation of *élections*.

The creation of *élections*, therefore, might imply the beginning of an assault on the provincial Estates; but it did not necessarily commit the government one way or another. A period of negotiation between the government and the province began. If the province demonstrated the capacity for unified resistance to the government–as did Provence in 1630–1, Burgundy in 1630–1, Languedoc in 1630–2, and Navarre-Béarn in 1632–3— then it might escape, usually at a price. If the province proved incapable of such resistance, the destruction of the representative institution was only a matter of time. In general, a distinction may be made between representative institutions in areas of income tax (*taille personnelle*) and those in areas of land tax (*taille réelle*).[1] In most—but not all—areas of *taille réelle*, representative institutions survived; in most—but not all— areas of *taille personnelle* they did not. The type of fiscal regime was not coincidental with the survival of the provincial Estates: the land tax was almost invariably administered by the Estates themselves and it was a dangerous venture to alter existing procedures. The only example of the successful creation of

offered 1·6 million: E 106b–107a, fo. 309, [?] July 1631. Both offers were ratified by the council. For the *traité* of Jacques Le Feroz, sieur de Saint-Marcel, and Claude Vanel for 22 *élections* in Languedoc (22 July 1629): cf. V6 73, no. 50, 28 Nov. 1629. The Estates eventually paid 2,885,000 *livres* to reimburse the tax-contractors: cf. E 117b, fo. 345, 17 June 1634.

[1] On land tax: Esmonin, *Études*, pp. 167–73. G. Frêche, 'Compoix, propriété foncière, fiscalité et démographie historique en pays de taille réelle (xvie–xviiie siècles)', *Revue d'Histoire Moderne et Contemporaine*, xviii (1971), 321–53. For an English comparison: W. R. Ward, *The English land-tax in the eighteenth century* (Oxford, 1953).

élections in an area of land tax were the eleven *élections* created in Guyenne in 1621–2. The procedure was carefully supervised by Séguier, the intendant,[1] and may have had a political rather than fiscal purpose.[2]

The assault on the local Estates was not new at the time of Richelieu. Henri IV had declared to Matignon, the lieutenant-general in Guyenne: 'il me semble que le temps n'est pas propre pour faire telles assemblées, lesquelles ordinairement tendent plus à descharger mes subjects de despenses qu'à me fortiffier et assister en mes affaires.' The king added that the great weakness of local asemblies was that 'chacun ne regarde pas plus loin . . . que à sa commodité particulière . . .' The king was at war with Spain. For this reason, he asked Matignon to defer the meeting of the Estates of Guyenne until a 'temps plus opportun'.[3] Henri IV and Sully later determined to establish *élections* in Guyenne, however, and the provincial estates— which were of recent origin—went into abeyance. Condé still referred to Guyenne as a *pays d'états* as late as 1638–9, but the meeting which he summoned at Bordeaux in November 1638 was composed of lieutenants-general of the *sénéchaussées*, not elected representatives.[4]

Henri IV's words with regard to Guyenne foreshadowed the assault on another representative institution: the Estates of Périgord. The assembly was never forgiven by the government for championing the grievances of the rural taxpayers at the time of the rebellion of the *Croquants* in 1593–5.[5] In 1606, the syndic of the Estates of Périgord presented a request to the council that the assembly should meet once again, and an executive committee of the institution survived until this date or

---

[1] E 74b, fo. 265, 16 May 1623.

[2] Bercé, *Histoire des croquants*, i. 88, argues that the area was predominantly protestant while the *élus* were catholic.

[3] *Recueil des lettres missives de Henri IV*, ed. M. Berger de Xivrey and J. Guadet (9 vols., 1843–76), iv. 343 (18 Apr. 1595). Major, 'Henry IV and Guyenne', p. 367, n. 7, reprinted in *State and society*, ed. Kierstead, pp. 18–19.

[4] Bercé, *Histoire des croquants*, i. 107. J. R. Major, 'French representative assemblies. Research opportunities and research published', *Studies in medieval and renaissance history*, *I.*, ed. W. M. Bowsky (Lincoln, Nebr., 1964), p. 202, n. 66. E 148b, fo. 280, 16 Feb. 1639.

[5] L. de Cardenal, 'Les derniers réunions des trois ordres du Périgord avant la Révolution', *Études présentées à la commission internationale pour l'histoire des assemblées d'États*, ii (1937), 118. Bercé, *Histoire des croquants*, i. 262.

thereabout. On 6 July 1611, however, Marie de Médicis announced that 'de telles réunions ne pouvaient résulter que de mauvais résolutions au préjudice au service du Roy et au bien et au repos des ses sujets'.[1] This was the last that was heard of the Estates of Périgord. The *Croquants* of 1637 demanded that the government should 'rend[re] cette province pays d'Estat' once more—but for obvious reasons, this demand was rejected.[2] The Estates of the Auvergne were in decline,[3] while those of Poitou had disappeared[4] by the time of Richelieu's ministry.

The clearest example of the destruction of a local representative institution in an area of *taille personnelle* at the time of Richelieu is provided by the Dauphiné, whose Estates did not meet between 1628 and 1788. The Dauphiné lost its Estates because the province was divided, with the Third Estate campaigning actively for the destruction of an institution which had operated against its interests since 1554. Originally, the Estates of the Dauphiné had deliberated and voted in one assembly—as did the Estates of Languedoc. In the course of the sixteenth century, however, voting by the separate orders had become the rule.[5] The origins of the conflict in the Dauphiné lay in a crucial decision of the Estates taken on 16 February 1554. The Estates declared on this occasion that future decisions would be binding if two of the three orders were in agreement, provided that there were an unspecified, but not necessarily large, number of votes in favour of the measure in the third order. At the same time, the clergy and nobility were declared exempt from taxation on all their existing landholdings—this exemption was extended into the future without time limit.[6] The functioning of the Estates and the nature of the fiscal regime in the Dauphiné were thus linked inextricably from 1554 onwards. The clergy and the nobility were determined to co-operate in the defence of their fiscal privileges. They would always be able to count on the votes of a few clients in the

[1] Cardenal, 'Les derniers réunions', p. 118.

[2] ibid., pp. 122–3. *Lettres . . . au Chancelier Séguier*, ed. Mousnier, ii. 1109. Bercé, *Histoire des croquants*, i. 418–19, ii. 754. The nobles requested a meeting of the provincial Estates in 1651: Bercé, op. cit., ii. 815.

[3] Though there are sporadic references to meetings of the Estates of both Bas and Haut Auvergne: E 153c, fo. 306, 14 Dec. 1639. E 200a, fo. 339, 8 Mar. 1645.

[4] J. M. Tyrrell, *A history of the Estates of Poitou* (The Hague–Paris, 1968). These Estates had not enjoyed significant fiscal powers after 1435, however.

[5] Dussert, *États du Dauphiné*, pp. 311–13.   [6] ibid., pp. 313, 336.

Third Estate. On the other hand, the majority of the Third Estate contested the legality of the decision, which had been taken by 43 members of the first two estates and only 13 members 'du tiers estat, les plus ignorans et les plus grossiers'.[1] The decision was against immediate precedent[2] and also against the medieval principle *quod omnes tangit . . .* ('ce qui se fait pour les affaires de tous doit être par tous supporté . . .').[3]

From the meeting of the Estates at Romans in 1575, when the Third Estate declared that the institution was not functioning properly, until the implementation of the land tax in 1639 the conflict remained a permanent feature in the Dauphiné. The Third Estate claimed that it had no representative of its own and demanded a *procureur spécial*.[4] It wanted a doubling of representation in the Estates to achieve numerical equality with the other two orders[5]—a demand which was not achieved until 1788. It wanted the abolition of new offices which carried fiscal exemptions.[6] Above all, it wanted the introduction of the system of land tax, since this would require the privileged orders to pay tax on their *terres roturiers*.[7] Attempts at conciliation in 1575 and 1579 failed. The cause of the Third Estate was gravely compromised by the revolt of the peasants of the Dauphiné (the *ligue des vilains*) in 1579–80. The problem became more acute as time passed. The amount demanded by the crown in taxes increased. So did the number of fiscal exemptions. There was thus less and less taxable land upon which to base the *taille*. By the end of the wars of religion, the problem had become desperate.[8] On 11 October 1597, the Third Estate agreed to forget disagreements and to pursue the case with vigour at the king's council. The result—the decree of 15 April 1602—was a disaster for the Third Estate. The exemptions of the first two orders were upheld, and were to apply to their peasant farmers too. The Third Estate had proved no match for Lesdiguières, the lieutenant-general, who had sided with the nobles.[9]

---

[1] ibid., p. 336, n. 3. A. Lacroix, 'Claude Brosse et les tailles', *Bulletin de la Société Départementale d'Archéologie et de Statistique de la Drôme*, xxxii (1898), 64–6.
[2] Dussert, 'Catherine de Médicis', p. 160.
[3] ibid., p. 131.   [4] ibid., pp. 132, 134, 142, 170.
[5] ibid., pp. 142, 168–9, 172.   [6] ibid., p. 133.   [7] ibid., pp. 160–1.
[8] P. Cavard, *La réforme et les guerres de religion à Vienne* (Vienne, 1950), pp. 398–405.
[9] Lacroix, 'Claude Brosse', *Bulletin . . . de la Drôme*, xxxii (1898), 142–60, 233–48.

After 1602, the cause of the Third Estate of the Dauphiné
was led by Claude Brosse. Brosse's dedication led him into
considerable personal sacrifice: between January and March
1631 he was imprisoned on orders of the *Parlement* of Grenoble.[1]
Brosse's first achievement was the abolition of the Estates in
1628. A variety of assemblies were held after this date until
perhaps 1670, but none had a comparable authority to that
enjoyed by even the divided Estates of the Dauphiné.[2] The
creation of *élections* in 1628, however, demonstrated that Brosse
had by no means won the battle to introduce the land tax. The
existence of *élections* implied the continuance of the system of
taille personnelle. On the other hand, Brosse won the crucial
argument which was that the province was too poor to reimburse the tax contractor if the *élections* were abolished.[3] On
21 December 1632, Brosse presented a *cahier* to the council of
state demanding the establishment of a land tax on the basis of
the lands held by the Third Estate in 1461.[4] On 4 August 1633,
the council ordered the first two Estates of the Dauphiné to
state their objections to Jacques Talon, the intendant. The
result was a decree issued on 31 May 1634 following the report
of Talon to the council. It was a substantial victory for Brosse
and the Third Estate, since the government ordered the
establishment of a system of land tax. The land register (*cadastre*)
was to be modelled on that of 1461, comprising 4,750 hearths.
The dates of clerical and noble landownership were relatively
unfavourable to the third estate, however.[5] Nevertheless, the
Third Estate had at last found its champion—in the person of
the intendant. The 'noblesse de l'une et l'autre robe' declared
Talon to be the 'partisan déclaré du tiers ordre'. They also
accused him of corruption. Since these accusations were a
direct criticism of government policy, they were rejected by the
council on 21 February 1637.[6] The nobles and office-holders

[1] ibid., xxxii (1898), 368; xxxiii(1899), 75–80. E 105b, fo. 55, 6 Mar. 1631.

[2] Major, 'French representative assemblies', p. 194.

[3] Rejection of the request of the *procureur-sindic* of the Estates: E 117a, fo. 106,
22 Apr. 1634.

[4] E 109b, fo. 421.

[5] Lacroix, 'Claude Brosse', *Bulletin . . . de la Drôme*, xxxiii (1899), 236. AD + 228,
31 May 1634.

[6] Esmonin, *Études*, p. 76. Lacroix, 'Claude Brosse', *Bulletin . . . de la Drôme*,
xxxiii (1899), 311–12. E 135a, fo. 454, 31 Jan. 1637. E 135b, fo. 464, 21 Feb.
1637.

organized assemblies at Grenoble in 1636–7, however; and tried to start riots against the land tax.[1]

It was scarcely surprising, therefore, that the ministers took considerable trouble between November 1637 and April 1638 in drawing up the commission for Helie Laisné, Talon's successor. The province of the Dauphiné was part of the departmental responsibilities of Sublet des Noyers. Sublet, or one of his chief clerks, drew up the commission of the intendant. Bullion, the *surintendant des finances*, then commented in detail on the proposed document. Sublet implied in the phrasing of the original commission that Laisné's commission had been desired by the Third Estate of the Dauphiné. Bullion pointed out that this was not the case. Laisné's proposals, which were enacted in the decree of 24 October 1639, marked a further retreat on the date of landownership—and a further concession to the nobles and office-holders. Sublet had allowed the possibility of 'plaintes et remonstrances' by the nobles to the intendant. Bullion objected that while general complaints might be permissible, to accept individual complaints would 'introduire une confusion'. The fundamental disagreement, however, was on the purpose of Laisné's commission. Sublet had conceived the purpose as 'le bien commun des trois ordres . . . et le restablissement du repos et d'une parfaitte union d'entr'eux'. Bullion's objections in this respect were much more far-reaching. He considered that such phrasing would re-open the whole issue of the land tax, which had been decided in favour of the Third Estate. Sublet's wording had allowed the possibility of assemblies in the Dauphiné. Bullion objected on three counts. Assemblies in the province had been prohibited because of recent disturbances. If assemblies were allowed, these would be used by the nobles and office-holders to escape payment of the *taille* on their *terres roturiers*. Assemblies would create 'une division perpétuelle' in the province and would reduce the Third Estate to despair.[2] The Dauphiné is thus an excellent example of the policy of divide and rule in action. The memory of the divisions between the privileged and non-privileged orders

[1] E 134c, fos, 197, 338, 20 and 31 Dec. 1636. E 139a, fo. 310, 22 Aug. 1637.
[2] For the discussion between Sublet and Bullion: A.G. A1 49, nos. 256, 258, 19 Nov. 1637 and 1 Apr. 1638. For the legislation: Lacroix, 'Claude Brosse', *Bulletin . . . de la Drôme*, xxxiii (1899), 314–17. E 150a, fo. 87, 6 Apr. 1639. E 155b, fo. 362, 12 May 1640. E 200a, fo. 288, 4 Mar. 1645. E 201a, fo. 373, 6 Apr. 1645.

was undoubtedly a major reason why there was no serious outbreak of the Fronde in the Dauphiné.

The Estates of Normandy were under severe assault during Richelieu's ministry too. The proliferation of *élections* in the sixteenth century had given the crown an alternative basis for fiscal administration and precluded the establishment by the Estates of a viable system of administration of its own. The Estates might protest against 'le nombre effréné d'officiers qui sont en chaque Élection' in 1624,[1] but by then it was too late to destroy the system of *élections* altogether. The Estates had their greatest moment in 1578, when they reduced the level of taxes to that of Louis XII's reign.[2] Thereafter, they frequently demanded a reduction of the *taille* but the royal commissioners ordered the levy of the full amount demanded by the government, although they temporarily suspended the levy awaiting further instructions. This activity of the royal commissioners clearly prejudiced the Estates' right of consent.[3] Under Henri IV the first clear evidence of a reluctance to summon the Estates became manifest, and this tendency was more apparent in the following reign.[4] The Estates clearly regarded the interruption in their meetings between 1639 and 1643 as a consequence of the revolt of the *Va-Nu-Pieds* 'dont le nom nous est terrible . . .'[5] There was no major revolt in Normandy between 1644 and 1648, yet the Estates were not summoned in those years. The duc de Longueville brought Normandy into the Fronde in 1649 and discredited the Estates still further by his action.[6] The decline of the Estates of Normandy may thus be seen as an indirect consequence of the Fronde,[7] its demise being the result of the assemblies of the nobility in 1657-9. The motives of the government in summoning the last three Estates of Normandy were scarcely conducive to a healthy survival of that institution. In 1638, the comte de Guiche

---

[1] *Cahiers . . . Louis XIII et Louis XIV*, ed. Robillard de Beaurepaire, ii. 150-1.

[2] Prentout, 'États de Normandie', ii. 150-1.   [3] ibid., ii. 153-4.

[4] The Estates were not summoned in 1615, 1621, 1625, 1628, 1632, 1635, 1636, 1639, 1640, 1641, and 1642.

[5] *Cahiers . . . Louis XIII et Louis XIV*, ed. Robillard de Beaurepaire, iii. 77.

[6] cf. the dismissal of Jacques Baudry, the *procureur-syndic* of the Estates, who was regarded as a supporter of Longueville: Prentout, 'États de Normandie', ii. 387-9.

[7] Logié, *La Fronde en Normandie*, iii. 145-8.

wanted an assembly because he had recently been appointed lieutenant-general of upper Normandy. In 1643 Longueville wanted them in order to 'concilie[r] les affections du peuple'— to make himself more popular in the province at the beginning of a royal minority. In 1655, it was Longueville who asked for them once more, presumably in the hope of restoring his reputation in Normandy which was somewhat tarnished as a result of his dealings during the Fronde. In no case did the pressure for representation come from the province itself. In 1657, Harlay, the archbishop of Rouen, a known opponent of Mazarin, demanded the summoning of the Estates. The Normans themselves were quiet. As Rouxel de Médavy, the bishop of Séez, told Mazarin, 'pour tous les cahiers refusés ny pour tous les Estats renouvelés n'en ayés jamais d'inquiétude'. The king was 'le maistre' in Normandy, he declared, unless the English arrived with a large and well-disciplined army, and unless Condé joined the invasion force—in this case there was a serious danger that they would be greeted with popular support.[1]

The demise of the Estates of Normandy may be attributed in part to a failure of the system of representation. Representation was based on the *bailliages*. At the sessions of 1643, there were seven representatives of the clergy, eight representatives of the nobles, and 35 representatives of the *vicomtés*, that is to say, members of the Third Estate.[2] The nobles in Normandy showed little inclination to participate in the electoral process. The *bailliage* of Rouen, the most important electoral area in the province, never had more than 37 nobles present at the time of elections to the Estates between 1610 and 1655. The record figure was in 1655, when the Estates were revived after an interval of twelve years. In 1630, when sessions were held more regularly, not one noble presented himself at the election in Rouen. In contrast, the nobles turned out to the national elections—132 nobles elected the representative of the Second Estate to the Estates-General of 1614.[3] Certainly the Third Estate was much more willing to participate in the electoral process. Since the office-holders were excluded, powerful

[1] P. Le Cacheux, 'Documents concernant les États de Normandie de février 1655', *Société de l'historie de Normandie. Mélanges. Documents.* 5th ser. (1898—published 1901), 140–1. Prentout, 'États de Normandie', ii. 366.
[2] *Cahiers . . . Louis XIII et Louis XIV*, ed. Robillard de Beaurepaire, iii. 291–5.
[3] ibid., iii. xviii–xix.

representatives could not be selected,[1] but there is evidence in 1600 that the representatives of the rural parishes as well as the towns participated in the elections.[2] During the reign of Henri IV, the franchise was thus wider geographically than was the case elsewhere in France, although it is an open question whether this was still the case during the reign of Louis XIII.

A crucial weakness of the Estates was the fact that they only met for a few days. The last session in 1655 was to have met only for three days 'en la manière accoustumée'. The meeting lasted for ten days, however, and because of this provoked the wrath of the ministers. Such a delay permitted seditious speeches, letters from the towns to their delegates, 'et tous les esprits s'eschauffent dans la discussion de tous leurs subjects de plainte, ce qui aliénera sans doute les esprits et nuira aux affaires du Roy'. Delay allowed issues to be debated. The ministers wanted short sessions, 'cela seulement pour la forme', their aim being to 'fermer la bouche à quiconque se voudra eschaper'. Such at least were the motives of the ministers in 1655.[3] Their motives during the earlier part of Richelieu's ministry may have been less clear-cut. After the Day of Dupes, however, there can be little doubt that fiscal necessity pushed the ministers towards the policy of abolishing the Estates of Normandy altogether. Taxes had to be increased and Normandy would have to contribute disproportionately towards the war effort. Yet in 1630 the Estates demanded a reduction of the *taille*,[4] a policy which they maintained consistently. The vote for the *généralité* of Caen provides a clear illustration. In 1631, the Estates voted 473,461 *livres* yet the government levied 1,075,140 *livres*. In 1634, the vote was reduced to 400,000 *livres* yet the government increased its levy to 1,908,993 *livres*. In 1638 and 1643, the Estates voted to halve the amount levied, which had risen to 3,198,742 *livres* and 3,233,799 *livres* respectively. The Estates realized that their assemblies under Richelieu and Mazarin were nothing more than 'une ombre de l'ancienne liberté . . .'[5]

---

[1] ibid., iii. xix–xx.

[2] M. Baudot, 'La représentation du Tiers-État aux États-provinciaux de Normandie', *Mémoires de l'Académie Nationale de Caen*, new ser., v (1929), 136.

[3] Le Cacheux, 'Documents', pp. 152–3. Prentout, 'États de Normandie', ii. 367–8.

[4] *Cahiers . . . Louis XIII et Louis XIV*, ed. Robillard de Beaurepaire, iii. 175–6.

[5] ibid., iii. 313.

The council of finance ordered the taxes for Normandy without reference to the Estates.[1] The Estates recognized the futility of their efforts bearing in mind that in the other *pays d'états* taxation was 'le sujet principal' of the assembly of the three orders.[2] By 1655 the ministers were demanding that the Estates should listen to the commissions of the *taille* when they were read out, and then depart without any deliberation at all.[3]

The decline of the Estates of Normandy was inevitable, perhaps, because any opposition, however weak, to highly unpopular war taxes in a vital province was feared by the ministers. Their demise was hastened by their opposition to the system of war finance and to the intendants. The Estates criticized the financiers in 1624 and 1634.[4] In 1638, the assembly declared Normandy to be 'rongé des partisans de toutes sortes d'inventions'.[5] The opposition of the Estates in 1643 was much more vocal, however, for the simple reason that by this date the system of war finance had been developed to its fullest extent. The Estates were no less vocal on the subject of the intendants. Already in 1638, they had denounced the *régalement* of the *taille* by the intendants as 'ce régalement prétendu' which had been nothing less than 'un vrai desreiglement'. They had also passed comment in that year on 'la direction d'une intendance qui ... a passé sur les formes pour attaindre au plustost au but de sa commission'. Five years later the Estates were much more explicit. They declared the commissions of the intendants to be 'tousjours au-dessous d'une compagnie souveraine', which denied the juridicial basis of the powers of the intendants. They wanted the decisions of the intendants on the *taille* to be subject to appeal in the *cour des aides* of Rouen. Finally, they wanted a deputy of the third Estate to assist in the assessments of the *taille*.[6]

Many of these issues were raised once more in the last session of the Estates in 1655. The reinstatement of the *receveurs-généraux* was again demanded; so too was the abolition of the levy of the *taille* by the financiers—this time 'à peine du crime de lèse-majesté'—and a renunciation of the use of force in the levy

---

[1] E 185b, fo. 78, 16 Dec. 1643.

[2] *Cahiers ... Louis XIII et Louis XIV*, ed. Robillard de Beaurepaire, iii. 109.

[3] Le Cacheux, loc. cit. Prentout, loc. cit.

[4] *Cahiers ... Louis XIII et Louis XIV*, ed. Robillard de Beaurepaire, ii. 81; iii. 3–4.

[5] ibid., iii. 72.   [6] ibid., iii. 55, 59, 105–7, 113–14, 116–17.

of taxation. The debates went further than the *cahiers*, however. The deputies were convinced that the only reason for the continuation of the system of war finance was that the ministers 'ont part dans les profits'. The deputies wanted the *élus* to be allowed to levy the *taille*, and to remit the interest paid to the financiers as a concession to the taxpayers. The deputies argued that as the victories of the king had increased so too had the amount of taxes he levied. They demanded the recall of the intendants who had acquired 'la haine universelle'. 'On ne peut détromper le peuple', the bishop of Séez wrote to Mazarin, 'que ces Messieurs [the intendants] n'aient intéressement dans les traittants et qu'ainsi qu'ils ne soient juges et parties tout ensemble.' Only after the intervention of the duc de Longueville was the article demanding the suppression of the intendants removed from the *cahier*.[1] The programme of the Estates of Normandy in 1655 was essentially that of the *Chambre Saint-Louis* in 1648— the abolition of the financiers, the recall of the intendants, a remission on the taxes equivalent to the interest rate charged by the financiers. It was rejected for the same reasons: the demands of the war and the defence of the king's sovereignty. The ministers could always argue that they were operating under emergency conditions, requiring prompt action, for as long as the war lasted. The test of their intentions would be in the years immediately after the signing of the peace of the Pyrenees. In the autumn of 1660, the commissions of the *taille* which were sent from Paris for the fiscal year 1661 made no mention of the Estates. The *procureur-syndic* presented a request to the council of finance, and obtained a decision, on 16 December 1660, that 'cela ne soit tiré à conséquence à l'advenir'.[2] But a precedent had been established. The Estates were not summoned. Only the *procureur-syndic*, the *trésorier*, and the *greffier* of the Estates remained. In 1666, Colbert bought out their offices and with them disappeared the last trace of the Estates of Normandy.

Not all the Estates in areas of *taille personnelle* suffered a similar fate to those of Poitou, the Périgord, Guyenne, the Dauphiné,

[1] ibid., iii. 135. *Cahiers des États de Normandie de février 1655 suivi des remontrances présentées au roi par les députés des États en décembre 1657*, ed. Robillard de Beaurepaire (Rouen, n.d.), pp. 6–7. Le Cacheux, 'Documents', pp. 130–1, 135, 139. Prentout, 'États de Normandie', ii. 364–6.
[2] E 340, fo. 265.

and Normandy. The Estates of Burgundy are a striking example of the survival of a representative institution even after the creation of *élections*. The case of Burgundy is all the more surprising because Henri IV singled out its deputies for violent criticism in 1608.[1] The Estates of Burgundy did not present great dangers to the government, however. The province was relatively small,[2] and the Burgundians were renowned for their 'politesse',[3] a characteristic which some members of the government might interpret as political ineffectiveness. The sessions of the Estates were, moreover, triennial. This made continuity of opposition to the government difficult to sustain, especially as the sessions of the Estates were short and rarely lasted twenty days.[4] In the interim between meetings of the Estates an executive committee called the *élus généraux* was supposed to defend the interests of the province,[5] although there was a suspicion about the political independence of this committee. The *élus généraux* negotiated with the government for the purchase of exemption for Burgundy from the winter quarter for the troops.[6] They regarded themselves as stewards for the province: 'les économes soubz le bon plaisir de Sa Majesté de la juridiction et entière administration des deniers qui se lèvent dans l'estendue desd[its] Estats . . .'[7] From the point of view of the government the revenues from Burgundy were relatively secure, and could be anticipated in the form of loans from financiers. The activities of the *trésorier* of the Estates of Burgundy thus became secondary to those of the financiers at Paris.[8]

[1] Major, 'Henry IV and Guyenne', p. 367, n. 7, reprinted in *State and society*, ed. Kierstead, p. 19.

[2] 'Un si petit pays . . .' A.A.E. France 1492, fo. 122, 22 June 1656.

[3] The expression of Bernard d'Épernon: A.A.E. France 1492, fo. 85, 16 May 1656.

[4] Drouot, *Mayenne et la Bourgogne*, i. 96. Thomas, *Une province*, p. 7. The sessions at Noyers in 1659 lasted a week (31 Mar.–6 Apr.). A.A.E. France 1492, fos. 227, 229.

[5] Their administration which lasted for three years between the sessions of the Estates was called the *triennalité*: A.A.E. France 1492, fo. 98ᵛ, 28 May 1656.

[6] E 294, fo. 223, *traité* for the *don gratuit*, *subsistances*, and exemption from the winter quarter, 11 Oct. 1655. E 274a, fo. 1, exemption from the winter quarter purchased for 75,000 *livres*, 1 Feb. 16[6]5, countersigned by Louis XIV and Colbert.

[7] E 364b, fo. 37, 14 July 1663. Cf. previous decrees of 16 Mar. 1641, 7 June 1651, 16 June 1660, and 18 Sept. 1660 cited by Thomas, *Une province*, p. 72, n. 1.

[8] E 349a, fo. 356, 25 Oct. 1661.

The political control of the Estates was facilitated by the fact that voting was carried out by the three orders separately. In the word of Baltazar, a *maître des requêtes* sent to Burgundy in 1658, 'les estatz n'ayant que trois voix, la noblesse et l'église estant pour le roy, elles emporteroient celle du tiers estat'.[1] The specific details of representation thus became of academic interest only. The Estates of 1656 were a clear illustration of Baltazar's argument since in that year the clergy and the nobility were in agreement. (However, Bouchu, the intendant, was obliged to 'venir aux extrémitez . . . avec le tiers estat'.)[2] Yet the alliance between the clergy and the nobility did not always occur. In 1650, the nobility was quiescent, but the clergy and the Third Estate co-operated to limit the money, grant to the crown.[3] At the Estates of Noyers in 1659, the clergy were the most recalcitrant of the three orders.[4] The government tried to forestall difficulties at the meetings of the Estates of Burgundy by organizing all the patronage forces at its disposal. Between 1631 and 1651 this consisted essentially of the enormous influence of the Bourbon princes of Condé,[5] ably assisted in the years 1635–8 and 1644–50 by two intendants— the brothers Charles and Louis de Machault, who were clients of the princes of Condé. Louis II de Bourbon, prince de Condé, held both the Estates of Burgundy and the *Parlement* of Dijon firm during the so-called 'constitutional' Fronde of 1648–9; the province was affected by civil war only when Condé was arrested and his supporters went into rebellion. In 1651, the patronage network was broken, when Condé was replaced as governor by the duc d'Épernon. Within a year, Épernon had created his own power base in the *Parlement* of Dijon;[6] by 1656, it was said that the province had such respect for its new governor that the Estates would refuse him only 'ce qui sera impossible d'accorder'.[7] During the Fronde, the crown had had to combat a second clientage network in Burgundy, that of Jean Bouchu, the *premier président* of the *Parlement* of Dijon, who

[1] Thomas, *Une province*, p. 9. A.A.E. France, 1492, fo. 201 [1658].
[2] A.A.E. France 1492, fo. 113ᵛ, 15 June 1656.
[3] A.A.E. France 1491, fo. 268, 2 Apr. 1650.
[4] A.A.E. France 1492, fo. 227ᵛ, 3 Apr. 1659.
[5] Thomas, *Une province*, p. 25.
[6] A.A.E. France 1491, fo. 355, 16 Feb. 1652.
[7] A.A.E. France 1492, fos. 80ᵛ, 229, 16 May 1656 and 6 Apr. 1659.

was a firm supporter of Condé and indeed had been appointed to his office as a result of the influence of Henri de Bourbon in 1638. Appreciating that it was safer to mobilize this clientage network rather than to destroy it, the government appointed Claude Bouchu, the son of the *premier président*, as intendant in 1656. Bouchu's appointment is thus a striking exception to the general rule that intendants were not natives of the provinces in which they served. Bouchu's clientage network was first put to the test at the Estates of 1656. On 16 May, the intendant informed Mazarin: 'j'employe avec tout le soing imaginable mon crédit, celuy de mes amis et de mes parents qui ont entrée en cette assemblée pour faire réussir les intentions du Roy.'[1] 'J'oserois assurer Votre Éminence', Bouchu wrote a month later, 'que sans les habitudes que j'ay parmy eux, la patience avec laquelle j'en ay usé il eust esté impossible de les porter à beaucoup prez de cette somme . . .' The fiscal demands of the crown in 1656 were so great—3 million *livres* was the original demand, reduced to 1·4 million over three years— that Bouchu and his clientage system became discredited for a time in the province.[2] The intendant nevertheless prepared the sessions at Noyers three years later with great care. 'J'ay traversé toute la Bourgogne', he informed Mazarin on 3 April 1659, 'et y ay veu tout ce que j'avois de parens et d'amys dans tous les ordres, et j[e les] ay disposé de se rendre aux Estats de Noyers pour donner satisfaction au Roy.' The outcome this time was much more successful. Without the activities of Bouchu's brother and two uncles in the chamber of the clergy, however, the negotiations would have been protracted and the outcome much less certain.[3]

The Estates claimed that no new taxes could be levied in Burgundy except with their consent, and after registration of the fiscal edicts in the sovereign courts. They argued that decrees of the council did not possess sufficient authority to order taxes in Burgundy[4]—a claim which the government did not accept. In 1656, Mazarin argued that the government demanded only 800,000 *livres* in taxes although it intended to levy an additional

---

[1] A.A.E. France 1492, fo. 81.
[2] A.A.E. France 1492, fos. 113ᵛ–114ʳ, 200, 15 June 1656 and 28 Nov. 1658.
[3] A.A.E. France 1492, fo. 227ᵛ, 3 Apr. 1659.
[4] A.A.E. France 1492, fos. 59, 236–7, 26 July 1655, Apr. 1659.

sum as a result of new fiscal edicts. Mazarin offered the province the opportunity of buying off these fiscal edicts. The chief minister criticized Bouchu for putting a figure—three million—on the total tax demand of the crown.[1] This was an important issue. There was considerable opposition in 1656, not merely to the size of the demand, but to the way the government sought to achieve its aims. Bouchu confessed to Mazarin that the proposals were 'si odieux en cette province . . . qu'il y a peu de personnes qui eussent peu insister comme j'y fais à ces establissements sans hazard'. The nature of the fiscal demands in 1656 and 1658 appeared as a threat both to the Estates and the *Parlement* of Dijon, and the great danger was that the two institutions would unite against the government. The Estates held at Dijon in 1658 refused a grant to the crown, while the *Parlement* demanded a political union with the representative institution. Finally, on 22 November 1658, it refused entry to Baltazar, a *maître des requêtes* sent to the court on the orders of the Chancellor.[2] The government transferred the Estates to Noyers and suspended the sessions of the *Parlement* in January 1659; previously, it had exiled the *premier président* and certain *conseillers*. The *Parlement* was not allowed to meet again until July 1659, after the Estates of Noyers had completed their sessions safely.[3]

The provincial Estates in areas of land tax were in a somewhat more secure position than their counterparts in areas of *taille personnelle*. They were, not however, immune from assault by the government. In Provence, the Estates were increasingly under threat from 1629 and were not summoned again after 1639. The demise of the Estates of Provence was foreshadowed by long-standing social tensions within the province. In this respect, the situation in Provence was the reverse of that in the Dauphiné. In the Dauphiné, the members of the Third Estate sought to abolish the representative institution because they considered the Estates to be controlled by the clergy and the

[1] A.A.E. France 1492, fo. 91, 22 May 1656.
[2] A.A.E. France 1492, fos. 196–200, 28 Nov. 1658. E 1708, no. 158, 24 Dec. 1658.
[3] F. Dumont, 'French kingship and absolute monarchy in the seventeenth century', *Louis XIV and absolutism*, ed. Hatton, p. 65. A.A.E. France 1492, fos. 239–40, 6 and 20 July 1659.

nobility in their own interests. They sought also to change the fiscal regime from *taille personnelle* to *taille réelle* so that the clergy, nobles, and office-holders would be required to pay taxes on recently acquired *terres roturiers*. In Provence, the situation was quite different because the *taille réelle* was already the fiscal regime in the province and the Third Estate had no wish to upset a *status quo* which worked in their favour. In 1611, they stated that they had lived for 'plus de cinquante ans en paix' and had no wish to enter a protracted lawsuit with their *seigneurs*. In contrast, the privileged orders considered that they had a grievance. The size of their estates had increased dramatically since 1471 (the date of the last land register [*affouagement*]) as a result of massive land purchases by the clergy, *nobles d'épée, nobles de robe*, merchants, and bourgeois. Yet because of the nature of the fiscal regime, the amount of taxable land held by the privileged classes had increased too. By 1549, the clergy, nobles, and office-holders of Provence were protesting against the situation, but the *Parlement* of Aix decided in favour of the Third Estate on 6 March 1549 and upheld the system of *taille réelle*. On 5 September 1552, as a concession, the *Parlement* worked out a complicated—and probably unworkable—system whereby the privileged classes would gain tax relief on *terres nobles* which had been sold off or rented to members of the Third Estate in order to compensate for taxes which they had to pay on recently acquired *terres roturiers*.[1] This long-standing conflict led the nobles to use their numerical preponderance in the Estates[2] to refuse taxes which in an area of land tax would fall partly on their own estates. They were able to do so because the three orders deliberated and voted together and the nobles holding fiefs were the most numerous of the three orders. In contrast, the First and the Third Estates were relatively under-represented—the clergy had only eighteen members and

[1] The history of the conflict comes from E 32b, fo. 147, 10 Sept. 1611. Legislation of the *Parlement* of Paris according to this document. Legislation of the *Parlement* of Aix according to Deyon, 'À propos les rapports entre la noblesse française et la monarchie absolue', translated in *State and society*, ed. Kierstead, p. 28.

[2] There were 160 nobles at Tarascon in 1631, 220 at Brignoles in 1632, and 166 at the last meeting at Aix-en-Provence in 1639. Pillorget, *Les mouvements insurrectionnels*, p. 103. Much material on the Estates, the Assemblies of the Communities, and the *procureurs du pays* is to be found in Kettering, *Judicial politics*. Cf. also R. Pillorget, 'L'Assemblée des communautés de Provence', *Les provinciaux sous Louis XIV. Actes du centre méridional de rencontres sur le xviie siècle* (1975).

the Third Estate thirty-seven members. Thus in 1628, 1629, 1633, and 1639 the Estates refused to grant a *don gratuit* to the crown. In a period when other provinces were experiencing a rapid increase in taxation, such action could not be justified. The refusals of 1628–9 forced the government to decide on the establishment of *élections* in Provence. The resistance of the nobles to this innovation found a response in the province as a whole. The seriousness of the rioting at Aix-en-Provence in the autumn of 1630 convinced the government that the *élections* were not a realistic political alternative to the Estates. There was some possibility that a new governor would be able to dominate the institution: in 1632, the maréchal de Vitry forced the Estates at Brignoles to vote 1,110,000 *livres* to the government. Increasingly, however, the government came to rely on an alternative form of assembly—the *assemblée générale des communautés* which comprised the Third Estate with one representative from each of the two privileged orders. Since the meetings of this assembly took place without any significant participation of the nobles, they were controlled much more easily by the government. In 1634, the assembly at Apt granted 975,000 *livres*. Three assemblies held between December 1635 and July 1636 resulted in a grant of 2·2 million.

The nature of representation changed: but some of the basic institutions in Provence survived. The *assemblée générale* had the same interim executive committee, called the *procureurs du pays*. The committee was drawn essentially from notables at Aix-en-Provence—the archbishop, three *consuls*, and an *assesseur*. It played a crucial role in organizing the three revolts of the city against the government in 1630, 1649, and 1659. From the point of view of the crown, therefore, it was essential that the *procureurs du pays* should be 'bien intentionnées'.[1] The *assemblée générale* retained the same fiscal machinery as that employed by the Estates. The *receveurs* of the communities collected the *taille* and paid it to the *receveur* of the *viguerie*. This official paid the money in turn to the *receveur* of the *taille*. Finally the money reached the *trésorier* of the *assemblée générale*. Between 1624 and 1651, under both the Estates and the *assemblée générale*, Gaillard was the treasurer. After his bank-

[1] B.L. Harleian 4493, fo. 80, memorandum of Oppède to Chancellor Séguier, 1659.

ruptcy in 1651, Gaillard was succeeded by Maurel de Pontèves. The intendants did not interfere with this fiscal machinery in normal years, and thus their role with regard to taxation in Provence was very limited.[1] In certain crisis years, however— notably 1625, 1628, 1633–4, and 1658—the governors and intendants attempted to levy taxation by ordinance without the approval of a representative institution of the province.

Before 1637, it was the governor who controlled the representative institutions of Provence. The maréchal de Vitry, for example, attended at least six and perhaps eight of the eleven meetings of the Estates and *assemblées générales* held during the period of his governorship. In contrast, the comte d'Alais, his successor, attended only four of the eleven assemblies convened between 1638 and 1648. Before the Fronde, therefore, the task of supervising the assemblies fell increasingly upon the intendants. François Bochart was present at all the assemblies held during his two terms as intendant (1638–40; 1643–7). Cazet de Vautorte had to supervise three sessions of the *assemblée générale* —in 1640, 1641, and 1643—without any help from the governor. On 7 April 1643, Vautorte informed the Chancellor that the governor's presence at the meetings was essential for their successful management. He implied that the comte d'Alais had failed to carry out his duties.[2] After the Fronde, the frequent absences of the duc de Mercœur at the war front introduced uncertainty once more with regard to the control of the assemblies. The problem was made worse by the fact that there was no permanent system of intendants in Provence. Maynier d'Oppède, the *premier président* of the *Parlement* of Aix, in his capacity as acting governor and acting intendant supervised the assembly of 1658. The failure of this meeting provided the background to the riot at Aix-en-Provence the following year.

There was no permanent system of intendants in Brittany either. In this province, the Estates were controlled jointly by the governor or lieutenant-general and by councillors of state sent directly from Paris. In 1636, 1647, and 1659 the councillors of state were also intendants. In 1636 and 1659 the Estates made no protest at the title of intendant being held respectively by

[1] *Lettres . . . au Chancelier Séguier*, ed. Mousnier, i. 512.
[2] ibid.

Estampes de Valençay and Louis de Boucherat.[1] In 1647,
however, they made a formal objection to this title being held
by Cœtlogon de Méjusseaume. Cœtlogon was a Breton and
was in serious conflict with the *Parlement* of Rennes. The
Estates declared that his commission ought not to be interpreted
as prejudicing the 'droits, franchises et libertés de la province'.[2]
In other years, the councillors of state were often men of great
standing, who served as intendants and commissioners elsewhere
in France. In this category may be included Mesmes de Roissy
(1610), Le Bret and Charles Machault (1625), André Lefèvre
d'Ormesson (1632), Laisnier (1634), Laubardemont (1638)
and Harouys (1640, 1647, 1649, and 1651). In the years after
the Fronde, Boucherat began to make this task virtually his
personal property.[3]

Before 1626, the duc de Vendôme, the governor of Brittany,
had dominated the Estates. Vendôme was disgraced in 1626 as
a result of his participation in the Chalais conspiracy, and his
governorship was transferred to the maréchal de Thémines.
Louis XIII presided over the Estates of Brittany in person in
1626. Thémines died in 1627, and after an interim in which
the Estates tried to obtain the governorship for the Queen
Mother, Richelieu was appointed governor (16 September
1631). Richelieu held the governorship until his death in 1642.
In 1645, it was taken up by Anne of Austria who held it until her
death in 1666. Neither Richelieu nor Anne of Austria visited
Brittany as governor. The real authority in the province,
therefore, was exercised by the lieutenant-general. From 18
March 1632 until his death on 8 February 1664, this office was
held by the duc de La Meilleraye. La Meilleraye was Richelieu's
cousin; he was also his political disciple. In 1632, he had
accompanied Condé to the Estates of Brittany, where he had
witnessed at first hand the dealings of the first prince of the
blood—Condé was Richelieu's ultimate sanction against the

[1] F. N. Baudot [Dubuisson-Aubenay], 'Journal das Estats de Bretagne com-
mencés à Nantes en décembre 1636', ed. A. Bourdeault, *Bulletin de la Société
Archéologique et Historique de Nantes et de la Loire-Inférieure*, lxvii (1927—published
1928), 352–3. A.A.E. France 1504, fo. 146, instructions to Estampes, 28 Nov. 1636.
[2] Canal, *Origines de l'intendance de Bretagne*, pp. 98 ff. Rébillon, *États de Bretagne'*
pp. 213–14. A.A.E. France 1507, fo. 54, instructions to Harouys and Coetlogon,
20 Feb. 1647.
[3] Boucherat was a royal commissioner to the Estates in 1657, 1659, 1661, 1667,
1671, and 1673.

pays d'états.[1] Having learnt from this experience, La Meilleraye was left in charge of all the subsequent sessions of the Estates until the personal rule of Louis XIV. He was instructed by Richelieu in 1634 to 'remettr[e] les Estatz en leur ancienne liberté'—to behave with more circumspection than Condé—and to allow them free votes provided that 'soubz ce prétexte il ne se fasse aucune chose qui puisse estre désagréable au roy'.[2] La Meilleraye was successful in 1634, although in later years his conduct was much more controversial. On some occasions, he favoured strong-arm tactics in dealing with the representatives of the province.[3] On other occasions he was accused by the ministers of siding with provincial resistance.[4] Colbert had no use for 'un homme si difficile'[5] and was probably responsible for the disgrace of his son, the duc Mazarin, in 1669.

After 1630 the sessions of the Estates of Brittany were biennial and they rarely lasted more than a month. In 1653, there was a demand for annual sessions, chiefly as a means of escaping 'l'oppression du Parlement [de Rennes] qui sera retenu quand il verra les Estatz se tenir tous les ans . . .' La Meilleraye opposed the measure, however, since the crown would not gain a larger money vote from annual meetings of the Estates, and would incur greater political risks. The idea was dropped.[6] The royal commissioners always contrasted the 'foiblesse dans les Estats' with the 'audace du costé du Parlement';[7] yet the Estates were by no means easy to control. Representation in the First and Third Estates was restricted numerically—to a maximum of 58 and 44 deputies respectively.[8] Yet the Second Estate was not restricted numerically: all nobles possessing fiefs in Brittany could enter the Estates. They did not always go to the meetings. Between 1576 and 1649 there were only seven occasions when the number of nobles

---

[1] A.A.E. France 1505, fo. 72ᵛ, La Meilleraye to D'Effiat, 25 Apr. 1632. 'Ils crient que M. le prince ne vient ici que pour les violenter dans leurs libertés . . .'

[2] *Lettres . . . de Richelieu*, ed. Avenel, vii. 728–9. A.A.E. France 1504, fo. 104, 2 Nov. 1634.

[3] A.A.E. France 1505, fo. 427, 25 Nov. 1638.

[4] For Foucquet's fears that La Meilleraye would support Breton grievances: B.L. Add. MS. 39673, fos. 60–1, 16 July 1655.

[5] *Lettres . . . de Colbert*, ed. Clément, iv. 27 (17 Sept. 1663).

[6] A.A.E. France 1508, fo. 185, 26 Nov. 1653.

[7] A.A.E. France 1506, fo. 263, 5 Nov. 1653.

[8] Rébillon, *Les États de Bretagne*, pp. 104–13.

present at the Estates exceeded one hundred. After 1649, however, there were never less than one hundred nobles present at the sessions of the Estates. At the crucial meeting of 1651, 226 nobles arrived at Nantes.[1] The Estates were thus dominated by the Breton squirearchy, whose ignorance was matched only by their lawlessness and sense of independence. The Bretons were quite different from the more placid Burgundians. 'L'esprit des Bretons est tellement aisé à blesser', remarked La Meilleraye, 'que la moindre nouveauté les chocque . . .'[2]

The size of the noble representation at the Estates of Brittany posed considerable political dangers to the government. At the Estates of 1634, the nobles split into factions and 'une recreue des cadets de la noblesse . . . donnerent leurs voix les espées hautes et quelques uns armez de pistolletz . . .'[3] The situation was particularly serious during the Fronde. La Meilleraye was probably the only man who could have kept the Breton nobles in order,[4] and fortunately for the government, his loyalty never wavered. On the other hand, he had quarrelled with the duc de Rohan-Chabot in 1647, and in the autumn of 1651 Rohan made a serious attempt to gain the leadership of the Breton nobles, and thus bring the province into the revolt of Condé. Rohan sought to achieve these aims by gaining the presidency over the nobles at the Estates, which was contested also by the duc de Vendôme. Rohan claimed that the Estates were in 'une dépendance absolue' on La Meilleraye and Vendôme, whereas he had the support of between 400 and 500 nobles— 'la plus saine partie de la noblesse de Bretagne'.[5] La Meilleraye ordered Rohan to leave Nantes and suspended the meetings of the Estates until he did so.[6] Rohan appealed to the *Parlement* of Rennes, which sided with his faction. Thus began a conflict between the *Parlement* and the Estates which lasted until 1655. The revolt of Rohan was a failure in Brittany, however, because La Meilleraye never lost control of the military situation. Rohan had to pursue his objectives in his former governorship of

[1] ibid., p. 93.

[2] A.A.E. France 1505, fo. 90, 21 Dec. 1634.

[3] A.A.E. France 1505, fo. 147, anon. memorandum.

[4] A.A.E. France 1506, fo. 174, 6 Mar. 1649.

[5] A.A.E. France 1508, fo. 76, manifesto of Rohan, 28 Sept. 1651, with signatures of nobles.

[6] A.A.E. France 1508, fo. 92, 29 Sept. 1651.

Anjou, where he was defeated decisively by La Meilleraye in the course of 1652.[1]

Fortunately for the government, in normal years the scale of representation was irrelevant to the functioning of the Estates. Voting was by the three orders separately as in Burgundy. As a rule, if two of the three Estates were in agreement on a proposal, the other Estate fell into line: 'deux ordres emportent tousjours le troisiesme . . .' was the Breton maxim. In 1653, there was a suggestion that this arrangement should be altered: the proposal was rejected on the grounds that without this arrangement there would be 'une confusion presque perpétuelle [dans] toutes les délibérations.'[2] The importance of this rule was that the clergy and nobility tended to coerce the Third Estate into agreeing the crown's tax demands. La Meilleraye stated in 1643 that the Third Estate 'n'a jamais rien consenti ce qu'il n'a peu éviter'; the clergy were more co-operative, but still reticent; the nobles, however, granted 1·2 million *livres* to the government 'avec grande cœur'.[3] This situation prevailed in most years. In 1649, La Meilleraye had to coerce the Third Estate 'avec une viollence extrême'.[4] The crown relied greatly on the 'bons sentiments' of the nobility to avoid 'les propositions incommodes des autres ordres' and to 'emporter la conclusion'.[5] This was why factions among the nobles as in 1651 were so dangerous to the government.

Despite the informal alliance between the lieutenant-general and the nobility, the Estates of Brittany had considerable bargaining power. In 1632 and 1634 the demands of the crown (1·4 and 1·5 million *livres* respectively) were accorded. In other years, however, they were not. As the demands of the crown increased, so too did the resistance of the Estates. Estampes de Valençay was instructed in the crisis year of 1636 to secure a money grant twice that which had been voted in previous years. He could not reach 2·8 or 3 million, however, and the best he could achieve 'sans une extrême violence' was two million.[6] The record vote before 1661 was 2·9 million in 1643—

[1] Débidour, *La Fronde angevine*, pp. 273–95.
[2] A.A.E. France 1506, fo. 273ᵛ, 16 Dec. 1653.
[3] A.A.E. France 1505, fos. 90ᵛ–93ʳ, 137, 14 and 21 Dec. 1634.
[4] A.A.E. France 1506, fo. 179, 26 July 1649.
[5] A.A.E. France 1506, fo. 393, 8 Aug. 1655.
[6] A.A.E. France 1504, fo. 146, 28 Nov. 1636.

but on this occasion La Massaye, the financier of the Estates, went bankrupt and the crown received only two million.[1] After 1636 there was always a gap between the demands of the crown and the money vote of the Estates. Sometimes—as in 1651—this gap approached 50 per cent.[2]

The crucial factor complicating relations with the Estates of Brittany was the attitude of the *Parlement* of Rennes. The sovereign courts of Brittany had substantial power because they registered the contract between the government and the Estates. Furthermore, the Bretons enjoyed the privilege—shared also by the Burgundians—that no taxes could be levied by fiscal edicts without the consent of the Estates and formal registration in the sovereign courts.[3] Tension between the Estates and the *Parlement* of Rennes was latent throughout Richelieu's ministry. On 17 April 1632, La Meilleraye noted 'les mauvaises volontés du Parlement lequel est composé du grand nombre de gens qui ont crédit et parmi la noblesse et toutes les communaultés . . .'[4] This latent tension burst into the open on 17 October 1651, when the *Parlement*—acting in support of Rohan—annulled the deliberations of the Estates at Nantes.[5] The king's council sided with the Estates, but the *Parlement* replied by refusing to register the contract of 1651. The question was whether the government would exploit this dispute to its own advantage. D'Espeisses and De la Court, the councillors of state at the Estates of 1653, thought the dispute was an ideal weapon for weakening the Estates, 'estant intollerable de veoir des subjets soubz prétextes de leurs prétendus privilèges se vouloir exempter de contribuer aux nécessitez de l'estat'.[6] La Meilleraye agreed. The dispute was an ideal application of the principle of divide and rule: 'le Roy demeure maistre entière-ment'.[7] By 1655, however, there was no doubt about the wisdom of continuing this policy. La Meilleraye opted for the defence of

[1] A.A.E. France 1506, fo. 366, 30 June 1655. A.A.E. France 1507, fo. 55, 20 Feb. 1647.

[2] B. Pocquet, *Histoire de Bretagne. La Bretagne province, 1515–1715* (Rennes, 1913), pp. 418–50. A.A.E. France 1504–8, *possim.*

[3] A.A.E. France 1504, fo. 192. La Meilleraye to Louis XIII, 4 Dec. 1638.

[4] A.A.E. France 1505, fo. 75, 17 Apr. 1632.

[5] Pocquet, *Histoire de Bretagne*, pp. 430–5. A.A.E. France 1508, fo. 100, *c.* 5 Oct. 1651. E 1697, nos. 229, 231, 249, 6 Nov. 1651.

[6] A.A.E. France 1506, fo. 263, 5 Nov. 1653.

[7] A.A.E. France 1506, fo. 271ᵛ, 6 Dec. 1653.

Breton privileges, arguing that it was in the crown's interests to secure a smaller but guaranteed revenue 'avec la bénédiction [des] peuples' than to rely on 'une division et un désordre' such as had existed for the last six months. La Meilleraye recognized the change in political attitudes that had occurred since the Estates of 1653.[1] The Estates were now convinced of the need for reconciliation with the *Parlement*. Guillaume de Lamoignon, the councillor of state at the meeting of 1655, confirmed La Meilleraye's analysis. 'C'est la persuasion de leur propre intérest qui les porte à cela', he reported, '. . . . ils croient que si ceste division dure on ruinera toute la province et on destruira tous leurs privilèges.'[2] The government made no serious attempt to prolong the conflict between the Estates and the *Parlement*, which was pacified at Vitré in 1655. By 1657, Boucherat considered that the *Parlement* had regained sufficient influence over the Estates to prevent the vote of a large money grant to the crown.[3] Divide and rule was an essential aspect of government in a period of crisis such as the Fronde. Yet in more normal circumstances, and especially in a distant province such as Brittany, it could pose as many dangers as it appeared to solve. Institutional conflict meant administrative confusion. Administrative confusion threatened the crown's tax demands just as much as an informal alliance between the *Parlement* and the Estates.

The Estates of Languedoc were the most important representative institution in France. Not only did the vote of the Estates tend to influence the size of money grants in Brittany, Burgundy, and Provence:[4] the Estates of Languedoc met more regularly, and for longer periods than any other assembly. The contrast between the Estates of Languedoc and Brittany is striking. After 1632, the first met annually, the second biennially. After 1645, the sessions in Languedoc were on average twice as long as those in Brittany. There were thirteen more sessions of the Estates of Languedoc than those of Brittany under Richelieu and Mazarin. The Estates of Languedoc were assembled for

[1] A.A.E. France 1506, fos. 355ᵛ–356ʳ, 16 June 1655.
[2] A.A.E. France 1506, fo. 377ᵛ, 13 July 1655.
[3] B.L. Harleian 4490, fo. 423, 10 Nov. 1657.
[4] *Histoire générale de Languedoc*, ed. Roschach, xiv. 334.

nearly three times as long as their counterpart in Brittany.[1]
These differences were crucial. It was generally recognized
that long sessions of the Estates were extremely dangerous.
François Foucquet, the bishop of Agde, informed Mazarin in
1655: 'je suis persuadé que la longueur des Estats et des
assemblées tumultueuses et des gens ramassez est toujours
préjudiciable au service du Roy'.[2] Delay always stiffened
resistance among the Third Estate. If the deputies of the
Third Estate had time to visit their towns, they arrived back at
the Estates 'plus obstinés qu'auparavant'.[3] If the Estates
stayed in sessions for any length of time, this gave the towns the
opportunity to 'affermir leurs députés en leur obstination par des
lettres . . .'[4] One purpose of the edict of Béziers, which was
imposed on Languedoc after the Montmorency rebellion in
1632, was to limit the sessions of the Estates to a fortnight. The
edict was never observed in this respect, however: even the
Montpellier Estates of 1633 lasted eighteen days. After 1635,
the Estates were allowed to meet for a month, which was a
more realistic time-limit. Between 1632 and 1645 no sessions of
the Estates lasted more than forty days. After 1645, however,
long sessions were the order of the day. When the edict of
Béziers was revoked in 1649, this removed all limitation on the
length of meetings.[5]

The contrast between the Estates of Brittany and those of
Languedoc was not confined to length and periodicity of sessions,
however. The crucial difference was that the Breton Estates had
only three votes, whereas those of Languedoc had 87 votes.
Since the fifteenth century, the Estates of Languedoc had
possessed an essential feature of genuine representation which
the Estates of the Dauphiné did not gain until 1788 and the
Estates-General of France did not gain until 1789: double
representation for the Third Estate. The Third Estate of
Languedoc was represented by 65 deputies holding 43 votes out

[1] Languedoc: 35 sessions, 1624–61, totalling 2,760 days. Average length of
sessions 78 days. Brittany: 22 sessions, 1624–61, totalling 928 days. Average length
of sessions 42 days.
[2] A.A.E. France 1636, fo. 379, 19 Jan. 1655.
[3] *Bnutrennyaya*, ed. Lublinskaya, pp. 123, 126.
[4] A.A.E. France 1634, fo. 180, memorandum of 1645.
[5] Twelve sessions, 1632–43, totalling 332 days. Average length of sessions, 27
days. Sixteen sessions, 1645–61, totalling 1,811 days. Average length of sessions, 113
days.

of a total of 101 deputies holding 87 votes.[1] In a period when absenteeism was frequent in all three orders, the Third Estate was often left as 'le maistre de toutes les délibérations'.[2] The crown thus had to deal in Languedoc with an institution that had a narrow representative basis yet which acted by the procedure of a democratic vote. As a result, a close vote was the order of the day except in rare sessions, such as those of 1647, when the money grant was passed with sixty votes for the government.[3] Disaster might sometimes strike the government, as at the Narbonne and Pézenas Estates of 1645–6, when no 'extraordinary' grant was forthcoming at all. At the Pézenas Estates of 1655 there was initially a majority of twenty-two against any grant being made[4]—although eventually the meeting was brought to reason.

In years of agrarian difficulty, years also when the movement of troops through the province and the billeting of troops added to the existing burden of taxation, there seems to have been a radical party in the towns of Languedoc which opposed the tax demands of the crown. The inequalities of the system of representation did not prevent the deputies acting as the spokesmen of radical movements in the towns and dioceses of the province. The intendants advised the government to hold the Estates of Languedoc in January, so that the municipal representatives would be leaving and not commencing their terms of office, and consequently feel free to consent to taxation. It was taken for granted that newly-elected deputies were unwilling to consent to 'extraordinary' taxation 'de peur que le peuple ne se prenne à eux durant l'année entière de leur consulat'.[5] There was an example at Toulouse in 1644 of a deputy whose rights as bourgeois of the town were removed because he consented to unpopular taxes.[6] The town applauded their deputies when they resisted the demands of the government.[7] The practice of municipalities issuing their

[1] Mariotte, 'Mémoire concernant la forme des assemblées des États de Languedoc' (1 Oct. 1704). A.A.E. France 1640, fos. 221f. Cf. Mousnier, *La plume*, p. 239.
[2] A.A.E. France 1636, fo. 450, 14 Dec. 1655.
[3] A.A.E. France 1634, fo. 283, 16 Apr. 1647.
[4] A.A.E. France 1636, fos. 444–5, 12 Dec. 1655.
[6] A.A.E. France 1634, fo. 59, 22 Nov. 1644.
[6] A.A.E. France 1634, fo. 77^v, 5 Feb. 1645.
[7] *Bnutrennyaya*, ed. Lublinskaya, pp. 123, 129.

deputies with instructions was one reason for the radicalism of
the third Estate of Languedoc. Governments in early modern
Europe always wanted deputies to be armed with wide powers
to accord the taxes that were demanded. But in 1645, the
Languedoc towns issued instructions to their deputies prohibiting them from agreeing to the winter quarter.[1] The towns did
not go this far in normal years, although Toulouse always
issued restrictive instructions to its deputies. The deputies of
Toulouse, who usually led the opposition of the Third Estate of
Languedoc, were instructed by their municipality to champion
the privileges of the province; in reality, however, their chief
concern was to defend the privileges of Toulouse. The government replied by revoking these privileges as punishment for
consistent opposition to royal policy at the Estates.[2] The
governor and intendants tried to circumvent the instructions of
the municipalities by forming their own clientage network
among the deputies of the Third Estate.

The cause of the government was far from hopeless in
Languedoc, however. As Pierre de Marca, the archbishop of
Toulouse, informed Mazarin in 1656: 'le secret pour réussir
dans les Estats consiste à réunir Messieurs les Evesques et les
barons en un mesme sentiment . . .'[3] This was the essential
strategy of the governor and the intendants. The clergy were
represented by 22 bishops. In some years, however, several of
the bishops failed to appear at the Estates. At Narbonne in
1645, the *grands vicaires* representing absentee bishops 'ne
pouvoient servir plus mal qu'ils ont fait'.[4] At the Pézenas
Estates in 1655–6, scarcely any bishops arrived: '[cela] remet
le pouvoir tout entier entre les mains du tiers estat', Bazin de
Bezons declared.[5] The opening of the Estates at Béziers in
1656–7 was delayed because of the absence of bishops and
barons,[6] while at the Pézenas meeting in 1657–8, Bazin de
Bezons informed Mazarin that he relied particularly on the

[1] A.A.E. France 1634, fo. 180, 7 Dec. 1645.

[2] Instructions for the deputies of Toulouse: *Histoire générale de Languedoc*, ed.
Roschach, xiv. 34–9, 120–1, 192–6, 247–50, 277–80. Revocation of the *abonnement*
of Toulouse: E 1703, fo. 378 and E 284b, fo. 474, 15 Dec. 1655.

[3] A.A.E. France 1636, fo. 468, 4 Jan. 1656.

[4] A.A.E. France 1634, fo. 76^v, 5 Feb. 1645.

[5] A.A.E. France 1636, fo. 425, 9 Nov. 1655.

[6] A.A.E. France 1636, fo. 506, 13 Nov. 1656.

efforts of the bishops.[1] Moreover, there were opponents as well as supporters of the government among the bishops.[2]

Each bishop weighed up the advantages of royal service— pensions, ecclesiastical preferment for oneself and one's relatives, letters as councillor of state, an ambassadorship, or perhaps under Richelieu a military command—against potential loss of popularity and power in the diocese. Would the bishop's local objectives—control of municipal elections, supplementary income from the diocesan *assiettes*, exploitation of the seigneurial relationship[3]—be furthered by support for the government? Certain bishops, such as Daillon du Lude, bishop of Albi, risked the consequences of alienating local support,[4] Equally loyal, but more prudent bishops such as Rebé, the archbishop of Narbonne and president of the Estates, had to have their doubts removed by the intendant.[5] The difficulty in controlling the Béziers Estates of 1656–7 resulted from the absence of Rebé, archbishop of Narbonne, and Marca, archbishop of Toulouse. The government had to rely instead on the less influential bishop of Lavaur.[6] The truth was, as Bosquet observed, that 'l'épiscopat est une fonction mixte en cette province'. The bishops of Languedoc were politicians. Vacant benefices thus needed to be filled with 'personnes autant exercées aux affaires publiques qu'à la dévotion'.[7] Above all, vacant benefices in Languedoc must not be filled with persons who were 'intéressés à la province'.[8] There was a great danger in appointing *dévot* bishops, since religious extremism might lead to political opposition. This seems to have been the case with Nicolas Pavillon, bishop of Alet, whose Jansenist activities coincided with a consistent opposition to the crown's tax

[1] A.A.E. France 1637, fo. 114ᵛ, 28 Aug. 1657.

[2] Among the opponents of the government in 1645–6 were the bishops of Agde, Alet, and Nîmes. There were accusations against the conduct of the bishop of Montauban in 1653, the bishop of Viviers in 1654, and the bishops of Alet and Comminges in 1656–7.

[3] For these objectives in the case of the bishop of Mende: B.L. Harleian 4494. For supplementary income from the *assiettes*: A.A.E. France 1634, fo. 254ᵛ, 21 Nov. 1646.

[4] He was beseiged in his episcopal palace during the Fronde: A.A.E. France 1634, fos. 312, 318, 7 July 1647. E 1700, no. 102, 22 Sept. 1652.

[5] A.A.E. France 1634, fo. 66 and B.N. MS.fr. 18830, fo. 200, 16 Dec. 1644.

[6] A.A.E. France 1637, fo. 42ᵛ, 29 Jan 1657.

[7] *Bnutrennyaya*, ed. Lublinskaya, p. 164.

[8] A.A.E. France 1636, fo. 510, 18 Dec. 1656.

demands. It was also the case with Pierre de Bertier, bishop of Montauban, whose family had both *dévot* and Jansenist connections. In 1653 Bertier championed a political union between the Pézenas Estates and the *Parlement* of Toulouse[1]—a policy which was anathema to the government.

Success for the government at the Estates of Languedoc did not depend merely on the bishops, however. The nobles had to be rallied too. This was the task of the governor, who was usually successful: in crisis years such as 1645, however, an occasional noble might vote against the government. The most serious problem was absenteeism. If the nobles were represented by *envoyés*, these were often 'sans bien et sans naissance' and might vote with the Third Estate.[2] The contrast between representation of the nobles in Brittany and in Languedoc is striking. Certainly the seigneurial regime was weaker in Languedoc; but this does not explain why, since the fifteenth century, representation had been limited to the holders of twenty-two specific baronies. These twenty-two nobles were only a small, unrepresentative element of the Languedoc nobility as a whole. In 1651 an attempt was made to broaden the representation of the nobility which—if it had been successful—would have altered decisively the character of the Estates of Languedoc. The agitation was doomed to failure, however, since the government regarded it as a local manifestation of the Fronde.[3]

The control of the Estates of Languedoc required the careful and selective use of a variety of weapons at the disposal of the government. A kernel of faithful royal supporters at the Estates might be interviewed at Paris by a minister even before the Estates were convened.[4] Before the first session, the governor and the intendant tried to ascertain the state of opinion by a series of social functions, dances, banquets, and other festivities.[5] The session was opened by a sermon from one of the bishops, a dangerous moment for the government, for these sermons frequently contributed towards resistance of the crown's tax demands.[6] Thereafter, a quick decision was needed. If it

[1] A.A.E. France 1636, fo. 144, 1 Apr. 1653.
[2] B.N. MS.fr. 18830, fo. 72, 27 June 1651.
[3] A.A.E. France 1636, fo. 108. B.N. MS.fr. 18830, fos. 71–2. E 1696, nos. 208, 227, 12 June, 22 July 1651.   [4] A.A.E. France 1634, fos. 150–1, 16 July 1645.
[5] A.A.E. France 1634, fo. 72, 23 Jan. 1645.
[6] A.A.E. France 1636, fo. 232, 22 Dec. 1653.

appeared that the royal commissioners were temporizing and intended to increase their demands later,[1] or if they pressed their demands too far,[2] the whole success of the meeting might be jeopardized. Bribery was at best an uncertain and expensive weapon which might misfire.[3] The billeting of troops on towns which opposed the government's demands might exacerbate relations in the next Estates.[4] So too might the summoning to Paris of leading opponents.[5] Ultimate sanctions—the transfer of the Estates to Tournon under the presidency of eleven royal commissioners,[6] or the presence of ministers at the Estates as in 1632 and 1659—were generally too hazardous to be contemplated. What mattered in the end was the vote, and if this went satisfactorily for the government, all else was forgotten. Between 1624 and 1629 the Estates of Languedoc voted very little money to the government.[7] Part of the difficulties of the government may be explained by the lack of continuity of royal commissioners in these years—the authority of the duc de Ventadour, the lieutenant-general, was not as great as that of Montmorency, the governor, and loans, not taxes, were raised in the years (1626, 1629) when he presided. In some years—1624, 1625, 1629—there was no intendant present at the Estates. Undoubtedly a second factor in explaining the loss of royal control over the Estates of Languedoc in these years was the war against Rohan and the devastation of the countryside by the troops: the deputies were unlikely to vote taxes in addition to sums being levied in kind by the army. When the Estates separated from Pézenas on 2 August 1629 the government turned to Jacques Le Feroz and Claude Vanel and their financial consortium to provide 3·9 million *livres* from the establishment of twenty-two *élections*.[8] In September 1631, the Estates reached a preliminary understanding with the

[1] A.A.E. France 1636, fo. 257, 17 Jan. 1654.
[2] A.A.E. France 1634, fo. 515ᵛ, 27 Nov. 1650.
[3] A.A.E. France 1634, fos. 217ᵛ–218ʳ, 5 Feb. 1646. A.A.E. France 1636, fo. 265, 27 Jan. 1654.
[4] A.A.E. France 1634, fo. 225, 13 Mar. 1646. A.A.E. France 1636, fos. 245–246, [?] Jan. 1654.
[5] A.A.E. France 1634, fo. 105ᵛ, 26 Mar. 1645.
[6] B.N. MS.fr. 18830, fos. 34–6, 6 and 13 Feb. 1646.
[7] Gachon, *États de Languedoc*, pp. 127–30.
[8] ibid., pp. 217, 288. A.A.E. France 1628, fo. 121, 1 May 1632. E 104, fo. 387, 18 Sept. 1630. Nicolas Mignot was the *prête-nom* of the financial consortium.

government to reimburse the financiers and thus escape the new fiscal jurisdictions. The compromise broke down in the course of 1632, however, and the establishment of *élections* was the reason why a minority of the Estates, including the provincial *syndics*, joined the revolt of Montmorency on 22 July. Montmorency was defeated at Castelnaudary on 1 September 1632.

The edict of Béziers, which was read out at the meeting of the Estates in October 1632, abolished the *élections* in return for the same amount of compensation that had been envisaged the previous year. The Estates were ordered to pay annually a minimum of 1,332,500 *livres* to the crown.[1] The edict was thus an attempt to extract a more regular source of income from Languedoc, and as such has been hailed by certain historians as the destruction of provincial independence. Far from bringing the revenues of Languedoc into line with those of other provinces, however, the edict hindered this effort. The figures were insignificant in a period when the costs of government were rising astronomically; although the edict set a *minimum* amount of taxation to be borne by the province, it was interpreted by the governor—notably in 1635 and 1637[2] —and by the Estates—notably in 1638, 1639, and 1640—as a *maximum*. The edict of Béziers thus became the best defence of the province against contributing towards the war effort, or participating in a more equitable tax structure for France as a whole. During the Fronde, pressure for the revocation of the edict of Béziers became irresistible and the government was forced to accede to this demand since it could not afford to lose control of an important province when its victory in the Fronde was far from certain. The concessions of 1649 nevertheless had a disastrous effect on the vote of the Estates in succeeding years: the situation was retrieved somewhat in the 1650s, but not fully until Louis XIV and his ministers presided over the

---

[1] 2,232,430 *livres* if income to defray local expenditure is included. The edict is printed in J. Albisson, *Loix municipales et économiques de Languedoc* (7 vols., Montpellier, 1780-7), i. 288-97. Commentary by Gachon, op. cit., *passim*. Baron Trouvé, *Essai historique sur les États-Généraux de la province de Languedoc* (1818), pp. 130-3. E. Delcambre, *Contribution à l'histoire des États provinciaux: les États de Velay des origines à 1642* (Saint-Étienne, 1938), p. 185-91.

[2] A.A.E. France 1629, fo. 387ᵛ, 10 Dec. 1635. A.A.E. France 1630, fo. 216, 7 Apr. 1637.

Estates at Toulouse in 1659. In 1653–4 Bazin de Bezons advised the reintroduction of the edict of Béziers;[1] Pierre de Marca, the archbishop of Toulouse, feared the same measure in 1655–6;[2] finally, two million out of a vote of three million *livres* were accorded by the Estates in 1659 to avoid the reimposition of this limitation on their powers. Throughout the ministries of Richelieu and Mazarin the Estates of Languedoc exercised their consent to taxation in an effective way. The Parisian financiers rarely felt sufficiently secure of the size of a forthcoming vote to make loans in anticipation of revenues from Languedoc. In 1643, Bonneau and Marin, under the *prête-nom* of Marin Hoquin, made a loan of 1·55 million *livres* to the government in anticipation of a grant that was scheduled for 1645. The Estates of Narbonne refused the grant, however, and Bonneau and Marin could not be reimbursed.[3] Finance in Languedoc thus retained a provincial character: by the second half of the century, the firm credit of the Estates contrasted sharply with the failing credit of the government.[4]

The Estates of Languedoc thus rarely agreed to the sums demanded by the government, and frequently they imposed conditions to their grant which the ministers condemned as seeming to emanate from 'des souverains plustost que . . . des sujets'.[5] In these years, the troops took what the Estates refused to grant. Faced with a demand for 1·06 million for the *subsistances* of the troops in 1638, the Estates of Carcassonne decided to 'se laisser manger jusques aux os plustost que d'imposer un escu pour la subsistance . . .'[6] Following the refusal of the Estates, the officials who composed the diocesan *assiettes* went on strike, leaving the tasks of collection to Schomberg the governor, and the intendants.[7] The Carcassonne Estates of 1639 refused to accord the winter quarter for the troops; but successive meetings

---

[1] A.A.E. France 1636, fo. 275ᵛ, 10 Feb. 1654.
[2] A.A.E. France 1636, fo. 448ᵛ, 4 Dec. 1655.
[3] E 208b, fo. 366, 28 Feb. 1646.
[4] The role of Languedoc finance in the years 1661–1715 is illuminated in the earlier pages of G. Chaussinand-Nogaret, *Les financiers de Languedoc au xviiiᵉ siècle* (1970).
[5] A.A.E. France 1636, fo. 245, [?] Jan. 1654. The comment was Servien's.
[6] A.A.E. France 1630, fos. 436–40, 19, 21, and 22 Dec. 1638.
[7] A.A.E. France 1631, fo. 319 and B.N. MS.fr. 3768, fos. 13ᵛ–14ʳ, 10 May 1639. A.G. A1 49, fos. 142, 218, 30 June and 29 Dec. 1638. Numerous minutes of the war minister in A.G. A1 50 and 50/2.

at Pézenas (1640, 1641), Béziers (1642), and Montpellier (1643) did so. In 1645 and 1646 Schomberg and the intendants levied the winter quarter directly and circumvented the fiscal machinery of the Estates. The Pézenas Estates of 1653 refused to make a grant while the troops remained in the province, with the result that the troops took 1·8 million for the winter quarter and probably much more besides.[1] The government did not repeat this mistake after 1653: whenever possible, the troops were kept in Roussillon until the deliberations of the Estates were completed. On 16 November 1656, however, the troops entered Languedoc on the very day that the Estates began their deliberations. Twelve days later, the Estates refused a money grant to the government, and they were not brought back to obedience until the middle of January 1657.[2]

The history of the provincial Estates at the time of Richelieu and Mazarin is thus in most cases a question of gain and loss. The Estates of Normandy and the Dauphiné disappeared. Those of Burgundy, Brittany, and Languedoc not only survived, but prospered. In some cases, notably Provence, the situation was less clear-cut because the nature of representation changed. Each province had to defend its representative institution; both geographical and social fragmentation had to be avoided. The fiscal regime was by no means the only factor in success or failure: the Estates disappeared in Provence, an area of land tax, but they disappeared in the Dauphiné also in the last years of the *taille personnelle*. Yet the fiscal system was of great importance. The land tax was relatively less corrupt, more efficient, and socially more progressive than the income tax in areas of *taille personnelle*. For these reasons, some intendants favoured an extension of the land tax into the whole of France.[3] The relative merits of the land tax favoured the survival of representative institutions, since the government could rely on the sums

[1] A.A.E. France 1636, fos. 167, 170, 20 and 31 May 1653.

[2] A.A.E. France 1637, fos. 12, 16, 30, 1[?], 8, and 16 Jan. 1657.

[3] *Lettres . . . au Chancelier Séguier*, ed. Mousnier, i. 248. Its problems were rigidity at the level of the province as a whole: G. Frêche, *Toulouse et la région Midi-Pyrénées au siècle des lumières, vers 1670–1789* (1974), pp. 496, 498–9, 501. Where adjustments were made, everything depended on who made them. Cf. the criticisms of Charreton de la Terrière of the land tax in Montauban, chiefly because of the adjustments brought about by the *élus*: Bercé, *Histoire des croquants*, ii. 800–1.

accorded by the Estates being levied effectively by their fiscal machinery.[1] In contrast, the inefficiency of the *élus* forced the government increasingly to circumvent these officials in the 1630s and 1640s. Much more money was demanded and levied from the *pays d'élections*: but the gap between the projected and the actual tax yield in these areas was much wider than in areas of land tax. The system of land tax thus allowed the intendant only a small role in the fiscal process, this role being limited to the revision of the land registers, which did not occur frequently.[2] The fiscal machinery of the Estates worked, however, because it relied on an element of consent; the same aspect of consent severely restricted the size of the revenues which the government could expect from the province. The increase in the *taille* in the *pays d'élections* was an authoritarian act, carried out without reference to the population as a whole. The Estates-General, which in any case had no power of the purse, had not met since 1614. The summoning of the Estates-General, and its being accorded fiscal powers, were live political issues under Richelieu and Mazarin—particularly during the Fronde. The government, when it was secure politically, had no intention of conceding the right of consent to taxation to the whole of France. This would have been regarded as a division of the king's sovereignty and thus was unacceptable politically to the ministers. Of more practical importance was the fact that where local Estates survived, the burden of taxation was relatively light and became proportionately lighter as the war progressed.[3] Brittany, Burgundy, Languedoc, and Provence were protected from the fiscal demands of the government because they possessed strong, although quite different, local institutions. In view of the strategic importance of most of the *pays d'états* as frontier provinces, there may have been some political gains for the government in protecting their privileges.

---

[1] With the notable exceptions of Brittany in 1643 and Provence in 1651.

[2] For example, Miron and Le Camus in the diocese of Lodève: E 122a, fo. 210, 20 Jan. 1635. Bosquet in the *élection* of Armagnac: E 171a, fo. 345, 14 June 1642. Pellot in the *généralité* of Montauban: E 374a, fo. 337, 8 Oct. 1664. For Boucault in the diocese of Lodève: E. Appolis, 'La confection d'un compoix diocésain en Languedoc au xviie siècle', *Anciens pays et assemblées d'états*, xl (1966), 151–2.

[3] Thus the diocese of Castres in Languedoc contributed 128,366 *livres* in 1635, 194,991 *livres* in 1648, yet only 118,102 *livres* in 1661: Frêche, *Toulouse*, pp. 503, 517. Provence contributed 2,222,287 *livres* in 1636 yet only 1,845,450 *livres* in 1657: Kettering, *Judicial politics*.

CHAPTER XVI

The Protestants

ALMOST EVERYONE involved in government at the time of Richelieu and Mazarin wanted ultimately to suppress Protestantism in France. The debate was over how best to achieve this aim, whether Protestantism should be proscribed officially, and whether coercion should be used. Many Catholics agreed with Cardin Le Bret when he described the edict of Nantes of 13 April 1598 as 'cette ombre de loi que la nécessité du temps a tiré par la force de la piété de nos Rois . . .'[1] On the other hand, there was a body of Catholic opinion which argued that the 'edicts of pacification'—that is to say, all royal edicts concerning the Protestants of which there were numerous examples after 1563[2]—were political concessions to secure the safety of the state. The future of Catholicism, according to this argument, was best guaranteed by the maintenance of public order rather than civil war. For these reasons, Chancellor Séguier argued as late as 1656 that 'les édits de pacification sont les fondements de la tranquillité publique qui ne doibt point estre branlés sans grande raison, et le changement que l'on y apporte doibt bien estre considéré'.[3] At the time of Richelieu particularly, French society was still obsessed by the issues of the wars of religion in the late sixteenth century and the lessons to be drawn from them. The development of the powers of the intendants over the question of Protestantism followed the public debate on this subject. All the intendants were Catholic, and some were hardline Catholics who were members of the *dévot* party:[4] it followed that the Huguenots regarded any increased authority of the intendants with great suspicion

1 Quoted by Picot, *Cardin Le Bret*, p. 189.
2 Edicts and treaties concerning the Protestants were issued in 1570, 1577, 1589, 1591, 1594, 1598, 1610, 1615, 1616, 1622, 1626, 1629, 1643, 1652, and 1656.
3 A.A.E. France 900, fo. 84 and B.L. Harleian 4489, fo. 2, 16 June 1656.
4 B.N. MS.fr. 14028, 'le portrait des maîtres des requêtes'. This suggests that Olivier Lefèvre d'Ormesson, Boucherat, Barrin, and Garibal, among others, were *dévots*.

unless Protestants were appointed as joint royal commissioners.[1]

Before 1629 the situation of the Protestants was complicated by the existence of their political and military organization which had been allowed by the secret articles of 30 April 1598. By the time of Louis XIII's reign, the royal subsidy to the Protestants, allowed by Henri IV on 3 April 1598, had been stopped. The defeat of any Protestant conspiracy or revolt would be used by the government as an excuse to undermine the Huguenot political and military establishment. The Protestants mobilized their forces in 1611–12 following the dismissal of Sully, Henri IV's Protestant minister,[2] who joined Condé's rebellion in 1615–16. On 10 May 1621, Rohan, the governor of Poitou, and Soubise, his younger brother, led a revolt of the Protestants following the enforced restoration of Catholicism in Béarn. The duc de La Force, the Protestant governor of Béarn, also joined the rebellion, which ended with the peace of Montpellier (19 October 1622). This treaty was a significant defeat for the Huguenots[3] since Béarn did not regain its former autonomy as a Calvinist stronghold, while Rohan and the duc de La Force were deprived of their governorships. The edict of Nantes and the secret articles of 2 May 1598 were both confirmed: but the secret articles of 30 April 1598, which had granted a political and military organization to the Huguenots, were not confirmed in full. Thus the Protestants lost nearly half their *villes de sûreté*. During the revolt of 1621–2 there had undoubtedly been much greater intervention in Protestant affairs by Catholic intendants than hitherto:[4] as a

[1] cf. the attitude of Elie Benoist, who thought the intendants were 'toujours amis du clergé et des Jésuites'. E. Benoist, *Histoire de l'édit de Nantes contenant les choses plus remarquables qui se sont passés en France avant et après sa publication* (5 vols., Delft, 1693), iii. 120. However, one intendant at least—Tallemant—was a *nouveau converti*: A.A.E. France 1634, fo. 585ᵛ, 29 Mar. 1652. Perhaps it was for this reason that he was recalled suddenly from Montpellier: E 1700, no. 67, 13 June 1652.
[2] For Sully's refusal to abjure: B. Barbiche and D. J. Buisseret, 'Les convictions religieuses de Sully', *Bibliothèque de l'École des Chartes*, cxxi (1963), 223–30. For Sully's participation in the rebellions of 1615–16 and 1621–2: *Négociations, lettres et pièces relatives à la conférence de Loudun*, ed. Bouchitté, p. 319. K 112, no. 5 [Musée AE II 798], 22 May 1622.
[3] cf. the judgement of Lublinskaya, *French absolutism*, p. 210.
[4] For example by Machault in the Limousin and later in Languedoc: V6 1212, no. 18, 30 Mar. 1621. E 72a, fo. 362, 21 July 1622.

concession to the Protestants, the terms of the peace were enforced in provinces such as Poitou and Guyenne by joint Catholic and Protestant commissioners,[1] comparable to those sent
out in 1599 and 1611 to enforce much more extensive privileges.[2] Nevertheless, in some areas dominated by the Huguenots, such as the Vivarais, the commissioners re-established
Catholic rights of worship which had been forfeited during the
rebellion.[3] The power of the crown in certain towns formerly
dominated by the Huguenots was strengthened after the peace.
At Montpellier, the *consulat* was divided between Catholics and
Protestants, with the *consuls* nominated by the crown. Estampes de Valençay, the governor of the town, was a partisan
of the Catholic cause. He interfered in the elections of 1623 and
arrested Rohan when he tried to support the Protestant cause.
A fortress was constructed at Montpellier in order to give
security to the Catholics. François du Faure, the intendant of
Languedoc, was one of those responsible for supervising the
completion of the fortifications.[4]

The appointment of Richelieu as first minister (13 August
1624) did not disrupt the peace with the Protestants established at Montpellier two years earlier. Richelieu was the
candidate of the *dévot* party, but while the *dévots* wanted the
destruction of the Huguenots as a priority above all else, and
the immediate revocation of the edict of Nantes,[5] Richelieu
thought it could safely be deferred. In Richelieu's view, decisions in French foreign policy could not be deferred in this
way: in particular the king could not abandon the Valtelline
without sacrificing his honour. Richelieu was thus prepared to
postpone the destruction of the Huguenot 'state-within-a-state'

---

[1] Instructions for the commissioners: Petracchi, *Intendenti e prefetti*, p. 25. Amelot
and Chalars in Poitou: E 76, fo. 179, 17 Aug. 1623. E 79b, fo. 395, 21 Aug. 1624.
Séguier and Pardalian in Guyenne: cf. V6 94, no. 59, 7 Mar. 1634.

[2] For the commissioners of 1599, the definitive study is F. Garrison, *Essai sur les
commissions d'application de l'édit de Nantes. I. Règne d'Henri IV* (Montpellier, 1950).
There is no comparable study in print for the later commissioners. For Boissize and
de la Caze in Guyenne: E 33b, fo. 125ᵛ, 17 Dec. 1611.

[3] By De la Croix and Chabrilles: cf. E 78c, fo. 142, 24 Apr. 1624.

[4] P. Gachon, *Quelques préliminaires de la révocation de l'édit de Nantes en Languedoc,
1661–1685* (Toulouse, 1899), p. 41. Lublinskaya, *French absolutism*, p. 215. Clarke,
Huguenot warrior, p. 111. *Les papiers de Richelieu*, ed. Grillon, i. 157–8. A.A.E. France
1627, fos. 124, 230, 19 Mar. 1623, 8 Feb. 1625.

[5] Allier, *La cabale des dévots*, p. 287. Cf. Marillac's speech to the king's council in
1626, cited above, chapter II.

indefinitely and was taken completely by surprise by the revolts of Rohan and Soubise in 1625. Richelieu had not expected them to exploit the opportunity presented by French intervention in the affairs of Italy and Switzerland in support of a Protestant ally of France,[1] and he never forgave them for doing so. The revolt was based on La Rochelle and the Huguenot towns in the Midi, but support was uneven. Rohan's control did not extend to all the Huguenot towns. At Montauban, the populace forced the rebellion on a reluctant municipality. Castres was prepared to consider a separate peace, and was prevented from doing so only by Rohan's personal intervention. The Huguenot party had thus lost a great deal of its momentum as a political force, and from Richelieu's point of view this was fortunate indeed. Even a relatively ineffective Huguenot rebellion posed a major threat to Richelieu, whose position at court was uncertain and whose foreign policy was desperately unpopular. Richelieu was forced to make peace with the Huguenots at Paris on 5 February 1626. The provisions of the peace of Montpellier were upheld, with the exception of La Rochelle. A conservative municipal constitution was imposed on La Rochelle, and a peace commissioner was to remain in the city during the king's good pleasure.[2]

The Huguenots had succeeded in making a dangerous enemy of Richelieu, but had gained nothing from the revolt of 1625–6. They would resume the offensive at a favourable opportunity; for his part, Richelieu was determined to destroy the Huguenot political and military organization during the next trial of strength. The treaty of Monzon, which was ratified on 2 May 1626, was in some respects a diplomatic defeat for Richelieu: but it eliminated the foreign diversion—

[1] Richelieu might have borne in mind the Valtelline difficulties of the Brûlarts shortly before the peace of Montpellier. Cf. Lublinskaya, *French absolutism*, pp. 209–10. He was certainly aware of Henri IV's difficulties with the Protestants during the siege of Amiens, which had been captured by the Spanish in 1597. In that year, the Protestants had gone into revolt and obtained concessions that were confirmed in the settlement of Nantes in 1598. *Les papiers de Richelieu*, ed. Grillon, i. 184.

[2] It is an open question whether this clause was implemented fully: Clarke, *Huguenot warrior*, p. 134. Lublinskaya, *French absolutism*, p. 217. For the debate over whether to make peace with the Protestants in 1625–6: *Les papiers de Richelieu*, ed. Grillon, i. 218–20, 226–33, 294–5. For difficulties of the government in obtaining registration of the settlement by the *Parlements* without modification: E 87a, fo. 368, 13 May 1626.

at least temporarily—and ensured that the full weight of the French army would be used in the forthcoming struggle with the Huguenots. The trial and execution of Chalais on a charge of high treason (18 August 1626) strengthened Richelieu's position at court. In 1625 and again in 1628 Richelieu demanded, and obtained, a grant from the clergy towards the costs of besieging La Rochelle. The Huguenot leaders recognized the need for allies in the struggle, however. The great hope lay with the English, who invaded the Île-de-Ré on 10 July 1627. Rohan resolved to go into rebellion shortly after this invasion, and on 10 September 1627 the rebellion was proclaimed by a general assembly at Nîmes. The trial of strength had begun.

Louis XIII and Richelieu conducted the siege of La Rochelle personally, while the command of the other forces in the Midi was given to Condé. The Condé of the 1620s was a very different political being from that of 1615–16. His hard-line attitude towards the Huguenots was proverbial. In his advice to the king on the 'moiens infaillibles de ruiner en peu de temps les Huguenots de Languedoc', Condé rejected the idea that the Protestants were divided and that some towns were neutral. He argued that all the Huguenot towns supported the rebellion financially, whether or not they joined in the military campaign. Condé thus proposed that the attack should be directed against all the Huguenot towns. He rejected all talk of truces and of a separate peace with Rohan. He wanted the sequestration of Rohan's property, the abolition of the *chambres de l'édit*—special courts dealing with Protestant cases set up by the terms of the edict of Nantes—and 'un degast générale de ville en ville, brusler leurs maisons voisines et en un mot procéder par une entière rigueur . . .'[1] In the long-term, these tactics were successful. In the short-term, however, they had the effect of stiffening resistance. Both Castres and Montauban had stood aloof from the rebellion before Condé put Realmont to the sword (30 March 1628). When the exiles from Realmont went to these two cities, they brought about a political revolution in Rohan's favour.[2] On 29 October 1628, Louis XIII and Richelieu achieved the breakthrough with the surrender

[1] A.A.E. France 792, fo. 221, n.d.
[2] Clarke, *Huguen otwarrior*, pp. 166–7. A.A.E. France 790, fo. 175, 12 May 1628— 'cela a pesé le coeur des habitans de Castres'.

of La Rochelle. The special privileges of the town were removed and the demolition of its fortifications was ordered. On 16 November, Coignet de la Thuillerie was appointed as its intendant. His powers included those of presiding over the municipality and municipal elections. He was ordered to carry out the terms of the capitulation of the city, and to supervise the demolition of the fortifications. The fall of La Rochelle meant inevitably that Rohan would lose control of the Huguenot towns in the Midi too.[1] He held an assembly at Nîmes in an attempt to counteract this trend, and in desperation signed an alliance with Philip IV of Spain on 3 May 1629. Rohan was to be paid 900,000 *livres* in three instalments by the terms of this treaty,[2] but the financial assistance did not arrive early enough to prevent the fall of Privas on 27 May. On 17 June the city of Alais capitulated: there was no choice but peace.

The peace of Alais (28 June 1629) ended eight years of intermittent civil war. The edict of Nantes was guaranteed; but the secret articles of 30 April 1598 and 2 May 1598 were abolished. Instead, all Protestant fortifications were to be razed and all cannon melted down and sold. The political and military organization of the Huguenots was destroyed. Moreover, Rohan was sent into exile, although his title of duke was restored and he received 300,000 *livres* in reparations. The troops of Rohan were to serve the cause of the king of France in Italy.[3] Although at first sight just one more in a long line of *édits de pacification*, there is no doubt that the edict of Alais broke with previous practice. Richelieu remarked that whereas previous edicts had secured a temporary peace by giving the Huguenots 'des avantages préjudiciables à l'état', the peace of Alais was an *édit de grâce*, an act of clemency on the part of the king: the Huguenots were allowed liberty of conscience and, within the limits of the edict of Nantes, freedom of worship.[4] As with the edict of Nantes, the edict of Alais had to be reg-

---

[1] Hanotaux, *Origines*, pp. 282–9. Clarke, *Huguenot warrior*, pp. 172–3. Lublinskaya, *French absolutism*, p. 219. A.A.E. France 791, fo. 214, 24 Dec. 1628: 'toutes les villes demandent la paix a quelle condition que ce soit . . .'

[2] Richelieu, *Testament politique*, ed. André, p. 108. Clarke, *Huguenot warrior*, pp. 174–5. B.L. Add. MS. 30599, fos. 254–62.

[3] Clarke, op. cit., p. 179. Edict of *abolition* for Rohan and Soubise (July 1629). Cf. P 2358, pp. 167–89, 21 Feb. 1630.

[4] Richelieu, *Testament politique*, ed. André, p. 107.

istered in the sovereign courts. Marillac, the Keeper of the Seals, regarded registration as indispensable. In his view, it was essential that there should be no modifications to the edict since 'leurs difficultez précédentes ont donné lieu ou prétexte au derniers mouvements . . .'—he was thinking almost certainly of the opposition of the *Parlement* of Rouen to the edict of Nantes between 1598 and 1609, and the general opposition of the courts to article 27 of the edict of Nantes, the right of the Protestants to enter royal, seigneurial, and municipal office.[1] Marillac added: 'ès affaires de paix et de traictez le Roy les ayant examinés et discutés, il veut que les édits en soient enregistrez simplement . . .' Marillac accordingly advised Richelieu to send Nicolas Vignier or Charles Machault to enforce the registration of the edict of Alais at the extremely pro-Catholic *Parlement* of Toulouse.[2] Machault, the intendant of Languedoc, appears to have carried out the task.[3] Marillac also regarded the demolition of fortifications as of crucial importance.[4] Though a *dévot*, Marillac favoured the use of commissioners of the two religions.[5] Thus the terms of the peace of Alais were implemented in certain provinces, such as Languedoc[6] and Guyenne,[7] by Catholic intendants assisted by Huguenot notables. Sometimes—as at Nîmes in 1629—the task of demolishing the fortifications was commenced by a *maître des requêtes*;[8] on other occasions, relations with the Protestants were left to a *subdélégué* of the intendant, as in Poitou in 1630.[9]

The demolition of fortifications appears to have proceeded without great difficulty.[10] The removal and melting down of cannons was another matter. At Nîmes this was opposed from 1629 until 1632 because it was regarded as the prelude to a general disarming of the population. Machault, the intendant,

---

[1] Mousnier, *La vénalité*, pp. 592–4, 638–45.

[2] A.A.E. France 794, fo. 99, 18 Aug. 1629.

[3] A.E.E. France 795, fo. 96, 2 Oct. 1629.

[4] A.A.E. France 794, fo. 97, 16 Aug. 1629.

[5] A.A.E. France 794, fos. 31, 87ᵛ, 20 July and 2 Aug. 1629.

[6] By Machault and Candiac: cf. E 111c–112a, fo. 120, 12 May 1633. A.A.E. France 1628, fo. 40, Candiac to Richelieu, 15 Mar. 1630.

[7] By Verthamon and De Saint-Privas: V6 78, no. 1, 20 Sept. 1630.

[8] By Le Grand: cf. E 117b, fo. 494, 30 June 1634.

[9] Commissions of 9 Jan. 1630 and 12 Aug. 1632 to Jean Pallet seigneur des Rousseaux: cf. V6 132, no. 30, 17 Sept. 1638.

[10] It was, of course, part of a general attack by the crown on independent and especially seigneurial fortifications. Bercé, *Histoire des croquants*, i. 50–1, 124.

and Candiac, his Protestant assistant, were accused of giving the king's council 'de faux advis pour se maintenir ... et régner icy [Nîmes] enfin pour complaire aux huguenots'. There was a demand for a separate intendant for the town of Nîmes, who would be changed from time to time so that he would not be bought off by the local inhabitants.[1] Machault, however, was well aware of the dangers presented by the Protestants' retaining their cannons. He appears to have experienced genuine difficulty at Nîmes: 'ils ont [les armes] dans leurs maisons particulières ... en grande nombre comme dans une ville de rébellion'.[2] Elsewhere in Languedoc and its border regions, notably the Vivarais, Machault was much more successful in implementing the edict of Alais.[3] The success of the commissioners in 1629–30 is best illustrated by a negative fact: the Huguenots did not join any other rebellion during the ministries of Richelieu and Mazarin. They were quiescent during the revolt of Montmorency,[4] the Soissons conspiracy of 1641[5]— the duc de Bouillon, one of the leading conspirators, was a former Protestant[6]—and again during the Fronde.[7] It was not until 1683 that further Protestant revolts—the risings in the Vivarais and the Dauphiné—began in earnest.

The second period of Richelieu's ministry—the years from 1630 to 1642—was thus quite different from the first with regard to policy towards the Protestants. Richelieu continued to seek a conference of the two religions at which the 'errors' of the Protestants would be demonstrated conclusively.[8] In the mean-

---

[1] A.A.E. France 1628, fo. 105, Alexandre Fichet to the archbishop of Arles, 10 Feb. 1632.

[2] A.A.E. France 1628, fo. 107, 21 Feb. 1632.

[3] A.A.E. France 807, fo. 30, an account of Machault's activities, 28 Sept. 1632–27 Feb. 1633.

[4] Despite the fears of some observers: A.A.E. France 799, fo. 285, 17 Dec. 1631. Cf. the loyal conduct of Nîmes: A.A.E. France 1628, fo. 149, 18 July 1632.

[5] Despite the fears of the government: A.G. A1 65, mins. 33, 37/2, 7 June 1641.

[6] Bouillon had abjured Protestantism on 5 June 1636.

[7] Despite the fears in the Midi: Pillorget, *Les mouvements insurrectionnels*, p. 614. Memoranda to Mazarin: A.A.E. France 869, fos. 121, 404, 8 Oct. and [?] 1650. Mazarin feared that Turenne would lead a rising of the Protestants: P. A. Chéruel, *Histoire de France pendant la minorité de Louis XIV* (4 vols., 1879–80), i. 128–9.

[8] Blet, 'Le plan de Richelieu'. J. Orcibal, 'Louis XIV and the edict of Nantes', *Louis XIV and absolutism*, ed. Hatton, p. 155. For irenical proposals at Nîmes: A.A.E. France 838, fos. 27, 42, 25 Jan. and 5 Feb. 1641.

time, the edict of Nantes was guaranteed, but interpreted in the narrowest possible way and in important respects redefined. The Protestants retained their own courts, the *chambres de l'édit*, until 1679: but they changed decisively in character. Under Henri IV, the deputies-general of the Protestants conferred annually with the Chancellor on the choice of *parlementaires* for service in the *chambres de l'édit*. While this happened, moderates were selected, and Catholic zealots excluded. However, this practice was dropped during the reign of Louis XIII.[1] The *premiers présidents* of the *Parlements* simply informed the Chancellor of the *parlementaires* who had been nominated by the courts.[2] In addition, measures were taken to ensure Catholic preponderance at all times. On 18 January 1635, the king's council decided that in the absence of the Catholic *président*, the most senior Catholic councillor should preside over the *chambre de l'édit*. This decision was accepted by the *Parlement* of Toulouse with enthusiasm and practised at Castres after 1637.[3] The claims of the Protestant *président* and of any Protestant councillors who might be more senior than their Catholic counterparts were thus ignored. The *chambres de l'édit* at Paris, Castres, Bordeaux, and Grenoble had been established to eliminate the danger of partisan legal decisions being taken by the sovereign courts, which were dominated by Catholics. However, their effectiveness depended on a constructive attitude on the part of both religious parties, which was not the case by the reign of Louis XIII. Even though the *parlementaires* formed half the membership of the *chambres de l'édit*, they were seen as a threat to the supremacy of the existing courts. The abolition of these chambers, and the incorporation of their personnel into the *parlements*, was thus a consistent aim of the Catholic office-holders in the seventeenth century.[4] Furthermore, the intendants regarded these courts as a nuisance. They considered the *chambres de l'édit* fit for registering legis-

---

[1] Benoist, *Histoire de l'édit*, i. 277–8.

[2] J. Cambon de Lavalette, *La chambre de l'édit de Languedoc* (1872), pp. 164–5. B.N. MS.fr. 17367, fo. 237, 24 May 1633. La Vrillière advised Séguier to accept the nominations of the *premiers présidents* of Bordeaux and Toulouse: A.A.E. France 898, fo. 211, 19 July 1656.

[3] Cambon de Lavalette, op. cit., p. 103. B.N. MS.fr. 17370, fo. 196, 30 Dec. 1636.

[4] For example, the *Parlement* of Toulouse: Cambon de Lavalette, op. cit., p.106. B.N. MS.fr. 17389, fo. 11, 22 Jan. 1648. The *Parlement* of Aix: Pillorget, *Les mouvements insurrectionnels*, p. 21.

lation concerning the Protestants, but little else.[1] Antoine
Le Camus, the intendant of Languedoc, commented that the
court at Castres 'empesche et ruine la pluspart des affaires par
les deffences qu'elle donne . . . à tous ceulx ausquels on faict le
procès quand ils sont de la relligion [prétendue réformée]'.[2]
A second way in which the situation of the Protestants deteriorated under Richelieu was in the nature of their political
power in certain towns in the Midi. Up to 1630, the Protestants
denied Catholics political power in the towns which they
controlled. The *Parlement* of Toulouse, zealous as ever of Catholic interests, was determined that article 27 of the edict of
Nantes should be redefined and that Catholics should be admitted into municipalities dominated by the Protestants. Le
Mazuyer, the *premier président* of the *Parlement* of Toulouse,
informed Richelieu on 28 October 1630 that 'il ne faut esperer
avoir un fruit des succès des armes du Roy si en toutes les villes
les Catholiques ne sont admis aux consulats . . . ' He insisted also
that the *chambre de l'édit* of Castres should be denied jurisdiction
in election disputes involving towns with a significant Protestant population. He alleged that any such jurisdiction held
by the *chambre* was 'contraire la teneur des édits'.[3] The *Parlement* won its campaign. On 19 October 1631, the king's council
ordered that Catholics should be admitted into a number of
municipalities previously dominated by the Huguenots.[4] This
decree was enforced in Languedoc by commissioners of the
chambre de l'édit of Castres in 1631–2 and 1634–5.[5] Nevertheless,
the Huguenots might retain real control of the town, despite
the introduction of the *consulat mi-parti*, unless the governor, the
intendant, and the local bishop could agree on Catholic candidates for municipal office. In some towns, such as Nîmes,
there were few Catholics and intermarriage took place between

[1] B.N. MS.fr. 17369, fo. 180ᵛ, 24 Oct. 1634.

[2] *Bnutrennyaya*, ed. Lublinskaya, p. 22.

[3] A.A.E. France 796, fos. 279, 289, 28 Oct. and 9 Nov. 1630. These letters bear
out Ligou's description of Le Mazuyer as the 'véritable chef du parti ultra en
Languedoc'. D. Ligou, *Le protestantisme en France de 1598 à 1715* (1968), p. 94.
Gilles Le Mazuyer had served as intendant in Burgundy in 1612 before becoming
premier président in 1615: E 34b–35a, fo. 286, 31 Mar. 1612.

[4] Gachon, *Quelques préliminaires*, pp. 30–2, 49.

[5] A.A.E. France 1628, fo. 113, 28 Feb. 1632—report of the commissioners
critical of the *Parlement* of Toulouse 'à quoy les voyes de douceur ne sont pas
agréables . . .' E 122d, fo. 9, 28 Mar. 1635.

Catholics and Protestants. In such a town, the Catholic converts were suspect to the bishop: 'la pluspart des officiers convertis pour l'intérest depuis 12 ou 15 ans sont encores dans l'âme de très fiers Huguenots', reported the bishop in 1640.[1] A similar situation arose from the new requirements that a Catholic magistrate should preside over all meetings of the Huguenots 'pour leurs affaires extraordinaires'. In Languedoc in 1633, Schomberg and the intendants considered that there were relatively few Catholic office-holders with suitable experience to perform such tasks.[2]

A third way in which the situation of the Protestants deteriorated under Richelieu was in the re-interpretation of clauses 8 and 9 of the edict of Nantes. In order to hold services, the Huguenots had to justify the right to do so from legal deeds. If they could not produce the requisite documents, the intendants judged that the Protestants had a 'possession abuzive' and prohibited services from being held. The bishop of Nîmes wanted illegal meetings to be investigated jointly by the intendant and the local bishop in the area where the meeting had been held.[3] Others—such as Schomberg, the governor— took a more moderate stance. The intendants, in his view, should investigate illegal meetings to 'leur faire peur seulement'. Schomberg proclaimed a cease-fire: 'en ce temps il ne seroit pas bon de les tormenter mais aussy ne voulons-nous pas leur faire voir qu'on relasche.'[4] Articles 8 and 9 of the edict of Nantes had stipulated the type of places where services might be held. The clauses made no mention of the residence of the pastors who held the Protestant services. Antoine Le Camus, the intendant of Languedoc, thus advised the Chancellor to have a decree drawn up prohibiting services from being held by pastors from outside the locality: 'vous pourriez en justice faire cette établissement sans vous départir en façon quelconque des édits de pacification . . .'[5] The intendant alleged that the legislation was already in practice in Languedoc; he merely suggested a general codification and the extension of the practice through-

[1] A.A.E. France 837, fo. 186ᵛ, 14 Aug. 1640.

[2] *Bnutrennyaya*, ed. Lublinskaya, p. 25.

[3] A.A.E. France 837, fo. 186ᵛ, 14 Aug. 1640.

[4] A.A.E. France 1629, fo. 50, memorandum of Schomberg, Apr. 1635 [?].

[5] *Lettres . . . au Chancelier Séguier*, ed. Mousnier, i. 220–1. B.N. MS.fr. 17368, fo. 168ᵛ. B.N. MS.fr. 17369, fo. 180, 24 Oct. 1634.

out France. Another area in which redefinition occurred was in the question of marriages between Protestants and Catholics. Pierre Fenouillet, the bishop of Montpellier, insisted on the abjuration of Huguenots who entered such marriages: in his diocese, therefore, the effective prohibition of mixed marriages was being enforced as early as 1637, although this was not enforced nationally until 1680. In 1638, Miron and Dupré, the intendants, issued an ordinance against the 'profaners of the sacrament of marriage' which Protestants saw as the source of all subsequent legislation on 'relapsed' Catholics.[1]

The deaths of Louis XIII and Richelieu led to no sudden change in the direction of royal policy with regard to the Protestants. On 8 July 1643 the previous edicts of pacification were confirmed. On 30 January 1645, the jurisdiction of the *chambres de l'édit* in cases involving Protestants was confirmed too. Mazarin was no crusader for the orthodox religion.[2] Mazarin's preoccupation with foreign affairs left the conduct of policy towards the Protestants largely in the hands of the secondary administrators. The attitude of the intendants was therefore of great importance. The intendants of Languedoc warned the government of the dangers posed by the Protestants during a royal minority. Bosquet, the moderate intendant, noted the Huguenots' 'pensées avantageuses pour leur party'. In his view, they wanted 'l'entière exécution de l'édict de Nantes . . . [et] descharge de l'obligation de toutes les déclarations, arrests et règlements postérieurs à l'édit'. The Protestants also wanted to hold services in all areas occupied during the revolts of 1621–9.[3] Baltazar, Bosquet's less moderate colleague, saw the situation as nothing less than a Protestant conspiracy. 'Il les fault humilier', he declared. In his view, Protestants should be excluded from office:[4] throughout his period as intendant, Baltazar maintained his opposition to the *chambre de l'édit* of

[1] F. Shickler, 'Les mariages mixtes. Lettre de l'évêque de Montpellier à M. de la Vrillière, 1637', *Bulletin de la société de l'histoire de protestantisme français*, xv (1866), 418–24. Cf. also Baltazar's ordinance of 25 Oct. 1644 against Protestants who abjured, married according to Catholic ceremony, and then returned to Protestantism. *Bnutrennyaya*, ed. Lublinskaya, p. 87.

[2] Blet, *Le clergé*, ii. 346–8. Cambon de Lavalette, *La chambre de l'édit de Languedoc*, p. 107.

[3] *Bnutrennyaya*, ed. Lublinskaya, pp. 38–41.

[4] ibid., p. 51. A.A.E. France 1634, fo. 254, 21 Nov. 1646.

Castres and the *cour des comptes* of Montpellier (which he wanted
to separate as a *chambre des comptes* and *cour des aides*).[1] Above
all, he formulated the doctrine that the intendant had ultimate
jurisdiction in cases involving Protestants, 'le droit commun
donnant l'autorité au premier magistrat d'y pourvoir'.[2] During Baltazar's intendancy, therefore, the principle of public
law was applied to the *chambres de l'édit*. The edict of Nantes had
assumed that the two religious groups at the *chambre de l'édit*
would attempt to co-operate, and when a division (*partage*)
along religious lines occurred for example at Castres, it would
be resolved at Grenoble. Ultimately, decisions on appeals were
to rest with a special commission of the *chambre de l'édit* of Paris.
The extension of the principle of public law into the area of
Protestant cases meant that divisions of opinion along religious
lines at the *chambre de l'édit* could be resolved by the king's
council in favour of the Catholic interpretation. Moreover, the
intendant became the watchdog of the government over all
Protestant activities. Bosquet's conduct was moderate, but he
refused to receive deputations from the Protestants.[3] Baltazar
received deputations, but harangued them and acted in an
overtly hostile manner. He refused to allow the Huguenots of
Montpellier a parish bell on the grounds that the secret articles
of 2 May 1598, which had conceded this right, had been
revoked. If the Protestants had won the right to parish bells at
Montpellier, Baltazar argued that they would have demanded
the same right elsewhere.[4] Baltazar intervened regularly in the
meetings of the synods and consistories of Languedoc.[5] Else-

[1] Although Baltazar proposed this measure to humiliate the court, the union of
the *Chambre des comptes* with the *cour des aides* in 1629 was a measure aimed at
diluting the Protestant control of the *comptes* who 'composoi[en]t plus que les deux
tiers de la compagnie . . .' A.A.E. France 1629, fo. 21, memorandum *c*. Dec. 1633.
The measure had originally been proposed by François Faure, the Catholic
intendant, in a memorandum to Chancellor Sillery of 18 Mar. 1623. A.A.E.
France 1627, fo. 122.
[2] '. . . Ceux de l'une et l'autre religion sont également leurs justiciables . . .',
he added. *Bnutrennyaya*, ed. Lublinskaya, pp. 138–9. On another occasion, Baltazar
declared that 'si nostre compétence dépendoit des chambres de l'édit et des parlements, nostre fonction seroit assez inutile dans les provinces et particulièrement
en celle-cy, tant à cause de la jalousie des autoritez, que parce que c'est icy où est
la pépinière des huguenots'. Ibid., p. 46.
[3] cf. A.A.E. France 1637, fo. 99, 4 July 1657.
[4] *Bnutrennyaya*, ed. Lublinskaya, p. 49.
[5] ibid., pp. 50–1, 100–4, 199–200. Porchnev, *Les soulèvements populaires*, pp.
640–1.

where, the intendants intervened in Protestant affairs, too. In 1647, Jean Lauzon, the intendant of Guyenne, was empowered to investigate alleged violations of the 'edicts of pacification' by the Protestants.[1]

The Fronde was a crucial period for the future of Protestantism in France. The Huguenots benefited from certain measures taken in the early stages of the Fronde, such as the recall of the intendants from all but six provinces. The rebellion of the *Parlements* in 1648–9 gave the Protestants hope that these institutions might become discredited—a state of affairs beneficial to the *chambres de l'édit* which in general supported the cause of the government during the Fronde.[2] The last year of the Fronde brought the prospect of real gains to the Huguenots. Condé's revolt of 1651–2 was based on Guyenne and the southwest of France. The government greatly feared the spread of the revolt into the Huguenot towns of Languedoc.[3] This development could be prevented with certainty only by a declaration favourable to the Protestants which would 'rétablir . . . l'estat où ils ont esté autrefois dans le Languedoc et dans le reste du royaume'. The result was the declaration of Saint-Germain (21 May 1652), issued shortly before Mazarin's second exile, which appeared to remove all the legal obstacles to a full interpretation of the edict of Nantes. The Protestants were to be 'maintenus et gardés en la pleine et entière jouissance de l'édit de Nantes' as a reward for their 'affection et fidélité notamment dans les circonstances présentes, dont nous demeurons très satisfait'. The declaration did not restore the *status quo ante* 1629: but it appeared to remove at a stroke all the measures taken by Louis XIII, Richelieu, Mazarin, the council, and the intendants after that date.[4] Other decisions of the council in the course of 1652 guaranteed the position of Protestants in the

---

[1] E 1692, no. 232, 19 Dec. 1647.

[2] For example, Castres: Cambon de Lavalette, *La chambre de l'édit de Languedoc*, pp. 110–13. More specifically, it would tend to strengthen the power of the Protestant members of the court against the Catholic *parlementaires*. Baltazar thought they were already strong enough: 'il est certain que les juges huguenotz sont beaucoup plus unis entr'eux que les catholiques.' *Bnutrennyaya*, ed. Lublinskaya, p. 139.

[3] cf. the instructions to Maugiron, corrected in Servien's hand: A.A.E. France 1634, fo. 556ᵛ, 3 Mar. 1652.

[4] Blet, *Le clergé*, ii. 350. E. G. Léonard, 'Le protestantisme français au xviiᵉ siècle', *Revue Historique*, cc (1948), 167–8.

Languedoc towns, including Montpellier.[1] The Protestant gains from the last year of the Fronde were thus substantial. What they could not gain from the king's council they attempted to take by force. In 1653 a band of seven or eight thousand Protestants tried to establish by force of arms the right to hold services at Vals in the Vivarais. They were prevented by the comte de Rieux, who had summoned a force of about six thousand retainers. Vals was a test case: if the Protestants has been strong enough to enforce their rights there, they would have asserted their claims to hold services in other localities.[2] In 1654, Louis de Boucherat and D'Escorbiac—the latter a Protestant— were commissioned to investigate alleged infringements of the 'edicts of pacification' in Languedoc, Haute Guyenne, and Foix as a direct response to these events.[3] The Estates of Languedoc of 1654–5 greeted this investigation with considerable relief, and the work of the commissioners marks the beginning of a hardening of attitudes towards the Protestants in the later years of Mazarin's ministry.

The declaration of Saint-Germain was extremely unpopular with Catholic opinion generally, and above all with the *dévots*, who applied pressure on the Assembly of Clergy to get the declaration revoked. On 8 June 1654, 2 April 1656, and 12 July 1656, the clergy presented remonstrances to the government.[4] Chancellor Séguier was highly critical of the stand taken by the Assembly. The clergy, he argued, was the most privileged of the three orders of France, but in such questions its assembly had no more authority than that of any other body such as the provincial Estates. Séguier had no wish to encourage Protestantism, or heresy 'au préjudice de l'église' as he termed it. However, he was against the government being forced to revoke the edict of Saint-Germain. In the event, however, he reluctantly agreed to a new declaration which would render

[1] E 1700, nos. 36, 44, 57, 18 Mar., 11 Apr. and 21 May 1652. Cf. E 1696, no 279, 26 Sept. 1651.

[2] A.A.E. France 890, fo. 298, 20 Sept. 1653. A.A.E. France 1636, fo. 219, 15 Nov. 1653. The Estates of Languedoc in 1656–7 voted the comte de Rieux a reward of 15,000 *livres*. Cf. B.L. Harleian 4442, fo. 169, 13 Apr. 1660: the Protestants, according to Bezons, had established services at Saint-Gilles 'soubs prétexte de la déclaration . . . [de] 1652'.

[3] cf. E 1706, no. 38, 28 Apr. 1656.

[4] Allier, *La cabale des dévots*, pp. 309–10, 315. Blet, *Le clergé*, ii. 351–2, 357, 359, n. 89.

that of 1652 'inutil en ce qu'elle pouvoit estre avantageuse à ceux de la R.P.R. audelà de l'édit de Nantes et autres déclarations depuis intervenus'.[1] The result was the declaration of 18 July 1656. This stated that the government had had no intention of innovating when it issued the declaration of Saint-Germain, which, it alleged, was merely a restatement of decisions taken during Louis XIII's reign.[2] The restrictive legislation and interpretations of legislation would thus continue to apply. The declaration also committed the government to send out Catholic and Protestant commissioners—Séguier had accepted this proposal on 26 June 1656 and La Vrillière had apparently issued commissions to the intendants by 12 February 1657. However, little effective work seems to have taken place.[3] Almost certainly it was Mazarin himself who prevented this investigation into alleged contraventions of the 'edicts of pacification'. A new declaration was acceptable to the chief minister. Its rigorous implementation was not: this would be a triumph for the policy of the *dévots*, whom Mazarin greatly feared.[4]

The declaration of 18 July 1656 pleased neither side. The clergy protested that it was not being implemented and that in any case it was too liberal with regard to the *chambres de l'édit*, which they wanted to abolish.[5] The Huguenots, too, protested against the declaration. The *chambres de l'édit* refused to register it until forced to do so by the council of state.[6] The full extent of the Huguenot opposition was revealed by the manifesto entitled the *Apologie des églises réformées du Languedoc*,[7] which circulated widely in the province 'par une infinité d'exemplaires imprimez'[8] and was declared seditious by the council of state.[9] The *Apologie* argued that the government was about to

[1] A.A.E. France 900, fo. 84 and B.L. Harleian 4489, fo. 2, 16 June 1656.
[2] Blet, *Le clergé*, ii. 359. To a certain extent the government may have been influenced by motives of foreign policy in issuing the declaration of 18 July 1656. It sought to distract domestic attention from the alliance with Cromwell: Orcibal, 'Louis XIV and the edict of Nantes', *Louis XIV and absolutism*, ed. Hatton, p. 156, n. 17 (at p. 168). [3] Blet, *Le clergé*, ii. 356, 361.
[4] For Mazarin's distrust of the *dévots*: Allier, *La cabale des dévots*, pp. 340, 346, 361.
[5] Blet, *Le clergé*, ii. 361.
[6] Cambon de Lavalette, *La chambre de l'édit de Languedoc*, pp. 117–19. E 1706, nos. 147, 161, 17 Feb. and 27 Mar. 1657.
[7] B.L. printed works 1019, fo. 19/4.
[8] A.A.E. France 1637, fo. 102, 1 Aug. 1657.
[9] E 1708, no. 5, 14 Jan. 1658.

abolish the *chambres de l'édit* and to revoke the edict of Nantes. The ultimate aim, it claimed, was to expel the Huguenots from the kingdom. The Protestants were being excluded systematically from the *consulats*, and the example of Montpellier was cited, where the all-Catholic *consuls* of 1652 had been continued in office each year by a decree of the council.[1] Once an all-Catholic magistrature was installed, the pamphlet argued, local administration became sectarian in character: in particular, poor relief was administered to Catholics only. The pamphlet complained bitterly against the comte de Roure, one of the lieutenants-general of Languedoc, who had brought a substantial number of troops into Montpellier on 5 March 1657 to ensure that only Catholics were elected.[2] By 1657, therefore, the Protestants of the Midi feared imminent persecution.

Almost all Catholic opinion in France sought to destroy Protestant civil rights in the years between 1630 and 1661. Above all, the clergy and the sovereign courts waged a persistent—and ultimately successful—campaign to achieve this end. It was unlikely that in the long term the crown could combat this common front successfully, even had it wished to do so. Both Richelieu and Mazarin made clear concessions to the anti-Protestant coalition: most of these measures had been implemented by the intendants. Mazarin had not applied the declaration of 1656 to the full because of his dislike of the *dévots*: perhaps also Mazarin felt that Louis XIV himself should determine the timing of the resolution of the Protestant problem. The anti-Protestant crusade in the years after 1661 was thus not inevitable: but the increasing restrictions exercised over them by the intendants of Richelieu and Mazarin made it not only possible but probable.

[1] cf. E 1706, no. 63, 28 Aug. 1656.
[2] The Protestants claimed 4,000 troops. Roure claimed to have brought in 800: A.A.E. France 1637, fo. 65, 5 Mar. 1657.

CHAPTER XVII

The New Provinces

FRANCE IN 1659 was a larger country than in 1598. A number of provinces had been acquired which added significantly to the territory ruled by the king of France. Louis XIV was to make more conquests—notably in the Low Countries and Franche-Comté: but the principle of an aggressive, expanding France had been established before he began his personal rule in 1661. This was somewhat surprising in view of Richelieu's emphasis on legitimacy in French foreign policy: Richelieu had argued that the Habsburgs constituted a threat to the balance of power in Europe and to the territorial integrity and independence of smaller states. Once the Habsburgs had reconquered Germany, he argued, they would 's'occuper en France à nos dépens'.[1] The war against the Habsburgs was legitimate, therefore, because it was defensive. Leagues would be formed in Germany and Italy to counter the policy of the Habsburgs and prevent a resurgence of their power after the peace settlements had been signed. However, there was always an element of paradox in Richelieu's foreign policy. He wanted to make Louis XIII 'le plus puissant monarque du monde et le prince le plus estimé'. France was not interested merely in the formation of defensive leagues: it also wanted reparations and territorial guarantees against Habsburg intransigence at a later date. The cause of peace, therefore, became linked inextricably with the issue of sovereignty. On 20 September 1641, Richelieu ordered the Chancellor to investigate the claims of the king of France to Milan, Naples, Sicily, Piedmont, and the county of Burgundy: 'j'en ai besoin pour l'instruction de la paix', Richelieu declared.[2] Richelieu may thus have come near to accepting Le Bret's maxim on the inalienability of the royal domain, and the applicability of this concept to areas of the former Carol-

---

[1] Richelieu, *Mémoires*, ed. Lacour-Gayet and Lavollé, v. 193. Certain aspects of Richelieu's foreign policy are well studied by H. Weber, 'Richelieu et le Rhin', *Revue Historique*, ccxxxix (1968), 265–80.

[2] *Lettres . . . de Richelieu*, ed. Avenel, vi. 877. Thuau, *Raison d'état*, p. 302.

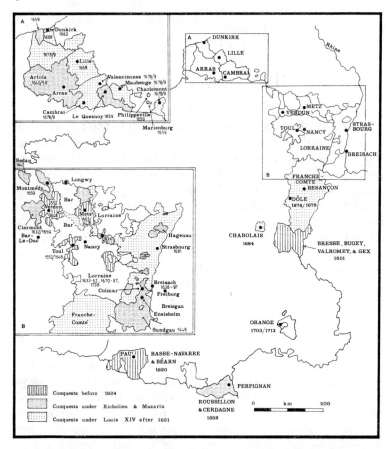

MAP. IV. Territorial annexations by France in the seventeenth century.

1632–62: period of occupation by French troops not leading to formal annexation
        at a peace treaty.
1703/1713: date of occupation/date of annexation at a peace treaty.
1678/9: duration of peace conference.

ingian empire which were no longer part of France.[1] There
were two ways in which new provinces might be acquired. The
first was through concessions by treaty—such as the acquisition
of Bresse, Bugey, Valromey, and Gex by the treaty of Lyon
(17 January 1601). The second was as a result of armed intervention and the establishment of a French administration—

[1] Above, chapter VI.

this was the method at the time of Richelieu. Military intervention arose from an overwhelming strategic consideration. Once the 'new provinces' were in French control, however, a claim to sovereignty gradually evolved. Ultimately, French control might be sanctioned by treaty. The intendants were the method by which French claims to sovereignty were enforced in the interim period.

The four provinces of Bresse Bugey, Valromey, and Gex were acquired from Savoy in 1601. Henri IV had declared war on 11 August 1600 on the issue of the marquisate of Saluzzo; he renounced this claim in return for these new provinces. In strategic terms, they were useful acquisitions—the city of Lyon itself was much better protected henceforth. The four provinces retained a considerable degree of administrative autonomy during the reigns of Henri IV and Louis XIII. One reason undoubtedly was that Bresse had its own representative institution.[1] A second factor was that when the intendancies were established in the 1620s and 1630s, there was genuine doubt whether these provinces should be linked with Lyon or Dijon. In 1621, Juyé de Moric included these new provinces in his enquiry comprising the farm of the *gabelle* in the Lyonnais.[2] Between 1628 and 1632, however, the provinces were administered independently, when Brûlart de la Borde verified the debts of the communities.[3] Yet in 1638 the area seems to have been linked with the intendancy of Lyon under Dreux d'Aubray,[4] while a new verification of the debts was carried out by commissioners from Burgundy.[5] By 1648, it appears that Bresse was firmly linked with the intendancy of Burgundy.[6] Part of the uncertainty resulted from the hostility of the lesser courts in Bresse to the *Parlement* of Dijon.[7]

The new provinces of Béarn and Basse Navarre similarly retained a considerable degree of autonomy. The religious

---

[1] Major, 'French representative assemblies', p. 191.

[2] E 69a, fo. 202, 27 Oct. 1621. E 70b, fo. 442, 22 Mar. 1622.

[3] cf. E 119a, fo. 269, 17 Aug. 1634.   [4] E 146a, fo. 423, 22 Sept. 1638.

[5] cf. E 151b, fo. 95, 18 June 1639.

[6] K 117b, no. 70, 1 Dec. 1648. The intendant ordered the *subsistances* for Bresse from 1636 until 1659: cf. A.A.E. France 1492, fos. 140, 148ᵛ, 26 Sept. 1656, 5 Jan. 1657. Bouchu, the intendant of Burgundy, established a *chambre souveraine* in Bresse in 1659: A.A.E. France 1492, fo. 227, 3 Apr. 1659.

[7] E 122c, fo. 103, 8 Mar. 1635.

situation was complex: Basse Navarre was overwhelmingly Catholic and hostile to the Protestant-dominated *vicomté* of Béarn.[1] In 1620, Louis XIII invaded Béarn, forcibly re-established Catholicism, and forced the *conseil souverain* to register the union of Béarn and Navarre to the crown of France. Robert Aubéry was subsequently sent to the area to enforce the edict of union since its validity was contested by the Estates of Navarre and of Béarn.[2] French language and French institutions were adopted only gradually, and met with considerable resistance. In May 1624 a predominantly Protestant *Parlement* was established at Pau, whose work was carried out in French. On 17 November 1631, Pierre de Marca, a *président* in this court, was appointed as intendant—chiefly as an assistant to the governor. By 1636, the *Parlement* had come to fear any increase in Marca's power as a loss of its own.[3] The appointment of Jean Gassion as intendant on 22 April 1640 brought this conflict to a head. The *Parlement*, arguing that it represented 'l'intérêt du roi et du public', asked that Gassion's commission be revoked. Gassion, however, was a *président* in the *Parlement*: he argued that no-one else would consider 'les intérestz de la compagnie comme luy'. In 1641, the Estates of Béarn sided with the *Parlement*. Gassion's commission, they asserted, 'pervertit les ordres antiens de ladite province pour la justice, police et finances'. They claimed that Gassion's commission was modelled on 'celles qui s'expédient pour les grandes provinces'—in short, that it was not suitable for Béarn.[4] The local politicians did not get their way, however. Gassion remained intendant until 1648,[5] chiefly because the governor considered him a useful agent in ordering the *subsistances* for the troops.[6] After 1644 his intendency comprised Navarre, Béarn, Bayonne,

[1] Estrée, *La Basse Navarre*, p. 132. The Estates of Navarre objected to the predominantly Protestant membership of the *parlement* of Pau, to its use of the French language, and to the implied subordination of Navarre to Béarn.

[2] P. Tucoo-Chala, *La vicomté de Béarn et le problème de sa souveraineté. Des origines à 1620* (Bordeaux, 1961), pp. 133, 200. Estrée, op. cit., p. 32. E 1685, fo. 26 and E 71c, fo. 309, 30 June 1622.

[3] Estrée, op. cit., p. 81. F. Loirette, 'L'administration royale en Béarn de l'union à l'intendance, 1620–1682. Essai sur le rattachement à la France d'une province frontière au xviie siècle', *XVIIe Siècle*, lxv (1964), 74. Gaquère, *Pierre de Marca*.

[4] Loirette, art. cit., pp. 77–81. For the commission in dispute: A.G. A1 62, no. 125, 22 Apr. 1640.

[5] E 228a, fo. 23ᵛ, 8 Jan. 1648.   [6] Loirette, art. cit., p. 79.

Bas Armagnac, Bigorre, Marsan, Foix, and the whole of the administrative area of the *chambre des comptes* of Navarre.[1] After the Fronde, however, there was very little activity by intendants in Béarn and Navarre. These provinces were linked on an *ad hoc* basis with Guyenne.

Between 1630 and 1659, French control was established in parts of Italy, Lorraine, Artois, Alsace, and Roussillon, all as a result of French intervention in the Thirty Years War and its aftermath, the protracted struggle with Spain. In addition, French control was established in Catalonia from 1641 until 1652, and an attempt was made to establish French control in Franche-Comté between 1636 and 1643 (the so-called TenYears War).[2] The commitment in Italy arose first, during the Mantuan Succession War of 1628–31. Abel Servien, the future war minister, was sent to Pinerolo immediately after its capture in 1630: he served both as intendant of the army and president of the *Conseil souverain au département delà les Monts*. He was succeeded on 10 September 1630 by Estampes de Valençay,[3] and in 1631 by Expilly, a *président* in the *Parlement* of Grenoble. The continuation of French rule was not left in doubt. The intendant was to 'leur faire cognoistre la douceur d'un juste gouvernement [et] les avantages qu'ilz ont acquis d'estre redevenus noz subjectz par la réunion desd[its] lieux à nostre couronne . . .'[4] The supremacy of French law was made quite explicit on 2 August 1634, when a decree of the council of finance, sitting at Paris, empowered Expilly, Servien, a *trésorier* at Grenoble, and Le Blanc, the *président* of the *élection* at Briançon, not only to verify the debts of Pinerolo but also to draw up a tax register: the intendant at Pinerolo had thus come to assume control of the municipal accounting and fiscal process.[5] The administration of an intendant at Pinerolo continued until 1696 when the fortress was returned to Victor Amadeus of Savoy.[6]

---

[1] E 189b, fo. 50, 20 Apr. 1644.

[2] The resistance to French intervention was led by the *Parlement* of Dôle, and in 1643 a compromise evolved whereby the neutrality of this area was bought by an annual payment of 120,000 *livres* per annum: this sum was paid until 1659. Several intendants of the army were appointed during the Ten Years War.

[3] cf. A.G. A1 13, no. 172, 10 Sept. 1630.

[4] A.G. A1 14, no. 164, 1631.   [5] E 119a, fo. 10.

[6] By article 12 of the treaty of Turin of 29 June 1696: Marquis de Roux, *Louis XIV et les provinces conquises*, p. 3. R. D. Handen, 'The end of an era: Louis XIV and

Intendants were also established in Lorraine after the French invasion of 1632. The issues of sovereignty were exceedingly complex because while Lorraine was a fief of the empire, the duchy of Bar was a fief of the king of France. Richelieu also contended that duke Charles IV of Lorraine and his predecessors had appropriated lands from the bishopric of Metz, lands which in his view formed an inalienable part of the domain of the king of France. A commission in 1624 under the presidency of Cardin Le Bret, the intendant of Champagne, and the three bishoprics of Metz, Toul, and Verdun, had investigated the 'usurpations du duc de Lorraine' and pronounced verdict against Charles IV.[1] The juridical dispute was of the greatest strategic importance: the disputed area included the fortresses of Vic and Moyenvic, which dominated the main road between Nancy and Strasbourg, and when the French forces invaded Lorraine in 1632 they effectively cut the most westerly of the remaining Spanish supply routes from Milan to the Netherlands.[2] Complicating these strategic concerns was the fact that Charles IV was a Habsburg client. In 1630, he allowed Imperial troops to occupy Vic and Moyenvic. He supported the conspiracies of Gaston d'Orléans and gave him refuge in his lands in 1630 and again in 1631–2. On 3 January 1632, Gaston married Charles's sister, Marguerite de Vaudemont, without the permission of Louis XIII. On two occasions—July 1632 and February 1641—Charles IV submitted to Louis XIII: yet each time he had rejoined his Habsburg allies within a few months. The bad faith of the duke was sufficient for Richelieu to claim sovereignty over Lorraine either 'en vertu du droit de conquête, soit à la suite du crime de félonie d'un vassal'.[3]

The intendancy of Lorraine operated in a similar way to

Victor Amadeus II', *Louis XIV and Europe*, ed. R. M. Hatton (1976), p. 255: 'the loss of Casale and Pignerol meant the end of all that France had worked for in Italy since the time of Richelieu.' Bréant, intendant at Pinerolo and Casale: E 1822, 1 Mar. 1683. A similar financial control was exercised by the intendant at Casale in Montferrat: A.G. A1 125, no. 197, 15 Nov. 1651.

[1] Above, chapter VI. Picot, *Cardin Le Bret*, pp. 48–9. B.L. Harleian 4463.

[2] G. Parker, *The army of Flanders and the Spanish Road, 1567–1659. The logistics of victory and defeat in the Low Countries' Wars* (Cambridge, 1972), p. 76.

[3] A. Leman, *Richelieu et Olivarès. Leurs négociations secrètes de 1636 à 1642 pour le rétablissement de la paix* (Lille, 1938), p. 59.

that in Italy. There were a series of intendants of the army.[1]
But in addition a *conseil souverain*, comparable to that of Pinerolo, sat at Nancy after 17 September 1634[2] and was dominated
by the intendant. The military occupation in 1632 had resulted
in a rapid assumption of complete financial control over the
two duchies of Bar and Lorraine. After 15 May 1634, Chantereau-Lefèvre, the *intendant des finances*, supervised the accounts
of the ducal officials in Lorraine, prohibiting them from paying
'aucune chose qu'en vertu des ordonnances de l'intendant'. The
ducal officials were forced to take an oath of loyalty to the
intendant, although they insisted that such actions should not
be interpreted as prejudicing the rights of Charles IV or their
loyalty to him.[3] The activities of Chantereau-Lefèvre were
reinforced by a decree of the French council of finance issued
on 30 December 1634. This referred to the duchies of Lorraine
and Bar as belonging to Louis XIII—the phrase '[nos] duchés'
was employed. It called the inhabitants of these duchies the
'subiectz du Roy' and the taxes levied there 'les deniers de Sa
Majesté'. The decree declared levies of taxation that had not
been authorized by the crown to be illegal and punishable by
death. The *conseil souverain* at Nancy, Barillon de Morangis, the
intendant of justice in the duchy of Bar, and Chantereau-
Lefèvre, the intendant of finance in the duchies of Bar and
Lorraine, were ordered to carry out the decree.[4] When Barillon
was appointed as intendant of justice earlier in the year, it
appears that French judicial control was to be exercised at
Saint-Mihiel, with the intendant acting as president of the
former ducal court of that town: there was certainly no clear
connection with the three bishoprics of Metz, Toul, and Verdun.[5] On 21 May 1637 Rigault was appointed as intendant at
Metz, while the duchies of Lorraine and Bar had their own
intendant in Mangot de Villarceaux after 1635.[6] It was not
until after Rigault's recall—and perhaps as late as 1640—that

[1] On the introduction of the intendants: G. Zeller, *La réunion de Metz à la France,
1552–1648* (2 vols., 1926), ii. 286–93. The earliest of the army intendants was
presumably Jean du Tillet, intendant of justice and finance in the duchy of Bar:
E 109a, fo. 175, 10 July 1632. He was succeeded by Barillon de Morangis on 16
July 1634.

[2] Livet, *L'intendance d'Alsace*, p. 58, no. 3.   [3] ibid., p. 64.

[4] E 121c, fo. 278.   [5] Hanotaux, *Origines*, pp. 327–9.

[6] For Rigault: Guyot and Merlin, *Traité des droits*, iii. 123, n. 1, 125, n. 1, 127,
n. 1. V6 129, no. 12, 23 Apr. 1638. V6 134, no. 78, 12 Nov. 1638.

in practice the intendancy of Lorraine and Bar was linked in the person of Mangot de Villarceaux with the three bishoprics. In July 1637 the *conseil souverain* of Nancy was abolished and Mangot was left in sole control.[1]

The commissions of Mangot de Villarceaux and Nicolas Vignier, his successor, demonstrate that the intendant dominated both financial and judicial administration in Lorraine and Bar. The existing administrative machinery continued to function, but the office-holders were to present their financial accounts before the intendant. In cases of fraud, corruption or mal-administration, the intendant could order 'telle punition ou amende . . . que vous verrez juste et raisonnable' and could appoint new officials on an interim basis.[2] Under Vignier, the intendancy was administered with a considerable degree of administrative uniformity. He referred to Lorraine as 'cette pauvre province' and pointed out the need for a verification and redemption of the debts:[3] indeed, the work on the debt, which was commenced by Vignier on 10 September 1644, applied to Lorraine and Bar as well as to the three bishoprics— the letters patent were not registered by the *Parlement* at Toul[4] (which opposed the whole scheme) but at the *bailliage* of Nancy, the ducal capital of Lorraine.[5] Vignier seems to have resided chiefly at Nancy, where he exercised absolute control over the major revenues—the farms of the ducal domains—which were administered by 'les formes dont on se sert en France, et celles qui ont esté gardées de tout temps en Lorraine'.[6] Caution was the watchword of the new intendancy. Vignier affirmed to Séguier on 28 May 1643 that La Ferté Seneterre, the governor, and he were in agreement that 'il fallait gagner les coeurs des peuples avec modération et le bon traictement et que la douceur estait un aussy bon moyen de les tenir dans le service du Roy que la violence et la force'.[7] Above all, the key to political control was

---

[1] Livet, *L'intendance d'Alsace*, p. 59. E. Duvernoy, 'Gouverneurs et intendants de la Lorraine au dix-septième siècle', *Annuaire-Bulletin de la Société d'Histoire et d'Archéologie de Lorraine*, xxxviii (1929), 21–5.

[2] Livet, op. cit., p. 918. A.G. A1 62, no. 258, 4 Dec. 1640.

[3] *Lettres . . . au Chancelier Séguier*, ed. Mousnier, i. 514, 573.

[4] A *Parlement* had been established at Metz on 15 Jan. 1633 which was transferred to Toul on 16 May 1636.

[5] Guyot and Merlin, *Traité des droits*, iii. 141.

[6] *Lettres . . . au Chancelier Séguier*, ed. Mousnier, i. 611. Were the two compatible?

[7] ibid., i. 606.

an alliance with the urban notables, taking into consideration their commercial and financial interests.[1] The French military occupation of Lorraine was effective, and political control was assured by the intendant. At the Pyrenees in 1659, Don Luis de Haro made Charles IV pay dearly for the Franco-Spanish peace: he had to surrender the duchy of Bar and the fortresses of Stenay, Montmédy, and Clermont; the fortifications of Nancy were to be razed, thus making Lorraine completely defenceless. The French force of occupation was withdrawn until 1670, however.[2]

The intendancy of Alsace was established in a very different way from that of Lorraine. In Lorraine, the French occupation arose from strategic necessity—the danger of Imperial occupation of the duchy—and from a juridicial claim to the duchy of Bar. The French occupation of Alsace was virtually inevitable because of the need to protect the eastern flank of Lorraine and the three bishoprics. Nevertheless, in marked contrast to the occupation of Lorraine, the French presence was actually demanded by the towns of Alsace.[3] These 'treaties of protection' presupposed a temporary transfer of administration in large areas of Alsace from the Emperor to the king of France, but did not envisage a transfer of sovereignty. Although an extension of French claims was probable, the success of any claims to sovereignty was not inevitable. The Emperor could have regained Alsace if French authority had collapsed there during the Fronde; the declaration of war by the German Diet against Louis XIV in May 1674, followed by an Imperial invasion of Alsace, offered a second opportunity. The Spanish, too, threatened the French position in Alsace and there was a further possibility that Alsace—perhaps linked with Lorraine—might become a semi-autonomous client state of the Habsburgs. Bernard of Saxe-Weimar may have intended the creation of such a 'Weimar state' between December 1638, after the

[1] ibid., i. 658.
[2] Between 1670 and 1697 the duchy of Lorraine was included in a French intendancy based at Metz. The intendant was Jacques Charuel: E 1822, 1 Mar. 1683.
[3] Livet, *L'intendance d'Alsace*, pp. 28–9, and *passim* for much of what follows. Cf. G. Livet, 'Louis XIV et les provinces conquises. État des questions et remarques de méthode', *XVIIe Siècle*, xvi (1952), 481–507. G. Livet, 'Royal administration in a frontier province: the intendancy of Alsace under Louis XIV', *Louis XIV and absolutism*, ed. Hatton, pp. 177–96.

capture of Breisach, and his death in July 1639. Harcourt, the
French governor of Alsace, may have had similar ideas between 1650 and 1654. Perhaps as a reaction to these dangers,
the commission issued to De Belesbat, the intendant, on 20
April 1639, described the towns of Alsace as 'sous nostre obéissance' rather than 'placés en nostre protection'.[1] Nevertheless,
a clear statement of French sovereignty was not enunciated
until 15 June 1661, when Louis XIV accorded a two-thirds tax
remission to the inhabitants of Alsace. Colbert de Croissy, the
intendant, declared that this remission was not 'une obligation'
but 'une grâce particulière' made by a king who could 'gouverner comme il luy plaît'. The inhabitants of Alsace paid their
taxes, he stated, as 'la reconnaissance d'un droit de souveraineté'.[2]

Almost from the outset, the intendant was the controller of
the troops and the master of the 'contributions' in Alsace.
Control over the financial and judicial machinery was established much more slowly. One reason for this was the traditional power of the Estates. The Estates were not summoned
during the French occupation and the last sessions—in 1631
and 1636—had demonstrated the hostility of the nobles to increased taxes. Nevertheless, the tradition of Alsace was that no
extraordinary tax was levied without the agreement of the
Estates. The assumption of complete financial control by the
intendant was thus delayed by considerations of political
prudence. It was felt that Habsburg rule had been marked by
respect for constitutional privileges and that this had left 'beaucoup de bonne volonté et inclination pour elle'. In leaving to
the intendant alone 'la faculté de faire les impositions', the
French crown was taking a calculated risk with the loyalties of
the inhabitants: it is not clear that this risk was taken before
July 1656.[3] The establishment of the intendancy as an administrative system was in any case imperilled by the existence
of a powerful governor after 1648 who wanted to allow the
crown 'l'économie d'un intendant en Alsace'; by the existence
of two intendants between 1640 and 1654, one of whom was

[1] Livet, *L'intendance d'Alsace*, pp. 69, 920.   [2] ibid., pp. 219–21.
[3] ibid., pp. 184, 213. But cf. ibid., p. 152: the 'contributions' for the troops were
closely linked (as in France) to other forms of taxation and were supervised by the
intendant.

resident at Breisach; and by the existence of other, archducal, institutions which the governor wanted to strengthen. Most notable of these was the archducal chamber at Ensisheim which had both a judicial and a financial section. The earlier intendants of Alsace were empowered to issue definitive sentences equivalent to those issued by the sovereign courts in France—but it was left enresolved whether appeals were to go to the king's council at Paris or to the surviving archducal institutions such as the chamber at Ensisheim. The intendants obviously preferred the first procedure because this was less likely to lead to a local institutional conflict and interference with their freedom of action.[1]

The situation was not clarified until a *conseil souverain* of Alsace was set up by an edict of September 1657. The financial section of the former archducal chamber was 'réuny en la personne de l'intendant' as a result of this edict. The judicial aspect of the chamber devolved on the *conseil souverain* which was composed of seven appointees of the intendant, four of whom were French. The intendant presided over this new institution.[2] The *conseil souverain* was thus designed as a permanent judicial tribunal under the presidency of the intendant, comparable to *ad hoc* tribunals summoned by the intendants elsewhere in France to deal, for example, with cases of sedition. As such it was extremely unpopular with the *Parlement* of Metz, which secured its abolition in November 1661 and the establishment of a much more acceptable *conseil provincial*.[3] Nevertheless, by 1661 fundamental changes had occurred which undermined the old archducal traditions and made Alsace much more akin to a French province. The intendant had been left in complete control of the fiscal system, although his interventions in the realm of private law were sporadic only. French law was dominant in administrative questions, and in private law it was well on the way towards gaining predominance in view of the appellate jurisdiction of *Parlement* of Metz—which was confirmed in 1661—and the crown's right to 'changer, corriger ou abolir les ordonnances

[1] ibid., pp. 104–5.　　　　[2] ibid., pp. 224, 236.
[3] More acceptable to the *Parlement* in that its members were not appointed by the intendant but (eventually) bought their offices. Moreover, it was reduced to the status of a *bailliage* or lesser court—the *Parlement* heard appeals from its sentences.

qui ont été pratiquées et d'en substituer d'autres'.[1] Although
Colbert de Croissy, the intendant between 1655 and 1663,
learnt German, the French language was clearly intended as
an additional weapon to enforce French claims to sovereignty.[2]
Between 10 May 1661 and May 1663, Colbert de Croissy
held the intendancy of Alsace jointly with that of the Three
Bishoprics and the duchy of Bar: it became clear that in administrative terms this was nonsense. Control of Alsace could
not be secured from Metz: it had to be gained in Alsace itself,
from Breisach, Ensisheim, or ultimately—after 1681—from
Strasbourg.[3] One remarkable feature of government in Alsace
in these years was that the province retained a highly influential
Protestant community. The intendants were instructed to
ensure that the Catholics were allowed freedom of worship,[4]
not to achieve their political predominance as was the case
elsewhere in France.

The attempt to establish French sovereignty in Catalonia, in
marked contrast to developments elsewhere, met with complete
failure. The French were invited to enter the principality by
the treaty of Ceret (24 September 1640), but early French
military successes were not followed up after 1643[5] and Catalonia proved extremely difficult to defend as a long-term
proposition. The French had hoped to use the revolt as a
means of attacking Philip IV 'dans son propre throsne', leading
to an invasion of Aragon and Valencia and the cutting of
Spanish naval communications with Italy.[6] Philip IV concentrated his resources and manpower on the reconquest at
a time when France was weakened domestically by the Fronde:
the surrender of Barcelona on 13 October 1652 marked the
collapse of resistance. The French position in Catalonia was
always weak because of the nature of the revolt itself.[7] The
Catalans had no wish to exchange a French form of absolutism
for the Castilian model which they had rejected. The early

[1] Livet, *L'intendance d'Alsace*, p. 238.   [2] ibid., p. 237.
[3] ibid., p. 233.   [4] ibid., p. 110.
[5] With the exception of Harcourt's capture of Rosas on 28 May 1645.
[6] J. Sanabre, *La acción de Francia en Cataluña en la pugna por la hegemonía de Europa, 1640–1659* (Barcelona, 1956), pp. 675–6.
[7] J. H. Elliott, *The revolt of the Catalans. A study in the decline of Spain, 1598–1640* (Cambridge, 1963).

negotiations with France had not marked a decisive break with Spain. Only when Philip IV and his advisers proved intransigent did Pau Claris and the other Catalan leaders establish an independent republic (16–23 January 1641). The republican experiment failed because Catalonia lacked social cohesion and political unanimity. Moreover, just as they had refused to contribute towards Olivares's Union of Arms, so the Catalans refused to come to their own defence. The need to defend the revolution pushed leaders such as Pau Claris towards the alternative of French rule. Richelieu distrusted the Catalans, and wanted them to break clearly with Spain before he was prepared to commit French troops on a large scale. The result was the decision of the Catalan leaders, on 23 January 1641, to place the principality under the rule of Louis XIII, 'as in the time of Charlemagne, with a contract to observe our constitutions'.[1] The details of the arrangements were negotiated by René I Voyer d'Argenson, the first French intendant in Catalonia, and they were ratified by Louis XIII at Péronne on 19 September.[2]

The strength of constitutional traditions in Catalonia gave this transfer of sovereignty a much more limited character than was the case with other territorial acquisitions by France during the Thirty Years War. Although the generals and administrators of Catalonia in the 1640s were French, concessions were made to the forms of Catalan government before the revolt. The French generals were called viceroys and were instructed to act in a similar manner to their predecessors when Catalonia was under Spanish rule.[3] The rapid turnover of viceroys had an unsettling effect on the conduct of government and tended to increase the already serious faction fighting.[4] There were, moreover, times when there was no viceroy on the province. The first of these periods, between May and December 1642, saw the predominance of Argenson, the intendant;[5] but in the second and third interregna (1649; January–June 1651), Pierre de Marca, the *visiteur-général* of Catalonia, was left in control.[6] Although this office was based

---

[1] Sanabre, op. cit., p. 134. Elliott, op. cit., p. 522.
[2] Sanabre, op. cit., pp. 164, n. 84, 185–7, 648–52.
[3] ibid., p. 688.   [4] ibid., pp. 676–80.
[5] ibid., pp. 207–17.   [6] ibid., pp. 431–52, 481-99.

on the precedent of Castilian rule in the principality, the *visita* had been essentially a temporary official. Pierre de Marca resided in Catalonia from 1644 until 1651 and made himself extremely unpopular in the process. At the time of his appointment, Marca had also received a commission as intendant of justice, police, and finance.[1] This commission, together with the appointment of a number of provincial and army intendants, led to divisions of responsibility which had a disruptive effect on administration. In 1645, for example, there were three intendants in Catalonia—Marca, Imbert, and Goury.[2] In any case, there was great uncertainty about judicial procedure and the language in which administration was to be carried out—in both instances, Catalan appears to have prevailed over French.[3] The political divisions of the Catalan leaders led to the collapse of the experiment of French rule. It was clear that the French regime operated in favour of a relatively small number of families who benefited from the offices and confiscated property of Philip IV's supporters.[4] This small circle of French supporters might have provided a satisfactory political base given military success: when the French crown declared bankruptcy in 1648 and the troops were forced to live off the land,[5] support for the French cause collapsed.

In contrast to events in Catalonia, French rule was established in Roussillon without great difficulty after 1642. Essentially, success in Roussillon came from French military ascendancy in the area. This ascendancy was reinforced, rather than weakened, by the collapse of resistance in Catalonia. Politics in Roussillon came to be dominated first by the French representatives and later by the Catalan *émigrés*. Just over a month after the surrender of Perpignan (9 September 1642), Hercule des Yvetaux was appointed as intendant of Roussillon: between 1642 and 1645, the area had its own intendant, who was concerned chiefly with fortifications, munitions, and the *subsistances* for the troops.[6] Ultimate military control rested with the lieutenant-general of the army, who was also viceroy of

[1] B.N. MS.fr. 4169, fos. 83, 93, 1644.

[2] A.G. AI 92, nos. 236, 245, 17 Jan. and 10 Feb. 1645.

[3] Sanabre, op. cit., pp. 655, 657.

[4] ibid., pp. 199–200, 424–7, 434–42, 608.   [5] ibid., pp. 612–13.

[6] A.G. AI 71, no. 150, 12 Oct. 1642. A.G. AI 85, no. 230, 22 Jan. 1644.

Catalonia. It thus made sense to link the intendancies of
Roussillon and Catalonia, which occurred between 1645 and
1649. An alternative solution, however, which was adopted in
1641–2[1] and 1649–56,[2] was to make the intendancy of Roussillon an ancillary task of the intendancy of Languedoc. This
made sound strategic sense, since the defence of Roussillon
rested essentially on the supply lines from Languedoc. During
the reign of Louis XIV, one intendant considered that it
would prove the best way to break down separatist tendencies
in Roussillon.[3] Yet this arrangement did not become permanent, and undoubtedly one reason for this was the special
position of the Catalan *émigrés* within Roussillon society. The
position of the *émigrés* was already significant by 1652, but was
reinforced by the failure of a pro-Habsburg revolt at Perpignan
in that year: the lands of the conspirators were confiscated and
granted out to the Catalan exiles. Thereafter, the Catalans
were the leading protagonists of the struggle of Roussillon
against Spain.[4] The *conseil souverain* of Roussillon, which was
established in 1660 following the peace of the Pyrenees, recognized this special position. The official head of the institution
was the governor of the province, but the *première présidence* was
held jointly by two prominent Catalan exiles—Sagarre and
Fontanella. Only one member of the *conseil souverain* was a
native of Perpignan: the other six members were Catalan
exiles, too. Thus it was almost inevitable that in 1660 the
province was given a separate, peace-time, intendancy.[5]

The establishment of French rule in Artois also resulted
from military conquest. Arras, its capital, surrendered on
terms in 1640. Among the articles of surrender was a clause to
the effect that liberty of conscience would not be permitted
and that the Catholic religion alone would be recognized:[6] the
regime of the edict of Nantes thus could not be extended to this

[1] A.E. A1 67, no. 100, 14 Mar. 1641.
[2] *Lettres . . . au Chancelier Séguier*, ed. Mousnier, ii. 1087–9. A.G. A1 125, no. 193,
25 Sept. 1651. A.G. A1 139, fo. 215, A1 138, fo. 400, and B.N. MS.fr. 4186, fo.
215, 21 May 1653.
[3] Raymond de Trobat, quoted by marquis de Roux, *Louis XIV et les provinces
conquises*, pp. 89–90.
[4] Sanabre, op. cit., pp. 704–5: protests of the Catalan exiles against the proposed
Franco-Spanish boundary in Aug. 1659.
[5] Livet, 'Louis XIV et les provinces conquises', p. 495, n. 1.
[6] Roux, op. cit., p. 205.

new province. A second important clause was the guarantee that 'on ne peult faire aucune levée dans le pays d'Artois sans . . . l'assemblée du pays'. This aspect of the treaty was abrogated, however, because the Estates were not summoned between 1640 and 1661.[1] Instead, the intendant carried out the levy of taxation. Jacques Chaulnes appears to have believed that the ruling of 22 August 1642 on the fiscal role of the intendants applied to Artois too.[2] On 5 February 1641, a *conseil souverain* was established at Arras. The intendant presided over this court, and rejected its claims to an independent financial jurisdiction.[3] Despite its title, the *conseil souverain* of Artois—unlike its counterpart in Roussillon after 1660—was not a sovereign court. Its decisions were equivalent to sentences issued by the *présidiaux* in France: appeals were heard by the *Parlement* of Paris. Thus the supremacy of French law in Artois was guaranteed at an early date. Between 1642 and 1645 it appeared that the government was going to create a separate intendancy for Artois;[4] after 1645, however, Artois was linked firmly with the intendancy of Picardy. In 1661, the Estates were revived and they continued to meet until 1789.[5] However, the fiscal role of the intendant ensured that the power of the Estates after 1661 was greatly reduced in comparison with the situation in the years before 1640.

France benefited from the successes of foreign policy and war by acquiring new territories and peoples. To a country of some 33,226 towns and parishes in 1624 a further 2,360 towns and parishes were added as a result of the various treaties and settlements between 1628 and 1662.[6] At the same time, the *petites souverainetés* belonging to the great magnates—of which

---

[1] For the Estates before the French occupation: C. Hirschauer, *Les États d'Artois de leurs origines à l'occupation française, 1340–1640* (2 vols., 1923).

[2] *Lettres . . . au Chancelier Séguier*, ed. Mousnier, ii. 744.

[3] O1 11, fo. 41ᵛ, commission of Brethe de Clermont, 1645.

[4] This would have confirmed a development towards smaller territorial units on the northern frontier, evidenced also by the intendancy of the counties of Ponthieu and the Boulonnais, which was created in 1637–40: A.G. A1 12, no. 51, 4 Feb. 1637. *Lettres . . . au Chancelier Séguier*, ed. Mousnier, ii. 1054–6.

[5] G. Bellart, 'L'organisation et le rôle financer des États d'Artois de 1661 à 1789', *Positions des thèses de l'École des Chartes*, cviii (1956), 23–8.

[6] B.N. 500 Colbert 261. The document dates from 1677, but the dates of the annexations are given. The figures must be regarded as approximate.

there were several in north-eastern France belonging to the prince de Conty, the duc de Nevers, and the duc de Bouillon among others[1]—were gradually subsumed into the patrimony of the king of France. Sometimes, this took place in a treaty which the magnate owning the principality entered into voluntarily.[2] On other occasions, expropriation was much more explicit. In 1642, the duc de Bouillon was forced to hand over his principality of Sedan because of alleged participation in the Cinq-Mars conspiracy: this act, together with the intervention of Frederick-Henry of Nassau, his uncle on the maternal side, saved Bouillon from execution.[3] However, not all the apanages, principalities, and *petites souverainetés* were confiscated or absorbed. The Comtat Venaissin remained independent of the crown and controlled by papal administrators until the time of Napoleon. The principality of Orange was not finally annexed by Louis XIV until 1703.[4] Most important of all, the *vicomté* of Turenne retained its autonomy and separate representative institutions until 1738: the writ of the intendants of Guyenne and the Limousin did not run in this area.[5]

The establishment of intendants in the 'new provinces' acquired before and after 1661 was a consequence of the *volonté assimilatrice* of the French crown. These lands had their own forms of administration, their own customs and traditions. The populations were not necessarily Francophile in attitude: Richelieu considered the bourgeois of Arras to be 'tous ennemis jurés des français et plus espagnols que les Castillians'.[6] Thus

[1] E 38b, fo. 84^{v}, 11 Dec. 1612.

[2] As in 1629, when the principality of Châteaurenard was bought from the duchesse de Conty for 1,720,000 *livres*: cf. E 159a, fo. 382, 16 Jan. 1641.

[3] B.N. MS.fr. 17331, fo. 105, 'abolition du duc de Bouillon', Sept. 1642. Cf. K 114b, no. 42/12 [Musée AE II 835], 10 Jan. 1643. For the intervention of Frederick-Henry: B.N. MS.fr. 17331, fos. 111^{v}–112^{v}.

[4] Though it had been occupied previously in 1673–8 and 1682–97 and was not part of a treaty until 1713: S. B. Baxter, *William III* (1966), pp. 185–6. W. C. Scoville, *The persecution of the Huguenots and French economic development, 1680–1720* (Berkeley–Los Angeles, 1960), p. 70.

[5] R. Fage, *Les États de la vicomté de Turenne* (2 vols., 1894), i. 27. Cf. Bercé, *Histoire des croquants*, i. 94, who argues–mistakenly—that Bouillon's revenues from the Estates were paid into the royal treasury. For the failure of the intendant's writ to run: R2 493, fos. 268, 295^{v}–296^{v}, 15 Dec. 1635, 22 Nov. 1638. The exception was the attempted levy of the forced loan which resulted in rebellion: E 144a, fo. 17, 5 June 1638; E 149a, fo. 439, 17 Mar. 1639.

[6] Quoted by marquis de Roux, op. cit., p. 47.

if the intention of the crown was to 'établir les moeurs françaises',[1] to 'conformer tous les jours autant qu'il sera possible et insensiblement les usages de ce[s] pais . . . à ceux de [France]',[2] in practice the greatest caution was needed. Honoré Courtin, the intendant of Picardy and Artois, was in no doubt that the 'new provinces' had to be treated virtually as a French *pays d'états*. In his view, the government had to 'conserver leurs privilèges, les bien traiter, leur faire tant de grâces qu'ils soient plus heureux sous [la] domination [de Louis XIV] qu'ils n'étaient sous celle de leur maître d'autrefois'.[3]

---

[1] Louis XIV, *Mémoires pour les années 1661 et 1666* . . ., ed. J. Longnon (1923), p. 110.

[2] Colbert quoted by A. Lottin, 'La fonction d'intendant vue par Louvois d'après sa correspondance avec l'intendant de Flandre, 1668–1683', *Mélanges historiques et littéraires sur le xviie siècle offerts à Georges Mongrédien par ses amis* (1974), p. 66.

[3] Quoted by marquis de Roux, op. cit., p. 49.

CHAPTER XVIII

Epilogue: The Personal Rule of Louis XIV

LOUIS XIV was already experienced in government when he declared his intention, on the day following the death of Mazarin (9 March 1661) of ruling without a chief minister. The young king had first presided over the council of state on 7 September 1649, at the age of eleven.[1] The first political decision taken on his own authority was the arrest of Cardinal de Retz (19 December 1652).[2] By 1653–5, Mazarin and Louis were going over government business for at least an hour every day. Morosini, the Venetian ambassador, noted that when Louis considered that the decisions taken in the council 'ne conviennent pas vraiment à son service, quoiqu'elles soient approuvées par les autres il les casse, en les désapprouvant résolument . . .' Mazarin had thus introduced Louis slowly, but progressively, to the process of government.[3] The *Frondeurs* had feared that Mazarin would use his position as *surintendant de l'éducation du roi* to indoctrinate the young king into Mazarin's 'fausse et pernicieuse politique'.[4] Their fears proved well-founded, but it was the position of chief minister rather than *surintendant de l'éducation* which had given Mazarin his opportunity to teach Louis his political principles. Louis not only liked Mazarin:[5] he greatly admired his political achievement. The guiding principles of Louis's first years of personal rule were thus in most respects a consolidation of the policies pursued by Mazarin before his death. Indeed, Louis implemented the principles formulated by Mazarin on his death-bed and dictated by Louis to one of his secretaries on 9 March 1661. Louis XIV was thus the political disciple of Mazarin.

[1] Mousnier, *La plume*, p. 154. B.N. Clairambault 651, fo. 341.
[2] Lacour-Gayet, *L'éducation politique*, pp. 184–5.
[3] ibid., pp. 117–18, 176.
[4] C. Joly, *Recueil des maximes véritables et importantes pour l'institution du roy contre la fausse et pernicieuse politique du Cardinal Mazarin* (1653).
[5] Lacour-Gayet, *L'éducation politique*, p. 136.

Mazarin advised Louis to respect the sovereign courts but to
'les obliger de se tenir dans les bornes de leur devoir'—the
direct result of this advice was the decree of 8 July 1661 confirming the supremacy of the king's council over the sovereign
courts.[1] The *Parlement* of Paris considered this decree 'un coup
fatal à la dignité des compagnies souveraines . . .' but Louis
reassured them that 'il n'avoit point entendu diminuer
l'authorité de la compagnie mais seulement régler ses fonctions
comme celles du conseil'.[2] Louis followed up this measure in
October 1665 by renaming the sovereign courts *cours supérieures*.
'Les compagnies . . . se regardaient comme autant de souverainetés séparées et indépendantes', Louis commented in his
memoirs. 'Je fis connaître que je ne souffrirais plus leurs entreprises.'[3] In 1673 the right of remonstrance was restricted, so
that remonstrances could be issued only after registration of the
relevant legislation. Louis may not have intended the measure
to be permanent, but merely a temporary response to a war-
time situation. However, France remained at war or on a war
footing from 1673 until Louis's death in 1715 and the edict
remained in force during his lifetime.[4] As the political role of
the courts declined, so too did their economic privileges. Up to
1665, offices had retained their investement value reasonably
well. It is true that the *gages* had been cut after 1639 and suspended altogether in 1648, and that in the 1640s the *parlementaires* of
Aix and Rouen had seen the value of their offices fall dramatically with the establishment of *semestres* which had virtually
doubled the membership of their courts.[5] Yet they had resisted
such measures by armed force in 1649 and obtained their
revocation. However, after 1652 no *Parlement* resorted to armed
force against the French monarchy,[6] while after 1661 very few

[1] Above, chapter I.
[2] Lacour-Gayet, op. cit., p. 131. X1a 8392, fos. 399, 431, 5 Aug. and 2 Sept.
1661.
[3] Glasson, *Parlement de Paris*, i. 409. Louis XIV, *Mémoires pour les années 1661 et
1666 . . .*, ed. Longnon, p. 86.
[4] R. Mousnier and F. Hartung, 'Quelques problèmes concernant la monarchie
absolue', *X Congresso internazionale di scienze storiche* (Rome, 1955), 10. Glasson,
op. cit., i. 434–7.
[5] For the fall in the value of offices at Rouen: Logié, *La Fronde en Normandie*,
i. 63.
[6] With the exception of the *Parlement* of Aix in 1659: but the *parlementaire* element
in the riot was small compared with ten years earlier. The *Parlement* of Brittany was

remonstrances were issued. The political decline was not permanent—the *parlements* were active in politics once more after 1715—but it was of crucial significance in the short term. It coincided with a government victory in the area of political theory: with the exception of Protestant theorists such as Jurieu after 1685,[1] ideas of resistance, and especially of resistance manifested by institutional means, virtually disappeared in France. There was no theorist of the office-holders to follow the path of Charles Loyseau, and argue the rights of the sovereign courts against the government of Louis XIV. Independent political thought by the office-holders was thus in abeyance,[2] and this decline was symptomatic of the general position of the sovereign courts—they were in no position to defend themselves in December 1665, when Colbert arbitrarily reduced the value of offices. Colbert argued that the capital value of offices was too high and deprived other sectors of the economy of productive investment. This measure attempted to reduce the value of certain existing offices by one-third.[3] Moreover, the courts saw their burden of cases being reduced as a result of several extraordinary royal commissions during the 1660s and 1670s (the *chambre de justice;* the *réformation de la noblesse;* the verification of the debts; the *réformation des eaux et forêts,* and so on). Members of the courts thus lost much of their income from cases (*épices*) which in turn confirmed the fact that office was a depreciating capital asset.[4] Louis XIV created innumerable new offices—including offices in the *parlements,* particularly in the 1690s—and reduced the salaries of existing office-holders, without meeting any resistance from the courts comparable to the 1640s.

---

exiled at Vannes between 1675 and 1690 for alleged complicity in the riot of 1675 at Rennes: J. J. Hurt, 'The Parlement of Brittany and the crown, 1665–1675', *French Historical Studies,* iv (1966), 411–33, reprinted in *State and society,* ed. Kierstead, pp. 44–66. L. Bernard, 'French society and popular uprisings under Louis XIV', *French Historical Studies,* iii (1964), 454–74, reprinted in *State and society,* ed. Kierstead, p. 170.

[1] G. H. Dodge, *The political theory of the Huguenots of the Dispersion with special reference to the thought and influence of Pierre Jurieu* (Columbia, N.Y., 1947).

[2] W. F. Church, 'The decline of the French jurists as political theorists, 1660–1789', *French Historical Studies,* v (1967), 1–40.

[3] Hurt, 'Les offices', pp. 18, 24. Meyer, La noblesse bretonne, ii. 937–41. Hamscher [*The Parlement of Paris after the Fronde,* pp. 14, 21–2] argues that *pots de vin*—illegal extra payments to the vendor—kept the real price of offices high in the 1670s.   [4] Hurt, 'Les offices', pp. 19–21.

Mazarin may well have warned Louis to beware of Foucquet's ambition;[1] he certainly told him that 'un roi qui ne pouvait gouverner n'était pas digne de régner . . .' The decision to rule without a chief minister, proclaimed by Louis on 10 March 1661, was thus the implementation of one of Mazarin's death-bed wishes.[2] Mazarin also recommended Louis to employ Colbert as Foucquet's assistant. While Colbert had served Mazarin faithfully since 1651 and thus appeared to personify continuity in government, his criticisms of Foucquet since 1659 implied a determination to break with some aspects of the past, notably the system of war finance and the excessive power enjoyed by the *surintendant*. Colbert, moreover, needed to destroy Foucquet: the immense fortune left by Mazarin on his death, amounting to about 37 million *livres*, required that Colbert eliminate all traces of a somewhat compromising political past as Mazarin's financial agent, and transfer all blame to Foucquet.[3] The arrest of Foucquet on 5 September 1661 was followed ten days later by the abolition of the *surintendance* and the establishment in its place of a *conseil royal des finances*.[4] This new council—which was below the council of state but superior to the lesser councils (the *conseil privé* and the *conseil d'état et des finances*) was created with the purpose of providing more effective direction than that of the *surintendant*, without any corresponding threat to the crown. Louis XIV presided over this council,[5] and thus unlike his father—and himself in the 1650s—was really informed about the detailed state of the finances and the routine working of government.

[1] R. Darricau and M. Laurain-Portemer, 'La mort du Cardinal Mazarin', *Annuaire-Bulletin de la Société de l'Histoire de France* (1960), p. 120 notes. Foucquet was warned that Mazarin had done so: E. Spanheim, *Relation de la cour de France en 1690*, ed. E. Bourgeois (1900), p. 304, n. 2. Colbert thought Mazarin had done so: *Lettres . . . de Colbert*, ed. Clément, ii, pt. i, 33.

[2] Lacour-Gayet, *L'éducation politique*, p. 132.

[3] D. Dessert, 'Finances et société au xviie siècle: à propos de la chambre de justice de 1661', *Annales E.S.C.*, xxix (1974), 868–9. Dessert, 'Pouvoir et finance au xviie siècle: la fortune de Mazarin', *Revue d'histoire moderne et contemporaine*, xxiii (1976), 161–81.

[4] *Lettres . . . de Colbert*, ed. Clément, ii. 749–50. E 1713, fo. 173 and A.A.E. France 911, fo. 166. A valuable recent discussion of this measure is provided by Antoine, *Le conseil du roi*, pp. 67–9.

[5] Its nominal president was the maréchal de Villeroy, Louis XIV's childhood governor and a client of Mazarin, who was no more than a figurehead. Real power in the council was held by Colbert: A.G. A1 170, min. 44, 12 Oct. 1661.

Louis jealously guarded his powers over this council. He struck off items of expenditure which he considered unwarranted.[1] When Louis left for the war front in 1672, the Queen was left to preside over the council in his absence.[2] Two years later, Louis was even more cautious. Colbert was to inform him each week of the important business of the council, but Louis reserved to himself, on his return, the power of verifying the accounts of the royal finances.[3]

The council of finance (*conseil d'état et des finances*) under the presidency of Chancellor Séguier between 1635 and 1661 had failed to provide a firm check on the authority of the *surintendant*, and was thus relegated to overseeing the details of financial administration and removed from the area of political initiative. As a result of the ruling of 15 September 1661, the Chancellor was no longer automatically a minister with entry to the council of state or the new *conseil royal des finances*. Le Tellier, who was appointed in 1677, and Pontchartrain, who was appointed in 1699, were Chancellors who enjoyed these rights. Séguier from 1661 until his death in 1672, Étienne III d'Aligre, who was appointed in 1672, and Boucherat, who was appointed in 1685, did not. This decline of the Chancellorship had been foreshadowed under Richelieu and Mazarin by its subordination to the requirements of a system of government based upon a chief minister. The new *conseil royal des finances* allowed freedom of action to a small inner group of the most able councillors—in the first instance, Colbert, Aligre, Sève, Marin, Le Tonnelier de Breteuil, and Hervart (all of whom had served as royal commissioners in the provinces, and three of whom had served as provincial intendants under Richelieu and Mazarin)[4]—without the debilitating influence of an ageing Chancellor and a large council membership. In the *conseil d'état et des finances*, Colbert as an *intendant des finances*—and, after 1665, as *contrôleur-général* as well—could merely act as *rapporteur* of decrees: by contrast in the new council he kept the registers of receipts and expenses and proposed measures of the greatest political and fiscal importance. Colbert exercised a real responsibility without

[1] B.N. Mélanges Colbert 295, fo. 314, 8 Dec. 1675.
[2] E 1766, fo. 273, 22 Apr. 1672.   [3] E 1775, fo. 359, 18 Apr. 1674.
[4] Aligre, Sève and Le Tonnelier de Breteuil (the last-named served under Mazarin only).

enjoying independent political power: on the rare occasions that he overstepped the mark, he received a sharp rebuke from the king.[1]

Colbert regarded the *conseil royal des finances* as the instrument by which a systematic reform of the finances of the French monarchy might be undertaken. The chief aspect of this reform was economy. Colbert managed to reduce total expenditure to 42 million *livres* in 1663. Such restraint could not be maintained, but when Colbert complained to Louis XIV in 1670 that increased expenditure was undermining his reforms, the figure he was criticizing—75 million—was lower than that of any year between 1636 and 1662 for which evidence is available. Colbert's reforms earned both political and financial advantages for the government in the short term. They were politically advantageous in that to Louis XIV and Colbert accrued the prestige of having achieved some of the more constructive aims of the *Chambre Saint-Louis*. They were financially advantageous in that the reduction of government expenditure and the fines levied on the financiers by the extraordinary financial tribunal (*chambre de justice*) of 1661 facilitated the balancing of the budget and further reductions in government expenditure.[2] At the same time as he was eliminating wasteful expenditure, Colbert set about reorganizing the income of the French monarchy. He appreciated that the *taille* could not be relied upon as the major revenue of the French crown.[3] Accordingly, he remitted the arrears from the last years of Mazarin's ministry,[4] and reduced the amount of the *taille* progressively. Even during the Dutch war of 1672–8, it was kept to 40 million *livres*, well below the level of 1658, and by 1680 it had been reduced again to 32 million.[5] Unfortunately, the effects of these cuts were largely nullified by the agricultural depression after 1670. Moreover, the corollary of Colbert's policy of reducing the *taille* was the expansion of the indirect revenues. In 1662, Colbert negotiated leases totalling 44 million. On his death in 1683, the figure was 65·8 million. The indirect taxes, therefore, brought in about 50

[1] Quoted by C. W. Cole, *Colbert and a century of French mercantilism* (2 vols., New York, 1939), i. 289–90.
[2] Bonney, 'The secret expenses of Richelieu and Mazarin', p. 835.
[3] *Lettres . . . de Colbert*, ed. Clément, vii. 237–8.   [4] Above, chapter X.
[5] Esmonin, *La taille*, pp. 513–32. E 1792, fo. 367, 7 May 1678. E 1798, fo. 84, 16 Aug. 1679. However, if one bears in mind the fantasy element in the nominal

per cent of the total revenues of the crown, whereas the *taille* had fallen to about 30 per cent of the total.[1] The lease negotiated with Fauconnet in 1680 marked the beginning of that most successful of financial institutions in eighteenth-century France, the *ferme-générale*, which brought together a number of indirect taxes into a single tax farm.[2] Linked to these measures were changes in the methods of tax collection. In 1661 Colbert substituted the *receveurs-généraux* and the *voies ordinaires* for the financiers and coercion by the troops. The government may well have been feeling its way towards this decision in the last months of Foucquet's ministry, but Colbert greatly accelerated the process. With relatively few exceptions, coercion of payment by the intendants and the special brigades was a thing of the past by the 1660s.[3] After 1661, Colbert was much more scrupulous than his predecessors about the recourse to troops for the purposes of tax-collection. It was above all as a result of his financial reforms and this new moderation on the part of the government that the prestige of the intendants rose after 1661. Colbert's financial reforms were only part of his overall economic measures which aimed at assisting French manufactures, commerce and agriculture in a period of economic depression. At a national level, this policy was marked by Colbert's 'tariff war' against the Dutch and his attempts to establish French trading companies. At a local level, Colbert encouraged the intendants to establish new manufacturing industries with government subsidies. The intendants also sought local investment for Colbert's commercial enterprises and came to play an important part in poor relief and in distributing grain, notably during the subsistence crises of 1693–4 and 1709–10.

Colbert's attitude to the intendants had been a subject of some controversy among historians, and his instructions to the *maîtres des requêtes* in September 1663 have frequently been

---

figures for the *taille* in the 1640s [above, chapter VIII] the cuts may not have been quite as significant as they seem at first sight.

[1] Bercé, *Histoire des croquants*, i. 67. Y. R. Durand, *Les fermiers-généraux au xviii* *siècle* (1971), p. 57.

[2] Durand, op. cit., p. 51. S. T. Matthews, *The royal general farms in eighteenth-century France* (Columbia, N.Y., 1958), p. 51.

[3] Esmonin, *La taille*, p. 500, n. 3. E 1713, fo. 57 and E 344, fo. 415, 30 Apr. 1661: 'soient payées par les voies accoustumées'.

misunderstood.[1] It has been argued that Colbert regarded the
intendants as no more than temporary investigators and that he
envisaged the possibility of doing without them altogether.
This view rests on one equivocal passage in the instructions[2]
and on the fact that they were issued to the *maîtres des requêtes*
and not the intendants as such. In reality, the terms *maître des
requêtes* and intendant had become virtually synonymous by
this date.[3] Although there was a rapid turnover of intendants
in the 1660s, this does not necessarily imply that the intendants
were regarded as no more than temporary investigators: the
need to appoint former intendants to serve as judges at the
trial of Foucquet, the patronage conflict between Colbert and
Le Tellier, and the military reviews of Louvois in 1666 were all
factors in this situation.[4] It is inconceivable that Colbert
envisaged the abolition of the intendants. As early as 1658 he
had appreciated the advantages of resident intendants,[5] while
in a memorandum of 1 October 1659 to Mazarin he had considered the intendants the essential instruments of fiscal
reform: 'toutes ces choses', he wrote, 'ne peuvent estre exé-
cutées dans les provinces que par le ministère des intendants.'[6]
Moreover, the government was unlikely to abolish the intendants for the very fact that in 1660–1 the *trésoriers* and *élus*
held illegal meetings to press this issue: the government
rejected the claims of the financial officials, left the intendants
with their fiscal powers intact, and indeed ordered the intendants
to ensure an end to the meetings of the *trésoriers* and the *élus*.[7]

[1] For a contrasting interpretation both of the date and the significance of the
instructions: Esmonin, *La taille*, p. 57. Esmonin, *Études*, pp. 37–8. Esmonin,
Voisin de la Noiraye. Mémoires sur le généralité de Rouen, 1665 (1913), p. xii. G. Pagès,
'Essai sur l'évolution des institutions administratives en France du commencement
du xvie siècle à la fin du xviie siècle', *Revue d'Histoire Moderne*, vii (1932), 129.

[2] It was hoped that 'par un travail assidu et une application extraordinaire'
the *maîtres des requêtes* would visit 'tout le dedans du royaume en l'espace de sept ou
huit années de temps . . . ' However, the intendant was to leave a memorandum to
his successor, which implied administrative continuity in the provinces: *Lettres . . .
de Colbert*, ed. Clément, iv. 27–43, at p. 42.

[3] cf. Séguier's comments to the *maîtres des requêtes* in Oct. 1665: Ormesson,
Journal, ed. Chéruel, ii. 399.

[4] Ormesson, *Journal*, ed. Chéruel, ii, *passim*, alludes to these issues when men-
tioning new appointments as intendants.

[5] *Lettres . . . de Colbert*, ed. Clément, i. 308. A.A.E. France 905, fo. 357, 8 Aug.
1658.   [6] *Lettres . . . de Colbert*, ed. Clément, vii. 177. Esmonin, *La taille*, p. 49.

[7] For the opposition of the *élus* in 1661: Esmonin, *La taille*, p. 124. The intendants were ordered to prevent assemblies of the *élus* 'soubz prétexte de retranch-

Thus Colbert confirmed the fiscal responsibilities of the intendants on 16 November 1661,[1] 12 February,[2] 25 August[3] and 6 September 1663.[4] Any authority retained by the *trésoriers* was essentially as a result of commissions received from the council:[5] not without reason might the *trésoriers* lament that 'nos charges sont tombés dans la dernière décadence' and that the intendants 'retiennent ce qui est de plus honnorable et plus effectif et ne laissent dans les bureaux que le fardeau du grand nombre d'expéditions pour le Roy'.[6] The *élus* retained most of their civil and criminal jurisdiction, but a number of cases of corruption involving the *élus* came before the king's council in the 1660s[7] which confirmed the need for close supervision by the intendants. All the intendants could hope to do was to prosecute those officials who committed serious offences when there was clear evidence against them: 'il faut s'appliquer', wrote Pontchartrain in 1689, 'à en faire des examples de sévérité qui soient rares à la vérité, mais qui servent à instruire et à corriger les autres . . .'[8]

After 1669, the intendants began to stay longer in the provinces than had previously been the case. In the fifty years between 1666 and 1716, the 'average' intendant stayed five years in his province, two years longer than his predecessor after the Fronde.[9] It thus appears that the 'three-year rule', after which an intendant appointed by Richelieu and Mazarin had to be re-appointed, sent to a new province, or recalled, was abandoned during the years of Louis XIV's personal rule. Each province might have expected to experience the administration of nine or more intendants in the fifty years between

---

ment de leurs gages et droitz': E 332a, fo. 56, 4 Feb. 1660. Louis XIV pronounced his verdict on the meetings of the *trésoriers* and *élus* within a month of Mazarin's death: E 1714, no. 62, 2 Apr. 1661.

[1] The intendants' powers to hold the assessments were confirmed at the same time as the loans contracted by Foucquet on the *généralités* for 1662 were abrogated: E 349b, fo. 91.

[2] Moreau de Beaumont, *Mémoires concernant les impositions*, ii. 24–5.

[3] 1718, fo. 111.   [4] E 1719, no. 102. Cf. E 366b, fo. 83, 20 Sept. 1663.

[5] Two *trésoriers* at Soissons were ordered to verify the arrears of the *taille* from 1647–56 and to countersign orders for coercion: E 346b, fo. 254, 25 June 1661. The *trésoriers* of Tours were given similar powers for the arrears from 1657–61: K 891, no. 7, 29 Dec. 1663.

[6] Dumont, *Bureau des finances de Moulins*, p. 134–5.

[7] Bonney, 'Intendants', p. 246.   [8] G7 5, 2 Sept. 1689.

[9] Bonney, 'Intendants', p. 334.

1666 and 1716. There was much less mobility in the *pays d'états* than in the *pays d'élections*. The *généralité* of Montauban saw eleven intendants; Alençon, Moulins, Poitiers, and Rouen experienced even more. In contrast, Bouchu served as intendant in Burgundy for 27 years (1656–83) while Basville served in Languedoc for 33 years (1685–1718). Why was it that the intendants tended to stay longer in their provinces? One reason was Colbert's investigation into the debts of the towns. Bouchu had observed in 1666 that it was not enough to liquidate existing debts: it was essential to prevent the communities from incurring new ones.[1] Colbert appreciated the point. In a memorandum to the intendants of 29 February 1680, he asked for suggestions on how this should be achieved.[2] The reports of the intendants were enacted in the decree of 18 November 1681[3] and the edict of April 1683. The edict transferred the control of municipal finance from the towns to the intendants, and with the exception of the years between 1764 and 1771, provided the framework of the relationship between the government and the towns until the French Revolution. The edict did not prescribe the audit of municipal accounts by the intendants and Colbert did not favour this procedure. He considered it 'un travail immense qui ne produiroit aucun avantage aux peuples'. However, this was the logical outcome of Colbert's legislation and it was this, more than any single factor, which led to the *tutelle administrative* over the towns. The amount of work carried out by the intendants was greatly increased as a result of this measure and its implications. The intendants had to rely on subordinate officials during the verification and liquidation of the debts 'pour avancer un travail si nécessaire'. By 1718 business concerning the towns had become the '[travail] ordinaire'[4] of the intendant who relied on a network of local *subdélégués* to establish whether projected expenditure by the towns was worthwhile.[5] The towns were deprived of political and financial independence,

---

[1] cf. E 393a, fo. 378, 24 Nov. 1666.
[2] Pagès, 'Essai sur l'évolution', p. 134.   [3] E 1810, no. 106.
[4] The phrase was that of Basville, the intendant of Languedoc: 'Mémoires secrets de Lamoignon de Basville . . .' *Les chroniques de Languedoc*, ed. L. de La Cour de la Pijardière (Montpellier, 1877), iii. 2.
[5] Basville, for example, had about fifteen *subdélégués*: Bonney, 'Intendants', p. 335.

and as a result the crown was able to exploit them even more ruthlessly and systematically than had hitherto been possible. After 1683, abuse and exploitation by local notables was replaced by the ruthless exploitation of the towns by the state. The fiscal demands of the Nine Years War and the War of the Spanish Succession began a process which was consummated during the Wars of the Polish and Austrian Successions.[1]

A second factor in prolonging the periods of residence of the intendants was the stricter control over the Protestants imposed by Louis XIV. By 1657, the Protestants of the Midi had feared imminent persecution. Events in the following years, and particularly after 1661, demonstrated that their fears were not ill-founded. A discussion between representatives of the clergy and Chancellor Séguier on 23 February 1661 resulted in agreement that the *commissaires pour l'exécution de l'édit de Nantes* envisaged in 1656 should be sent out. No action was taken before Mazarin's death on 9 March. Within a month or so of the death of the chief minister, however, the first commissions were drawn up. On 15 June 1661, Louis XIV gave the clergy a further assurance that the declaration of 1656 would be implemented in full.[2] Ironically, at a time when the political influence of the *dévots* was on the wane their policy triumphed: Louis XIV was able to destroy the *dévot* movement by making the anti-Protestant crusade government policy.[3] The king recalled in his memoirs that in 1661 he had sought to restrict the concessions accorded by the edict of Nantes.[4] The way in which he did this was through the work of commissioners in not less than thirteen provinces throughout France.[5] In Languedoc, the work of Bazin de Bezons and De Peyremales constituted a systematic assault on the rights of the Protestants to participate in municipal government through the *consulats mi-partis*. In 1663, Catholic control was reimposed at Sommières Bédarieux, Montpellier, and Mazamet. The Protestants sometimes retained their rights, but the ground work had been laid: the new theory, as expressed in 1666, was that 'la com-

---

[1] Pagès, 'Essai sur l'évolution', p. 135. Temple, 'Control of French towns', *passim.*   [2] Blet, *Le clergé*, ii. 367–8. Allier, *La cabale des dévots*, pp. 318, 321.
[3] Allier, op. cit., p. 428.
[4] Louis XIV, *Mémoires pour les années 1661 et 1666 . . .*, ed. Longnon, p. 116.
[5] Bonney, 'Intendants', pp. 329–32. Fourteen if Béarn is included: Loirette, 'L'administration royale en Béarn', p. 104.

munauté ne peut être divisée ni partagée. Elle est toute catholique.'[1] The rights to hold Protestant services, as defined in articles 10 and 11 of the edict of Nantes were severely restricted.[2] Generally, the Protestant commissioner was anxious to retain royal favour and followed the view of the Catholic intendant.[3] The intendants sometimes summoned additional Huguenots to assist in the work—men who were their clients and whom, they hoped, would weaken the resolve of the Protestant commissioners. Thus Bazin de Bezons summoned Anoul, the *juge royal* of Uzès, to assist in the investigation in 1661.[4] Even if the Protestant commissioner did not follow the Catholic intendant, a commission of the council of state heard the appeals.[5] This commission of the council was, of course, composed exclusively of Catholics including two prominent members of the *dévot* party (Ormesson and Boucherat) and the son of an acting intendant (Bazin de Bezons). Thus the procedure was from the start weighted heavily against the Protestants. It resulted in the declaration of 2 April 1666, which severely limited the edict of Nantes.[6]

The judicial persecution of the Huguenots had begun. On 21 January 1669, the *chambres de l'édit* of Paris and Rouen were suppressed; that of Castres was transferred to the Catholic town of Castelnaudary. Ten years later, the remaining *chambres de l'édit* were abolished and incorporated into the local *parlements*.[7] A flood of restrictive legislation was passed after 1679 in a sense rendering the edict of Fontainebleau (18 October 1685)—which revoked the edict of Nantes—unnecessary.[8] The

---

[1] The theory argued by Pierre Bernard, a *conseiller* in the *présidial* of Béziers, in his treatise entitled *Explication de l'édit* (1666). Quoted by Gachon, *Quelques préliminaires*, p. 62.

[2] Public services had to have been held regularly at the place in question from 1577 until 1597: B. L. Harleian 4442, fo. 361ᵛ, 9 Sept. 1661. Even if this could be proved, the Chancellor could contest the evidence: Blet, *Le clergé*, ii. 384.

[3] Gachon, op. cit., pp. 37–41.

[4] B.L. Harleian 4442, fos. 361ᵛ–362ʳ, 9 Sept. 1661.

[5] E 1723, no. 129, 12 Sept. 1664.

[6] Blet, op. cit., ii. 385–7. P. Blet, 'Le conseil d'état et les Protestants de 1680 à 1685', *Bibliothèque de l'École des Chartes*, cxxx (1972), 138. However, the declaration of 1666 was revoked on 28 May 1669 and the offensive against the Protestants was suspended for a decade.

[7] Cambon de Lavalette, *La Chambre de l'édit de Languedoc*, pp. 143–5.

[8] Blet, 'Le conseil d'état et les Protestants'. J. Orcibal, *Louis XIV et les Protestants. La cabale des accommodeurs de religion. La caisse des conversions. La révocation de l'édit de*

forced conversions of the Protestants in Poitou and elsewhere after 1681 had of course created a new situation;[1] so too had Louis XIV's deepening conflict with the Papacy.[2] The revocation of the edict of Nantes was thus produced by a particular set of circumstances, foreign and domestic. However, it could not have been implemented effectively without the elimination of Protestant civil rights in the years before 1685. After that date, the work of the intendants concerning the *nouveaux convertis*—as the Protestants were now called—was greatly increased.[3] The intendants were ordered to prosecute Protestants captured trying to flee abroad.[4] They were ordered by a decree of the council of state, dated 13 May 1686, to supervise the drawing up of inventories of the possessions left behind by Protestant exiles, as a preliminary measure to the confiscation of such property.[5] The intendants prosecuted those *nouveaux convertis* who remained in France in the hope of practising their old religion and who were captured by the troops at illegal Protestant prayer meetings.[6] The intendants even carried out posthumous prosecutions of *nouveaux convertis* who refused to receive the Catholic sacraments on their death-bed.[7] The influence of certain intendants in the formation of government policy towards the Protestants was great. Basville engaged in a long controversy with Bossuet, the greatest Catholic mind of the age, on whether or not the *nouveaux convertis* should be forced by the intendants and the troops to attend Mass—significantly, the intendant thought that the converts should be forced to attend.[8] Basville came to have doubts about the policy of

Nantes (1951). D. Robert, 'Louis XIV et les Protestants', *XVIIᵉ Siècle*, lxxvi–lxxvii (1967), 39–52.

[1] André, *Michel Le Tellier et Louvois* (2nd ed., 1943), pp. 485–8.

[2] J. Orcibal, *Louis XIV contre Innocent XI. Les appels au future concile de 1688 et l'opinion française* (1949). J. Orcibal, 'Louis XIV and the edict of Nantes, *Louis XIV and absolutism*, ed. Hatton, pp. 158–67.

[3] Indeed, the importance of Protestant affairs almost certainly led to the establishment of a permanent intendancy in Béarn after 1682: Loirette, 'L'administration royale en Béarn', p. 107.

[4] For example, Languedoc, the Dauphiné, Poitiers, Soissons, and Rouen: E 1835–42, *passim*.   [5] E 1836, no. 52.

[6] Decrees affecting Orléans, Bourges, Provence, the Dauphiné, Paris, Caen, Bordeaux, Alençon, Rouen, Poitiers, Montauban, and Soissons: E 1835–92, *passim*.   [7] For example, Basville in Languedoc: E 1853, no. 38, 8 Mar. 1689.

[8] P. Gachon, 'Le conseil royal et les Protestants en 1698. L'enquête, la question de la messe et le rôle de Basville', *Revue Historique*, lxxxv (1904), 252–70: lxxxvi

coercing Protestants—but this was later, during the long struggle with the *Camisard* rebellion in the Cévennes after 1702.[1]

It has been suggested that while Louis XIV was the political disciple of Mazarin, he adopted certain new policies in the 1660s: a new council was established; an attempt was made to reform the finances of the French monarchy; the verification and redemption of municipal debts was carried out; the Protestants lost all civil rights, and later were coerced to abjure their faith. As a result of this combination of factors, the intendants came to stay longer in the provinces than had been the case before 1661. Had Louis XIV opted to maintain peace, he would have enjoyed much greater freedom of action, and—if he had so wished—might have renounced the legacy of Richelieu and Mazarin. Colbert's financial reforms were geared essentially to the exceptional conditions of twelve years of peace between 1660 and 1671.[2] So too were his plans to strengthen French manufactures, commerce, and agriculture in a period of economic depression. Colbert was probably not an advocate of war,[3] which was in flat contradiction to his policy of retrenchment and reform. Yet Louis had no intention of maintaining peace for its own sake. He had designs on the Spanish Succession;

(1904), 225–41. J. Lemoine, *Mémoires des evêques de France sur la conduite à tenir à l'égard des réformés, 1698* (1902).

[1] Armogathe and Joutard, 'Basville et la guerre des Camisards'.

[2] With the exception of the War of Devolution, 1667–8.

[3] Most historians argue that Colbert wanted the war against the Dutch in 1672. For one such view: P. Goubert, *Louis XIV et 20 millions de Français* (1966), pp. 85–95, 103–8. Yet the evidence is less clear-cut. Undoubtedly Colbert's tariffs of 1664 and 1667 exacerbated relations with the Dutch, but they seem to have been a subsidiary issue, not the *casus belli*: H. H. Rowen, *The ambassador prepares for war. The Dutch embassy of Arnaud de Pomponne, 1669–71* (The Hague, 1957), pp. 185–96. [But cf. S. Elzinga, 'La prélude de la guerre de 1672', *Revue d'Histoire Moderne* (1927), 349–66.] Colbert is known to have opposed Louvois's military reviews in 1666, the overall costs of government in 1670, and the costs of the Dutch war once it was undertaken: it remains to be demonstrated that he was more bellicose in 1671–2. Colbert's violent language should not be confused with the championing of open war. He argued that Holland should be 'destroyed' in maritime rivalry with the French, but thought in terms of 'une guerre d'argent'. In his view, trade was a peaceful activity although warlike in the sharpness with which it was waged: *Lettres . . . de Colbert*, ed. Clément, vi. 269. Rowen, *Ambassador*, pp. 195–6. None of this denies that Colbert was a pragmatic politician, who—unlike Pomponne—did not speak out openly against the war, but maintained his position in the government by accepting the king's decision. Cf. P. Sonnino, 'Louis XIV and the Dutch War', *Louis XIV and Europe*, ed. Hatton, pp. 157, 167.

he wanted to reinterpret the Westphalian settlement of 1648 in the interest of France; above all, in 1672 he wanted to punish the Dutch for having formed the Triple Alliance against him four years earlier.[1] The Dutch war rapidly escalated into a German war as well. By 1674, total expenditure reached 113 million *livres*, approximately the level in 1653. The debt left by the war accounted for expenditure of over 130 million in 1679 and 1681.[2] After Colbert's death in 1683, his reforms were completely undermined. In 1689, Louis XIV began the first of two major struggles with the formidable financial resources of England. The council established in 1661—the *conseil royal des finances*—now rarely met. When it met at all, it merely ratified decisions taken by the *contrôleur-général des finances*, acting as a latter-day *surintendant*.[3] Colbert had hoped that the indirect revenues would provide the basis of a more equitable distribution of taxation: but the successful levy of indirect taxes depended on the maintenance of peace. With the outbreak of war in 1689, the income from the indirect revenues quickly fell[4] and the government had once more to fall back on the *taille* and creations of offices as the means of financing the war. There was once more a widening gap between expenditure and revenue. The crown thus had no choice but to rely on the service of financiers such as Samuel Bernard and Antoine Crozat—and to pay the high rates of interest the financiers demanded for their services. Louis XIV set his course along the path of war rather than of continued retrenchment and reform. Louis thus believed that the demands of French foreign policy had to take precedence over all domestic considerations, and in this respect the later years of his reign form a direct link with the ministries of Richelieu and Mazarin. It meant that the chief concerns of government in the years after 1672 were essentially similar to the concerns of government in the years 1653–61: how could the war be financed without provoking a major insurrection of the French taxpayers? Concern for the welfare of the peasant taxpayers of France had been an aspect of government emphasized by Mazarin on his

[1] Rowen, *Ambassador*, *passim*. H. H. Rowen, 'John de Witt and the Triple Alliance', *Journal of Modern History*, xxvi (1954), 1–14.

[2] Bonney, 'The secret expenses of Richelieu and Mazarin', p. 835.

[3] Antoine, *Le conseil du roi*, p. 69.

[4] Matthews, *The royal general farms*, pp. 54–60.

death-bed, and the remission of the arrears of the *taille* in the early 1660s suggest that the idea had some influence on Louis XIV.[1] Yet prolonged war meant higher taxes and the lot of the peasant could only worsen in a period of economic depression. Even in the years of peace there had been major revolts, such as those of the Bénauge in 1661–2,[2] of the *Lustucru* in the Boulonnais in 1662,[3] of Audijos in the Chalosse in 1663–5,[4] and of Roure in the Vivarais in 1670.[5] There were further riots and revolts following the outbreak of war in 1672, most notably at Agen in 1673[6] and Bordeaux[7] and le Mans[8] two years later. The revolt of the *Bonnets-Rouges* or *Torrében* of Brittany in 1675 witnessed perhaps the greatest degree of social antagonism in any peasant rebellion in seventeenth-century France.[9] The later wars brought major rebellions in their wake, too, notably the Protestant *Camisard* rising of 1702 (which was in part a rebellion against taxation)[10] and the revolt of the *Tard-Avisés* of Quercy in 1707.[11] While 'tax rebellion' took place on a significant scale during the personal rule of Louis XIV, and on occasion

[1] For example, the phrasing of the decrees remitting arrears: E 1714, no. 60, 2 Apr. 1661. E 350, fo. 14, 5 Jan. 1662.

[2] F. Loirette, 'Une émeute paysanne au début du gouvernement personnel de Louis XIV: la sédition de Bénauge (déc. 1661–janv. 1662)', *Annales du Midi*, lxxviii (1966), 515–36.

[3] A. Hamy, *Essai sur les ducs d'Aumont, gouverneurs du Boulonnais, 1622–1789 Guerre dite de Lustucru, 1662 . . .* (Boulogne-sur-Mer, 1906–7). P. Heliot, 'La guerre dite de Lustucru et les privilèges du Boulonnais', *Revue du Nord*, xxi (1935), 265–318. André, *Le Tellier et Louvois*, pp. 107–11. E 1720, no. 53, 17 July 1662.

[4] A. Communay, 'Audijos. La gabelle en Gascogne', *Archives historiques de la Gascogne*, ser. i, xxiv, xxv (1893–4). O'Reilly, *Pellot*, i. 437–520. E 1726, fos. 183, 283, 13 May, 22 Aug. 1665. E 1728, no. 120, 3 July 1665. E 1732, no. 210, 17 Aug. 1666.

[5] Leroy-Ladurie, *Les paysans de Languedoc*, i. 609–10. E 1758, nos. 157, 191, 12 July and 9 Aug. 1670.

[6] E 1772, no. 2, 3 Jan. 1673.

[7] Bercé, *Histoire des croquants*, i. 517–23. E 1781, nos. 151, 235, 26 June and 24 Nov. 1675.

[8] E 1781, no. 106, 3 May 1675.

[9] A. de la Borderie, *La révolte du papier timbré advenue en Bretagne en 1675. Histoire et documents* (Saint-Brieuc, 1884). J. Lemoine, 'La révolte dite du papier timbré ou bonnets-rouges en Bretagne en 1675', *Annales de Bretagne*, xii–xiv (1896–9). Y. Garlan and C. Nières, *Les révoltes bretonnes de 1675. Papier timbré et bonnets rouges* (1975).

[10] Leroy-Ladurie, op. cit., i. 627–9. H. Bosc, *La guerre des Cévennes, 1705–1710, d'après les archives du Depôt de la Guerre à Vincennes et les mémoires du temps* (2 vols., Lille, 1974), i. 34–43.

[11] Bercé, *Histoire des croquants*, i. 524–33.

involved the intendants,[1] the scale was much less than under Richelieu and Mazarin. There is no simple explanation why this was the case, because in part it was the result of a change in peasant attitudes.[2] By forcing the peasants to concentrate above all on scratching a livelihood, the agricultural depression may actually have hindered rather than encouraged active protest: the peasants at the time of Richelieu and Mazarin were somewhat more prosperous and thus in a sense had more to lose from increased taxation paid to the state.[3] The greater strength of government, especially in terms of the availability of troops in most years, the more certain status of the intendants after 1661, and the more savage punishment meted out to rioters[4] were other contributory factors.

The relative quiescence of the nobles certainly assisted the government in its task of isolating and suppressing rural rebellions. Mazarin on his death-bed had counselled Louis XIV to preserve the privileges of the nobles, and Louis certainly did so with regard to their social and economic privileges.[5] Yet Louis did not allow nobles from the older and more established families to enter government except on an occasional, individual basis—the most notable example being the duc de Beauvillier after 1691.[6] The remarkable fact about Louis XIV's personal rule, and the great contrast with the situation in his minority, is that the magnates did not rebel at their exclusion.

[1] Apart from the instances cited, cf. Machault in the *généralité* of Soissons: E 1780, fo. 66, 3 Aug. 1675. Béchameil de Nointel and Larcher at Villenauxe: E 1878, fo. 27, 16 Feb. 1692. Maupeou d'Ablieges in the *élection* of Issoire: E 1882, 3 Apr. 1694. Sanson near Villefranche-en-Rouergue: E 1893, no. 78, 4 Oct. 1695.

[2] E. Leroy-Ladurie, 'Révoltes et contestations rurales en France de 1675 à 1788', *Annales E.S.C.*, xxix (1974), 6–22.

[3] cf. recent local economic studies, most notably: P. Goubert, *Beauvais et le Beauvaisis de 1600 à 1730. Contribution à l'histoire sociale de France du xviie siècle* (2 vols., 1960). Leroy-Ladurie, *Les paysans de Languedoc*. J. Jacquart, *La crise rurale en Ile-de-France, 1550–1670* (1974).

[4] For example, after the defeat of the *Lustucru* at Hucqueliers (11 July 1662), 584 rebels were taken captive. Those over seventy and under twenty years of age were pardoned and set free. Another twelve were to be prosecuted by the intendant as ringleaders. Four hundred persons were sent to the galleys: E 1720, no. 53, 17 July 1662.

[5] Although, of course, he was forced to infringe them with the establishment of the *capitation* in 1695 and the *dixième* in 1710. These taxes were not a success, however. Cf. J. Meuvret, 'Fiscalism and public opinion under Louis XIV', *Louis XIV and absolutism*, ed. Hatton, pp. 218–22.

[6] J. Lizerand, *Le duc de Beauvillier, 1648–1714* (1933).

The conspiracies of the chevalier de Rohan in 1674[1] and of Schomberg in 1692[2] were abortive although they produced the usual manifestos proclaiming the need to restore the privileges of the nobility, the *Parlements*, the provinces, and to reduce the burden of taxation. Louis XIV's foreign policy and his domestic religious policy combined to prevent all but a tiny minority of the population from active subversion. The *dévot* argument of the 1620s that the war was unjust because it divided Catholic Europe at a time when there was a significant Protestant minority at home was scarcely applicable after 1666 and incorrect after 1685: Louis XIV fought the Protestant English and Dutch and forced the abjuration of his Huguenot community. The willingness of the Emperor to partition the Spanish inheritance with France after 1668[3] removed the possibility of a strong 'Catholic' alliance of Habsburg Spain and Austria against France.

Within the provinces, the lesser nobility was gradually transformed in the 1660s and 1670s as a result of conscious royal policy. A highly seditious and ill-defined social group at the time of Richelieu and Mazarin, they became during the personal rule of Louis XIV a highly independent but nevertheless legally-defined, and increasingly law-abiding, group of privileged persons. The *réformations* of the nobility undertaken by the intendants on the orders of Colbert were extremely important, not least because they were desperately unpopular with the nobles themselves.[4] There were clear precedents for the investigation into titles of nobility: in 1598, 1634, 1640, and

[1] P. Clément, *La police sous Louis XIV* (1866), pp. 151–5, 411–26. A. Maury, 'Une conspiration républicaine sous Louis XIV', *Revue des Deux Mondes*, lxxvi (1886), 376–406, 756–84. K. Malettke, *Opposition und konspiration unter Ludwig XIV. Studien zu kritik und widerstand gegen system und politik des französischen königs während der ersten hälfte seiner persönlichen regierung* (Göttingen, 1976).

[2] C. Bost, *Les prédicants protestants des Cévennes et du Bas-Languedoc, 1684–1700* (2 vols., 1912), ii. 515. Leroy-Ladurie, *Les paysans de Languedoc*, i. 614–15.

[3] J. Bérenger, 'Une tentative de rapprochement entre la France et l'Empereur: le traité de partage secret de la succession d'Espagne du 19 janvier 1668', *Revue d'Histoire Diplomatique*, lxxix (1965), 291–314, translated in *Louis XIV and Europe*, ed. Hatton, pp. 133–52.

[4] For example, rebellions against the *réformation* in the *généralité* of Paris to be investigated by Auguste-Robert Pommereu de la Bretesche and Foucault: E 399a, fo. 296, 13 July 1667. Sieur de la Hubardière to be prosecuted by Barentin for 'mauvais traitements' when asked to present his titles of nobility: E 395b, fo. 30, 21 Mar. 1667.

1655 recent letters of *anoblissement* had been revoked and investigations of claims to nobility had been undertaken. In the *généralité* of Caen, for example, this had resulted in two armorials of nobility being drawn up—respectively by Mesmes de Roissy in 1598–9 and by Étienne III d'Aligre in 1634–5. In other provinces, however, the investigation was probably less thorough or else the records of the enquiry were subsequently lost. Colbert's survey was much more complete, extending at various times throughout most of France.[1] One aspect of the enquiry had a fiscal purpose, to ensure that all false titles were annulled so that 'le fardeau de la taille soit porté avec égalité par tous ceux que la naissance y assujetit'.[2] Yet there was also a political aspect to the enquiry.[3] However uneven the results of the investigation into noble titles, there were three important consequences. The first was that throughout France—the chief exceptions were Brittany and Provence—the intendant, in close contact with the king's council (but without reference to the governor), became the arbiter of what was, and what was not, a legal title to nobility. In every province there were 'false nobles' whose claims were dismissed (*déboutés*) and who were required to pay a fine of not less than 100 *livres*. Many illustrious noble families (*nobles d'ancienne extraction*), on the assumption that their lineage was beyond dispute, had not bothered to keep archives. Accordingly, they found themselves in great difficulty when faced with the intendant's desire for the *preuves nobiliaires*. The search for relevant documents at the local law-courts, among the church records, and the records of notaries was both an expensive and an uncertain procedure. By contrast, the *noblesse de robe* had little difficulty in proving a claim to nobility that did not often reach back beyond 1550: the dates of provisions to offices conveying nobility were known, and the recent *anobli* was likely to have been more methodical in conserving his documents. A second consequence of the investigation was a new definition of nobility: the nobleman was no longer he who claimed to be a noble, he who was

---

[1] The investigations by the intendants resulted in a series of armorials. Many of these are cited by G. Saffroy, *Bibliographie généalogique, heraldique et nobiliaire de la France* (3 vols., 1968–74) chiefly s.v. *recherches de noblesse*. For a discussion of the investigation: Meyer, *La noblesse bretonne*, i. 29–61; Constant, 'L'enquête de noblesse de 1667'.

[2] E 393b, fo. 197, 6 Dec. 1666.   [3] cf. above, chapter XIII.

thought of as a noble, or he who enjoyed exemption from direct taxation. The nobleman became the person who had obtained an *ordonnance de maintenu de noblesse* from the intendant, a legally binding document after an enquiry into written evidence. A third consequence of the investigation, and other associated government measures, was a closing of the ranks of the nobles after the 1660s. Increasingly, the distinction between *nobles de robe* and *nobles d'épée* began to disappear. In part, this was because of the decline in the profitability of office during the reign of Louis XIV: the majority of the *noblesse de robe* had to rely on their lands for the major part of their income to offset the loss of revenues from law practice and the depreciating capital asset represented by the ownership of most of the expensive offices.[1] At the same time, the investigation into noble titles made it much more difficult to gain new exemptions from taxation. The 'usurpation' of nobility—or gaining nobility through prescription without a clear title—was always possible in the *ancien régime*: but the intendants' control of the *taille* was meant to reduce false claims to fiscal exemption as much as possible.[2] Noble independence was never completely undermined by the Bourbon monarchy: but through the *recherches de noblesse* undertaken by the intendants, and through other associated forms of judicial and political control, the threat posed by the nobles to the body politic between 1624 and 1661 was removed. At the same time, the peasants lost their champions in 'tax rebellion' against the crown, and the potentially rebellious governor lost his power base.

The extent of Louis XIV's innovations after 1661 should not be exaggerated. In most respects, his changes did little more than consolidate the political achievement of Richelieu and Mazarin. The threads of continuity were strengthened by the fact that substantially the same families dominated government and the intendancies before and after 1661. Louis XIV's ministers before 1700 were drawn predominantly from families which had risen to prominence under Richelieu and Mazarin.[3]

---

[1] Hurt, 'Les offices', pp. 25–8. Hamscher [*The Parlement of Paris after the Fronde*, p. 37] argues for a clear distinction between *noblesse de robe* and *noblesse d'épée* in the earlier part of Louis XIV's personal rule. But what of the later years?

[2] Cf. D. J. Sturdy, 'Tax evasion, the *faux nobles* and state fiscalism: the example of the *généralité* of Caen, 1634–35; *French historical studies*, ix (1976), 549–72.

[3] Bluche 'L'origine sociale des secrétaires d'état de Louis XIV'.

Colbert, his brother Colbert de Croissy, Colbert's son Seignelay, and Croissy's son Colbert de Torcy formed one group of ministers. Michel Le Tellier, his son Louvois, and Louvois's son Barbezieux formed a second group. There were few ministers —such as Pontchartrain and Chamillart—who were not allied with one or other group.[1] Lionne, Louis XIV's foreign minister from 1663 until 1671 was the nephew of Servien and had been a member of the government since at least 1651. Pomponne, who succeeded Lionne, had been a *protégé* of Foucquet[2] and had served as an intendant of the army in the 1650s. Similarly, several intendants appointed by Mazarin served during Louis XIV's personal rule. Bazin de Bezons did so in Languedoc until 1673, Bouchu did so in Burgundy until 1683, Hotman de Fontenay did so at Paris until 1681, and Pellot did so at Bordeaux and Montauban until 1669. Pommereu de la Bretesche, the first intendant in Brittany when the intendants were re-established in that province in 1689,[3] had served as intendant of Moulins in 1660. In addition to intendants appointed by Mazarin who continued to serve during Louis XIV's personal rule, there were also sons and grandsons of intendants appointed by Richelieu and Mazarin: over twenty intendants came into this category.[4] For such reasons alone, it would have been difficult for Louis XIV to have formulated and implemented radically different policies from those pursued by Richelieu and Mazarin.

[1] *Le conseil du roi*, ed. Mousnier, p. 173.   [2] ibid., p. 160.

[3] H. Fréville, *L'intendance de Bretagne, 1689–1790. Essai sur l'histoire d'une intendance en pays d'états au xviiie siècle* (3 vols., Rennes, 1953), I. 45–65.

[4] For example, Thomas-Alexandre Morant, Pierre Cardin Le Bret, Cardin II Le Bret, Claude Méliand, Antoine-François Méliand, Anne Pinon, François II Le Tonnelier de Breteuil, Henri Aguesseau, Guillaume Sève de Châtillon, Charles Faucon de Ris, Louis Bazin de Bezons, Étienne-Hyacinthe Foullé, François Lefèvre de Caumartin, André Harouys, Étienne-Jean Bouchu, Anne Turgot, Jean-Étienne Turgot, Marc-Antoine Turgot, Henri Nesmond, André II Lefèvre d'Ormesson, Antoine d'Aubray comte d'Offémont, Jean Phélypeaux, Louis II Machault, Jean II Le Camus.

Conclusion

DOMESTIC POLITICS were subordinated to foreign policy at the time of Richelieu and Mazarin. There is little doubt that with foreign policy this order of priorities achieved its purpose. The threat of encirclement of France by the Austrian and Spanish Habsburgs was removed decisively. The power of the Emperor in Germany was checked in 1648 and this success was followed up by a French-organized League of the Rhine which imposed a stringent 'election capitulation' on the Emperor Leopold I in 1658. The power of Philip IV was checked, too, notably once France and England were allied after 1655. The duchy of Lorraine, formerly allied with the Habsburgs, was demobilized. Dutch independence from Spain was recognized—although from the French point of view the Dutch proved themselves unreliable allies by making a separate peace in 1648. Sweden gained an empire in north Germany largely as a result of French military and diplomatic support in the 1640s: this empire was extended in the 1650s partly as a result of continued French diplomatic support. The peace of the Pyrenees substituted a French for a Spanish hegemony in Europe and left open the distant possibility of France gaining part or all of the Spanish succession. Yet as a result of what appeared to be a 'defensive' war against Habsburg aggression, French prestige was high in Europe. It was not until Louis XIV initiated his two early wars (1667–8, 1672–8) that it appeared that France might threaten the balance of power and the peace of Europe equally as the Habsburgs had done.

However, these successes in French foreign policy were not inevitable. The Spanish invasion of 1636–7 was a great trauma for the populations on three war fronts—the north and east in 1636 and the south the following year. Little went right for France in the Thirty Years War until Bernard of Saxe-Weimar, a French ally, captured Breisach in December 1638. It was not until Portugal and Catalonia seceded from Spanish rule in 1640 that the prospects of a French victory appeared less distant. As late as 1647–8, however, Spanish intransigence combined with the domestic political difficulties of Mazarin to threaten the direction of French foreign policy. The most important factor in domestic politics was that there was no majority support for the war effort among the propertied classes.[1] The French armies were commanded by members of the *noblesse d'épée*: but certain nobles at least were prepared to argue that profound changes had occurred in French society as a result of the war effort, and that these changes should be reversed. The changes were indeed profound. In political terms, France in 1661 was scarcely recognizable as the same country that had survived the trauma of Henri IV's assassination and the troubles of Louis XIII's minority. Louis XIV chose to govern without a chief minister: but he was able to do so realistically because he inherited a government which was far stronger and better organized than that inherited by Louis XIII in 1610. It was certainly true that Louis XIV also took over extremely serious fiscal problems as a legacy from Mazarin's ministry. Nevertheless, the resources of the French monarchy were much greater in 1661 than they had been in 1610 or even 1624. Other political changes had taken place which were of great importance. The nobles were defeated as a political force acting independently of the crown and resorting to the sanction of armed rebellion. The independence of the governors was undermined: a governor could no longer expect to mobilize his province against the crown with impunity. The political power of the Huguenots was destroyed. The towns lost some, but not all, of their independence. In certain provinces (Normandy, the Dauphiné, and Provence) the Estates disappeared. In others (Languedoc, Brittany, and Burgundy) they survived, but operated in a rather more orderly way. In 1676 John Locke could comment on the Estates of Languedoc 'that they never doe, and some say dare not, refuse whatever the king demands'.[2] This comment would have been inconceivable thirty years earlier. The enormous wave of rural and urban disturbances, linked to the massive increase in taxation, was held in check. The government opted for an executive-style

---

[1] 'Le sentiment d'icelle est en peu d'esprit . . .' A.A.E. France 256, fo. 108ᵛ, anon. memorandum to Richelieu, 1637.
[2] *Locke's travels in France, 1675–1679 . . .*, ed. J. Lough (Cambridge, 1953), p. 30.

administration: accordingly the claim of the sovereign courts to participate in affairs of state was undermined, and the lesser courts lost a great deal of their administrative powers. The establishment of the intendants as an administrative system was crucial to all these processes of political change. The great advantage of the intendant—and of the commission which formed the basis of his power—was flexibility. Additional powers could be conferred according to the requirements of a new political situation. When the political situation returned to normal, certain of those powers could be removed. The intendant was thus a remarkably useful agent for effecting political change. Unlike the other institutions in seventeenth-century France—the sovereign and lesser courts, the governors, and the Estates—the intendants could not become an alternative source of power to the crown. By the 1630s and 1640s the king could not rely on his office-holders to administer his policies and instead he had to turn to royal commissioners to implement measures which were against the *officiers'* political, economic, and social interests. Although the intendants might be termed 'autant de rois dans les provinces',[1] and although each intendant might have political principles of his own, perhaps even independent ideas, the similarity in their social origins and career patterns ensured a common approach to their work and acted as a guarantee of their loyalty. Even had this not been the case, the flexibility of the commission could come to the rescue of the government. The theory of the king's *justice retenue*—that part of the king's justice that could be granted out and then revoked at will—meant that the intendant, unlike the law court, or the representative institution, could be dismissed. Moreover, unlike the governor, the intendant could be dismissed without risking grave political dangers. The career of the intendant was quite unlike that of magnates such as Gaston d'Orléans, Condé, and the other governors: his career was entirely in the hands of the ministers. From the start, the career of an intendant could be broken if he gave bad service: when Richelieu introduced this concept into the governorships in the 1630s, it was an innovation which was greatly resented. The system of intendants thus had an inbuilt check against action taken independently of the crown.

[1] Bercé, *Histoire des croquants*, ii. 796: 'autant de pouvoir que le Roy mesme . . .'

The importance of French domestic political change under Richelieu and Mazarin is illuminated by comparison with Spain. If Richelieu 'succeeded' and Olivares 'failed'—and this was true for their respective successors, Mazarin and Don Luis de Haro—this was only in part due to the outcome on the battlefield. Richelieu had great advantages over his Spanish counterpart. The French kings of the later fifteenth and sixteenth centuries had made taxes permanent; in theory almost completely, and in practice absolutely, they had abolished the right of consent to taxation in the *pays d'élections*. There was thus no legitimate opposition to Richelieu's vast increase of taxation in the 1630s. There were *soulèvements populaires*, it is true: but these were a less dangerous proposition than the sort of constitutional conflicts that Languedoc experienced. If all France had been *pays d'états*, the Thirty Years War could not have been won. Even as it was, Richelieu feared a general insurrection comparable to the revolt of the Catalans. The purpose of the intendants was to destroy opposition to the French war effort. Both in their political role of suppressing revolts, and in their financial role of collecting taxes, the intendants were indispensable, and it is difficult to imagine the two peace settlements of Westphalia and the Pyrenees being achieved on such advantageous terms for France without them. No matter how shaky the political and financial structure in France, vast sums were mobilized at the right moment to pay for the war. The credit market in France was a domestic one: in 1648, at a moment of crisis, Mazarin could bring pressure to bear upon it. The French financiers were willing to lend the government money at favourable rates of interest in the hope of securing compensation for their losses in the bankruptcy of 1648. This was not the case in Spain: when Philip IV went bankrupt in 1647, the Portuguese financiers withdrew their services and the break was irrevocable.[1] The French state remained intact until 1648 at a time when the Spanish state all but fell apart. Thereafter Spain was too weak to be able to exploit effectively the difficulties of the Regency government and the divisions of the Fronde. The political and financial position of Spain was undoubtedly worse than that of France. Catalonia was

---

[1] A. Castillo, 'Dans la monarchie espagnole du xviie siècle: les banquiers portugais et le circuit d'Amsterdam', *Annales E.S.C.* xix (1964), 311–16.

reconquered in 1652, but Philip IV was forced to confirm its constitutional position—that is to say, he had to renounce Olivares's programme of reform. It was not until 1707 that Philip V abolished the privileges of Aragon and Valencia, introduced a uniform administration—including intendants—and increased taxation in the outlying regions of the Iberian peninsula. The reforms of Amelot, Bergeyck, and the rest came over half a century too late.

The achievements in terms of French domestic political change were thus so important that other questions must be asked: could they have been prevented? Once they were initiated, could they have been reversed? Both Richelieu and Mazarin had to survive many political crises, but there is little doubt that the most serious threats to the continuance of political change occurred in the years 1630–2 and 1648–53. The events of the Fronde were the more serious because as a result of the bankruptcy in July 1648 Anne of Austria and Mazarin lost control of events and were forced to concede legislation which they were committed to reverse at a later date, while Mazarin's position in 1648–51 was much weaker than that of Richelieu in 1630–2 since he was the chief minister of a Regent, not a king who had come of age. The Fronde was the most serious crisis of the French monarchy, certainly under Richelieu and Mazarin, and probably in the seventeenth century. Its outcome was not predetermined: once the break-down had occurred, almost any outcome was possible. Yet in the end, the Fronde failed, and thus far from temporarily halting or weakening the political changes of Richelieu and Mazarin, it consolidated them and made them irreversible. As a result, at the end of the civil war, the crown was left considerably stronger than before in domestic political terms. How had this situation come about? Short-term factors, the divisions among the office-holders, the divisions between the office-holders and the nobles, the failure of noble leadership, and the faltering support from Spain, were undoubtedly important.[1] Yet there were long-term, structural, causes too. Even in 1648–53 the French monarchy was sufficiently self-confident in ideological terms, and sufficiently strong militarily,

---

[1] R. J. Bonney, 'The French civil war, 1649–53', *European Studies Review*, viii (1978), 71–100.

to win an armed conflict against domestic faction—although the outcome of prolonged civil and foreign war was less certain. There was little prospect of successful opposition to the crown by non-violent means. France lacked a forum for constitutional opposition to the crown. There were great—and probably misguided—hopes of the Estates-General during the Fronde, which was summoned in 1649 and 1651, although it did not actually meet. Many politicians wanted an Estates-General to oust Mazarin from power and establish a broader-based council in his place: certain nobles thought this was the way their participation in government could be secured and the political changes imposed by Richelieu and Mazarin reversed. Yet profound constitutional innovations would have been required for the Estates-General to have participated in government in this way, and much greater social unity and political resistance would have been needed to force regular sessions on the crown.

The sovereign courts were not an effective substitute for the failure of a national representative institution. Before 1661, the courts certainly opposed taxation resulting from the war, especially when their members had to contribute in the form of taxes on office-holding. They opposed the strengthening of central government and the establishment of the intendants. They did not agree with Le Bret's argument that the king could change the constitution if he so wished. They certainly did not accept the implications of Le Bret's distinction between 'public law' and 'private law', with the office-holders confined to cases between contending parties where the interests of the state were not directly affected. In the exceptional years of 1648–9, the objectives of the office-holders were reasonably coherent and might seem perfectly sensible and indeed attainable. The declarations of July and October 1648 were a move towards the ideal polity from their point of view. Yet the ideal was not the only polity which the office-holders would accept: their essential political requirements were much more limited. They were concerned less with opposing political change for its own sake than with attempting to control it in their own interests. Most *parlementaires* thought of high politics only occasionally, at moments of political crisis, or when their own interests were severely threatened. For the rest of the time, they tended to think in terms of their *intérêts particuliers*, their corporate interests as *parlementaires* or their private interests as office-holders and landowners. It was this sentiment which the government tried to foster by offering favourable treatment to the sovereign courts when renewing the *droit annuel*, a tactic which in most years—with the exception of the disastrous year of 1648—was successful. The crisis of 1648 arose in part from the fact that the *gages* of all courts with the exception of the *Parlement* of Paris were to be suspended for four years in return for the renewal of the *droit annuel*. The defence of a vital private economic interest of the office-holders[1] forced them into the public arena of high politics. However, sooner or later the government would be in a position to offer the office-holders concessions which would undermine their resistance. Resistance to political change was also undermined by the fact that there were always office-holders who were prepared to accept royal commissions. They might claim that they had not demanded them from the government: but once they had received these powers they were obliged to act upon them. The resistance of the *maîtres des requêtes* to the government in 1648 was particularly short-lived. Far from the courts preventing 'the progression from Henry IV to Louis XIV . . . [toward] a much more powerful monarchy'[2] to a considerable extent they brought about the rise of a much more effective and authoritarian system of government. The *Parlements* played a major part in destroying any system of national representation in France: it was their hostility to the Estates-General which encouraged the government to resist demands for the summoning of this body. Yet the events of the Fronde and of Louis XIV's personal rule demonstrated that the courts could not influence the conduct of government when a chief minister or a powerful and self-confident king were committed to a particular line of action.

Could the nobles have reversed the process of political change and acted in a more decisive manner than the office-holders? As provincial governors and military leaders in their own right, the magnates were perhaps in a better position to do so. However, the government was usually strong enough after 1630 to put down armed rebellion by force. Since assemblies

---

[1] The importance of the *gages* before 1665 is demonstrated convincingly in Hurt, 'Les offices'.   [2] Moote, *Revolt of the judges*, p. 375.

of the nobles were usually declared illegal[1] they lacked a constitutional forum in which their views could be expressed by peaceful means. Of course, even more than the office-holders, the nobles were open to the charge of acting from motives of self-interest and the *demandes particulières* that followed their taking to arms provide ample evidence that political principle was closely allied to personal gain. Individual nobles might lose political power as a result of the political changes imposed by Richelieu and Mazarin but they registered economic gains. There is little doubt that the wealth of great magnates such as Condé, Conty and Longueville increased almost in direct relation to the failure of their rebellions, a process which was in most instances consolidated by the settlement of the Fronde. Magnates were too dangerous not to be rewarded with pensions, lands and military commands. Although the grants were made by the king, they were actually at the expense of the French taxpayer, predominantly therefore the peasants. As a result, it is probable that wealth was distributed more rather than less inequitably by 1661. However, the nobles were not a homogenous economic group. There was no similarity of interests between the magnates and the lesser nobles. Sometimes the lesser nobles would follow the lead of a magnate and join in rebellion; as often, they did not. The traditional ties of patronage were severely tested by the fact that the wealth of the lesser nobles did not increase in the seventeenth century as a concomitant of their loss of political power with the introduction of the intendants as a disciplinary force in the provinces. Quite the reverse: there is much evidence to suggest that many of the lesser nobles were no more than squires and *hobereaux* and that their economic position declined in the seventeenth century.[2]

The net effect of these developments may have been to increase social tensions. Such tensions were obvious, not merely between the privileged orders of the clergy and nobility and the unprivileged, but at certain moments—particularly the Fronde —between the privileged themselves (for example, the mutual antagonism of the nobles and office-holders). In the towns

---

[1] Certain of the legal or semi-legal assemblies are discussed in J. D. Lassaigne, *Les assemblées de la noblesse de France au xviie et xviiie siècles* (1965-6).

[2] Goubert, *Beauvais et le Beauvaisis*, i. 206-22. Deyon, 'À propos des rapports entre la noblesse française et la monarchie absolue'.

there was a residual conflict between those who enjoyed the privileges of urban life—relative fiscal immunity, participation in town government, and so on—and those who did not. In the rural parishes there was a similar conflict between the *coqs de paroisse*, those who enjoyed higher standards of living than the majority and claimed the right to fiscal immunity—either because they held office or because they worked or administered lands belonging to the nobility—and the majority of the peasants, whose landholdings were drastically reduced in size as a result of economic developments during the seventeenth century. Indeed many independent peasants were dispossessed or pauperized as a result of these changes.[1] Did the French monarchy exploit such social tensions as a long-term policy of divide and rule? It seems unlikely, for in constitutional theory the king was ruler of all his subjects, not some. There was always a government 'party' comprising certain members of the clergy, certain *nobles d'épée*, certain *nobles de robe*, certain municipal officials, certain village notables, and so on. Sometimes the crown could rely on more support than at other times and in the spring of 1652 support reached a nadir, probably for the entire period of Richelieu and Mazarin's rule. It is certainly true to say that the government recognized that social discontent might arise from the iniquities of the fiscal system: this was one reason why the administration of the *taille* was conferred on the intendants in 1642.[2] The illogicality of the government's position was that although it conceded that in a war-time emergency fiscal immunities might be abrogated, it was committed to the continuation of privilege as a long-term policy. Indeed, privileges were justified as specific concessions of previous kings: they could not easily be dispensed with, because to do so was unpopular and dangerous and left the government open to the charge of acting in bad faith. For this reason, the French monarchy was incapable of self-sustained political, social, and fiscal reform. The crown was not the prisoner of any one social group in terms of the broad direction of policy: but in practice 'absolutism' was limited by the

[1] cf. particularly the studies of Leroy-Ladurie, *Les paysans de Languedoc* and Jacquart, *La crise rurale*.
[2] cf. article 7 of the ruling of 22 Aug. 1642: the intendants 'taxeront et cottiseront les fermiers des gentilshommes et seigneurs des parroisses lesquels jusques à présent n'ont que peu ou point porté desdites impositions . . .'

existence of different hierarchies of privilege. In terms of fiscal policy the crown was in a cleft stick. It could not hope to increase the yield from taxation without the reform of abuses, thus to some extent a reduction of fiscal privileges. Yet the mere suggestion of redistribution, the slightest hint of an assault on the privileges of the more prosperous parishes, the merest indication of heavier taxes on the richer peasants, was a *casus belli*, a signal for rebellion by those whose interests were affected: the lesser nobles could not stand idly by in such a rebellion. If fiscal, social, and economic inequalities were a cause of certain revolts, it is also true to say that there were rebellions in areas where the seigneurial regime and the impact of urbanization were weak and where the peasantry was relatively prosperous. Indeed, some of the *foyers insurrectionnels*—such as the *vicomté* of Turenne[1]—were precisely the most privileged areas where the political changes of Richelieu and Mazarin had made least headway. Overall, it is probably true to say that 'vertical' allegiances between the privileged and less privileged— sometimes including the poor—were a more frequent cause of revolt than social divisions at town or parish level, the elements binding the rural community usually proving stronger than those which divided it.[2]

Most contemporaries considered that there was a fundamental contradiction between the policies of domestic reform and the pursuit of an aggressive foreign policy. This contradiction was expressed most clearly by Marillac in his speech to the king's council in 1626, which advocated the policy of 'la réforme au dedans du royaume'. To a certain extent, this viewpoint is

---

[1] Bercé, *Histoire des croquants*, ii. 650–3. Although it is true that Bouillon's reven- ues from his 111 parishes rose during the 1630s and 1640s [cf. ibid., i. 94] the amount paid was still small. When in 1650, in order to pay for his Fronde, Bouillon asked for exceptional effort, he received a grant of only 119,192 *livres*—and this anticipated his revenues three years in advance. Cf. ibid., i. 465. Fage, *Les états de la vicomté de Turenne*, i. 241; ii. 161–4. R2 493, fos. 108ᵛ, 337, 18 May 1650.

[2] cf. the percipient, though ideologically motivated, comments of D. Parker, 'The divided village', *Times Literary Supplement* (1 Aug. 1975). Cf. the rebellion at Beuzeville caused by the sieur Barlemaigne de Boullé, a *conseiller* in the *cour des aides* of Rouen, and the *curé*, his relative, who tried to ensure that their thirty farmers paid no more than 12 *livres* in *taille* each: E 347a, fo. 17, 7 July 1661. The sieur de Sousternon 'exempted' his farmers from paying the *taille* at Saint-Rémy- en-Rollat and attacked the collectors: E 1711, no. 107, 14 Aug. 1660. Opposition of both the lesser nobles and peasants to the fen drainage scheme at Niort and Fontenay-le-Comte: E 297a, fo. 35, 4 Jan. 1657.

followed by those historians who see the years of peace (1598–1610 and 1660–71) as years of missed opportunity. War certainly exacerbated the abuses in fiscal administration, although it might force the government through desperation to abrogate fiscal privileges on a temporary, emergency basis. Yet was the policy of resisting foreign adventures, of reform and retrenchment—presumably through the operation of 'mercantilist' policies, the recovery of alienated crown lands, the strengthening of the guilds, the creation of trading companies and a navy—was this a viable alternative? Increased intervention of the state in economic matters was inevitable and imperative because of the weakness of French commerce and the merchant classes in France: yet it was not regarded favourably by the majority of property-owners in an economy and society which remained stubbornly agricultural in emphasis. Given the size of the military establishment and the nature of the fiscal system financing it, Louis XIV would have had great difficulty—even had he so wished—in adopting the policy of a Charles XI of Sweden and resisting foreign adventures. Many nobles and office-holders invested in the fiscal system, relatively few in commercial and manufacturing enterprises. *Ancien régime* society was a society of the privileged that was qualitatively less advanced than the Dutch Republic and England as an economic and social system.[1]

In one important respect there was no alternative policy for the government, since the old hierarchial system of law and finance courts could not be abandoned because of the enormous financial investment in offices. Office-holders could not be expropriated because this would be interpreted as an attack on property and a justification for rebellion. Office-holders could not be bought out on the massive scale that was needed because the crown would be bankrupted in the process.[2] The political changes introduced by Richelieu and Mazarin developed French 'absolutism' to its natural limits, namely the continuance of privilege and the existing social structure. The crown had no wish to reverse these political changes, with

[1] Cf. R. B. Grassby, 'Social status and commercial enterprise under Louis XIV', *Economic History Review*, 2nd ser., xiii (1960–1), 19–38, reprinted in *State and society*, ed. Kierstead, 200–32.

[2] According to Colbert's figures in the 1660s, 419·6 million *livres* in compensation would have been necessary: B.N. 500 Colbert 259, fo. 1.

the result that the system was continued despite disadvantages that became more apparent with the passing of time. Even when certain aspects of the system were modified—as in 1715, when the restriction on the right of remonstrances was withdrawn—there was no great advantage to the government: the *Parlements* used their newly regained powers to oppose the crown's fiscal and religious policies. The theory of absolutism left the king dangerously exposed. He was the ruler of all his subjects, the 'protector' of his poor peasants who in most years had to suffer increased taxes to support the regime. One day the king, and not his evil counsellors, would be blamed for the faults of a system which in theory he was able to control—as early as 1652 there were radical pamphlets which blamed the fourteen-year-old Louis XIV for the civil war then raging. The political system could be justified in terms of the need for supreme national effort and sacrifice in order to support the war. Indeed, in the context of 1610, 1624, or even 1652 a stronger monarchy and a more authoritarian system of government could be said to be relevant to the problems of French society: under a *roi de Bourges* the French state could have fallen apart.[1] But what of the system after 1672, 1688, or 1702? The system remained essentially the same in new conditions of war, a war which in each case could probably have been averted. The argument of 'necessity' and the need for domestic sacrifice must have appeared threadbare by the last years of Louis XIV's personal rule: it was in shreds by the time of the wars of the later eighteenth century.

The intendants proved to be much more effective as agents of an authoritarian government than as the instruments of reform. Of course, there was a reforming element to their work throughout the seventeenth and eighteenth centuries, and there were distinguished *intendants éclairés* under Louis XVI.[2] Above all, however, the intendants of Richelieu and Mazarin were *agents de combat*, the agents of a central government which was insensitive—indeed diametrically opposed—to the fiscal

[1] For Gaston's fears that Louis XIV would be reduced to the position of a Charles VII: 'Journal inédit du Parlement de Paris . . .', ed. Courteault, p. 226.
[2] Useful studies on the intendants in the eighteenth century: M. Bordes, 'Les intendants de Louis XV', *Revue Historique*, ccxxiii (1960), 45–62, and Bordes, 'Les intendants éclairés de la fin de l'ancien régime', *Revue d'Histoire Économique et Sociale*, xxxix (1961), 57–83.

interests of the provinces. The intendants of Louis XIV were much more sensitive to local interests but still predominantly fiscal and political agents of central government. By the eighteenth century, however, the intendants had strong local connections since they tended to stay much longer in the provinces:[1] in a sense they had become a half-way house between the commissioner and the office-holder. It was this transformation which gave significance to the reform plan of the marquis d'Argenson, who in the mid-eighteenth century would have turned the clock back to the ministries of Richelieu and Mazarin by making the intendants triennial.[2] The system itself had begun to stagnate: the choice was to abandon it altogether (the outcome of 1789) or to tinker with it half-heartedly and late in the day (the establishment of the *assemblées provinciales* by Necker in 1787). The political changes inaugurated by Richelieu, and continued by Mazarin, ultimately removed the freedom of action of the crown: their very short-term success perhaps constituted their ultimate danger to the Bourbon monarchy.

[1] The 'average' intendant in the years between 1715 and 1790 stayed ten years in his province. Fifty intendants—one-fifth of the total appointments—stayed fifteen years or more in one province: Mead, 'The administrative *noblesse*', i. 284–6. Bonney, 'Intendants', p. 336.

[2] René Louis Voyer de Paulmy, marquis d'Argenson, *Considérations sur le gouvernement ancien et présent de la France* (Amsterdam, 1765), p. 244, article 34.

Appendix

Notes concerning the Map of France at the Time of Richelieu and Mazarin

MAPS PURPORTING to show the administrative boundaries of France at the time of Richelieu and Mazarin or Louis XIV are often based on inaccurate information[1] or show the boundaries existing after 1716.[2] There is a serious difficulty in obtaining accurate information since seventeenth-century cartography was primitive[3] with improvements taking place locally rather than nationally.[4] Successive creations and abolitions of offices and jurisdictions add to the difficulties. It is thus virtually impossible to draw a map of the *bailliages*[5] or the *élections*[6] of France at the time of Richelieu and Mazarin. Rather than embark on this hazardous exercise it is preferable to list the *élections* in each *généralité* in the early 1660s, viz.:[7]

Name of *généralité*

Alençon [created 1636]	(9)	Alençon, Argentan, Bernay, Conches, Domfront, Falaise, Lisieux, Mortagne, Verneuil.
Amiens	(6)	Amiens, Doullens, Montdidier, Péronne, Ponthieu, Saint-Quentin.

[1] Thus the map in R. Mandrou, *Louis XIV en son temps, 1661–1715* (1973), p. 103, is based on the imperfect evidence in *Lettres . . . de Colbert*, ed. Clément, ii. pt. i, cclxxiv–cclxxix.

[2] Thus the map in *La France au temps de Louis XIV*, ed. G. Mongrédien *et al.* (1966) and *Louis XIV and absolutism*, ed. Hatton, p. xii.

[3] As is shown by the maps of Melchior Tavernier and Pierre d'Avity, both dating from 1637, and of Guillaume de l'Isle (1703).

[4] F. de Dainville, 'Cartes anciennes du Languedoc', *Bulletin de la Société Languedocienne de Géographie* (1960).

[5] However, for 1790, cf. A. Brette, *Les limites et les divisions territoriales de la France en 1789* (1907).

[6] Dupont-Ferrier lists 228 *élections* existing at some stage between 1356 and 1790: G. Dupont-Ferrier, 'Essai sur la géographie administrative des élections financières en France de 1356 à 1790', *Annuaire-Bulletin de la Société de l'Histoire de France*, lxv (1928), 193–342; lxvi (1929), 223–390. But cf. the remarkable map appended to Dupâquier, 'Essai de cartographie historique', for the *élections* of ten *généralités* in northern France and his comments (p. 982) on the changes and enclaves.

[7] B.N. 500 Colbert 259, 260. *Élections particulières* omitted.

Bordeaux	(8)	Agen, Bordeaux, Cognac, Condom, Les Lannes, Périgueux, Saintes, Sarlat-la-Canéda.
Bourges	(5)	Blanc en Berry, Bourges, Châteauroux, Issoudun, Saint-Amand-Mont-Rond.
Caen	(9)	Avranches, Bayeux, Caen, Carentan, Coutances, Mortain, Saint-Lo [suppressed in 1662], Valognes, Vire et Condé
Châlons	(10)	Bar-sur-Aube, Châlons, Chaumont, Epernay, Langres, Reims, Rethel, Sézanne, Troyes, Vitry.
Dijon	(5)	Auxerre, Bar-sur-Seine, Bellay, Bourg, Mâcon.
Grenoble	(6)	Gap, Grenoble, Montélimar, Romans, Valence, Vienne.
Limoges	(6)	Angoulême, Bourgneuf, Brive-la-Gaillarde, Limoges, Saint-Jean d'Angély, Tulle.
Lyon	(5)	Beaujolais, Lyon, Montbrison, Roanne, Saint-Étienne.
Montauban [created 1635]	(11)	Armagnac, Astarac, Cahors, Cumenge, Figeac, Loumagne, Millau, Montauban, Rodez, Rivière-Verdun, Villefranche.
Moulins	(8)	Châtea-chinon, Combrailles, Franc-aleu, Gannat, Gueret, Montluçon, Moulins, Nevers.
Orléans	(12)	Beaugency, Blois, Chartres, Châteaudun, Clamécy Dourdan, Gien, Montargis, Orléans, Pithiviers, Romorantin-Lanthenay, Vendôme.
Paris	(20)	Beauvais, Compiègne, Coulommiers, Dreux, Etampes, Joigny, Mante, Meaux, Melun, Montfort, Nemours, Nogent-sur-Seine, Paris, Provins, Rosoy, Senlis, Sens, Saint-Florentin, Tonnerre, Vézelay.
Poitiers	(9)	Châtellerault, Fontenay-Le-Comte, La Rochelle, Mauléon,

		Niort, Poitiers, Les Sables d'Olonne, Saint-Maixant, Thouars.
Riom	(6)	Aurillac, Brioude, Clermont, Issoire, Riom, Saint-Flour.
Rouen	(13)	Les Andelys, Arques, Caudebec, Chaumont-et-Magny, Évreux, Gisors, Lyons-la-Forêt, Montivilliers, Neufchâtel, Pont de l'Arche, Pont-Audemer, Pont l'Évèque, Rouen.
Soissons	(7)	Château-Thierry, Clermont, Crépy-en-Valois, Guise, Laon, Noyon, Soissons.
Tours	(16)	Amboise, Angers, Baugé, Château-Gontier, Château-du-Loir, Chinon, La Flèche, Laval, Loches, Loudun, le Mans, Mayenne, Montreuil-Bellay, Richelieu, Saumur, Tours.

Total: 171 *élections*.

Bibliography

I. MANUSCRIPT SOURCES

A. *Archives Nationales*

1. *Fonds du conseil d'état.*
In terms of size and importance, this was the most important series used. Eight hundred volumes or so were utilized in the section *conseil d'état et des finances:* E 26/27a–414b, (1610–68). Many of these volumes contain 400 or more folios and all are without inventory. About two hundred volumes of *arrêts en commandement* emanating from the *conseil d'en haut:* E 1684–1904 (*c.* 1635–97). About 32 registers and 160 cartons of documents emanating from the *conseil privé:* V6 1189–1220 (1610–29); V6 45–195 (1624–45); V6 228–38 (1648–9).

2. *Parlement* of Paris.
About 15 registers and cartons, viz.: X1a 8387–92 (1636–41); X1b 8854–7 (1644–52); U 25–30 (1617–54).

3. *Cour des aides* of Paris.
About 17 registers: Z1a 159–64 (1605–61); Z1a 77a–88 (before 1645).

4. *Trésoriers* of Paris.
About 42 volumes: Z1f 174–7 (1623–7); Z1f 189–226 (1634–61).

5. *Contrôle-général des finances.*
About 30 cartons: G7 4–8, 71–5, 85–91, 103–4, 493–502, 1127, 1132.

6. *Maison du Roi.*
About 31 volumes: O1 1–30.
Occasional forays into other series, for example: *Grand conseil* (V5 1076–9), *Maîtres des requêtes de l'hôtel* (V4 63), *Fonds privé* (120 ap. 16–18), AD + and AD IX, and so on.

B. *Château de Vincennes*

1. *Expéditions.*
About 30 volumes (1631–58), important for the commissions of the intendants: A1 14, 26, 32, 41–2, 49, 56, 62, 67, 71, 78–80, 85–6, 92, 96, 101, 111, 113, 121–2, 124–5, 132, 138, 141, 142, 146, 147, 151.

2. *Minutes.*
About 50 volumes (1631–61): A1 12–13, 15–19, 22–3, 24–5, 26–31, 34–41, 43–8, 50–6, 57–61, 63–6, 68–70, 73–6, 81–4, 161–3, 168–70.

C. *Archives des Affaires Étrangères*
About 170 volumes in the series *Mémoires et Documents, France*: 790–912 (1628–61); 1626–1637 (Languedoc); 1701–19 (Provence); 1504–8 (Brittany); 1491–2 (Burgundy).

D. *Bibliothèque Nationale*
Many of the volumes of the *Manuscrits Français* are indexed which facilitates consultation: 3768, 4168–24, 7007, 7686, 16218, 17311, 17367–94, 18510, 18830, 32785, 32786, were consulted among others. The fiscal sources are important: *Nouvelles acquisitions françaises* 164–170 and *Mélanges Colbert* 264–310.

E. *Departmental archives*
About ninety items were consulted through the loan system of the Archives Nationales:

Aisne B 681, 682, 1505, 1905
Allier B 740
Bouches-du-Rhône B 3339, 3351–2, 3354 (photocopies). C 4766
Cher C 913–22
Gironde C 3877–81, 3902–11
Haute-Garonne B 1913, C 2301–2.
Hérault C 6460–2
Puy de Dôme B Clermont 94 (photocopies).
Rhône C 528–33, 561–75
Seine Maritime C 1148–61, 1164, 1696.
Somme 1B 21, 24, 27–9
Tarn C 534
Vienne C 77–85

F. *British Library*
Particularly the Séguier collection: Harleian 4442, 4466, 4489–91, 4493.

G. *Sources specifically related to the social background of the intendants*
1. *Bibliothèque Nationale, pièces originales*
[Name of intendant followed by volume numbers in the series.][1]
AGUESSEAU, ANTOINE D', seigneur de Puiseux: 14

[1] This list comprises 128 provincial intendants appointed under Richelieu and Mazarin and excludes: i. Specialized commissioners without general powers as *intendant de la justice*. ii. Commissioners sent out during the Fronde, but who did

ALIGRE, ÉTIENNE III D', seigneur de La Rivière: 36–7
ALIGRE, MICHEL D', seigneur de Boislandry
AMELOT, DENIS, seigneur de Chaillou: 52
AMELOT, JACQUES, seigneur de Beaulieu
AUBRAY, DREUX D', seigneur d'Offémont: 128
BALTAZAR, JEAN-BAPTISTE, seigneur de Malherbe: 180
BARRIN, JACQUES, seigneur de Rezé and la Galisonnière: 204
BAUTRU, GUILLAUME III, comte de Serrant: 230
BAZIN, CLAUDE, seigneur de Bezons: 235–6
BÉNARD, CYPRIEN, seigneur de Rezé: 287, 323, 2470
BESANÇON, CHARLES, seigneur de Jaligny: 319–21
BOCHART, FRANÇOIS, seigneur de Sarron and de Champigny: 375–6
BOCHART, JEAN, seigneur de Sarron and de Champigny
BORDEAUX, GUILLAUME, siegneur de Génitoy: 416–17
BOSQUET, FRANÇOIS: 424
BOUCAULT, PIERRE, seigneur de Teyran: 428
BOUCHERAT, LOUIS, seigneur de Compans: 436
BOUCHU, CLAUDE, seigneur de Lessart: 438
BRAGELONGNE, JEAN: 490
BRETEL, NICOLAS III, seigneur de Grémonville: 503
BRIES, JEAN: 517
BRÛLART, NOEL, baron de Sombernon: 535–7
CAZET, FRANÇOIS, seigneur de Vautorte: 609, 631
CHAPONAY, HUMBERT, seigneur de Lisle: 676
CHARRETON, JACQUES, seigneur de La Terrière: 687
CHAULNES, JACQUES II, seigneur d'Épinay: 714
CHOISY, JEAN, seigneur de Beaumont: 758
CŒTLOGON, LOUIS, seigneur de Méjusseaume: 798
COIGNET, GASPARD, seigneur de La Thuillerie: 802–3
CORBERON, NICOLAS, seigneur de Tourvilliers: 850
DANÈS, JACQUES II, seigneur de Marly: 968, 969
DUGUÉ, FRANÇOIS, seigneur de Bagnols: 1422–3
DUPRÉ, BARTHÉLÉMÉ, seigneur de Chatulé: 2372
DYEL, JACQUES, seigneur de Miroménil: 1045, 1544–5, 1972
ESTAMPES, JEAN D', seigneur de Valençay: 1076
FAUCON, JEAN-LOUIS, seigneur de Ris: 1103
FAURE, FRANÇOIS: 1107–8

not receive commissions between 1624 and 1648 or between 1653 and 1661. iii. Intendants of the army who did not receive commissions as provincial intendants.

French names in the seventeenth-century pose particular problems to the historian. An individual might be called by his family name, or the name of his lands. He might use the preposition 'de' before both names (e.g. Jean de Martin de Laubardemont). To avoid repetition and for greater clarity the extra preposition has been removed (thus Jean Martin de Laubardemont).

FAVIER, JACQUES, seigneur du Boullay-Thierry: 1111–12
FAVIER, JACQUES, seigneur de Méry-sur-Seine
FORTIA, BERNARD, seigneur du Plessis Clereau: 1204
FORTIA, FRANÇOIS, seigneur du Plessis Clereau
FOUCQUET, NICOLAS, vicomte de Melun and marquis de Belle-
   Isle: 1217–19
FOULLÉ, ÉTIENNE, seigneur de Prunevaux: 1215
FREMIN, GUILLAUME, seigneur de Couronnes: 1241
GALLARD, GALLIOT, seigneur de Poinville: 1264, 1269
GAMIN, HENRI: 1274
GARGAN, PIERRE: 1281
GARIBAL, JEAN, baron de Saint-Suplice: 1282
GASSION, JEAN: 1289
GAULMIN, GILBERT, seigneur de Montgeorges: 1294
GOBELIN, CLAUDE, seigneur d'Aunoy: 1340
GRANGER, MAXIMILIEN, seigneur de Sousiarière: 1396
HAROUYS, LOUIS, seigneur de La Seilleraye: 1486
HAY, PAUL, seigneur du Châtelet: 1495
HEERE, DENIS III, seigneur de Vaudois: 987, 1502
HOTMAN, VINCENT, seigneur de Fontenay: 1535
IMBERT, PIERRE: 1556
JEANNIN, NICOLAS, seigneur de Castille: 616–17, 1578
JOUBERT, JACQUES, seigneur de Bouville: 1596
JUYÉ, ISAAC, seigneur de Moric: 1602
LAFFEMAS, ISAAC, seigneur de Beausemblant: 1616
LA GUETTE, HENRI, seigneur de Chazé; 1619
LAISNÉ, HELIÉ, seigneur de La Marguerie: 1621
   LAISNÉ, LOUIS, seigneur de La Marguerie
LAISNIER, FRANÇOIS, seigneur des Ferrières: 1655
LAUZON, JEAN, seigneur de Liré: 1666–7
LE BRET, CARDIN, seigneur de Flacourt: 1677
LE CAMUS, ANTOINE, seigneur d'Esmery: 582–3, 1677
   LE CAMUS, JEAN
LEFÈVRE DE CAUMARTIN, JACQUES, seigneur de Saint-Port:
   1139
LEFÈVRE DE LA BARRE, ANTOINE: 1139
LEFÈVRE D'ORMESSON, ANDRÉ: 1139, 1145, 1679
   LEFÈVRE D'ORMESSON, OLIVIER
LE GRAS, FRANÇOIS, seigneur du Laurt: 1682
LE JAY, CHARLES, baron de Tilly: 1683
LE LIÈVRE, THOMAS, marquis de Fourilles: 1717
LE MAISTRE, LOUIS, seigneur de Bellejambe: 1807
LE PICARD, JEAN-BAPTISTE, seigneur de Périgny: 2262–3
LE PRÉVOST, JACQUES, seigneur d'Herbelay: 2382

LE ROY, Charles, seigneur de La Potherie: 2581
LE TONNELIER, François, seigneur de Conty: 2582
LE TONNELIER, LOUIS, seigneur de Breteuil
LIGNY, JEAN, seigneur de Greugneul: 1721
LUILLIER, GEOFFROY, seigneur de la Malmaison and d'Orgeval:
    1773
MACHAULT, CHARLES, seigneur d'Arnouville: 1786
MACHAULT, LOUIS, seigneur de Fleury
MANGOT, ANNE, seigneur de Villarceaux: 1827–8
MANGOT, JACQUES, seigneur d'Orgères
MARC, SCIPION, seigneur de La Ferté: 1834
MARTIN, JEAN, seigneur de Laubardemont: 1871–3
MÉLIAND, NICOLAS, seigneur d'Egligny: 1914
MESGRIGNY, JEAN, seigneur de Briel and marquis de Manœuvre:
    1939
MESMES, JEAN-JACQUES IV, comte d'Avaux: 1941–3
MIRON, ROBERT, seigneur de Tremblay: 1973
MOLÉ, JEAN-ÉDOUARD, seigneur de Champlâtreux: 1980–2
MONTESCOT, FRANÇOIS, seigneur de Courteault and du Plessis:
    2015
MORANT, THOMAS, baron du Mesnil-Garnier: 2042
NESMOND, FRANÇOIS-THÉODORE, seigneur de Saint-Disant:
    2097
OLIER, FRANÇOIS, seigneur de Verneuil: 2138–9
PAGET, JACQUES, seigneur de Villemomble: 2180
PARIS, CLAUDE: 2197–9
PELLOT, CLAUDE, seigneur de Portdavid: 2228
PHÉLYPEAUX, ANTOINE, seigneur du Verger: 2257
PINON, CHARLES, seigneur de Villeneuve: 2285
POMMEREU, AUGUSTE-ROBERT, seigneur de la Bretesche: 2322
    POMMEREU, FRANÇOIS, seigneur de la Bretesche
PUSSORT, ANTOINE-MARTIN: 2400
RANCÉ, ANDRÉ, seigneur de la Perche: 2431
RÉNOUARD, JEAN-JACQUES, seigneur de Villayer: 2463–4
SÉGUIER, PIERRE V, seigneur d'Autry: 2671–3
SERVIEN, ABEL, marquis de Sablé: 2695
SÈVE, ALEXANDRE, seigneur de Chatignonville: 2698
SEVIN, LOUIS, seigneur de Quincy: 2700
TALLEMANT, GÉDEON: 2788
TALON, JACQUES: 2789–91
THIERSAULT, PIERRE, seigneur de Conches: 2827
TRONCHAY, CLAUDE, seigneur de Ceinechaux: 2887
TURGOT, JACQUES, seigneur de Saint-Clair: 2897
TURQUANT, JEAN, seigneur d'Aubeterre: 2900

VAUQUELIN, HERCULE, seigneur des Yveteaux: 2946
VERTHAMON, FRANÇOIS, marquis de Manoeuvre: 2976
VIGNIER, CLAUDE, marquis de Mirebeau: 2995
VILLEMONTÉE, FRANÇOIS, marquis de Montaiguillon: 3008
VOISIN, DANIEL, seigneur du Plessis-au-Bois: 3037
VOISIN, JEAN-BAPTISTE, seigneur de la Noiraye
VOYER, RENÉ I, seigneur d'Argenson: 89, 3041
VOYER, RENÉ II, seigneur d'Argenson
YVON, PIERRE, seigneur de Lozières: 3059

2. Marriage contracts of intendants

[References to the *Archives Nationales*, except where otherwise indicated.]

AGUESSEAU, ANTOINE D', to Anne Ginet: Y 175, fo. 90ᵛ, 13 May 1634.
ALIGRE, ÉTIENNE III D', to Jeanne Luillier: Minutier Central XXXVI 103, fo. 144, 5 Feb. 1617.
ALIGRE, MICHEL D', to Genevefe Guynet: Y 184, fo. 305, 14 May 1645.
ALIGRE, MICHEL D', to Catherine Machault: Y 187, fo. 478, 29 Jan. 1651.
ALIGRE, MICHEL D', to Magdelaine Blondeau: Y 196, fo. 275ᵛ, 24 Feb. 1659.
AMELOT, DENIS, to Marguerite du Drac: Y 143, fo. 253, 12 Sept. 1604.
BALTAZAR, JEAN, to Barbe Guyon: A.D. L'Yonne, Dépôt de M. André Guimard 33, no.51, 24 Feb. 1626.
BALTAZAR, JEAN, to Anne Hémard: Chambre départementale des notaires de Sens, Étude Villiers, liasse 1171, 21 Feb. 1632.
BARRIN, JACQUES, to Elisabeth Le Boulanger; Y 175, fo. 267ᵛ, 20 May 1635.
BAUTRU, GUILLAUME III, to Marie Bertrand: Y 184, fo. 42, 8 Dec. 1644.
BÉNARD, CYPRIEN, to François Méliand: Y 229, fo. 228, 19 Feb. 1645.
BOCHART, FRANÇOIS, to Magdelaine Luillier: Y 169, fo. 45ᵛ, 31 Aug. 1628.
BOUCHERAT, LOUIS, to Françoise Marchant: Minutier Central LVII 56, fo. 92, 15 Feb. 1640.
BOUCHERAT, LOUIS, to Françoise de Loménie: Y 192, fo. 412ᵛ, 7 Oct. 1655.
BOUCHU, CLAUDE, to Louise Guérin: Y 205, fo. 76, 6 Mar. 1655.
CAZET, FRANÇOIS, to Marie Marcel: Minutier Central LI 491, 30 Jan. 1634.

CHOISY, JEAN, to Claire de Jesse: Y 167, fo. 442, 8 Feb. 1628.

ESTAMPES, JEAN D', to Marie Le Guel: Y 167, fo. 336, 26 Nov. 1627.

FAUCON, JEAN-LOUIS, to Bonne Royer: Minutier Central XLI 181, 15 July 1638.

FAVIER, JACQUES, seigneur du Boullay-Thierry, to Elisabeth Vallée: Y 179, fo.172 and Minutier Central LXXV 33, 24 Jan. 1637.

FOUCQUET, NICOLAS, to Marye Magdelaine de Castille: Minutier Central XIX 443, 4 Feb. 1651.

GOBELIN, CLAUDE, to Elisabeth Ardier: Y 173, fo. 440^v, 16 Jan. 1633.

HEERE, DENIS III, to Catherine Nicot: Y 170, fo. 235, 27 Nov. 1626.

HEERE, DENIS III, to Nicolle Lignage: Y 170, fo. 237, 10 Jan. 1630.

JEANNIN, NICOLAS, to Claude de Fieubet: Y 176, fo. 101, 21 Jan. 1636.

JUYÉ, ISAAC, to Françoise Giroult: Minutier Central CVII 170, 12 June 1645.

LAFFEMAS, ISAAC, to Jehan Marie Haultdesens: Minutier Central LXXXVII 426, 10 Nov. 1608.

LA GUETTE, HENRI, to Lyée Bochart: Minutier Central XXVI 35, 11 Feb. 1619.

LAISNÉ, HELIÉ, to Anne Camus: Y 151, fol 215^v, 15 May 1611.

LAISNÉ, LOUIS, to Anne Marcel: Y 178, fo. 42^v, 18 Jan. 1637.

LEFÈVRE DE CAUMARTIN, JACQUES, to Geneviefve de la Barre: Minutier Central CVII 210, item 48, 28 Jan. 1624.

LEFÈVRE DE LA BARRE, ANTOINE, to Marie Mandat: Minutier Central CVIII 94, 10 Sept. 1645.

LEFÈVRE D'ORMESSON, ANDRÉ, to Anne Le Prévost: Minutier Central LIV 463, 10 July 1604.

LEFÈVRE D'ORMESSON, OLIVIER, to Marie de Fourcy: Minutier Central XIX 420, 22 July 1640.

LE JAY, CHARLES, to Gabrielle de Lesrat: Y 180, fo. 251, 20 Feb. 1640.

LE LIÈVRE, THOMAS, to Anne Faure: Y 179, fo. 304^v, 28 Jan. 1639.

LE PICARD, JEAN-BAPTISTE, to Catherine Talon: Y 180, fo. 492^v, 2 Sept. 1640.

LE ROY, CHARLES, to Françoise Frezon: Minutier Central LXVI 59, 11 Feb. 1630.

MACHAULT, CHARLES, to Marie Sevin: Y 186, fo. 59, 16 Aug. 1647.

MANGOT, ANNE, to Marye Phélypeaux: Y 165, fo. 55, 19 Feb. 1625.
MESGRIGNY, JEAN, to Huberte-Renée de Bussy: Y 175, fo. 217, 29 Jan. 1635.
MORANT, THOMAS, to Catherine Bordier: Y 180, fo. 389ᵛ, 23 May 1640.
PELLOT, CLAUDE, to Claude Le Camus: Y 181, fo. 319, 13 Aug. 1640.
PHÉLYPEAUX, ANTOINE, to Marie de Villebois: Minutier Central XC 215, 18 Feb. 1652.
POMMEREU, AUGUSTE-ROBERT, to Agnes Lesné: Y 192, fo. 56ᵛ, 19 Dec. 1654.
SÉGUIER, PIERRE V, to Magdelaine Fabry: Y 155, fo. 129ᵛ, 30 Jan. 1614.
SÈVE, ALEXANDRE, to Marie Marguerite de Rochechouard: Y 177, fo. 259, 3 Jan. 1637.
TRONCHAY, CLAUDE, to Françoise Sain: Y 172, fo. 193, 15 Feb. 1624.
VERTHAMON, FRANÇOIS, to Marye Boucher: Y 165, fo. 117, 30 Jan. 1625.
VOISIN, DANIEL, to Jeanne Broé: Y 182, fo. 1, 5 Jan. 1642.
VOYER, RENÉ I, to Helaine de la Font: Y 167, fo. 146ᵛ, 18 July 1622.

PRINTED SOURCES

Note. All printed works in French are published in Paris unless otherwise stated. All printed works in English are published in London unless otherwise stated.

ALLIER, R., *La cabale des dévots, 1627–1666* (1902, repr. Geneva, 1970).
ANDRÉ, L., *Michel Le Tellier et l'organisation de l'armée monarchique* (Montpellier, 1906).
ANDRÉ, L., *Michel Le Tellier et Louvois* (2nd ed., 1943).
ANDRÉ, L. (ed.); A. J. du Plessis, Cardinal de Richelieu [?], *Testament politique* (1947).
ANTOINE, M., *Le conseil du roi sous Louis XV* (Paris and Geneva, 1970).
ARBOIS DE JUBAINVILLE, H. d', *L'administration des intendants d'après les archives de l'Aube* (1880).
ARMOGATHE, J. R. and JOUTARD, P., 'Basville et la guerre des Camisards', *Revue d'Histoire Moderne et Contemporaine*, xix (1972), 44–67.
AVENEL, D. L. M. (ed.), *Lettres, instructions diplomatiques et papiers d'état du Cardinal de Richelieu* (8 vols., 1853–77).

BAEHREL, R., *Une croissance. La Basse Provence rurale, fin du xvie siècle en 1789. Essai d'économie historique statistique* (2 vols., 1961).

BARBICHE, B., 'Les commissaires pour le "régalement" des tailles en 1598–9', *Bibliothéque de l'École des Chartes*, cxviii (1960), 58–96.

BARBIER, A., 'Les intendants de province et les commissaires royaux en Poitou de Henri III à Louis XIV', *Bulletin et Mémoires de la Société des Antiquaries de l'Ouest*, 2nd ser., xxvi (1902), 293–637.

BAXTER, D. C., 'French intendants of the army, 1630–1670' (University of Minnesota Ph.D., 1971).

BAXTER. D. C., *Servants of the sword. French intendants of the army, 1630–1670* (Urbana, Illinois 1976).

BEIK, W. H., 'Magistrates and popular uprisings in France before the Fronde: the case of Toulouse', *Journal of Modern History*, xlvi (1974), 585–608.

BEIK, W. H., 'Two intendants face a popular revolt: social unrest and the structures of absolutism in 1645', *Canadian Journal of History*, ix (1974), 243–62.

BERCÉ, Y. M., *Histoire des croquants. Étude des soulèvements populaires au xviie siècle dans le sud-ouest de la France* (2 vols., Paris and Geneva 1974).

BERCÉ, Y. M., *Croquants et nu-pieds. Les soulèvements paysans en France du xvie au xixe siècle* (1974).

BERCÉ, Y. M., *Fête et révolte. Des mentalités populaires du xvie au xviiie siècle* (1976).

BERCÉ, Y. M., 'Aspects de la criminalité au xviie siècle', *Revue Historique*, ccxxxix (1968), 33–42.

BERCÉ, Y. M., 'De la criminalité aux troubles sociaux. La noblesse rurale du sud-ouest de la France sous Louis XIII', *Annales du Midi*, lxxvi (1964), 41–59.

BERCÉ, Y. M., 'La bourgeoisie bordelaise et le fisc sous Louis XIII', *Revue Historique de Bordeaux*, new ser., xiii (1964), 41–66.

BERGER DE XIVREY, M., and Gaudet, J. (eds.), *Recueil des lettres missives de Henri IV* (9 vols., 1843–76).

BLET, P., 'Richelieu et les débuts de Mazarin', *Revue d'Histoire Moderne et Contemporaine*, vi (1959), 241–68.

BLET, P., 'Le plan de Richelieu pour la réunion des Protestants', *Gregorianum*, xlviii (1967), 100–29.

BLET, P., 'Le conseil d'état et les Protestants de 1680 à 1685', *Bibliothèque de l'École des Chartes*, cxxx (1972), 131–62.

BLET, P., *Le clergé de France et la monarchie. Étude sur les assemblées générales du clergé de 1615 à 1666* (2 vols., Rome, 1959).

BLUCHE, J. F., 'L'origine sociale des secrétaires d'état de Louis XIV, 1661–1715', *XVIIe Siècle*, xlii–xliii (1959), 8–22.

BLUCHE, J. F., *L'origine des magistrats du Parlement de Paris au xviiie siècle* (1956).

BLUCHE, J. F., *Les magistrats du Parlement de Paris au xviiie siècle, 1715–1771* (1960).

BLUCHE, J. F., *Les magistrats du grand conseil au xviiie siècle, 1690–1791* (1966).

BOISLISLE, A. M. DE (ed.), *Correspondance des contrôleurs-généraux avec les intendants des provinces, 1683–1715* (3 vols., 1874–9).

BOISLISLE, A. M. DE [untitled communication], *Revue des Sociétés Savantes*, 7th ser., iii (1881).

BOISLISLE, J. M. DE (ed.), *Mémoriaux du conseil de 1661* (3 vols., 1905–7).

BOISSONNADE, P., 'L'administration royale et les soulèvements populaires en Angoumois, Saintonge et en Poitou pendant la ministère de Richelieu, 1624–1642', *Bulletin et Mémoires de la Société des Antiquaires de l'Ouest*, 2nd ser., xxvi (1902), xix–liii.

BONNEY, R. J., 'The secret expenses of Richelieu and Mazarin, 1624–1661', *English Historical Review*, xci (1976), 825–36.

BONNEY, R. J., 'The intendants of Richelieu and Mazarin, 1624–1661' (Oxford University D.Phil., 1973).

BONVALLET, A., 'Le bureau des finances de la généralité de Poitiers', *Mémoires de la Société des Antiquaires de l'Ouest*, 2nd ser., vi (1883), 139–424.

BOSCHERON DES PORTES, C. B. F., *Histore du Parlement de Bordeaux depuis sa création jusqu'a sa suppression, 1451–1791* (2 vols., Bordeaux, 1877).

BOUCHITTÉ, L. F. H. (ed.), *Négociations, lettres et pièces relatives à la conférence de Loudun* (1862).

BOURGEON, J. L., *Les Colbert avant Colbert. Destin d'une famille marchande* (1973).

BOYER DE SAINTE-SUZANNE, BARON C. V. E., *L'administration sous l'ancien régime. Les intendants de la généralité d'Amiens (Picardie et Artois)* (1865).

BUISSERET, D. J., *Sully and the growth of centralized government in France, 1598–1610* (1968).

BUISSERET, D. J., 'Les précurseurs des intendants du Languedoc', *Annales du Midi*, lxxx (1968), 80–8.

BUISSERET, D. J., 'A stage in the development of the intendants: the reign of Henry IV', *Historical Journal*, ix (1966), 27–38.

CAILLARD, M., 'Recherches sur les soulèvements populaires en Basse Normandie (1620–1640), et spécialement sur la révolte des Nu-Pieds', *À travers la Normandie des xviie et xviiie siècles. Cahiers des Annales de Normandie*, iii (1963).

CAMBON DE LAVALETTE, J., *La chambre de l'édit de Languedoc* (1872).

CANAL, S., *Les origines de l'intendance de Bretagne. Essai sur les relations de la Bretagne avec le pouvoir central* (Rennes, 1911).

CERTEAU, M. DE, 'Politique et mystique. René d'Argenson, 1596–1651', *Revue d'ascétique et de mystique*, xxxix (1963), 45–82.

CHARLÉTY, S., 'Lyon sous le ministère de Richelieu', *Revue d'Histoire Moderne et Contemporaine*, iii (1901–2), 125–36, 493–507.

CHARMEIL, J. P., *Les trésoriers de France à l'époque de la Fronde. Contribution à l'histoire de l'administration financière de l'ancien régime* (1964).

CHAULEUR, A., 'Le rôle des traitants dans l'administration financière de la France de 1643 à 1653', *XVIIe Siècle*, lxv (1964), 16–49.

CHENAYE, AUBERT DE LA, and BADIER (eds.), *Dictionnaire de la noblesse* (3rd ed., 19 vols., 1863–76).

CHÉRUEL, P. A. (ed), *Journal d'Olivier Lefèvre d'Ormesson et extrait des mémoires d'André Lefèvre d'Ormesson* (2 vols., 1860–1).

CHÉRUEL, P. A., and AVENEL, G. D', (eds.), *Lettres du Cardinal Mazarin pendant son ministère* (9 vols., 1872–1906).

CHÉRUEL, P. A., *Histoire de France pendant la minorité de Louis XIV* (4 vols., 1879–80).

CHÉRUEL, P. A., 'Les carnets de Mazarin pendant la Fronde, sept. en oct. 1648', *Revue Historique*, iv (1877), 103–38.

CHURCH, W. F., *Richelieu and reason of state* (Princeton, N.J., 1972).

CHURCH, W. F., *Constitutional thought in sixteenth-century France. A study in the evolution of ideas* (Cambridge and Harvard, 1941).

CHURCH, W. F., 'The decline of the French jurists as political theorists, 1660–1789', *French Historical Studies*, v (1967), 1–40.

CLARKE, J. A., *Huguenot warrior. The life and times of Henri de Rohan, 1579–1638* (The Hague, 1966).

CLÉMENT, P. (ed.), *Lettres, instructions et mémoires de Colbert . . .* (10 vols., 1861–82).

CONSTANT, J. M., 'L'enquête de noblesse de 1667 et les seigneurs de Beauce', *Revue d'Histoire Moderne et Contemporaine*, xxi (1974), 548–66.

COURTEAULT, H. (ed.), 'Journal inédit du Parlement de Paris pendant la Fronde (1 déc. 1651–12 avril 1652)', *Annuaire-Bulletin de la Société de l'Histoire de France [année 1916]*, (1917), 163–315

CUBELLS, MME., 'Le Parlement de Paris pendant la Fronde', *XVIIe Siècle*, xxxv (1957), 171–99.

DÉBIDOUR, A., *La Fronde angevine. Tableau de la vie municipale au xviie siècle* (1877).

DÉGARNE, M., 'Études sur les soulèvements provinciaux en France avant la Fronde. La révolte du Rouergue en 1643', *XVIIᵉ Siècle*, lvi (1962), 3–18.

DELAUME, G., *Le bureau des finances de la généralité de Paris* (1966).
DENT, J., 'An aspect of the crisis of the seventeenth-century. The collapse of the financial administration of the French monarchy, 1653–1661', *Economic History Review*, 2nd ser., xx (1967), 241–56.
DENT, J., *Crisis in finance. Crown, financiers and society in seventeenth-century France* (Newton Abbot, 1973).
DENZER, H. (ed.), *Jean Bodin. Proceedings of the international conference on Bodin in Munich* (Munich, 1973).
DESSERT, D., 'Finances et société au xviiᵉ siècle: à propos de la chambre de justice de 1661', *Annales E.S.C.*, xxix (1974), 847–81.
DESSERT, D. and JOURNET, J. L., 'Le lobby Colbert: un royaume ou une affaire de famille?', *Annales E.S.C.*, xxx (1975), 1303–36.
DESSERT, D., 'Pouvoir et finance au xviiᵉ siècle: la fortune de Mazarin', *Revue d'Histoire Moderne et Contemporaine*, xxiii (1976), 161–81.
D'ESTRÉE, A., *La Basse-Navarre et ses institutions de 1620 à la Révolution* (Zaragoza, 1955).
DETHAN, G., *Gaston d'Orléans. Conspirateur et prince charmant* (1959).
DEVÈZE, M., *La grande réformation des forêts sous Colbert, 1661–1683* (1954).
DEYON, P., *Amiens. Capitale provinciale. Étude sur la société urbaine au xviiᵉ siècle* (Paris and The Hague, 1967).
DEYON, P., 'À propos des rapports entre la noblesse française et la monarchie absolue pendant la première moitié du xviiᵉ siècle', *Revue Historique*, lxxxviii (1964), 341–56.
DOOLIN, P. R., *The Fronde* (Cambridge and Harvard, 1935).
DROUOT, H., *Mayenne et la Bourgogne, 1587–1596. Contribution à l'histoire des provinces françaises pendant la Ligue* (2 vols., 1937).
DUBÉDAT, J. B., *Histoire du Parlement de Toulouse* (2 vols., 1885).
DUBUC, P., *L'intendance de Soissons sous Louis XIV, 1643–1715* (1902).
DUMONT, F., *Le bureau des finances de la généralité de Moulins* (Moulins, 1923).
DUPÂQUIER, J., 'Essai de cartographie historique: le peuplement du bassin parisien en 1711', *Annales E.S.C.*, xxiv (1969), 976–98.
DUVERNOY, E., 'Gouverneurs et intendants de la Lorraine au dix-septième siècle', *Annuaire de la Société d'Histoire et d'Archéologie de Lorraine*, xxxviii (1929), 1–32.
ESMONIN, E., *La taille en Normandie au temps de Colbert, 1661–1683* (1913).
ESMONIN, E., *Études sur la France des xviiᵉ et xviiiᵉ siècles* (1964).
ESMONIN, E., 'Un épisode du rétablissement des intendants après

la Fronde. Les maîtres de requêtes envoyés en chevauchée', *Revue d'Histoire Moderne et Contemporaine*, xii (1965), 219 ff.

FAGE, R., *Les états de la vicomté de Turenne* (2 vols., 1894).

FEILLET, A., *et al.* (eds.), *Œuvres de Retz* (10 vols., 1870–96).

FLOQUET, A. M., *Histoire du Parlement de Normandie* (7 vols., Rouen, 1840–2).

FLOQUET, A. M. (ed.), *Relation du voyage du Chancelier Séguier en Normandie* (Rouen, 1842).

FOISIL, M., *La révolte des Nu-Pieds et les révoltes normandes de 1639* (1970).

FRÊCHE, G., 'Compoix, propriété foncière, fiscalité et démographie historique en pays de taille réelle (xvie–xviiie siècles)', *Revue d'Histoire Moderne et Contemporaine*, xviii (1971), 321–53.

FRÊCHE, G., *Toulouse et la région Midi-Pyrénées au siècle des lumières (vers 1670–1789)* (1974).

FRONDEVILLE, H. DE, *Les conseillers du Parlement de Normandie sous Henri IV et sous Louis XIII, 1594–1640* (Paris and Rouen, 1964).

FRONDEVILLE, H. DE, *Les conseillers du Parlement de Normandie de 1641 à 1715* (Rouen, 1970).

GACHON, P., *Les états de Languedoc et l'édit de Béziers, 1632* (1887).

GACHON, P., *Quelques préliminaires de la révocation de l'édit de Nantes en Languedoc, 1661–1685* (Toulouse, 1899).

GALLET-GUERNE, D., 'Une conséquence des troubles féodaux sous Louis XIII: les confiscations royales de 1629 à 1641', *Bibliothèque de l'École des Chartes*, cxxvii (1969), 329–54.

GAQUÈRE, F., *Pierre de Marca, 1594–1662. Sa vie, ses œuvres, son gallicanisme* (1932).

GARRISON, F., *Essai sur les commissions d'application de l'édit de Nantes. I. Règne d'Henri IV* (Montpellier, 1950).

GLASSON, E., *Le Parlement de Paris. Son rôle politique depuis Charles VII jusqu'à la Révolution* (2 vols., 1901).

GODARD, C., *Les pouvoirs des intendants sous Louis XIV, particulièrement dans les pays d'élections, 1661–1715* (1901).

GOUBERT, P., *Beauvais et le Beauvaisis de 1600 à 1730. Contribution à l'histoire sociale de France du xviie siècle* (2 vols., 1960).

GOUBERT, P., 'Les officiers royaux des présidiaux, bailliages et élections dans la société française du xviie siècle', *XVIIe Siècle*, xlii–xliii (1959), 54–75.

GRILLON, P., (ed), *Les papiers de Richelieu. Section politique intérieure. Correspondance et papiers d'état. I. 1624–1626* (1975).

GRUDER, V. R., *The royal provincial intendants. A governing élite in eighteenth-century France* (Ithaca, N.Y., 1969).

GUYOT, G. A. and MERLIN, P. A., *Traité des droits, fonctions, franchises, exemptions, prérogatives et privilèges annexés en France à chaque*

Bibliography 469

dignité, à chaque office, à chaque état, soit civil, soit militaire, soit ecclésiastique (4 vols., 1786–8).

HAMSCHER, A. N., *The Parlement of Paris after the Fronde, 1653–1673* (Pittsburgh, Pa., 1976).

HANOTAUX, G. *et al.* (eds.), 'Maximes d'état et fragments politiques du Cardinal de Richelieu', *Mélanges historiques. Choix de documents* (3 vols., 1880).

HANOTAUX, G., *Origines de l'institution des intendants des provinces* (1884).

HANOTAUX, G., and LA FORCE, DUC DE, *Histoire du Cardinal de Richelieu* (6 vols., 1893–1947).

HATTON, R. M. (ed.), *Louis XIV and Europe* (1976).

HATTON, R. M. (ed.), *Louis XIV and absolutism* (1976).

HAYDEN, J. M., *France and the Estates-General of 1614* (Cambridge, 1974).

HENRY, P., *François Bosquet. Intendant de Guyenne et de Languedoc. Evêque de Lodève et de Montpellier. Étude sur une administration civile et ecclésiastique au xviie siècle* (1889).

HIGOUNET, C. (ed.), *Histoire de l'Aquitaine. Documents* (Toulouse, 1973).

HURT, J. J., 'Les offices au Parlement de Bretagne sous le règne de Louis XIV: aspects financiers', *Revue d'Histoire Moderne et Contemporaine*, xxiii (1976), 3–31.

IMBERT, J. (ed.), *Quelques procès criminels des xviie et xviiie siècles* (1964).

JACQUART, J., 'La Fronde des princes dans la région parisienne et ses conséquences materielles', *Revue d'Histoire Moderne et Contemporaine*, vii (1960), 257–90.

JACQUART, J., *La crise rurale en Île-de-France, 1550–1670* (1974).

JARRY, L., *La guerre des Sabotiers de Sologne et les assemblées de la noblesse, 1653–1660* (Orléans, 1880).

JOURDAN, A. L. J., DECRUSY, and ISAMBERT, F. A. (eds.), *Recueil général des anciennes lois françaises depuis l'an 420 jusqu'à la révolution de 1789* (28 vols., 1821–33).

KETTERING, SHARON, *Judicial politics and urban revolt: the Parlement of Aix, 1629–1659* [forthcoming at Princeton, N.J.]

KIERSTEAD, R. F. (ed.), *State and society in seventeenth-century France* (New York, 1975).

KOSSMAN, E. H., *La Fronde* (Leiden, 1954).

LA BARRE, P. DE, *Formulaire des esleuz auquel sont contenues et déclarées les functions [sic] et devoirs desdits officiers et sommairement ce qu'ils sont tenus scavoir et faire pour l'acquit de leur charge . . .* (Rouen, 1627).

LACOUR-GAYET, G. and LAVOLLÉ, R. *et al.* (eds.); A. J. du Plessis, Cardinal de Richelieu, *Mémoires* (10 vols., 1907–31).

LACOUR-GAYET, G., *L'éducation politique de Louis XIV* (2nd ed., 1923).

LACROIX, A., 'Claude Brosse et les tailles', *Bulletin de la Société Départementale d'Archéologie et de Statistique de la Drôme*, xxxi (1897), 181–90, 289–99, 388–96; xxxii (1898), 54–68, 142–60, 233–48, 363–71; xxxiii (1899), 75–80, 234–7, 307–23.

LAIR, J., *Nicolas Foucquet. Procureur-général, surintendant des finances, ministre d'état de Louis XIV* (2 vols., 1890).

LASSAIGNE, J. D., *Les assemblées de la noblesse de France au xviie et xviiie siècles* (1965–6).

LE BLANT, R., 'Notes sur Jean de Garibal, associé de Notre-Dame-de Montréal. Vers le 24 juillet 1619–17 juillet 1667', *Revue d'Histoire de l'Amérique Française*, xv (1961), 104–22.

LE BRET, CARDIN, *De la souveraineté du roy* (1632).

LEBRUN, F, (ed.), *L'histoire vue de l'Anjou, 987–1789. Recueil de textes d'histoire locale pour illustrer l'histoire générale* (Angers, 1963).

LEBRUN, F., 'Les soulèvements populaires à Angers aux xviie et xviiie siècles', *Actes du 90e congrés national des sociétés savantes* [1965] (1966), 110–40.

LEBRUN, F., 'Les intendants de Tours et d'Orléans aux xviie et xviiie siècles', *Annales de Bretagne*, lxxviii (1971), 287–305.

LE CACHEUX, P., 'Documents concernant les états de Normandie de février 1655', *Société de l'histoire de Normandie. Mélanges. Documents*, 5th ser. (1898—published 1901), 121–58.

LEFEBVRE, A. and TRIBOUILLARD, F., 'Fiscalité et population dans l'élection de Valognes de 1540 à 1660', *Annales de Normandie*, xxi (1971), 207–33.

LEGRELLE, A., 'Les assemblées de la noblesse en Normandie, 1658–9', *Société de l'histoire de Normandie. Mélanges*, 4th ser. (1898) 307–46.

LÉGUAI, A., 'Les "émotions" et séditions populaires dans la généralité de Moulins au xviie et xviiie siècle', *Revue d'Histoire Économique et Sociale*, xliii (1965), 44–65.

LE PESANT, M. (ed.), *Arrêts du conseil du roi. Règne de Louis XIV. Inventaire analytique des arrêts en commandement. I. 20 mai 1643–8 mars 1661* (1976).

LEROY-LADURIE, E., *Les paysans de Languedoc* (2 vols., 1966).

LIVET, G., *L'intendance d'Alsace sous Louis XIV, 1648–1715* (Strasbourg, 1956).

LIVET, G., *Le duc Mazarin. Gouverneur d'Alsace, 1661–1713* (Strasbourg and Paris, 1954).

LIVET, G., 'Louis XIV et les provinces conquises. État des questions et remarques de méthode', *XVIIe Siècle*, lxv (1964), 66–108.

LOGIÉ, P., *La Fronde en Normandie* (3 vols., Amiens, 1951).

LOIRETTE, F., 'Un intendant de Guyenne avant la Fronde: Jean de Lauzon, 1641–1648', *Bulletin philologique et historique jusqu'à 1715 du comité des travaux historiques et scientifiques* [*année 1957*] (1958), 433–61.

LOIRETTE, F., 'L'administration royale en Béarn de l'union à l'intendance, 1620–1682. Essai sur le rattachement à la France d'une province frontière au xviie siècle', *XVIIe Siècle*, lxv (1964), 66–108.

LOIRETTE, F., 'Une émeute paysanne au début du gouvernement personnel de Louis XIV. La sédition de Benauge, déc. 1661–janv. 1662', *Annales du Midi*, lxxviii (1966), 515–36.

LONGNON, J. (ed.), *Mémoires de Louis XIV pour les années 1661 et 1666* . . . (1923).

LUBLINSKAYA, A. D. (ed.), *Bnutrennyaya politiyka francuzkovo absolutizma, 1633–1649* [= *The internal policy of French absolutism*] (Moscow and Leningrad, 1966).

LUBLINSKAYA, A. D., *French absolutism: the crucial phase, 1620–1629* (Cambridge, 1968).

MAILFAIT, H., *Un magistrat de l'ancien régime. Omer Talon, sa vie et ses œuvres, 1595–1652* (1902).

MAJOR, J. R., 'French representative assemblies. Research opportunities and research published', *Studies in medieval and renaissance history*, ed. W.M. Bowsky (Lincoln, Nebr., 1964), i.182–219.

MAJOR, J. R., 'The crown and the aristocracy in renaissance France', *American Historical Review*, lxix (1964), 631–45.

MAJOR, J. R., 'Henri IV and Guyenne. A study concerning origins of royal absolutism', *French Historical Studies*, iv (1966), 363–83.

MALETTKE, KLAUS, *Opposition und konspiration unter Ludwig XIV. Studien zu kritik und widerstand gegen system und politik des französischen königs während der ersten hälfte seiner persönlichen regierung* (Göttingen, 1976).

MALLET, J. R., *Comptes rendus de l'administration des finances du royaume de France* (London, 1789).

MATTHEWS, G. T., *The royal general farms in eighteenth-century France* (Columbia, N.Y., 1958).

MAUGIS, E., *Histoire du Parlement de Paris dès l'avènement des rois Valois à la mort d'Henri IV* (3 vols., 1913–16).

MEAD, G. J. DE CUSANCE, 'The administrative *noblesse* of France during the eighteenth-century, with special reference to the intendants of the *généralités*' (London Univ. Ph.D., 1954).

MEYER, J., *La noblesse bretonne au xviiie siècle* (2 vols., 1966).

MICHAUD, J. F. and POUJOULAT, J. J. F. (eds.); A. J. du Plessis, Cardinal de Richelieu *Mémoires* . . ., 2nd ser., viii (1838).

MICHAUD, J. F. and POUJOULAT, J. J. F. (eds.); Omer Talon, *Mémoires* . . ., 3rd ser., vi. (1839).

MONGRÉDIEN, G., *Le bourreau du Cardinal de Richelieu. Isaac de Laffemas* (1929).

MONGRÉDIEN, G., *10 novembre 1630. La journée des Dupes* (1961).

MOOTE, A. L., *The revolt of the judges. The Parlement of Paris and the Fronde, 1643–1652* (Princeton, N. J., 1971).

MOOTE, A. L., 'The French crown versus its judicial and financial officers', *Journal of Modern History*, xxxiv (1962), 146–60.

MOOTE, A. L., 'The Parlementary Fronde and seventeenth-century robe solidarity', *French Historical Studies*, ii (1962), 330–55.

MOREAU, C. (ed.), *Choix de Mazarinades* (3 vols., 1853).

MOUSNIER, R. É. (ed.), *Lettres et mémoires adressés au Chancelier Séguier, 1633–1649* (2 vols., 1964).

MOUSNIER, R. É., LABATUT, J. P., and DURAND, Y. R., *Problèmes de stratification sociale. Deux cahiers de la noblesse pour les États Généraux de 1649–1651* (1964).

MOUSNIER, R. É. (ed.), 'Les règlements du conseil du roi sous Louis XIII', *Annuaire-Bulletin de la société de l'histoire de France* (1948), 93–211.

MOUSNIER, R. É. (ed.), *Le conseil du roi de Louis XII à la Révolution* (1970).

MOUSNIER, R. É., *La vénalité des offices sous Henri IV at Louis XIII* (2nd ed., 1971).

MOUSNIER, R. É, *La plume, la faucille et le marteau. Institutions et société en France du moyen âge à la Révolution* (1970).

MOUSNIER, R. É., *Fureurs paysannes. Les paysans dans les révoltes du xviie siècle. France, Russie, Chine* (1967).

MOUSNIER, R. É., *Les institutions de la France sous la monarchie absolue, 1598–1715. I. Société et état* (1974).

MOUSNIER. R. É., *L'assassinat de Henri IV. 14 mai 1610* (1964).

MOUSNIER, R. É., 'Sully et le conseil d'état et des finances', *Revue Historique*, cxcii (1941), 68–86.

MOUSNIER, R. É., *La stratification sociale à Paris aux xviie et xviiie siècles. L'échantillon de 1634, 1635, 1636* (1976).

NÉRAUD, J., *Les intendants de la généralité de Berry* (1922).

O'CONNELL, D. P., *Richelieu* (1968).

O'REILLY, E., *Mémoires sur la vie publique et privée de Claude Pellot . . . 1619–1683* (2 vols., Paris and Rouen, 1881).

PAGÈS, G., *La monarchie d'ancien régime en France de Henri IV à Louis XIV* (1928).

PAGÈS, G., 'Le conseil du roi et la vénalité des offices pendant les premières années du ministère de Richelieu', *Revue Historique*, clxxxii (1938), 245–82.

PAGÈS, G., 'Autour du "grand orage"'. Richelieu et Marillac. Deux politiques', *Revue Historique*, clxxix (1937), 63–97.

PAGÈS, G., 'La vénalité des offices dans l'ancienne France', *Revue Historique*, clxix (1932), 477–95.

PAGÈS, G., 'Essai sur l'évolution des institutions administratives en France du commencement du xvie siècle à la fin du xviie siècle', *Revue d'Histoire Moderne*, vii (1932), 8–57, 113–37.

PALLASSE, M., *La sénéchaussée et la siège présidial de Lyon pendant les guerres de religion. Essai sur l'évolution de l'administration royale en province au xvie siècle* (Lyon, 1943).

PARKER, D., 'The social foundation of French absolutism, 1610–1630', *Past and Present*, liii (1971), 67–89.

PETIT, J., *L'assemblée des notables de 1626–1627* (1936).

PETRACCHI, A., *Intendenti e prefetti. L'intendente provinciale nella Francia d'antico regime. I. 1551–1648* (Milan, 1971).

PICOT, G., *Cardin Le Bret (1558–1655) et la doctrine de la souveraineté* (Nancy, 1948).

PILLORGET, R., *Les mouvements insurrectionnels de Provence entre 1596 et 1715* (1975).

PILLORGET, R., 'Les "cascaveoux". L'insurrection aixoise de l'automne 1630', *XVIIe Siècle*, lxiv (1964), 3–30.

PILLORGET, R., 'Vente d'offices et journée de barricades du 20 janvier 1649 à Aix-en-Provence', *Provence Historique*, xv (1965), 25–63.

PILLORGET, R., 'Les luttes de factions à Salon de 1608 à 1615', *Provence Historique*, xviii (1968), 293–311.

PILLORGET, R., 'Luttes de factions et intérêts économiques à Marseille de 1598 à 1618', *Annales E.S.C.*, xxvii (1972), 705–30.

PORCHNEV, B. F., *Les soulèvements populaires en France de 1623 à 1648* (1963).

PRENTOUT, H., 'Les états provinciaux de Normandie', *Mémoires de l'académie nationale des sciences, arts et belles-lettres de Caen*, new ser., i–iii (1925–7).

RANUM, O. A., *Richelieu and the councillors of Louis XIII. A study of the secretaries of state and superintendants of finance in the ministry of Richelieu, 1635–1642* (Oxford, 1963).

RANUM, O. A., 'Richelieu and the great nobility. Some aspects of early modern political motives', *French Historical Studies*, iii (1963), 184–204.

RAVENEL, J. (ed.), *Lettres du Cardinal Mazarin à la Reine, à la princesse palatine . . .* (1836).

RÉBILLON, A., *Les états de Bretagne de 1661 à 1789. Leur organisation. L'évolution de leurs pouvoirs. Leur administration financière* (Paris and Rennes, 1932).

RENAUD, H., (ed.), 'Correspondance relative aux provinces d'Aunis, Saintonge, Angoumois et Poitou . . .', *Archives Historiques de la Saintonge et de l'Aunis*, vii (Saintes, 1880), 285–350.

RICOMMARD, J., 'Les subdélégués des intendants aux xviie et xviiie siècles', *L'Information Historique*, xxiv (1962–3).

ROBILLARD DE BEAUREPAIRE, C. DE (ed.), *Cahiers des états de Normandie sous les règnes de Louis XIII et de Louis XIV. Documents relatifs à ces assemblées* (5 vols., Rouen, 1876–8, 1883, 1891).

ROSCHACH, E., DEVIC, C., and VAISSETTE, J. (eds.) *Histoire générale de Languedoc*, vols. xiii, xiv (Toulouse, 1876).

ROUX, MARQUIS DE, *Louis XIV et les provinces conquises. Artois, Alsace, Flandres, Roussillon, Franche-Comté* (1938).

RULE, J. C. (ed.), *Louis XIV and the craft of kingship* (Columbus, Ohio, 1969).

SANABRE, J., *La acción de Francia en Cataluña en la pugna por la hegemonía de Europa, 1640–1659* (Barcelona, 1956).

SCHMIDT, C., 'Le rôle et les attributions d'un "intendant des finances" aux armées. Sublet des Noyers de 1632 à 1636', *Revue d'Histoire Moderne et Contemporaine*, ii (1900–1), 156–75.

SOMAN, A., 'Press, pulpit and censorship in France before Richelieu', *Proceedings of the American Philosophical Society*, cxx (1976), 439–63.

TAPIÉ, V. L., *La France de Louis XIII et de Richelieu* (2nd ed., 1967).

TAPIÉ, V. L., *La politique étrangère de la France et le début la guerre de Trente Ans, 1616–1621* (1934).

TEMPLE, N., 'Control and exploitation of French towns during the *ancien régime*', *History*, clxxi (1966), 16–34.

THÉRIVE, A. (ed.); Guy Patin, *Lettres pendant la Fronde* (1921).

THOMAS, A., *Une province sous Louis XIV. Situation politique et administrative de la Bourgogne de 1661 à 1715* . . . (Paris and Dijon, 1844).

THUAU, E., *Raison d'état et pensée politique à l'époque de Richelieu* (1966).

TUCOO-CHALA, P., *La vicomté de Béarn et le problème de sa souveraineté, des origines à 1620* (Bordeaux, 1961).

VALOIS, N. (ed.), *Inventaire des arrêts du conseil d'état, règne de Henri IV* (2 vols., 1886, 1893).

VANNIER, J., *Essai sur le bureau des finances de la généralité de Rouen, 1551–1790* (Rouen, 1927).

VINDRY, F., *Les parlementaires français au xvie siècle* (4 vols., 1909–12).

WESTRICH, S. A., *The Ormée of Bordeaux, A revolution during the Fronde* (Baltimore, Md., 1972).

ZELLER, G., 'L'administration monarchique avant les intendants. Parlements et gouverneurs', *Revue Historique*, cxcvii (1947), 180–215.

ZELLER, G., *La réunion de Metz à la France, 1552–1648* (2 vols., 1926).

Index

intendants
—provincial: significance, 442; origins, 29, 30, 32, 81–4, 140–1; as temporary investigators, 32, 34, 119; change in title before 1648, 32, 45, 141–4; change in title after Fronde, 70–1, 154–6; commissions, *135–58*; later evolution of powers, 451–2; length of service, 49–50, 71, 108, 204, 427–8, 452; family, *76–89*; earlier careers, 93; career as int. not an end in itself, 105–6; age when appointed, 106; political attitudes, *112–34*; remuneration, 109, 127, 212–13; disgrace and recall, 132–4, 159; not natives of the provinces in which they served, 203–4; listed, 457–61; collapse of government predicted if recalled (1648), 30, 191–2; demand for their recall, 54–5, 191–2; recalled 61, 227, 311, 330; six provinces excepted from recall, 59–61, 153, 279–80; legislation of Fronde concerning not revoked, 68; arguments in favour of restoration, 68–9, 197–8, 331; Colbert and, 425–7; Richelieu and, 34; Mazarin and, 58–9
—fiscal powers, 33, 147, 176, 178–83; levy forced loans on towns, 43–4, 72, 325–7; levy *subsistances*, 44–5, *274–6*, *280–1*; levy *taxes des aisés*, 327–8, 330; levy *sol pour livre*, 45, 328–30; given control of *taille*, 49, 184–90, 219–20, 276, 448; this control removed (1648), 55–6, 191–2; returned (1653), 69–71, 198–203; relationship with financiers, 208–10; suppress tax rebellion, 214–37; and the *cours des aides*, 252–8; verify debts of towns, *337–43*
—administer by judicial process, 135; date of becoming administrators, 49, 70; ordinances equivalent to those of sovereign courts, 141, 158; preside over lesser courts, 246–7; and the *Parlements*, *244–52*; and Protestants, 384–5, 395–7, 400, 429–32; size of areas, 46–7, 72–3; joint ints. 47–8, 72; administration of army, *271–83*; suppress urban riots, *323–32*; relations with govs., *299–306*; police lesser nobles, *309–13*; and assemblies of nobles, 315–17;

right of entry into sovereign courts, 148, 250; sons and grandsons ints. of Louis XIV, 439 n. 4; total number appointed under Richelieu and Mazarin, 30, 78
intendants des finances, 18–19, 62, 208, 226, 256, 281, 349; as royal commissioners during the Fronde, 60, 62–3, 153, 266
interest, rate of on loans to crown, 54, 360; on municipal loans, 339, 341
invasion, *see* France, invasion of
Issoire, 435 n. 1
Italy, 37, 43, 51, 58, 138, 224, 259, 264, 269–70, 276, 279, 387, 389, 401, *405*, 412

Jacques, Philippes; *prête-nom*, 188
Jailly, 312
Jaligny, *see* Besançon
Jansenism, 112–13, 127, 377–8
Jarnac, the sr. de, 312
Jars, chevalier de, 125
JEANNIN, Nicolas, sr. de Castille: family, 78 n. 7, 131, 208; buys office, 95; int. at Châlons (1642–4), 147–8, 224, 271
Jeannin, Pierre (1540–1622); *contrôleur-général*, later *surintendant des finances*, 14, 23, 180
Jenatsch, Georg, 43
Jesuits, 90, 121
Joannis, Paul de, sr. de Châteauneuf, 324
Joigny, 232, 234 n. 5, 235, 331 n. 7
jointure (*douaire*), 86–7
Jons, 310
JOUBERT, Jacques, sr. de Bouville (1616–56): family, 79 n. 1; int. at Bourges (1656), 331 n. 7
juge royal, 85, 249, 430
jurats, 318
juridiction contentieuse, 26; ints. denied, 55; *trésoriers de France* denied, 167 n. 1; of *élus*, 166–7; of the *Parlements*, 245–6; of the *cours des aides*, 257–8
Jurieu, Pierre (1637–1713), Protestant propagandist, 421
JUYÉ, Isaac, sr. de Moric (1583?–1657): commissioner in Bresse and the Lyonnais (1621), 403; int. at Moulins (1629), 324; int. at Paris (1637), 273; int. at Grenoble (1640), 272

Index 493

LE MAISTRE, Louis, sr. de Bellejambe (?–1666): family, 78 n. 7; int.
at Angers (1630), 324; commissioner
in Languedoc (1631–3), 40, 248 n.
5, 338; int. at Orléans (1634–5), 253
n. 5; int. at Amiens (1636–43), 42,
147, 166, 218, 247 n. 6, 248, 271–2,
329
Le Mans, 83, 434
Le Mazuyer, Gilles, int. in Burgundy
(1612), 32 n. 6, 393 n. 3; *premier
président* in the *Parlement* of Toulouse,
393
Leopold I, Holy Roman Emperor, 440
Le Peletier, Claude, sr. de Morfon-
taine (1630–1711), *contrôleur-général
des finances* (1683–9), 163
LE PICARD, Jean-Baptiste, sr. de
Périgny (?–1653): family, 78 n. 7;
buys office, 95; int. at Soissons
(1643–6), 150–1, 189, 224; loans,
210
LE PRÉVOST, Jacques, sr. d'Herbelay (?–1653): family, 78 n. 7; int.
at Aix (1635), 340; int. at Lyon
(1635–8), 139 n. 3; int. at Orléans
(1639–41), 327
Le Puy, 323
Lérida, 51
Lérins islands, 259, 332
LE ROY, Charles, sr. de la Potherie
(?–1661): family, 79 n. 3, 88; int.
at Aix (1630–3, 1635), 300, 324, 332,
340; at Caen (1639–46), 49 n. 1,
189, 218, 221, 311, 327
Le Roy, Louis (?–1577), jurist, 91
Lescot, confessor to Richelieu, 123
Lesdiguières, Francois de Bonne, duc
de (1543–1626); Constable of France,
3 n. 2, 144 n. 1, 288, 353
Lesdiguieres, Jean-Francois de Bonne,
duc de; gov. of the Dauphiné, 308
Lesparre-Médoc, 229
Lessart, *see* Bouchu
lessees, 207
Le Tellier, François, marquis de
Louvois and de Courtenvaux (1641–
91), secretary of state for war, 13 n.
3, 283, 439
Le Tellier, Michel Ier, sr. de Chaville,
Mayenne's int. in Champagne (1591)
84–5
Le Tellier, Michel II, marquis de Bar-
bezieux, sr. de Chaville and de

Louvois (1603–85), 23, 64 n. 6, 204,
206, 209 n. 9, 228, 257, 262–5, 267–
8, 270, 281, 283, 315, 439; int. in
army of Lombardy (1640–3), 17 n.
1, 84, 105, 268, 278; secretary of
state for war (1643–77), 13–14;
attitude to provincial ints. 69, 73,
277–9; Chancellor of France (1677–
85), 423
Le Tellier, Nicolas, sr. de Tourneville,
receveur-général des gabelles, 208
Le Tillier, Jacques, *intendant des finances*,
63 n. 2
Le Tonnelier, François, sr. de Breteuil,
int. at Amiens (1674–83), 157
LE TONNELIER, François, sr. de
Conty (1584–1638): family, 78 n. 7;
int. at Rouen (1633–4), 209, 325;
int. at Limoges (1637), 136 n. 1, 147,
300
LE TONNELIER, Louis, sr. de
Breteuil (1609–85), int. of Languedoc (1647–53), 59–61, 271 n. 3;
int. in Roussillon (1649), 153, 270;
int. at Paris (1653–7), 72, 198, 200,
331 n. 7; king's councillor, 107, 423
lettre d'anoblissement, 77, 79, 181
lettre de cachet, 60 n. 5, 152–3, 240, 332,
334
lettre de jussion, 240
Le Vayer, Roland, sr. de Boutigny
(?–1685), int. at Soissons (1682–5),
157
licence ès lois, 90–2
Lieurey, 314
lieutenant-général: of a province, 61, 142,
217, 282, 302, 305, 307, 326, 334,
351, 353, 357, 367–8, 371, 400; in
the *bailliages*, etc., 99, 126 n. 2, 351
LIGNY, Jean, sr. de Greugneul:
family, 78 n. 7, 94; int. at Riom
(1647–8), 89
Ligny-en-Brionnais, riot at (1642), 208–
9, 329
Limoges, 41, 44–5, 48, 70 n. 1, 73, 108,
128, 135–6, 145, 150–1, 155, 157,
205–6, 214, 236, 329, 336
Limousin, 40, 46, 63 n. 2, 138, 143,
145–7, 153, 210, 217, 219, 222, 226,
231, 234–5, 273, 297, 299–300, 306,
309, 314, 385 n. 4, 417
Lionne, Hugues de, marquis de Berny
(1611–71), secretary of state for
foreign affairs (1663–71), 439

Parlements—contd.

88 n. 2, 93, 107, 133, 241; grievances in 1648, 53; attempted union with Paris (1649), 64; age of entry, 93; opposition to edict of Nantes, 390
—*Parlement* of Toulouse, 65 n. 2, 99 n. 4, 119, 242–3, 244 n. 4, 245 n. 1, 248–9, 299, 378, 390; remonstrances (1648), 334; hostility to Foullé, 63; and Protestants, 392–3; attempted union with Paris (1650), 64 n. 6; allows intendants entry, 148 n. 4; and tax remissions, 225

partage, of inheritence, 77; along religious lines, 396

Particelli, Michel, sr. d'Hémery [Particelli d'Emeri] (1596?–1650), 129, 340, 342; *intendant des finances* in Languedoc (1631–2), 105 n. 2, 299–300; *contrôleur-général des finances* (1643–7), 254, 330; *surintendant* (1647–8, 1649–50), 15, 17, 61–2; borrowing, 51–2

Particelli, Michel, II, *trésorier de France*, 340

partis, see traités

Pascal, Étienne; *trésorier de France*, 187–8

Patin, Guy (1602–72), 22

Pavillon, Nicolas (1597–1677); bishop of Alet, 377

pays d'élections, 33, 44–9, 59, 61–2, 64, 70–1, 108, 148, 155, 163, 174, 178, 181, 185, 188, 198, 203–4, 219, 224–5, 227, 234, 236, 244, 327, 383, 428, 443; bears heaviest burden of *taille*, 48, 214

pays d'états, 41, 44–6, 48, 59, 70 n. 4, 71, 107–9, 209, 227, 344–83, 418, 428, 443

pays nouvellement conquis, 153

peace, foreign, Richelieu's belief in a firm treaty, 37; negotiations with Spain, 51–2, 58, 314–15

peasants, more prosperous types of, 181, 449; pauperization, 448

peculation, 169, 194, 305; prosecutions by ints., 140–1, 145, 185, 202, 254, 256 n. 4

Peiresc, Nicolas-Claude Fabri de (1580–1637), *conseiller* in the *Parlement* of Aix and *savant*, 92, 341

PELLOT, Claude, sr. de Portdavid (1619–83); family, 89; *conseiller* in

the *Parlement* of Rouen, 97; political attitudes, 131; int. at Grenoble (1656–8), 73, 250; int. at Limoges (1658–64), 73 n. 6, 130, 234–5, 331, n. 7, 336, with Poitiers (1658–63), 73 n. 6, 202, 234–5; int. at Bordeaux and Montauban (1663–9), 383 n. 2, 439; *premier président* in the *Parlement* of Rouen (1669), 130, 251 n. 1

Perche, 273, 314

Perier, *conseiller* in the *Parlement* of Aix, 341

Périgny, *see* Le Picard

Périgord, 148, 210, 217, 221, 230, 237, 248, 273, 360

Périgueux, 325

Péronne, 413

Perpignan, 270, 414–15

personal rule, of king, 3, 419, 422

Peyremales, Protestant commissioner in Languedoc, 429

Pézenas, 347, 375–6, 378–9, 382

PHÉLYPEAUX, Antoine, sr. du Verger (1604–65): family, 78 n. 7, 86; int. at Moulins (1643–8), 223, 225 n. 2

Phélypeaux, Louis III, marquis de la Vrillière (1636–99); secretary of state, 13 n. 3, 88, 107, 392 n. 2, 399

Phélypeaux, Raymond II, sr. d'Herbault (1560–1629), financier and secretary of state, 83–4

Philip IV, king of Spain (r. 1621–65), 52, 58–9, 284, 298, 389, 412–14, 440, 443–4

Philip V, king of Spain (r. 1700–46), 444

Philipsbourg, 267

Picardy, 42, 55, 60–1, 84, 89, 107, 139, 142, 149–50, 152–3, 182, 210, 218, 226, 231, 259, 262 n. 3, 272, 279, 281, 287–8, 293–5, 304, 309–11, 314, 416, 418

Piedmont, 114, 401

Pietre, Julien (?–1686): *trésorier de France*, 166, 226; interim int. at Amiens (1656), 280

Pignerola [Pinerolo], 52 n. 5, 342, 405

Pilloys, lieutenant-general in the Sologne, 233

PINON, Charles, sr. de Villeneuve (?–1672): family, 78 n. 7, commissioner at Soissons (1650), 63

Pinon, Jacques, sr. de Vitry-sur-Seine, 85